String Processing
and Text Manipulation In C

Selected Data Structures and Techniques

String Processing
and Text Manipulation In C

Selected Data Structures and Techniques

Bernice Sacks Lipkin

P T R Prentice Hall
Englewood Cliffs, New Jersey 07632

Library of Congress Cataloging-in-Publication Data
Lipkin, Bernice Sacks.
   String processing and text manipulation in C: selected data structures
and techniques / Bernice Sacks Lipkin.
     p.   cm.   Includes index.   ISBN 0-13-121443-8
   1. C (Computer program language)   I. Title.
QA76.83.C15L56 1994
005.15'3--dc20   94-1457
                                                CIP

Editorial/production supervision: **Ann Sullivan**
Manufacturing manager: **Alexis R. Heydt**
Acquisitions editor: **Paul W. Becker**
Editorial assistant: **Maureen Diana**

©1994 by Bernice Sacks Lipkin

Published by PTR Prentice Hall
Prentice-Hall, Inc.
A Paramount Communications Company
Englewood Cliffs, NJ 07632

Apple is registered by the Apple Computer, Inc. Brief is a text editor for DOS and Windows, developed by
Underware, Inc. and marketed by Borland, Inc. It has many of the features of Richard Stallman's Emacs. (DOS is
an operating system and Windows is a user's interface. Both trademarks are registered by Microsoft, Inc.) C is a
programming language designed by Dennis Ritchie in the 70s and implemented on the UNIX operating system.
The basic reference for C is *The C Programming Language*, by B W. Kernighan and Dennis M. Ritchie. It was
first published in 1978. References to it in this book are to the Second Edition published in 1988 by Prentice-
Hall, Inc. CodeView is a debugging program for the Microsoft compiler. It is registered by Microsoft, Inc. Fortran is an acronym for FORmula TRANslating System. It was developed in the 50s at IBM under the direction of
John Backus. Its forte continues to be numerical computation. MaTEXT is a set of string processing programs
written in Sail. It is registered by Bernice Sacks Lipkin. Microsoft. The Microsoft Compiler Version 7 is the
compiler referenced in the text, unless otherwise indicated. It is registered by Microsoft, Inc. Pascal is a high
level a language emphasizing structured programming. It was developed by Niklaus Wirth in the late 1960s.
"The Programming Language Pascal" appeared in *Acta Informatica* in 1971. PC for Personal Computer and IBM
are registered by International Business Machines, Inc. SAIL, an acronym for STANFORD ARTIFICIAL
INTELLIGENCE LANGUAGE, was developed by Dan Swinehart *et al* in the 1960s at the Stanford Artificial
Intelligence Project. TXT is a set of string processing programs written in C. It is copyrighted by Bernice Sacks
Lipkin. UNIX is a registered trademark of UNIX System Laboratories, Inc. (a wholly-owned subsidiary of Nov-
ell, Inc.) in the United States and other countries. VENTURA, a desktop-publishing package, is registered by
Xerox, Inc.

Limits of Liability and Disclaimer of Warranty: The author and publisher of this book have used their best
efforts in preparing this book and software. These efforts include the development, research, and testing of the
theories and programs to determine their effectiveness. The author and publisher make no warranty of any kind,
expressed or implied, with regard to these programs or the documentation contained in this book. The author and
publisher shall not be liable in any event for incidental or consequential damages in connection with, or arising
out of, the furnishing, performance, or use of these programs.

The publisher offers discounts on this book when ordered in bulk quantities.
For more information, contact: Corporate Sales Department, PTR Prentice Hall, 113 Sylvan Avenue,
Englewood Cliffs, NJ 07632; Phone: 201-592-2863; Fax: 201-592-2249

Printed in the United States of America
10 9 8 7 6 5 4 3 2 1

ISBN 0-13-121443-8

Prentice-Hall International (UK) Limited, *London*
Prentice-Hall of Australia Pty. Limited, *Sydney*
Prentice-Hall Canada Inc., *Toronto*
Prentice-Hall Hispanoamericana, S.A., *Mexico*
Prentice-Hall of India Private Limited, *New Delhi*
Prentice-Hall of Japan, Inc., *Tokyo*
Simon & Schuster Asia Pte. Ltd., *Singapore*
Editora Prentice-Hall do Brasil, Ltda., *Rio de Janeiro*

DEDICATION

This book is for Lew, my husband

CONTENTS

PREFACE

This book is intended as a resource for the C programmer who works with text data. It takes as given that text data are as important if not more important than numeric data in providing a basis for plans, hypotheses, strategies and decisions. It takes as given that text data can be turned into information much as numerical data are manipulated to provide meaningful patterns not apparent in the individual numbers.

Text processing, as contrasted to word processing, turns text data into information. It can extract a group of text phrases whose commonality may be as simple as a sequence of characters or as complex as a user-articulated class definition. Text processing is capable of categorizing the elements of raw text into meaningful subsets. And text manipulation is important in the tasks involved in database management and data input. In each of these cases, the text is subjected to various operations that analyze it, organize it, restructure it, and reshape it. As a text fragment takes new form, its contents may often bear little resemblance to dictionary words or grammatical phrases. So we employ the more neutral term *string processing* to describe the operations performed on text.

Implementing text procedures in C has many advantages. The C language is deservedly a very popular language. And it provides a reasonable platform for shunting programs across a variety of machines. It is not noted, however, for providing string constructions and utilities for text manipulation and analysis. It lacks strong string utilities. It has few powerful string-handling primitives and functions. In addition, the rapid increase in availability of large bodies of text in machinable form makes processing demands on C it was not designed to treat. These demands exacerbate the problems of dealing with storage, stack size and information extraction.

This book explores the implications of C's concept of *string* in context of other basic C language features. The goal is to develop a repertoire of basic data structures customized for text and a knowledge of some fundamental computing techniques adapted to operate on these data structures.

The book builds a foundation for string programming by providing an expanded formulation of the concept of *string*. It characterizes and contrasts different ways of representing the text strings that embody the data. It examines some of the techniques that are currently available. It fashion tools from C primitives to meet string processing requirements. And it illustrates how to adapt and develop supplementary robust string-handling utilities.

The first chapter outlines the basic data objects and programming resources available in C. It serves as a general review of the C language and grammar, its control mechanisms and its operators. It identifies data types of significance in string processing: the char, the char array, the pointer to the array and the struct. It begins the detailing of C language differentiations that have consequences in string processing: literal strings versus variable strings, preset string storage versus on-the-fly allocation, local buffers versus global arrays. The relationships of variable to function, function to file, file to running program are developed.

In the next two chapters we look at a fundamental way that a text stream, i.e., a sequence of characters, can be represented in C; namely, we explore in detail the relationship of the char to the char array and the relationship of the char array to the char pointer that both represents the array and operates on it. The metaphor is a stream of characters that come to rest in a buffer, where the order in which they arrive is carefully preserved. Ways of working with the character array, the character pointer and the pointer to the character pointer are developed, including how to stop the stream at a particular position, how to delete the initial part of the array, how to give the text stream a home and how to relocate it.

While still focused on text as a stream of characters, in Chapter 4 we examine the setbreak utility. It admits only particular character values from a file to memory—or from one array to another—and stops text entry on any of a group of specified values. The setbreak controller is implemented as twin matrices that function as gatekeepers acting directly on the contents of the stream. A special construction, the setbreak table, succinctly tells the program to: (1) stop entry of the stream of characters if it reaches any character listed as a break character; (2) prevent all characters on its omit list from entering; (3) leave case as is or change the case of those characters allowed entry to upper case or to lower case; and (4) dispose of the break character in one of several ways. Use of the setbreak tool increases our versatility in dealing with several string representations. Bitmapping, an integral part of the setbreak implementation, is discussed.

In chapter 5, we look at ways to maintain the associations of a community of strings during processing by grouping them: (1) within two-dimensional (2D) arrays that are sized uniformly or unequally; or (2) inside one very large buffer, the one-dimensional (1D) array. Variations on the 1D and 2D arrays are shown to be capable of mimicking a true 2D string array—what in C would be a three-dimensional array; i.e., they can deal with a cluster of strings, each of which travels with a retinue of associated information.

The versatility of the struct, which can handle a complex representation of the text string, is examined in Chapter 6. It can be used to store a string or the components of the disarticulated string; and, like the array, it fosters access to these components. The struct is better suited than the array to database records where fields are composed of subfields that themselves are compounded of still smaller subunits. In general, the struct is an excellent data structure for keeping sufficient information about the string to reconstruct its original state or some amplified or reduced version of the original. Within the context of collating a group of related structs, we deal with the linked list and the array of linked lists. Hashing, a basic computing tool, is used as a way to facilite locating any one of the linked structs.

Chapter 7 provides functions for modifying the string. Operations on the single string include stripping away extraneous characters, extracting portions such as bracketed text, changing string content by single characters or by overwriting, changing the string to some other data type and augmenting the string with stylized text. Substring formation may depend on location, size or content. Clones can be created by copying the string with or without modification. Multiple strings can be compared for an exact match, for an identical substring or by a fuzzy match. Strings can be swapped, combined or reconstructed from substrings. Pains have been taken to assure procedural integrity, so it should be easy to incorporate these individual utilities into increasingly complex functions.

Procedures used or referenced in the book are to be found in compilable form in LISTINGS, the disk that accompanies this book.

ACKNOWLEDGMENTS

I would like to express my gratitude to Gary Knott, who is CEO of Civilized Software, Inc., for reading the manuscript. MLAB, his program for mathematical and statistical analyses, is a model for what an interactive program can do and how it should communicate with the user. I would like to thank the editorial and production staff at Prentice-Hall, and in particular Sophie Papanikolaou for her tactful advice on turning a manuscript into proper book format. I thank my husband, children and grandchildren for their patience, understanding and humor.

TYPOGRAPHY

Typographic conventions used in this book are:

- A program or part of a program is in **bold** ordinary-sized font. Glosses within a program are written as comments in plain text; i.e., **/*....*/**.

- In the text, names are in *italics*. This includes function names, macro names, program names, file names and variable names.

- File names cited in include directives are capitalized; e.g., **#include <COMLIB.H>.**

- In the text, quoted program code is written in bold ordinary-sized font, as in this sentence: Given that *x* is of the appropriate data type, **x = 1;** and **x = 111E-5;** and **x = NewStruct;** use the same simple assignment format.

- In the text, **BOLD** is the font used instead of quote marks; e.g., The display reads: **x = 10; y = 20;.** Directives such as **Push <ENTER> Key.** are bolded. Characters and phrases that might ordinarily be put in single quote marks are usually bolded.

NOTATION

Sections in a chapter begin with the chapter number; e.g., 2.1 refers to the first section in Chapter 2 and 5.3.2 refers to the second subsection of the third section of Chapter 5.

A () terminates procedure names; e.g., *ttyin*() in this sentence: The arg transmitted to *ttyin*() is examined a character at a time.

Macro names are similarly terminated with a (), as in this sentence: *RDINVIS(p,l,x)* is a macro.

All function arguments are referred to as args—either when reference is to the argument in the calling function or to the argument in the called function.

In the text, *char* and *character* are used interchangeably. So are *int* and *integer*. *float*, *floating point number* and *real* are interchangeable.

Even though a program may define an integer variable as an int, on some machines the variable may need to be reconfigured as a long. This is particularly important when bit operations are involved that are predicated on a 32-bit word as are the setbreak operations detailed in Chapter 4.

When used in the text, the term *string* (lower case) is equivalent to a character array containing text. Used in a program and always capitalized, *STRING* is typedef'ed as the character pointer; e.g., the definition **STRING ptr;** is the same as **char *ptr;**.

In a program, *PTRADR* is typedef'ed as the pointer to a character pointer; e.g., the definition **PTRADR padr;** is the same as **char **padr;**.

Special keyboard characters are written in CAPS and bracketed with triangular brackets. Thus, the Escape key is written as <ESC>.

When control characters are to be entered at keyboard, they are written as CTRL#, as in **CTRLd**. When they are elements of a string literal, they are written in ASCII; e.g., **"ABC\04"**.

Examples involving *main()* are usually prototyped as **int main(void);** and written as **main();**. Example procedures in the text will seldom have a **return (0);** or **exit(0);** statement in *main()*, even though it should be inserted just before *main()* successfully terminates. Compilers complain if it is omitted.

NOTES ON ZERO

- As is conventional, *NULL* represents the null pointer constant; e.g., **if (fileptr != NULL)....** Depending on implementation, the constant has a system-defined macro value of **0, 0L** or **(void *)0**. This does not mean that the pointer is pointing to memory address zero; instead, it means the pointer is not pointing to a defined variable or function. *NULL* is portable across systems, no matter what the internal representation. From a programmer's point of view, it is sufficient to know that a pointer with a value of NULL is guaranteed not to be pointing at a memory location that contains a C language object.

- *FALSE* (*NO*) is #defined as 0 in relational expressions, where outcomes can only be zero or one; i.e., all non-FALSE outcomes are set to TRUE (YES). As example, the outcome of the if conditional **if (p > 0 && r < 10)** is either TRUE or FALSE, depending on the values assigned p and r.

- Text in a character array must be terminated by the null character constant **'\0'**, which is ASCII 0, the symbol that represents the byte whose bits are all zero. For example, if the character array *a*[10] holds the string *ABC*, then: **a[0] = 'A'; a[1] = 'B'; a[2] = 'C'; a[3] = '\0';**. In this book, SNUL is the alias for the null character constant; the usual substitute, NUL, is too similar to NULL.

- An empty string literal is written as **""** with no space between the quote marks; e.g., **setbreak(&Tbl, "", "", "is");**. A string variable with a '\0' as first element is functionally empty to operations that halt string examination at the SNUL; e.g., **newstr[0] = SNUL; printf("%s",newstr);** would print nothing.

- The single text character '**0**' is octal 60 in ASCII; e.g., **"AB01234"**.

- Integers and floating point numbers can have a numerical value of zero, written as *0* or *0.0*; e.g., **x = 0;** for integers and **x = 0.0;** for floating point numbers.

NOTES ON USING THE DISK

The disk is called *LISTINGS*. It contains the code for the programs and functions used in the text.

As a minimum, a file holds a small but complete program for what may be just a few lines of example code in the text. Some of the files include exercises and expanded examples. Some contain complete programs, rather than just example functions.

Most programs has the same format: an INCLUDE FILES list, an extern list of the functions in the program, macros and #defines specific to the program, the program functions, the main() procedure.

The include files are in LISTINGS\include.

- Macros and definitions of constants are filed as LISTINGS\include\define.h.

- The few global variables that are referenced are in LISTINGS\include\globals.c.

- String processing utilities are in LISTINGS\include\comlib.c.

- Setbreak and input/output utilities are in LISTINGS\include\comset.c.

Make sure that the LISTINGS\include files are available to the chapter subdirectories when compiling. A comprehensive linkage would include the object code of the main program, globals, comlib and comset. globals.obj subsumes define.h. define.h subsumes the library files: *ctype.h*, *stdio.h*, *stdlib.h* and *limits.h*. When *string.h* is used (Chapter 4), it appears in the main program.

Programs are filed under the chapter subdirectories in which they are discussed; chap1 refers to Chapter 1, chap2 to Chapter 2, and so forth. A program is filed according to the chapter section in which it was discussed or referenced. Thus, 1-6-1.c is material associated with the first chapter, Section 1.6.1. If several procedures are in the same section, the files are called, for example, 1-6-1a.c and 1-6-1b.c.

Aside from the header files, an individual program is completely stored in a single file. In addition, in each chapter subdirectory, there is one file with a dot C extension that contains all the listings.

When a program calls for a specific database, change the name, if you want to try a real database of your own. For convenience, databases of the right name, if of trivial content, are usually provided. Output files usually have a ".tmp" extension so they should be easy to find and delete.

Print Products are labeled: /*PrintProduct:*/ or /*PP:*/. Print macros are in *define.h*. PD prints an int, PC a char, PS a string and PJ a comment.

All examples were tested using both the Microsoft C Compiler (MSC) Version 5.1 and the fully ANSI C Version 7, using the HUGE library and EMULATION mode under DOS 5 on a 80386 PC clone with full 640K memory and 16M extended memory, 64 Kb cache memory, a 200M hard disk and a 80387 floating pointing processor. Pragma commands, extended language facilities and optimizations were NOT used. Where results differ between the two compilers, the examples shown are those compiled by Version 7. To convert examples for use with pre-ANSI and not fully-ANSI compilers: (1) do NOT initialize a local char array or a local int array; and (2) do NOT assign one struct to another or use a struct as a function argument. To fill a local array with some example text, copy a string literal to the array. Unix machines will need to inspect CRLF input/output and integer size.

CHAPTER 1

A REVIEW OF BASIC CONCEPTS IN THE C LANGUAGE

1.1. INTRODUCTION

1.1.1. GENERAL COMMENTS

This chapter recapitulates information on the C language[1]. The intent is to establish a foundation for examining C constructs from the point of view of string processing. It also provides a quick reference to C language objects so that the book may be used as a stand-alone document. It assumes a general knowledge of programming. It makes no pretense of being a general text for the C language or grammar.

C is a deceptively simple language. On the one hand it has a stylistic penchant for terse statements. On the other hand, it is capable of forming complex structures that are the elaborate products of multiple data types that are composed of data types that are themselves accretions of simpler data types. Assembly language and Fortran programs can be patched in.

---

1 This chapter has been checked against the second edition of *The C Programming Language*, written by Brian W. Kernighan and Dennis M. Ritchie (K&R) and published by Prentice-Hall, Englewood Cliffs, NJ, 1988. The other reference document is *American National Standard for Programming Languages—C*, copyright in 1990 by the American National Standards Institute, New York City, NY, and published as *ANSI/ISO 9899-1990* in 1992. The rules stated in the text attempt to conform to ANSI C standards, bearing in mind there is still much room for different compiler implementations and different user interpretations. Inaccuracies where present are of course my own doing. Comparisons of C to other high level programming languages are based on notes written with Earl Smith, now at OpenVision, Inc., NYC, NY. A large part of Section 1.10 on portability is adapted from **Portability Guideline Issues For C** by Karanjit S. Siyan, published in the *C Users Journal*, R&D Publications, Lawrence, KS, December, 1989, pp. 65-68.

C combines low level concerns with high level power. It has become a truism that compared to other high level languages, C is on a lower level. In any language, attention to data type, to data conversion and to the rules governing binary operations is necessitated by storage requirements. In C, the skeleton shows more clearly than in Sail or Fortran In C, we are never allowed to forget storage concerns. String processing seems particularly difficult because there is nothing defined as *string*, except in the trivial sense of a sequence of characters in double quotes; i.e., the string literal. To store text, characters can be brought into memory one at a time and stored in sequence in a char array. That's what happens in any language? Perhaps. But it is nicer when the system[2] handles housekeeping details such as memory allocation transparently, under all conditions. In Sail, we could reference a string as an entity just as we do an int or a double. In C, because a string is not a data type in the way an int is, we are constantly reminded we are dealing with a set of entities, characters, not with a single entity. We can never neglect the chores of arranging for enough string space or erasing a string that may have considerably changed its size and contents, housekeeping jobs those who deal for the most part with numbers are spared.

C's error checking capability is abysmal. The user has responsibility for preventing over-flow and overload, restricting the size of the integer or floating point number permitted entry, and so forth. In string processing this translates to chronic concerns with staying within array limits and treating pointers with the respect we give to any potentially deadly weapon. The problem is exacerbated by stack limitations in present day Microsoft DOS-class operating systems. Large string processing programs, particularly those that require parsing and interpretation of input strings, often will initially cause runtime errors, forcing the programmer to trim buffer sizes and resort to overlays.

On the other hand, C is (relatively) portable, well supported, and available on a large and growing number of machines. Indeed it is the relatively low level of C that makes the language machine-independent and its full utilization machine-dependent, the compiler supplying input and output capability. To enhance portability, we should forget being clever about using machine architecture efficiently. The better the program will fit one machine, the poorer it is likely to fit all others.

Once primarily run under the UNIX operating system, C is available on a range of machines from the small computer—the APPLE and under DOS in IBM-style machines—to mainframes. UNIX has the accumulated advantage of man eons of software development but many of its facilities are more or less available in the other operating systems.

---

2   We will use the term *system* to indicate any aspect of the software system(s) that makes a program run and that is not specifically a compiler task. It is more or less equivalent to *execution environment*. It includes heap allocation during runtime.

1.1.2. FORMAL DEFINITION OF C

We define a C **language object** as any object[3] in the language that: (1) is provided space in memory (whether, depending on its storage class, this storage is for the life of the program or temporary or at recurring intervals); and (2) is given an explicit name, is denoted by membership in a named object as is, for example, an individual element of an array, or is stored as a constant. Entities in the C language include: functions, function arguments, constants, void, integer variables, floating point variables, pointers, arrays, structs, unions and enums.

Data objects or data types are a restrictive subset of the set of C language objects. The primary data types are the integer and floating point variables. After receiving an initial value, they may be re-valued by a single assignment statement. Pointers, which are derived from these types, may also be re-valued by a single assignment statement. Most recently, structs and unions have been given some of the characteristics of the primitive data types[4]. The primary types, pointers and, in a restricted sense, the structs and unions are **lvalues**[5]. Compound data types are arrays, structs, unions and any user-developed complex unit that is composed of simpler data types. Compound data types have rules of governance over and above the rules that control their member elements. Pointers will be discussed together with the compound data types because of their close association with arrays and structs.

Expression[6] is a general term denoting any language component together with its allowable punctuation (such as square brackets or parentheses or dot or arrow) or a grouping of such components. An **arithmetic expression** is any group of operands and/or arithmetic operators and/or constants and parenthesis punctuation acceptable to the language; in C, **i++** is an expression. **keyfind(char *str, char *wrd)** is an expression involving a function.

A **constant** is a particular numerical or ASCII[7] value or string of ASCII values that is asserted rather than created by a processing operation.

---

3   We make no distinction between object, entity, unit, element, component or any other word that conveys: **this is something we talk about and have rules about**.

4   In ANSI C the entire struct, not just individual struct elements, can be assigned the member values of another struct of the same type, suggesting there is no intrinsic reason other aggregates such as arrays could not also join the ranks of objects that can be treated as a single entity.

5   **lvalue** derives from left-side value. In the assignment statement **x = 4;**, the variable x is the lvalue. An lvalue is allocated space in memory. The contents at that location are the **rvalue**; in this example, **4** is the rvalue. Note that in an array, an individual element is an lvalue, the entire array is not.

6   In discussing grammatical constructions below, note that an expression is written as **e**, a name or identifier as **id**, a variable as **v** and a constant as **K**.

7   A mnemonic for American Standard Code for Information Interchange.

To illustrate C features, we will sometimes compare them to features in other programming language. We will gloss programs as does C, using the /* to begin a comment and */ to terminate it; e.g., /*This is a comment*/. Only single spaces or, where appropriate, the language-reserved separators ([](){},;:) are required to separate language elements in C; multiple spaces and white space characters (tabs, blanks, NewLines, vertical tabs, form feeds and carriage returns) are allowed and aid readability.

In the discussion that follows, bear in mind that the general format for defining a variable (i.e., giving it an address, a home), is, reading from left to right:

<storage type> <data type> <id>

Briefly, the storage type determines whether a variable is recognized over several files or just a single file or just within a single function. Ints, floats, chars, and so forth are data types. The data type determines the amount of memory storage delegated to the variable; conversely the contents of a memory address are interpreted according to its data type. The identifier is the name of the variable.

The general format for defining a function is:

<storage type> <data type returned> <id> ([{<arg data type><arg id>]})[8]

In actuality, we will discuss the parts that go into creating a definition in reverse order, starting, in Section 1.3, with the rules on naming identifiers.

1.2. THE PROCEDURE

1.2.1. THE PROCEDURE AS THE BASIC UNIT IN C

Let us begin by diagramming what is both the simplest procedure as well as the simplest program in C that is compilable:

main()
     { }

A C program is a sequence of independent procedures.

---

8 Throughout this book, we will use **arg** indiscriminately to denote a function argument, both the dummy argument and the actual calling variable, relying on context to make clear which is referenced. Alternative terms in use are: **parameter** (as in K&R, p. 25) or **formal argument** for the dummy argument; **argument** or **actual argument** for the calling variable.

A program consists of one or more individual procedures, called functions. One of the functions must be named *main*. A function consists of a function name followed by parentheses enclosing optional formal parameters, followed by braces enclosing the body of the function. The function body consists of optional declarations, followed by simple and/or compound statements. Individual statements are terminated by semicolons. Compound statements consist of unnamed braces surrounding optional initial declarations and one or more simple statements. Simple statements call other functions or assign a value or control execution.

Languages such as Pascal are block-structured. A block is a compound statement, where a compound statement is one or more statements—declarations, definitions and simple statements—surrounded by a pair of delimiters and an optional associated name. So a block is a unit that has an optional name and is delimited by reserved BEGIN and END symbols. The BEGIN symbol is followed by declaration of the variables that pertain just to that block, and the declarations are followed by processing statements, which in turn are terminated by the END symbol. A processing statement may itself be compound; i.e., it may itself contain statements bound into a unit by a BEGIN END pair of symbols and containing their own local variables.

C is a procedure-structured language. A procedure is a specialized block with formal parameters and a name that is required and not optional. A block is executed where defined. A procedure may be executed anywhere it is recognized; i.e., within the scope of its definition and/or declarations.[9] Procedures in C must be individual; one procedure can not encompass the definition of another.

A procedure in C may be called before it is defined (its definition may be in another file), providing it is first declared to be a procedure by means of an extern statement. The type of variable returned by the procedure must be declared or is defaulted to an int. There is a specialized return statement, written with or without an arg. **return(v);** simultaneously terminates the procedure and returns to the calling function the result of evaluating some variable *v*. A function with multiple contingencies may have a separate return statement in each branch; if any one of them is encountered, the procedure terminates. If no return statement is written, it is implicit, with computed values undefined except in very simple cases.[10]

Languages such as Fortran make a distinction between procedures that are subroutines and procedures that are functions, based on whether the procedure returns the value of a

---

9 The definition of a procedure is its compilable code. The scope of the definition is from the beginning of the code to the end of the file in which the code resides. At a minimum, the declaration of a function is the assertion of its name, the type variable it returns and its logo, the paired parentheses (and). The scope of a declaration is from the declaration statement to the end of the file.

10 Such as the function *mult*() below. Even if *mult* returns no formal variable, **result = mult(first, second);** would likely have the correct value. But it is poor practice to assign to a variable the value of a function that does not formally return a value.

specified variable. C *does* not. In C all procedures are called functions. In C, the BEGIN and END delimiters are { and }. As in blocks, the { and } create a unit from a sequence of statements.

To flesh out our simplest C programming example:

```
main()                        /*Program execution starts at block named main.*/
    {
    int    new;               /*A definition.*/
    int old;                  /*Another definition.*/

    old = 3;                  /*An assignment statement.*/
    new = 2 * old;            /*Another assignment statement.*/
    }
```

The following is an example of a program composed of a sequence of two functions. In this example the variable *result* will be given the value of the dummy variable *e* when the statement **return(e);** is processed.

```
int mult(int c, int d)
    {
    int    e;

    e = c * d;
    return(e);
    }


main()                          /*The program starts at the block labeled main.*/
    {
    int    result      = 0,
           first       = 5,
           second      = 2;

    result = mult(first,second);
    }
```

1.2.2. FUNCTION FEATURES

A function in C is the equivalent of a subroutine in Fortran. In both languages the source code for a program can be spread among several files. However, in Fortran, within a single file, the main routine must precede the subroutines. In C, functions can both precede and follow the main function; C does not specify in which order functions are written. But, as noted, one, and only one, of these functions must be called *main*. It serves as the module that calls other functions in the order prescribed in the main block. In C a program starts at *main* and ends when *main* terminates.

All functions are automatically recursive, not just, as in Sail, those labeled recursive. A recursive function is one that may call itself and may call functions that call it.

Any lvalue data object and only an lvalue data object may serve as function argument. This is truly a treacherous statement. It is accurate, even though it appears to ignore the apparent use of arrays as args in the calling routine. Appearances aside, an array arg is treated as a pointer-to-array of type whatever. In a similar vein, functions may not be used as args; only pointers-to-function may. But there is nothing to prevent the programmer from using the name of the function as a pointer-to-function arg[11], as this example illustrates.

extern void FName(int num, char *numbuf, void (*NewName)(int , char *));

prototypes[12] a function called *FName* that has three args: an int, a pointer-to-char and a pointer-to-function. The third arg, *NewName*, points to a function that has two args and returns no value.

The definition of *FName* (i.e., the actual code) would include a statement using *NewName*. For example:

```
void FName(int num, char *numbuf, void (*NewName)(int , char *))
    {
    .........
    NewName(num,numbuf);
    }


void SuperFct(int a, int b)/*SuperFct() is a function that call FName().*/
    {
    char buf[10];
    ...........................
    FName(a+b, buf, stitoa);13
    printf("\nbuf = %s", buf);        /*PrintProduct: buf = 7*/
    ...........................
    }
```

---

11 Except in sizeof and unary & constructions, a function returning *type* is "converted to an expression that has type 'pointer to function returning *type*'". An array of *type* is implemented as a "..pointer to *type* that points to the initial element of the array object and is not an lvalue". See ANSI/ISO 9899-1990, p. 36. As a consequence, array and function names can function as what we might call constant pointers; i.e., they have some of the attributes of an ordinary pointer variable, including the ability to serve as function args. See also Sections 1.5.2 and 3.3.1.

12 To prototype a function is to declare its arg types. As in the prototype of the last variable *NewName*, only the types are necessary. The compiler ignores arg names, but they are useful cues for the programmer; e.g., *fname* for file name, *num* for number, and so forth.

13 *stitoa* is the name of an actual function and is prototyped as: **void stitoa(int , char *)**. Any function with a similar prototype—same number, types and order of function args; same return data type—would be an acceptable arg in *FName*. Like the library function *itoa*(), *stitoa* writes the character version of a number into a character array. Note that the name of the function *stitoa* serves as a pointer to the function *stitoa*(). Similarly, the name of the character array, *buf* serves as a pointer-to-char.

```
main()
    {
    int x = 3;
    int y = 4;
    SuperFct(x,y);
    }
```

A function may return a value or not. If it does, unless the data type returned is an int, the data type must accompany the function name; e.g., **float FName()**.... If *FName* returns no value, we would write **void FName()......** A function may only return a data object. A function, therefore, may not return a function but it may return a pointer to a function. Similarly a function may not return an array, but it may return a pointer to an array.

If a function contains no args and returns no value, we would write:

PROTOTYPE   **extern void FctName(void);**
DEFINITION   **void FctName(void) {..}**
USAGE   **FctName();**   /*Do NOT leave off the parens.*/

If the function contains args and returns values, we could write, as example:

PROTOTYPE   **extern char *FctName(char *pa, int b);**
DEFINITION   **char *FctName(char *pa, int b) {...}**
USAGE   **pb = FctName(pch, num);**

Function arguments are passed by value; that is to say, copies of the variables are faxed to the called function. The originals remain secreted at their home addresses. Within the called function, operations are performed that may change the values of these variables, but the original values of the variables remain undisturbed. Nevertheless, ordinarily, the outcome of passing an array is equivalent to passing by reference[14] because arrays are not passed as such; instead, a pointer to the memory address of the first element of the array is transmitted. Similarly, passing the name of a function is the same as passing the address of the function.

Functions generally have a fixed number of args. When indeterminacy is expected, in printf and scanf statements, the compiler handles the problem. Otherwise, there is a gothic construct called *va_arg* available to the programmer when a variable number of args is likely. Used in a loop, *va_arg* will handle one arg each call.

Function names may always be followed immediately by the left parenthesis. Alternatively, intervening spaces or tabs are permitted by many compilers; e.g., **main()** and **main ()** are equivalent. Whichever style is followed, consistency is helpful during debugging.

---

14 To pass an argument by reference means that the variable's address is passed to the called function, not just its value. So if the value of the variable is changed in the function, the change in value is permanent; i.e., the variable has this new value even after the function ends. See discussion beginning at Section 3.2.

1.2.3. MACROS

In addition to functions, C allows #define statements with arguments[15]. Called macros, these do what functions do. Though code size is increased, they are faster because they interfere less than do subroutines with the pipelined sequence of instructions. Nor do data types need to be specified for macro args.

The function *mult*() in Section 1.2.1 can be written as a macro with two args as:

#define mult(c,d) c * d

If this macro is substituted for the called procedure *mult*(), *main*() needs no modification.

```
main()
    {
    int    result,
           first,
           second;

    first = 5;
    second = 2;
    result = mult(first,second);
    }
```

result, first and *second* could just as easily be floats and still make use of the *mult*() macro. Like functions, macros permit local variables in the expanded definition.

#define CLRPCHAR(x) {char *pnew = x; while (*pnew) {*pnew = SNUL[16]; pnew++;}}

Unlike functions, macros may not contain explicit return statements; thus:

#define BADMACRO(x,y) {if (x < y) return (x); else return (y);}

Attempting to use a *return*() statement will result in warnings or in error messages depending on the compiler. Yet it is possible within a #define statement to use a function that has a return statement as part of its definition. For example, the library function *strcmp*(), compares two strings by ASCII values. It returns a zero if the args match; otherwise it returns the difference in value. If x is closer to the A end of the alphabet than y, the function will return a minus, as in this case.

#define LESS(x,y) (strcmp((x),(y)) < 0)
void main(void)
**   {**

---

15 A #define is a single statement text rewrite rule. In the simplest case, **#define x y** means that *x* is an alias for *y*, as in **#define NEWNUM 10**. The compiler will rewrite *y* where ever it finds *x* at the end of the preprocessing stage of compilation.

16 SNUL is #define'ed as '\0', ASCII zero, the char whose bits are all zeros. See *Notes on Zero*.

```
        char a[50] = "ABCD";
        char b[50] = "LMNO";
        if (LESS(a,b)) printf("a is less."); else printf("a is higher.");
        }
```

LESS may be #define'd before *strcmp*() is declared. Similarly, a set of macros functions may use each other without regard to the order in which the macros are listed.

```
#define ITALPHA(x) ( ((x) >= 'a' && (x) <= 'z') II ((x) >= 'A' && (x) <= 'Z') )
#define ITALPNUM(X) ( ITALPHA(x) II ITDIGIT(x) )
#define ITCONSONANT(x) ( ITALPHA(x) && (! ITVOWEL(x) ) )
#define ITDIGIT(x) ( (x) >= '0' && (x) <= '9' )
#define ITVOWEL(x) ((x)=='a'II(x)=='A'II(x)=='e'II(x)=='E'II \
        (x)=='i'II(x)=='I'II(x)=='o'II(x)=='O'II(x)=='u'II(x)=='U')
#define GET(x) ((x) = getchar())
#define GETIT(x) while ( ((x) = getchar()) != EOL )
```

#define'd macros are also useful for eliminating the need to write phrases that are the typing equivalents of tongue twisters, e.g., *GET(x)* and *GETIT(x)*, shown above. An example of usage is:

```
char        buf[20] = {SNUL};
int         c = SNUL;
int         i = 0;

printf("\nType some letters. Break with a <RETURN>");
while (GET(c) != EOL)[17]
        {
```

/*Next, if the variable *c* is a consonant, its value is assigned to the array element *buf*[i]; then *i* is incremented.*/

```
        if (ITCONSONANT(c)) buf[i++] = c;
        if (i == 10)
                break);
        }
```

1.2.4. BUILT-IN FUNCTIONS

Strictly speaking, except for *sizeof*, there are no built-in compile-time functions. Instead, C has what has been colorfully described as a toolkit; i.e., library functions that mimic built-ins. Coding may be machine specific, but each library function has particular args in a prescribed order. These can themselves be written in C and are portable except for the

---

17 If two operators are used with the same set of expressions, the precedence rules determine
   which operator is evaluated first. The equality operator **!=** is of higher precedence than
   the assignment operator = (see Table 1.8). So without parentheses, the system would first
   evaluate whether **getchar()** **!= EOL**, a 1 or 0 possibility. This 1 or 0 would then be
   assigned to *c*. EOL is the end-of-line value, '\n'.

parts that are machine-dependent. Such functions include input/output statements, string operations and data conversion from ASCII representation to numerical form and the reverse.

C compilers include a rich collection of library routines that input and output text and binary data under a variety of conditions. To move data to or from a file on disk, the system has first to make a connection to the file to control READING FROM it and/or WRITING TO it. **fopen("LexFile","r");** directs that a connection be established to read from a text file named *LexFile*. To both read from the file and also write to it is accomplished by a statement such as **fopen("LexFile","r+");**. Among the tasks involved in opening a file, the system creates an individual system struct of type _iobuf for the file. FILE (capitalized) is short for *struct of type _iobuf*. The struct for the particular file is user-transparent. It keeps track of such matters as whether the file is open for reading or writing or both, and the location of the next char to be read from or written to the file. Any library function that can command the opening of a file returns a pointer-to-FILE, i.e., the integer address of the struct. In analogy to the notion of *channel number*, this unique value can be used by system and user functions as readily as the file's name to identify that particular file as long as the file remains open. (In this book, we will frequently call the pointer-to-FILE associated with a particular file its channel number.)

The system reserves five such pointers-to-FILE: (1) *stdin* to connect to the standard input device, usually the keyboard; (2) *stdout* to connect to the standard output device, usually the screen; (3) *stderr* to write error messages, usually to the screen; (4) *stdaux* to connect to some auxiliary device; and (5) *stdprn* to connect to a printer. *stdin* and *stdout* can be redirected to other file. To calculate how many files can be open at one time in a program, these five 'files' must be deducted from the number allowed by the operating system. Handling peripheral devices as specialized files is an elegant idea that derives from UNIX.

Data move as a stream of characters to and from: (1) files on disk, (2) variables in memory and (3) peripheral devices, particularly screen and keyboard.[18]

The basic functions are machine-dependent but maintain the same syntax from compiler to compiler:

getchar()	READ an ASCII character FROM the keyboard
getc(fptr)	READ an ASCII char FROM a file whose channel number is *fptr*
putchar(c)	WRITE an ASCII character TO the screen
putc(c,fptr)	WRITE a char variable TO the file whose channel number is *fptr*

The *printf()* functions are WRITE TO functions. They copy the values of memory-resident variables to the display, to disk or to other variables.

---

18 C compilers currently have a large group of unbuffered UNIX-style I/O functions with integer file descriptors that are incompatible with buffered I/O functions. Unbuffered functions are not used in this book and will be ignored here.

printf(<text>,arg,...)   WRITE TO the display
fprintf(fptr,<text>,arg,...)   WRITE TO a file on disk
sprintf(&var,<text>,arg,...)   WRITE TO a char array in memory

The first arg in a *fprintf*() statement is the channel number of the disk file to which text will be written; in *sprintf*(), the first arg is the address of the character array in memory to which text will be written. *printf*() has no equivalent arg; one screen is assumed so it doesn't need to be identified. The second arg in *print*() and *sprintf*() and the first in *printf*() is text enclosed in double quotes. Within these quotes, the % symbol signals that a variable follows: **%i** or **%d** for int, **%o** for octal representation of ints, **%x** for hexadecimal; **%ld** for long, **%f** for float, **%c** for char, **%u** for unsigned and **%s** for a string array. Otherwise the text is output as written including spaces and tabs. The final args in any print function map memory-resident variables one by one to the % symbols. If the variable is a string, the name of the char array may serve as arg.

The *scanf*() functions are READ FROM functions. They read from keyboard, a memory variable or disk and deposit the values into memory variables.

scanf(<text>,&var,...)   READ FROM the keyboard
sscanf(&var,<text>,&var,...)   READ FROM a character array in memory
fscanf(fptr,<text>,&var,...)   READ FROM a file on disk

scanf(**"%s %d",&buf,&newnum**) transports a sequence of non-white characters from the keyboard to *buf* and converts a march of numerical ASCII characters bracketed by white space to a numerical value. Input values may be assigned to any memory variables that are active; i.e., a scanf statement within a function may access both external variables and the function's local variables.

The first arg in *sscanf*() is the address of the string in memory that is being read. The first arg in *fscanf*() is the channel number of the file being read. The first arg in *scanf*() and the second in *sscanf*() or *fscanf*() is a format statement that includes % symbols that assert the data types of the subsequent args, which are listed by address (e.g., not *newnum* but &*newnum*).

The following code opens two files on disk; reads text from the first file to an array located in memory; writes it from the array in memory to the screen and to another file; and closes the files. Note that *fscanf*() ignores initial white space and then reads in up to 29 characters. It stops prematurely at EOL or white space.

```
main()
    {
    FILE *fptr1, *fptr2;        /*Two channel numbers are defined.*/
    char wrd[30] = {SNUL};      /*A 30-char array in memory is defined and cleared.*/

    fptr1 = fopen("file1","r");    /*Returns the channel number for file1.*/
    fptr2 = fopen("file2","w");    /*Returns the channel number for file2.*/
    fscanf(fptr1,"%29s",&wrd);     /*Reads 29 chars from file 1 to wrd: wrd[0]:wrd[28]*/
    printf("%s",wrd);              /*Writes the text in wrd to the screen.*/
    fprintf(fptr2,"%s",wrd);       /*Writes the text in wrd to the 2nd file.*/
```

fclose(fptr1);   /*Closes the first file.*/[19]
fclose(fptr2);   /*Closes the second file.*/
}

1.3. NAMING C LANGUAGE OBJECTS

Language objects in C are identified by names that are unambiguously defined over the particular block, range of blocks, set of functions or set of files in which they are active. In general, names may be 31 characters long[20] if the file is not linked with another file. Variables or functions defined over several fiIes should be no longer than 6 significant characters. Identifiers must begin with a letter or the underscore character (_). The rest of the name is composed of letters, digits and underscore characters; for example: *in_2file* or *_newf10*. System libraries tend to use an initial _ to avoid duplicating names assigned by programmers.

C reserves a set of words called keywords, which may not be used as identifier names. For the most part, as Table 1.1 shows, these are data types, type modifiers, control directives, and a built-in function (sizeof).

asm	enum	short	
auto	extern	signed	
break	float	sizeof	
case	for	static	
char	fortran	struct	
const	goto	switch	
continue	if	typedef	
default	int	union	
do	long	unsigned	
double	register	void	
else	return	volatile	while

Table 1.1.   C-reserved keywords.

Names are case sensitive in most compilers, formally so in ANSI C. But it is poor practice to use the same word with different mixtures of upper and lower case to represent different

---

19 Files are automatically closed when a program ends, but it is still a good idea to close disk files explicitly.

20 The name may be any length, but ANSI compilers read only the first 31 characters.

entities. It is customary to write variable names in lower case; upper case names are reserved for macros, #define'd and typedef'ed expressions. Names, keywords and operators MUST be separated from each other by at least one white space character, except that a function name or macro name may be followed immediately by the left parenthesis.

1.3.1. NAMING FUNCTIONS

A function may have the same name as a static variable in some other file. It may have the same name as a local variable in some other function even in the same file[21], providing the function is not also called within that other function. (This may cause confusion to program readers, if not to the compiler.) A function may not have the same name as an external (global) variable; the compiler sees this as a redefinition. By eliminating a description of a system function's prototype, a function may use the name of a system function, but this is risky, unless it is certain the system function is not even indirectly involved in the program.

During recursion, when the same function calls itself repeatedly, the system creates different temporary names for the changing values of the recycling function arg. When the procedure finally halts, the program performs the indicated processing in reverse order. There had better be some break statement in the function such as **if (i < 20) RecursFct();** or the program will run as long as the machine is powered.

1.3.2. NAMING VARIABLES

The objects that procedures operate on are called variables. In a variable the identifying name persists while the value assigned to the identifier may change, depending on the operations performed on it within procedures.

Several variables may share a name, providing they are defined inside different functions or in separate blocks within a function or if they are members of different structs or if they serve as args in different functions. External static variables[22] may share a name with different external static variables in other files. There is no ambiguity even when the files are linked. Similarly, the name of a static global variable can be that of a dummy variable in some function in which the global variable is not used as such. (See Section 3.3.1, Method

---

21 Technically, when two or more language objects have the same name, it is called *overloading the name*. There's never conflict assigning the same name to a member of a particular struct type and a struct tag and an enum tag and a goto label and a preprocessor macro and a function. In this chapter, we call attention to some less obvious permitted overloadings.

22 An external static variable is a variable defined outside any function and known only within the file in which it is resident.

2, for an example.) When several variables of the same name are active in a particular block or function, the one defined in the innermost block is the one the program will process, thus:

```
void newfct(void)
    {/*OutsideBlock*/
    int       i = 0;                        /*Defines i as an int.*/
    char      call = SNUL;                  /*Defines call as a char.*/

    for (i = 1; i < 5; i++)                 /*Starts a loop with i = 1.*/
        {/*InsideBlock*/      /* Inside a loop: i is 70, call is 'd' (ASCII decimal 100).*/
        int   i = 70;                       /*Redefines i for InsideBlock only.*/
        char call  = (char)i + 30;          /*Redefines call for InsideBlock only.*/
        }/*InsideBlock*/
    call = (char)(i + 30);                  /*After looping: i is 5, so call is '#'.*/[23]
    }/*OutsideBlock*/
```

Names are case sensitive. As with other data objects, if the variable is used just in a single file or as a local variable in a function, it may have up to 31 significant characters; but if it is active over several files, so that linking of files is involved, it should be kept to 6 significant characters to make sure it will satisfy all compilers.

1.3.3. NAMING CONSTANTS

Any expression that can be variable can be constant; hence there are integer constants, long constants, character constants and, as a special case, string constants. Data types can be assigned constant values. Constant expressions can be given an alias by way of a #define statement. String constants are retained as written permanently. Named constants have the same size restrictions as do named variables. And the name need offer no clue that it is a constant and not a variable.

1.4.　THE PRIMITIVE DATA TYPES AND RELATED CONSTANTS

In C, how you are stored is what you are. Or as K&R put it, 'An object is a named region of storage;' (K&R, p. 197). The data types discussed in this section—chars, ints, floats and doubles—are primitives because they can be mapped directly to storage space; their storage

---

23 Note that casting (see Section 1.4.5.2) with (char)(i + 30) and (char)(i) + 30 are the same. But without the cast, the compiler may complain about data conversion from a larger sized variable to a smaller sized one.

requirements are well defined and exactly known. And they do not, like the pointer, need to be tied to another variable to be useful. They are not, like arrays, built from a sequence of primitive elements.

Defining the data type of a numerical variable determines the storage requirements of the assigned number; and the proper base representation is used at input and/or output. A local variable may be initialized with a constant expression.[24] It can also be assigned an expression if the expression's variables have values. In this example, *i* is defined first.

```
void call(void)
    {
    int    i = 10;
    char  cc = (char) i * 7/3 + 14;   /*PrintProduct: % */
    int    foo = 50*i - 4;            /*PrintProduct: 496 */
    }
```

The value of an external variable and the size of an external array MUST be a numerical constant. A numerical constant, though decimal representation is the default, may be 'coded' for both the data type and base; e.g., 01234UL is an octal unsigned long integer; 0X123.4F a hexadecimal single precision floating point number.

1.4.1. INT

The int in C is equivalent to the integer in Fortran. But C gives the programmer greater control over the size of variables. For example, 123L is read in as a long int, even though it is short in size.

ints may be qualified as short or long; so the integer types are: char, short int, int and long int. They are usually but not necessarily signed by default; i.e., they are capable of taking both positive or negative values. Writing **int newnum;** is the same as writing **signed int newnum;**. Consequently, if an unsigned int is desired, it must be stated; e.g., **unsigned int newnum;**. No absolute size checking is done by the compiler. Size of *int* is machine-dependent, but we can usually assume, in small machines, a short int and an int are both 2 bytes long and a long int is 4 bytes long, unless otherwise stated. On some machines an int and a short int are equal in size; on some an int equals a long int. If an integer constant is not explicitly labeled, it may be given the storage of the smallest integer data type that can hold it. When the incoming integer has a higher value than the largest possible short int, the machine may override instructions and store it as a long.

---

24 It seems appropriate to discuss constants together with variables in this section, even though this contradicts the definition of data types formulated in Section 1.1.2.

Octal constants begin with zero; e.g., 010. Hexadecimal constants in C begin with 0x or 0X; e.g. 0X10. Long integer values end in l or L, unsigned (where values are either zero or positive) integers in u or U, and unsigned long integers in ul or UL. 2343L is an example of a decimal constant considered as long. 02343U is an unsigned octal and 0x23343ul an unsigned long hexadecimal.[25] A 0 or 0x prefix signals what the base is. Appending L or U is useful when a constant is given an alias; e.g., #define NEWVAL 234ul. Otherwise, assigning the constant value to an lvalue integer variable labeled long or short or unsigned will force the value to the proper kind of integer.

In addition to the usual way of assigning a value to an int, e.g., **i = 3;** or **k = i = 3;** or **i = i+1;**, C provides idioms. One is **i++** as in **k = i++;**, which means that k takes the value of i and then i is incremented by 1. Another, **++i**, as in **k = ++i;**, means that i is incremented by 1 and then k is assigned this incremented value. Assignments such as **i = i++;**, although not illegal, are ambiguous; they should be avoided.

There are also arithmetic idioms. The format **(new lvalue) OPERATOR (right value)** is read as: **(new lvalue) = (current lvalue) OPERATOR (right value)**. The operators are **+=** as in **i += 1;** (another way of incrementing i by 1); **-=** as in **i -= 10;**, which is the same as **i = i-10;** the multiply operator, ***=**, as in **i *= y+5;**, which is the same as **i = i*(y+5);** and the divide operator, **/=**, as in **i /= y*2;**, which is the same as **i = i/(y*2);**.

1.4.2. CHAR

The character is the basic building block of text. The char is the basic data type that represents the text character. In string processing, the char variable is the basic unit. A char can be given a value; its value can be changed; it can be placed in sequence with other chars; its home can be entered; it can be relocated or copied to other locations.

A char is a 1-byte integer, whether it is declared signed or unsigned. A byte is 8 bits; so 4 chars can be compacted into a 32-bit machine word. A grouping of chars embodies the text and is the object of the available library string operations. Physically, a string is a bulk set of individual bytes stored sequentially in a memory region. Viewed as a data structure, a string is basically a uni-directional sequence of 1-byte elements in a character array (actually, a vector). Each symbol in the language has a unique encoding.

When C was developed, it assumed a 7-bit character set for expressing all of C's code and all the data on which the programs would operate. The set of 128 different bit patterns that can be created with 7 bits is sufficient to represent all the upper- and lower-case letters, digits and punctuation used in the English language. Seven bits is even enough to provide representation for control characters used as meta characters and as printing operators. Many C library routines are designed to work particularly well with symbols coded in 7-bit

---

25 Note that general programs to extract numbers from text can not rely on scanning for digits 1-9 as this example, shown in K&R, p. 37, makes clear: **0xful** is 15 in long unsigned hexadecimal.

ASCII, in which the notion that '2' follows '1' and 'b' follows 'a' in the character set is ingrained. Using 8 bits (a single unsigned byte) doubles the number of available representations, making it possible to map a variety of graphical characters as well as to mimic specialized characters in other languages—the accent grave in French, the umlaut in German.

Geographic differences have had more profound consequences on the expansion of C than simply the addition of a few symbols. A new set of library procedures prototyped in *locale.h* deals with differences in the way time is expressed, currency and other numeric information written. The down-side of this expansion is that in alphabetizing or otherwise sorting a set of strings, we can no longer take ordinary collation rules for mapping characters (i.e., English dictionary order and ASCII representation order) for granted. As example, procedures for erasing bracketed text from a string can no longer necessarily take advantage of the fact that if the left bracket is greater than or equal to ASCII '<', then the matching right bracket is the left char's ASCII value plus 2.

Even an 8-bit character set is insufficient to represent the multiplicity of symbols in languages such as Kanji[26]. ANSI C supports wide-character individual characters and wide-character string constants, both of which are typed as **wchar_t**, rather than as **char**; the definition of wchar_t is in *stddef.h*. The transition is not seamless. It involves the use of an extended syntax for encoding, in that wide-character types require an initial L and an elaborate mapping. Transmitting wide characters to output devices that read character streams one byte at a time is jury-rigged. Specifically, wide characters are written in multibyte character format and a multibyte character set is very much implementation-specific; the major requirement being that a system be able to hold the largest extended character set of all the locales supported. Dealing with multibyte characters also means accepting the disturbing fact that a familiar I/O library function that only affected a discrete byte under all conditions may now *en passant* be manipulating other data objects as well. How other bytes are affected depends on how an initial byte of the extended character is interpreted. Ordinary string constants and wide-character arrays can not be amalgamated into a single entity.

In this book we will for the most part assume standard 1-byte ASCII representation.

1.4.2.1.   Char Constant.

C uses single quote marks to bracket char constants. A char constant is an enclosed: (1) ordinary character (decimal ASCII zero to 127); or (2) character in a backslash format.

Examples of backslash notation are:

char eop = '\014';   /*The End Of Page or form feed in octal.*/

---

26 Thanks are due to Dr. Xiaowei Sherwin Yang of Cambridge Research Associates, McLean, VA, for a critical reading of this section.

char eop = '\xC';   /*The End Of Page or form feed in hex.*/
char eop = '\f';   /*The End Of Page or form feed in backslash idiom.*/

Any single character may be made special by using its ASCII octal code following the backslash; e.g., **'\051'** is the code for the character 3. Hexadecimal equivalents of octal values are written with an **x** following the backslash, not **0X**.

The backslash also provides a simple means to indicate special characters such as the space, tab and underscore. In this format, the backslash and the character that follows it are counted as a single character during string operations. Some will be taken as meta commands in print statements; these include **\n**, which forces a new line, and **\t**, which produces a tab. The **\f**, on the other hand, just writes a form feed symbol that later is a command to the hard copy printer. The backslash constants are listed in Table 1.2. The **\?** is only necessary when a string literal contains a double ? that might be confused with the start of a trigraph character[27].

\a	is sound alert	****	is line continuation
\b	is the backspace	****	is the backslash
\r	is the carriage return	**\t**	is the horizontal tab
\v	is the vertical tab	**\?**	is the question mark
\'	is a literal single quote	**\"**	is a literal double quote
\f	is the form feed	**\n**	is NewLine

Table 1.2.   Backslash character constants.

If \ isn't followed by a recognized character, it will be ignored. The single \ acts as a concatenate symbol in a string constant written across two lines as in:

printf("\nfirst half of str
ing. second half\n");

It is probably more convenient to use the newer method of concatenating parts of string constants into a single string.

printf("\nfirst half of str"
**   "ing. second half\n");**

Either format would display the following on the screen:

first half of string. second half.

---

27 ANSI C recognizes a minimal C character set that lacks symbols such as the tilde. A trigraph sequence is a double question mark followed by a character available in the set. For the tilde it is **??-**. So **"ABC??-"** prints as **ABC~**. String processing could happily do without the trigraph construct.

1.4.2.2.   Char Variable.

Chars are defaulted to signed or unsigned, depending on the system. We can specify whether a particular char is signed or unsigned. For either signed or unsigned chars, the basic characters represented by ASCII zero to 127 are guaranteed to be positive. Signed chars may take values between -127 and 127. Objects in the signed char other than the basic set are implementation-dependent. For printing graphics, the char should be declared unsigned (positive values only), so that it can take ASCII values from 0 to 255.

A char variable is initialized by giving it the value of a char constant or of another char variable or of a cast'ed integer expression. A char can be emptied by assigning it the value \0; i.e., **char new = SNUL;**.

A char should be treated as a signed integer when reading characters from a file, so that a single character can be compared to EOF, the end-of-file value, which is usually written as **-1**. Chars once were automatically converted to ints when used as function args. Since ANSI C was adopted, this is no longer necessarily true, so the char function arg should be specifically cast to an int. Alternatively, the character that tests for EOF can be declared as an local int variable, thus:

```
void ReadStoreChars(void)
    {
    FILE *inchn = fopen("data", "r");
    int    ch = 0;
    char buf[LRGSZE] = {SNUL};          /*A home for the incoming chars.*/
    int    i = 0;

    while (ch = getc(inchn))            /*stops at line a below.*/
        {
        if (ch == EOF)                  /*Triggers action to stop the character stream.*/
            break;                                              /*a*/
        else buf[i++] = (char) ch;
        }
    printf("\n%s",buf);
    fclose(inchn);
    }
```

Each letter, digit and punctuation mark has a unique representation in ASCII notation. But to ensure exportability to machines using other mappings, char notation (e.g., **'A','0', '$'**) should be used whenever possible, rather than the corresponding ASCII value.

1.4.3. FLOAT AND DOUBLE

The C *float* is a single precision floating point number and is equivalent to the Fortran Real*4. The C *double* is a double precision floating point value and is the equivalent of the Fortran Real*8. The long double is a new construct in C that extends precision. Assume a floating point number is 4 bytes and a double is twice as long. But float, double and long double may be the same size or three separate sizes with float the smallest, long double the largest, without violating ANSI C requirements, because representations of floating point numbers differ on different machines.

The E format, which writes floating point numbers with exponents in Fortran (e.g., +1234.5E-1), and the F format, which has only the decimal (e.g., 123.450000), are lumped as *float* in C. Floating point constants ending in **f** or **F** are typed float, those ending in **l** or **L** are long doubles—the decimal point and/or **E** makes it clear this is a floating point number, not an long int. Unspecified float constants default to double.

1.4.4. SIZES OF SIMPLE DATA TYPES

Table 1.3. lists the sizes to expect for the different variables on current machines.

signed	char	1 byte	-127 : 127
unsigned	char	1 byte	0 : 255
	int	2 bytes	-32767 : 32767
short		2 bytes	-32767 : 32767
unsigned	short	2 bytes	0 : 65535
long	int	4 bytes	-2147483647 : 2147483647
unsigned	long	4 bytes	0 : 4294967295
float		4 bytes	~ -3.4E-38 : 3.4E38 (7 digit precision)
double		8 bytes	1.797E-308 : 1.797E308

Table 1.3.   Likely sizes of variable types.

1.4.5. CONVERSIONS OF SIMPLE DATA TYPES

1.4.5.1.   Automatic Conversions.

Conversions are automatic in: (1) assignment statements; (2) expression evaluation; and (3) function arg transmission; i.e., in functions with char and float args, chars are handled as ints, floats as doubles.[28] The data type returned by a function must be of the type stipulated by the prototype or to int by default. But before the variable is returned to the calling function, the compiler attempts (and usually succeeds) to convert it to the type of the variable to which it is assigned. Even so, it is never wrong to make the conversion explicit by casting when the variable returned by the function is of different type than the lvalue (See Section 1.4.5.2 on casting.) This is particularly true for pointers to the various types.

---

28 In ANSI C chars and floats are not expanded if the function is prototyped. Knowing what the arg types are also makes it possible for the compiler to attempt to convert the actual variables in the calling function to the types demanded by the function.

Ordinarily, if a char is changed to an int and is then changed back to a char, there is no change in the char. However, if a char is changed to an int and the value of the int is increased over 255 for an unsigned char or over 127 for a signed char, the compiler must decide how to change the value when the int is changed back to a char. Usually, the high order bits are dropped, leaving a value within the char range. Indeed, C guarantees that the reincarnated char will have a non negative value. However, during the time the char is assigned to int space, it suffers the hazards of unstandardized system implementations of the int; i.e., depending on how high order bits are treated on the particular machine, the int may be positive or negative and the bit patterns will of course differ.

A float arg used to be automatically handled as a double but it may now be declared as a float and not be converted, unless it is processed together with another operand that is a double. An unspecified floating point number still defaults to a double.

In general, the interactions of two operands of different signs is complicated. Table 1.4 summarizes conversion rules when an arithmetic operation involves disparate variables. It is based on Section A6.5, K&R, p. 198.

---

v1 and *v2* are two operands. *v1* is a data type that uses less storage that *v2*.

CONVERTO means *is converted to a*

if (v2 == long double)	v1 CONVERTO long double;
else if (v2 == double)	v1 CONVERTO double;
else if (v2 == float)	v1 CONVERTO float;
else if (v2 == unsigned long int)	v1 CONVERTO unsigned long int;
else if (v2 == long>max unsigned int)	unsigned int v1 CONVERTO long[29];
else if (v2 == long int)	v1 CONVERTO long;
else if (v2 == unsigned int)	v1 CONVERTO unsigned int;
else /*default*/	{v1 CONVERTO int; v2 CONVERTO int}

Table 1.4.   Automatic arithmetic data type conversions.

Examples.

(1) **if ((v1 == char || v1 == short) && v2 == int) v1 CONVERTO int**

(2) **if (v1 == float && v2 == double) v1 CONVERTO double**

If a float is forced to an int and then changed back, it is truncated. The chopped float must be no larger than available integer space and ensuring that this is so is the programmer's responsibility. A double is converted to a float by rounding or by truncation, depending on implementation. A float converted to a double and then back again to a float is unchanged. A long int is converted to a char/int by dropping high order bits.

---

29 if (v2 == long) on a machine in which the long int can not represent all values of an unsigned int, both v2 and v1 are converted to unsigned long ints.

In calling a function with parameters, the proper data types must be used as instantiators of the args. Faced with wrong data types, the compiler usually issues what seems a mild warning (such as: 'data conversion'). But, as example, using a short integer as a counter, when a long integer is needed, could prove ruinous during the execution of the program. A short integer on PC's has a maximum value of 32767 or two bytes. So after the 32767th record of a database, the program will partially recycle the count and do interesting binary conversions, but the count of the total number of records in the database is guaranteed to be wrong.

(3) Conversions within a *printf* statement.

When a value is defined as a char, it can be printed out using the *printf()* statement with its character value (%c) or with its octal value(%o), or with its decimal value (%d). However, neither an int nor a char will convert to a string (%s). A %f will print a float as a double.

(4) The if-else triad converts to the highest storage required.

rez = e1 ? e2 : e3

Suppose e2 is a float and e3 is an integer. If e1 is false, we might expect e3 and therefore rez to be integer. But e3 is changed to a float before e2 is evaluated.

1.4.5.2.   Casting.

In C, the programmer has the ability to use a variable other than the type expected in the function arg by casting the variable as the required data type; i.e., by doing an explicit conversion. Casting is a UNARY operation. The arg for the library function *sqrt()* should be a double. So the int *n* is cast as a double, thus:

int n = 435;
int rez;
rez = sqrt((double) n);

sqrt() return a doubles and *rez* is an int. This might be sufficient to convert the returned double to an int. Or the compiler might issue a warning about the data conversion. To prevent warning messages, this following cast would force the double calculated in the function to an int.

rez = (int) sqrt((double) n);   /*PrintProduct: rez = 20*/

There is no change in the storage type of *n* or of the actual value of *n* because C passes function args by value, unless *n* is assigned the value of the evaluated function. In the next example, *n* is permanently changed, because it is assigned the result of processing *sqrt*(n).

n = (int) sqrt((double)n);

Casting a char to an int and back obeys the same rules as does the automatic conversion of a char to an int and back.

Note that pointers (see Section 1.5.2) of different types need to be cast to the proper type. In ANSI C a function such as *malloc()* that can serve various data objects is written canonically as (void *). When used for a particular data type it is cast to the specific pointer-to-data type.

1.5. COMPOUND OR DERIVED DATA TYPES AND RELATED CONSTANTS

This section deals with compound data types and other derived types. The data structures of major importance to string processing are in this group: the character array and the struct, together with the pointer-to-char and the pointer-to-struct. The struct and union have rules for the struct gestalt independent of the rules for the individual members, but in many string operations they must be responsive to the data types of their members.

A compound variable can not be recast into another data type. Pointers are also derived types. Not only can they be cast from one pointer type to another, much of programming revolves around converting the pointer returned by a function to the needed pointer type. This is particularly true when using the dynamic allocation functions. The enum type, a set of integer constants, which syntactically resembles the struct and union class constructs, is also discussed in this section.

1.5.1. ENUM

An enumeration is a set of integer values. An enum has some of the flavor of a compound type such as the struct, in that a class name is given to a set of ordered members. Moreover, in ANSI C, each distinct enum is a different enumerated type, just as each struct of a particular type is distinct from structs of another type. But an enum is a set of constants, not variables. The enum construct is a named set of ordered integer constants, where the first int is equal to zero, unless assigned a different value, and each int in the list is automatically incremented by one unless specifically given a value. Defining an variable as related to the construct, such as enum winter *coldmos* in our example below, does not produce a replica of the enum complete with storage. Instead, *coldmos* is an integer variable that may be assigned any single value of the enum set.

```
enum team     {jane = 1, martha, edith, may} morning = jane, evening;
enum winter   {december = 12, january = 1, february};
enum winter   coldmos;
```

In the first example, an enum of type team is declared with four values: 1,2,3,4. By *declared* we mean a template has been created but no storage is assigned. At the same time, two enum variables of type team are defined, *morning* and *evening. morning* has been initialized, evening has not but it may be assigned any of the values of the template enum; e.g., **evening = may;** would give it the value of 4. Once assigned a value, it may used in any appropriate construction—the construction needs to be appropriate, not the semantics; e.g.

while (evening > jane) evening--;   /*Final PrintProduct: 1*/

winter is another enum. In a separate statement, *coldmos* is defined as an enum variable of type winter. It may be assigned the value of any member of enum *winter*.

```
float mos;
coldmos = december;
mos = (float) coldmos;              /*PrintProduct: 12.000000*/
```

Unfortunately or not, enums are not checked, so an enum variable may suddenly acquire a value not among the enum set without raising an alarm. In the following example, coldmos is incremented to 13, which is out of the range of the enum.

```
if (december == 12)
     coldmos = december;
coldmos++;                          /*coldmos is now equal to 13.*/
```

In text processing, enum constructions are valuable in case statements to direct processing by task or menu item. They do away with having to define each int constant separately. And if a new member is inserted into an enum class, its value is automatically assigned. These #define statements:

```
#define add         1
#define alphabetize 2
#define delete      3
     and so forth
```

can be replaced by:

```
enum whattask {add = 1,alphabetize, check, delete, index, label, merge, rearrange,
sort, search, update} task = add;

switch(task)          /*task was assigned the value 1*/
     {
     case delete:     {printf("\nIn delete");break;}
     case add:        {printf("\nIn add");break;}
     /*....and so forth.......*/
     }
```

1.5.2. POINTER

A pointer points to a language object: to a char, to an int, to the first byte of an array, to the start of a struct, to the beginning of a function. A pointer is not classed as a primitive data type. It holds an integer value corresponding to the entire address of a simple data object or to the address of the first element of a C compound language object.[30]

---

30 This definition emphasizes that a variable pointer always points to a single element, not to an entire array. C print notation is idiomatic. If **pa = &a[0];**, either **printf("%s",a);** or **printf("%s",pa);** will print out the chars from *pa* to the terminal SNUL in an implicit loop. But *pa* does not point to the entire array.

The pointer is discussed with the compound data types because of its close association with arrays. In string processing, we are particularly interested in its linkage to the character array. Even when the pointer points to simple data types, the interest is (usually) in processing the variable to which the pointer points, not in the pointer itself.

A pointer is itself a variable, a variable whose value is the address of some other variable. Go to the address stored in the pointer and there is the variable of interest. Two special symbols, **&** and *, are used to handle the relationship between a pointer and the variable to which it points. Loosely, **&v** means **the address of v** and *p means **the variable pointed to by p** (see USAGE in Table 1.5). Writing and interpreting the local or global definition of a pointer requires acclimation. Table 1.5 shows how to define a pointer to an int (*pi*), a pointer to a char (*pa*) and a pointer to a struct (*ps*).

DEFINITION:	int i;	char a[10];	struct nm new;
DEFINITION:	int *pi;	char *pa;	struct nm *ps;
USAGE:	i = *pi;	a[0] = *pa;	new = *ps;
USAGE:	pi = &i;	pa = &a[0];	ps = &new;

Table 1.5.   Relationship of pointers and their data objects

The only allowable arithmetic operations on pointers are those that: (1) measure the number of units between two pointers that point to the same data object, e.g., **pa = pb** or **pa - pb**; or (2) find the address of a pointer some number of units distance from the reference pointer, e.g., **pa+i** or **pa-i**. Note that in the second case, *pa+2* will access an address two units from *pa*, no matter whether *pa* is a pointer-to-int, a pointer-to-char or a pointer-to-struct. The system's housekeeping services keep track of the number of bytes it takes to move a pointer to the next element, independent of data type. On the surface, if a pointer is an address, it seems illogical to force a pointer to be identified as pointing to a particular data type. But different data types take different amounts of storage, so the program needs to know what kind of pointer it is dealing with to move the pointer from one element of a particular array to the next.

To pass an array to a function, the compiler transmits a pointer that has been assigned the address of the first element of the stored array. If *a* is an array and *pa* is a pointer-to-char, then **pa = &a[0];** means that the value of *pa* is the address of *a*[0]. Given that *pa* is anchored to the top of the array, any element of the array may be accessed through an offset of *pa*. For example, the 8th array element, *a[7]*, may be accessed through *pa+7*. *a[7]* is the same element as *(pa+7)*. So either **a[7] = 12;** or *(pa+7) = 12;** will assign the value 12 to the 8th character element of the array. Symmetrically, *pa+7* contains the address of *a*[7]; *pa+7* and *&a[7]* are two ways of writing the address of the 8th element of the array. A pointer can also be assigned or reassigned directly to any array element; e.g., **pa = &a[7];**. In addition, C has an idiom using the name of the array so that **pa = a;** is the same as **pa = &a[0];** but this format can only be used to assign the pointer to the top of the array.

Arrays in C are virtual in that the concept of an array is conventional but access to array elements is actually in terms of offsets. In other words, an array element may be thought of as being one element after another array element or as one element before the next array element but the system handles it as the contents of an address that is an offset from the address of the start of the array. This means we can write **a[7] = 'Z';** or ***(a+7) = 'Z';**. Both mean: **the value of the 8th element is the contents of the element that is 7 units from the first element of the array a**. Or more generally, **a[i] == *(a+i)**. Applying the address operator **&** to both sides results in another identity: **&a[i] == a+i**. Using similar notions, a defined pointer-to-char such as *pa* may be set to the actual value of the 8th element of the array by writing ***(pa+7)** or **pa[7];** or more generally, **pa[i] == *(pa+i)**.

ROW 1:	a[i]	I	*(a + i)	I	*(pa + i)	I	pa[i]
ROW 2:	&a[i]	I	a + i	I	pa + i	I	&pa[i][31]

Table 1.6.   Ways of indicating pointers and array elements.

In sum, in Table 1.6, formats in row 1 all describe an element i units from the top of the array *a* and row 2 formats are ways of writing the associated pointer to the element i units from the top of the array.

The *pa*[i] form is of particular interest. We have been insisting that arrays are submitted to functions as pointers. So how do we make sense of this function adapted from K&R, p. 29, which not only seems to be transmitting two char arrays, *to* and *from*, but assigning values to array members *to*[i] and *from*[i]. In actuality, *to* and *from* act as pointers that point to the beginnings of their respective arrays. And *to*[i] and *from*[i] are not array elements but subscripted pointers that function as array elements; i.e., the *pa*[i] format defined above.

```
void copy(char to[], char from[])
    {
    int    i = 0;
    while ((to[i] = from[i]) != SNUL)              /*a*/
        i++;
    }
```

A popular use of the pointer-to-char is to: (1) point to an array element; (2) copy that character to an element in some other array (as in line *a* above); (3) move the pointer to the next element; and (4) possibly move an element onward in the output array. These steps can be done in C with a single statement as in line *b* in this next function, which rids a string of tabs and NewLine's.

```
void cleanb(char *st)      /*The arg st is a pointer-to-char holding the address of the*/
    {                      /* source string.*/
    char buf[100] = {SNUL};   /*buf will store the accumulating clean string.*/
    int    i = 0;
```

/*Note that the null pointer constant in C is written as NULL. It is defined in *stddef.h* as 0, 0L or (void *)0, depending on implementation. Hence, for universality it is written as NULL rather than as a character value. C guarantees NULL is never a valid memory address for

---

31 For example: **static char a[6] = "12345"; char *pa = a; printf("%s",&pa[2]);** would display **345**.

data; i.e., a pointer whose value is NULL is not pointing to any language object in memory. So functions that return a pointer to a memory location can return NULL to signal error or malfunction.*/

```
char *p = NULL;      /* p is defined as a yet unassigned pointer-to-char.*/
p = st;              /*p points to where st does, to the first character in the array.*/
```

/*This next line starts a loop in which st is incremented one character each cycle. It will continue until st points to the terminal SNUL in the source string. Line a makes the condition: if the character pointed to by st is neither a tab or a NewLine...*/

```
while (*st)
    if (*st != '\t' && *st != '\n')            /*a*/
```

/*In the next line, a buf element is filled with the character to which st points. Then st is incremented by 1, as is i, so that st points to the next character in the source string and buf[i] is the next character in the destination string.^{32}*/

```
        buf[i++] = *st++;                      /*b*/
            else st++; /*The if test in line a failed but st still needs to move to the next char.*/
    buf[i] = SNUL;  /*SNUL marks the end of a string.*/
```

/*The next statements show a way of sending back a clean version of the input string: the cleaned string is copied to the start of the array; i.e., to where st initially pointed. We first regain st's original value (the address of the top of the array), which we stored in p during initialization. Then we copy the cleaned string to it.*/

```
    st = p;
    strcpy(st,buf);
    }
```

As an example of usage:

```
char str[10] = {SNUL};                          /*c*/
strcpy(str, "\t\t\tH\t\tI");
cleantb(str);
printf("\n%s",str);          /*PrintProduct: HI*/
```

When the array *str* is defined in line *c*, the compiler does two things: (1) it allocates array space and (2) it creates a pointer, *str*, that we may think of a constant pointer, in that the name of the array *per se* is a constant and may not be incremented; e.g., we may not write **str++;**. The name can, however, be used (without size dimension) as a function arg. Inside the function, it is treated as a variable pointer; i.e., the name of the array is used as a pointer to the first array element. In this example, *cleantb*() is handed the address in memory of *str*[0]—the value of the pointer arg *str* is a memory address, specifically, it is the starting address of the character array *str*. This may sound schizophrenic, but it works.

---

32 ++ and * are equipotent and associate from right to left. ***++st** increments the pointer and then examines the contents at the new pointer position. But **(*st)++** or **++*st** increments the character pointed to by *st*; e.g., the letter d would become e. Similarly, ***st--** and ***--st** decrement the pointer, while **(*st)--** or **--*st** decrease the value of the character to which *st* points.

Indirect addressing through pointers allows the programmer easily to probe any data structure. It is one of C's strongest features. On the other hand, using pointers properly requires discipline. They can point anywhere. It seems to take no effort to point to unintended portions of memory. When combined with the ease with which array borders can be breached, pointer facility can prove fatal. Local pointers should either be assigned immediately or be NULL'ed immediately upon entering a procedure, even if (particularly if) they are likely to be assigned in some inner block. During the procedure, if the object referenced by the pointer is deleted, the pointer should be NULL'ed.

External static pointers are often used for variable continuity, hence they are not often deleted. But problems may arise when a second pointer is assigned to the same variable, perhaps during a called procedure. Pointers to dynamically stored arrays are often troublesome, especially when the pointer becomes a function arg to a function arg to a function arg, threading its way through a hierarchy of called functions.

When dynamic memory allocation (see Section 2.5.2) is requested, either allocation function, *calloc*() or *malloc*()[33], returns the memory address of the start of the block where the system has stored the reference data object. The formal prototype for the allocation function, *malloc*() is:

void *malloc(size_t);

where size_t is typedef'ed as an *unsigned integer*. The specific integer data type is specified in the *stddef.h* include file. The MS compiler for DOS defines size_t as an unsigned int. In ANSI C the void pointer, (void *), is the neutral interface, replacing (char *) as generic pointer cast. The (void *) cast is capable of pointing to any type variable, capable of being assigned to or compared with any type of pointer in a relational expression. This said, it should also be noted that void pointers have no built-in information on data type, so they can't be directly dereferenced and the rules for pointer arithmetic can't be applied. To use the function, the returned pointer is cast to the data type of the pointer used; e.g.

int   *pnum;
pnum = (int *) malloc(50);

would reserve space in memory for 50 integers. *pnum* points to the start of this space. Similarly, if *psave* were defined as some other type of pointer, a pointer-to-struct of type EXAMINE, say, then (struct EXAMINE *) would serve as pointer cast. The pointer-to-char is the pointer of major importance for string processing.

If *psave* is a pointer-to-char and *s* is the string array to be stored by the system, the calloc allocation function can be written as:

psave = (char *) calloc((unsigned) strlen(s)+1, (unsigned) sizeof(char));

---

33 *calloc*() and *malloc*() provide the same service. *calloc*() is safer than *malloc*() for string processing because the space is initialized to zero.

1.5.3. ARRAY

An array is a sequence of variables with a common name. More accurately, an array is a sequence of variables of the same data type, where the variables do not have individual names but are identified through the array name. The lower limit of an array in C is always 0, NOT 1. If a is the array name, $a[0]$ is always the first element (i.e., an element is a single variable but partakes of the group identification), $a[1]$ is the second element of the array, and so on. The location of any element relative to the first element in the array is built in to the element identifier; e.g., $a[5]$ is 5 elements past the first element of the array a, consequently it is the sixth element of the array. An array may be a group of ints, floats, chars, pointers, structs, or unions. It may not be a group of functions. The value of an array element may be any value appropriate to the array type.

An array is not a primary data type. An array element is. If a is an integer array, **a[10] = 7;** means the 11th element in a is an int with value 7. Defining and initializing a as **int a[100] = {0};** means the array a can store up to 100 integer variables, from $a[0]$ to $a[99]$; all the elements of a have been assigned a value of zero. There is no element $a[100]$. Except for char arrays, all one-dimensional (1D) arrays can store items from $a[0]$ to $a[n-1]$, where n is the size of a. A character array can store value in $a[0]$ to $a[n-2]$. $a[n-1]$ is reserved for the terminal SNUL, if all elements are filled. An array element is denoted by its location within the vector in a 1D array or by tracking systematically through n vectors for n-dimensional arrays. There is an imposed order such that $a[1]$ comes before $a[2]$, $a[1,3]$ comes before $a[1,4]$.

Because arrays may involve large amount of data, instead of passing a copy of the array to the function, the program passes the address of the first element of the array to the function. And all array elements are accessed as offsets to this starting address. Therefore, even though function calls are by value, the end result in this case is the equivalent of a call by reference—with a copy of an address available to it, the function can change the value residing at that address permanently.

The compiler takes care of scaling; i.e., it takes into account the storage requirement of the data type when an array element is incremented by one. To increment a vector element by one means to shift from examining the variable $a[3]$, say, to examining the variable $a[4]$; or more precisely, to move from the address of the element 3 units after the first element of the array to the address of the element 4 units away.

There are major conceptual differences between *array* in C and *array* in other languages, differences that tend to discourage the use of multidimensional arrays. In C, arrays are viewed as vectors, not as matrices. By definition, a vector is a 1D array. Multidimensional arrays may be visualized as adjacent vectors where the elements of the far left vector point to the next right vector and so forth. Each element of the first vector points to a separate vector; each element of this second vector points to a separate vector, and so forth. Suppose an array a that is 3 by 4 by 2, i.e., $a[3,4,2]$; and 4 pointers, $p0$, $p1$, $p2$ and $p3$. How, mimicking the program, would we access the last element in the array, $a[2,3,1]$, or in C vector notation, $a[2][3][1]$?

We begin with *p0*, where **p0 = &a[0][0][0];**. In our example, the first vector has 3 elements. The last element of the first vector begins the last row, in matrix terms.

p1 = p0 + 2   p1 points to the last element in the first vector; i.e., to the start of the last row of the matrix (the cell with the value 18).

p2 = p1 + 3   p2 points to the last column of the last row. It points to the last element within the 2nd vector (the cell with the value 21).

p3 = p2 + 1   p3 points to the correct element within the 3rd vector.

*p3 is **a[2][3][1]**.

Table 1.7 is an example of a 3 by 4 by 2 array, shown with values for the first two dimensions and a single 3rd dimension vector. The elements of the first vector are valued at 10,14,18. The element whose value is 18 points to a row vector whose elements are valued at 18, 19, 20, 21. The element whose column value is 21 points to the vector whose elements are valued at 21, 22.

row 0:	**10**	**11**	**12**	**13**	
row 1:	**14**	**15**	**16**	**17**	
row 2:	**18**	**19**	**20**	**21**	
					22

Table 1.7.   An example of a 3 by 4 by 2 array.

In our example, *a*[2][3][1] is 22.

We have been illustrating how arrays are conceptually structured as vectors. In actuality, all the array elements are stored sequentially. The compiler maps this list to the conceptual structure. The critical information for the system is how many memory slots to make available between elements of the first vector. In our example, the distance from p0+0 to p0+1 is 4*2 elements, the sizes of the 2nd and 3rd vectors. Given a list of values, the system would store the first number in *a*[0][0][0], the second in *a*[0][0][1] then in *a*[0][1][0] (the cell with the value 11), then in *a*[0][1][1], then in *a*[0][2][0] (the cell with the value 12), and so forth through *a*[0][3][1]. If there are unused numbers, it would start another module of 8 slots, beginning with *a*[1][0][0] (conceptually, the 2nd element of the 1st vector). For this operation, it does not need to know the dimension of the first vector, so *a*[3][4][2] may as easily be written as *a*[][4][2] or (**a*)[4][2].[34] The complete storage mapping function in our example is **(3-1)*4*2 + (4-1)*2 + 2**. In more general terms, if the array *a* is sized at [i][j][k], then the last element, *a*[i-1][j-1][k-1], is calculated to be in the (i-1)*j*k + (j-1)*k + k th position, where the element *a*[0][0][0] is in the first position.

In sum, to access an element of a multidimensional array, its location can not be given relative to the corner element of the array. Instead, a pointer must be accessed for each dimension of the array. The correct element of the leftmost vector must be calculated, then

---

34 In Fortran, the left column varies most rapidly (storage by column). In C, the rightmost vector varies most rapidly (storage by row, as in Pascal and Sail.)

the left+1 vector element, and so forth, and the array element located from this. Thus, while *A[i,j,k,l]* denotes a single cell in a 4-dimensional matrix, the closest equivalent in C is *A[i][j][k][l]*, which denotes accesses to four separate vectors to get at the single cell. This access has no relationship to the mathematical concept of matrix. Rather, the overriding emphasis appears to be on storage considerations. This unduly complicates the programmer's task of algorithm translation, while making the compiler's task easier.

1.5.4. STRING CONSTANT

A string constant is a set of characters and/or backslashed ASCII symbols enclosed in double quotes and stored by the compiler as written, including white space and control characters[35]. Endowed with static storage, string constants are retained for the life of the program, but whether two identical string literals are distinct is implementation-dependent. ANSI C explicitly frowns on tampering with the contents of a string constant. It does, however, foster the concatenating of neighboring string constants[36].

Defined character arrays may be initialized by a string literal in a single assignment[37], the same way that an integer is initialized by an int constant. Or the string constant can be accessed through a defined pointer.

char keep[] = "Error. Redo";   /*Initializing an array.*/
char *pkeep = "Error. Redo";   /*The pointer holds the address of the string literal.*/

A unnamed string constant can serve in a *printf* statement such as: **printf("Error. Redo.\n")**; or in a #define statement: **#define ERRPR printf("Error. Redo.\n")**. More generally, the quoted character string can be used as a function arg whenever the function calls for a string.

When a string constant is defined, as when it was assigned to *keep[]* above, the system obligingly finds permanent storage for it in memory and terminates it by adding a SNUL. Access to the string is by way of an explicit or implicit pointer to the first character of the array.

A set of string constants can be grouped, with each element of an array of pointers accessing a separate string.

char   *flower[] = {"arbutus", "carnation", "lilac", "rose", "tulip"};

---

35 Note that a string literal is implemented as a constant pointer to the memory area holding the constant text. A constant pointer is not an lvalue, so we can not write **"ABC" = x;** But we can use the constant pointer as a function arg and we can assign it to a variable pointer; more precisely, we can assign the address of the constant text to the variable pointer by writing **char *x = "ABC";**.

36 See Section 1.4.2.1 on *printf*() and Section 1.9.1.5 on stringizing, i.e., concatenating strings in a #define statement.

37 Global and static character arrays could always be initialized by a string literal, and in ANSI C so can local character arrays.

defines *flower* as an array of pointers-to-char, such that *flower*[0] points to the string constant **arbutus**, *flower*[1] to **carnation**, and so forth. Making each pointer element specific to a particular string has the advantage of random access; i.e., *flower*[2] always points to **lilac**.

This would write out the list of flowers in reverse order:

```
for (i = 4; i >= 0; i--)
    printf("\n%s", flower[i]);
```

```
char       **pflower = flower;
```

defines *pflower* as a pointer-to-pointer-to-char; i.e., the value of *pflower* is the address of the pointer, *flower[0]*, the first element of the array *flower*.

So, to access the individual strings, we can also write:

```
for (i = 0; i < 5; i++, *pflower++)
    printf("\n%s",*pflower);
```

pflower first points to the pointer that indirectly references the first char at the top of the char array; i.e., to the **a** of **arbutus**. The print statement outputs the chars from this **a** to the first SNUL terminus. When incremented by 1, *pflower* moves to the next element of the pointers-to-char array, *flower[1]*, which is pointing to the char **c** that starts the string **carnation**, and so forth.

A backslash within the string constant signals that the next character is special, just as it does in a char constant. The empty string is written as **""**, not as **" "** (which is a string consisting of a space), not as **"\0"** and not as **NULL**. Literal single and double interior quote symbols need to be preceded with the backslash to differentiate them from the C meta characters that bracket string and char constants; e.g., **printf("\"Hi\", he said.");**.

Decimal numbers are written directly, not after a backslash; e.g., **7**. Octal numbers are written as 1, 2 or 3 chars following the back slash; e.g., **\007** or **\07** or **\7**. When only one digit is significant, the initial zeros aren't necessary. Hexadecimal numbers are written with an x following the backslash; e.g., **\x7**.

A SNUL is automatically added by the program as it stores the string constant in memory. This final SNUL counts as a char for storage but not when calculating string length (i.e., the number of characters in the string.) White spaces are counted. The outer quote marks are not. Note that **/*** does not signal the start of a comment; comments are not acknowledged within a string constant (nor within any variable). So this string is 20 characters long.

"\"Hi/*ho*/,\", he said."

It would print as:

"Hi/*ho*/,", he said.

It reduces portability, but for legibility and visibility, some punctuation marks are often written as octals rather than literals within a string constant or within a char constant: **\40** (space), **\45** (%), **\54** (comma), **\073** (;) **\173** ({), **\175** (}) and all chars below octal 40.

1.5.5. STRING VARIABLE

A string in C is stored as a vector, a character array of defined size. If we abide by the definition in Section 1.1.2 that a primary data object is an entity that can be re-valued in a single operation, then obviously there is no primitive string data type in C. Nevertheless, given pointer facility, substringing is readily accomplished, at least for char arrays with predefined storage space. Concatenating (i.e., adding B to the tail of A) is facilitated by a library function called *strcat()*, again for strings with predetermined storage space. The large set of standard string operations includes *strcmp()* that compares two strings by ASCII values and *strcpy()* that copies a string to another char array. In addition, there is a set of supplied functions that operate on blocks of data in memory. They always handle a specific number of characters and they ignore the terminal SNUL that signals the end of a string in the string processing functions. *memmove()* can be used, for example, to move a chunk of data to the video memory area. The mem functions also include *memcpy*, which copies a specified number of characters from one area to another; *memcmp( )*, which compares two memory areas; and *memchr()*, which searches an area for a specified character. They can be used with care on strings but are less suitable for substring and concatenating operations than the system-supplied string processing functions. Prototypes for all these functions are to be found in *string.h*.

Character arrays store chars from *a*[0] to *a*[n-2], where *a*[n-1] holds SNUL and *n* is the size of the array *a*. The size of the array can be determined using *strlen()* which returns the number of chars in the array up to but not including the first (or only) SNUL encountered.

C is sensitive to the differences between a single char and a string of length 1 (i.e., a 2-element char array) and doesn't allow substitutions in type or casting from one to the other. This may become particularly awkward when a function arg is prototyped as a char array or a pointer-to-char, but only a char constant is available. The value of the single char can be assigned to the first element of an array, as in this example.

char stop = '!';   /*A single char*/
char endit[2];   /*A 2-element char array*/

endit[0] = stop;   /*The 1st element of the array is assigned the value of stop.*/
endit[1] = SNUL;   /*This terminates the one-char string.*/

1.5.5.1.   Writing To A Char Array.

A character array can be defined and initialized in one operation with a string constant using a double quotes format; i.e., it can be assigned a group of chars in the same way an integer, say, is given a multi-digit value in a single assignment. Otherwise, a string is filled a character at a time. (Several of the built-in functions for introducing text from disk do, it is true, create the illusion that the entire string is handled as a single entity.)

(1) The characters are streamed into a memory buffer individually from disk.

Some library functions, *fscanf()* and *fgets()*, have built-in halts so they can read in a string of characters in a single function call. *fgets()* reads in a specified number of characters or halts at the NewLine or at the EOF, whichever comes first, and terminates the string with a SNUL. If the NewLine is the halt character, it is added to the input text.

Others, *fgetc()* and the library macro *getc()*, read in a character per call, making them particularly useful for examining characters as they arrive. They reject no character and return EOF when the end of the file is reached. They add no SNUL. These functions are prototyped as

```
int    fscanf(fptr, <format instructions>, &var1, &var2...);
char *fgets(char *string, int n, FILE *fptr);      /*n-1 chars are read in from the file.*/
int    fgetc(FILE *fptr);      /*A character converted to an int is read in from the file.*/
int    getc(FILE *fptr);       /*Like fgetc, getc returns the next char from the file.*/
```

The scanf functions were discussed in Section 1.2.4. In this section, we will illustrate usage for some ***get***-based functions.

(1a) The array can be filled with a single call to fgets().

Given an open file (represented by IN in this example), *fgets()* fills the first nine elements of the array, a[0]:a[8], with characters from the file unless it encounters a NewLine, which halts entry. It sets the 10th element, *a*[9], to SNUL.

```
char       a[10];
fgets(a, 10, IN);
```

(1b) The array can be filled character by character using *fgetc()*.

This next piece of code opens a file and reads characters from it to a buffer. *fgetc()* does not add a terminal SNUL so that is done as a separate operation for string closure in line *a*.

```
char       a[10];
int        i;
FILE       *IN = NULL;

if ((IN = fopen("data.tmp", "r")) == NULL)
     {
     printf("\nProblem opening file.");
     exit(2);
     }
for (i = 0; i < 9; ++i)
     a[i] = (char) fgetc(IN);
a[i] = SNUL;                                                    /*a*/
```

There are characters in a[0] through a[8], so string length is 9. The SNUL in *a*[9] is not counted by *strlen()*.

(1c) Filling the array from disk can conveniently be done using pointers.

```
char       a[10], *pa;
FILE       *IN = NULL;
pa = a;
```

pa is a pointer-to-char assigned to point at the top of the array *a*. In the next code, the string variable that *pa* references is filled. Because *getc*() allows examination of the individual characters as they arrive, entry can be stopped at a particular character. The halt character can be included or excluded from the string. The loop shown prevents flooding the array; it brings in characters up through the percent sign or until the pointer reaches *a*[9]. It replaces the percent sign, if present, with a SNUL. Otherwise, *a*[9] holds the string termination symbol.

```
while (TRUE)
    {
    *pa = (char) getc(IN);
    if (pa == &a[9] || *pa == '%')        /*Breaks after chars have been entered into*/
        {                                  /* a[0:a[8] or if the char is a %.*/
        *pa = SNUL;
        break;
        }
    pa++;
    }
```

(2) The characters are typed directly at the keyboard.

Characters are read in from the keyboard, using *scanf*() or one of the *get* functions that are capable of reading from a file. When handling keyboard input, they take the arg *stdin*. In addition, there is a variant of *getc*() specific to the keyboard called *getchar*(). The next program illustrates some valuable library routines for keyboard input. Included is *puts*(char *), a macro that displays the text in a buffer on the screen, adding a terminal NewLine. (Other output functions include *putc*, which writes to the display, one character at a time, and a variant of *putc* specific to the keyboard called *putchar*().) *gets*(), the macro version of *fgets*(), accepts entry from the keyboard or whatever the standard entry device is, stopping at the NewLine and replacing it with a SNUL.

These functions are prototyped in *stdio.h* as:

```
char *fgets(char *string, int n, FILE *stdin);   /*Read n-1 characters from the keyboard.*/
char *gets(char *string);                        /*Read a line from the keyboard. Add SNUL.*/
int   getc(FILE *stdin);                          /*Read a char at a time from the keyboard.*/
int   getchar(void);                              /*Read a char at a time from the keyboard.*/


void getin(STRING s, int lim)
    {/*BP*/[38]
    int   c = 0;
    int   i = 0;

    s[0] = SNUL;
```

---

[38] Commented BP is used in this book to denote the BEGINNING of an individual procedure. Similarly commented EP marks the END of the procedure.

```
     while ((c = getchar()) != EOL)
          {
          if ( (c == TAB || c == SPACE || c == VT || c == FF) )
               continue;
          else break;
          }
     if (c == EOL || c == ESC)
          s[0] = SNUL;
     else
          {
          s[0] = (char) c;
          for (i = 1; i < lim-1 && (c = getc(stdin)) != EOL && c != ESC; ++i)
               s[i] = (char) c;
          s[i] = SNUL;
          }
     }/*EP*/

int main(void)
     {
     char      buffer[SMLSZE] = {SNUL}, temp[SMLSZE] = {SNUL};
     int       ii = 0;

     printf("\nPlease type your registration code.\t");
     while (TRUE)
          {
          ii++;
          getin(buffer,SMLSZE);
          if (ii == 5)
               {
               printf("\nSorry. Session is over.");
               exit(2);
               }
          else
               {
               printf("\nThis is the code you typed in.\t");
               puts(buffer);               /*Writes the text from buffer to the screen.*/
               printf("\nIf it's wrong, retype it. Otherwise push <ENTER>.\n");
               gets(temp);                 /*Writes the text from the keyboard to temp.*/
               if (temp[0] == SNUL)
                    break;                 /*gets replaces the NewLine with a SNUL.*/
               else
                    {
                    strcpy(buffer,temp);
                    break;
                    }
               }
          }
     }
```

(3) A library copying function such as *strcpy*() copies one string to another, char by char; e.g.

```
char a[9] = {SNUL};
strcpy(a,"Hi there");
```

if *a*[2] is later assigned the value SNUL, then the characters in *a* would be "hi\0" and *strlen*(a) would be 2. *a* would still be sized at 9.

Some version of *strcpy*() is needed whenever a string is cloned or a string is modified in size or character.

1.5.5.2.   Value Versus Reference.

As with int and float arrays, string arrays are transmitted as args to functions by sending the pointer to the address of the first array element. Hence the individual characters can be changed as if the array elements were sent by reference. But the pointer itself is passed by value; i.e., the address where the pointer resides is not sent. What is sent is a copy of the value of the pointer, which is the address of the first array element. So the contents of an array (i.e., the individual characters) can be permanently changed in a function, but when control is returned to the calling routine the pointer snaps back to the top of the char array; it does NOT stay at the terminal SNUL where it was last pointing. In sum, the effect of passing a pointer by value is to restore the pointer to its original value on exit from the function. (See Section 3.2.3.1 for details.)

```
void strcpy(char *dsn, char *src)
    {
    while (*dsn++ = *src++) ;
    }


void copyit(void)
    {
    char      line[] = "good morning";
    char      copyofline[200] = {SNUL};

    strcpy(copyofline,line);
    printf("\n%s",copyofline);        /*PrintProduct: good morning*/
    printf("\n%s",line);              /*PrintProduct: good morning*/
    }
```

Inside *strcpy*(), at the end of the while statement, the pointer *src* that stands for *line* is pointing to the SNUL that terminates the string **good morning.** This is also true for the pointer *dsn* that stands in for *copyofline*. But function args are transmitted by value, so that when *strcpy*() is done and control reverts to the calling function *copyit*(), the pointer is where it always was, pointing to the top of the string. Hence both *line* and *copyofline* contain the fill-in text.

Another consequence is less pleasing. Suppose the first half of a string is deliberately erased during processing. The char array returned would have SNUL's in these positions. But the returned string would begin exactly at the same address as before it was processed. So, instead of the new string being the second half of the old string, it would have a SNUL in its first char element and appear to be empty, while still taking up storage space. To change the starting address of the string so that the beginning of a string can be erased cleanly, the address of the pointer to the character array needs to be accessed. Or the second half of the string has to be rewritten to the top of the array before the function is returned (e.g., *cleantb*() in Section 1.5.2.)

1.5.6. STRUCT

A struct has some of the attributes of a primitive variable in that it can be assigned as a single entity, just like the int or float or char. And it can serve as a function arg. But functionally a struct is a frame that holds together a group of variables of the same or of different data types listed in a particular order. A struct resembles a structured ASCII database record, except that the variables (the information fields) are immediately stored according to their data types (i.e., as ints or char arrays) and not as ASCII text. More formally, structs are hierarchical labeled templates for data item association. Field order and data types within fields are preassigned; the template is a complete representation of the format of each 'record'. To say that *s* is a struct of type *t* is to say that the members of *s* are the same data types and in the same order as those in the template identified by the tag name *t*. To say that *r* and *s* are structs of the same type is to say that the members of *r* are of the same data types and in the same order as those of *s*; and that *r* and *s* have a common template. Member values, of course, may differ.

Struct implementation suffers from the same problems as array implementation. The virtual framework is NOT a matrix. Hence, a data item, a struct element, can not be simply located as the row, column equivalent to record *r*, field *f*. Instead, the item is located by its hierarchical position in the struct template following a top down pathway. If a set of structs are elements in an array, the struct may be referenced as an array element; but the members of the struct still need to be reached through the top level of the struct. If *st* is the struct's name and *ix* is an int field, then *st.ix* represents the int field. Alternatively, if *pst* is a pointer-to-struct, *pst->ix* represents the int field. As does *(*pst).ix*. The pointer is parenthesized, otherwise the program would read it as *(pst.ix) because of the superior binding power of the period. And pst.ix is meaningless in C syntax.

The struct is an excellent data type for representing individual records in ASCII databases, where some fields are numerical, others text. The data types of the members[39] of a struct are unrestricted, except that a struct may not contain a member that is a struct of the same type as the struct. But a member may be a pointer to a struct of the same type (or of a different type). And a struct of a different type may be a member.

---

[39] The data objects comprising the struct are usually referred to as members rather than as elements, perhaps to suggest that the elements of the struct may be of disparate types.

Creating just the struct template is a declaration; it provides no storage. Storage for structs is obtained by naming structs that replicate a declared struct template or by requesting space for a newly created struct when the program is run. Storage for numerical members of a struct is handled by the system as part of setting up storage for the struct. Storage for string members is immediate if they are defined as character arrays of fixed size. However, if the member is a pointer-to-char, only the pointer is stored; some string will likely later be associated with the pointer. It will need to acquire storage space from the system in a separate request.

This is a simple example of a creating a struct template and of defining actual structs of that type.

struct simple
```
    {
    char      i;
    char      j;
    } new, *ps;
```

A struct template is declared by writing its data type, i.e., *struct* followed by an ordered list of the data types of the struct members enclosed in brackets. Like any declaration, this reserves no storage. The present example also defines a struct, *new*, and a pointer-to-struct, *ps*, by associating these variables with the struct template. These defined variables acquire immediate storage. Note that *ps* is defined—hence has storage—but it not as yet assigned to point to any particular struct. The name *simple* which follows the keyword struct is called a struct tag. It provides a way to refer to our example struct template. Variables can hereafter be defined to be *structs of type simple*.

new.i = 'x';   /*In this line and the next, the members of new are assigned values.*/
new.j = 'y';

ps = &new;   /*ps now points to new, a struct of type simple.*/
printf("new.i=%c;new.j=%c",ps->i,(*ps).j); /*Ways of referencing the members of new.*/

This second example shows how struct templates can be interconnected. We begin by constructing a globally-declared template for a two-member struct of type nm.

struct nm   /*nm, which follows immediately after struct, is the struct tag;*/
**   {**   /*i.e., we have just established a new data type: a struct of type nm.*/
**   char lastname[30];**
**   char initial;**
**   } newname = {"Jones, ", 'L'};**   /*newname is a struct of type nm, defined */
                                              /* and even initialized.*/
struct nm ed;   /*ed is an empty struct of type nm.*/

Next we develop another template, the ground plan for a struct of type biblio. Its first member is a struct of type nm and another member, *peditor,* is a pointer-to-struct of type nm. No storage is provided for the biblio template. On the other hand, bib[100] defines (i.e., provides storage for) an array called bib, which has 100 elements. Each element is defined as a struct of type biblio.

struct biblio   /*This establishes a new data type, a struct template tagged as biblio.*/
    {
       struct nm auth;   /*auth is a member of biblio. auth is a struct of type nm.*/
       char initial;   /*This can later be valued as the period.*/
       int year;   /*This can later be valued as some default year.*/
       char journalname[10];   /*A 10-element unfilled char array.*/
       struct nm *peditor;   /*peditor is a pointer-to-struct of type nm.*/
       char titlename[30];   /*A 30-element unfilled char array.*/
       int page;   /*An integer value.*/
    } bib[100], *pbib;

In this example, we created a template for a struct of type nm. Put another way, we created a new data type called *nm*. We defined *newname* and *ed* as structs of type nm just we would define a particular integer as **int newint;**. And in defining them, we caused the system to provide them with storage space. *newname* was immediately initialized. *ed* is as of now empty, but it could be filled, for example, in this way: **strcpy(ed.lastname, "Brown, ");** and **ed.initial = 'M';**.

We also created an array sufficient to hold 100 structs of type biblio, and in doing so we acquired storage for 100 structs of type biblio, including storage for the struct members. Included among *biblio*'s members are *auth*, which is a struct of type nm, and *peditor*, a pointer-to-struct of type nm. *auth* has unfilled storage space for its members (lastname and initial). *peditor* itself has been provided with storage space, but it is unattached to any particular struct. An unnamed struct of type nm can, however, be acquired dynamically and *peditor* used to reference it, thus:

bib[1].peditor = (struct nm *) calloc(1, sizeof(struct nm));

bib[1].peditor now contains the address of unfilled space in memory sufficient for storing a struct of type nm. The pointer *peditor* for *bib*[1] is distinct from the *peditor* for *bib*[0], and so forth.

A struct can not have two members with the same name; e.g., biblio could not have char *initial* and int *initial* (instead of int *year*, say). But different structs can have the same member names, just as variables in different blocks can have the same name, because there is no ambiguity about which one is meant. Thus, char *initial* is a member of structs of type biblio and of structs of type nm. Similarly, a struct member may have the same name as any local or external variable or function arg.

Suppose *pbib* defined above as a pointer-to-struct of type biblio is assigned to the second array element: **pbib = &bib[1];**. A record equivalent to row *bib*[1] printed out with this command:

printf("\n%s%c%c %d %s %s %c %s %d", pbib->auth.lastname, pbib->auth.initial, pbib->initial, pbib->year, pbib->journalname, pbib->peditor->lastname, pbib->peditor->initial, pbib->titlename, pbib->page);

might look like this:

Graham, C. 1932 J Physiol Smith, R The Limulus Eye 65

A struct is a data type; hence a struct of type nm can be typedef'ed[40]. In this next example we typedef a struct without instantiators.

typedef struct nm LNAME;

and the following would create a struct of type nm:

LNAME *pauthor;
pauthor = (LNAME *) calloc(1, sizeof(LNAME));

Note that the first term is a cast, for automatic type conversion of the pointer returned by *calloc*(). Each struct type requires its own pointer type when a block of memory is allocated dynamically

While the primitive types in C (int, float, ..) are few in number, general in their usage and easily separable in concept, the types of structs may be as narrowly separated and even more profuse in number than French sauces, the difference in a single member of a struct being sufficient to occasion the naming of a new struct. And while classes of structs may be sorted out by examining individual struct types—those useful as coordinate systems in graphic displays or those that provide links between elements affiliated chronologically—there is no generality in the label *struct*. The word conveys only that it binds together a set of often disparate variables of all types, both simple and compound and including pointers to other structs of the same or different type. But what is a disadvantage from the point of view of mathematical elegance is an advantage in dealing with fields of very diverse databases. Fields and subfields, consisting, say, of counts that are ints, payments that are floats and names that are char arrays, are free to mimic any order established in the mind of the database creator, unrestricted in concept, bound only by C's syntactic rules for processing anything labeled as struct.

We may assign to members of a local or external struct. And we may initialize a struct during its definition by listing the values of all the members of the struct in sequence within braces. In ANSI C a struct may be passed by value directly as a function arg; e.g., **check-str(bib[10]);**. And we may assign to the struct as a whole, and copy the struct as a whole to another struct of the same type. This following would copy the example record in *bib*[1] to the struct array element *bib*[5]: **bib[5] = bib[1];**. All the data would be copied into all the component variables. Two structs may NOT be directly compared; but their members may.

1.5.7. UNION

A union is a structure in which all members have offset zero. A union is a storage dump with possible holes, and is fixed at a size dictated by the different data types it may contain at different times. This is where we can disobey all rules. We can rotate a float, call an integer a string, and so forth. A union provides an easy way of redefining a datum, so that we can put in an integer and take out a float. Or take out an int only under some conditions and

---

40 See Section 1.5.9.

floats otherwise. At one extreme it is an easy way to get garbage from data. Alternatively, it provides an elegant though risky way of comparing entities that have many similarities with only a few differences. This struct type, for example, maintains information about the location of the sort key for a single record. (The text of the database record upon which the record is sorted /alphabetized is called its sort key or just its key.) A key may be numerical or alphabetic.

```
struct alpnum
    {
    union
        {
        char *akey;       /*Pointer to the alphabetic key of this record.*/
        float nkey;       /*The numeric key for the record.*/
        } key;
    long bgnrec;          /*Where the record begins as offset in the database file.*/
    } ;
```

Either *key.akey* or *key.nkey* is assigned a value (but not both), depending on whether the end user had picked an alphabetic sort or a numeric one. Thus:

```
if (task == ALPHABET)
    printf("%s-%ld|\n",p->key.akey,p->bgnrec);
else
    printf("%f-%ld|\n",p->key.nkey,p->bgnrec);
```

would display the key and where the record is located (in byte offsets) in the database. If the sort is alphabetic and the key is **whale**, then **whale-8057|** would be a possible output.

1.5.8. MORE COMPLEX DATA TYPES

C allows the construction of individualized compound data types.

<u>RULE for reading complex definitions:</u>

Find the innermost identifier.

Work within the confines of the innermost parentheses that enclose the innermost identifier.

Look to the right of the identifier for a pair of [] brackets or a pair of () parentheses.

Interpret a pair of [] brackets as **array**, a pair of () parentheses as **function**. *id*[] or *id*[10] is an array, *id*() or *id*(arg1, arg2 ..) is a function.

Look to the left for one or more asterisks. Interpret * as pointer, ** as pointer to pointer.[41] ***id(arg1, arg2)** declares id to be a function that returns a pointer to.....

But a parenthesized id such as **(*id)(arg1, arg2)** indicates id is a pointer to a function that ....[42] And (**id)() is a pointer to a pointer to a function that.....

*id[] declares id to be an array of pointers to .... But a parenthesized id such as (*id)[] indicates id is a pointer to an array of .... And (**id)[] is a pointer to a pointer to an array of ...

Look to the right again: if the next item is a right unpaired parenthesis[43] you should be through with the innermost enclosure. Branch out to the items within the next outer (....) parentheses, again reading the right side, then the left side. Keeping doing this until all the symbols are read.

Fortunately an array of functions is illegal, so you WON'T have to interpret this: int id[](arg1, arg2). And a function that returns an array is illegal, so you WON'T have to interpret this: int []id().

On the other hand, following the rules:

int *(*id[])(arg1, arg2);

legitimately defines *id* as an array of pointers to functions that return pointers to int. Similarly,

struct p * (*(*id)[5])();

is supposed to inform us that *id* is a pointer to an array of 5 pointers to functions that return pointers-to-structs of type p.

RULE for writing very complex definitions: don't.

1.5.9. TYPEDEF

The typedef statement provides a way to nickname a data type in terms of previously defined data types. A typedef accepts a simple name for what can be a very complex data

---

41 If you encounter ***, you are dealing with a pointer that points to a pointer that points to a pointer. Give up. It won't get any better.

42 Remember the precedence rule that array and function symbols take precedence over pointer symbols. Because () has higher binding power than *, without the parens around *id, the program would attach id to (arg1, arg2), which would not be what is wanted. Of course, it would be less confusing if the function symbol was not the same as the parenthesis separator.

43 The right and left hand innermost brackets have been located and paired.

type. Hence the TYPEDEF alias is most useful for identifying a long and involved complex data structure. The TYPEDEF construct is classed with storage types, but it does NOT create new storage.

The typedef format is

typedef x y;

typedef's do not start with a # as do #define's. The x is a defined data type, the y an additional name for this data type. This does not preclude a typedef being extremely complex in that a data type may be defined in terms of a data type that has been typedef'ed in terms of a simpler data type. Examples used in this book are:

```
typedef char        *STRING;      /*A pointer-to-char is typedef'ed as STRING.*/
typedef STRING      *PTRADR;      /*PTRADR is char **; pointer-to-pointer-to-char.*/
typedef struct in_stat    FSTAT;  /*FSTAT is short for struct of type in_stat.*/
typedef FSTAT       *PALFSTAT;    /*A pointer-to-struct of type in_stat.*/
typedef PALFSTAT *PPALFSTAT;      /*A pointer-to-pointer-to-struct of type in_stat*/
```

PALFSTAT is now typedef'ed as a pointer-to-FSTAT; hence, **PALFSTAT pnew;** defines *pnew* just as **struct in_stat *pnew;** would. Similarly, **PPALFSTAT r;** can be written in place of the definition: **struct in_stat **r;**

1.6. STORAGE: DEFINITIONS, DECLARATIONS AND INITIALIZATION

We have talked about defined variables, without making clear just how this occurs. The statement:

int   x = 0;

defines *x* because by means of this statement *x* receives a name, is typed as an int and, simultaneously, the system receives instructions to find *x* a place in memory of int size. In this example, the variable is also assigned an initial value at the time it is defined; this is called initialization.

The statement is exactly equivalent to:

int   x;
x = 0;

This section will discuss in detail how a C language object is stored.

1.6.1. VARIABLES

Before a variable can be used, the program must be told its data type and id by means of a definition statement. Local variables, i.e., those that reside within a single function, must be explicitly defined. Global variables, i.e., those that are common to several functions, must first be defined explicitly or be declared by way of an extern declaration.[44]

To **define** a variable is: (1) to name the variable; and (2) to assert the data type. When the variable is defined, it may, in the same statement, be initialized (i.e., given a value), but this is not required. When a variable is defined, the system is given the information it needs to store the variable. Indeed, to define a variable is to assign it a place in memory, to see to its storage.

To **declare** a global variable is also to assert the data type of a named variable. But the variable is not assigned a value and the system does not assign it storage. A declaration notifies the program that the variable is defined further down in the current file or it is in some other compilable file and will be made available to the compiler when the files are linked. A declaration statement differs from a definition statement in that it starts with the keyword *extern*. In theory and in clean practice, an indefinite number of declarations about a single variable may be made, but there can exist only one definition of that variable. In loose practice, if only declarations about the variable exist (i.e., the linker is unable to find a definition among the various linked files that constitute the program), the declaration statements collectively become the definition of the variable, with an initial value of zero.

As an example of the customary way to define and declare global variables, consider these variables in File A, written outside of any function and usually prior to any function code.

```
int sample1[12]    =    {1,3,5,7,9,0,11,13,0,15,17,19};
int sample2[100]   =    {0};
int sample3[]      =    {1,3,5,7,9,0,11,13,0,15,17,19};

char samp1[7]      =    "hi ho.";
char samp2[100]    =    {SNUL};
char samp3[]       =    "hi ho.";
```

A global int array called *sample1* is defined as having 12 elements, from A[0] to A[11]. If these are initialized (as here), the values assigned must be listed in order. If the values listed are fewer than the number of elements in the array, the unassigned elements are zeroed. Listing more values than the space available is an error. In string mode, the values of the char elements are listed in sequence bracketed by double quote marks. In the char array *samp1*, letters fill the array from *samp1*[0] to *samp1*[5]. The 7th element of the array, *samp1*[6], is assigned a SNUL by the compiler. If an array is too small for the number of values assigned, the compiler will complain that the array bounds have overflowed. Char arrays may be defined and filled with SNUL's and int arrays with zeros, as are *samp2* and *sample2*. Or they may be partially filled; e.g.,*samp1* could have been defined as: **char samp1[100] = "hi ho."**. An alternative way of defining an external array is to provide the values of the elements and let the program calculate the size of the array, as in *sample3* and

---

[44] C has no common area as does Fortran. Declaring a variable external enables the referencing by multiple functions of the same memory store.

samp3. *samp1* and *samp3* are exactly equivalent to and could have been written cumbersomely as: **char samp1[] = {'h','i',' ','h','o', '.'}.**

In C, if the global variable is initialized, the initial values must be constants or constant expressions; e.g., **int sample = new;**, where *new* is a variable, is not allowed. Note that this is more restrictive than the data types that can be assigned to a local variable.

In File B, prior to using these variables in the different functions resident in File B, they would be declared as

extern int sample1[12];
extern int sample2[100];
extern int sample3[];

extern char samp1[7];
extern char samp2[100];
extern char samp3[];

Note that no values are asserted in declarations and that declare statements begin with the keyword *extern*.

1.6.1.1.   Storage Types.

Once a variable is defined, its scope depends on its storage type. Storage classification has two dimensions: (1) external versus local and (2) static versus ... [its opposite depends on whether storage is external or local]. The lease of life in memory of any variable depends on where it is defined (i.e., inside a particular function or outside any function) and whether it is labeled static or not.

LOCAL: The scope of any local variable, whether static or auto, is the function in which it resides. It is unknown outside the function. It is often stated that a local variable is initialized each time the function is entered. This doesn't mean that it is reset to zero, only that the previous value has not been retained. Local variables are commonly known as automatic variables because the system sets them up with addresses automatically when the function is called and they are discarded and their addresses made available for reassignment when the function finishes. When the function is run again, the variable will have whatever accidental value happens to be in its new address, unless there is an explicit initialization or assignment of a value.

A variable within a function does not need to be labeled auto, and rarely is. Indeed, within a function, if a variable is not explicitly labeled extern or static, it is automatic by default. A local variable is defined by setting its data type. In ANSI C, all variables can be typed and initialized in the same statement[45]. Initial values of local variables may be constants, previously defined variables or functions, whose prototypes are known. *am* in line *d* is a

---

45 In earlier compilers, local compound variables such as line *a* could not be initialized in a single assignment.

pointer that is given a value by *dssave*(), a function that obtains storage from the system dynamically and saves the text in the allocated space.

```
void newfct(void)
    {
    char      aa[10] = {SNUL};              /*PrintProduct: (null)*/      /*a*/
    char      bb[100] = {"abcdefghijklmn"}; /*PrintProduct: abcdefghijklmn*/
    int       i = 20;
    int       j = i + 50;              /*PrintProduct: 70*/                /*b*/
    char      a = SNUL;
    char      b = (char) j +10;        /*PrintProduct: P*/                 /*c*/
    char      ac;
    float     ft;
    char      *am = dssave(bb);        /*PrintProduct: abcdefghijklmnopq*/ /*d*/
    char      *pb  = &bb[0];           /*PrintProduct: abcdefghijklmnopq*/
    int       xa   = FALSE;            /*PrintProduct: 0*/
    }
```

FALSE has the integer value of zero. SNUL is the null character constant, **\0** (ASCII zero). The pointer *pb* is set to point to the just defined char b[46]. These variables will be reset to these initial values each time the function is called. In contrast, *ac* and *ft* are not initialized and will have random values each time *newfct* is called.

A static local variable, on the other hand, is initialized once at the start of the program. It keeps its address. Any change in value that occurs during the running of a function is sticky; i.e., the variable has this value when the function is called again. However, it can not be accessed except while the function is active. Static local variables like global variables can be initialized only by constant values. And they can not take the value returned by a function. Lines *c* and *d* could not be used with static variables. Otherwise the same format applies except they begin with the keyword *static*.

```
static    char      aa[10] = {SNUL};               /*PrintProduct: (null)*/
static    char      bb[100] = {"abcdefghijklmn"};  /*PrintProduct: abcdefghijklmn*/
static    int       i = 20;
```

If a local variable is defined in an inside block of a function, it is not recognized outside that block. Blocks may nest within blocks to any depth; i.e., an outer block begins before an inner block and extends beyond it. Two variables that are defined in the same block may not have the same name, but two variables defined in separate blocks of a function may. If two variables with the same name are recognized in the same block, the variable defined in this block is the one processed. If a set of nested blocks contains two (or more) variables of the same name, the variable defined in the (relatively) innermost block is the one processed. (See Section 1.3.2 on naming variables.)

---

46 If a pointer is defined before its associated variable, it should be given the value NULL. It can later be assigned the address of the variable.

EXTERNAL: An external (i.e., global) variable is defined outside of any function. An external variable is defined once, thus acquiring storage space for the life of the program. Its storage space is not erased or replaced. An external variable whose scope is a set of linkable files must be defined or at least declared before any of the functions that use it. (Examples of external definitions and declarations are shown in Section 1.6.1.) External variables are initialized once at the beginning of the running program with some constant value or constant expression provided by the programmer or implicitly to zero.[47] The initial value is retained until it is changed in some function.

Static external variables, like static local variables, retain their values over the life of the program. Static external variables reside outside any function but are accessible only to those functions that (1) are within the same file and (2) are written after the variables are defined or declared. A static external variable may be defined and assigned a value in a single statement, even if it is a compound variable; for example, we can write **static char newval[100] = {SNUL};** (not **extern static char ...**) The corresponding declaration is **static char newval[100];**. Typically, static variables are defined somewhere near the top of the file and declarations are unnecessary.

If the variable is not a local variable inside a procedure and is not typed static outside a function, it is an ordinary global variable; i.e., a variable that is defined once but that is potentially callable from any where within its own file or from any other file for the life of the program. If the definition of a variable comes later than its use, perhaps because the definition is in another file that is not used until later in the program, it must be declared prior to use by way of an extern statement. For example, if the definition is **char newval[100] = {SNUL};** then the corresponding declaration is **extern char newval[100];**. The extern statement is not assigned a value. It is placed: (1) in an include file composed of extern statements; or (2) at the top of the file where the calling function is written; or (3) within the calling function itself.[48]

1.6.1.2.   Defining A Variable As Global Versus Local.

An external variable defined globally across files or statically within a file can reduce the number of args needed by a function. For example, suppose an array called *buf*.

static char   buf[] = "SOME WORDS";

buf is eventually used in the calling function *callingfct()* and the called function *countchar()*. Thus:

void callingfct()
       {

_____

47 It is always safer to make the initial value explicit.

48 It can be a bit of a nuisance looking for the statement that defines an external variable, it being the one NOT labeled extern. In Sail, the definition statement was labeled Internal, a more reasonable approach.

```
        int i = 0;

        i = countchar();
        printf("\nd",i);              /*PrintProduct: 10*/
        ... do something with buf.....
        }

int countchar(void)
        {
        int i = 0;                    /*a*/

        while (TRUE)
                if (!buf[i++])        /*i will count an extra char before the loop breaks.*/
                break;
        printf("\nd",i-1);            /*PrintProduct: 10*/
        return(i-1);
        }
```

Alternatively, *buf* may be made a local variable in the calling function and its value used by *countchar()* as function arg, thus:

```
void callingfct(void)
        {
        char buf[100] = "SOME WORDS";
        int i = 0;

        i = countchar(char *buf);
        }

int countchar(char buf[])          /*buf is a dummy variable and different*/
        {                                      /* from that in callingfct().*/
        /*... same body as in countchars above, starting line a....*/
        }
```

As this example indicates, there is usually a choice where to define a variable that is processed in several functions. It can be defined either as a global variable or as a local variable in a function that will transmit its value to some called function. The global definition of a variable has the advantage that it cuts down on stack space used and on the number of args that the programmer needs to remember and to type. A change made in the value of a variable in one function will be permanent when it is processed by another function. This might be what is wanted. Often it is not. Yet is it precisely this ease of transmitting the value of a variable that makes an external definition the method of choice when the variable participates in a number of functions, some of which call each other, some of which do not, but all of which have an effect on changing the value of the variable.

Alternatively a variable may be defined as a local in the calling routine so that its value must be transmitted as a function arg if it is to participate in the operation of the called function. Using the value of the variable as a function arg permits more control on what changes in value are allowable and is faster. Moreover, variables that have the same name are less likely to interfere with each other. On the other hand, the number of args can grow unreasonably.

1.6.1.3. Register Variables.

When memory registers provide storage for frequently used local variables, execution is faster. The compiler is asked to make a register available, using the register format (e.g., **register int c;**) but it need not comply. Registers may be requested for integer types and pointers. But the address of the variable may not be used. Thus:

```
register int     i;
register char    *p;
char a[] = "Print some words fast."

for(i = 0, p = a; *p; i++, p++)                /*Allowed.*/
    {
    if (*p == 'r') printf("\ni = %d\n", i);      /*Allowed.*/
    if (&p == 1456) printf("no way");            /*Not allowed.*/
    }
```

1.6.1.4. Preset Versus Dynamic Storage.

We preset the amount of storage required by a struct by associating the name of the particular struct with a struct template; in the example used to illustrate structs in Section 1.5.6, **struct nm ed;** sets up storage for a struct of type nm called *ed*. Similarly, the size of an array can be preset by making it explicit; e.g., **char new[100];**. In this example, the array has 100 bytes reserved for it in memory. However, when the size of an incoming string is unknown, it is costly in space to assign a fixed amount of storage for it; e.g., **char new[100];**, when the string may be only 10 bytes in size. This is true whether the variable is local or external.

C provides an alternative to explicit storage called dynamic storage, whereby only a pointer to the potential space needs to be defined. When space is needed, a request is made to the system for a specific amount, using either *malloc*() or *calloc*(). A defined pointer is set to point to this space; this pointer is the ONLY contact with the stored string. Once the variable is stored, storage is forever while the program is running unless the user deallocates the stored variable with a *free();* statement. If the pointer to the stored variable is temporary or is erased, the variable is no longer accessible to the program but it still occupies space. A local static pointer can access the stored string whenever the function is run. To obtain two structs of the type defined above:

pstr = (struct nm *) malloc(2 * sizeof(struct nm));

or

pstr = (struct nm *) calloc(2, sizeof(struct nm));

Dynamic storage of strings is discussed in Chapter 2.

1.6.1.5.   Illustrating Storage Types.

```
extern char newfile1[100];          /*Declaring a variable outside any function and*/
                                    /* defined elsewhere.*/
char newfile2[100] = {SNUL};         /*Defining a variable outside any function. newfile2*/
                                    /* is accessible to all files.*/
static char newfile3[100] = {SNUL}; /*Defining a variable outside any function. newfile3*/
                                    /* is accessible only within the file.*/
char *ptr = NULL;                    /*Defining a global pointer-to-char that can access*/
                                    /* an array stored dynamically.*/


extern char newproc1(char newfile); /*The function newproc1 is defined elsewhere,*/
                                    /*in this or another file.*/


static char newproc2(char newfile)  /*A function known just in the current file.*/
    {
    auto char buf[100];             /*An ordinary local variable. auto is unnecessary.*/
    register   *ptr;                /*A register variable, a local variable*/
    static char *pi;                /*A static local variable.*/
    char *pb = buf;                 /*A local pointer assigned to point to the start of buf.*/
    }
```

Note that if a static local pointer such as *pi* in *newproc2*() is assigned to point to some dynamically stored array, it will retain the address of the stored array from one call on the function to the next.

```
char newproc3(char newfile)    /*A function known to any file in which it is declared.*/
    {
    int   i = 0;               /*A local variable known to all of newproc3.*/
    char buffer[100];          /*Another local variable.*/

    while (i < 5)
        {
        int i = 0;             /*A local variable known only in this block.*/
        i++;                   /*Infinite loop.*/
        }
    return( char(i));
    }
```

1.6.2. FUNCTIONS

Similar to the scope of a static variable, a static function can be accessed just within a single file. Otherwise the function is globally external. There are no internal functions; i.e., one function may not be written (i.e., given a name, args and function body) within another function, as it can in Pascal. A function may of course call functions external to itself. C puts no restrictions on the order in which functions are written. But the compiler does need some immediate information on the characteristics of a procedure when it is called; specifically, what type of variable the procedure returns. **return(int);** NOT **return(void);** is the default and is assumed by the compiler in the absence of an extern declaration.

If the variable returned by the function is not an int, and the procedure has not yet been written within the file or it is in another file that isn't available to the program until files are linked, the function must be at least minimally characterized by an extern statement such as **extern char *newfct();** prior to being called. The extern statement may be placed: (1) in a separate file, whose name is placed in an include statement at the top of the file; (2) at the top of the file; or (3) within the calling function itself. ANSI C encourages amplifying the minimal extern statement by prototyping, whereby the extern statement also describes the arg types; e.g., **extern char *newfct(int i, char *call);**. The compiler can errorcheck calling variables against the prototyped dummy args. We routinely use prototyping in this book.

1.6.3. ISOLATING A GROUP OF PROCEDURES AND VARIABLES

As noted, unlike Pascal, C does not permit nesting of functions; i.e., it is illegal to write a function block within another function block. To write the equivalent of nested blocks (a group of functions in which one function may encompass another that encompasses still another, with a set of global variables defined only across that group of functions and not recognized outside of that group), the group can be isolated in a separate file and thus made semi-independent of the rest of the program. A global variable must precede the functions that use it and it must be defined as static; e.g., **static char newbuf[100] = {SNUL};**. Just as with any external variable, static variables are defined once and retain their addresses for the life of the program. The functions are also declared as static. A procedure labeled static as in **static float secretproc();** can not be called from any procedure outside of the file in which it is resident. Of course, at least one function that uses these static procedures must be callable from another file; else the exercise is pointless.

It is a good idea to provide extern prototypes for static functions at the top of the file because, even in a single file, one static function may call another static function that is defined later. An alphabetic list of function prototypes can be written early in the file. In this example, *closeup()*, *dsinput()* and *intscan()* are accessible to procedures in other files, the others are not.

/*ALPHABETIZED LIST OF FUNCTIONS IN THIS FILE*/

```
extern    void     closeup(void);
extern    char     *dsinput(FILE *ifptr, BITMAP tbl, int *pbrk);
static    int      DULcase(int c);
static    int      filehash(FILE *numb, int prime);
extern    int      intscan(char *psrc, int *pbrk);
```

1.7. OPERATORS

1.7.1. OPERATOR PRECEDENCE

Table 1.8, adapted from the Table in K&R p. 53, lists C's operator symbols. In most cases, when several operators of the same binding power are in the same expression, they associate left to right. Line by line, the operators are reduced in precedence in the order listed in the table. The operators most strongly linked to their associated language objects are in line 1 and the weakest operator, the comma, is listed in the final line.

Line 1 contains notation for functions, arrays and two ways to express struct membership, reading from left to right. The next most binding operators are in line 2: the unary reversals, incrementing/decrementing operators, unary signs (+ and - are not arithmetic here), pointer notation, the cast and sizeof operators. Lines 3 and 4 are the arithmetic operators; line 5 lists the bit shifts; and lines 6 and 7 the relational operators. The next three lines are bit operators, followed by the 2 regular boolean operators. The **?:** is the idiomatic triad if-else operator. Assignment operators are next, including bitwise boolean and shift assignments. The lowest in precedence is the comma operator, which is used mainly in the first and third terms of for constructions as in **for (i=1, y=0, z=1; i < 10; i++,y--,z+2)**. The comma operator guarantees left to right evaluation. The commas found between function args and between definitions of variables are NOT comma operators.

ANSI C protocols guarantee that the program will finish evaluating a statement before looking at the next program statement. More precisely, in segmented statements such as **e1 && e2** or **e1 ‖ e2** or **e1 ? e2 : e3**, *e1* will be completely evaluated before *e2* is examined. There is no restriction, however, on the order in which associative and commutative operators (such as plus, minus, greater, less than) within *e1* are evaluated. Left to right or right to left order is compiler determined. So cutesies such as **j = i++ - ++i;** or **j = (i = 2) + (i = 3);** or **j = f(i) + g(i);** or even **s[i] = i++;** are best avoided. Note also, as this example from K&R (p. 53) makes clear, that the ordering of args in a print statement does not control evaluation, even though ordinary args are supposed to be evaluated before functions are called.

printf("%d %d\n", ++n, power(2, n));

should be rewritten as:

++n; printf("%d %d\n", n, power(2, n));

In many cases, it is possible to control the order of evaluation within segments by liberal use of parentheses. But it is not clear how general this is. At one extreme, parentheses are not effective in **j = f(i) + g(i);** where *g()* is liable to be evaluated first. At the other extreme as in **j = ((i + 2) / (i -2));**, parentheses act as segmenters to maintain order.

Operator	Associativity
() [] -> .	left to right
! ~ ++ -- + - * & (cast) sizeof	right to left
* / %	left to right
+ -	"
<< >>	"
< <= > >=	"
== !=	"
&	"
^	"
|	"
&&	"
||	"
?:	irght to left
= += -= *= /= %= &= ^= |= <<= >>=	"
,	left to right

Table 1.8. Precedence of operators.

1.7.2. TYPES OF OPERATORS

1.7.2.1. Assignment Operators.

```
=    +=   -=   *=   /=
&=   !=   ^=
```

When an assignment is concluded, the type is the type of the left variable.

1.7.2.2. Arithmetic Operators.

```
*    /    %    -    +
```

where / is used for ordinary division and % is the modulus divisor. For integers, x/y yields an integral value, with the fractional part truncated; x%y yields the truncated fractional part. % is undefined for floating point values. Like Fortran, C uses * as the multiplication operator. Unlike Fortran, C has no ** to indicate raising a value to an exponent.

Reading left to right, the precedence is: (1,2,3) > (4,5), meaning that * / and % all take precedence over - and +.

1.7.2.3.   Relational Operators.

Within a single expression that has two or more operands, the relational operators are:[49]

>   >= <   <=   ==   !=

>	**is greater**		<=	**is less than or equal to**
>=	**is greater or equal to**		==	**is equal to**
<	**is less than**		!=	**is not equal to**

Reading left to right, the precedence is: $(1,2,3,4) > (5,6)$, meaning that the first 4 operators are equipotent and they each take precedence over the last two.

Examples of single expressions are: **(a == t*2)** or **(a != b+1)** or **(a < b < c)**

The relational operators are of lower precedence than the arithmetic operators, so in the second example it is not necessary to write **(a != (b + 1))**. + will bind *b* with 1 before the != operator is assessed.

Each expression can be individually tested for TRUE or FALSE in the conditional component of an if() or while() control statement. Note that FALSE is integer 0 and any other result is TRUE and equal to integer 1.

1.7.2.4.   Boolean Or Logical Operators.

NOT is a unary boolean operator that reverses the TRUTH value of the expression. And two boolean operators are available for the relationship between two or more expressions, evaluating each expression separately, beginning with the leftmost one. For an AND relationship to be TRUE, all the component expressions must be TRUE. For an OR relationship, only one of them need be TRUE. The program stops the evaluation as soon as the end result is inevitable.

NOT	**!(e1)**	as in:	**if (!r)**
AND	**e1 && e2**	as in:	**while (r >= 7 && s <= 2)**
OR	**e1 || e2**	as in:	**if (r == 7 || s != 2)**

f = 6;
if (a == b && c != d && !g) f = 10;[50]

Let *e1* be (a == b), *e2* be (c != d) and *e3* be !g. *e1*, *e2* and *e3* are separately evaluated to TRUE or FALSE, the evaluation stopping if any of them is FALSE. For *e3*, if *g* is TRUE

---

49 K&R (p. 41) reserve the term relational for the first four operators. The other two are called equality operators and have a lower precedence than the relational operators.

50 Equality and relational operators have higher precedence than boolean operators, so the individual expressions do not need to be parenthesized. Note that it MUST be **if (a == b)** and not **if (a = b)**, which is an assignment statement and is unconditionally TRUE.

(has a value other than zero), then !g is FALSE, and visa versa. If e1, e2 and e3 are all TRUE, *f* is assigned the value of 10. If any expression is FALSE, *f* remains 5.

Because the AND operation stops at the first FALSE expression, expressions can be prioritized, so that a more critical term is assessed first. As example, to determine if a char variable **c** is a vowel followed by **h** or **s** or **b**, considerable processing time is saved if it is first determined that *c* is a vowel. Given that *pc* points to *c*:

if (ITVOWEL(*pc) && (*++pc == 'h' || *pc == 's' || *pc == 'b')) .....

Note that the NOT symbol is **!**. Given: **int Smode, Amode, Rmode, Tmode;**

To write: **if (not (e)) { }:**

WRONG: **if (~Smode && ~Amode && ~Rmode) Dmode = TRUE;**
RIGHT: **if (!Smode && !Amode && !Rmode) Dmode = TRUE;**

Using ~ instead of **!** is an error that often is not caught. **~(e)** is the bitwise complement of **(e)**; see Table 1.9.

Some boolean equivalences are:

!(e1 && e2)	is the same as	**(!e1 || !e2)**
!(e1 || e2)	is the same as	**(!e1 && !e2)**

1.7.2.5.   Bit Shift And Logical Bit Operators.

Given any type of number, the usual operations performed on it are arithmetic. We add it to another number, we integrate it, we find some corresponding value on a graph. But if we regard the binary representation of numbers solely as unique patterns of 1's and 0's, we can use particular patterns to trigger a specific processing action or to express the coded field data of a database record or to summarize within a 32-bit word the YES-NO responses of an interviewee to a 32-item questionnaire. Bit operators may be applied to the binary representation of integral data types such as ints and chars. The binary pattern of the ASCII character **v**, for example, is 01110110 or octal 166. Bit manipulations can not be done on floats directly; they must first be converted to integers.

In Table 1.9, *b* is a single bit position in *e*, where *e* is a number or an expression that results in an integer. The lowest bit position in *e* (i.e., the rightmost) is called bit 0, the second lowest bit position in *e* is bit 1, the third is bit 2, and so forth. For example, using single-digit octal numbers, from 000 to 111, and *b* at bit 1, then *b* would be 1 in integer **2, 3, 6**, and **7** and zero otherwise. When two expressions are involved, *b1* and *b2* are the bits in the same location in *e1* and *e2*, respectively.

The bit operator precedence is:

~   <<   >>   &   ^ |

Reading left to right, the precedence is: **1 > (2,3) > 4 > 5 > 6** meaning that logical inversion has precedence over shifting which in turn has precedence over bit AND'ing. AND'ing is done before eXclusive OR'ing in an ambiguous situation. XOR'ing, in turn, takes precedence over ordinary OR'ing.

~e	Unary. **Logical inversion**. If b is 1, the result is 0; if b is 0, the result is 1.
e1 << n	Shift e1 left n bits.
e1 >> n	Shift e1 right n bits.
b1 & b2	**Logical AND.** If both b1 and b2 are 1, the result is 1. Else 0.
b1 ^ b2	**Logical XOR, (exclusive OR).** If one and only one of the b bits is 1, the result is 1. Else 0.
b1 I b2	**Logical OR.** If either (or both) bit b is one, the result is 1. Else 0.

Table 1.9.   Bitwise shifts and logical bit operations.

Shifting to the left by 1 bit is the same as multiplying by 2, shifting to the right by 1 bit is the same as dividing by 2. Shifting to the left may result in overflow; shifting to the right operations are generally not portable. For portability, use **(e & ~1)** for setting the lowest bit to zero, NOT **0177776**, which will only work on 16-bit machines. Similarly, using **~0** when shifting will drag along a stream of 1's. When shifting an int, be sure to declare the int as unsigned.

0177 is the same as the 2-byte bit pattern 0000000001111111. It can be used to delete the high order bits in an int when a char is changed back from an int to char (see Section 1.4.5.1), thus:

c & 0177

Suppose MASK8 is a 8-element int array in which each element in the array is assigned a 1 in a single bit position and a zero in every other position. Written as the actual bit patterns in the byte, this is *MASK8*[8]:

MASK8[0] = 00000001;   MASK8[1] = 00000010;   MASK8[2] =00000100;
MASK8[3] = 00001000;   MASK8[4] = 00010000;   MASK8[5] = 00100000;
MASK8[6] = 1000000;   MASK8[7] = 10000000;

What we are describing in arithmetic terms is assigning MASK8[0] the value 1; MASK8[1] 2, MASK8[2] 4, MASK8[2] 8 and so on. In terms of bit patterns, we have listed all the ways that one bit in a byte is 1 and the rest 0. The set of masks contains all the patterns that can be formed by shifting this 1 bit from bit position 0, the extreme right, to bit position 7 on the left.

Should we need to query one particular bit in some integer, the masks we have so laboriously described would become useful. In bit operations on two numbers, if one of them is a known number—one of our prepared masks—we have stacked the deck. AND'ing MASK8[4] with a number is guaranteed to isolate the 5th bit in that number, because AND'ing two bits yields a 1 only if both bits are 1. And our mask is zero except for that one particular bit.

The results of the AND'ing operation can be used to direct further processing; thus, if *e* is an integer:

if ((e & MASK8[4]))

Process1();
else Process2();

In addition to AND'ing, these are other operations doable with masks that have a single 1 bit and are everywhere else zero. As before, e is an integer number and b is the bit in e located at the same position as the single bit in a MASK that is set to 1:

- **(e = e & ~MASK)** First, the bits in MASK are reversed and b becomes 0. So when e and the inverted MASK are AND'ed, the b th bit in e is set to 0; the other bits in e don't change.

- **(e = e | MASK)** sets b to 1; the other bits don't change.

- **(e = e ^ MASK)** reverses the value of b, setting 1 to 0, 0 to 1; the other bits don't change.

Bitwise boolean equivalents are listed in Table 1.10.

~(e1 & e2)	==	(~e1 | ~e2)
~(~e1 | ~e2)	==	(e1 & e2) NOT(NOT (boolean of line 1)) returns the original
~(e1 | e2)	==	(~e1 & ~e2)
~(~e1 & ~e2)	==	(e1 | e2) NOT(NOT (boolean of line 3)) returns the original
e1 ^ e2	==	(e1 | e2) & (~(e1 & e2))

Table 1.10. Bitwise boolean equivalents.

Also useful are bit fields, typed as unsigned ints and written as: **unsigned int x : 2**, meaning that **x** is equal to the two least significant bits in the word. Bit fields are easy to maintain as struct members, but they are not portable.

1.8.   CONTROL STATEMENTS

1.8.1. BRACES

The { } pair indicates that a group of sequential statements is to be treated as a single unit. Either all are done or none are done. Unless, of course, one of the statements contains a break, continue, return or goto directive. Or if one of the statements contains a call to a function that terminates the program or moves it outside the domain of the bracket pair.

1.8.2. WHILE (e == TRUE) { } or WHILE(e) { }

Testing takes place at the beginning of the while structure, so if e immediately evaluates to FALSE, no processing of the bracketed material takes place. Expressions may be arithmetic or be pointers, such as **while (*pstr++)**, where *pstr* points to an element within a char array; the while() will recycle until *pstr* points to the terminal SNUL of the array. A while expression, e, is reevaluated each time at the start of the loop. In the next configuration, e1 will pass the while (e1 == TRUE) test and drop into the body of the while statement.

```
e2 = 0;
e1 = 5;
while (e1)
     {
     ......
     e1 = e2;
     };
```

Within the loop, **e1 = e2 = 0**. Processing will stop when it is time to reenter the loop.

while (TRUE) is acceptable; processing will continue forever unless terminated within the bracketed text. More generally, if the expression in the parens evaluates to NOT ZERO, the expression is TRUE and the material in the brackets is processed. Otherwise, the program begins to examines the first non-comment statement just after the final brace of the while construction.

while () may contain a set of expressions; e.g., **while (((r-s)/(t*l) >= ft || (r+s)/l <= t) && *pstr != 'X')....** Each expression is individually evaluated to TRUE or FALSE; i.e., any evaluated expression that is NOT zero is TRUE. If the expressions are linked by a boolean OR (||) and any expression is determined to be TRUE, then the later expressions are not examined; **while()** is set to TRUE. If the expressions are linked by a boolean AND (&&) and any expression is FALSE, examination of the later expressions stops and **while()** is set to FALSE. In our example: **(e1 || e2) && e3**, if either *e1* or *e2* is TRUE, the () is TRUE, and the program proceeds to ascertain the TRUTH of *e3*. If *e3* is TRUE the entire phrase is TRUE.

do { } while () is a while() variant, which evaluates after the do { } rather than at the beginning of the construction. Hence the format guarantees that the { } statements will be done at least once.

1.8.3. FOR ()

FOR() is a WHILE statement with initializers and incrementers/decrementers.

for (e1; e2; e3) { } ;

where e1 is one or more initializers, separated by commas and terminated by a semicolon; e2 is a while statement; e3 is one or more indices, separated by commas and NOT terminated by a semicolon. It is not necessary to give values to all the e's. All the work can be done by just e2, incrementing taking place in the predicate of the statement. If all 3 e's are empty (e.g., **for (; ;)**), then the break condition must be in the predicate of the for statement. For example:

```
int x = 0;
for (; ; )
     {
     x += 10;
```

```
if (x > 200) break;     /* or return(x);*/
}
```

1.8.4. IF-ELSE ()

(1) **if (e1 == TRUE) s1; else s2;**

or

(2) **if (e1 == TRUE) s1; else if (e2 == TRUE) s2 ; else if (e3) s3; .... else if (en-1) sn-1; else sn;**

In the simplest case (#1 above) if (e1) evaluates to TRUE, the statement s1 is carried out and processing stops. If e1 is FALSE, then s2 is processed.

The construction may achieve considerable complexity starting with a single if () followed by any number of else if () conditionals—which may themselves contain nested if else conditionals—followed terminally and optionally by a final conditional or unconditional else (). Each segment is examined in turn. Processing of the entire construction ends when an if (e) expression evaluates to TRUE.

There is also an idiomatic if-else construction: **(e) ? s1 : s2** This is read as: **if (e) is TRUE, process s1. Otherwise do the statements in s2.**

1.8.5. SWITCH()

```
switch(v)
    {
    case <value of v is v1>:   {.........; break;}
    case <value of v is v2>:   {.........; break;}
    case <value of v is v3>:   {.........; break;}
    case <...............
    case <value of v is vn>:   {.........; break;}
    }
```

The test variable is given a value in switch (v). This is matched to various integer values of v listed in the individual case statements. <value of v> is actually a label. When a match is found, the instructions within the { } are carried out. However, unlike Sail, C has no automatic break at the end of a case statement. So the program goes on to examine the next case statement, unless the case statement ends with a break, as in the example shown. Or unless there is a return() statement to prevent fallthrough.

```
switch(a)
    {
    case 4 :         { .........; break; }
    case 1 :
    case 2 :         { ..................}
    case 3 :         { .....; return(a); }
    default:         break;
    }
```

This example illustrates several points: (1) values need not be ordered, the case of *a* equal to 4 is written first (though not necessarily handled first by the compiler); (2) each case must be a unique value of *a*; (3) several values can force the same processing as in case 1 and case 2; (4) if only one of the case statements is to be processed, case statements need to be terminated by a break or a return statement. Otherwise as with case 2, processing continues through to the next case (case 3); and (5) it is a good idea to use a default statement, where default is a keyword, to cleanly terminate the switch construction when no case is matched.

A case statement in a switch construct may itself contain a switch construct, as this next piece of function code shows. Note, however, that a case statement may not contain a continue instruction. The continue in case 0, if allowed, would recycle the program back to the for (i = 1....) statement, exactly the effect the break statements have. The return statement is read after the for() loop is completed and breaks the program out of the entire switch(keeprcd) construction by returning control to the calling function.

```
switch(keeprcd)
    {/*WhichMode*/
    case 'M':
        {/*Mixed Mode*/
        for (i = 1; i <= numfields; i++)
            {/*WhichFieldToUse*/
            switch(Mlist[i]) /*Mlist[i] can contain the value 0, 1 or 2*/
                {
                case 0:
                free(fieldA[i]);
                continue;        /*WRONG. Not grammatical*/

                case 1:
                free(fieldB[i]);
                break;

                case 2:
                fieldB[i] = dssave(fieldA[i]);/*dssave()saves an array dynamically.*/
                free(fieldA[i]);
                break;
                }
            }/*WhichFieldToUse*/
        return (TRUE);
        }/*MixedMode*/

    case 'F':
    ...............
    }/*WhichMode*/
```

The control constructions terminate processing when some test condition is met.

1.8.6. ADDITIONAL CONTROL MECHANISMS

1.8.6.1.   Break.

A break is used to force a break out of the current loop in for(), while(), do() and switch() constructions. A statement such as **if (x > 5) break;** is not legal except in context of an allowed loop, such as, in this example, the inner of two nested for() loops:

```
for (z = 0; z < NUM; z++)
    {
    for (i = z+2, x = 1; i < 100 ; x++, i++)
        {
        ..............
        if (x > 5) break;
        }
    z = i+10;
    }
```

Control is given to the first statement that follows the loop in which the break resides. In this example, **z = i+10;** is part of the outer loop.

1.8.6.2.   Continue.

A continue is used to force the program to start the next loop in a for(), while() or do() loop. Typically it is used with an if() format within a loop; as in:

```
int i = 0, x = 0;
for (i = 0; i < 10 ; i++)
    {
    .....processing statements involving x...
    if (x < 0) continue;
    .....more processing....
    }
```

The continue statement forces the program to go immediately to the start of the for() or while() construction in which the continue resides and perform the next cycle. In the for() construction, it will first increment variables that are listed for incrementing. Then the while expression is tested.

1.8.6.3.   Goto.

In Sail, blocks could be labeled, and the label acts as an identifier. So in a multiple loop, it was possible to break from one level and jump to any level. Because the labeled block facility does not exist in C, a simple alternative is the goto statement where a location is named in the goto statement and that place is marked somewhere else within the same function, some place that is not part of a loop. The program will immediately jump there. Note that the Begin-End comments are just that, comments, not labels.

```
int doA(arg1, arg2)
    {/*Procedure*/
    for (e1; e2; e3)
        {/*level1*/
        for (e4;e5;e6)
            {/*level2*/

            .............
            while (e7)
                {/*level3*/

                .........
                if (arg1 == 9) goto LEVEL1;

                .............
                }/*level3*/
            ................
            }/*level2*/

        ...........
        }/*level1*/
    LEVEL1:

    ...........
    return(arg2);
    }/*Procedure*/
```

For those with religious scruples against the GOTO, the previous code can be rewritten with a toggle, thus:

```
int doC(arg1, arg2)
    {/*Procedure*/
    int toggle = 0;
    for (e1; e2; e3)
        {/*level1*/
        for (e4; e5; e6)
            {/*level2*/

            ............
            while (e7)
                {/*level3*/

                ........
                if (arg1 == 9)
                    {
                    toggle = 1;
                    break /*level3*/;
                    }

                .............
                }/*level3*/
            if (toggle == 1)
                break /*level2*/;

            ...............
```

```
        }/*level2*/
    if (toggle == 1)
        break /*level1*/;

    ...................
    }/*level1*/

    ...............
return(arg2);
}/*Procedure*/
```

1.9. PROGRAM STRUCTURE AND COMPILATION

1.9.1. PREPROCESSING

The compiler begins transforming a C program into machine-readable code well before it reads a line of the actual program. As in the format for a single file program (see Table 1.11), the start of the main file of a large program usually contains a list of include files. Include files are files that contain definitions and aliases of constants that the main program may use, files that declare variables defined in still other files, files that contain prototypes of library routines and files that contain prototypes of user-created functions that may be called in the main program. The main file may also contain define statements for constants specific to the program, hence not contained in the header files. These are all preprocessed by the compiler before it attends to the main program.

Preprocessor statements begin a line with **#** as the first significant character and stop at the end of the line unless the line is extended by a \.[51] Preprocessing statements are commonly written at the top of the file(s) but they may be written anywhere in the program files and can reference variables retroactively.

Preprocessor statements include the following:

1.9.1.1.   #define.

as in: **#define x y**

---

51 The compiler will delete the backslash and NewLine, thus attaching the line to the next line. A space is not added, so use a space just prior to the backslash to keep the first word on the next line separate.

Very generally, the #define statement is a way of establishing that a term x is a place holder where ever it appears for the text of y[52]. A constant may be defined by a simple #define statement format, where x is a name whose data type need not be given and y is a value:

#define OPENFILE 20

Copies of #define OPENFILE 20 can be scattered throughout the files that will be compiled together without violating C syntax.

If y is blank, as in

#define then

it is equivalent to instructing the program to ignore **then**, so we can write with impunity:

if (TRUE) then r = 10; else r = 20;

#define OPENFILE 30

is a redefinition of OPENFILE. This is an error.

1.9.1.2.   #undef.

#undef undoes a previous definition legally; as in:

#undef OPENFILE
#define OPENFILE 30

A macro can be #undef'ed even if it is not certain the macro exists. This is protection against inadvertently but illegally using the same name as one possessed by a macro in some library file, particularly when the library macro is not wanted.

1.9.1.3.   #include.

It is sensible and customary to write the functions and external variables that are used by a program in separate files. A file called *genio.c* might contain a group of general input/output routines, a few of which will almost certainly be used by any new program. *genio.c* can be compiled by itself and thereafter be available to a large group of programs. It does not need to be recompiled each time the main program is rewritten. Conversely, when a file whose functions are prototyped in an include file is recompiled, all the program files that use any of the include file's functions need to be recompiled.

Include statements name the files that contain prototypes and declarations. They are of two types:

#include <FILENAME>

---

52 Section 1.2.3 illustrated the #define'd macro, which contains args just like a function and is a compact way of writing a function.

#include "FILENAME"

Triangular brackets signal the file is a system file; as in **#include <STDLIB.H>** Quoted brackets are used for user-created files; as in **#include "GENIO.H"**. The preprocessor introduces the text listed in the include file at the point where the #include ... is stated. Note that these files are NOT the files that contain actual functions; i.e., they are not source code files.[53] But when a file of functions is developed (e.g., *genio.c*), it is customary simultaneously to create a sister file that contains the function prototypes (e.g., *genio.h*). The prototypes of referenced functions that reside in other files enable the compiler to compile a source file.

1.9.1.4.   Conditional Compilation.

Several formats are available. Note that args do not have to be parenthesized.

#if !defined DELIM   /*If DELIM has not been #define'ed, then do it now.*/
#define DELIM '~'
#endif

Nesting is allowed, with a separate #endif required to close each nested if phrase. The next example is read: If EME is #defined but RECEND and FLDEND are not, then define RECEND as ~ and FLDEND as **!**.

#if defined EME
#if !defined RECEND
#define RECEND '~'
#endif
#if !defined FLDEND
#define FLDEND '!'
#endif
#endif

This next example shows how to select machine-dependent file parameters. One of the set of constants linked to different operating systems is set to YES before the processor examines the conditional statements.

#define UNIX57 YES   /*UNIX57 has the value 1.*/
#ifdef MSC   /*If MSC was defined in a #define statement.*/
     #define INFILE 1

---

[53] Source files contain C language code: the actual functions and some specific definitions of variables. Compiling a source code file generates a file of object code. An object file is machine-readable, but is not relocatable or executable. Moreover, it probably does not contain some necessary functions and variable definitions that are to be found in other files. When the several object code files needed by the program are linked together by the linker, the result is a portable execute file. If *add.c* is source code file and *add.obj* is object code, generation of the runtime file, *add.exe*, is done by linking *add.obj*, *genio.obj*, *stdlib.obj* and so forth.

```
         #define OUTFILE 10
#elif defined(UNIX57)              /*Equivalent to: else if previously #defined'd*/
         #define INFILE 1
         #define OUTFILE 25
#elif defined(SUN)
         #define INFILE 1
         #define OUTFILE 25
#else
         #define INFILE 1
         #define OUTFILE 10
#endif
```

which is read as: if MSC has been #define'd and therefore is not zero, the constant INFILE is set to 1 and the constant OUTFILE to 10, and the compiler moves to the point after #endif. Otherwise it evaluates whether UNIX57 is TRUE (which it is in this case), and if so, INFILE is set to 1, OUTFILE to 25, and examination of the statement ends. Otherwise the next #elif is examined, and so forth. The construction ends with a #endif. Shown next is the complementary version, which is read as: if MSC is not TRUE (i.e., if MSC is zero because it has not been #define'd), then #define it.

```
#ifndef MSC
#define MSC 1
#endif
```

Comments in C may not be nested. This next code can be used to comment out a piece of code that may itself contain comments. Note, however, that the compiler can't handle unpaired single and double apostrophes, which signal the start of char and string literals, respectively. Which is why an apostrophe is inserted after the **t** in *Don't* while the code is inactivated.

```
#if 0
/*............/*comment*/
printf("\nDon't' know."); ............ /*comment*/ */
#endif
```

1.9.1.5.   Stringizing, Creation Of Strings From Args.

Ordinarily, there is no expansion of the macro arg inside a quoted string, as in

#define Ename(Earg) "Error message: Earg"

The Earg inside the replacement code is not replaced. But ANSI C allows the virtual equivalent of replacing code inside a string. A **#** preceding the macro arg inside the replacement text (**"Error message "** #Earg in our example) is a signal that the arg is to be expanded; e.g., Ename(E5) would become: **"Error message: E5"**.

#define Ename(Earg) printf("\nError message: " #Earg) Ename(Variable undefined.);
        /*PrintProduct: **Error message: Variable undefined.**/

This replacement within quotes may be used together with the automatic concatenation of a sequence of strings.

Thus:

#define cloz(chan, fn) {fclose(chan); printf("\n" #fn ".tmp is closed.");}

then cloz(F1,dbA1) would be rewritten as:

fclose(F1); printf("\n" "dbA1" ".tmp is closed.");

Adjacent strings are concatenated, so the end result is

fclose(F1); printf("\ndbA1.tmp is closed.");

1.9.1.6.   Pasting Tokens In A #Define Statement.

#define rez(x,y) x##y

is equivalent to concatenating two tokens, x and y, to produce a third token, xy. Thus:

int   i, j, k, ij;

i = 7; j = 8; k = 56; ij = i * j;
if (k == rez(i,j))
**   printf("\nHIT");**
else printf("\nNO");

1.9.1.7.   Pragma Directives.

#pragma statements extend preprocessor capability. They are compiler specific, implementation dependent and not universally supported. They are analogous to command line parameters in that they allow the programmer to change parameters for a particular compilation without needing to enter the file and rewrite parameter definitions. They enable language extensions, optimize loops or not, write utilities such as *max* and *min* as functions or as macros, default the char data type to unsigned or signed, check stack space, and so forth.

1.9.2. FORMAT OF A SIMPLE PROGRAM

A simple one-file C program written for a single machine might have the format shown in Table 1.11.

1.9.3. FORMAT OF A COMPLEX PROGRAM

A program that runs over several files has a more complicated format. The major differences are: (1) the program functions are written across several files; (2) include files can define values that should be uniform for all the files that constitute the program and values that should change depending on what compiler and/or machine is used. Customizing programs is made possible using available preprocessing statements.

Initial header comments. The comment illustrated includes the name of the program, the version, date and remarks about the program.

/*PROG.C: VERSION 2.1, Single user, PC 5May.93*/

The next list contains prototypes of the basic utility functions provided by the system. These files are encased in triangular brackets. They are examined by the compiler before the program file.

#include <STDIO.H>
#include <STRING.H>
#include <STDLIB.H>

Next is a list of #include files that contain prototypes of basic user-developed functions, some of which will be used by the current program. They are bracketed in double quotes. These are examined by the compiler before the program file.

#include "COMLIB.H"
#include "GENIO.H"

Next is a list of #defines. The first two provide alternative names of constants. The third is a function macro that clears an int array.

#define TOT 10
#define VOWELS AEIOUaeiou
#define CLRINT(i,x,y) for (i = 0; i < y; i++) x[i] = 0

Next is a list of the variables available to all the functions that follow.

static int new[TOT] = {0};
static int old[TOT*2] = {0};

The next is an alphabetized list declaring the program procedures. Each function in the program is prototyped. This has the advantage of eliminating the need for extern statements within the individual procedures. If a program is contained in one file, they can be labeled static.

static char *infct(char *a);
static int main(void);
static void match(int a, int b);
static int nsort(int a, int b);

Procedures are written alphabetically, in clusters or haphazardly. Among these actual procedures is a procedure called *main*() that marks the start of the running program. When *main*() terminates, the program terminates.

Table 1.11.   A simple one-file C program written for a single machine.

1.9.3.1.   File Of Constants And Macros.

This is a user-created file that will be included in all the other files. We will call it *define.h*.

#include "DEFINE.H"   /*User include files are in quotes.*/

This collects the symbolic constants, preprocessor instructions and #define'd macros used by all the files in the program. It has no variables so this file does not need to be compiled. *define.h* is included in the modules that are eventually linked. Hence if any statement in *define.h* is changed, any file that calls it MUST be recompiled. These constants and macros are traditionally written in upper case. The top of *define.h* itself contains include files that prototype functions supplied as a library by the compiler; *stdio.h* and *stdlib.h* are commonly used. Other library functions are used for graphics, string manipulation, I/O and mathematical calculations. If the compiler library function prototypes are in a directory called *include*, we would write at the top of *define.h*:

#include <\INCLUDE\CTYPE.H>   /*System library files are in triangular brackets.*/
#include <\INCLUDE\STDIO.H>
#include <\INCLUDE\STDLIB.H>

1.9.3.2.   File Of Machine Dependencies.

We can redo a whole set of parameters and sizes depending on machine and compiler type and maintain all the critical values for a particular machine in a single file. There is a separate file for each machine/compiler. At the beginning of the file of definitions, *define.h* in our example, we would write:

#define MSCDOS 1   /*The compiler-machine used.*/
#if ZNTH486
#include "ZNTH486.H"
#elif MSCDOS
#include "MSCDOS.H"
#elif PSBRLND
#include "PSBRLND.H"
#else
#include "NOSUCHFILE.H"
#endif

For any particular machine/compiler, this next is the only notation that needs to be changed PRIOR to compiling the other modules. Change:

#define MSCDOS 1

to

#define PSBRLND 1

or whatever. Then recompile.

Including a non-existent *nosuchfile.h* ensures that if none of the listed possibilities was set, the compiler will issue a fatal error message such as: **Can't open include file 'NOSUCHFILE.H'**.

The specific file would specify sizes and dimensions appropriate to the machine. On one machine, int may be 16 bits and long 32 bits; on another machine int may be 32 bit. Suppose a 4-byte int is needed because the program does a considerable amount of bitmapping, where ints are masked with a 32-bit mask. In versions intended for 16-bit machines, one could set up an alias called *INTEGER*, thus:

typedef long INTEGER;

In machines with a larger size int, we would write:

typedef int INTEGER;

For portability, each print statement also needs individual long and int alternatives. For example, **if (cpu16) printf("32 bits = %ld",i); else printf("32 bits = %d",i);**. This can be done by macros, thus:

```
#define cpu16 1
#define PCD(c, x) printf("\n" #c ": " #x " = %d", x)
#define PCL(c, x) printf("\n" #c ": " #x " = %ld", x)
#define P(c,x) if (cpu16) PCD(c,x); else PCL(c,x)

int main(void)
    {
    INTEGER i;

    P(32 bits, i);
    return(0);
    }
```

1.9.3.3.   File Of Global Variables.

A file we will call *globals.c* is reserved for global variables. *globals.c* collects all the variables that are common between many program modules. In programs involving databases, *globals.c* would contain default field and record delimiters, limits on the number of fields and subfields, and an array of input and output pointers-to-FILES. A graphics program would define coordinates and keyboard key definitions. The variables are defined and initialized in *globals.c*. *globals.h* contains the prototypes of the variables listed in *globals.c*; *globals.h* variables are extern. And they are assigned no values.

GLOBALS.C:

```
long dbreccnt = 0;                    /*A long integer.*/
char difields[SZE(4)] = {SNUL};       /*A char array. Each element is SNUL'ed.*/
char *field[MAXFIELDS +1] = {NULL};   /*An array of MAXFIELDS pointers-to-char.*/
                                      /*All the pointers are NULL'ed.*/
int   numfields = 0;                  /*A single int is set to zero.*/
```

GLOBALS.H:

```
extern    long     dbreccnt;
extern    char     difields[SZE(4)];
extern    char     *field[MAXFIELDS+1];
extern    int      numfields;
```

Later, in the files that contain the program functions, *globals.h* should be listed just after *define.h*, the file used for constants. Positioning *globals.h* this close to the top precludes the need for additional extern statements in the separate files in which the global variables are used. *globals.c* is compiled by itself and *globals.obj* will be made available to the linker.

1.9.3.4.   Utility Files.

Utility files are user-created files that contain input-output functions, string manipulation functions, graphics functions and so forth. One or more of these will be used by any new program. In the utility files, the actual function code should be preceded with an (alphabetized) list of prototypes of the functions in the file. Then it doesn't matter in what order functions are written.

Writing explicit extern declarations over and over again in calling functions is a nuisance. To use a function in another file: label the function an extern in the calling file and place the extern statement above all the functions that will be referencing it. What is even simpler, particularly with utility files that are constantly accessed is simply to prepare a file of externs for all the functions in the file as we did with *globals.c*. Suppose two files, *io.c* and *strings.c*, which contain heavily used functions. Moreover, functions in these files call each other. If extern files are written, then

the top of strings.c would be:

```
#include "DEFINE.H"
#include "GLOBALS.H"
#include "IO.H"
```

and the top of io.c would be:

```
#include "DEFINE.H"
#include "GLOBALS.H"
#include "STRINGS.H"
```

1.9.3.5.   The Main File.

The top of the main file is:

```
#include "DEFINE.H"          /*define.h includes reference to C library files.*/
#include "GLOBALS.H"
#include "IO.H"
#include "STRINGS.H"
```

followed by an alphabetized prototype list of the extern and static functions in the file. Then it doesn't matter in what order functions are written.

This file may include a sizable number of functions. One of them must be called *main*. The program starts at this function and terminates when *main*() terminates, if it has not already exited by some other route.

Note that like any function, *main*() may contain args. These args reference text directly entered from the keyboard when the program is called. By convention, there are three command line args: (1) int argc counts the number of separate 'words' typed when calling a program; (2) char *argv[] is an array of pointers-to-char, where each pointer points to the start of one of the 'words' (The machine finds space for the actual text just as it does when an external array of pointers to string constants is defined. See Section 1.5.4.); and (3) char *envp[] stores the machine environment detailed, in a DOS environment, in *autoexec.bat*. If a program called *addit* is to operate on an input file called *dbjune* and send results to an output file called *dbjune.rez*, then typing **addit -idbjune -odbjune.rez** would mean *argc* is 3; *argv*[0] points to *addit*; *argv*[1] points to *-idbjune* and *argv*[2] points to *-odbjune.rez*. Keyboard-entered terms can be used to initialize parameters, state the input and output file names, select a particular subset of available functions or set the degree of help a program will offer a novice.

1.9.4. LINKING FILES

By this point the system knows which functions are used in each file and, if some of the functions are not defined, the compiler has prototypes for these functions. At link time the linker shuffles through the object files that are to be linked finding the cited functions. If any function is missing, an error message is issued. Combining the object files with the code for functions called from the system's library, it produces an executable file. This next is a file called *txtadd.lnk*, which instructs the Microsoft linker to link *txtadd.obj, globals.obj, comlib.obj, comset.obj* and functions from the *llibce.lib* library in the lib directory. Parameters and options begin with the **/** or **-** symbol. *txtadd.map* will contain all the symbols found by the linker.

/I /F /PAC /M /NOD -E -CP:0x1111 /ST:0xA000 txtadd globals comlib comset
txtadd
txtadd.map
\lib\llibce

To run the linker, the programmer would type:

LINK @TXTADD.LNK

When a program overruns the available stack space or is too large for the available memory, it sometimes helps to divide the program into portions that are executed at different times. These non intersecting segments can occupy the same place in memory at different times. These are said to overlay each other. For a file that will be an overlay: its *include* files must include the functions that the current overlay file calls. If *a*, *b*, and *c* are sufficiently discrete so that they can overlay each other and if they all call *d* and *e*, then: **link d e (a) (b) (c)** will link the files. The beginning of *a* or *b* or *c* is: **#include "d"** and **#include "e"**.

1.10. PORTABILITY

For maximum portability, it is well to stay close to K&R as being the minimum standard supported by almost all C compilers. These are some sensible rules for dealing with different compilers, particularly those not at current ANSI standard.

When naming identifiers, keep external identifiers that will be resolved by the linker unique in the first 6 chars. Keep internal and local variables unique in the first 6 chars to maintain compatibility with some older compilers, even though 31 chars are now allowed. Don't use the same name for a struct/union tag and an enclosed member.

With backslash notation, don't use \xHHH where HHH are Hex digits; use \ddd octal digits. Don't use **\a** (alert) or **\v** (vertical tab), which are in the latest standard only. Don't use underscore as the first char in a variable's name; it might conflict with a system name. Don't use a restricted character set and trigraph construct.

Initialize predefined global and local variables to zero, even though they are supposed to default to zero. Initialize all pointers to NULL; this is no place to save execution time.

The difference between two pointer values can be more than an unsigned int, so make the difference a long int[54]

```
char       *pBegin;
char       *pEnd;
long       Size = pEnd - pBegin;
```

Use portable size terms defined in *limits.h* for the particular compiler and machine. Use **INT_MAX** and **UINT_MAX** instead of the particular maximum signed/unsigned int value on a particular machine. Similarly, use **LONG_MAX** and **ULONG_MAX** for the maximum signed/unsigned long value on a particular machine. On 2's complement implementations that don't supply *limits.h*, do this:

```
#define INT_MAX ((int) (((unsigned) -1) > 1))
#define UINT_MAX ((unsigned) - 1)
#define LONG_MAX ((long) (((unsigned long) -1L) > 1))
#define ULONG_MAX ((unsigned long) -1L)
```

---

54 To be precise, the difference between two pointers is defined as ptrdiff_t, where ptrdiff_t is either int or long. The particular data type for the compiler used is to be found in *stddef.h*.

```
int MaxValue1 = INT_MAX;
long MaxValue2 = LONG_MAX;
```

Similarly, for low or high byte, use a portable macro definition such as LOBYTE defined as:

#define LOBYTE(y) ((y) & 0xFF)

Make use of *ctype.h* for char definitions such as *isupper*() and *islower*(). Don't write:

if ((c >= 'A') && (c <= 'Z'))

When using the right shift operator on signed quantities, mask them with the bitwise AND operator, if you don't want the sign extended bits.

```
char Char1 = -8;
unsigned char Byte1;
Byte1 = (unsigned char) (Char1 > 3) & 0x1F;
```

Be careful comparing char and int types. This will never evaluate to TRUE on a system that sign extends the char types but treats hex numbers as unsigned:

```
char CharValue;
if (CharValue == 0x80) printf("This won't be executed.");
```

An implementation may chose to sign extend a char to int type and then convert it to unsigned. Or the compiler may convert *CharValue* to an unsigned type of the same size and then zero extend it to unsigned int length.

Hence the following code is tricky:

```
char CharValue = (char)-7;
unsigned UnsignedValue;
if (UnsignedValue == (unsigned) CharValue)
     printf("Result is compiler-dependent");
```

Because C guarantees that all members of the character set are treated as positive, this is safe:

```
int CharValue;
if (CharValue == 'X')
     printf("Safe comparison");
```

As suggested in Section 1.9.3.2, it is a good idea to typedef INTEGER in a preprocessor conditional so that it represents an int on larger machines and a long integer on small machines. It is less simple to create a char for all languages. Transforming a character from a char representation (using a 1-byte character set) to a wide-character representation retains the ASCII configuration, but multiple mappings become possible during multibyte character transformations, and these are implementation-dependent. Even moving from ASCII to EBCDIC, a classic problem, breaks up representation sequences that after long use have begun to seem instinctive and upon which searches and sorts may depend.

Machines differ in how they respond to register variables. So don't use 'register' to optimize code.

Never use a variable with side effects more than once as an arg to a function/procedure call. This is ambiguous code:

FunctionCall(i, i++);

To ensure that the program will handle structs and arrays on outdated compilers:

- Don't directly assign structs/unions through the assignment operator.

- Don't pass structs/unions by value to/from functions. Instead, use pointers and explicitly assign each member of the struct/union.

- Don't use initializer lists with union type objects.

- Don't initialize local variables that are arrays or struct/unions.

Don't use the newer defined operator in #if and #elif directives. Use the older #ifdef, #ifndef and #else operators. Similarly, the stringizing operator (#) and the token-pasting operator (##) may not be supported.

Don't use the enum construction; use a set of macro #defines instead.

Volatile and **Const** are new keywords. **Const int pulse** declares that the variable integer *pulse*, once initialized, can NOT be changed in value by the program; i.e., the value at the address of *pulse* can not be changed. **volatile int pulse** declares that the variable integer *pulse* is subject to change by the operating system in ways that may frustrate optimization, so the compiler should not attempt optimization. **const volatile int pulse** says the program may not change *pulse*, the operating system may.

volatile and *const* can be used if they are nulled for non-ANSI compilers, thus:

```
#ifdef VOLATILE        #ifdef CONST
#define volatile       #define const
#endif                 #endif
```

Always include a type specifier with each const or volatile declaration; e.g., write: **volatile int k**. Don't write: **volatile k**.

CHAPTER 2

TEXT AS A SINGLE STREAM: ENTRY AND STORAGE

2.1. INTRODUCTION

Strings as such do not exist in C. In C, a string is not a thing. It is not a single variable. From the start, it is viewed as a composite object. By definition, a string is a sequence of characters, each of which has an ASCII representation[1]. The sequence must be terminated by the character \0[2]. Indeed, \0 can not be part of viable text, because its presence signals the immediate functional termination of the string.

That a string is markedly different from the other C data types is not just a matter of definition. Its particular structure affects ease of handling. We do not within very large limits need to assign different storage sizes to integers. Or to different sized floating point numbers. Or to a compound data type such as a struct of type whatever, even though the struct may contain a variety of different data types. Given that x is of the appropriate data type, **x = 1;** and **x = 111E-5;** and **x = NewStruct;** use the same simple assignment format. But **x = OldString;** is not a compilable assignment because a string begins life as a vector, i.e., a one-dimensional (1D) array, not as a single entity. Indeed, strings are always one dimension more than any simple data type. A set of related integers may be gathered into a 1D vector but a group of strings requires a two-dimensional (2D) array, where the number of rows is determined by the number of strings and the number of columns by the size of the largest string[3]. Higher-dimensional string arrays are not encouraged by the resources available in C.

---

1 As noted in Section 1.4.2, originally C assumed a 7-bit ASCII character set, which is sufficient for English language representation, but can now address the requirements of languages with larger symbol sets. In this book, we use 1-byte ASCII representation.

2 To highlight that '\0' is special, we will use SNUL as alias for \0, the character constant in C that signals the termination of a string. SNUL is ASCII zero, the character whose bit representation is all zeros.

3 As an exercise, consider the representation of values **11, 13, 150, 2** as an array of integers and as an array of strings.

There is no built-in standard size for strings as there is for ints or floats or structs or pointers. Ints take 8 bits or 16 bits or 32 bits, depending on the machine. Floats take 32 or 64 bits. Chars take 8. Strings? We don't know until we have actually composed the string. We can't calculate how many chars of space the string will take, until it actually takes it. At best, we can define a buffer—a character array—of a particular size, which provides one piece of information in that the string must not be larger than the buffer that will hold it. Each string, except for string literals, must state its capacity, its upper limit for storing characters. Sizing is not automatic as it is in a language such as Sail, where we could write **STRING new;** and leave it to the system to provide sufficient storage for however many chars *new* contains, no matter how or how often *new* is reassigned.

In this chapter we will begin the discussion of ways and means of getting around these handicaps. Our goal will be the implementation of a construct: the flexible string; i.e., a data type that is responsive to the demands placed on it by programs that deal with text as data and text as information. We will examine in greater detail than in Chapter 1 the char array, the pointer-to-char and the pointer-to-pointer-to-char. These are all data types in C. To do what we want to do with text strings, sometimes we will have to make use of the properties of the char array. Other times only the pointer-to-char will allow us to do what we want. Or the pointer-to-pointer-to-char may be the right tool. Or none of these will do, so we should implement the string(s) using data structures discussed in later chapters. No one of them, unfortunately, does it all.

If we could design a new and wonderfully useful data type called **string**, how would we characterize its features? Our ideal string would surely have some of the attributes of a char array, in that we would be able, if we chose, to reach immediately any character in the string, independent of any other character. It should be like a 2D array, so that we can group a cluster of strings that belong together. Its size should be instantly available, without us or some program having to start at the top and count to the end of the string before its size can be stated. We would like to chop it at will into neat same-sized packets or unevenly, stopping at a particular character or at one of a set of halt indicators. We would like the ability to clump it with other strings in a simple fashion. We don't always know ahead of time how many other strings will be merging, but it would be nice if we could just name the strings, however many there are, in a single concatenate statement and without making arrangements to store the now enlarged string. We would also want the string to be transparently addressable so we can immediately and permanently chop off chars at the beginning of the string, or anywhere else in the string. Getting it storage should requires no special arrangements. And when we have no further use for it, it should quietly vacate the premises, leaving its living quarters clean and immediately usable by other strings.

More formally, we have proposed the features of a primitive data type *string* with the characteristics needed in text manipulation and analysis. But there is no such unit package. So let's look at what we have to work with. And let's figure out how string features we need can be expressed in C. In a later chapter, we will explore more complex data structures such as the struct and the linked list, all in the service of designing tools to make the string malleable, to make the string easy to use and responsive. And we will present *setbreak*(), a utility adapted from the Sail language that can be used to recreate aspects of the Sail string's flexibility.

In a language such as Sail, a string is an entity to be dealt with directly. We don't need to request storage from the system or predeclare the amount of storage required. When the variable is no longer needed or has acquired a different number of characters, the system quietly takes care of junking the old value of the variable without bothering the programmer. 'Ah', you might say, 'there is no real difference. In your ideal system, the system, poor thing, is the one that is forced to find space for this string and return a pointer. It's a matter of dealing with pointers, not strings at all.' 'And you', I would respond, 'miss the point. I am talking of the items the programmer has to deal with. I care nothing about improving working conditions for the machine or the compiler. A reasonable system should allow me to think directly of the strings I manipulate. I should not be forced to think of filling out papers on how many characters I will need well ahead of time. I should not need to count how many characters have accumulated and ask the system to find this group of chars that would like to live together a home somewhere. And please, sir, would you let me know their address when you're done.'

The string seems to bring out the worst in C. An array of ints is a lot of ints. But an array of chars is only a single string. Most data types are well behaved. To make a permanent change in an int or a float or even a struct, we know we need to use its address as function argument. The address is expressed as **&var** or else a separate datum, a pointer such as ***pvar***, is assigned the address of the variable. Simple and consistent. But a string is an array and arrays have an additional way, an idiomatic format whereby on occasion the name of the array can stand in for its own pointer value. Consistency would have been preferable. Uniformly writing the pointer to the first element of the array as &*var*[0] or as pvar does not seem a hardship. But since idioms are a fact of the C string programmer's life, we will discuss how to deal with them—when a pointer seems to be an array and when an array name substitutes for its own pointer.

String functions shown in this book are, for the most part, consistently labeled.

- The prefix **st** indicates that the function is appropriate for either preset or dynamically stored strings or that it is a rewriting of a standard C library function such as *strcat(), strcpy(), strlen() or strcmp()*.

- The prefix **ds** indicates the procedure expects a dynamic string or will create a dynamically-stored string. Only one of the strings is changed and/or created.

- The prefix **ps** indicates the function deals with a preset mother or daughter string that will be modified.

- When both the source and destination strings are changed by the function, then the function has a double prefix; e.g., *psdsscan()* indicates that the preset mother string is modified and the daughter string is created dynamically within the function and *dspsscan()* means that the portion extracted from the dynamically-created mother string is stored in a preset char array. (See Chapter 7 for syntax.)

Function args have, where appropriate, the following sequence: **source string, arg 2, arg 3, ... arg n-1, destination string**; i.e., the mother string is listed first, followed by auxiliary args and finally the name of the daughter string. In functions dealing with dynamically stored daughter strings, no destination string arg is needed, because the daughter string is created within the function. Instead, a pointer to where the string is stored is returned.

Actual program functions used as illustrations are taken from TXT [4]. To maintain TXT function argument syntax, several of the C library string processing have been rewritten with reversed arg order. As example, **stcat(arg 1, arg 2)** appends arg 1 to the end of arg 2 in contrast to **strcat(arg 1, arg 2)**, which appends arg 2 to the end of arg 1. Similarly, **stcpy(arg 1, arg 2)** copies arg 1 to arg 2, overwriting arg 2. This is in contrast to the library function *strcpy()*, which writes to arg 1 from arg 2.

Some typedef'ed synonyms for common data types that will be used throughout the book are shown in Table 2.1.

typedef short	**BOOL;**	/*Sets switches: TRUE/FALSE or YES/NO.*/
typedef unsigned long	**BITMAP;**	/*On small machines, sets a 32-bit word size.*/
typedef char	***STRING;**	/*A pointer-to-char is typedef'ed as STRING.*/
typedef STRING	***PTRADR;**	/*PTRADR: char **, a pointer-to-pointer-to-char.*/

Table   2.1. Some typedef synonyms used in this book.

2.2.   ACQUIRING STRINGS

To speak of a program manipulating a string presupposes an existing string. This section is preliminary to the discussion of how strings become available. The intent is to make a clear and workable distinction between two kinds of strings: constant strings and variable strings.

A word on terminology. Much of the writing on C strings deals mainly with the string literal, with emphasis on storage considerations. In the summary of C language changes formalized in the ANSI standards, K&R (p. 260) note that "Strings are no longer modifiable, and so

---

4   TXT is a set of interrelated C programs for working with text data formatted as notes, as documents or as database records. It derives from an earlier system called MaTEXT (an acronym for Manipulation and Analysis of Text), written in the 1970s in Sail. The TXT system extracts strings/records from database files, where the critical element for selection is location or keyword or user-defined class name or stylized text. TXT procedures alphabetize and otherwise sort serial strings/records; assign numeric values to sets of text phrases for on-line coding and table-making; annotate text; substitute phrases; restructure files; compact, rearrange and tabulate the information in records; and conditionally or unconditionally generate subfiles according to specific text, class name, or program-created badges.

may be placed in read-only memory.", a statement which is true because the term *string* in C refers specifically to a sequence of characters enclosed in double quotes. To talk of a library function such as *strcpy()* as a string processing function is, strictly speaking, a misnomer, in that it operates on arrays that contain characters, not C-defined strings.

Newer compilers expect a quoted character string not to change contents during a program run. In fact, a compiler is free to put string constants in a read-only area or not; and when string constants are read-only, a compiler may store identical constants in one location.

What happens when a string literal is used to initialize a character array, which is of course a variable? The program is allowed to change the individual characters of the initialized array. This next code is legal.

char new[] = "OldString";
new[6] = 'o';   /*a*/

Is this inconsistent with the notion that a string constant is not to be changed? Not from the point of view of implementation. The compiler stores the string constant in a static (possibly read-only) location and then copies the characters to a separate memory location of sufficient size to house the elements of the array. So the array can not affect the string constant.

The array is, however, subject to the same rules of overflow that apply to pre-sized arrays. The next code is illegal, but the compiler is unlikely to prevent us from modifying the contents of the array, even if the new text is longer than the previous text. We could—but should not—write:

stcpy("This is a second string designed to overflow new.",new);

Depending on the compiler this will appear to work or it might create errors or produce unusual machine behavior.

A string literal can be directly accessed through a pointer-to-char. The pointer is given the actual address of the stored string literal. It is therefore in a position to manipulate the string. As noted by K&R (p 104): "...the pointer may subsequently be modified to point elsewhere, but the result is undefined if you try to modify the string contents." Illegally modifying one of two identical string constants adds another layer of uncertainty. In compilers that store them as one, modifications in one string also modify the other. Despite the consequences, the compiler might not complain when the contents of the string constant are changed.

The pointer is linked to the string constant thus:

char *pold = "OldString";

All in all, compilers expend a great deal of attention on string literals. Certainly, once a literal character string is defined, the system keeps aware of it, not just where it is, but what it is. Each time, the system knows it is dealing with the same character string, in that the addresses of relevant strings pop up on the stack whenever the function is called. For example, as shown in Section 3.1.4, a non-static local pointer is reunited with the same string literal each time the function is invoked. This is in marked contrast to the linkage of a local pointer and a string dynamically-stored in the heap, where strings are also static and also stored by the system in a location of its own choosing (see Section 3.1.3).

From the user's point of view, there is a functional distinction to be made between arrays we want to overwrite and those that we do not. We want to treat some strings as read-only with assurance that such strings once defined will not change. We want assurance that our string variables can always change, subject to array size limits. To create a working distinction, we need terms and procedures that *functionally* separate the constant string from the variable string. These procedures of course depend on implementation details of storage and accession that are reasonably uniform across compilers.

First, terminology. *string literal* and *quoted character string* and *character string literal* retain the base meaning of the string constant; e.g., **"This is a string literal."**. We will reserve the term *string constant* for a defined character array that is initialized with a string literal[5]. The compiler handles this at compile time. A *variable string* is a character array of any storage class that is filled by characters by way of stream functions or string copy functions. The system handles this at run time.

A *string literal* is a set of characters enclosed in double quotes. It need not be defined explicitly; for example, the string literal constitutes the essence of one of the printf() or scanf() args—it is all the characters enclosed in bracketing quotes including white space characters and the percent signs that mark where values will be entered in the print output. More generally, it can serve any function as an arg whenever text is needed; e.g., **ttyin("td");**

A *string constant* is either a char array initialized by a string literal or a pointer-to-char that points to a string literal. The amount of storage need not be stated. Nor is the terminal SNUL written into the string literal. String constants have obvious use in naming files or devices or fixed classes.

The distinctive feature of the string constant is that, once written, we treat it as **read-only** text for the life of the program. The text can be printed or it can be copied to variable strings but we will never intentionally change the original text of the string constant. Whether or not the compiler sets it aside in a read-only area isolated from that used by strings where changes in content are expected is irrelevant.

Given that what we call a string constant is a character array, how do we set the string constant apart from the string variable, taking into account likely compiler implementation?

First: string constants have permanent storage; they may request static global, static local or external global storage. They are never written as local arrays. Variable strings, on the other hand, are unrestricted in scope.

---

5   C makes no such distinction between string literal and string constant.

Second: the array containing the string constant can be sized or not, while the char array for the variable string is always sized; thus, **char Kstring[] = "Stuff";** versus *char varstring[10] = {SNUL};*

Third: the string constant is initialized when it is defined; it should be completely determined at compile time. Filling the array is achieved by writing characters inside double quote brackets. A variable string is NOT initialized when it is defined, except with {SNUL}, where appropriate.

Fourth: we do not terminate the string constant with a SNUL. The compiler will do that. String processing operations that we write must add the terminal SNUL for the variable string.

Fifth: a variable pointer-to-char that is assigned the address of a string constant will not be revalued with another address. In contrast, when a pointer to a variable string is defined, it is either valued at NULL or at the address of a variable string and it can be revalued. Ways to revalue the variable string depend on whether the array is preset or dynamically allocated.

Sixth: the constant string will be complete and filled at compile time. The variable string can always be filled (and refilled) at run-time. Copying text from a string literal to a variable string is, however, allowed at compile time; e.g., **char varstring[20] = {SNUL}; stcpy("string literal", varstring);**. Nevertheless, *varstring* is a variable string. It is defined without an initializer and it can, as shown in line *a* above, be modified.

Turning these statements around, we can assert that for our purposes any character array stored as a static local or static global or external global object AND initialized with a value other than SNUL is a string constant.

As an additional but unnecessary safeguard, we can use *const* to prevent a function from permanently changing the contents of an array element. Suppose at the top of the file:

const char keep[20] = "Don't Change";
const char new[25] = "SeparateString";

and later in some function, there is the instruction:

keep[3] = 'X';

The compiler will issue an error message and not compile. So the const construction does, in a sense, prevent a permanent change in the array element. Unfortunately, the compiler may let *keep* overwrite another const string such as *new*; but it will issue a warning.

2.2.1. STRING CONSTANTS

If we decide to name the file to which, say, we send intermediate status reports *temp.log*, the name can written into an unsized global char array with the statement:

char nfile[] = "temp.log";

Or into a static local array with this statement:

static char nfile[] = "temp.log";

We need not specify the number of characters to be made available. The compiler sets the right amount of space aside. We may of course, if we wish, size the array.

char nfile[9] = "temp.log";   or   char nfile[8] = "temp.log";

The first format is obviously correct. We allowed eight spaces in the array for the name: *nfile*[0] to *nfile*[7]. *nfile*[8] holds the terminal SNUL, filled in by the compiler. Interestingly enough, in some compilers, *nfile*[8] also works.[6] These compilers rectify array dimensionality when the string is stored. This is a boon for the programmer who works mostly with systems or numerical arrays and uses strings mainly to hold error messages and file names. He is spared the need to remember to provide space for the terminal SNUL.

As shown in the previous chapter, C provides the programmer a choice whether to use ASCII or octal code to represent a character in a string constant. For the most part, it is easier to recognize **?;.**, and so forth, than to decode their ASCII equivalents. Also, given the differences among compilers and the demands of porting programs to non-ASCII systems, K&R (p 19) recommend writing ASCII chars in character mode rather than in octal; i.e., to write the comma as **,** rather than as **\54**, the double quote as **\"** rather than as **\42**, and the single quote as **\'** rather than as **\47**. Thus:

#define regpunc ",.?;: \"\'\n\t"

However, where portability and char extensibility are not considerations, quotes may be simpler to pick out in octal. A **\40** certainly stands out more clearly than a space. And a comma is so common, it might be ignored if not listed in octal. This is the same as the previous definition:

#define regpunc "\54.?;:\40\42\47\n\t"

We can define a pointer to a string literal, just as we define a pointer to a string variable. By language rules, the pointer is a variable and can be reassigned. In our restricted usage, once a pointer is affiliated with a string literal, it remains attached for the life of the program.

In the next example, *fname* is defined as a pointer-to-char and assigned the address of the literal string. This seems to be doing things backwards, in that the string is still homeless. But the compiler will find a place for the string and put its address in *fname*. The string can be retrieved by way of its pointer.

---

6 See K&R, p. 261: "Character arrays with an explicit size may be initialized by a string literal with exactly that many characters (the \0 is quietly squeezed out."

STRING fname = "temp.log";   /***STRING** is typedef'ed as **char * ***/

Suppose we have a struct called *db*, which contains information about a database and one member of *db* is an array called *name*, which will store the name of the data file. We could copy the text **temp.log** to the empty struct member thus:

struct dbtype {char type[20]; char fn[20];} db;
stcpy(fname,db.fn);[7]

To handle a set of constants, we can define an array of character pointers, each pointer in the array in turn pointing to the next string literal in the list. Instead of writing:

printf("This is an error. The function should have 3 args.\n");
printf("Consult the handbook, 4.16.5, for examples of usage.\n");

we could use this next construction, which holds a fixed message, separated in line-sized chunks that can be separately changed or rearranged. There are three pointers, with each pointer assigned the address of a different string. *mesg*[0] points to **This is an error....**, and so forth.

int   i;
static char *mesg[] =
        {
        "This is an error. The function should has 3 args.",
        "Consult the handbook, 4.16.5, for examples of usage.",
        ""
        };

The size of the array need not be stated, making it easy to add lines to the text if necessary. The compiler adds a SNUL to each piece of text when storing it in memory.

The pieces are ready to be issued as a single message when an error is uncovered or they can be used to explain the purpose of the program, when a program is initiated.

The messages may be delivered with this statement:

for (i = 0; stlen[8](mesg[i]) != 0; ++i)

---

7 As noted in Section 2.1, TXT utilities have standardized notation. Specifically, where appropriate, the first arg is the string source, the second the string destination, the sink. *stcpy*(arg A, arg B) reads: **copy the source, arg A, to the destination, arg B**. Otherwise, it is similar to the library string function, *strcpy*(arg A, arg B), where the args read: **copy to the sink, arg A, from the source, arg B.**

8 *stlen*() does what the C library function, *strlen*() does; i.e., it calculates the number of chars in the array.

```
    printf("%s\n", mesg[i]);
```

A drawback to this way of halting the display of a message is that the stop condition depends on an empty string that must be present as the last line of the message. Alternatively, we could count the number of non empty lines and write:

```
for (i = 0; i < 2; i++)
    printf("%s\n",mesg[i]);
```

Better still, we dispense with an empty last string and let the system calculate the number of pointers, thus:

```
int pakets = 0;
pakets = sizeof(mesg)⁹/sizeof(mesg[0]);
for (i = 0; i < pakets; i++)
    printf("%s\n",mesg[i]);
```

Or if we #define a macro that would print out the message.

```
#define LOOP(i,m) for (i = 0; i < (sizeof(m) / sizeof(*m)); ++i) printf("%s\n", m[i])
LOOP(i,mesg);
```

The undimensioned array of character pointers format is also useful in defining a set of unrelated messages:

```
char *bomb[] =
    {
    "Unrecognized token.",
    "Syntax error.",
    "Divide error.",
    "Struct member missing."
    };
```

Later in the program, if *db.fn* is empty, this code

```
if (stlen(db.fn) == 0)
    printf("%s\n",bomb[3]);
```

would write the message pointed to by bomb[3] to the display, namely:

Struct member missing.

Typically, string constants such as *bomb* or *mesg* will have external storage over the file or over the set of files that constitute the program. The specific text to be installed in the char array is defined either at the top of the program or in a file accessible to any program module that will make use of this string. As a much less likely possibility, the string constant is static

---

9   Each array element (e.g., mesg[0]) is a character pointer, where the size of the pointer in bytes is fixed for the particular machine. The size of the array in bytes is usually the size of an element in bytes multiplied by the stated size of the array in elements. In the present case, where the definition of *mesg*[] is undimensioned, the compiler calculates the size of the array from the number of filled elements.

and local inside a function. As with a static variable, it remains unchanged when the function is inactive and can be used whenever the function is reactivated. If a string constant is defined through an automatic pointer variable, it will be accessible through that pointer each time the function becomes active. The string is written once and retained permanently. The pointer is inactivated at the end of the function and is (possibly) relocated when the function is recalled. Yet, as a consequence of how string literals are handled on the stack, it is reunited at each function call with the single copy of the string. So, in this one case, defining the pointer as an automatic local variable or as a static local variable has the same effect.

In this example, string literals are used directly. All error message are maintained in a single function. The first function arg indicates whether the error is describing an integer or float or struct error, the second arg indicates which error message is targeted.

```
void ErrorSweep(char K, int ii)
    {
    switch (K)
        {
        case 'I':
            switch (ii)
            {
            case 1: {printf("Divide by zero.\n"); break;}
            case 2: {printf("Exceeded maximum value.\n"); break;}
            case 3: {printf("Not an integer value.\n"); break;}
            }
        case 'F':
            switch (ii)
            {
            case 1: {printf("Divide overflow.\n"); break;}
            case 2: {printf("Exceeded maximum value.\n"); break;}
            case 3: {printf("Roundoff error.\n"); break;}
            }
        case 'S':
            switch (ii)
            {
            case 1: {printf("Member unrecognized.\n"); break;}
            case 2: {printf("Member missing.\n"); break;}
            case 3: {printf("Wrong type pointer.\n"); break;}
            }
        }
    }
```

In some other function, we could write:

ErrorSweep('S',3);

and the screen would immediately display the message: **Wrong type pointer.** This format has the advantage that we are not dealing with arrays, and so the first case can be labeled case 1, not case 0.

In string programming, string constants are used minimally, aside from their efficiency in storing error messages and file names. It is the string variable that concerns us in this book.

2.2.2. STRING VARIABLES

Particularly if we work with text databases and manuscripts, string variables are what we commonly think of as strings. Like the string constant, a variable string can be made available at compile time, simply by copying a text phrase as part of a function; e.g., **char errhold[100]; stcpy("Error. Start again.",errhold);**. Most often, however, the contents of the string are not known at compile time. As with other variables, we assume that text will be assigned in the course of running the program and we assume that the text is likely to change. A string is typed in from the keyboard or is the result of converting some number to its ASCII representation. To process an ASCII database, typically the text of a single record is brought into from disk file to memory; the text is subjected to small or large amounts of processing; the transformed string is released to some output file; and the next stream of chars (the next record, usually) is brought in. The char array that holds the record text will change contents each time a new record is brought into memory.

Strings in memory can generate strings. One string can be copied to another. Or a single string can give rise to a very large number of substrings. One substring, say, is the original string until a comma is encountered; this might extract the last name from a *person* field. Another is the part of the string that starts with the first letter following a space and ends with the letter before the next space. The result would be a single word extracted from the string. Another might be all the text enclosed by square brackets, when database material is glossed by informal bracketed material. In each such case, just as the result of a numerical subtraction operation is stored in another numeric variable, so we expect that partitioning a string will be followed with the assignment of text to other strings. Similarly, the result of concatenating strings, like adding numbers, will show up in some string variable.

2.2.2.1.   Array Size.

In C the natural data structure for string storage is a char array. To deal with the string, the system needs two pieces of information: (1) an upper limit to the number of characters the array can store; and (2) the size of the particular string stored in the array. This is done by: (1) sizing the array—at a minimum it must be sufficiently large to store the text; and (2) by terminating the text with \0. With string variables, in contrast to string constants, it is the programmer's obligation to make sure the string ends with a SNUL. Either he adds it himself. Or he copies the string from an existing string that has a terminal SNUL. Later in our discussion we will be dealing with string pointers and dynamic storage by the system. But even there, the user must somehow either know how many chars are to be stored or he must collect the entire incoming text in some temporary buffer before requesting storage space from the system.

The size of any array is the number of elements it contains. Given an array of size 50 (e.g., $a[50]$), values may be stored in $a[0]$ to $a[49]$. The size of the array is the index value of the highest element that is fillable plus one; in this example, the size is 49 plus 1.

To provide space for 50 int items or 50 float items or 50 structs or 50 unions, defining an array as $a[50]$ allows us to put 50 items in $a[0]$ to $a[49]$. There is no $a[50]$ element.

If the items are pointers-to-char (or pointers to anything else), defining a pointer array as $a[50]$ allows us to put 50 pointer values in $a[0]$ to $a[49]$. There is no $a[50]$ element.

If, however, $a[50]$ is defined as a char array and we fill the entire array, we may put 49 chars into $a[0]$ to $a[48]$ but $a[49]$ must be reserved for the SNUL value that terminates the string. Note that this does not mean that all the elements or any of the elements need to be filled with chars. It does mean that the actual text must end in a SNUL. It does mean that the text can be no more than 49 visible and/or control chars located in $a[0]$ to $a[48]$.

When the domain is months or student rankings or fields in a record and so forth, it is natural to place the first item in $a[1]$ rather than in $a[0]$. To start counting elements from $a[1]$, then, with the exception of the char array, the size must be one larger than the maximum number of elements to be filled. For 50 pointers or 50 integers, the size is 51; i.e., the array is defined as $a[50+1]$; and $a[1]$ to $a[50]$ can be filled. But for a 50-element char array, the size is 52; i.e., the array is defined as char $a[50+2]$. Elements $a[1]$ to $a[50]$ can be filled with significant chars; and $a[51]$ contains the terminating SNUL in a completely filled array. (See Section 2.4.2 for some consequences of ignoring $a[0]$.)

The compiler maintains local variables on a stack. Using too much local buffer space, particularly in a PC, may prevent a fairly large program from linking, or if it does link components, the program may soon stop with a runtime error indicating stack overflow. Reducing buffer size often circumvents limited stack size. Hence, although compilers may accept arrays as large as or larger than 64K bytes, often even 5K local buffers—if many are in use—may need to be trimmed. As a general rule, it is a good idea to program defensively. As one approach, sizes can defined as HUGESZE or LRGSZE in an initial accessible file of macro definitions where the size can be universally changed by a single retype. Thus:

#define HUGESZE 10000

and the char array would be sized as

char a[HUGESZE + 1];

The array can hold up to HUGESZE values in $a[0]$ to $a[HUGESZE-1]$ plus a terminating SNUL in $a[HUGESZE]$. This works well if only a few values such as SMLSZE, MEDSZE, LRGSZE and HUGESZE are sufficient. The problem with this approach is it is not fine-scaled, it is not flexible and it is not easy to remember how big HUGESZE is relative to LRGSZE, and so forth. Another approach is to #define a macro on top level such as:

#define SZE(x) x

so that char $a[SZE(31)]$ is the same as char $a[31]$. It is easy to search for **SZE**, should it become necessary to reduce storage space.

Using *SZE*(30+1) or *SZE*(30)+1, as in *a*[SZE(30) +1], to plug in 30 integer items starting at *a*[1], has much to recommend it. It is easy to find, should the size needs to be changed. Moreover it has a built-in reminder that there are 30 items of interest. In the same way, a char array that will store values in *a*[0] through *a*[30] would be sized as char *a*[SZE(31) + 1]. The same-sized char array intended to be filled with values in *a*[1] through *a*[30] would be sized as char *a*[SZE(30)+2]. In both cases, *a*[31] is valued at SNUL.

2.2.2.2.   Initializing Variables.

Global and static variables can be initialized as part of the definition, and should be.

```
int            intbuf[SZE(10)]    =    {0};
BOOL           mark               =    FALSE;
char           new[SZE(100)]      =    {SNUL};
static char    old[SZE(100)]      =    {SNUL};
char           *pnew              =    NULL;
```

new and *old* are defined and initialized as empty global char arrays, each capable of holding up to 99 ASCII values starting at *new*[0] or 98 values starting at *new*[1]. *old* is a static global array, accessible to all functions in the file. *new* is available to all functions in all files that compose the program.

The effects of NOT initializing local variables are not as dramatic, but just as real and trouble-producing.

Primitive data types and pointers to these types can be zeroed as part of the definition, thus:

```
char           a    =      SNUL;
int            i    =      0;
double         f[SZE(10)] =      {0};
STRING         p    =      NULL;
PTRADR         pa   =      &p;
float          interfl[SMLSZE];
static char    lnew[SMLSZE] = {SNUL};
STRING         pset[SMLSZE] = {NULL};
char           regbuf[LRGSZE] = {SNUL};
int            subtotals[SZE(5)] = {0};
```

A local array—whether int, float, char or pointer—can be cleared as part of its definition.

When a char array is always examined or filled from the first element and there is a guaranteed terminal SNUL, it is easy to convince ourselves that the text will be overwritten by new text, as in a cassette tape.

The assumption is usually correct. But there are unhappy consequences the rare times it is not. Consider a function that assumes the string will be overwritten by new material before it is sent out. This pseudo-code describes bringing text into a buffer called *new* and processing it, if an indicator, *mark*, is TRUE. Then outside that block, the text in *new* is output unconditionally. Obviously, at the start of the function run, there may be junk in *new* that will not be cleared or overwritten should *mark* be FALSE. The extraneous junk will later be output.

```
void fctdanger(void)
    {
    BOOL      mark = FALSE;        /*BOOL is typedef'ed as a short int.*/
    char      new[SZE(100)];                                            /*a*/
    if (mark == TRUE)              /* Test mark.*/
        {
        Bring in text to new;
        Do some processing;
        }
    output(new);
    }
```

Rewriting line *a* as: **char new[SZE(100)] = {SNUL};** prevents such problems.

If array elements will be examined randomly later in the function, the array can be cleared 'by hand'. CLRINT sets an int array to zeros, and CLRFLT sets a float array to zeros. CLRCHAR sets each char in a char array to SNUL. CLRPTR sets each pointer in a pointer array to NULL. In all of these macros, the first arg, *i*, is the loop counter, *x* is the name of the array and *y* is the size of the array.

```
#define CLRINT(i,x,y)       for (i = 0; i < y; i++) x[i] = 0
#define CLRFLT(i,x,y)       for (i = 0; i < y; i++) x[i] = 0
#define CLRCHAR(i,x,y)      for (i = 0; i < y; i++) x[i] = SNUL
#define CLRPTR(i,x,y)       for (i = 0; i < y; i++) x[i] = NULL
```

Using the variables defined, these are examples of usage:

CLRINT(i,subtotals,SZE(5));   would zero the int elements of the array *subtotals*
CLRFLT(i,interfl,SMLSZE);   would zero the float elements of the array *interfl*
CLRCHAR(i,regbuf,LRGSZE); would SNUL the character elements of the array *regbuf*
CLRPTR(i,pset,SMLSZE);   would NULL the pointer elements of the array *pset*

The importance of initializing a pointer as part of its definition can not be overstated. A safety feature in the C protocol guarantees that a NULL-valued pointer will not point to a memory location that contains a language object. So the pointer should either be assigned to point to a previously-defined variable or set to NULL. A NULL-valued pointer MUST be reset to point to a variable before it is used in a processing statement, but a NULL-valued pointer can serve as function arg in the expectation that it will be assigned to a string that will be dynamically created inside the function.

In working with strings, it is important initially to:

•   set each STRING (pointer-to-char; e.g.: char *ptr) to NULL

•   set each PTRADR (pointer-to-pointer-to-char; e.g.: char **pptr) to NULL

•   set at least the first char of each char array to SNUL

With dynamic string allocation (see Section 2.5.2), a pointer needs to be re-valued to NULL after it is freed. Else we could have a helpful pointer suddenly pointing at random; i.e., to obscure spots in the heap or even outside the heap.

Having proselytized so intensively for preliminary NULL'ing of pointers, we should point out it is poor practice to NULL a pointer function arg representing a string whose text is to be examined in the called function. In this next example, *psent* is the pointer to a preset char array and has the effect of bringing in the comparison string. If we NULL *psent*, we wipe out the connection to this string.

```
static STRING preps[10] =
{"above","at","for","in","of","on","over","out","to","under"};
```

```
static BOOL checkforprep(STRING psent)
    {/*BP*/
    int i = 0;
```

/*THIS NEXT STATEMENT IS THE WRONG THING TO DO HERE. The pointer should NOT be NULL'ed.*/

```
    psent[0] = SNUL[10];
```

/*Next, the keyfind() function glides through a string represented by the pointer arg psent, attempting to match a string literal accessed by an element of the pointer-to-char array preps. Under control of a for() loop, the sentence is compared to each of the prepositions in turn.*/

```
    for (i= 0; i < 10; i++)
        if (keyfind(psent, preps[i]))
            return(TRUE);
    return(FALSE);
    }/*EP*/
```

Usage:

```
if (checkforprep("Do it for the gipper."))
    printf("\nFound one.");
else printf("\nNo such luck.");
```

2.2.2.3.   Interchanging String Literals and String Variables.

When a function arg is a string literal, we can create a string variable that may be used interchangeably with it. The reverse is also true.

---

10 In the *psent*[i] format, the pointer functions as a char array element (see Section 1.5.2) and is equivalent to ***psent = SNUL;**. This is to be differentiated from the same-looking but very different construction, *preps*[i], which is a pointer element in an array of pointers. *preps*[i] is not idiomatic; it acts as an ordinary pointer to a string. The two constructions can be differentiated by context.

The TXT function *sttidy()* is a general string filter that produces a modified and cleaned string. It can change a set of characters to a particular character; it can prevent a run of spaces or a run of any other character; it can clean the beginning or the end of a string; it can remove field and record delimiters; it can change case; and it can prevent entry of particular characters into the revised string. It is prototyped as:

extern STRING sttidy(PTRADR s, STRING nchar, STRING changestr, STRING omitstr, STRING feuldm)

where:

arg 1:   the address of the pointer to the string that is to be tidied.

arg 2:   a pointer to the particular character that substitutes for the characters of arg 3.

arg 3:   a pointer to a set of characters, all of which are to be changed to arg 2.

arg 4:   a pointer to a set of characters, all of which are to be deleted.

arg 5:   feuldm is a mnemonic; each letter represents a separate task. 'F' cleans the front of the string; 'E' cleans the end of the string; 'U' changes string elements to upper case; 'L' changes them to lower case; 'D' prevents a run of arg 2 in the revised string; and 'M' deletes field and record markers.

At its simplest, substituting a string variable for a regularly used string literal is a safeguard that some letter is not left out, changing the meaning of the directive. In this example, the string literal "FUD" would be siphoned into the string variable **VFUD**.

```
char      dbr[100];
char      *pdbr = dbr;
char      VFUD[7];

stcpy(" Smith# R,T,# 1914#  1978# NYC#  NY~",dbr);
printf("\n[%s]", pdbr);     /*PrintProduct for the original record:
                            [ Smith# R,T,# 1914#  1978# NYC#  NY~]*/
stcpy("FUD",VFUD);          /*Reminder: stcpy() copies arg A to arg B.*/
sttidy(&pdbr,"-","#","\40",VFUD);   /*The variable, VFUD, serves in place of the*/
                            /*string constant, "FUD".*/
printf("\n[%s]", pdbr);     /*PrintProduct for the revised record:
                            [SMITH-R,T,-1914-1978-NYC-NY~]*/
```

Conversely, it often simplifies a program to substitute a specific string literal for a variable, particularly in try-out programs, when we need to test a small piece of code and don't want to set up an elaborate infrastructure.

In the general case, to open a set of files usually requires establishing arrays of pointers to the input and output file names and to their associated channel numbers such as these:

STRING	**infile[MAXIF]** [11] **= {NULL};**	/*Pointers-to-char array for file names.*/
		/*Read from these files.*/
STRING	**outfile[MAXIF] = {NULL};**	/*Pointers-to-char array for file names.*/
		/*Write to these files.*/
FILE	***inchan[MAXIF] = {NULL};**	/*Pointers-to-FILE array for read files.*/
FILE	***outchan[MAXOF] = {NULL};**	/*Pointers-to-FILE array for write files.*/

In addition, in the general case, interactive routines need to written to determine the names of the files to be processed and where the processed material is to be put. This can be circumvented by using a specific file name.

To read a file, we could write:

```
FILE *inchn = NULL;
inchn = fopen("db14feb.db","r");
```

And to write it out:

```
FILE *outchn = NULL;
outchn = fopen("feb.tmp","w");
```

2.2.2.4. Non-Interchangeability of Char and Char Array.

An int can be cast into a float or double or char. But a char and a char array can not be cast one to the other. Nor can they be interchanged as function args. If, in our example in the previous section, we needed only a single char as function arg—say, we wished the uppercase version of the input—it would seem reasonable to write:

```
sttidy(&pdbr,"","","",'U');
```

But this would be an error. We need to use a char array not a char, thus:

```
sttidy(&pdbr,"","","","U");
```

---

11 *outchan*[MAXIF] and *outchan*[MAXOF] are pointers-to-FILE arrays. *outfile*[MAXIF] and *infile*[MAXOF] are pointers-to-char arrays. MAXIF (equal to 5) and MAXOF (equal to 7) are values defined in *define.h* as the most input and output files I'd keep simultaneously open on a DOS system.(In machines with larger capacity, they can be redefined.) The actual limit is FOPEN_MAX, a value defined in *stdio.h*. From this, the system reserves 5 'files': stdin, stdout, and so forth. Additional auxiliary and communication devices and printers may siphon off still more file slots.

In C, a char and a char array are entirely different entities, even if the char array contains only a single character. An element of the char array may be assigned the value of a char, but direct substitution of one for the other is not possible.

It is often clumsy to develop the proper arg for a function such as *sttidy*() that demands a char array or pointer-to-char as arg, if all we have available is a single char variable or single char constant. In the example shown next, the second arg to *callingfct*() is a single char, *in*, that determines how the string is to be tidied. It has to be changed to an array before it can serve as arg to *sttidy*(). *change*() is a leveler function that converts a single char, *SC*, to a char array, *CA*. (*CA* is defined for convenience as static global and used and reused as needed.)

Inside *change*(), we can not write **CA = SC;**, because we can not make a single assignment to an entire char array. To transfer the char *SC* to *CA*, we write the two statements shown; the first assigning a char to the first element of the array *CA*, the second terminating the string with a SNUL.

```
static char      CA[2];      /*A minimum-sized string given scope over the whole file.*/
void change(char SC)
     {
     CA[0] = SC;
     CA[1] = SNUL;           /*CA is now a single-element string.*/
     }
```

Usage:

```
void callingfct(STRING db, char in)
     {
     change(in);
     sttidy(&db,"","","",CA);
     ..................
     }
```

Our example is admittedly trivial. The problem, however, is commonly encountered and more serious in database management, when record and field delimiters, decoded and returned as single characters by one function, are to be used by another function that demands a character array as arg.

2.3. ARRAY INPUT

Section 1.5.5.1 demonstrated some major library routines for transactions between disk, keyboard and memory. They provide the kernels around which amplified input/output functions are written. Even a simple function such as *getin*(), in (2) in 1.5.5.1, provides other services beyond storing keyboard characters; namely, it rids the entry string of initial white space, it identifies blank entry, it has some flexibility in how to halt input, it prevents array overflow and it adds the terminal SNUL for string closure.

2.3.1. CUSTOMIZING KEYBOARD ENTRY ROUTINES

Text data brought in for processing are almost always streamed from disk. Transmitting a text file for processing implies relatively large amounts of memory storage and the expectation is that, barring error, the program will sweep the data through the procedures in accordance with some preset schedule. In contrast, preliminary keyboard entry during a program run is typically used to initialize program options, requires small data storage and is intensely interactive. It may also be noted that keyboard entry is probably the last stronghold of the notion that the NewLine is the way to terminate a string.

A general-purpose library function such as *scanf* can handle all data types but ignores some of the routine problems specific to keyboard entry of text. As example, we shouldn't assume array space is sufficient or even available for the entering string; often there is only a pointer waiting to hook on to an incoming string that has no preset storage. And the need to delete the white space that brackets the string is almost always part of the preprocessing of keyboard entry. Moreover, whenever the end user is allowed to type his answers to requested information—the name of an optional sort module, say—in upper case or lower case or any case combination, the letters of the entry must be converted to a uniform case to check the entry text. In addition, in a geographic mapping or polar coordinate universe, we might wish to convert the string immediately to an integer or float value and modify it relative to specific coordinates. In an environment where incoming text needs to be formatted in one of several optional database styles, the basic data would be modified upon entry.

Example 1.   A general keyboard input acceptor.

ttyin() is an example of a customized *get*-based[12] workhorse routine that attends to some major requirements of keyboard text entry. It transfers input from the keyboard to a char array defined as **char ttystr[TTYSZE];**. *ttystr* is a convenience buffer for temporary storage. To save stack space, it can be defined as a global variable and saved in a file of global variables; e.g., *globals.c*. TTYSZE can be #defined in a file such as *define.h*.

---

12 *ttyin*-style functions, based on some version of the *get* library utility, can not be mixed with *scanf*()-based string input functions. *ttyin*() brings in ALL the characters typed (assuming it doesn't overflow the 132-byte buffer), and relies on later code to decipher text that might be a composite of multiple variables (see Section 3.). *scanf*() deletes initial white space but it doesn't flush typed characters that, for one reason or another, are not accepted into the current memory array. Hence noise and other characters remain in the input channel, waiting to be eliminated at the next call to *scanf*(). If **ttyin("");**, which instructs the function to bring in whatever is typed without deleting initial white space, is called between *scanf*() calls, an error decoding the input text is a likely possibility. Conversely, *ttyin*() will delete the unused end of a typed string that *scanf*() expects to process the next cycle.

ttyin() takes a single arg from the set {u, t, d, l} written inside double quotes; e.g., **ttyin("dut");**. Each letter sets a separate switch. These switches change the case of the incoming string, clean up white space at the beginning of the string, and direct the system to store the string dynamically. No explicit statement is needed to set a switch to 'NOT SET'. The procedure adds a terminal SNUL.

These switches are:

Case: 'u' or 'U' for upper case; 'l' or 'L' for lower case.

Case Default: each char is stored in the case received.

Tidy: 't' or 'T' deletes initial spaces, vertical tabs, horizontal tabs and form feeds.

Tidy Default: all chars entered are stored except the terminating RETURN or ESC key.

Dynamic save: 'd' or 'D' dynamically stores the string written into ttystr. It uses *calloc*() and returns its storage address.

Save Default: writes the text into *ttystr*; it doesn't call *calloc*().

ttyin() returns a pointer-to-char. When the string in *ttystr* is stored dynamically by the system, this pointer becomes the only access to it. Otherwise, the return pointer serves no purpose except to satisfy a particular compiler's fretful insistence on complete syntax. To prevent wasting stack space on nonessential pointers, *ptemp* is defined as a global pointer-to-char in *globals.c*. It is never NULL'ed. It is just reused. For example, suppose the text typed into *ttystr* determines the value of some permanent variable; e.g., **if (ttystr[0] == 'Y' || ttystr[0] == 'y')) usenum = 1; else usenum = 0;**. As soon as the statement is processed, the text in *ttystr* has no meaning. And the returned pointer has no meaning.

The single arg is case and order independent; e.g., **lut == TLU**.

Examples of syntax: **ptemp = ttyin("LT");** or **ptemp = ttyin("td");** or **ptemp = ttyin("");**

However, the arg can NOT be left blank. These are NOT ALLOWED: **ttyin; ttyin(void); ttyin(NULL);** [13]

In this example of *ttyin*() usage, the program has a set of tasks it performs. The user selects one. *taskintdecode*() checks that the task number is within the range of possibilities indicated by arg 2. Note that a for() or while () loop is essential in that there is no point continuing if the task information is incorrect. This is some code from *txtsort.c*, which sorts processed records in a variety of ways, including *lazyboy*, where the program develops its own sort categories based on the data received. *task* is an integer whose value is determined by the end user.

```
enum tasktype {LS = 1, NS, LP, NP, LAZYLET} ;
printf("\nPress <RETURN> for menu or type in command number.\n\t");
```

---

13 *ttyin*(NULL) bombs using the Microsoft compiler (MSC). *ttyin*() and *ttyin*(<space>) appear to work with MSC but should probably not be used.

```
while (TRUE)
    {/*GetCommands*/
    ptemp = ttyin("T");   /*Delete whatever white space starts the keyboard response.*/
    if (ttystr[0] != SNUL)
        {
        if (taskintdecode(ttystr,SZE(5),&task))
            break /*GetCommands*/;
        else
            printf("\nRetype command or press <RETN>\n.");   /*The program*/
        }                                                    /*needs to know what to do.*/
    else
        {
        printf("\nSORT BY:\n");
        printf("\n%d-1st letter? %d-same-sized number classes?", LS, NS);
        printf("\n%d-preset text class keys? %d-preset number classes?",LP,NP);
        printf("\n%d-lazyboy text category sort?\n", LAZYLET);
        printf("\n\nType in command number.\t");
        ptemp = ttyin("T");
        if (taskintdecode(ttystr,SZE(5),&task))
            break /*GetCommands*/ ;
        else
            printf("Retype command number or press <RETN>.\n");
        }
    }/*GetCommands*/
```

Example 2.   Opening read and write files during keyboard interaction.

The essential routine for file opening is *fopen*(), declared as follows:

```
FILE *fptr = NULL;
fptr = fopen(<filename>,"x");   /*where "x" represent r for read, w for write,*/
                                /* a for apend, etc.*/
```

Amplified file-opening routines can ensure that an existing file is not opened unintention-
ally—where opening it for writing would wipe out the data currently in the file. They can
be written to notify the user that a specified file doesn't exist or can't be overwritten. They
can be enlarged to create a struct that will store statistics on what types of characters come
into a file during the time the file is open; e.g., words are counted by tracking spaces and
NewLines. They can check restrictions on what part(s) of the file the particular user can
access in public-private files. These next two functions, *read1* and *write* are examples of
such file opening routines. They return the channel number of the opened file or NULL to
indicate the file could not be opened.

read1() opens a file for reading. It notifies the user if the named file doesn't exist. And it
creates a struct of type in_stat for maintaining statistics on what characters enter the file
during the program run. It assumes multiple files may be simultaneously open. The pointer
to a struct specific for this file is kept in an array of pointers-to-struct called *IN_KEEP*.
i_lookup() and *i_install*(), the functions that create the statistics struct, are discussed in
Section 6.9.2. In addition, Section 6.6.2 contains a simple procedure for opening a single
input file and a single output file interactively.

```
/*PROCEDURE*/ FILE *read1(STRING filename)
    {/*BP*/
    FILE        *fileptr = NULL;
    struct      in_stat *pstr = NULL;

    fileptr = fopen(filename,"r");
    if (fileptr != NULL)
        {
```

/*Thanks to the previous statement, if we get here, we have the reassurance the file is open. Now we must determine whether the statistical struct for the file has been installed in the array of structs. In line a, if the file struct is installed, i_lookup() will return its pointer value and no more is done. If NULL is returned, there is no struct, so i_install() installs it and provides it with a pointer value. MAXIF is maximum number of files that can be kept in the array. See Footnote 11.*/

```
        if ((pstr = i_lookup(fileptr,IN_KEEP,MAXIF)) == NULL)     /*a*/
                pstr = i_install(fileptr,IN_KEEP,MAXIF,filename);
        return(fileptr);
        }
    else
        {/*return_empty*/          /*The file can't be opened.*/
        printf("\nCan't open %s. Doesn't exist OR is read-protected.",filename);
        return(fileptr);
        }/*return_empty*/
    }/*EP*/
```

write1() protects the file from being overwritten accidentally. If the function determines overwriting will occur, the user must confirm that overwriting is acceptable. If the user doesn't want overwriting, the program returns a NULL file pointer that must be dealt with by some other function—*init*() in our example—that allows the user to rewrite the name or exit the program.

```
FILE *write1(STRING filename)
    {/*BP*/
    FILE *fileptr = NULL;

    while (YES)
        {/*check!before!writing*/
```

/*Preventing overwriting is a two-stage process. First, the function opens the specified file for reading; this does not destroy the data in it. If no such file exists, fopen returns a NULL. The function can now safely open the file for writing.*/

```
        fileptr = fopen(filename,"r");
        if (fileptr == NULL)
                {/*Lookup!succeeded*/
                fclose(fileptr);
                fileptr = fopen(filename,"w");
                if (fileptr != NULL)
                        break;
                else        /*The next block doesn't apply to DOS machines.*/
```

```
                    {/*likely!protected*/
                    printf("\nCan't open %s. It may be write-protected.",filename);
                    fclose(fileptr);
                    return(NULL);
                    }/*likely!protected*/
              }/*Lookup!succeeded*/
         else                    /*If the initial fileptr isn't NULL, the file already exists.*/
              {/*OpeningFileWillDestroyContents*/
              printf("\nDo you want to overwrite %s if possible? (y/n) [n]",filename);
              ptemp = ttyin("TU"); /*Tidy the front end and uppercase the answer.*/
              if (ttystr[0] == 'Y')
                    {/*overwrite*/
                    fclose(fileptr);
                    fileptr = fopen(filename,"w");
                    if (fileptr == NULL)   /*The file is read-only. Not on DOS machines.*/
                         printf("\nCan't open %s. May be write-protected.",filename);
                    return(fileptr);
                    }/*overwrite*/
              else
                    {/*don't overwrite*/   /*Any answer except YES is taken as NO.*/
                    fclose(fileptr);
                    return(NULL);
                    }/*don't overwrite*/
              }/*OpeningFileWillDestroyContents*/
         }/*check!before!writing*/
    }/*EP*/
```

Usage.

An example of using read1() and write1().

```
void init(void)
    {
    FILE *inchn = NULL, *outchn = NULL;

    while (TRUE)
         {
         printf("\n Name of file to be processed?\t");
         ptemp = ttyin("TU");
         inchn = read1(ttystr);
         if (inchn == NULL)
              printf("\nChoose another input file name.\t");
         else break;
         }
    while (TRUE)
         {
         printf("\n Name of output file?\t");
         ptemp = ttyin("TU");
         outchn = write1(ttystr);
         if (outchn == NULL)
              printf("\nChoose another output file name.\t");
```

```
        else break;
        }
    }
```

Clearly, we can create a repertoire of functions similar to *write1*() that would open a file for appending or reading, with or without notification that the file does not exist, with or without the creation of a struct for maintaining statistics, and so forth. When a set of functions are concerned with the same task, and have essentially the same prototype, it is often useful to create a class function for ease of cataloguing the individual functions. As example, *io*() is a class function in which its first arg is the arg of any function constructed like *write1*() and its second arg is a pointer to the specific function. *io*() is prototyped as:

extern FILE *io(STRING filename, FILE *(*filefct)(STRING filename));

Accessed through *io*(), a call to *write1*() in the previous example would be written as:

outchn = io(ttystr,write1);

2.3.2. CONTROLLING ARRAY INPUT FROM DISK

Once an input file is open, characters can be streamed in by one of the *get*-based library functions. *getc*() is a passive filter, accepting each character as is, until the end of the file. As such, it is a good base on which to build routines in which the entry of particular characters or types of characters have different consequences and the stream stops at any one of a set of characters. The halt character can be deleted or added to the string in memory. Other characters can be excluded from entry. For the next examples, the input procedure, *psin*() disposes of each entering character in accordance with rules written into setbreak tables[14].

If you notice unexpected text or added-on incorrect phrases in processed text, the routine that created the text may not be appending the terminal SNUL that prevents accretion from an adjoining memory area. The string processing routine should also prevent the entry and/or the accumulation of more chars than the buffer can store. Typically, this is done by a function arg that states array size so that the procedure can stop input or string growth when the limit is reached.

Routines that input char arrays from disk also need built-in limits to buffer size, unless the size of entry text has an imposed limit, as is the case for fixed-size records, and this limit is maintained for all local buffers in functions that handle the entry text.

---

14 The setbreak utility, which allows a set of operations to be performed on the entering stream of characters simultaneously, is discussed in Chapter 4. The code for *psin*() is listed in Section 4.11.

If the buffer limit is made one of the function args, then overload can be prevented in several ways:

(1) A warning message is displayed and the stream is chopped at the buffer limit[15].

For example:

printf("\nRECORD %ld has been chopped. The program can't handle more than %d chars per record.", reccnt, lim);

(2) If chopping the flow at the buffer limit would make the rest of the program nonsense, a warning is issued that the text needs to be preprocessed for size and the program exits.

(3) If the text is some defined entity such as a database record, the program takes what it can of the text into the buffer provided. It then handles the remainder of the record in whatever way makes sense. If, say, all the words of the files are to be counted as part of the program run, then the oversized record[16] can be brought into memory in segments for processing.

inandchop() is an all-purpose utility that brings in a single ASCII-delimited record from disk into a HUGESZE-sized local buffer, and chops it into its component fields, using the record and field delimiters written into args 2 and 3. It stores these fields dynamically, using the elements of a globally defined pointer array to point to the individual fields. (The array of pointers-to-char is named *field*[MAXFIELDS+1] and is defined in globals.c.) The fourth arg is a pointer to this pointer array. The record and field delimiters and the expected number of fields per record (*nfields*) are told the program interactively by functions such as *majorfile*(), discussed in Sections 3.6.2 and 5.2.2.3. *inandchop*() compares *nfields* and the actual number of input fields (*infields*) and, if necessary, sends an error message to the file represented by *outerrchn*. The procedure returns an integer variable, *endf*. A zero *endf* indicates that the record currently in memory (record number *reccnt*) is incomplete; it was chopped because it was too large for the buffer. The rest of the record is still on disk and will be brought in the next cycle for processing.

```
while (TRUE)
    {/*ExamineARecord*/
    endf = inandchop(inchn, Tterstop, Ttrastop, pf0,nfields, &infields,
                        outerrchn, reccnt);
    if (endf == 0)
        fprintf(outerrchn,"Record %ld was more than %d chars.",reccnt,HUGESZE);
    .....do regular processing on the portion of the record currently in memory.......
    continue;          /*Fetch the next record or the rest of the current record.*/
    }/*ExamineARecord*/
```

---

15 The warning can also be sent to some error collecting file that is (re)opened whenever the program is run. See the example in (3). The error messages are then available for examination when the program terminates.

16 ASCII-delimited files rely on separating fields and records by delimiters not used in the text of the record. Note fields of unrestricted size can cause intake problems.

The next is an alternative way of handling the oversized record when only the first part of the record is needed for processing, as when file records are to be reordered alphabetically, say, by the text in field 3. It is particularly suitable for semi-stylized records of unrestricted size, where the first part of the record is structured as informational fields and the last part of the record is a set of informal notes of unlimited size.

If, in line *b* below, *endf* returned by *inandchop*() is zero, it means the record is not completely input. So at line *c* the program sets *TOOBIG* to YES and processes the part of the record currently in memory. In the NEXT cycle, handled starting at line *a*, the rest of the record will be brought in and junked. Note the auxiliary switch, *brkN*. If *brkN* is NULL, there is still more of the record sitting on disk that must be brought in and junked. All of the current record will be brought in before a new record is fetched via *inandchop*().

```
BOOL TOOBIG = NO;      /*TOOBIG will mark a record that is larger than HUGESZE*/
while (TRUE)
     {/*ExamineARecord*/
```

/*If in the PREVIOUS loop the entire record could not be brought in, TOOBIG was set to YES. In the current cycle, this signals that the rest of the record is to be dealt with. The program is to take it in but not use it.*/

```
    if (TOOBIG == YES)                                                      /*a*/
         {/*PullinRestofRecord*/   /*This cycle brings in the too-large residue.*/
         psin(inchn,Tterstop,&brkN,HUGESZE, buf);   /*Bring in the rest of the*/
                                                    /*record; but don't use it.*/
         if (&brkN == NULL)  /*Some of the record is still out on disk, so fetch it.*/
              continue /*ExamineARecord*/;
         else if (endf == 0)   /*End of the file has been reached.*/
              break /*ExamineARecord*/;                    /*Stop processing records.*/
         else TOOBIG = NO;  /*No more residue. Fetch the next record at the*/
                            /* next instruction, which is at line b.*/
         }/*PullinRestofRecord*/
```

/*This is where a new record is brought in. In the next line of code, if endf returned by inandchop() is zero, the program will set TOOBIG to YES as indicator that in the following cycle the rest of the current record is to be brought in and junked. Then it processes the part of the record that did fit into the memory buffer.*/

```
    endf = inandchop(inchn, Tterstop, Ttrastop, pf0,                       /*b*/
         nfields, &infields, outerrchn, reccnt);
    if (endf == EOF) break;
    if (endf == 0)
         TOOBIG = YES; /*In the NEXT cycle, input the rest of record
              but don't use it.*/                                          /*c*/
    ......Process the part of the record currently in memory.
    }/*ExamineARecord*/
```

2.3.3. STRING CONTENTS IN FILES AND IN MEMORY

In this Section we detail changes that occur in the stored representation and/or meaning of some characters in a text string as it is moves from an ordinary ASCII data file to a memory buffer under control of a C program. The characters of interest are the backslash characters (see Section 1.4.2.1), particularly backslash ('\\') and the double quote ('\"'), both of which have special meaning in print statements. The conversion from the carriage return ('\012') and line feed ('\015') combination (collectively, CRLF) to a NewLine ('\n'), common in many implementations, is also discussed.

Suppose that as part of writing ordinary text—program documentation, say—on any non-wrap-around ASCII word processor, these three lines (including the backslashes) are typed on the keyboard and installed directly in an ordinary ASCII file named *in.db*:

**printf("\\na\tb
c\fd
ef\"");**

the text in *in.db* would be mapped as: **printf("\\na\tb\015\012c\fd\015\012ef\"");**

Note that within the file C-idiomatic backslash notation is not operative. The sequence of \ and **n** does not signal NewLine; doubling the backslash does not make it a literal or special symbol. On the other hand, there is a CRLF added by the word processor to represent the End-Of-Line (EOL) [17] on the first two lines.

This next is a complete program, *charprint.c*, that brings the entire contents of *in.db* into memory—into an array called *buf*. The CRLF combination is translated by C into the NewLine character. The backslash chars are stored as is. A terminal SNUL must be added by the programmer; it is not done automatically. In this case, it is done by *psin*(), a procedure that brings in characters from a file, stopping input in accordance with directions set forth in the setbreak table *Tstop*. Setbreaks are discussed in the Chapter 4. For now, it is sufficient to know that the directions embodied in *Tstop* on line *a* tell the program to let all the characters into the file until it reaches the End-Of-File (EOF) character, which in the Brief text editor is located a line or two after the final character typed.

```
#include "DEFINE.H"      /*A file of macros and #define'ed constants*/
#include "COMSET.H"      /*The prototypes of the components of the setbreak utility.*/


main(void)
     {/*BP*/
     int brk = 0;                    /*Will indicate the character on which input stopped.*/
     char buf[SZE(100)] = {SNUL};
     int i = 0;
     FILE *inchn = fopen("in.db","r"); /*Opens in.db and connects it to a system struct*/
                                       /*pointed to by inchn. (see Section 1.2.4).*/
     BITMAP Tstop = 0;        /*Tstop is the setbreak table constructed in line a.*/

     setbreak(&Tstop, "", "", ""); /*Sets up the setbreak table labeled Tstop.*/   /*a*/
     psin(inchn,Tstop,&brk,SZE(100),buf);
```

---

17 The present description of the conversion of EOL (produced by pushing the <ENTER> key) to a CRLF is true for DOS machines, not UNIX.

```
    for (i = 0 ; buf[i] != SNUL; i++)                                        /*b*/
        printf("\nchar i = %d;\tchar = %c;\tchar = %o", i, buf[i], buf[i]);
    printf("\n\nbuf[i] in char = %c; in octal = %o", buf[i], buf[i]);        /*c*/
    printf("\n\n\n%s",buf);                                                  /*d*/
    printf("\\na\tb\                                                         /*e*/
c\fd\
ef\"");
}/*EPmain*/
```

The instruction starting on line *b* would display the contents of *buf* char by char, both in character mode and in octal.

```
char i = 0;       char = p,   char = 160
char i = 1;       char = r;   char = 162
char i = 2;       char = i;   char = 151
char i = 3;       char = n;   char = 156
char i = 4;       char = t;   char = 164
char i = 5;       char = f;   char = 146
char i = 6;       char = (;   char = 50
char i = 7;       char = ";   char = 42
char i = 8;       char = \;   char = 134
char i = 9;       char = \;   char = 134
char i = 10;      char = n;   char = 156
char i = 11;      char = a;   char = 141
char i = 12;      char = \;   char = 134
char i = 13;      char = t;   char = 164
char i = 14;      char = b;   char = 142
char i = 15;      char =
;        char = 12
char i = 16;      char = c;   char = 143
char i = 17;      char = \;   char = 134
char i = 18;      char = f;   char = 146
char i = 19;      char = d;   char = 144
char i = 20;      char =
;        char = 12
char i = 21;      char = e;   char = 145
char i = 22;      char = f;   char = 146
char i = 23;      char = \;   char = 134
char i = 24;      char = ";   char = 42
char i = 25;      char = ";   char = 42
char i = 26;      char = );   char = 51
char i = 27;      char = ;;   char = 73
char i = 28;      char =
;        char = 12   /*Elements 28 and 29 reflects the extra lines in the file before EOF*/
char i = 29;      char =
;        char = 12
```

The next statement, at line *c*, prints out the final character of the string; i.e., buf[30] contains SNUL; i.e.,

buf[i] in char = ; in octal = 0

Note that a backslash char such as \t is brought in as two characters. SNUL and ASCII 1, ASCII 12 and ASCII 15 are non-printing chars. The system does not transfer the carriage return; it acts it out. The line feed is transmitted as a NewLine. If the example text were to be shipped back to a file using *fprintf()*, a CRLF would be substituted for the NewLine symbol, and it would look exactly as it did in the original file. The terminal SNUL would not be transmitted.

The exchange of CRLF and NewLine becomes important in retrieving a record from disk randomly rather than sequentially. Almost certainly, except in systems such as UNIX, there are fewer chars in the memory copy than in the disk version.

If, instead of displaying the individual characters in *buf*, we request the program to display the entire data string in *buf*, as in line *d*, this would be the print product:

```
printf("\\na\tb
c\fd
ef\"");
```

Note that this reproduces the looks of the original text in *in.db*. The newline is treated as a metacharacter; i.e., it is taken as a display instruction. The other backslash characters, however, are treated as regular data characters when they are part of the string constant, except that the backslash diphthong is counted as a single character. Thus, **stlen("a\tb");** is three, not four, characters long.

Line *e* is a source code statement. It duplicates our data string, except that continuation backslashes have been added to indicate it is a single print statement.[18] The print product is:

```
\na b c♀d ef"
```

The backslash characters have now become printing and control instructions, except that the initial double \\ compels the printout of a literal \. Note that the form feed symbol will not become an actor until the string is sent to a responsive formatter program or a hard copy printer, when it will force a shift to the next page.

2.4. POSITIONING CHARS: ARRAY NOTATION VERSUS SENTENCE NOTATION

2.4.1. TWO WAYS TO LOCATE AN ARRAY ELEMENT

Formally, when we have a sequence of semantic tokens 1,2,3,4 and so forth that can be expressed as exact quantities, we are using cardinal numbers. When we point to a set of objects and arbitrarily sequence them as first, second, third, we are using ordinal numbers. When **1** and **first** refer to the same object in an array, there is no conflict and no need to trouble ourselves which system we are using. But in C, it is always the case that the top end of an array is *a*[0], not *a*[1]. So the first char is in array element zero, not in array element 1. Given, **His father is a doctor.**, if we were asked to state the first two letters, we would say **Hi**, because ordinarily we think of the chars in ordinal position, or, in the present terminology, sentence position. But we must program in C in array position. If we forgot and asked for *array*[1] and *array*[2], the system would return **is**, not **Hi**.

---

18 A final backslash on a line of a *printf* statement forces a continuation to the next line, negating the NewLine.

The programmer often finds it convenient to store a string starting at a[1]; as in this segment that copies a string to an array in memory called *buf*.

```
void fctstoreA(void)
     {
     char       buf[SZE(50)+2];
     char       *pbuf = &buf[1];
```

/*In these definitions, buf is an array that will hold 50 chars starting at buf[1] plus the terminal SNUL. pbuf is a single pointer-to-char, pbuf, is set to point to the second element in buf, buf[1], not buf[0]. The next line puts the string into buf, starting at buf[1]. Note that accessing the string via pbuf writes the string properly; accessing it from buf[0] writes whatever random character is in buf[0].*/

```
     stcpy("All Gaul is divided into three parts.",pbuf);
     printf("\npbuf = [%s]", pbuf);    /*PrintProduct: pbuf = [All Gaul is divided into*/
                                        /*three parts.]*/
     printf("\nbuf = [%s]", buf);      /*PrintProduct: buf = [zAll Gaul is divided into*/
     }                                  /*three parts.]*/
```

To tailor the notion of cardinal and ordinal mapping to our particular concerns, we will use array notation to mean either that the program starts an array in *a*[0] or that it begins a counter at *i* = 0. Sentence notation will indicate that significant chars are stored in an array beginning at *a*[1] and counters begin counting at one, not zero.

2.4.2. USING SENTENCE NOTATION

Sentence notation is civilized. *a*[1] holds the first element, *a*[2] the second, and so on. We can focus on the task without needing to shift each char mentally by one. Operationally, changing the top end of an array is possible. But we need to be aware of the consequences.

(1) If the array doesn't begin on zero, the array name can't be used as the arg in such functions as *stlen* and *printf*(). With stlen and print statements, if *a*[0] is SNUL, the string would be assumed to be empty. It is true that we can finesse these problems. Providing *a*[0] is not SNUL, we can subtract one from the *stlen*() count. Or, better still, we can assign a pointer to *a*[1]. Using the pointer as arg would force *stlen*() to provide us an accurate count starting at *a*[1]. And *printf*() would write out the string starting at the pointer, not at the actual start of the array, thus:

```
STRING   pa = {NULL};
char       a[SMLSZE] = {SNUL};

pa = &a[1];
printf("\nstlen(\"%s\") = %d.",pa, stlen(pa));
```

(2) It isn't enough just to change dimensionality of the defined arrays to provide for the shift in starting element. Any procedure that deals with string length and compares one string to another will need shifts of one element. As example, the loop in *stmfind*() in Section 3.2.4.2, which tries to find a *wrd* within *str*, would need to be changed from:

```
for (start = str; str - start <= (length(str)-length(wrd); str++)
```

to:

for (start = str; str <= (length(str)-length(wrd)+1); str++)

And, at the beginning of the search, *start* is set to one, not zero.

In general, these modifications are necessary:

- The array must be increased in size.

- An array can no longer be functionally cleared by placing a zero in *a*[0], if the string starts in *a*[1].

- A pointer to the array is written **ptr = &a[1];** not **ptr = a**;

- All loops involving array chars must start at **a[i] == 1;**, not **a[i] == 0;**.

- Counting backwards in a loop must stop before the first element in the array.

With some care, we can resist the forces that encourage indexing the first element of a character array as zero, whether we wish to or not. But if we choose to use sentence notation, we need always to keep in mind that the language and the compiler and the library routines are geared to starting an array in *a*[0]. So extreme care must be taken to ensure that an item (or a lack of an item) in *a*[0] doesn't cause trouble. In this odd-appearing but fairly realistic next example, the *pgroup* array of character pointers is reused to store addresses of substrings of the strings currently referenced by these pointers. This, as they say, is a true story.

trim(STRING str, int AMT, STRING substr) is the generic name of functions that, in this case, chop out the first AMT chars from a string referenced by *str*, store this substring dynamically and place its address in *substr*. In this example, it extracts the first 7 chars of the string referenced by *pgroup*[j], gets storage space for this substring from the system, then puts the address of this substring into the previous pointer element, *pgroup*[j-1]. The original string referenced by *pgroup*[j] is then freed and *pgroup*[j] becomes available to reference the substring created from the string whose address is in *pgroup*[j+1].

The scheme is straight forward, but the programmer, me, forgot that the first significant substring pointer would be *pgroup*[0], not *pgroup*[1].

```
for (j = 1; j < SZE(50)+1; j++)
    {
    trim(pgroup[j], SZE(7), pgroup[j-1]);       /*File 2-4-2.c in LISTINGS\chap2 uses*/
                                                /*dssubst() as the trim routine.*/
    free(pgroup[j]);
    }
```

The problem came in the next stage. Ironically, the problem was due in part to an automatism, the conscientious NULL'ing of the first element of "unused" arrays, forgetting that in this case *pgroup*[0] was meaningfully occupied. The substring whose address was in *pgroup*[0] could no longer be accessed. The problem was discovered far downstream, when some function in a different file was told to print out the list of substrings and to stop when *pgroup*[j] was NULL. Because *pgroup*[0] was NULL, nothing was printed. Thanks to the ripple effect, it took time to backtrack and find the cause.

Because many of the utilities used by me for text manipulation are based on functions originally written in Sail, where the top element of an array can be 1 (or any other value), I was highly motivated to use sentence notation. It would make working with arrays more natural. Several ways to accomplish this sprang to mind. But most seemed to suffer from the gold bug effect, where, as in Edgar Allen Poe's story, a minute difference in array format can lead to multiple revisions and complexity. Going counter to so fundamental a language characteristic is risky.

We could decree that all char arrays start on a[1], leaving the first char random. This would simplify char ordering: a[1] and first would reference the same char. But then indicating array position by offsetting would become difficult. Also, a[0] might by chance contain a SNUL, poor usage in a language that called a string all chars UP TO the SNUL.

We could create a struct for each string with three members: (1) string name, (2) string length and (3) memory address of the dynamically stored string. If both dynamic and preset strings are created, then a fourth member would be needed to indicate string type. Conceptually, this is a fine idea. But the practical consequences of tracking a string that is handed to a function that calls a function that calls a function, each of which can change the character of the string, is a formidable deterrent to using this as a general approach.

Forgoing a sweeping change in array structure, limited solutions are available that require no secondary shoring up of functions.

As one possibility, suppose that we wish to store a set of strings permanently, referencing them through an array of pointers-to-char called *pgroup*. It doesn't much matter that a string begins in array[0]. But we do want the pointer list to begin at *pgroup*[1], so that pgroup[1] references the first string entered, *pgroup[2]* references the second string, and so on. This has the advantage that we can think pointer 1 for first string, pointer 2 for second string, and so forth, while storing strings in the customary array fashion.

store contains a local temporary holding buffer, *buf*. A group of character pointers called *pgroup* is defined permanently prior to calling *store*. In each cycle of the loop, *store* obtains dynamic storage for a single string, assigning its address to the next *pgroup* pointer in line. As set by *Thalt*, an entry string is all the text up to a space, tab, or NewLine; i.e., this next piece of code brings in a word at a time and stores it as a separate entity.

```
static char *pgroup[SZE(50)+1];        /*This array can hold 50 pointers,*/
                                       /*  starting with pgroup[1].*/

static FILE *inchn = NULL;
BITMAP Thalt = 0;


void store(void)
    {
    char      buf[SMLSZE];
    int       i, brkchar;

    setbreak(&Thalt,"\40\t\n","",""); /*psin() and setbreaks are discussed*/
```

```
                                        /* in Chapter 4.*/
    for (i = 1; i < SZE(50)+1; i++)     /*pgroup[0] won't be filled with an address.*/
       {
```

/*The next line of code, *a*, writes text into buf from a file whose channel number is inchn. Input stops at any character mentioned in the second arg of the Thalt table—at a space, NewLine or tab. Sufficient storage for the string in buf is allocated dynamically at line b. The current i th pointer is set to point to this memory location and the string in buf is copied to it.*/

```
            psin(inchn, Thalt, &brkchar, SMLSZE, buf);    /*a*/
            pgroup[i] = dssave(buf);                       /*b*/
            }
       }
```

Or functions can be written user-transparent, so the end user can say **use the first five letters** and the function translates this into **a[0]:a[4]**. In Section 3.2.4.2, which examines *stmfind*(STRING str, STRING wrd, long *place), an integer array pointed to by *place* stores the start position of every place *wrd* appears in *str*. The results are issued, in current terminology, in array mode. If we change one line of code to: ***place++ = str-start+1;**, processing wouldn't change, but results would be presented in sentence notation. So given the string **the theme of mathematics is therefore this.** and the phrase **the**, the elements of *place* would read **1 5 16 29**, a natural way to think about text.

But to deal with twin notations in a general way, we need twin function options. Array position notation is the more likely to be used for actual programming. It is compatible with C's usual programming style and requires no adjustments when a function using array notation calls another function and so forth. Sentence notation, on the other hand, is appropriate for interactions with the end user in that it permits him to react normally; as, for example, when a program elicits user choices from the available task options. The program takes on the responsibility of *subtracting one* from the natural sentence order to keep the array count correct. When args are written in sentence notation, the function converts these values to array notation during processing. The results appear in sentence notation.

2.4.3. TWIN FUNCTIONS TO MAP ARRAY ELEMENT LOCATION

To illustrate the use of twin functions to bypass arguments on whether it is better to map strings in sentence position or array position, consider these variants of a single function:

```
char stchara(STRING str, int str_position)    /*Array mode*/
char stchars(STRING str, int str_position)    /*Sentence mode*/
```

Give either routine a position in the string and it will return to the calling function the char in that position; i.e., *stchara*() is the converse of the C library function *strchr*(), which returns the address of a char arg. *stchar* functions examine both predefined and dynamic strings. Essentially, they display the equivalent of: **printf("%c",str[i]);**, where **i** is *str_position*.

If the first arg is **This Sentence.** and the second arg is **2**, then *stchars*() would return **h**, *stchara*() would return **i**. *stchara*() uses array notation, where **2** means *array*[2]. *stchars*() uses sentence notation, where **2** means the 2nd char in the string.

```
char stchara(STRING s, int num)        char stchars(STRING s, int num)
  {/*BP*/                                {/*BP*/
                                         num = num - 1;
  if (num >= stlen(s) || num < 0)        if (num >= stlen(s) || num < 0)
     {                                      {
     printf("\nString length is %d.",stlen(s)); printf("\nString length is %d.",stlen(s));
     return(SNUL);                          return(SNUL);
     }                                      }
  else                                   else
     {                                      {
     printf("\nString length is %d.",stlen(s)); printf("\nString length is %d.",stlen(s));
     return(s[num]);                        return(s[num]);
     }                                      }
  }/*EP*/                                }/*EP*/
```

Usage:

```
static char   cc[] = "abcdefgh";
int    i;

for (i = 0; cc[i]; i++)
    if ( (newchar = stchara(cc,i)) == 'e')
         break;
```

stchara(cc,0); prints: **a**   stchars(cc,0); prints: **String length is 8.**
stchara(cc,3); prints: **d**   stchars(cc,3); prints: **c**
stchara(cc,8); prints: **String length is 8.**   stchars(cc,8); prints: **h**
stchara(cc,13); prints: **String length is 8.**   stchars(cc,13): prints: **String length is 8.**

The disadvantage of this approach is a proliferation of functions. Indeed, aside from variations due to string storage type, position ambiguity is the major reason for writing multiple versions of a single function.

2.5. STRING STORAGE

Storage for string variables is either predefined or dynamic.

2.5.1. PRESET (PREDEFINED) STRING STORAGE

A string variable is brought in from file or via keyboard; or it is created from one or more strings already in memory. Coming under the control of the program, it is often stored in a predefined buffer. In shorthand fashion, we refer to strings written into defined and dimensioned char arrays (into fixed-size buffers) as predefined strings or as preset strings. To assign 100 bytes to a char array called *ttystore*, we would write: **char ttystore[100];**. What is preset is the allocation of character space, not the characters themselves or the number of characters in the string that will fill the array, providing the number is not greater that the space provided.

With the string constants discussed in Section 2.2.1, it was sufficient to simply state the contents of an undimensioned array; e.g., **char nfile[] = "temp.log";**. But a variable char array such as *ttystore[100]* must be sized. All string variable may be initialized as empty in a single statement in ANSI. In pre-ANSI compilers, a local array can be made operationally empty by SNUL'ing its first char. Whatever its storage type, because SNUL signals the end of a string, many a function will not examine a string beyond the first SNUL it encounters.

During processing, text will be written into the defined array, character by character. These characters can be exchanged for others or partially erased or the entire buffer may be emptied. But the buffer itself endures. Its life span depends on where and when the programmer chooses to define it.

An empty char array that is declared at the top of a file prior to a set of functions is accessible to all these functions. It can store a string indefinitely. Alternatively, it can be reused to hold various strings during the life of the program. If our example array, *ttystore*, is defined as a static char array early on, it becomes invisible to all other files holding program procedures, while remaining accessible to the routines within its own file. If it is not static, a variable defined at the beginning of a file is by default considered externally global, potentially visible to all the other modules of the program.

With external global variables, an efficient strategy is to assemble in a single file all the variables, including char arrays and pointers-to-char, used in common by the separate modules of the program; call this file something like *globals.c*. These variables are given values in *globals.c*, meaning they are defined here and nowhere else; e.g., **char ttystore[SZE(100)] = {SNUL};**. This file is compiled separately. *globals.h*, a sister file to *globals.c,* would DECLARE the same variables, prefixing each prototype with the descriptor: *extern*; e.g., **extern char ttystore[SZE(100)];**. (Note that these declared externs are not given values.) Reference to the variables listed in *globals.h* would be by means of an **#include "GLOBALS.H"** statement in each of the other program files.

Alternatively, our example char array may be defined within a particular function. A string stored in a local array remains accessible for the run of the function. When the function is completed, the string is no longer known to the program. However, it does not need to be specifically deleted. The space it occupies is immediately available to store other data. The exception is when a variable char array within a function is labeled static. It also disappears when the function terminates. But the system guarantees that no other text will overwrite that area in memory during the time the function is inactive. When the function is recalled, the text of the string is as it was. Because it is a variable and not a string constant, the contents of the string may be intentionally rewritten by the program any time the function is active.

Major uses for preset memory space (i.e., predefined char arrays) are:

1.   to maintain a separate and permanent char array for each expected string, or string source, particularly when string size is fixed or at least is within a narrow range

2.   to afford temporary storage for each of a sequence of strings, brought in one at a time for processing before moving to permanent quarters. These strings are likely to be of varied sizes

3.   to house as a unit a set of independent strings that will be processed together or in a fixed sequence

The first case—maintaining a set of buffers for a limited set of strings—is efficient if we are able to make an educated guess about how much space to allocate for each expected string because the strings are the names of database files or they are limericks or we have knowledge about how large a record is allowed to grow, or we are dealing with fixed-size database records, and so forth. Some extra bytes will provide flexibility in changing string size as a result of processing.

In the second case, space allocation is based on the anticipated size of the longest string that might eventually occupy the array, even though most of the strings stored in the array may be significantly smaller. Allocating a lot of space has the advantage that this space will likely be enough even if the string is concatenated with several other strings. But this is wasteful of space, still a consideration when working on the typical microprocessor.

Nevertheless, a fixed buffer in which to dump text temporarily is a necessity in many situations[19]. As example, in a program with a user language where user instructions need to be decoded and checked for syntax, each instruction is separately interpreted. A copy of the original instruction is placed in a small char array—and replaced with the next instruction if it passes inspection. Error boilerplate is maintained in a permanent buffer. If an error is discovered, the incorrect string can be immediately displayed and the program terminated. Another typical use of the temporary buffer is to bring in a string that is to be cleaned of control chars and white space. Once this is done, the string can be relayed to other functions for further processing or stored dynamically in memory space cut exactly to size.

In the third case, a permanent large buffer stores strings sequentially in the order they are input or created. This uses space efficiently and is fine for a set of strings that will not change over the course of the program run. A fixed set of questions to be presented on the screen face cyclically in a Question-and-Answer program makes good use of a fixed-size buffer.

---

19 Almost every function that participates in the intermediate steps whereby a string is shaped from the original text may need a local preset buffer that is as large as the compiler's stack allows. Such buffers are particularly needed when a dynamically stored string is expanded or markedly contracted.

Prestoring string space has advantages:

- It saves code-writing time. Storage doesn't need to be gotten as needed and then released when not needed. The programmer is freed from needing constantly to assign and to free space for strings. The space is immediately available within the block(s) in which the char array is known; the occupied space disappears, i.e., the string no longer is allocated space when the block is exited.

- It saves thinking. The programmer doesn't have always to consider whether to save/destroy the original text, part of the original text, a copy of the original text, and so forth.

An ideal situation is when storage needs to be prepared for just a few strings ahead of time and these buffers are used and reused again and again. An example is a program that brings in one record at a time, stores it in one of these predefined arrays, does things to it that requires sending material to a few others such buffers. Finally, it sends the record out to a file or to the display and brings in the next record, overwriting the strings.

Unfortunately, except for such limited cases of small demand on storage space, it is almost impossible to do things simply. Preset string handling is usually procrustean; the string may be too large for the space available and need to be chopped. Alternatively, a 3-letter string resident within a global array will remain the life of the program, wasting most of a 100- or 1000- or 10000-element array. If a small number of strings are stored in a fixed-size 2D array sized to hold the largest string it might ever need to hold, the amount of wasted space is mind boggling.

But when presetting space works, when there is sufficient storage for all the string variables, no matter how we change them, there is every reason to use predefined string storage exclusively, if only so we will never need to allocate storage dynamically. Then happily, we will never need to free the allocated space—an occupation aptly called garbage collecting, and almost as much fun as the real thing. Because incoming strings are seldom so considerate, let us next examine dynamic allocation, a type of string storage that may be more tricky but is certainly more flexible.

2.5.2. DYNAMIC STRING STORAGE

We refer to storage that is allocated only when it is needed as dynamic. (This shorthand seems easier than continuously needing to write: a string that are not stored until the exact space it needs is known; at which time it is stored in space allocated to it by the system following a call to a library allocation function). Dynamic string storage is a convenience, if not a necessity, in many situations. It allows us to be responsive to changing storage requirements.

When strings are subject to potential shifts in size because they undergo splitting or coalescing, fixed-size buffers becomes impractical. When a string is brought in from a file or keyboard, we seldom know ahead of time how much space to set aside. Even when a string stays a particular size for the life of the program, it is often advantageous to set aside just the space required, rather than storing it in some large fixed-size buffer. So the ability to acquire specific amounts of storage as needed is a major programming requirement. Typically, a string is collected character by character in a temporary over-sized buffer and stored after the program calculates how many bytes of space are required to store it. The user either writes his own buffer allocation and reorganization routines or relies on C library allocation functions. In the first case, the programmer requests a large piece of memory from the system and then parcels out pieces of it himself, keeping track of usage and reorganizing space that is no longer needed in order to avoid fragmentation. More typically, he will ask the system for space customized to a particular string. It is this method we will discuss here.

There are advantages in doling out storage space on-line. Space waste is reduced in that only a pointer to the destination space needs to be predefined, either globally or in the calling function. We do not need to declare a particular array or to state its size. The program will accurately supply just enough storage space, somewhere. Our only interaction with this allocated memory area is by way of the predeclared char pointer that stores the address of the first character of the array. As with any variable, where we define the pointer to the system-secluded array determines its accessibility. Defined at the top of the file above all the functions, the pointer is available to all functions within the file if it is declared static and to functions in other files if it is not tagged as static. If it is defined as static within a function, it will reinstate communication with the array whenever that particular function is active.

Dynamic string storage is sparing of storage space for the individual string. Defining a character pointer rather than a character array provides the convenience of not having to guess how much storage will be needed by some oddball database text sometime in the future. We don't need to dimension multiple arrays with some large value that soaks up memory. Alternatively, we don't need to figure out what to do with data slopover that doesn't fit the size array we provided. The knowledge we will never have to worry about data overflow or memory under-utilization makes the use of char pointers and dynamic storage very attractive.

The basic tasks in obtaining dynamic storage are:

STEP 1: Preset a pointer that will be active during the period that its associated string is needed.

STEP 2: Preset a temporary huge buffer large enough to hold the largest string expected. Defined as a local variable, this temporary buffer will go away by itself. If, however, the program doesn't compile because of stack overflow, it sometimes helps to establish a permanent global buffer that can be used on a fill-and-spill basis by any string destined for dynamic storage and needing a one-time temporary home.

STEP 3: Input the string into this buffer from disk, keyboard or another string[20].

---

20 In these examples, we will mostly obtain a string by copying a string constant.

STEP 4: Ask the compiler for enough memory to store the string that is in the temporary buffer. This must include space for the string's terminal SNUL. The address where this space is located will be written into the preset pointer.

STEP 5: Copy the string to the allocated memory location.

As an example of the procedure for acquiring dynamic storage:

step 1:   **STRING p = NULL;**
step 2:   **char vararray**[21]**[SMLSZE];**
step 3:   **stcpy("A bit of string.", vararray);**
step 4:   **p = (STRING) malloc(stlen(vararray)+1);**
step 5:   **stcpy(vararray, p);**

When the system receives a request for string space, it finds enough space to satisfy the request and keeps a record of the starting address and the number of bytes of storage allocated. This information is kept on a list together with information about the other blocks of memory that have been assigned. If the request for storage is conveyed via one of the library allocation functions, the function returns the address of the first byte. Note that filling the memory area, Step 5, is not handled by the compiler allocation function; it is up to the programmer to write into the allocated space. All the compiler does is the equivalent of making a notation that that particular space is on the *space taken* list and no longer on the *space available* list.

When the system is requested to free the space, the information on where the first byte of the string is located and how many bytes were assigned is erased from the *space taken* list. The block is back on the *space available* list. The contents of the now-available space are NOT physically erased.

2.5.2.1. Library Functions to Allocate and Free Dynamically-Stored Strings.

The chief library functions that handle dynamic storage are *calloc*() and *malloc*(). They are similar, except that *calloc*() also cleans out the requested space; i.e., it sets each char to '\0', a useful precaution in string processing. Both return NULL if no space is available

---

21 Note the different operational meanings of *vararray*, depending on context and on the specifics of the function in which it is processed. In step 2, it is SMLSZE bytes of space in memory. In steps 3 and 5, it is a sequence of chars plus a terminal SNUL. In step 4, it is sequence of chars without the terminal SNUL.

Applied to strings, *calloc()* has two args and for the general case is prototyped as:

(void *) calloc(size_t number_of_chars, size_t[22] sizeof[23](char));

As noted in Section 1.5.2, (void *) can not be directly dereferenced. Hence, this next formula should be used to assign the address of a string stored via *calloc()* to a pointer-to-char. If *p* is a predefined pointer-to-char, then:

p = (STRING) calloc(size_t number_of_chars, size_t sizeof(char));

This next formula will also work when, as is usual, a char is one byte in size: **p = (STRING) calloc(size_t number_of_chars, 1);**.

The allocation functions may be used for any data type: structs, integers, and so forth. The assignment prototype for the general case for *calloc()*, where p is a predefined pointer-to-data_item is: **p = (data_item *) calloc(size_t number_of_data_items, size_t sizeof(data_item));**

malloc has one arg and is prototyped as:

(void *) malloc(size_t number_of_chars);

The assignment prototype can be written:

p = (STRING) malloc(size_t number_of_chars);[24]

In addition, *realloc()* is available to reallocate memory if the string increases or diminishes in size. It is prototyped as:

(void *) realloc(pointer-to-char, size_t number_of_new_chars);

For strings, the assignment prototype can be written as:

p = (STRING) realloc(pointer-to-char, size_t number_of_new_chars); [25]

And the system provides *free()* to deallocate dynamic strings, written as:

free(pointer-to-char);

---

[22] ANSI C typedef's **size_t** as *unsigned integer*, where the specific integer data type is set by the system and is declared in stdlib.h; size_t is likely to be an unsigned int in compilers for DOS class operating systems.

[23] The *sizeof* operator calculates the size of data types, primary or compound, in bytes.

[24] More generally, the arg for *malloc()* is the number of bytes of space to reserve. The general assignment prototype is: **p = (data_item *) malloc (size_t number_of_data_items * sizeof(data_item));**

[25] The general prototype is: **p = (data_item *) realloc(pointer-to-data-item, size_t number_of_new_data_items * sizeof(data_item));**

where the function arg is the address of the dynamically stored string.

The system has knowledge of the address of the first byte of the space and of how many bytes are available as a result of freeing the string. It made no connection between its list of free space and the name of the pointer whose value is the address of that space. So it doesn't have the resources to NULL the pointer to the space. Nor does it clear the characters in the now unassigned space. Therefore, after a string is freed in the sense that the system can reassign the space, its pointer and contents have not been erased. They continue to show the values they had when the space was on the allocated list. So if we inspect the location by a print statement or by using CodeView, the variable appears unchanged. In the next code, *p* is a pointer-to-char that holds the address of a dynamically-stored string.

char keep[] = "This is a string.";   /*Write this as a global string constant.*/
p = (STRING) malloc(sizeof(keep)^{26});
printf("\nString is located at = %i", p);   /*PrintProduct: **String is located at -7086***/
stcpy(keep,p);
free(p);
printf("\nString is located at = %i", p);   /*PrintProduct: **String is located at -7086***/
printf("\nString contents: %s", p);/*PrintProduct: **String contents: This is a string.***/

To ensure that a dynamically-allocated variable is still storaged before attempting to free it, use a macro such as NULLIT(x), which tests that the pointer has a value other than NULL before *free()* is called to deallocate memory area.

#define NULLIT(x) if (x) { free((x)); (*x) = SNUL; (x) = NULL;}

NULLIT() also eliminates the danger of the dangling pointer (i.e., a pointer that continues to point to memory that has been freed) by NULL'ing the pointer as soon as its string has been freed. NULLIT resets the pointer variable to NULL, which guarantees the pointer is not aimed at any accessible memory address. And it SNUL's the first char of the string so that it is displayed as an empty string.

The next piece of code illustrates usage. Note that *buf* serves as a temporary buffer to collect chars. It is the chars in buf through the terminal SNUL that are stored by the system, after

---

26 The system adjusts the size of the unsized array *keep* so that it is just large enough to store the string plus its terminal NULL. Therefore, the sizeof() function, which returns the dimension of an array, is capable, in this case, of acquiring just enough character space to store the string.

it has found some empty space, not *buf*. The analogy is valet-parking a car. The car is carted off, not the concrete under it, to some unknown destination, our only contact with it a ticket. The similarity breaks down in that if we lose the ticket, we will eventually recover the car.

```
char      buf[SMLSZE] = {SNUL};
FILE      *inchn = NULL;
FILE      *outchn = NULL;
STRING    p = NULL;
```

/*In the next lines, note that stcpy() copies the terminal SNUL from buf to p[27], but stlen()[28] does not count the terminal SNUL as a char, so we must request an additional byte of space to store the SNUL that ends the string[29].*/

```
stcpy("Tape1: In testing 1Dec93", buf);
p = (STRING) calloc(stlen(buf)+1, sizeof(char));
if (p == NULL)            /*If p is NULL, the system is out of storage space.*/
     exit(2);             /*So terminate the program.*/
else stcpy(buf,p);


stcpy("Tape2: Shipped 5Dec93.", buf);
NULLIT(p);
p = (STRING) malloc(stlen(buf)+1);
if (p == NULL)
     {
     printf("\nOut of memory. Check program.");
     exit(2);                  /*Terminates the program after issuing an error message.*/
     }
else stcpy(buf,p);


stcpy("Tape1: Checked 6Dec93. Shipped 7Dec93.", buf);
p = (STRING) realloc(p, stlen(buf)+1);
if (p == NULL)
     {
```

/*In a program such as TXTalphabetize when there's no more string storage space, rather than terminating the program, the alphabetized records are sent to a temporary file, and the freed memory is available for alphabetizing the next batch of records. Of course, at some point, the different batches of stored records have to be merged.*/

```
     dumpmem(outchn);
```

---

27 More accurately, any SNUL will terminate the array, in that *stcpy()* ignores characters to the right of the first SNUL it encounters.

28 *stcpy()* and *stlen()* are run time functions. In contrast, *sizeof()* is a compile-time function. It returns the size of the array; it can't return the exact number of chars the array may eventually contain.

29 Another advantage of asking for one char more than the size of the string is that it guarantees we never ask for zero space; i.e., requesting no space—**p = (STRING) malloc(0);**—is undefined.

```
        fclose(inchn);
        startagain(inchn);
        }
else stcpy(buf,p);
```

All three allocation functions return a pointer or, if there is no space to store the string, a NULL. Procedures that amplify the basic save routine are useful in monitoring a possible NULL return and acting on it. One such is *dssave*(), which closes files before exiting.

```
STRING dssave(STRING s)
    {/*BP*/
    int        i = 0;
    STRING    save = NULL;

    if (save = (STRING) calloc((unsigned) stlen(s)+1, (unsigned) sizeof(char)))
        {
        stcpy(s, save); /*Copy the text referenced by s to the memory area*/
                        /*whose address will be stored in save.*/
        return(save);
        }
    else
        {
        printf("\nIn dssave(). No more calloc() storage available.");
```

```
/*If the program is interrupted, this next code saves data files. As discussed in Section
2.2.2.3, MAXIF is the most input files and MAXOF is the most output files that can be open
simultaneously. They can be redefined in define.h.*/
```

```
        for (i = 1; i < MAXIF; i++)
            if (inchan[i]) fclose(inchan[i]);
        for (i = 1; i < MAXOF; i++)
            if (outchan[i]) fclose(outchan[i]);
        exit(2);
        }
    }/*EP*/
```

2.5.2.2.   Enlarging the Dynamically-Acquired String.

Consider the case of the single string that is processed in some fashion that increases its size. As example, suppose a string **This is the forest primeval.** that, at line *a*, is stored dynamically and referenced by *p*, a pointer-to-char. Suppose we wish to append to it the next line of Longfellow's poem, stored in *addstr*.

```
static char addstr[] = "\nThe murmuring pines and the hemlocks.";
```

```
main()
    {
    char       buf[LRGSZE] = {SNUL};
    STRING    p = NULL;
```

```
if ( (p = dssave("This is the forest primeval.")) == NULL)        /*a*/
    exit(2);
```

There is the disadvantage in dynamic storage that even a single additional character can not be casually added. We can not append additional chars directly to a dynamically allocated string because that would overflow and overwrite neighboring memory locations not assigned to the string.

THIS WOULD BE WRONG: **stcat**[30]**(addstr,p);** If new space must be allocated because the string is about to outgrow its initial boundaries, then as shown next: (1) the string is shunted to a temporary buffer and its dynamic storage deleted. In its temporary home, it is increased or reconstructed or revamped and the new entity is dynamically installed in memory; or (2) a procedure such as *realloc()* is invoked to free the old space and find enough room for the enlarged string. Then the pieces that compose the enlarged string are concatenated in the allocated memory position.

Method 1.

```
stcpy(p,buf);        /*buf now contains: This is the forest primeval. plus terminal SNUL.*/
stcat(addstr,buf);   /*addstr is appended to the tail of the string in buf, starting on the*/
                     /*terminal SNUL.*/
NULLIT(p);           /*Releases the memory space occupied by the original string:
                       This is the forest primeval.*/
```

/*In the next line of code, the system sets aside enough space to store the expanded string that is currently stored in buf; i.e., space in memory is set aside and p points to the start of that space. But no string is as yet written into the allocated memory area.*/

```
p = (STRING) malloc(stlen(buf)+1);
```

/*This next command copies the string in buf including the terminal SNUL to the memory area whose address is the value of p.*/

```
if (p != NULL)
        stcpy(buf,p);
printf("\n%s",p);        /*PrintProduct:  This is the forest primeval.
}                                        The murmuring pines and the hemlocks.*/
```

Method 2.

```
p = dssave("This is the forest primeval.");    /*Starting from scratch. Like line a above.*/
stcpy(p,buf);        /*buf now contains: This is the forest primeval. plus terminal SNUL.*/
```

/*Next, the system sets aside enough space for the two strings that have not yet been concatenated. Because they are to be united into a single string, only 1 terminal SNUL is necessary. If, for some reason, the strings were to be kept separate, then this would be the code: **p = (STRING) realloc(p, stlen(p) + stlen(addstr) + 2);**/

```
p = (STRING) realloc(p, stlen(p) + stlen(addstr) + 1);
```

---

30 *stcat()* adds arg 1 to the tail of arg 2. Otherwise, it is similar to the C library procedure *strcat()*, which adds arg 2 to the tail of arg 1.

```
if (p != NULL)
    {
    stcpy(buf,p);          /*The first string is copied to the allocated memory area.*/
    stcat(addstr, p);      /*The line in addstr is added to the tail of the first line,*/
    }                      /* starting on the terminal SNUL.*/
printf("\n%s",p);          /*PrintProduct:  This is the forest primeval.
}                                         The murmuring pines and the hemlocks.*/
```

2.5.2.3.   Contracting the Dynamically-Stored String.

Conversely, if a dynamically stored string is markedly reduced in size as a result of local processing, the space for storing the string does not automatically shrink. The original space needs to be freed and smaller quarters issued. In the next examples, *p* points to the dynamically stored string, **This is the forest primeval**, of which the first half is to be retained.

Two methods to shrink the string are shown. They make use of different versions of a TXT utility that creates a substring from the original string, from the *bgn*th element of the string to the *ndd*th element; the string itself is not modified.

The two versions for producing an independent substring are prototyped as:

extern STRING dssubst(STRING str, int bgn, int ndd)
extern void pssubst(STRING str, int bgn, int ndd, STRING dsn)

In the first method, *p* is freed after a copy of the string is copied into a holding buffer, *buf*. *dssubst*() gets dynamic space, places the first half of the string into it and writes the location of the string into *p*. In the second method, *pssubst*() copies a substring into a preset array; in this case, it copies the first half of the string addressed by *p* into *buf*. A smaller amount of space is reallocated. The halved string is then copied into its new home.

Method 1.

```
stcpy(p,buf);                   /* p reads: This is the forest primeval.
                                buf reads: This is the forest primeval.*/

NULLIT(p);
p = dssubst(buf,1, stlen(buf)/2);   /* p reads: This is the fo*/
```

Method 2.

```
pssubst(p,1, stlen(p)/2, buf);   /* p reads: This is the forest primeval.*/
                                 /*buf reads: This is the fo*/
p = (STRING) realloc(p, stlen(p)/2 + 1);
stcpy(buf,p);                    /*p reads: This is the fo*/
```

Note that in the prototypes for either version of the substringing function, the original string is referenced by a pointer-to-char, *str*. The second arg is the starting position of the substring within the string. Similarly, the third arg indicates the position of the last element of the string to be written to the substring. Both the second and third args are written in sentence notation (see Section 2.4); e.g., as **1** for the first char in the string or **10** for the 10th char in the string. The function reduces this value by one to make it compatible with array notation;

e.g., if the substring is to begin with the third char of the string, the substring would begin with the char, *str*[2]. If the third arg is 10th, this substring ends with *str*[9].

pssubst() copies a portion of arg 1 directly to the array whose address is in arg 4. In *dssubst*(), a home for the substring doesn't exist until it is made available by the system. So the function uses a temporary local buffer, *dsn*, to store the evolving substring. The functions are fairly similar, except that *pssubst*() doesn't need to return a value because the substring is directly streamed to the array named in arg 4. *dssubst*() returns a pointer to where the substring is located, if a substring is formed; *pssubst*() needs only to make sure the daughter string has a terminal SNUL. If no substring can be formed, the daughter string is automatically SNUL'ed in *pssubst*(). In *dssubst*(), in contrast, if no substring can be formed, the function needs to return a value, NULL, to alert the calling function that space was not allocated.

/*PROCEDURE*/ void pssubst(STRING str, int bgn, int ndd, STRING dsn)
    {/*BP*/

```
int   ls = stlen(str);
dsn[0] = SNUL;    /*Clears the first char of dsn, which is preset space external*/
                  /* to this function.*/
if (bgn < 1)      /*Guarantees no minus array elements; the first char is in str[0].*/
    bgn = 0;
else bgn--;       /*Subtracts 1 to describe the element's position in array notation.*/
if (ndd > ls)     /*str[ls] is reserved for the terminal SNUL.*/
    ndd = ls - 1;
else ndd--;
```

Table 2.2.   This Section is common to both pssubst and dssubst.

/*Arg 2 must be equal to or less than arg 3 and the string must be at least 1 char in size for processing to take place. If it is possible to extract a substring, this next loop will copy the designated portion of the mother string to a preset buffer, creating a daughter string.*/

```
if (ls != 0 && ndd >= 0 && bgn <= ndd)
    while (bgn <= ndd)
        {
        *dsn++ = str[bgn++];    /*The pointer str[bgn] is functioning as an */
        }                        /* array element. See Section 1.5.2.*/
```

/*Any time a substring is created, the function must make sure the substring terminates in a SNUL. Hence the next statement.*/

```
        *dsn = SNUL;
    }/*EP*/
```

/*PROCEDURE*/ STRING dssubst(STRING str, int bgn, int ndd)
    {/*BP*/
    char dsn[LRGSZE];
    STRING   pdsn = dsn;   /*dsn can't serve as its own pointer in the copying*/
                                        /* loop below. See Section 3.3.2.*/

> See common section in pssubst.

if (ls == 0 || ndd < 0 || bgn > ndd)
    return(NULL);   /*The substring will be empty so no request for*/
while (bgn <= ndd)   /* system-allocated space is made.*/
    *pdsn++ = str[bgn++];
*pdsn = SNUL;

/*In the previous code, pdsn pointed to the predefined local array. In the next line, it is reused to store the address of the dynamically-stored string that is a copy of the string in dsn. There is no conflict; a pointer does not need to be freed from its attachment to a preset array. dssave calls calloc(), which finds memory space to store a string.*/

    return(pdsn = dssave(dsn));
    }/*EP*/

2.5.2.4. Freeing Obsolete Strings.

Suppose we wish to process a different record from a data file each time a particular function is called. Were we dealing with preset char arrays, when the function finished one cycle, we would not need to worry about deleting the text in the buffer. We would simply overwrite it in the next cycle (with the proviso that we do not fill the array beyond its capacity). With dynamic storage, however, replacing one string by another has the same problems encountered in processing a single string. When the function is recalled in the next cycle in the loop, memory space is still assigned for the amount of characters taken up by the first string. We could define the pointer to this first string as static and then simply overwrite the text of the first string. If, however, the second incoming string takes only a small part of the allocated memory space, we have undone the advantages of conserving space. If, on the other hand, the first string is shorter than the second, the second string will swamp the space devoted to the first string, overflowing to memory locations likely holding other data. If we simply ignore the first string, which is now obsolete, and create new space for the second string by reassigning the pointer, sending records from a hefty database just through a scan function can wipe out much of the available dynamic data storage space.

A severe disadvantage of dynamic storage is that a variable stored by the system is stored permanently. If the string becomes obsolete, its space must be specifically released; it does not automatically disappear. If left to its own devices, a dynamically assigned string continues to occupy memory space after the program exits the block(s) in which the string has definition. When a function finishes, the pointer-to-char that is the programmer's link to a dynamically saved string or a modified dynamic string may no longer be accessible. But the system-stored string itself continues to occupy its allocated area, which is therefore unavailable to the program for storing other strings.

Underlying the difficulties in using dynamic storage is that C has no automatic garbage collection, or, to put it more delicately, obsolete dynamically-stored strings are not automatically deallocated. In C, only local automatic preset variables are trashed by the system when the function finishes. Otherwise, a system does no garbage collecting; i.e., it does not scavenge for no-longer-used bytes. And while it will coalesce adjoining blocks of unused space, it has no squisher, such that the stored strings are on occasion moved close together in memory, leaving a large mass of free space.

Instead, it is the responsibility of the programmer to delete a string by formally freeing it; i.e., by alerting the system that the string's space can be reused. Moreover, the programmer is able to free allocated space only within the function blocks in which the pointer to the string is a known symbol, not at some convenient time. It is a nuisance to forever be freeing text that is no longer needed. Garbage collecting may not be what we envisioned when dreaming up new procedures, but it needs to be done and done scrupulously. Rather than reusing string space, we need to free this space and then allocate new space customized for the new or refashioned string.

There are some occasions when NULL'ing may be safely deferred as in this example, where each input string is represented by a separate pointer for the duration of the cycle in which the strings interact. These strings are not rewritten to other locations during that time.

In this task we accumulate a cluster of 100 strings, many of which, depending on their text, will be compared to each other. But no new strings are to be considered until all the comparisons are completed. As the comparisons continue, more and more strings drop out of the race. Deleting the strings that are no longer needed in the comparisons is delayed until the cycle terminates. The advantage is that we don't need to keep track of which strings are ready to be NULL'ed and which are still in use. The next example shows how to free the old strings when their pointers are required for the next set of input strings.

```
int        i, j = 0;
STRING     ptr[SZE(100)];
char       tmpbuf[LRGSZE] = {SNUL};
#define    NUMGRPS 25

for (j = 0; j <= NUMGRPS; j++)  /*Starts a new comparison of the group of strings.*/
    {
    for (i = 0; i < SZE(100); i++)
        {
        NULLIT(ptr[i]);        /*Free the previous string pointed to by ptr[i].*/
        ...bring in a string, clean it of white space, and store it in tmpbuf....
        ptr[i] = dssave(tmpbuf);
        }
    .......do a set of comparisons.....
    }
```

Aside from such local opportunities, as a general rule it is advisable to free strings and their pointers as soon as they are no longer needed. It must be admitted, however, that when a pointer to a dynamic string serves as arg to a function within a cascade of functions, even adopting a conscientious attitude may not be effective. Tracking a chameleon-like string through its peregrinations, worrying about possible changes in its size and whether some imbedded function has quite legitimately erased it, is never a simple matter in C, especially in serious programs rich in multiple and interconnecting pathways.

The danger of using a pointer carelessly or in an abstracted manner is high. Two particularly painful possibilities are: (1) the string that is disengaged from its pointer; and (2) the ambiguous string, i.e., the string that is both assigned and not assigned.

First the broken engagement between a string and its pointer. Consider that a char pointer provides the only connection to the dynamically-stored string. Legitimately deleting a string in one function and needing it later in another is a common occurrence. Or suppose by mistake we delete the pointer; or, if it is defined within a function, we forget to make it a static variable, so that at the end of the function it disappears. Or, suppose, because we customarily recycle pointers in order to keep down the number of pointer variables on the stack, absent-mindedly we reassign a still active pointer, linking it to another string. In all these cases, the original string will remain where it is for the rest of the program run, taking up space, because there is no way to address it. Defining essential pointers as static global so they stay resident and available helps avoid some mishaps. As does the generous use of separate and individual pointers, which keeps the reassignment of pointers to a minimum.

The second disaster, the ambiguous string, is all too easy to create. Its basic cause is the lack of a strong runtime system. Which translates to a split-brain working arrangement. The system keeps track of addresses and amounts. The programmer manipulates pointers and strings. Suppose, as in the next example, that two pointers point to the same string—the first pointer created in the calling function and the second pointer a temporary pointer created in the called function. Suppose further that during processing the string is freed via the temporary pointer. The system frees the string, i.e., it erases the string's address from its list of *taken*. But the string is physically present to the other pointer and visually present to any query through either pointer. So the unwary programmer may continue to use the mirage of a string, a string that is actually homeless, an apparition in space that can be rented to another string at any time. As in the next example.

```
void calledfct(STRING p)
    {
    STRING p2 = p;
    free(p2);
    printf("\np2 = %d", p2);        /*PrintProduct: p2 = -7310*/
    printf("\np2 = %s", p2);        /*PrintProduct: p2 = ABCDEFG*/
    }


void callingfct(void)
    {
    STRING p1 = NULL;

    p1 = dssave("ABCDEFG");
    printf("\np1 = %d", p1);        /*PrintProduct: p1 = -7310*/
    printf("\np1 = %s", p1);        /*PrintProduct: p1 = ABCDEFG*/
    calledfct(p1);
    printf("\np1 = %d", p1);        /*PrintProduct: p1 = -7310*/
    printf("\np1 = %s", p1);        /*PrintProduct: p1 = ABCDEFG*/
    }
```

Several solutions exist to prevent or at least identify the dangling pointer. First, using *NULLIT()* (see Section 2.5.2.1) rather than *free()* provides visual evidence within both *calledfct()* and *callingfct* that the string has been freed.

```
void calledfct(STRING p)
     {
     STRING p2 = p;
     NULLIT(p2);
     printf("\np2 = %d", p2);          /*PrintProduct: p2 = 0*/
     printf("\np2 = %s", p2);          /*PrintProduct: p2 = (null)*/
     }
```

NULL'ing the first character of the string in *calledfct()* will make the string appear empty when control returns to *callingfct()*. However, the pointer *p1* in the calling function still points to where the string was allocated space.

```
void callingfct(void)
     {
     STRING p1 = NULL;

     p1 = dssave("ABCDEFG");
     printf("\np1 = %d", p1);          /*PrintProduct: p1 = -7310*/
     printf("\np1 = %s", p1);          /*PrintProduct: p1 = ABCDEFG*/
     calledfct(p1);
     printf("\np1 = %d", p1);          /*PrintProduct: p1 = -7310*/
     printf("\np1 = %s", p1);          /*PrintProduct: p1 = (null)*/
     }
```

When a string is freed through one pointer, the other pointers to it must be separately NULL'ed. As shown in the next piece of code, in the current example it is simple to rewrite *calledfct()* to return the NULL'ed value to the first pointer in *callingfct()*[31]. Usually, given a cascade of functions, it is not.

```
void callingfct(void)
     {
     STRING p1 = NULL;

     p1 = dssave("ABCDEFG");
     printf("\np1 = %d", p1);          /*PrintProduct: p1 = -7310*/
     printf("\np1 = %s", p1);          /*PrintProduct: p1 = ABCDEFG*/
     p1 = calledfct(p1);
     printf("\np1 = %d", p1);          /*PrintProduct: p1 = 0*/
     printf("\np1 = %s", p1);          /*PrintProduct: p1 = (null)*/
     }
```

---

31 An alternative method permanently to NULL a pointer when its associated string is freed is to operate through the address of the pointer rather than through the pointer itself. This is discussed beginning in Section 3.5.

```
STRING calledfct(STRING p)
    {
    STRING p2 = p;

    NULLIT(p2);
    printf("\np2 = %d", p2);        /*PrintProduct: p2 = 0*/
    printf("\np2 = %s", p2);        /*PrintProduct: p2 = (null)*/
    return(p2);
    }
```

To sum up, it is possible to be a purist and use nothing but dynamic storage. This has the decided advantage that there is no built-in overhead; i.e., large amounts of space allocated in anticipation of possible, not necessarily guaranteed, use. But the convenience of dynamic storage can, as shown, unfortunately, be easily obviated. If, as the pointer threads through a hierarchy of routines, its connection to the string is accidentally lost, the string hibernates for the rest of the program run. It is there, but there is no way of addressing it. The same process repeated over several hundred cycles soaks up a great deal of memory. Obviously a string we have finished processing needs to be erased, or memory storage will soon be completely filled with 'dead' strings. So maintaining string and pointer connection is critical. Stringent discipline is needed to avoid the dangers in working with pointers to dynamically stored strings.

2.5.2.5.   Rules of Thumb for Working with Dynamic Strings.

Extracting from code for various string processing tasks—the amount of debugging time being a rough indicator of what is troublesome and insidious—some rules for working with dynamic strings become evident:

- The importance of initializing both static global pointer variables and local pointer variables can not be overstated. Compilers may ignore global and static variables that are not initialized. If a program is giving trouble, look at the list of variables in the link map. In my experience, probably when stack space was getting tight, uninitialized variables were occasionally ignored by the compiler.

- To avoid pointers that point to unpredictable spots in memory, assign all locally defined pointers that can't be immediately assigned to a particular string to NULL before processing begins. Do this even if the pointer will be assigned to some string in an upcoming processing step. Some condition will arise you never thought of and that processing step will not be entered. In the same way, unless pointers-to-pointers-to-char are function args, they should be set initially to NULL. A char array should be cleared when defined. In loops where the char array may be refilled each cycle, the first element of the array should be set to SNUL at the beginning of each cycle; e.g., **badgerep[0] = SNUL;**. All ints that will act as char counters should be set to 0. This is the wrong time to cut processing steps.

- If, within a function that returns a pointer, a local copy of the pointer arg is NULL'ed, returning the value of that local pointer will NULL a pointer in the calling function. As in the example in Section 2.5.2.4, this may be what we intend. On the other hand, if processing in the called function was not intended to affect the string in the calling function, then create new storage space in the called function for the temporary processing.

- It is a mistake to assume an allocation request is always honored. Provide for the contingency that the system will return a NULL to indicate it is out of space. Using a NULL pointer to copy or concatenate or interrogate its non-stored string could hang the system or, worse, lead to erratic results.

- Be on the lookout for multiple pointers to the same string, a common occurrence in string processing programs, where an army of functions call other functions and themselves. As we create substrings, partial strings, or add parts of separate strings, we often copy the value of the original pointer to other pointers.

- It takes strong character—or masochism—to work out and keep straight all the combinatorics of the variety of small to huge memory models, 16-bit and 32-bit int machines, the coordination of near and far pointers. Where it necessary, its necessary, but for a set of reasonably compatible machines—assume, say, a batch of 386's and 486's in a DOS 3 or better environment where end users do pretty much the same type of work—we can reduce complexity. It would be nice if, in these easier circumstances, we could stick to a 32-bit actual or virtual environment, if all ints and addresses could be declared as 32 bits. Unfortunately, it is dangerous to play around with 16-bit C library functions without knowing what they imbed, but making pointers 32-bit reduces some of the difficulty of working with pointers to strings. If the compiler doesn't, the NULL for pointers can be redefined as long ASCII zero. Also, restricting programs to the huge memory model wipes out the need to label pointers as near and far and well as decreasing the risks of wrong-sized pointers at memory segment boundaries[32]

- When several pointers to a string are separately defined, NULL'ing one will undo its connection to the string and free the string space associated with that pointer—by *free*, we mean making its space available via another allocation request. But the connections between the stored string and the other pointers remain. When space is freed by one pointer, the chars in the string are not physically erased and the pointer is not NULL'ed by the system. Even if we were to NULL this pointer, the other linked pointers are treated as independent entities. So depending on the pointer through which it is accessed, like the Cheshire cat, the string will appear and disappear.

---

[32] See **Pointer Arithmetic At Memory Segment Boundaries** by Daniel and Nancy Saks, *C Users Journal*, October 1989, pp. 27-35. Both far and huge pointers are not 32-bit integers. Each type is composed of two 16-bit integers, one for the segment and the other for the offset. But huge pointers are virtual 32-bitters in that the system does enough arithmetic to prevent wraparound on the offset by incrementing the segment integer.

- When several pointers to a string are separately defined and left dangling when one of the pointers frees the space, they can become a menace to the next string that occupies that space. Or to other data held in memory. This occurs when the precariously stored string—i.e., a string freed by one pointer but that is still physically present and that appears to be linked to another pointer—is combined with other strings. Or when the string is converted to a substring that is then used in still other expressions. Somewhere down the line, a perfectly ordinary string will suddenly change character—because its space was legitimately overwritten. The dangers inherent in having multiple pointers all pointing to the same string are reduced if each of the concatenated strings or each daughter string (i.e., a string created from the original string) has a separate pointer and a separate location in memory.

- Have a set procedure for working with functions with imbedded dynamic allocation; e.g., *dssubst*() in Section 2.5.2.3 contains *dssave*(), which calls *calloc*(). If one string is to replace a previously-saved dynamic string, the pointer to the string that is to be replaced needs to be freed. Then this pointer is reset to point to the new string. Indeed, a large part of debugging consists of examining functions that directly or indirectly call *calloc*() or *malloc*() to make sure the string product is still available or to determine whether it should be copied to some other space and the string formed by the function released.

- If a string will be subject to wild variations of size, but maintaining a huge permanent buffer for it will seriously compromise the available memory, it is advisable to store it dynamically, even if this means continuous and tedious freeings and resavings of the variable as it undergoes processing by multiple subroutines. In the same vein, when a dynamic variable shrinks just a little in size at the tail, it is tempting not to rewrite the variable, but if this happens often enough, these assigned but unused bytes may make for considerable space waste.

2.5.3. DYNAMIC AND PRESET STRING ARGS: CONVERSIONS AND INTERACTIONS

2.5.3.1. Conversions.

To summarize the preceding sections, the fundamental difficulty in using C to manipulate strings is that C does not automatically take care of string storage, so deciding which type of string storage to use is an important part of constructing any string-handling function. To put it more strongly, it is often the most important consideration.

Storage considerations are so important in string manipulation procedures that we often write multiple functions that do exactly the same job except that storage requirements for the args differ. Changes in the structure of a procedure are most often occasioned by the need to have a particular storage type for the output string. The type of the input string usually isn't of concern, in that its size was fixed, whether it is preset or dynamic, before it became a function arg. The exception is the function designed to change the size of the input string, such as scan functions that extract the daughter string rather than copy it; for example, *pspsscan*() transfers the first part of a preset string to a preset array and *psdsscan*() rewrites a predefined string when it transfers the first part of the string to dynamically-allocated space.

If a procedure was designed for a preset output string and must be redone to work for dynamic storage, there's several ways to handle it.

A common string function format is

p = fnct(STRING FromStr, arg 2,... arg n-1, STRING ToStr);

where the input string *FromStr* is processed and the resultant string stored in *ToStr*. Often *p* is unnecessary, because all the work is done inside the function. Or *p* is an additional handle on a specific variable.

The simplest way to revamp the function is to add a dynamic save statement inside the function to create a dynamic string that is the equivalent of *ToStr*. The final arg is now unnecessary, because the dynamically stored string needs no name. *p* is returned, as before. But now *p* is vital as the communication link to the stored string. The function is prototyped as:

p = fnct(STRING FromStr, arg 2,... arg n);

In cases where a function designed for a preset string does not return a pointer, the function would need to be modified to return a char pointer. As before, a dynamic save statement is incorporated into the function body.

When a dynamic string is reworked for use with preset storage, the tasks are reversed. An additional buffer for ToStr must be preset and a final arg added to the function. Most often the pointer that is returned by the function becomes unnecessary.

To generalize the modification of a function for use with different output string storage:

- To change to preset storage: predefine an output char array. Create a separate dummy arg for the output string. Delete dynamic save statements.

- To change to dynamic storage: add a dynamic save statement. Assign the return pointer to the storage dynamically obtained while running the function. Delete the dummy function arg that represents present storage for the output string.

To illustrate, the following are sister functions, both of which reverse a string **ABCD** to read **DCBA**. *dsreverse*() obtains new storage space from the system and writes the reversed string into this new space, thus preserving the original. *psreverse*() writes the reversed string to predefined storage. It preserves the original text, unless the original string is also the predefined storage. Note that in *dsreverse*(), the output string is stored by a *dssave*() statement and the returned pointer is vital to retain contact with the reversed string. In *psreverse*(), the returned pointer is not necessary, because the reversed string is stored in preset storage.

```
STRING dsreverse(STRING s)              STRING psreverse(STRING s, STRING d)
    {/*BP*/                                  {/*BP*/
    char     d[LRGSZE] = {SNUL};
```

```
STRING   pd = d;                          STRING   pd = d;
STRING   ps = s+stlen(s)-1;               STRING   ps = s+stlen(s)-1;

if (stlen(s) > LRGSZE - 1)                if (stlen(s) > LRGSZE - 1)
    {                                         {
    printf("\ndsreverse() can't handle "      printf("\npsreverse() can't handle"
    "a string longer than %d chars.\n"        "a string longer than %d chars.\n"
    LRGSZE-1);                                LRGSZE-1);
    exit(2);                                  exit(2);
    }                                         }
while (ps >= &s[0])                        while (ps >= &s[0])
    *pd++ = *ps--;                            *pd++ = *ps--;
pd = dssave(d);
return(pd);                               return(pd = d);
}/*EP*/                                   }/*EP*/
```

Usage:

```
STRING   p;                               STRING   p;
char     str[SMLSZE];                     char     str[SMLSZE];
                                          char     revstr[SMLSZE];


stcpy("cat",str);                         stcpy("cat",str);
p = dsreverse(str);                       p = psreverse(str, revstr);
printf("\n%s",p);      /*Prints: tac*/    printf("\n%s",revstr);    /*Prints: tac*/
```

dsreverse() points out the need of a temporary buffer (such as *d*) for working with dynamic strings, even with those that do not change in size or content but that give rise to (partial) copies of themselves. Such an accumulation buffer is even more necessary in a procedure that operates within a loop, adding a piece to a string, doing some processing, and adding some more chars. Without the buffer, the string must be stored and freed each time chars are added. This busyness may happen in languages that handle storage automatically, but the user doesn't absorb the cost consciously. In C, it stares us in the face, another consequence of having to do a large part of the housekeeping.

2.5.3.2. Interactions.

A general rule derives from the previous discussions of what happens when a string is changed in size or is used to create a daughter string: (1) if it and the daughter string are dynamic, storage for the string(s) needs to be handled on-line by the programmer; (2) if space for it and the daughter string has been predefined, changes in size require no restructuring of storage, providing that enlarging the string doesn't swamp the preset space. And the system takes care of the trash.

This would appear to give us a way of dealing with either dynamic or predefined string storage. What complicates this simple rule is its application. What if we are combining static and dynamic strings into a larger whole? What if a string shaping function calls another function that calls another that calls another that calls another, and so forth, all of which change the string somewhat. In this case, the pointer to a newly formed string becomes a function arg in another function concerned with reshaping the string, where again the process of shaping, freeing and resaving the string occurs. The pointer variable or one of its equivalents may take any of a number of convoluted paths, so that tracking it is painful if not, where there are many possible routes, almost impossible.

In other words, what if we can't be sure we are dealing with a sole-source dynamic or predefined string and not with a hybrid.

It sometimes seems we need to have the entire genealogy for each variable. We can't reallocate a changed string or free an empty or no longer needed string without being sure of its parentage. This is not easy when the original is some ten routines removed. Did it start life as preset storage or dynamic? It is not sufficient to say that if the function is one written for a dynamically obtained output string, the function arg must have been dynamic. The same ultimate routine might be called by a function where the string starts out dynamic OR by one where the string starts out preset and eventually calls the function through intervening functions.

Possible ways of maintaining awareness of what storage type is at issue suggest themselves:

(1) Have a function arg that states storage type: **P** for preset or **D** for dynamic. If you consider that in copying all or a portion of string A to string B, either string can be preset or dynamic, there has to be at least two letters in the function arg to indicate storage type for both strings; i.e., **MD** or **PS** or **MS** or **PD**. One of the args is a string literal that would include a subset of these letters:

m = dynaMic storage of input string.   **p** = Preset storage of input string.
f = Free (alter or destroy) original string.   **k** = Keep original string intact.
d = Dynamic storage of output string.   **s** = Static (preset) storage of output string.

as in:

```
#define Tstop ";., "
scan(&inbuf, Tstop, "PFS", outbuf);
```

inbuf is the string scanned. *Tstop* is a list of chars, any one of which will halt the scan. *outbuf* is the array that holds the first part of *inbuf* up to the halt char. **PFS** indicates that storage for both *inbuf* and *outbuf* is predefined, and that the piece of *inbuf* that is sent to *outbuf* is deleted from *inbuf*. Some hardworking utility function would interpret **PFS** or **MKD**.

This technique is reasonable and has the practical advantage of reducing the number of functions resident in user include files. But when three or more strings are involved in a hierarchy of function calls, where one function calls another calls another, this method requires sustained discipline.

(2) Use only preset OR only dynamic variables. It might be feasible using just dynamic variables. But it might be very difficult getting at all the places where reallocating string space sometimes will and sometimes will not need to be done; i.e., where ever the string has the opportunity to change size. To handle the potential size change that may occur at many points during string processing, the string must be constantly tested for size change. Or the programmer may adopt the position that if there is a possibility of size change, the string is automatically restoraged.

(3) Be very careful. Keep a temporary large predefined buffer in the calling function. Call the same procedure for either kind of storage. If string space won't overflow, take care of end product in the calling function; that is, once the string is modified and returned to the calling function, storage can be reissued if the string is dynamic. This is not helpful where there is a hierarchy of calling functions, so that the string is submerged in the depths of a set of interrelated functions. By the time these functions have operated on the variable, it might be too late to handle storage, the string having long since outgrown its confines.

(4) If the source string is the critical variable, have sister functions, one handling preset storage of the source string, the other operating on a dynamically stored source string. If the revised string is the critical variable, have sister functions, one sending the revised string to prearranged storage, the other storing the revised string dynamically as part of the procedure. A few functions, usually scan/lop functions, may modify both source and sink strings. Here, as in Sections 3.7.1.2 method 5, the appropriate notation is, say, *dsdslop()* or *psdslop()* This isn't problem-free, but it works for me. Most of the time.

With the best intentions in the world, there will be some basic functions that are used by functions that call functions through layers of other routines traveling multiple collateral routes, so that it is almost impossible to write them specifically for dynamic or for preset strings. If such a basic function is written so that it modifies the original string by sliding a same-sized or shortened revision up to the starting address, we can usually treat the source string, whether preset and dynamically-stored, as preset. For an example, see the last section of code for *pspsscan()* in Section 4.11.2, which scans a preset string. It copies the first part of the string (arg 1) up to some halting character to a daughter string (arg 4) and erases the copied section from the mother string. Rewriting the mother string is accomplished by sliding the unexamined part of the string up to the top of the array. If the mother string was a dynamically-stored string, the worst that is done is to waste some bytes. But the starting address of the string is still available so that the system can free the string when it is no longer needed, perhaps ten functions twice removed.

CHAPTER 3

TEXT AS A SINGLE STREAM: POINTERS AND ARRAYS

3.1. LINKING STRINGS AND POINTERS

3.1.1. WHERE CHAR ARRAYS AND THEIR POINTERS RESIDE

In the previous chapter, we discussed how strings are brought into memory and how they are stored, contrasting the predefined string, where space is set aside when the program is compiled, and the dynamically allocated string, which acquires a home when the program is run. Now we focus on character pointers, variables that can be assigned the addresses of these strings.

To set the stage, we begin with an example showing the physical locations of a char array and several pointers and how linkage between these variables is effected.

Suppose within a function, we are given these definitions of local variables:

```
int          i;
char         new[6];
char         *pditto;
static char  *pdyne
char         *pnew;
```

When a variable is defined, the compiler is put to work finding the variable storage. As shown in Table 3.1, in this example, the integer *i* is stored at address 30. *new*, a char array, is given storage starting at address 300 through address 305. The compiler finds the space and assigns the space but it does not clean out the space. So *new*'s space contains whatever garbage was in there at the time the space was assigned; in our case **OMPILE**. *pditto*, *pdyne* and *pnew* are unassigned char pointers and are given storage at address 200, 40 and 250, respectively. They contain whatever was previously there.

136

Address	ID	Contents
[30]	i	z
[40]	pdyn	-1275
[200]	pditto	S
[250]	pnew	C
[300]	new	O
[301]		M
[302]		P
[303]		I
[304]		L
[305]		E

Table 3.1. Illustrating where strings and pointers reside in memory.

The next code cleans out some of the variables. The first three bytes of *new* are SNUL'ed in the for() loop. The rest of the space occupied by *new* is still filled with garbage. At the completion of the loop, *i* is 3. The results are shown in Table 3.2.

```
pditto = NULL;
pnew = NULL;

for (i = 0; i < 3; i++)
    new[i] = SNUL;
```

Address	ID	Contents
[30]	i	3
[40]	pdyn	-1275
[200]	pditto	0
[250]	pnew	0
[300]	new	0
[301]		0
[302]		0
[303]		I
[304]		L
[305]		E

Table 3.2. A table illustrating where strings and pointers reside in memory.

In the next code and in Table 3.3, the string constant **CAT** is copied to *new*. A terminal SNUL is added as part of running *stcpy()*. The rest of the space assigned to *new* is still filled with junk that does not affect *new*, because anything after the SNUL in *new*[3] is ignored.

The char variables are linked to each other. *pnew* is set to point to *new*, which is shorthand for saying that the value of *pnew* is no longer NULL but is now the address of the first char of *new*. Indirect referencing is possible in C. By indirect referencing, we mean that the system does not stop once it has *pnew*'s value. Instead, it treats the value as an address; it goes to that address and uses what is there. The indirect referent of *pnew*, written as **pnew*, is the variable *new*[0], whose value is **C**.

pditto is given the value of *pnew*, which is 300. It becomes another pointer to *new*, because *new* is at address 300. So we can also reference *new* through *pditto*.

For dynamic storage, having assembled a string such as **CAT**, we would request storage using *calloc*(). The system would sequester the string in a separate memory area accessible only to it. To maintain contact with this unnamed string, we would assign its address as the value, say, of *pdyn*. The local pointers to *new* would not be affected.

stcpy("CAT",new);
pnew = &new[0]; /*This also defines the converse relationship: **new[0] = *pnew.** */
pditto = pnew;
pdyne = dssave(new);

Address	ID	Contents
[30]	i	3
[40]	pdyn	9450
[200]	pditto	300
[250]	pnew	300
[300]	new	C
[301]		A
[302]		T
[303]		0
[304]		L
[305]		E

Table 3.3.   Illustrating where pointers and strings reside in memory.

3.1.2.   POINTERS AS VARIABLES; POINTERS AS REPRESENTATIVES OF STRINGS

Earlier (see Footnote, Section 2.5.2), we made note that a char array has multiple *contextual* meanings: it is a buffer to hold characters, it is the string residing in the buffer, it is the actual characters in the text, it is the text complete with a terminal SNUL. The pointer-to-char is similarly invested with several meanings even though we tend to emphasize its built-in ability to reference indirectly the value of another variable. In longhand:

- The value of the pointer is an integer address; e.g., **pnew = 300;**.

- The variable resident at that address has a value, which is the value of interest; for example, **&new[0] = 300; new[0] = 'C';**.

- The pointer indirectly references this value; e.g., ***pnew = new[0] = 'C';**.

There is nothing in the way the pointer is assigned an address that is unique or directive. But **p = &a;** or **a = *p;**, when p has been defined as a pointer, is informative. The system 'knows' that it is to carry out a two-stage process: first, it looks up the address that is the pointer's value and, second, it goes to that address to access the value of the variable that resides there. As a short cut, we say that the pointer points to the variable—referring to the variable and its value by way of its address—as we might say **the deli is sure ...**, referring to the man who runs the deli, or even more portentously, **the White House insists**, referencing the words of some anonymous person who, presumably, is stating the views of the president who resides in the White House.

Because of the reversibility of array and pointer notation, the pointer is enabled to play several different roles. To exemplify the meanings of p, a pointer-to-char, consider this piece of code:

```
void pfct(void)
    {
    char      field[SMLSZE] = {SNUL};
    int       i;
    STRING    p = NULL;                                              /*a*/

    p = field;                                                       /*b*/
    printf("\np = %d", p);      /*PrintProduct: p = 3420*/           /*c*/
    i = 2;
    p = p+i;
    printf("\np = %d", p);      /*PrintProduct: p = 3422*/           /*d*/
    p = &field[0]; stcpy("The old brown cow.", p);                   /*e*/
    printf("\np = %s", p);      /*PrintProduct: p = The old brown cow.*/  /*f*/
    p = dssave(field);                                               /*g*/
    free(p);                                                         /*h*/
    }
```

Pointer-to-char as integer variable:

First, at its most simple as in line a, p is an independent variable, whose value is either NULL or an address. When p is assigned to reference *field* in line b, p contains the address of the first byte of *field*, as shown in line c. Pointer values—memory addresses—may be compared to other addresses in memory and, in the context of an **if (A OP B)** conditional, the results of this comparison may be used to determine which of the alternative paths is to be followed.

Second, as an integer variable anchored to a char array, p is capable of limited but flexible arithmetic maneuvering: it may be incremented (the value is shown in line d), decremented or its value may be fixed relative to the value of another pointer to the same array. Unlike the previous case which involved absolute addressing, comparing pointers relative to a specific array is restricted to operations compatible with anchor and offset operations.

p's major power, however, derives from the operations that can be performed because of its built-in linkage to whatever data object resides at the address that is *p*'s current value. As example, in its role as pointer-to-char, when it is transmitted as function arg to *stcpy*() in line *e*, it will course systematically through the set of addresses occupied by *field*. (Note that if we did not reset p, it would have printed: **e old brown cow.**.) As *p* is incremented by one, it becomes the address of the next byte in memory, where the next element of *field* has residence. At each stop, a char value is copied to the referenced element of *field*. In this way, the text of *field* is constructed, one char at a time.

Pointer-to-char as string representative:

Upon the completion of *stcpy*(), *p*, returns to the position assigned in line *b*: the start of *field*. *p* can substitute for the text in *field*, as in the *printf* statement of line *f*, because the compiler views the characters following the character targeted by *p* up to a SNUL as an entity. The idiomatic **p = field;** can be substituted for **p = &field[0];** as in line *b*, but otherwise the longer form must be used. For example, to write the string starting at the word **old**

```
p = &field[4];
printf("\nNew String = %s", p);
```

More generally, because in C an array serving as a function arg is conveyed to the called function as the address of its first element (see Section 3.2.3.1), the pointer-to-char can always serve as arg substitute for its associated array.

In line *g*, *dssave*() reassigns *p* to hold the address of a system-saved memory location that contains a *copy* of the text collected in *field*. Here, *p* plays its second major role to the full. It represents a string that can not be accessed except through a pointer. Nor can the string be deleted except thro ugh a pointer. *p*'s value is a memory address. Hence, when *p* is the arg of *free*() in line *h*, the system removes the block of memory that begins at the address that is *p*'s value from its list of not-available-space, allowing that portion of memory to be reused. The end result is that the string in that location is no longer viable.

3.1.3. POINTERS LINKED TO DYNAMIC STRINGS

In reading a program, when we see a char pointer construction not associated with a buffer, quite often it means that sooner or later there will be a function or a statement in which the pointer is attached to a string that does not yet exist. Space for the string will be provided by the system.

C makes it convenient for the system to store a string, with access to it through a defined pointer. The user has named this pointer and it is there as stand-in for the actual string, which does not have and does not need a name. In the same manner, an array of pointers can stand-in for a set of system-stored unnamed strings. A good example is the set of phrases (i.e., informational fields) that result from the decomposition of a record, with each substring referenced by a separate pointer. The record can be reconstituted by concatenating the set of pointers in sequence. After a while in string programming, often we begin to feel as if these pointers are the actual substrings, a feeling encouraged by the similarity of array and pointer notation.

When a pointer-to-char is defined, there may be the intention of connecting it with the storage of a specific string. But defining the pointer does not create storage for its associated string. For a proper assignment, the material that will be stored by the system is first collected in a temporary store. When its size is known, permanent storage is found and then, and only then, is the address of the storage location assigned to the pointer. Finally, the string is copied to that address.

A disparity in scope occurs when a local pointer is assigned to a string that is stored dynamically. The pointer is known only when the function is running but the string is stored for the life of the program. As example, consider the function, *dynamic()*, whose layout is shown in Table 3.4. (Note that *define.h* itself starts with a list of required C library files: *ctype.h, stdio.h, malloc.h, limit.h.*)

```
#include "DEFINE.H"
#include "GLOBALS.H"
#include "COMLIB.H"
extern void   dynamic(void);
extern int    main(void);

void dynamic(void)
    {   }

main(void)
    {
    int   i = 0;

    for (i = 1; i <= 3; i++)
        dynamic();
    }
```

Table 3.4.   Table showing layout of program
                 featuring *dynamic()*.

```
void dynamic(void)
    {
    char *pbuf;
    pbuf = dssave("All Gaul is divided into three parts.");
    printf("\nADDRESS: %ld; TEXT: %s\n", pbuf,pbuf);
    }
```

In Table 3.4, once the function finishes, the pointer *pbuf* 'dies' and so is permanently separated from its string, an unfortunate circumstance because the pointer is the only means of communicating with the string. The results of running the loop shown in the layout box are:

ADDRESS: 683409526; TEXT: All Gaul is divided into three parts.
ADDRESS: 683409566; TEXT: All Gaul is divided into three parts.
ADDRESS: 683409606; TEXT: All Gaul is divided into three parts.

Each time *pbuf* is assigned the address of a dynamically stored string copy of the string literal **All Gaul is divided into three parts.**, the stored string is a different string. The way to prevent wasting space storing the same string over and over again is clear: we should free the string before the function terminates, as is done next in *revdynamic()*.

```
void revdynamic(void)
    {
    char *pbuf;
    pbuf = dssave("All Gaul is divided into three parts.");
    printf("\nADDRESS: %ld; TEXT: %s\n", pbuf, pbuf);
    NULLIT(pbuf);
    }
```

3.1.4. POINTERS LINKED TO STRING CONSTANTS

For a string constant, if the pointer is global or static, the pointer may be defined and assigned the address of the string literal in a single statement and the pointer and string literal are mated for the life of the program, unless the pointer is revalued[1]. For example:

```
static char *instring = "All Gaul is divided into three parts.";
```

A differences in scope of the pointer and the static string literal can complicate what seems a simple rule. Unless a local pointer is a static local variable or is defined at the beginning of *main()*, it will disappear when the function finishes. Conversely, the string literal, even if defined inside a function, is retained for the life of the program. Now, if the local pointer is assigned the address of the string literal each time the function is called, is it a new string each time? As noted in Section 2.2.1, because the address of the string literal appears on the stack when the function is recalled, compilers can reassign the local pointer to the original string each time it comes into use, making the pointer a *de facto* static variable.

In this next example, a pointer-to-char is defined and then assigned the address of a string literal. Note the difference from the example in Section 3.1.3, where individual string variables are saved dynamically.

```
void statstr(void)
    {
    char *pbuf = "All Gaul is divided into three parts.";

    printf("\nADDRESS: %ld; TEXT: %s\n", pbuf, pbuf);
    }

int main(void)
    {
    int   i = 0;
```

---

1 More precisely, as noted in Section 1.5.4, the string literal is implemented as a constant pointer. This address is assigned to the variable pointer.

```
    for (i = 1; i <= 3; i++)
        statstr();
}
```

The results are:

ADDRESS: 440467522; TEXT: All Gaul is divided into three parts.
ADDRESS: 440467522; TEXT: All Gaul is divided into three parts.
ADDRESS: 440467522; TEXT: All Gaul is divided into three parts.

3.1.5. POINTERS LINKED TO PRESET STRING VARIABLES

If the operation performed on a string is extracting a substring or deleting bracketed text, obviously a buffer large enough to store the original string will be adequate for changes in the size of the string. Such a buffer can be preset and, if need be, its address assigned to a local pointer to represent it. Transmitted as a function arg, the pointer can thread through as complex a labyrinth of subroutines as any dynamically saved variable. If, weaving through layers of subroutines, the analogs are themselves preset, no care needs to be taken with any of the permutations of the local variable (represented by *pbuf* in the next example).

```
void startfct(void)
    {
    char buf[SMLSZE] = {SNUL};
    STRING    pbuf = buf;
    STRING    pnew = NULL;

    stcpy("StartStr",buf);
    pnew = callfct(pbuf);
    }
```

callfct(**pbuf**) calls
      nextproc(**pbuf analog)** which calls
          polish(**pbuf analog**) and so forth ...

When *startfct*() terminates, *buf*, *pbuf* and *pnew* will disappear, taking up no permanent storage space.

Given a preset buffer, a separate pointer is useful for probing the array directly, searching for a particular char or a particular type of char, a digit, say. The pointer to this array ripples down the array. This function counts the number of digits in the string.

```
void ripple(void)
    {
    char collect[SZE(100)] = {SNUL};
    STRING        pcol = collect;
    int           coldigit = 0;

    stcpy("ABC101DEF212GHI323III",collect);
    while (*pcol)
        {
```

```
        if (isdigit(*pcol))
            coldigit++;
        pcol++;
        }
    }
```

The act of defining a char pointer does not create storage for its associated string. For a proper assignment, the value of a char pointer has to be the address of an existing array. This holds true for all preset strings: globally defined strings, strings created locally that last only while the function is active, or static char arrays that are accessible only in the file in which they are written.

For the pointer to be gainfully employed, three conditions need to be met:

(1) the string is defined (i.e., given an address) but not necessarily initialized

(2) the pointer-to-char is defined

(3) the pointer-to-char is assigned the address of the string.

Pointers, such as *pdsn* in the next example, do NOT create string storage. Conditions 1 and 3 have not been met.

```
void somefnct(void)
    {
    STRING pdsn;

    .......
    }
```

In the next example, the local pointer and array are defined (i.e., given addresses in memory), but condition 3 is not met: the pointer *pdsn* is not assigned to the array *dsn*. It is an error copying to an unassigned pointer, as this example, where the string *instring* is copied to *pdsn*, illustrates.

```
static char *instring = "All Gaul is divided into three parts.";

void somefnct(void)
    {
    STRING        pdsn = NULL;
    char          dsn[SMLSZE] = {SNUL};

    stcpy(instring, pdsn);
    PS(dsn);                    /*macro to print string. Defined in define.h*/
    }
```

Depending on compiler version, the compiler may trap this as a null pointer assignment. Or the machine might hang. This holds true whether the attempt to copy to an unassigned pointer is made using a global constant, as we just tried, or a local string.

Still worse is this next version, where *pdsn* is not NULL'ed and lodges some random value that might well be an address containing text that *instring* will overwrite. Or it might hang the system.

```
void somefnct(void)
    {
    STRING        pdsn;
    char          dsn[SMLSZE] = {SNUL};

    stcpy(instring, pdsn);
    PS(pdsn);                     /*macro to print string. Defined in define.h*/
    }
```

In this next version of *somefnct*(), conditions 1, 2 and 3 are met.

```
void somefnct(void)
    {
    char          dsn[SMLSZE] = {SNUL};
    STRING        pdsn = dsn;

    stcpy(instring,pdsn);       /*pdsn was assigned the address of dsn above.*/
    PS(dsn);
    }
```

This section has focused on linking a pointer and a preset array by assigning the pointer a value, specifically the address of the char array of interest. A corollary is: if a char pointer is reassigned, it no longer points to the first array. Yet, given the need to minimize the number of local variables occupying stack space, pointers are often reused, as in the next example.

```
char       more[SMLSZE] = {SNUL};
STRING     pmore = more;                                                    /*a*/
char       new[SMLSZE] = {SNUL};

stcpy(instring, more);                    /*more reads:
                                          All Gaul is divided into three parts.*/
stcpy("A separate sentence.", new);       /*new reads: A separate sentence.*/
pmore = dscase(new, 'U');                 /*dscase is in comlib.c*/           /*b*/
printf("\n pmore: %s\n",pmore);      /*pmore reads:A SEPARATE SENTENCE.*/
printf("\n more: %s\n",more);        /*more reads: All Gaul is divided into three parts.*/
```

In line *a*, *pmore* is defined as pointing to the first char of the string *more*, which obtained storage when it was defined in the previous statement. In line *b*, *pmore* is reassigned the value returned by the function *uppercase*(); i.e., *pmore* is assigned the address of the beginning of the string that was uppercased. There is no longer a connection between *more* and *pmore*, despite the association suggested by their names. To establish one, *pmore* would need to be reassigned:

pmore = more;

A reassigned pointer is a hard bug to find. The tendency is to check carefully that the pointer was assigned when the local variables are initialized but pay little attention to the possibility that the pointer may have been indirectly reassigned.

The pointers examined in this section are used to represent strings. They do important service. Other pointers, used as variables returned by functions, may do little except satisfy the syntax of a called subroutine; some compilers will complain if a function is prototyped as returning a pointer and then doesn't. One solution is to define a single permanent junk pointer-to-char as a global variable in a file dedicated to global variables. (In this book, we call this file *ptemp*.) *ptemp* is never NULL'ed. It is just reused as needed. It is never queried. And no variable is ever referenced through it.

3.2. FUNCTION ARGS: STRINGS BY VALUE; STRINGS BY REFERENCE

This section will analyze the practical consequences of using args by value and args by reference. It will also serve as introduction to permanent changes (destructive), partially destructive and temporary changes in a string.

Any variable may be passed as an argument to a function by value or by reference. To start at the very beginning, let us briefly review the difference between sending a value to a function versus sending an address.

3.2.1. THE SINGLE CHAR FUNCTION ARG BY VALUE

If the variable is passed by value, a copy of the variable's value is transmitted to the called function. The variable itself can not be affected because the function has no access to where the variable is stored. Inside the called function, the value of the variable may be modified or even NULL'ed without affecting the actual value in any way. For example:

```
void try(char note)
    {
    note = 'a';
    }
main()
    {
    char charvar = 'z';
    try(charvar);
    printf("\ncharvar = %c\n",charvar);        /*PrintProduct: charvar = z*/
    }
```

One way to re-value the variable with the new value is to assign the value to it by means of a return statement. (The returned value may, of course, be assigned instead to another variable.)

```
char try(char note)
    {
    return(note = 'a');
    }
```

```
main()
    {
    char charvar = 'z';
    charvar = try(charvar);
    printf("\ncharvar = %c\n", charvar);        /*PrintProduct: charvar = a*/
    }
```

3.2.2. THE SINGLE CHAR FUNCTION ARG BY REFERENCE

To pass a variable to a function by reference means that the memory address of the variable is transmitted. Therefore, the function can store a different value at this address. This modification is 'real', it is permanent; i.e., the variable keeps the new value even after the function terminates.

For example if the function *try*() above is rewritten as:

```
void try(STRING note)          /*Passing the address of a char variable.*/
    {
    *note = 'a';                /*The char indirectly referenced by note is permanently*/
    }                           /* given the value a.*/

main()
    {
    char charvar = 'z';
    try(&charvar);
    printf("\ncharvar = %c\n",charvar);        /*PrintProduct: charvar = a*/
    }
```

try() expects the value of a pointer as arg, where the value of a pointer is an address. **try (&charvar);** directs the program to use the address of *charvar* as pointer value. This could also be written with an independent pointer as:

```
    char       charvar = 'z';
    STRING    pchar = charvar;
    try(pchar);
```

3.2.3. CONVEYING AN ARRAY TO A FUNCTION

A variable is passed by value. The way to perform the equivalent of passing an arg by reference, as the example in Section 3.2.2 illustrates, is to make a copy of its address accessible to the called procedure. Note that so far we have demonstrated the difference in effect of passing a variable by value and by reference for individual variables, NOT for arrays of variables. We consider the array as function arg next.

3.2.3.1.   Pointers-To-Char As Function Args.

As we know from Chapter 1, when we pass an array by value, the system does not respect the injunction that changes in array text be confined to the called function. Instead of utilizing array index notation, the system uses pointer notation to describe the array and its component elements[2]. The address of the first char in the array is what is sent to the called function. So, in effect, the actual array, rather than a copy of it, is passed. Regarded as a practical measure, this non duplication of the array saves header space, memory and overhead.

Hastily, we may conclude that, at least for strings, the string variable is transmitted by reference. This notion is reinforced when we are told that the array name and the pointer to the array are interchangeable as args; where ever a function expects a pointer to the start of the string as arg, the name of the string may be substituted. If:

char   a[SMLSZE] = {SNUL};
STRING   p = a;

then both

p = a; and p = &a[0];

assign *p* exactly the same value, the address of the first char of the array *a*. And if the function *dofct* calls for a char pointer arg, then both

dofct(p); and dofct(a);

are correct. They are functionally equivalent. However, despite appearances, the use of the string name as pointer value signifies only that we are dealing with one of the short cuts in C. To point to the fifth element in the array, we may NOT write:

p = a[4];

It must be

p = &a[4];

If *p* now points to *a*[4]; and we wish to operate on the portion of the array beginning at *a*[4], we can write:

dofct(p); or dofct(&a[4]);

Char pointers and char arrays may be interchangeable function args, but the only leger-demain is in the arbitrary decree that pointer notation be used in dealing with arrays. The pointer to an array of chars does not, in fact, accomplish what we expect of a pointer to a discrete char. Rather than signifying that string args are by reference, it may with more justice be claimed that the capability of the pointer is weakened for arrays, not that strings are made more robust. When a pointer effects a change in a single variable, the change is complete. When a pointer effects changes in an array, the individual elements of the array

---

2 In pointer notation an array is expressed in terms of the address of its first element. The elements of the array are located relative to this anchor value. The first element of the array, a[0], has an offset of zero. a[1] has an offset of plus 1, and so forth. Assumed in this is that the elements are sequential and that there is a halting criterion—the terminal SNUL.

can be modified, but, as we shall see, positional information is not affected; the location of the array in memory is not changed.

Suppose we start with the relationship between *a*, a char array and *p*, a pointer to the char array. These are shown in Table 3.5. *a* is not completely filled. It contains the text: **scratch**, then a SNUL, then some garbage left over from previous use.

```
char      a[10] = {SNUL};
STRING    p = &a[0];
```

C is consistent in that function args are always sent by value. Hence, if the called function is prototyped as **void dofct(char *);**, and if we write: **dofct(p);**, what is sent to the function is a COPY of the value of p; i.e., **300**. However, the value of the pointer is an address. In this case, it is the actual memory location of the first char of the string. So, yes, *dofct*() can make a real change in the value of the first char of the array.

Address	ID	Contents
[200]	p	300
[300]	a[0]	S
[301]	a[1]	C
[302]	a[2]	R
[303]	a[3]	A
[304]	a[4]	T
[305]	a[5]	C
[306]	a[6]	H
[307]	a[7]	\0
[308]	a[8]	z
[309]	a[9]	T

Table 3.5   Illustrating a string in memory.

Moreover, because all the addresses of all the elements are guaranteed to be in sequence with the first element of the array, *dofct*() may change the other chars of *a*. The pointer can be legally incremented. (To increment *p* by one is to re-value it with the address of the next element in the array.) The pointer can be directed to traverse the array. By utilizing the pointer, *dofct*() is given access to the actual locations of the elements that constitute the array, so it can permanently change the contents of the elements. By permanent, we mean that the change persists, even when control is returned to the calling function. Suppose first, as in lines *a* and *b*, we SNUL *a*[5] and *a*[6]. The text would then read: **SCRAT**, because the system would ignore any chars after a SNUL, even though the size of *a* has not changed.

Suppose next, as in line *c*, we do an ordinary string processing task, chopping off the beginning of the string to reshape it. In this example, we delete the first two chars of the array, setting them to SNUL.

```
void dofct(STRING p)
    {
    int   i;

    p[5] = SNUL;                              /*a*/
```

```
p[6] = SNUL;                          /*b*/
for (i = 0; i < 2; i++, p++)          /*c*/
      *p = SNUL;
printf("\n%s",p);                     /*PrintProduct: RAT*/
}
```

Inside *dofct*(), *p* is redefined to point to *a*[2]. And the print statement reads: **RAT**, the substring we want to keep. Have we permanently changed the starting address of the array?

The answer of course is NO. To effect a permanent change in the starting address of the array from within *dofct*(), we need the ability to redefine the array; i.e., give it a new location *vis a vis* the other variables written in memory. This is a system capability, not available to us. Or we need to be able to re-value *p*, our only contact with the array. *p* holds the array's address[3]. But *p*'s home address (i.e., 200) is NOT known inside *dofct*(). A copy of the pointer's value was transmitted to the function. The unreachable (from *dofct*()) pointer itself continues to contain its original value, i.e., 300.

So changes that occur in the starting address of the array inside the function have no permanence. Once out of *dofct*(), if the array is transmitted to another function as &*a*, the program uses its knowledge of the location of the array; i.e., the address of *a* is 300. If the array is later transmitted to another function using *p* as function arg, *p*'s value is the one stored at address 200. And that value is 300, not 302. A **printf("\n%s", p);** would be empty—because *a*[0] was SNUL'ed inside *dofct*(). It would not, as we had hoped, read: **RAT**.

We have then the interesting situation that the pointer variable is transmitted to the function by value, but because this value is the address of its associated array, we can get at the contents of the individual elements of the array. Within the called function, discrete characters can be changed permanently—e.g., changing **rat** to **rut** is sticky—because the called function accesses actual addresses as offsets from the pointer value. But the called function can't permanently change the amount of storage assigned to the array. Nor can it modify the starting address of the array referenced by the pointer. Even if all the chars in the first part of a string are SNUL'ed, there is no way for the called function to assign the starting address of this reduced string to the pointer; it has no access to the pointer.

Suppose a text **This is a X inner string.**, in which we wish to delete the first chars up to but not including the **X**, and then change **i**'s to **Y**'s. In *modify*(), the pointer **s** moves down the array until it encounters an **X**, where it stops. Another pointer *ss* is used to examine the rest of the string; *s* remains pointing to the beginning of the part of the string we wish to keep.

Note that the loop starting in line *a* will break when a local int *i* has reached the length of the original size of *s*, whether an **X** is encountered or not. This is protection against running past the space allocated to *s* when the text has no **X** to break the loop.

---

3 Ways to change a string's starting address are discussed in Section 3.7.

```
void modify(STRING s)
    {
    int      i    = 0;
    STRING   ss   = NULL;
    int      t    = stlen(s);

    for (i = 0; i < t; i++, s++)                    /*a*/
        if (*s == 'X') break;
    ss = s;
    while (*ss != SNUL)
        {
        if (*ss == 'i') *ss = 'Y';
        ss++;
        }
    printf("\n in modify: %s\n",s);  /*PrintProduct: in modify: X Ynner strYng.*/
    }

main(void)
    {/*MAIN*/
    char      str[SZE(100)] = {SNUL};

    stcpy("This is a X inner string.",str);
    modify(str);     /*The array name, a constant pointer, is used as pointer to itself.*/
    printf("\n in main: %s\n",str);  /*PrintProduct: in main: This is a X Ynner strYng.*/
    }/*MAIN*/
```

modify() does two things: it shifts the start of the string; then it changes **i**'s to capital **Y**'s. The changes to capital **Y** are permanent. And we can eliminate the first part of the string inside *modify*() by assigning the address of the char **X** to the pointer *s*. We do this by breaking the loop when the element the pointer *s* references is **X**. But the array itself has not shifted its address. It begins at the same address as before *modify*() was run. After *modify*() terminates, the string will read: **This is a X Ynner strYng**.

3.2.3.2.   Creating A Virtual String.

In the previous section, we temporarily changed the beginning of the text within the *modify*() routine. If we were to call another function within *modify*(), the text transmitted to this new function would be the lopped text, because it remains lopped until *modify*()terminates. This is an important concept. It means that we can create a virtual string[4] that operates as any other string during the lifetime of the function. It can be passed as a function arg to another function, which can transmit it through an entire series of functions. But once

4 It is not real in that it loses the boundaries it acquires inside the function when the function, *modify*() in this example, stops being active. Changes in its contents persist, but even though the string was defined outside the function, it reverts in size and location to its pre-function state.

we leave the function in which the virtual string was created, changes in the starting address of the string are not retained. It is easier to see this, if we rewrite *modify*() as two functions, where *modify* calls *inmod*(). The results are as before: a shift in the start of the text within *modify*(); a return to the extent of the original string after *modify*() finishes. Only the values of the individual elements are permanently changed.

```
void inmod(STRING s)
    {
    while (*s != SNUL)
        {
        if (*s == 'i') *s = 'Y';
        s++;
        }
    }


void modify(STRING s)
    {
    int   i = 0;
    int   t = stlen(s);

    for (i = 0; i < t; i++, s++)
        if (*s == 'X') break;
    inmod(s);
    printf("\n in modify: %s\n",s);        /*PrintProduct: in modify: X Ynner strYng.*/
    }
```

3.2.4. MORE ON THE CONSEQUENCES OF POINTER-TO-CHAR SYNTAX

3.2.4.1.   Char Pointers And Char Arrays As Interchangeable Function Args.

As another example of the consequences of the use by the system of pointer syntax when the function arg is an array, consider the function *stcpy*(), a single-statement function based on the C library function *strcpy*(). *stcpy*() copies a string into another string; specifically, the first arg of *stcpy*() is copied into the second, character by character.

Using pointer args, *stcpy*() may be written as:

```
void st1cpy(char *from, char *to)
    {
    while ((*to++ = *from++) != SNUL) ;
    }
```

or, using char array args, as:

```
void st2cpy(char from[], char to[])
    {
    int   i = 0;
```

```
    while ((to[i] = from[i]) != SNUL)
        i++;
}
```

Using either version, *stcpy()* is handed two args—char arrays or char pointers—by the function that calls it. Both arrays and pointers are authorized by the language to act as pointers when passed as args. Inside *st2cpy()*, *to* and *from* are pointers-to-char, not array elements. Recall, however, from Section 1.5.2, that *to*[i] and *from*[i] are pointers-to-chars that are syntactically functioning as array elements. So the comparison is to SNUL, not NULL[5].

In the next example, we get the same text in *new* using either version of *stcpy()* and either the array name, *new*, or its pointer, *pnew*, as function arg.

```
void somefct(void)
    {
    char     new[SMLSZE] = {SNUL};
    char     old[SMLSZE] = {SNUL};
    char     *pnew = new;
    char     *pold = old;

    stcpy("New and blue.", old);
    st1cpy(old,new); printf("\n%s",new);      /*PrintProduct: New and blue.*/
    st1cpy(pold,pnew); printf("\n%s",pnew);   /*PrintProduct: New and blue.*/
    st2cpy(old,new); printf("\n%s",new);      /*PrintProduct: New and blue.*/
    st2cpy(pold,pnew); printf("\n%s",pnew);   /*PrintProduct: New and blue.*/
    }
```

Within the called function, transmitted arrays are used as pointers. Moreover, as *new* illustrates, an array name (implemented, as we know from Section 1.5.2, as a constant pointer) may be used when the function arg specifically calls for a pointer; the array name acts as a variable pointer inside the called function. Once we accept this idiomatic concept, the legal equivalence of pointer and array name and char array can provide us with a powerful programming tool[6].

At the finish of the while statement, the *to* pointer points to SNUL. Yet when *stcpy()* terminates and the program returns to *somefct()*, *pnew*, represented by the dummy arg *to*, regains its original value and points to its original position, the top of the array *new*, not to *new*'s final SNUL.

---

5 The same result we'd have gotten if we had incorrectly assumed *to* and *from* were arrays, not pointers.

6 Much of the exposition of this section repeats what was expounded in somewhat different language in the previous section. The hope is that repetition will aid familiarization. I base this pedagogical strategy on a principle taught by a chemistry professor back in college. He always said that if something is repeated often enough, you may not really understand it, but you will get so familiar with it, you will think you do. More to the point, you will use it properly.

It is as if we had written the function in this way:

STRING stcpy(STRING from, STRING to)
    {

/*In the next line, top is assigned the address of the first character element of the array to. It does not change value. To, functioning as a pointer, is incremented as it rolls down the string.*/

    STRING   top = to;

    while ((*to++ = *from++) != SNUL);
        to = top;
    return(to);
    }

This last version is stilted to a C programmer, but it is correct. In addition to filling *to* with the contents of *from*, it will also return the address of the top of the char array. But it is not necessary. The earlier versions will do as well.

We know that if the function knows the address of a variable, it can change the contents at that address and the change sticks, even when the function finishes. If the function knows only the value of a variable, it can change the value within the function. But when the function terminates, changes made inside the function do not affect the old value residing at the address of the variable.

As applied to char pointers, when a function is handed a pointer, it is given a copy of the address of a single char, specifically, the first char in the array pointed to by the pointer. The address of the first char defines the address of the entire string, because all the following chars are considered part of this string until a SNUL is reached, marking the end of the string. So a copy of the address of the string is as good as the real thing. As it ripples down the array, the pointer is re-valued successively with the addresses of the consecutive chars. Hence, when the value of a char is changed, the change is real, permanent. But the function does not know the address of the pointer; i.e., the pointer itself was passed by value. So even though the pointer is incremented within the function, these changes in the pointer are not known outside the function. When the function ends, the original value of the pointer is restored; see, for example, the string processed by *modify()* in Section 3.2.3.1. Operations on the pointer within the function are as ineffective as the attempt to erase a blot on a slide by erasing the copy of the blot on a print of the slide.

This trick of virtual equivalence between the name of the array and the pointer to the array works because C immediately converts array index notation into address plus offset notation, and operates within the context of pointer grammar. The same operation is unacceptable for single ints or single chars. A function that receives a single char as arg receives only a copy of that char's value. Any and all changes to the value within the function are NOT transmitted to the calling char. As demonstrated in Section 3.2.2, the function must be given the address of the single char to change its value permanently.

3.2.4.2.   Deliberate Resetting Of The Pointer To The Top Of The String.

Usually it is not necessary to reset the pointer-to-char to the start of its char array. As shown in the last section, when a pointer to the top of a string is passed as a function arg, the pointer snaps back to the top of the string when the function is finished.

However, within the called function the entry address of the pointer, *p* in the next example, is lost as it begins to thread its way down the char array. If on occasion it is necessary to return to the top of the original string within a called function, a local variable can be set to point to the top of the string. In the next function shown, *dofct()* examines a string char by char. If it encounters a control char, it switches to another procedure to examine the entire string.

```
BOOL dofct(STRING p)
    {
    STRING   q;

    q = p;      /*This assigns q the value of p: the address of the first char in the array.*/
    while (*p != SNUL)
        {
        if (iscntrl(*p))    /*Prototyped in ctype.h: if the char is a control char*/
            {
            p = q;      /*This reset p to point to the top of the string.*/
            doctrlfct(p);
            return(YES);
            }
        else p++;
        }
    return(NO);
    }
```

Next is a program that highlights *stmfind()*, a procedure that examines a string (whose dummy arg is *str*) for copies of a string fragment (whose dummy arg is *wrd*). *stmfind()* does not examine each char. If *wrd* is matched, the function skips past the copy before renewing the search for the next copy of it in *str*. The program layout is in Table 3.6.

The function returns the int *hit*, which records the number of times *wrd* occurs. The starting position of each copy of *wrd* is listed as an element in the array referenced by the integer pointer *place*. In the sentence **the mathematics team then went home.**, there are three copies of *wrd*: **the** is at *str*[0], *str*[6] and *str*[21].

In the calling function (*callstmfind*) the name of the array holding the string queried (i.e., *sentence*) serves as its own pointer when it is used as function arg in *stmfind()*. Within *stmfind()*, this pointer moves down the array of char elements. The memory address of the character referenced can be determined immediately, but we want to relate the start of *wrd* to some array element, not to some address in memory that becomes a meaningless location once the function terminates.

```
/*Layout of stmfind file:*/

#include "DEFINE.H"7
#include "GLOBALS.H"
#include "COMLIB.H"
#include "COMSET.H"

extern  void    callstmfind(void);
extern  int     main(void);
extern  BOOL    stequ(STRING s1, STRING s2);
extern  int   stmfind(STRING str,STRING wrd, long *place);

BOOL stequ(STRING s1, STRING s2)  { }

int stmfind(STRING str, STRING wrd, long *place) { }

void callstmfind(){ }

int main()
    {
    callstmfind();
    return(0);
    }
```

Table 3.6   Layout of a program featuring stmfind().

Is the start of *wrd* on array element 2 or 4 or where? There is no immediate way to determine where the pointer is in terms of array elements, unless we keep a running count of the number of chars examined, or, as in this case, we calculate the relative difference of the address of the first char of *wrd* and the address of the top of the array, legitimate pointer arithmetic. For this purpose, before examination of the array was begun, a local pointer *start* was set to point permanently to the top of *str*.

```
int stmfind(STRING str, STRING wrd, long *place)
    {/*BP*/
    int        hits = 0;
    int        ls = stlen(str);  /*So the string's length won't have to be recalculated.*/
    STRING     start = NULL;
    int        lw = stlen(wrd);      /*Calculates word fragment length once only.*/

    if (ls < lw || ls == 0 || lw == 0)
```

---

7 *define.h* holds macro definitions and macro routines. *globals.c* has the global variables used by almost all the programs. *comlib.c* contains a set of string processing utilities. *comset.c* contains a set of scan and setbreak utilities. (See Chapter 4.)

```
        { /*Next, place returns -2 if wrd is longer than str OR if str or wrd is empty.*/
        *place = -2;
        return(hits);                          /*There are zero hits.*/
        }
for (start = str; str - start <= ls - lw; str++)      /*start will store the address of the*/
        {                                      /* first char of str.*/
        if (*str == wrd[0] && stequ(str, wrd) == TRUE)
                {
                *place++ = str - start;        /*The difference between the pointer values, */
                                       /* str and start, indicates the number of chars passed.*/
                str = str + lw - 1;   /*To jump lw chars. -1 negates str++ in the for() loop.*/
                hits++;
                }
        }
if (hits > 0)
        return(hits);
else
        {
        *place = -1;               /*Returns -1 to indicate no wrd was found.*/
        return(hits);              /* place can't be zero, because 0 stands for str[0].*/
        }
}/*EP*/
```

stmfind() utilizes *stequ*(), a function that compares two strings. *stequ*() differs from *strcmp*() in that *stequ*() matches a string fragment *s2* to a substring of the same size in the specified location in *s1*; it does not compare two complete strings. Terminal SNUL's are ignored. As *str* in *stmfind*() traverses the original string, it points further and further into the string. So its dummy, *s1*, represents only at the portion of the initial string that *str* has not yet examined. In *stequ*(str,wrd), *str* is a substring of the original *stmfind*() arg, *str*.

```
BOOL stequ(STRING s1, STRING s2)      /*s1 is the search space; s2 is specific text*/
        {/*BP*/
        int    i ;
```

/*i < stlen(s2) in the next line ensures the comparison of the chars of the two arrays doesn't include the terminal SNUL of s2.*/

```
        for (i = 0; i < stlen(s2); i++)
                {
                if (s1[i] != s2[i])      /*Note: pointers are functioning as array elements.*/
                        return(FALSE);
                }
        return(TRUE);               /*If it falls through the for() loop, s2 is part of s1.*/
        }/*EP*/
```

An example of *stmfind*() usage is:

```
void callstmfind(void)
        {
        int         bingo = 0;
        int         i = 0;
        char        phrase[SMLSZE] = {SNUL};
```

```
char      sentence[LRGSZE] = {SNUL};
long      where[SZE(20)+1] = {0};
long      *pt = &where[1];      /*As personal preference, starting entries at where[1],
                                /*so 1st hit is in where[1], 2nd hit is in where[2], etc.*/

stcpy("the mathematics team then went home.",sentence);
stcpy("the",phrase);
bingo = stmfind(sentence, phrase, pt);
if (bingo == 0 && where[1] == -2)
        printf("\nEither the match phrase or the sentence was empty."
               "\nOR the match phrase was longer than the sentence.");
else if (bingo == 0)            /*where[1] is -1.*/
        printf("\n%s could not be matched.", phrase);
else for (i = 1; i <= bingo; i++)
        printf("\nwhere[%i] = %i. This is substr %i: %s",i,where[i],i,\
               &sentence[where[i]]);
}
```

In *callstmfind()*, *stmfind()* is directed to located up to 20 occurrences of **the** in the string **the mathematics team then went home.** If **the** is found, it prints the substrings that begins with **the**. In our example, it will print:

where[1] = 0. This is substr 1: the mathematics team then went home.
where[2] = 6. This is substr 2: thematics team then went home.
where[3] = 21. This is substr 3: then went home.

3.2.4.3.   A Way To Substitute A Substring For A String.

As an example of usage, suppose in the previous section, we wanted to substitute for the original string the substring starting at the final location of the comparison word; i.e., the substring starting at *sentence*[where[3]]. One way is to overwrite the string with the substring as in line *a* in *revisedcallstmfind()* below. This is a permanent change. The size of the array hasn't shrunk; but the viable text it contains is reduced. It doesn't much matter for local strings, but for dynamic strings, it means unused space is not returned for recycling. Note also the idiomatic use of *sentence* to represent the pointer to the entire string. But to extract a substring, the pointer to the substring must be written out in full; i.e., *&sentence[where[bingo]]*.

In line *b*, *bingo* is 3, *where*[bingo] is 21, and the substring that starts at *sentence*[21] is **then went home..** This substring, including the terminal SNUL, overwrites the first part of the original string. The array will contain: **then went home.'\0'team then went home.'\0'.** But the system will disregard all chars after the first '\0' when asked to produce *sentence*. So the *printf* statement will read: **where[3] = 21; This is substr 3: then went home..**

```
void revisedcallstmfind(void)
    {
    int       bingo = 0;
    char      phrase[SMLSZE] = {SNUL};
    char      sentence[LRGSZE] = {SNUL};
```

```
long      where[SZE(20)+1] = {0};
long      *pt;

pt = &where[1];
stcpy("the mathematics team then went home.",sentence);
stcpy("the",phrase);
bingo = stmfind(sentence, phrase, pt);
if (bingo != 0)
    {
    stcpy(&sentence[where[bingo]],sentence);          /*a*/
    printf("\nwhere[%i] = %i; This is substr %i: %s",
        bingo,where[bingo],bingo,sentence);           /*b*/
    }
}
```

3.2.4.4.   Forcing A Pointer To Point To The End of the String.

One way to concatenate two strings into a large buffer is to use *stcpy*() to copy the first string into the buffer and then attach the second string with *stcat*(), creating one large string. Alternatively, we can employ a single function, *psnext*(), a version of *stcpy*() that returns a pointer pointing to the SNUL terminus of the copy. Inside a loop, it can, like *stcat*, operate as a sequential concatenation function, adding one piece of text to the seed string each time it is called, to create a longer strip of text. In addition, because it locates the end of the first string, the second string can be placed beyond the SNUL so that the strings are independent, even though they occupy the same array.

psnext() assumes, as does *stcpy*(), that there is predefined storage space sufficiently large to copy the pieces that accumulate as *psnext*() is repeatedly run. The first version of *psnext*(), which we label as *ps1next*(), is written as:

```
char *ps1next(char *from, char *to)
    {
    while (*from)
        *to++ = *from++ ;
    *to = SNUL;
    return(to);
    }
```

ps1next() copies *from* up to but not including the terminal SNUL, because it break the while() loop as soon as *from* is SNUL. Hence a SNUL needs to be appended. *to* will point to this terminal SNUL.

Given that different compilers may handle postfixing in somewhat different ways, it is always safe to write *psnext*() thus:

```
char *ps2next(char *from, char *to)
    {
    while (*to = *from)
        {
        from++;
```

```
        to++;
        }
    return(to);
    }
```

In this second version, *to* is eventually passed a SNUL and this terminates the while() loop. *to++* is not performed, so *to* points to the terminal SNUL when the function ends.

More cryptically or, depending on your viewpoint, more elegantly, *psnext()* can be written as:

```
char *ps3next(char *from, char *to)
    {
    while (*to++ = *from++) ;
    return(to-1);
    }
```

In *ps3next()*, the *to++* (and *from++*) expression consists of two inseparable operations. Inside the while() loop, the char pointed to by *to* is assigned the character pointed to by *from* AND *to* is incremented so that it points to the next char in the array. Only then is it examined for its TRUTH value. Hence, during what is the last entry into the body of the while() loop, even though *to* is set to stop when *to* is assigned a SNUL, it will nevertheless have traveled one char position beyond the SNUL. So we return (*to*-1), which repositions the pointer on the terminal SNUL.[8]

Note the difference between *psnext()* and *stcpy()*. In *stcpy()*, there is no return statement involving the pointer. Both pointers snap back to the top of the char array when the function falls through. (In the library function *strcpy()*, the function returns the dstination pointer.) In *psnext()*, the function returns the value of the pointer when it stopped moving; i.e., it returns the address of the char byte containing the terminal SNUL of the string that was represented in *psnext()* by *to*. In *cpyfct()*, this address is assigned to *pnxt*.

```
void cpyfct(void)
    {
    char    first[SZE(100)] = {SNUL};
    char    addon[SZE(100)] = {SNUL};
    STRING  pnxt = NULL;

    stcpy("\tOccasionally.",addon);
    pnxt = ps1next("All Gaul is divided.",first);
    printf("\n%s", first);          /*PrintProduct: All Gaul is divided.*/
```

/*The number of chars in first is given by stlen(first); i.e., if stlen(first) is 20, first[0]:first[19] hold the chars and first[20] holds the terminal SNUL. Hence, in the next line of code, first[stlen(first)] should be SNUL. It is.*/

---

8 Overshooting occurs in some library versions of *strcpy()*, but it doesn't matter because our interest is in copying characters, not in the final position of the pointer.

```
        printf("\n%o", first[stlen(first)]);
```
/*The next line of code reads: copy the contents of addon to the SNUL terminus of first, which is represented by the right-hand pnxt. Return the result of this operation—the new location of the terminal SNUL—to the left-hand pnxt.*/

```
        pnxt = ps2next(addon,pnxt);                                /*a*/
        printf("\n%s",first);        /*PrintProduct: All Gaul is divided. Occasionally.*/
        pnxt = ps3next(addon,pnxt);  /*The same reasoning as for line a*/
        printf("\n%s",first);        /*PrintProduct:
        }                  All Gaul is divided.  Occasionally.        Occasionally.*/
```

3.3. RULES ON USING AN ARRAY NAME AS ITS OWN POINTER

Success in getting the compiler to accept an array name as part of an expression often seems random chance. Sometimes using the array name or a char array works. Other times, the compiler is cranky and refuses to handle anything but a certified and independent pointer variable. Despite appearances, C is consistent in its rules, again with the proviso that pointer notation substitutes for array notation when a variable serves as function arg; i.e., the system transmits the address of the first char of the array, not the array itself. This holds true no matter how we write the arg. Therefore, given these definitions in the calling function:

```
char          a[SMLSZE] = {SNUL};
STRING        p = &a[0];
PTRADR        pa = &p;
```

if the called function requires a pointer arg, e.g., **dothis(STRING ptr);**, these are equivalent and appropriate:

dothis(a[]); = dothis(a); = dothis(p); = dothis(*pa);

What this says is that if the function arg is a character pointer, the programmer is free to transmit a char array or a char array name or a pointer to a char array or the value of a pointer-to-pointer-to-char. Whichever he uses, the system will treat the arg as a pointer variable inside the called function. Even the name of the array, which is a constant, can be subjected to pointer arithmetic within the called function in which it serves as arg. Except for this pointer-array equivalence idiom, ordinary C rules apply:

•   Variables such as pointers and pointers to pointers are lvalues.

•   Array names are constants and hence can not be used as lvalues.

•   The chars in a char array are lvalues, the char array itself is not.

As shown next, *a* is a char array name defined in *howmany*(). A name is a constant and not an lvalue. So we can not assign to it directly within *howmany*(); e.g., we could not write: **a**

= **somevalue;**. (Assigning to a single char of the array, e.g., **a[2] = 10;**, is of course acceptable.) But *a* can legally serve as a function arg to *significantchar*(), which requires a STRING arg. Inside *significantchar*() *a*, the analog of the char array, acts as pointer-to-char to the array *a* defined in *howmany*().

As an aid to making comparisons, we will use the variable names defined above—**a** for char array, **p** for STRING and **pa** for PTRADR—in both functions shown. It is understood that the dummy args in the called function are independent of the defined variables in the calling function.

```
void howmany(void)
    {
    char      a[LRGSZE] = {SNUL};
    int       i;

    stcpy(" 1213 !=+1415 [and] 16172 @#$ 34542 ",a);   /*A way to fill the array a.*/
    printf("\ni = %d", i = significantchar(a));          /*PrintProduct: i = 18*/
    }

int signficantchar(STRING p)
    {
    int    i = 0;

    while (*p)
        {
        if ( !ispunct(*p) && !isspace(*p) && __isascii(*p))  /*Library functions*/
            i++;                                              /* prototyped in ctype.h*/
            p++;
        }
    return(i);
    }
```

3.3.1. GLOBAL STRING VARIABLES

In the next example, *globvar* is a static global string variable. As such, it may legitimately serve as function arg and be used as a char pointer arg in functions such as *stcpy*() and *printf*(). But to use *globvar* as a pointer *directly* in *callingfct*() results in a major error.

globvar is defined over the entire file, including *callingfct*(). The name is a constant. So, in line *c*, **globvar++;** is instructing the compiler to increment a constant. The compiler won't but will usually indicate that this is an attempt to increment something that is not an lvalue.

```
static char globvar[SZE(100)] ;
static void callingfct(void)
    {
    char      localvar[SZE(100)] = {SNUL};
    STRING    plocalvar = localvar;

    stcpy("in the end, all Gaul isn't divided all that much.",globvar);
    while ( (*plocalvar = *globvar) != SNUL)        /*a*/
```

```
          {
          if (*globvar == 'a' || *globvar == 'i')          /*b*/
                *plocalvar = 'X';
          plocalvar++;
          globvar++;                                        /*c*/
          }
     }
```

If we were to comment out **globvar++;** in line *c*, the code would (unfortunately) compile. In both line *a* and line *b*, **globalvar* is acceptable usage; it refers to the first character in *globalvar*. As discussed in Sections 1.2.2 and 1.5.2, in the example using *cleantb()*, the name of a global array is treated as a pointer in a restricted fashion. When a character array, such as *globvar*[100] is defined, two things happen: (1) the compiler creates a vector with 100 elements; and (2) it creates a constant pointer—*globvar*, in this case. *globvar* is not an lvalue so its value can not be incremented but it has other properties of a pointer: it can represent the array in a function arg and it can indirectly reference the first element of its associated character array, as it does in line *a*. But the operation takes place in a loop. So **plocalvar* is continuously given the same first letter of *globalvar*, and an infinite loop is the result.

We can correct the basic problem in two different ways: (1) by assigning an independent variable pointer to *globvar*; and (2) by creating a second function, to which the name of the global char array can be transmitted as function arg.

Method 1. Global Variables as Lvalues:

```
static char     globvar[SZE(100)];          /*The array MUST be defined*/
static STRING  pglobvar = globvar;          /*before its pointer is assigned.*/

void callingfct(void)
     {
     char       localvar[SZE(100)] = {SNUL};
     STRING   plocalvar = localvar;

     stcpy("in the end, all Gaul isn't divided all that much.",globvar);
     while ( (*plocalvar = *pglobvar) != SNUL)
          {
          if (*pglobvar == 'a' || *pglobvar == 'i')
                *plocalvar = 'X';
          plocalvar++;
          pglobvar++;
          }
```

```
/*When processing by the while() loop is completed:*/
     printf("\nglobvar = %s",globvar);      /*globvar reads: in the end, all Gaul isn't*/
                                            /* divided all that much.*/
     printf("\npglobvar = %s",pglobvar);    /*pglobvar is empty, because it points to*/
                                            /* the terminal SNUL.*/
     printf("\nlocalvar = %s",localvar);    /*localvar reads: Xn the end, Xll GXul Xsn't*/
                                            /* dXvXded Xll thXt much.*/
```

```
        printf("\nplocalvar = %s",plocalvar);  /*plocalvar is empty, because it points to the*/
        }                                        /*terminal SNUL.*/
```

Method 2: Global Variables as Function Args:

```
static char     globvar[SZE(100)];

void callingfct(void)
        {
        char localvar[SZE(100)] = {SNUL};

        stcpy("in the end, all Gaul isn't divided all that much.",globvar);
```

/*In the next line, there is no conflict between the global variable globvar and the dummy variable globvar in calledfct(). Or between the local variable localvar and the dummy variable localvar.*/

```
        calledfct(globvar,localvar);
        printf("\nglobvar = %s",globvar);     /*globvar reads:
                                in the end, all Gaul isn't divided all that much.*/
        printf("\nlocalvar = %s",localvar);   /*localvar reads: Xn the end, XII GXuI Xsn't */
        }                                      /* dXvXded XII thXt much.*/

void calledfct(char *globvar, char *localvar)
        {
        while (*localvar = *globvar)
            {
            if (*globvar == 'a' || *globvar == 'i')
                 *localvar = 'X';
            localvar++;
            globvar++;
            }
        }
```

3.3.2. LOCAL STRING VARIABLES

The rules are the same as with global variables.

- If an array is defined as a local variable, the array name can not reflexively act as its own pointer in the same function. An additional independent pointer is required, just as in Method 1 in Section 3.3.1.

- A local variable, whether a pointer, a char array, the name of a char array or the value of a pointer-to-pointer-to-char can serve as a function arg and be used as a character pointer within the function to which it was transmitted as an arg.

Local Variables as Lvalues:

The next example demonstrates the first rule. *localvar*() is a buffer that is to collect a modified version of a dynamically stored string whose pointer is *pdynamvar*. As constructed, the function won't compile, which is just as well, because it is full of errors.

localvar is not an lvalue and can not be incremented; **localvar++;** in line *c* is wrong. The compiler error message will indicate it is not an lvalue. Without the ability to increment a pointer to traverse *localvar* the **while (....)** conditional in line *a* and the **if (.....)** conditional in line *b* won't work properly. Note also that *pdynamvar*, the properly defined pointer to a dynamically saved string, will, because of its participation in the while() loop (line *d*), be on the terminal SNUL of its string. Hence it will have lost connection to its system-stored string. Because it is defined in the function, the loss is permanent.

```
void callingfct(void)
    {
    char      localvar[SZE(100)] = {SNUL};
    STRING    pdynamvar = NULL;

    pdynamvar = dssave("in the end, all Gaul isn't divided all that much.");
    while ( (*localvar = *pdynamvar) != SNUL)      /*a*/
        {
        if (*localvar == 'a' || *localvar == 'i')      /*b*/
            *localvar = 'X';
        localvar++;                                /*c*/
        pdynamvar++;                               /*d*/
        }
    }
```

The next example is a revision of the previous function, using an independently defined pointer to the char array *localvar*. The program now runs, but the statement starting on line *b* is still incorrect. At the termination of the while() loop in line *a*, *localvar* reads: **Xn the end, all Gaul isn't divided all that much.**, showing that only the first letter was changed. Yet it is certain the loop went to completion because both *pdyn2* and *plocalvar* read empty, because both are on the SNUL terminus of their respective strings[9]

Note also that we now have two pointers to the dynamically stored string: *pdynamvar* holds onto the address of the string and *pdyn2* is incremented as needed. Thanks to *pdyn2*, the loop starting in line *a* goes to completion—in contrast to the loop starting in line *a*, Section 3.3.1.

```
void RevisedCallingFct(void)
    {
    char      localvar[SZE(100)] = {SNUL};
    STRING    pdynamvar = NULL;
    STRING    pdyn2 = NULL;
    STRING    plocalvar = localvar;

    pdyn2 = pdynamvar = dssave("in the end, all Gaul isn't divided all that much.");
```

---

9 As shown in Section 3.3.1, because of system implementation, the name of the array has the limited ability to behave as pointer to its first element. This can be useful when requesting a Yes-No answer to a query; e.g., **if (*ttystr == 'Y') doscan();**. The user can type **YES** or **NO**, but only the first letter is captured by the *ttystr construction.

```
    while (*plocalvar = *pdyn2)                              /*a*/
        {
        if (*localvar == 'a' || *localvar == 'i')            /*b*/
            *localvar = 'X';
        plocalvar++;
        pdyn2++;
        }
    printf("%s",localvar);        /*PrintProduct: Xn the end, */
                                  /* all Gaul isn't divided all that much.*/
    printf("%s",plocalvar);       /*plocalvar and pdyn2 point to the terminal SNUL's*/
                                  /* of their respective strings.*/
    }
```

For the function to work correctly, an lvalue must be used in the statement in line *b*. The revision reads:

```
    while ( (*plocalvar = *pdyn2) )
        {
        if (*plocalvar == 'a' || *plocalvar == 'i')          /*b*/
            *plocalvar = 'X';
```

Then

```
        printf("\n%s", localvar);   /*localvar reads: */
                          /* Xn the end, XII GXul Xsn't dXvXded XII thXt much.*/
        } /*plocalvar and pdyn2 point to the terminal SNUL's of their respective strings.*/
```

Local Variables as Function Args:

To demonstrate the use of a local variable as function arg, in this next example *callingfct*() calls *calledfct*(), in which the char array name *localvar* now legally serves as a function arg. Within the called function, the dummy pointer, *localvar*, is given the address of a string that is saved dynamically. It is also used to modify **e**'s and **u**'s in this string. The address of the stored string is returned to *pkeep* and *plocalvar*. Then, while *pkeep* maintains contact with the starting address of the string, *plocalvar* traverses it, changing each **a** and **i** to **X**.

```
void callingfct(void)
    {
    char      localvar[SZE(100)] = {SNUL};
    static    STRING   pkeep = NULL;
    STRING    plocalvar = NULL;

    pkeep = plocalvar = calledfct(localvar);
    printf("\n%s", pkeep);     /*PrintProduct: in thY Ynd, */
                          /* all GaYl isn't dividYd all that mYch.*/
    while (*plocalvar != SNUL)
        {
        if (*plocalvar == 'a' || *plocalvar == 'i')
            *plocalvar = 'X';
        plocalvar++;
        }
    printf("\nplocalvar = %s", plocalvar);     /*plocalvar points to the SNUL terminus*/
```

```
                                          /* of the dynamically stored string.*/
    printf("\n= %s", pkeep);              /*PrintProduct: Xn thY Ynd, XII GXYI Xsn't*/
    }                                     /* dXvXdYd XII thXt mYch.*/

STRING calledfct(STRING localvar)
    {
    STRING        pkeep = NULL;

    pkeep = localvar = dssave("in the end, all Gaul isn't divided all that much.");
    printf("\n%s", localvar);             /*PrintProduct: in the end, all Gaul isn't */
                                          /* divided all that much.*/
    while (*localvar)
        {
        if (*localvar == 'e' || *localvar == 'u')
            *localvar = 'Y';
        localvar++;
        }

    printf("\n%s", localvar);             /*localvar is empty.*/
    printf("\n%s", pkeep);                /*PrintProduct: in thY Ynd, all GaYI isn't*/
                                          /* dividYd all that mYch.*/

    return(pkeep);
    }
```

3.3.3. MACROS

A macro is not the same as a function. The macro rewrites its expansion statements *in situ* at compile time; it is not a separate entity on the stack. As a practical consequence, this means that, within the function in which it is defined, a char array or char name can NOT serve as a macro arg when a pointer is required. A separately defined pointer is necessary. In other words, this is just a reformulation of the rule that the name of a local variable may not serve as an variable in ordinary code in the same function in which it is defined. For example:

SLENGTH(int i, STRING p) is the macro equivalent of the *strlen*(STRING p) library function. *PD*, *PC* and *PS* are print macros. Note that *PS*() will surround the string output with square brackets.

```
#define SLENGTH(i,p) { i = 0; while ( *(p)++ != SNUL) (i)++; }
#define PC(x) printf("\n" #x " = %c", x)
#define PD(x) printf("\n" #x " = %i", x)
#define PS(x) printf("\n" #x " = [%s]", x)

void SomeFct(void)
    {
    int        ii;                        /*ii is a counter.*/
    char       new[SMLSZE] = {SNUL};
    STRING     pnew = new;
```

```
stcpy("CountChars",new);
PS(pnew);                              /*PrintProduct: pnew = [CountChars]*/
SLENGTH(ii,pnew);
PD(ii);                                /*PrintProduct: ii = 10*/
}
```

Lvalues as Macro Args:

In the next example, *str* is a locally defined char array and so may not be a macro arg within *lopchar()*.

lopchar() makes use of *LOP* which reads a string left to right, points to a single char in the string, and moves the pointer onward by one char.

LOP() is defined as:

#define LOP(x) ((x) == NULL || (*(x)) == SNUL) ? SNUL : (*(x)++)

Used as part of a loop statement that takes care of the halting criterion (such as the one in line *a*), *LOP* makes it possible to examine a sequence of substrings, formed by shifting the start of the string one char to the right each time. The macro does a virtual lop; i.e., the characters are not permanently lost. If line *b* were to read:

LOP(str);

the compiler would issue some error message, such as **++ needs lvalue**, meaning that it is not possible to increment *str* inside *LOP*, because the name of an array is not a variable. Instead, a separately defined char pointer must be used as arg to *LOP*; *pstr*, in this example.

Incrementing the pointer, usually done as a separate statement within the while() loop, is done as part of *LOP()*, where the expression *(x)++ points to a char and immediately increments the pointer. Note the sequence: (1) **print the char;** and (2) **LOP();.** If we lopped first, then because of the immediate incrementing of the pointer inside the macro, the first char of the string would not be printed.

```
void lopchar(void)
    {
    char      str[SMLSZE] = {SNUL};   /*The variables aren't alphabetical,
    STRING    pstr = str;      /* because we can't point pstr to str before defining str.*/

    stcpy("This is a new string.",str);
    while (*pstr)                  /*while (*str) would be an infinite loop*/        /*a*/
        {
        PC(*pstr);                 /*1st loop displays: *pstr = T*/
        LOP(pstr);                                                                   /*b*/
        PS(pstr);                  /*1st loop displays: pstr = [his is a new string.]*/
        }

    PS(str);                       /*PrintProduct: str = [This is a new string.]*/
    PS(pstr);                      /*Nothing to display: pstr = []*/
    }
```

Macros such as *LOP()* or *SLENGTH()* that manipulate pointers can cause unpleasant surprises. Within a function, incrementing a pointer does actually move its position. A pointer incremented in a macro also moves. In consequence, using another version of *callingfct()*, we can show two places that trouble can occur because the pointer moves its position as a result of serving as a macro arg: the first with a pointer addressing a dynamically saved string, the second with a pointer pointing to a predefined string.

```
void callingfct(void)
        {
        int        ii = 0;
        char       localvar[SZE(100)] = {SNUL};
        static     STRING pdynamvar = NULL;
        STRING     pdyn2 = NULL;
        STRING     plocalvar = localvar;

        pdynamvar = dssave("in the end, all Gaul isn't divided all that much.");
```

/*The next two statements together find the length of pdynamvar and prints out this size. We can not write: **(printf("\n%d",ii = SLENGTH(ii,pdynamvar));**. Macros don't return values[10].*/

```
        SLENGTH(ii,pdynamvar);                                        /*a*/
        PS(pdynamvar);               /*PrintProduct: pdynamvar = []*/
        PD(ii);                      /*PrintProduct: ii = 49*/
        while ( (*plocalvar = *pdynamvar) != SNUL)                    /*b*/
            {
            if (*plocalvar == 'a' || *plocalvar == 'i')
                *plocalvar = 'X';
            plocalvar++;
            pdynamvar++;
            }
        SLENGTH(ii, plocalvar);                                       /*c*/
        PD(ii);                      /*PrintProduct: ii = 0*/
        }
```

The first trouble spot is in line *a*. *pdynamvar* will point to the terminal SNUL of the string when SLENGTH() is completed. Contact to the string linked to *pdynamvar* will be lost for the rest of the run of *callingfct()*. Line *a* should be rewritten to use an additional pointer such as *pdyn2*, which has the value of *pdynamvar*. This will preserve *pdynamvar* for the excursion through the string, starting at line *b*.

```
pdyn2 = pdynamvar;
SLENGTH(ii,pdyn2);
```

---

10 Similarly, because macros can have no built-in return statements, we may not write:
   if (SLENGTH(i,pa) > SLENGTH(j,pb))

The second place to be careful is at line *c*, which is just after the while() loop. By the end of the while() loop, *plocalvar* is on the terminal SNUL of *localvar*. *plocalvar* needs to be repointed to *localvar* before it is used in *SLENGTH*, thus:

plocalvar = localvar;
SLENGTH(ii, plocalvar);

Names of Variables as Macro Args:

The name of a char array defined as a local variable may not serve as a macro arg within its own function. However, the same array name legitimately transmitted as an arg to some function may indeed serve as a macro arg within that function. Suppose the statement: **ptemp = ttyin("TLD");**[11] This means that within *ttyin()*, "TLD", represented by the dummy arg *cond*, can serve as macro arg to the macro *LOP()*.

This next is the piece of code from *ttyin()* involving LOP(). The arg transmitted to *ttyin()* is examined a character at a time, until there are no more chars left to examine. But the arg is not destroyed. When *ttyin()* finishes, the arg, a pointer-to-char, snaps back to pointing to the start of *cond*.

```
while (*cond)
    {
    switch(LOP(cond))
        {
        case 'D':
                saver = 'D';          /*Save the string using calloc().*/
                break;
        case 'L':
                ttyup = 'L';          /*Convert the string to lower case.*/
                break;
        case 'T':
                tidy = 'T';           /*Tidy up. Delete initial spaces, tabs, form feeds.*/
                break;
        case 'U':
                ttyup = 'U';          /*Convert the string to upper case.*/
                break;
        default: break;
        }
    }
```

Recall from Section 3.2.3.2, that in functions, virtual strings behave like real strings when transmitted to other functions. If fctA transmits a string as function arg to fctB, then, while fctB is in force, by pointing to a location within the string, we can create a temporary substring that may be used as function arg in fctC. When control returns to FctA, barring

---

11 Recall from example 1, Section 2.3.1, that the function prototyped as **STRING ttyin(cond);** brings in keyboard information and, depending on the contents of the arg *cond*, cleans the text, saves it dynamically and/or changes its case.

intentional permanent modifications, the original string is intact. This is also the case with macros.

RDINVIS(p,l,x) is a macro that can be included in a program's source code to highlight invisible and control characters. Its parameters are:

ParameterDefinitionComment

p	STRING p = &x[0];	p is a pointer-to-char.
I	I = %s in a printf statement;	I is a comment.
x	char x[];	x is a char array.

When the program is run, *RDINVIS*() will display a string, whether it was read in from a file or was composed by the program. The analogs for the *RDINVIS*() arguments must be predefined in the program. *RDINVIS*() writes the contents of the third arg, a char array, including its invisible chars, to the screen when the program is compiled. Non-printing chars are shown within <> brackets.

RDINVIS() transmits a virtual arg to another macro, *MAKEVIS*(), which in turn calls *ITINVIS*(). The connections between the macros are as follows:

```
#define ITCCCHAR(x) ( ((x) <= '\37' && (x) >= SNUL) II (x) == '\177') /* control chars*/
#define ITINVIS(x) ( ITCCCHAR(x) II (x) == SPACE )
#define MAKEVIS(x) (ITINVIS(x)) ? printf("<%o>",x) : printf("%c",x)
#define RDINVIS(p,l,x) printf("\n{%s}==",l); for (p = x;*p;p++) MAKEVIS(*p);printf("\n")
```

Usage:

```
void debuginvis(void)
     {
     char      answer[100] = {SNUL};
     STRING    pa;

     pa = answer;
     stcpy("All sentences\bare composed\tof\nchars.", answer);
     RDINVIS(pa,"DEMO:", answer);
     }
```

When *RDINVIS*() runs, the screen would display:

{DEMO:}==All<40>sentences<10>are<40>composed<11>of<12>chars.

When **RDINVIS**() terminates, the original contents of *answer* become available.

3.4. LOOPING AND TERMINATING LOOPS

In string processing, terminating a loop often involves the value of a pointer-to-char or the value of the variable referenced by the pointer. Using a loop and halting a loop are not, of course, unique to string processing, but knowing how to devise adequate halt conditions is a necessity when partitioning and trimming strings. Terminating a loop in string processing is usually more complicated than in processing numerical data, because a character array is not a single-valued integer. It is composed of many elements, including, very possibly, characters that are debris from previous string occupants. If one of these elements by chance matches the halt criterion, the loop will be unexpectedly terminated. The presence of multiple SNUL's in a string, as in the string shown in line *a* Section 3.4.1, may also halt a loop before its time.

On the whole, using pointers as terminators beats counting on our fingers but does introduce some difficulties. This next section deals with these problem areas and with related topics.

3.4.1. USING CHAR POINTERS TO BREAK LOOPS

In string processing, obviously, a major concern is how to stop the processing when the text has been deleted or completely chopped up or finally changed to our satisfaction. The role of the pointer representing that string is critical.

Suppose an informational field in a record is pointed to by a char pointer appropriately called *rcdfield*. *rcdfield* accesses text dynamically stored.

In this example, part of a program that forces text into columns, a field is chopped up into lines of proper width as long as a counter, *linecnt*, is less than *TOTLINES*, where *TOTLINES* is the most lines allowed in the frame. We wish to stop the loop when: (1) *rcdfield* is empty because it has been completely chopped into lines; or (2) we have reached the limit of the number of lines allowed in a single frame.

In pseudo-code:

```
while (rcdfield && linecnt < TOTLINES)
        {/*send lines in field to CollectingFile*/
        Send the first WIDTH chars from rcdfield plus an EOL to CollectingFile.
        Cut these first WIDTH chars from rcdfield. rcdfield now starts from the previous
                WIDTH+1 th char.
        Increment linecnt.
        }/*send lines in field to CollectingFile*/
```

This will recycle until TOTLINES have been read, but it doesn't stop—and it should—when the field is empty of text. The text is indeed diminished each iteration until there is no text left. But the pointer, *rcdfield*, has a value other than zero, because it is still assigned to a particular memory location. This is an important point: if a pointer is assigned to an address in memory and is not reassigned, it continues to point to that location even when the contents at that address are empty.

This next bases the halting criterion on the contents of rcdfield, which is helpful. But this version is still not what we want to say.

```
while (*rcdfield) for (i = 0; i < TOTLINES; i++)
        {/*send lines in rcdfield to CollectingFile*/
```

while (*rcdfield) ensures there is text in the string pointed to by *rcdfield*. Once. Then the program will merrily scan *rcdfield* TOTLINES times, even after the text is long gone.

To break the loop when the field is empty, we should write:

> **while (*rcdfield && linecnt < TOTLINES) ....**
> **{/*send lines in field to CollectingFile*/**

which reads: while the character pointed to by *rcdfield* is not SNUL, continue the loop. The loop will halt when the text is gone or when TOTLINES lines have been written.

As another example, recall the macro in Section 3.3.3 for lopping a character from the start of a string:

#define LOP(x) ((x) == NULL II (*(x)) == SNUL) ? SNUL : (*(x)++)

The change in the string is not permanent unless actual changes are made during processing.

LOP() is not capable, by itself, of terminating a loop. In this example using the text in line *a,* **while (ptext)** acts as loop controller. The loop should stop after the **y** in **Very**. Instead, this will go on forever, because the pointer will continue to hold some address, even if the contents at that address are empty. When *ptext* points to the SNUL in *text*[], the loop will emit one NULL after another.

```
char text[] = "  This Is A Very\0Long String.\0";                    /*a*/
char *ptext = SNUL;
..........
ptext = text;
while (ptext)
      {
      PC(*ptext);
      LOP(ptext);
      }
```

The correct statement is

while (*ptext)

which breaks the loop when the char that ptext points to is SNUL.

Along the same track, if

```
char           rcd[MEDSZE] = {SNUL};
STRING         prcd = rcd;
```

prcd will contain the address of *rcd*, even if *rcd* is empty. *prcd* will have a value, when *rcd* does not. Therefore, if performing an activity depends on the record being empty, we want:

if (*prcd == SNUL)...

not:

if (prcd == NULL) ...

3.4.2. ENCROACHING BEYOND DEFINED SPACE WITH A POINTER

A common way to examine each element in a character array is to use a char pointer to access the element, do something to the char, and then increment the pointer. It is obvious that this pointer must not be allowed to point past the string's terminal SNUL. It is less obvious that it is possible to encroach on memory locations preceding the string.

Example 1.

countback() examines each char of an array. In this example we use a string constant with a built-in SNUL. In line *a*, *p* is assigned to point at the character in the array positioned just before the terminal SNUL. *p* ascends towards the top of the array—*p*'s address is decreased by one each time through the loop at line *c*. The intent is to stop processing at *new*[0]. However, as written, line *b* instructs *p* to stop at a 0, so it stops at the char just after 'x'. It would do the same if the instruction was: **while (*p != SNUL)**.

```
static char new[] = "This is new tex\0t%987654321";
void countback(void)
        {
        STRING   p = &new[26];          /*a*/
        while (*p > 0)                   /*b*/
             p--;                        /*c*/
        }
```

Writing line *b* above as: **while (*p > '0')** would stop the process at any character represented by an ASCII value less than octal 60. The procedure would stop at the %. Again, this is not what is wanted. To stop the pointer at a particular element of the array, we need to specify an exact stopping address. So we should test pointer values—addresses—not char values.

The test at line *b* should read:

while (p != &new[0])   /*b*/

p will eventually equal the address of the top element of the array *a* and stop. This halting function ignores SNUL chars, so it is a way of examining all the characters in the array, a useful feature in an array that contains several individual strings in sequence.

Suppose we want to search the first part of the array, not necessarily the whole array, but the portion counted by *stlen()*, which returns characters up to a terminal SNUL. This is the general way to start a pointer at the last significant character and examine each character until the first character in the string is reached.

```
static char new[] = "This is new text%987654321";
void countback(void)
        {
        STRING p = &new[stlen(new)-1];
        while (p != &new[0])
             p--;
        }
```

Example 2.

The next example demonstrates the possibility of unknowingly examining memory locations prior to the one holding the first character of the array. (The encroachment problem is prevented at line *a*.) *cleanstr*() brings in a string, *from*, and store its cleaned version in *to*. It changes each space/tab/NewLine in *from* to a space in *to* unless the previous character in *to* is a space. As each character is examined, these are the possibilities:

(condition 1)   It is an ordinary char: it is copied to the next empty slot in *to*.

(condition 2)   It is a tab or space: the previous *to* element is checked.

    (condition 2a)   The previous char is not a space: the element in *to* is
                     assigned a space. The pointer is incremented.

    (condition 2b)   The last byte in *to* is a space: the while() loop recycles
                     to examine the next char.

```
#define PS(x) printf("\n" #x " = [%s]", x)
#define WHITE(x) (x) == '\40' || (x) == '\t' || (x) == '\n'


void cleanstr(STRING from, STRING to)
    {
    STRING start = to;                /*start points to the same char as does to.*/

    for (; *from != SNUL; from++)
        {
        if (WHITE(*from))             /*Condition 2*/
            {
```

/*The next line reads: if to is not at the first character in the string AND the character that is at the previous position of to is not a space. The first expression is to prevent a tricky intermittent error. Occasionally, we will find that a string starts with an ordinary char, when we expected it to start with a space. The problem is that while we checked that the previous char was not a space, tab or NewLine, we did not check that the previous char was part of the string. If we are at the first element in the array, the preceding char, which isn't part of the array, may be a space.*/

```
                if (to != start && *(to - 1) == '\40')    /*Condition 2b*/         /*a*/
                    continue;
                else                                      /*Condition 2a*/
                    *to++ = '\40';
                }
            else                                          /*Condition 1*/
                *to++ = *from;
            }
        *to = SNUL;
        }
```

```
void callingfct(void)
    {
    char        a[MEDSZE] = {SNUL};
    char        b[MEDSZE] = {SNUL};
    stcpy(" new            string ",a);
    cleanstr(a,a);
    PS(a);                              /*PrintProduct: a = [ new string ]*/
    }
```

Inside *callingfct()*, space can be allocated for two buffers. If the cleaned string is copied to buffer *b*, the original string is unchanged. In the current example, the cleaned string overwrites the original string.

3.4.3. REDEFINING A VARIABLE INSIDE A LOOP

This illustrates the error of permanently defining a variable that should be repeatedly redefined.

endbyperiod() is a prettify function that takes a database record with terminal punctuation and meta symbols and transforms it into a presentable manuscript sentence. Specifically, it deletes from the end of the record all characters that are not letters or digits; e.g., periods, spaces, commas, NewLine's, record delimiters, field delimiters and subfield delimiters. It then adds a final period.

ISALPNUM is #defined as:

#define ISALPNUM(x) (isalpha(x) || isdigit(x))

where *isalpha()* and *isdigit()* are prototyped in the library file ctype.h. *isalpha()* includes all the letters, upper and lower case; *isdigit()* includes all the decimal digits.

The first version of *endbyperiod*, is incorrect. *ss* is defined as having the value of the final char in the string, but is never put under the aegis of the loop, where it could be redefined. The loop tells the program to continue to drop the final char of the string until an alphanumeric is encountered; at which point processing of the loop instruction terminates. Suppose the final char in the string is a comma. So *ss* is valued as a comma the first time through the loop. The program wipes out the final char, BUT IT DOES NOT CHANGE the value of *ss*. Suppose the final char is now an **e**. The program checks *ss*, which is still a comma and wipes out the **e** and so forth. Each time through the loop, the string is shortened by one char, even though the final char of the string may be a legitimate stopping char. Eventually the whole string is destroyed.

```
static STRING endbyperiod(STRING ps)  /*THIS IS WRONG*/
    {/*BP*/
    char        ss = {SNUL};

    ss = *(ps+stlen(ps)-1);      /*Positions the pointer at the char just before*/
                                 /* the terminal SNUL.*/
    while (*ps)
        {/*StripFinalCommaSpacePeriod*/
```

```
        if ( ISALPNUM(ss) )
                break;
        else
                {
                ps[stlen(ps)-1] = SNUL;
                continue /*StripFinalCommaSpacePeriod*/;
                }
        }/*StripFinalCommaSpacePeriod*/
ps[stlen(ps)] = '.';
ps++;
ps[stlen(ps)] = SNUL;
return(ps);
}/*EP*/
```

The solution is to move *ss* under the loop.

```
while (*ps)
    {/*StripFinalCommaSpacePeriod*/
    ss = *(ps+stlen(ps)-1);
    if ( ISALPNUM(ss) )
            break;
    else
            ps[stlen(ps)-1] = SNUL;
    }/*StripFinalCommaSpacePeriod*/
```

The rest of the code is fine though klutzy. This next version is simpler. It doesn't bother SNUL'ing the end char until after the loop.

```
static STRING endbyperiod(STRING s)
    {/*BP*/
    STRING   ps = s + stlen(s) - 1;

    for ( ; ; ps--)
            if ( ISALPNUM(*ps) )
                    break;
    *++ps = '.';
    *++ps = SNUL;
    return(s);
    }/*EP*/

void callingfct(void)
    {
    char a[LRGSZE] = {SNUL};

    stcpy("LastField@.#,%!,",a);
    endbyperiod(a);
    PS(a);                              /*PrintProduct: a = [LastField.]*/
    }
```

3.4.4. BREAKING OUT OF THE RIGHT BLOCK

A program might be just breaking out of the inner of two loops, when it appears to be breaking out of the outer one, as in this next example, which is query code to determine what field in the database record is to receive an accession number. Incorrect labeling, a lot of intervening code and poor code formatting obscures the error. The original commented brackets have been changed to **Level 1** and **Level 2**. Quite often, a prettify program for C code, which is not influenced by user comments, will by the way it indents statements help spot the problem area. I use an excellent one written by Chuck Forsberg, and distributed, if memory serves, by the *C User's Group*.

```
while (TRUE)
    {/*Level 1*/
    printf("Type components of accession number:\n");
    ttyin("t");
    if (!acnumdo(ttystr))
        continue /*Level 1*/;
    [.....lots of processing code.....]
    if (nfields == 1)                          /*a*/
        {
        accnfield = 1;
        break /*Level 1*/;                     /*b*/
        }
    else while (TRUE)                          /*c*/
        {/*Level 2*/
        printf("\nAttach accession number to which field? ($$) [1]\t");
        ttyin("T");
        if (ttystr[0] == SNUL)
            {
            accnfield = 1;
            return(TRUE);                      /*d*/
            }
        else if (intdecode(ttystr, MAXFIELDS+1, &accnfield));    /*Repeat the */
                                                            /*level 1 while() loop*/
            break /*Level 1*/;                 /*e*/
        }/*Level 2*/
    [The level 2 break jumps here.]
    }/*Level 1*/
```

When there's just a single field, as on line *a*, there is no problem. The program breaks out of the outer loop at line *b*. As it should. But when there are multiple fields in the record, the program starts another while() loop, labeled **Level 2**. The break statement on line *e* is incorrectly labeled **Level 1**. If the program reaches this break statement, it breaks out of the Level 2 while() loop and restarts the Level 1 while() loop.

If the work of the function is done, the best thing to do is to substitute return statements for the break commands, as is done starting on line *d*. But this is not always possible. As an alternative way to break out of multiple blocks, a switch with only two values, 1 or 0, can be set. This is illustrated next redoing the code that started at line *c*. OUT is the switch name. The break levels are correctly labeled.

```
while (TRUE)
     {/*Level 1*/
     BOOL OUT = 0;

     ...........................
     else while (TRUE)                              /*c*/
          {/*Level 2*/
          printf("\nAttach accession number to which field? ($$) [1]\t");
          ttyin("T");
          if (ttystr[0] == SNUL)
               {
               accnfield = 1;
               return(TRUE);
               }
          else if (intdecode(ttystr, MAXFIELDS+1, &accnfield));
               {
               OUT = 1;
               break /*Level 2*/;
               }
/*If program gets here it is equivalent to OUT = 0;. So continue the while() loop on Level
2.*/
          }/*Level 2*/
     if (OUT == 1) break /*Level 1*/;
     }/*Level 1*/
[If OUT is 1, the program comes here.]
```

Alternatively, a goto statement can be substituted for a break statement. The goto has the advantage that it can cut through multiple levels quickly.

The break switch and the goto are usually dependent on an implicit TRUE or FALSE condition. But they may just as easily depend on a counter. For example:

```
for (i = 0; i < SMLSZE; i++)
     {
     if (i == VALUE) goto SOMEPLACE;
     }
```

In for () statements, the counter is incremented (or decremented) at the start of the for block. As one consequence, **VALUE** can not initially be larger than **SMLSZE** or the preemptive break will not happen. The problem doesn't occur within a while (TRUE) statement, because the counter is within the while block and when it reaches **VALUE,** the goto directive is immediate, as in:

```
while (TRUE)
     {
     i++;
     if (i == VALUE) goto SOMEPLACE;
     else DoSomeProcessing().
     }
```

3.5. POINTERS-TO-POINTERS-TO-CHAR

This entire chapter has emphasized the centrality of the pointer-to-char in accessing and manipulating text stored in char arrays. When the pointer-to-char serves as function arg, it transmits a copy of the address of its associated char array so individual chars within an array can be changed permanently[12], without violating the rule that default variables are transmitted to functions by value. (See Sections 3.2.3 and 3.2.4 for a discussion of the relationship of the pointer-to-char and its associated character array.)

The memory address of the pointer-to-char, which is not available to the called function, continues to store the pre-transmission value of the pointer. This value is the pre-transmission address of the associated char array.

There are two major consequences of the fact that the pointer-to-char is transmitted to the called function by value:

(1) Text created and dynamically stored during the running of the called function and referenced solely by that pointer arg will not be retrievable when control returns to the calling function.

(2) Any change to the starting address of a char array that occur in the called function is temporary and does not change the location of the char array when control returns to the calling function.

In both cases, the pointer-to-char is predefined but is given a new value in the called function. When the called function terminates, the value of the pointer-to-char reverts to whatever it was before the pointer was transmitted as function arg. Hence, modifications other than changes to the contents of the array elements are good only within the called function.

Ensuring permanence for dynamically acquired text requires the ability to retain the starting address of the array. Ensuring permanence for selected portions of the text requires the ability to redefine the starting address of the array. For these purposes, the major resources available to us within the called function are the variables transmitted as function args. Which is what makes the address of the pointer-to-char so valuable a function arg. If we know where the pointer-to-char resides, if we can invade its home, we can change the furnishings, the contents of the pointer's home being the memory address of the referenced char array. To make use of the address of the pointer-to-char as function arg, we transmit it as **&p**. Or we use the value of an independent variable, a pointer that points to *p*.

---

12 By *permanent*, we mean that the value is retained even after the termination of the called function in which the char received that value.

An independent variable that contains the address of a pointer-to-char is typedef'ed as PTRADR, to emphasize it is the address of a pointer, not the address of a character array.

typedef char *STRING;
typedef STRING *PTRADR;

Given these uninitialized definitions:

char   a[SMLSZE];
STRING   p;
PTRADR   pa;

we can establish these grammatical relationships linking the variables:

p = &a[0];   /* Meaning that the value of p is the address of the first char of a*/
pa = &p;[13]   /* Meaning that the value of pa is the address of p.*/

and inversely, though not really symmetrically:

a[0] = *p;   /* Meaning that the value of a[0] is indirectly referenced by p. */
p = *pa;   /* Meaning that the value of p is indirectly referenced by pa. */

A memory chart of the relationship of these variables might look like Table 3.7.

We would read the table as: 250 is an address that holds a variable *pa*, whose value (550) is the address of a variable *p*, whose value (725) is the address of a variable *a[0]*, whose value is **A**.

p has a key position in the hierarchy. Its address is the value of *pa*. Its value is the address of *a*.

When a function arg calls for the address of a pointer, transmitting either *&p* or *pa* as function arg will allow us to manipulate the memory contents of the variable *p*. Inside *calledfct*(), *&p* or *pa* may as a result of processing indirectly point to another position in the character array, and this new starting address of the array is retained when control is returned to the calling function.

We may also indirectly reference the contents of the contents of *pa* as ***pa**, which is *a[0]*. As Table 3.7 indicates, the value of *pa* is the address of a variable *p* whose value is the address of *a*[0]. They make this next *implicit* relationship true

a = **pa;

and we can reference (i.e., determine the value) of an element of *a* by writing ***pa**, as in:

while (pa++ != SNUL)**
dosomething();

---

13 Not so subtle a point: if the definition of a PTRADR variable assigns it to a single pointer, it is written: **PTRADR pa = &p;**. If it is assigned to an array of pointers defined, say, as **STRING p[SMLSZE];**, it is written: **PTRADR pa = &p[0];** or idiomatically as **PTRADR pa = p;**

Memory Address	Variable ID	Value of the Variable
250	pa	550
550	p	725
725	a[0]	A
726	a[1]	B
727	a[2]	C
728	a[3]	D
729	a[4]	E
730	a[5]	F
731	a[6]	G
732	a[7]	H
733	a[8]	I
734	a[9]	J
735	a[10]	K
736	a[11]	L
737	a[12]	M

Table 3.7. Illustrating a string in memory.

But if a function requires the address of a pointer-to-char as function arg, we can not write &&*a*. We can NOT make use of the implicit linkage of *pa* and *a*

pa = &&a;[14]   /*NOT COMPILABLE.*/

by writing as function arg:

calledfct(&&a);   /*NOT COMPILABLE.*/

despite the fact that the array *a*[] has an address. But whether its address is or is not a value in some explicitly defined pointer or indirectly in some PTRADR variable, && syntax is incorrect. In formal terminology, &&*a* is not considered an lvalue. It is not a variable. It can not syntactically exist.

The relationships between a PTRADR and the char to which it ultimately points can not be written as symmetrical statements. If the address of *p* is required, we must either write:

calledfct(&p);

or, if *pa* was defined as a pointer to *p*,

calledfct(pa);.

---

14 One suspects that C's early childhood within underpowered minis did not encourage indirect addressing in depth.

As the value of a STRING is the address of a char, so the value of a PTRADR is the address of a pointer-to-char. The value of a PTRADR is the address of the address of a character or of a char array.[15] With a STRING, we are once removed from the char variable of interest. With a PTRADR, we are twice removed from the same variable. We stalk the variable by means of this indirect addressing as we would in an ordinary treasure hunt game. In fact, compared to most treasure hunts, the tracking from the PTRADR to the pointer-to-char to the array is minimal indirection. The value of PTRADR is an address. When we go to the address, it contains another address, this time the address of a character. And there we are: accessing the char variable.

The next sections investigate ways to change some aspects of the text permanently. Section 3.6 deals with different ways of retaining dynamically-created text when threading through multiple functions. Section 3.7, in contrast, discusses several ways in which the initial characters of an existing string can be permanently deleted, both in dynamic and in static strings. Manipulating the address of the pointer-to-char transmitted as function arg—actually a copy of the address of the pointer—has the power to effect permanent changes in the referenced string. While not the only way to obtain this result, it is often the method of choice.

3.6. HOW TO SAFEGUARD DYNAMICALLY ACQUIRED STRINGS

3.6.1. USING A POINTER-TO-CHAR

In the next set of examples, *keep* has access to some permanent text. Whenever we need example text, we will copy it from *keep*.

static STRING keep = "What is a sentence but words.";

Suppose that we wish to extract the first word from a string and store it dynamically. To set the stage, let us start with a version that does NOT work. A pointer, *p*, is defined in *callingfct*() in line *a*. It is not to receive its assigned value until the word is stored, so very properly it is set to NULL. Transmitted as function arg to *wordsplit*(), it acquires the address of the substring **What** when the substring is stored dynamically.

```
void callingfct(void)                /*THIS VERSION IS WRONG.*/
    {
    char a[SZE(100)] = {SNUL};
    char *p = NULL;                                        /*a*/
```

---

15 As we would write **int x = 3;**, meaning the value of *x* is 3. Similarly, the value of a pointer is an address. And the value of a pointer to the pointer is an address.

```
        stcpy(keep, a);
        printf("\naddress: %d. p = [%s]",p,p);   /*PrintProduct: address: 0. p = []*/
        wordsplit(a,p);                                                       /*b*/
        printf("\naddress: %d. p = [%s]",p,p);   /*PrintProduct: address: 0. p = []*/ /*c*/
        }

void wordsplit(STRING str, STRING p)
        {
        int      i;
        char     buf[SZE(100)] = {SNUL};        /*The chars of the 1st word in str will*/
                                                /* be copied to buf one at a time.*/

        for (i = 0; *str; i++)
            {
            if (*str == '\40' || *str == '\n')       /*Signals that the word is complete.*/
                {
                buf[i] = SNUL;          /*Terminate the word with a SNUL.*/
                p = dssave(buf);        /*A copy of the word in buf is saved dynamically.*/
                break;
                }
            buf[i] = *str++;                                                    /*d*/
            }
        printf("\naddress: %d. p = [%s]",p,p);     /*PrintProduct: address: 72. p = [What]*/
        }
```

In this example, in line *b* we transmit a pointer-to-char, *p*, that is not linked to an array. It acquires a value in the called function. But with the termination of *wordsplit()*, in line *c* the value of the pointer has reverted to its actual value of NULL. Access to the stored text is irretrievably lost. As is the use of the text.

In examining this example and the examples that follow, bear in mind that we are dealing with a pointer to a dynamic string, not a pointer to a predefined array. In both cases— dynamic or preset—the prototypic format for the called function is **void wordsplit(STRING from, STRING to);**. In both cases, when *wordsplit()* finishes, the pointer-to-char representing the *to* string reverts to the value it had before its utilization in the called function. The difference is that in the predefined case, the prior value of the pointer-to-char is the address of an existing array—it would be an error to transmit a NULL pointer. And this array continues to exist when the function terminates. The preset array might already contain a string. Or, inside *wordsplit()*, the *to* string will twin some of the *from* array by means of an operation similar to the operation in line *d* in the current example. In the dynamic case, in contrast, the array is unnamed, its address is known only to the system, its only contact is a pointer-to-char, whose *calloc()*-bestowed value disappears the moment the function terminates.

It is, nevertheless, possible to transmit a pointer-to-char as function arg, assign it to a dynamically stored string and produce an indelible pointer-to-char value. The simplest way is to return the acquired pointer value and reassign the pointer with this value when control returns to the calling function, as in line *e*.

Method 1.   Revalue the pointer with the value returned by the called function.

```
void callingfct(void)
    {
    char       a[SZE(100)] = {SNUL};
    char       *p = NULL;

    stcpy(keep, a);
    printf("\naddress: %d. p = [%s]",p,p);      /*PrintProduct: address: 0. p = []*/
    p = wordsplit(a,p);                                                /*e*/
    printf("\naddress: %d. p = [%s]",p,p);      /*PrintProduct: address: 72. p = [What]*/
    }

STRING wordsplit(STRING str, STRING p)
    {
    char       buf[SZE(100)] = {SNUL};
    int        i;

    for (i = 0; *str; i++)
        {
        if (*str == '\40' || *str == '\n')
            {
            buf[i] = SNUL;
            p = dssave(buf);
            break;
            }
        buf[i] = *str++;
        }
    printf("\naddress: %d. p = [%s]",p,p);      /*PrintProduct: address: 72. p = [What]*/
    return(p);
    }
```

The substring will be accessible for the life of *callingfct*(). If the pointer is redefined in line *a* as **static STRING p = NULL;**, the substring would be available the rest of the program run. The disadvantage is that we may return only one value from a function, making this method unsuitable when several values are calculated in the called function. Or when the return value is needed to decide the next processing step.

Method 2.   Make the address a global variable.

The function is rewritten to take advantage of the scope of a global variable, i.e.,

```
static STRING p = NULL;
void callingfct(void)
    {
    char       a[SZE(100)] = {SNUL};

    stcpy(keep, a);
    wordsplit(a);
    printf("\naddress: %d. p = [%s]",p,p);      /*PrintProduct: address: 72. p = [What]*/
    }
```

```
void wordsplit(STRING str)
    {
    char      buf[SZE(100)] = {SNUL};
    int       i;

    for (i = 0; *str; i++)
        {
        if (*str == '\40' || *str == '\n')
            {
            buf[i] = SNUL;
            break;
            }
        buf[i] = *str++;
        }
    p = dssave(buf);      /*p was defined as a static global variable,*/
    }                     /* accessible to all the functions in the file.*/
```

Generality is lost, but it is a way to create a string that stays alive for the life of the program.

3.6.2. USING A POINTER-TO-POINTER-TO-CHAR

Manipulating the address of the pointer-to-char guarantees that the value acquired by the pointer-to-char remains when the function terminates; i.e., the pointer-to-char stays locked on the address of the string of interest. We rewrite our example function as:

```
void callingfct(void)
    {
    char      a[SZE(100)] = {SNUL};
    char      *p = NULL;

    stcpy(keep, a);
    printf("\np's value: %d. p = [%s]",p,p);   /*PrintProduct: value: 0. p = []*/
    wordsplit(a,&p);
    printf("\np's value: %d. p = [%s]",p,p);   /*PrintProduct: value: 72. p = [What]*/
    }

void wordsplit(STRING str, PTRADR pa)                              /*a*/
    {
    char      buf[SZE(100)] = {SNUL};
    int       i;

    for (i = 0; *str; i++)
        {
        if (*str == '\40' || *str == '\n')
            {
            buf[i] = SNUL;
            *pa = dssave(buf);                                     /*b*/
            break;
            }
```

```
            buf[i] = *str++;
         }
   printf("\npa's value: %d. *pa = [%s]",*pa,*pa);  /*PrintProduct:*/
   }                                                /* value: 72. *pa = [What]*/
```

The pointer to the not yet existing string that will be stored dynamically is passed by address. The pointer is linked to the string by indirect referencing in line *b*. The value of *pa* represents the address of *p*. So ***pa = dssave(buf);** is read as: the pointer-to-char that is referenced through *pa* is assigned the address of the string copied from *buf* and dynamically saved by the system. Indirect addressing is a major way in which a dynamically stored string can be permanently captured. When it is used, linkage of pointer and string is immediate and permanent. It does not require returning the value to another pointer, as in Method 1, Section 3.6.1. The return value can therefore be used instead to confirm that the system was able to store the string or to relay a critical value that will decide which of several alternatives to do next.

When text such as a file name is to be used in a program in multiple functions, some resident in different files, it is useful to preset a global pointer that will be given a non-null value when the input file is named by the user and stored by the system. It and its channel number will thereafter be accessible to all modules in the program. Note that in contrast to Method 2 in Section 3.6.1, where a particular pointer is specified in the body of the function, this next is a general function with values transmitted by dummy args. The global variables are:

```
STRING   infile =   NULL;    /* infile is a global pointer-to-char that will point to the array*/
                             /* whose text is the name of the file.*/
FILE     *inch =    NULL;    /* inch is a global pointer-to-FILE.*/
BOOL     InfoRec = NO;
```

#define PJ(x) printf("\n" #x)   /*PJ is short for print jabber.*/

Recall from Section 2.3.1, that *ttyin*() uses a global array called *ttystr* to store keyboard information supplied interactively by the end user. In this example, *ttystr* has received the essential information the program needs to process a database: the name of the database, the number of fields each record contains, the record and field delimiters; e.g., **Jun-File,7,~,#,**.

The function *majorfile*() decodes the characteristics of the database selected by the user for processing. It is prototyped as:

extern BOOL majorfile(STRING finfo, FILE **pchan, PTRADR pfile);

majorfile() extracts the name of the file from *ttystr*, stores its address dynamically and places this address in the analog to **pfile*. To ensure that the returned pointer sticks, the transmitted arg is the address of **pfile*, namely, *pfile*. In our example, the code would be written as:

InfoRec = majorfile(ttystr, &inch, &infile);

Given our focus on string processing, this section has concentrated on PTRADR's. But as the second function arg of the current example illustrates, the technique of manipulating the pointer to a pointer is not just for strings. The second function arg of *majorfile*() is a pointer-to-pointer-to-FILE. It permits the value of the pointer-to-FILE to be assigned permanently in *majorfile*() using this line of code:

if (*pchan = fopen(*pfile, "r")) return (TRUE); else return (FALSE);

If all goes well, the name of the string and its channel number are immediately and permanently set for the life of the program. But if the file name was mistyped by the user or is read-only or if the limit on open files has been reached, the return value can alert the next echelon function to hold its processing guns until the matter is settled.

3.6.3. USING A POINTER TO AN ARRAY OF POINTERS-TO-CHAR

The same concept of using the address of the pointer-to-char to ensure that the pointer is permanently valued can be extended to an array of pointers.

```
#define PS(x) printf("\n" #x " = [%s]", x)
#define PJ(x) printf("\n" #x)

void callingfct(void)
     {
     char          a[SZE(100)] = {SNUL};
     int           i;
     STRING        p[SZE(20+1)];  /*An array of 21 pointers-to-char*/
     PTRADR        pa = p;     /*pa points to the first pointer element of the array: p[0].*/

     stcpy(keep, a);
     wordsplit(a,pa);               /*The address of the first pointer element acts*/
                                    /* as function arg.*/
```

/*Next, looping through the pointers in the array at line a, if the word pointed to contains a non-NULL char, then the referenced word is displayed. In this example, the first 4 lines displayed would be:

```
pa[i] = [What]
pa[i] = [is]
pa[i] = [a]
pa[i] = [sentence]
*/
     for (i = 1; *pa[i]; i++)                                        /*a*/
          PS(pa[i]);
     }

void wordsplit(STRING str, PTRADR pa)
     {
     char          buf[SZE(100)] = {SNUL};
     int           i, ii;

     for (i = 1; *str; i++)          /*i is 1 so that pointer 1 will be the first pointer.*/
```

```
          {
          buf[0] = SNUL;
          for (ii = 0; *str; ii++)
               {
               if (*str == '\40' || *str == '\n')
                    {
                    buf[ii] = SNUL;
```

/*In the next line, pa[i] functions as one of the pointer elements of the array, NOT as a pointer-to-pointer-to-char. It is analogous to writing a char array element by utilizing its pointer-to-char index. (See Section 1.5.2.)*/

```
                    pa[i] = dssave(buf);
                    str++;            /*To move the pointer to the start of the next word.*/
                    break;
                    }
               buf[ii] = *str++; /*This fills the next element of buf with a char of the*/
               }                /* particular word to be referenced by pa[i].*/
          }
```

/*As in line a, this next statement will display the words referenced by each pointer in turn. *(pa+i) is a pointer element, as is pa[i] in line a. And **(pa+i) is the character referenced by *(pa+i), corresponding to *pa[i] in line a.*/

```
     for (i = 1; **(pa+i); i++)                              /*b*/
          PS(*(pa+i));
     }
```

The next example is another way to chop text into its constituent components, storing each word dynamically and saving its memory address in a separate member of an array of pointers-to-char. The technique can be used to create a set of global text phrases that will be used throughout a multi-file program.

In line *a*, *pwrd* is defined as a pointer to an array of pointers-to-char and is set to point to the first element of the array, i.e., *wrd*[0], even though, for convenience, wrd[0] is not used. Assigning *pwrd* to the top of the pointer array will save trouble dealing with the array of pointers, which are normally addressed by offsets from the top element of the array.

pf in line *b* is the dummy arg for *pwrd*. Each time *psdsscan*() in line *c* breaks off a piece of text from *buf*, the text is dynamically saved and its address is placed in the next element of the array referenced by *pf*. At each cycle of the loop *pf* is incremented and moves down the array in units of pointer-to-char, just as a pointer-to-char traverses an array in char units. Note that in line *c*, *pf[i]* functions as a pointer-to-char.

Much of the work done in the previous example is subsumed by *psdsscan*(),a general purpose function which chops a string according to a halting rule prescribed by, in this case, TBrkAtDelim (The mechanics are explained in Chapter 4.). As a portion of the string is broken off, a copy of the piece is saved dynamically and its address is installed permanently in the pointer analog of *pf[i]*.

Permanent change is forced in two ways in the loop involving line *c*.

(1) By way of the return statement, each pointer-to-char element is given a permanent value developed in *psdsscan*().

(2) *psdsscan*() is destructive; intentionally, it chews up the original string. To make this obliteration permanent, the *address* of a pointer to *buf* is what is transmitted as function arg. It can be applied to a dynamic string, because the string is destroyed, not its location. So the system can free it.

```
static BITMAP  TBrkAtDelim = 0;
static STRING  wrd[SZE(20+1)] = {NULL};
static PTRADR pwrd = &wrd[0];                              /*a*/

void dofct(PTRADR pf)                                      /*b*/
    {
    int       brk = 0;
    char      buf[HUGESZE] = {SNUL};
    int       i = 0;
    STRING    pbuf = buf;

    stcpy(keep, buf);
    for (i = 1; i <= 20 && *pbuf; i++)
        {
        pf[i] = psdsscan(&pbuf,TBrkAtDelim,&brk);        /*c*/
        PS(pf[i]);        /*When i = 1: pf[i] = [What]. When i = 6: pf[i] = [words.].*/
        }
    PS(buf);                /*PrintProduct: buf = [].*/
    }

void callingfct(void)
    {
    setbreak(&TBrkAtDelim,"\40\n","","is");
    dofct(pwrd); /*pwrd is a PTRADR, pointing to the top of wrd, an array of pointers.*/
```

/*The next command when acted upon will demonstrate that the pointer elements of wrd retain the values acquired in dofct(). Read this statement as: if *pwrd (*pwrd is the pointer element that is currently referenced by pwrd) has a non-NULL value, display the text located at that address and go to the next pointer. Note that even though the first used slot in the array is wrd[1], nevertheless, in line a we initialized pwrd with the address of wrd[0]. Things work better that way.*/

```
    for (pwrd = &wrd[1]; *pwrd != SNUL; pwrd++)
        PS(*pwrd);
    }
```

3.7. HOW TO CHANGE THE STARTING ADDRESS OF A STRING

String scanning is a general method for examining each character in the string in turn, looking for a particular value or for one of a set of values or for a value a certain distance from a particular character. Once that value is found, the examined portion of the string or the unexamined part can be copied to a separate daughter string. The examined portion can be eliminated from the mother string or the mother string can remain intact. Scanning is fundamental to all string processing procedures.

Lop functions, exemplified by the generic *delchar()* shown below, are specialized string scanning and chopping routines that actually or temporarily delete characters, one by one, starting at the head of the string. Some lop functions effect permanent changes in the string by deleting the examined part of the string, some do not. Done in a loop, lop functions can extract a set of substrings.

These are some tasks dependent on changing the string's starting address:

- repeatedly chopping the mother string into segments, starting from the beginning of the string. The original string is destroyed. This is a typical task when output substrings are to be of a standardized size. Or, if halting occurs when particular chars are encountered, the set of resultant substrings can be compared or shaped and then reconcatenated. The functions in Section 3.6.3 sliced a sentence into words. Similar procedures would serve to bring in an ASCII-delimited record from disk, chop it into its constituent informational fields, process one or more of these fields and output a reconstructed record.

- deleting characters starting from the beginning of the string in order to form a permanent substring of the original string to be returned to the calling function. The original string is reduced in size. The prototypic task is cleaning white space and diacritic markers from the front of a string.

- inspecting a string char by char for particular characters. When such a halt character is found, either the top part or the bottom section of the mother string is copied to a daughter string. The original string may be modified, destroyed or left intact. This is a fundamental technique for almost any search and/or sort task.

This section deals with ways of re-addressing the string when its beginning text is lopped to create virtual or real substrings. We will demonstrate manipulating the address of the pointer-to-char in context of other methods that are capable of deleting the first part of the string to enable substringing. The burden of this section is that while other methods are available and useful, manipulating the address of the pointer to the char array is a fool-proof way to modify permanently the beginning of the string of interest. A function can readily and permanently change a set of related or unrelated pointers-to-chars, if it has access to their addresses. Indeed, perhaps the major reason for using a PTRADR as function arg in string processing is to ensure access to the starting address of a string in order to erase unwanted text and retain its changed size across functions.

3.7.1. CHANGING THE STARTING ADDRESS OF A DYNAMIC STRING

Various methods are available for deleting the beginning part of a stored dynamic string and developing a substring that begins at what was an interior character of the original string. Recall from Section 2.5.2.1, however, that we can not be as cavalier as with preset string arrays. In making changes in dynamic strings, we can not casually perturb the address of the string because the system is able to free a system-stored string ONLY from the pointer to the first character of that string.

In the examples that follow, a global variable, *keep*[], (a string constant in our terminology) permanently accesses the example text: **ABCDEFGHIJKLMNOPQRSTUVWXYZ**. Whenever we need a fresh copy of the string, we take it from *keep*. Using *keep* in such statements as the one on line *a* in Method 1, Section 3.7.1.2 is law-abiding. We are not manipulating the string literal through *keep* but creating a copy that is stored dynamically and accessed through an associated pointer-to-char.

static STRING keep = "ABCDEFGHIJKLMNOPQRSTUVWXYZ";

3.7.1.1.   Using A Pointer-To-Char.

This section shows ways to eliminate the first part of text using a pointer to the text.

If the reference string is stored dynamically, functions to eliminate some of the text can be written cleanly so that no bytes are wasted; i.e., the space for the modified string is reallocated and so string modifications are permanent. The pointer value survives because it is reassigned to the pointer defined in *callingfct*(). Several ways to do this are shown, using the generic name *delchar*.

Method 1.   Overwrites the string with the substring. Uses realloc to store the substring.

Recall that the system must be asked for reallocation space before the new string is copied into the new space. Yet *stcpy*() in line *a* of *delchar*() writes a SNUL at the end of the new—and shorter—string before storage space is requested. This doesn't interfere with reallocation in line *b* by the system, which has a record of how many chars it gave *str* initially. The substring is shown in line *c*.

```
void callingfct(void)
    {
    STRING   p = NULL;        /*This will eventually be used to reference*/
                              /* the first element of a character array.*/
    p = dssave(keep);
    p = delchar(p,10);
    PS(p);                    /*PrintProduct: p = [KLMNOPQRSTUVWXYZ]*/
    }
```

```
STRING delchar(STRING str, int howmany)
    {
    STRING p2 = str;

    p2 += howmany;      /*Increments p2, so it points to the howmany th + 1 char in str.*/
    stcpy(p2,str);      /*This overwrites the top of str with the */
                        /* portion of str pointed to by p2. */              /*a*/
    str = (STRING) realloc((STRING) str, stlen(str) + 1);                   /*b*/
    PS(str);            /*PrintProduct: str = [KLMNOPQRSTUVWXYZ]*/          /*c*/
    return(str);
    }
```

<u>Method 2.</u>   Variant of Method 1 for virtual strings. It keeps a separate pointer to the 'real' string.

If the string, again represented by *str*, is virtual[16] and the real address is retained in a separate variable such as *pstart*, then *delchar()* may be rewritten so that the string is reallocated relative to the virtual string. In *delchar()*, *pstart* provides the system with the information it needs to delete the original string. Upon returning to the calling function, pstart is no longer valid.

The virtual string is created in line *a*. In line *b* (in *delchar()*) the virtual string is copied into the space occupied by the original string. This is a reduced string, so it doesn't overflow its boundary. Nor does it interfere with the system's ability to deassign the space of the original string. Several things happen in line *c*: (1) pstart is shifted howmany bytes, so that it now points to the desired start of the string; (2) *stlen()* calculates how much space is needed for the new string; (3) using *pstart*, the system reallocates space for the shifted virtual string; and (4)the address of the re-stored and reconstructed string is stored in *str*.

```
void callingfct(void)
    {
    STRING    pstart, p;        /*Both initially will point to the first element of*/
                                /* the char array.*/
    p = pstart = dssave(keep);  /*PrintProduct:
                                [ABCDEFGHIJKLMNOPQRSTUVWXWZ]*/
    p += 7;                     /*PrintProduct:
                                [HIJKLMNOPQRSTUVWXWZ]*/       /*a*/
    p = delchar(p,pstart,3);
    PS(p);                      /*PrintProduct: p = [KLMNOPQRSTUVWXYZ]*/
    }
```

---

16 By *virtual*, we mean the pointer-to-char *p* points to a new initial position in line *a* in the calling function but the actual location of the string has not been formally shifted by the system. This is a simplified instance of what typically occurs; namely, the apparent shifting of string position as a result of local processing.

STRING delchar(STRING str, STRING pstart, int howmany)
```
{
stcpy(str,pstart);                                          /*b*/
return(str = (STRING) realloc((STRING) pstart,stlen(pstart+=howmany)+1));/*c*/
}
```

In our example, the number of chars returned to the system are set by *howmany*. Most strings that change size, however, do so because a chunk has been chopped out of the string or it is merging with other text or specific chars are added or subtracted to the result of internal processing. So in most cases there needs to be a temporary buffer in which to collect the string undergoing modification before its revised size can be stated. So usually, as in the next example, it is just as efficient to use that buffer to handle the string without involving *realloc()*. The string is copied into some local large array where modifications and additions are made, the original string is freed, and the new version of the string is dynamically saved, reusing the char pointer from the original string.

Method 3.   Temporarily stores the substring while deleting the string. Saves the substring, reusing the pointer to the string.

The method shown uses *dssave()*, which calls *calloc()*, so the space is emptied before the string is re-stored. (The *realloc()* function calls *malloc()*, so the string space is not cleared.) The disadvantage is that a local buffer of sufficient magnitude has to be defined, making further inroads in the meager stack space set aside for local variables. The calling function of method 1, Section 3.7.1.1 can be used again. When *delchar()* finishes, as in Method 1, **p = [KLMNOPQRSTUVWXYZ]**.

STRING delchar(STRING str, int howmany)
```
{
char      tempbuf[SMLSZE] = {SNUL}
STRING    ptemp = str + howmany;

stcpy(ptemp,tempbuf);
NULLIT(str);
return(str = dssave(tempbuf));
}
```

3.7.1.2.   Using A Pointer-To-Pointer-To-Char.

Permanently changing the beginning of a string by manipulating the pointer-to-pointer-to-char that points to the character pointer that points to the first char of the array is a general and useful technique with dynamically stored strings, one whose utility grows as the function becomes more complex.

We begin by rewriting *delchar()* from Section 3.7.1.1, using the address of a pointer-to-char as arg. As in method 1 above, this is a straighforward change in the starting address by re-storing the text in the called function. An advantage of using a PTRADR as arg, even in this simple function, is that the return value is available for monitoring the reallocation.

<u>Method 1.</u>   Overwrites the string with the substring. Uses realloc to store the substring.

```
void callingfct(void)
    {
    STRING   p = dssave(keep);
    BOOL     CHANGE = FALSE;

    CHANGE = delchar(&p,10);
    PS(p);                    /*Print Product: p = [KLMNOPQRSTUVWXYZ]*/
    PD(CHANGE);               /*Print Product: CHANGE = 1*/
    }

BOOL delchar(PTRADR pa, int howmany)
    {
    STRING   p2 = *pa;

    p2 += howmany;
    stcpy(p2,*pa);
    if (*pa = (STRING) realloc((STRING) *pa, stlen(*pa) + 1))
        return (TRUE);
    else
        {
        printf("\nNo more calloc space.");
        return (FALSE);
        }
    }
```

<u>Method 2.</u>   Variant of Method 1 for virtual strings. It keeps a separate pointer to the 'real' string.

As does Method 2 in the previous section, this handles virtual strings. It frees the original allocation cleanly and stores the changed string using *realloc()*. Note that the second arg in *delchar()* is a pointer-to-char. This is sufficient to inform the system of the location of the original string so that the space can be deallocated. The first arg is a pointer-to-pointer-to-char to make the change in address of the new string sticky when control returns to the calling function. As line *a* indicates, the original address stored in *pstart* is no longer valid.

```
void callingfct(void)
    {
    STRING   pstart, p;  /*Both initially will point to the first element of the char array.*/
    BOOL     CHANGE = FALSE;

    p = pstart = dssave(keep);
    p += 7;
    PS(p);                         /*PrintProduct: p = [HIJKLMNOPQRSTUVWXWZ]*/
    CHANGE = delchar(&p,pstart,3);
    PS(p);                         /*PrintProduct: p = [KLMNOPQRSTUVWXYZ]*/
    PS(pstart);                    /*PrintProduct: pstart = [H]*/              /*a*/
    PD(CHANGE);                    /*PrintProduct: CHANGE = 1*/
    }
```

```
BOOL delchar(PTRADR str, STRING pstart, int howmany)
    {
    stcpy(*str,pstart);
    if ((*str = (STRING) realloc((STRING) pstart, stlen(pstart += howmany) + 1)))
        return(TRUE);
    else return(FALSE);
    }
```

<u>Method 3.</u>   It temporarily stores the substring and then resaves it.

As in Method 3 in 3.7.1.1, the new string is held in a temporary buffer while the original string is deallocated. This method has the advantage of working properly with any size of reconstructed string, not just a shortened version of the original string.

```
void callingfct(void)
    {
    STRING   p = NULL;
    BOOL     CHANGE = FALSE;

    p = dssave(keep);
    PS(p);                   /*PrintProduct: p = [ABCDEFGHIJKLMNOPQRSTUVWXYZ]*/
    CHANGE = delchar(&p,7);
    PS(p);                   /*PrintProduct: p = [HIKLMNOPQRSTUVWXYZ]*/
    PD(CHANGE);              /*PrintProduct: CHANGE = 1*/
    }
```

```
BOOL delchar(PTRADR pa, int howmany)
    {
    char        tempbuf[SMLSZE] = {SNUL};
    STRING ptemp = *pa + howmany;
    stcpy(ptemp,tempbuf);
    NULLIT(*pa);
    if (*pa = dssave(tempbuf))
        return(TRUE);
    else return(FALSE);
    }
```

<u>Method 4.</u>   Ways of using two pointers, so that string and substring occupy the same space.

The next example illustrates a less orthodox technique involving two pointers. In the calling function, the pointer *p* is the contact to a system-stored string. As shown in line *a* in *delchar( )*, resetting the value of *p* to some address that corresponds to an inside character of the string and storing this new address as the value of a PTRADR deletes the start of the string permanently and with less fuss than in the previous methods.

Unfortunately, we no longer have the address of the original string to hand the system so its space can't be freed. One way out of this dilemma is to define two pointers in the calling function. Using one pointer, we alter the substring with impunity. When processing is completed, the pointer to the original string, *pstart*, still points to the original address of the stored string and is available to free the string. This is shown next. Note that, in contrast to method 2 of Section 3.7.1.1, the original address is not involved in the processing of the substring. This technique works for virtual strings.

```
void callingfct(void)
    {
    int          i = 0;
    STRING       p = NULL;
    STRING       pstart = NULL;

    pstart = p = dssave(keep);
    PD(pstart);               /*PrintProduct: p = -7502*/
    delchar(&p,10);
    PD(p);                    /*PrintProduct: p = -7492*/
    PS(p);                    /*PrintProduct: p = [KLMNOPQRSTUVWXYZ]
    ....do some local processing or submit p as arg to other functions ...
    PD(pstart);               /*PrintProduct: pstart = -7502*/
    PS(pstart);               /*PrintProduct: pstart =
                                 [ABCDEFGHIJKLMNOPQRSTUVWXYZ]*/
```

/*As the previous line shows, pstart continues to address the original string. p points to the portion of the string that begins the substring, the letter K. Although they didn't interact during processing, the two pointers are not independent—the substring was not saved as an independent entity. Freeing pstart by NULLIT() will free the substring space.*/

/*NULLIT() removes the string from the allocated-space list. However, as explained in Section 2.5.2.4, deallocation does not erase characters, so p will still appear to contain the substring. To demonstrate that p is affected when pstart is deallocated, the next line of code wipes clean the memory area accessed through pstart. Then pstart is deallocated. As shown, this also deletes p. Note that pstart[i] functions as the ith character of the array pointed to by pstart.*/

```
    for (i = 0; i <= 25; i++)
        pstart[i] = SNUL;
    NULLIT(pstart);
    PS(p);                    /*PrintProduct: p = []*/
    }


void delchar(PTRADR pabuf, int howmany)
    {
    *pabuf += howmany;                                        /*a*/
    PS(*pabuf);               /*PrintProduct: *pabuf = [KLMNOPQRSTUVWXYZ]*/
    PD(*pabuf);               /*PrintProduct: *pabuf = -7492*/
    }
```

Alternatively, the lopped string can be rewritten to the original address. We again start with two pointers to the beginning of the array, *pstart* and *p*. *p* changes in value in *delchar*(), i.e., it points to a different memory location. In line *c*, the part of the string that starts at the new location is copied to *pstart*, i.e., to the original address. However, *p* and the substring are now disassociated. *delchar*() started the substring addressed by *p* 10 characters into the string. As line *b* indicates, the interval between the pointers is maintained. So we can assign the value of *pstart* to *p* on line *c* to re-associate *p* and its substring. Or we can have two 'fingers' in the string, one at a fixed interval from the other.

```
void callingfct(void)
    {
    STRING        p = NULL;
    STRING        pstart = NULL;

    pstart = p = dssave(keep);
    delchar(&p,10);
    PD(pstart);              /*PrintProduct: pstart = -7502*/
    PS(pstart);             /*PrintProduct: pstart =
                                  [ABCDEFGHIJKLMNOPQRSTUVWXYZ]*/
    stcpy(p,pstart);                                           /*a*/
    PD(pstart);              /*PrintProduct: pstart = -7502*/
    PS(pstart);             /*PrintProduct: pstart = [KLMNOPQRSTUVWXYZ]*/
    PS(p);                  /*PrintProduct: p = [UVWXYZ]*/       /*b*/
    p = pstart;
    PS(p);
            /*PrintProduct: p = [KLMNOPQRSTUVWXYZ]*/  }
```

In this last solution, the final few chars are now unused but they will not be released until the rest of the string is. The good news is that all the system needs to free the string is the starting address. So even if we SNUL all the last part of the string, it won't interfere with completely releasing the space when the time comes.

<u>Method 5.</u>   Uses TXT library LOP utilities.

Most of the previous methods reduced the original dynamic string to a single substring fashioned from a part of the mother string. The next technique, performed in a loop, is suitable for the virtual slicing of either a preset or a dynamic string systematically into equal-sized dynamic substrings. At line *b*, *dslop()* returns a pointer to where in the mother string the next substring is to begin cloning. After processing—line *d*—the original string is unscathed.

No space needs to be set aside in the calling function to hold the daughter strings. In the present example, an array of pointers (*pnew*, defined in line *a*, will contain their eventual addresses. It is to be emphasized that the daughter strings are written at memory locations independent of the original string and must be separately freed. Line *c* shows the text of the first substring. The last substring, *pnew*[3], would read: **VWXYZ**.

```
void callingfct(void)
    {
    int           i = 0;
    STRING        pbuf = NULL;
    STRING        pnext = NULL;
    STRING        pnew[5] = {NULL};                    /*a*/

    pbuf = dssave(keep);
    pnext = pbuf;
    PD(pbuf);              /*PrintProduct: pbuf = 12*/
```

```
for (i = 0; *pnext; i++)
    {
    pnext = dslop(pnext, 7, &pnew[i]);
    PS(pnext);      /*PrintProduct: pnext = [HIKLMNOPQRSTUVWXYZ]*/  /*b*/
    PS(pnew[i]);    /*PrintProduct: pnew[i] = [ABCDEFGHIJ]*/            /*c*/
    }
PS(pbuf);   /*PrintProduct: pbuf = [ABCDEFGHIKLMNOPQRSTUVWXYZ]*/ /*d*/
}
```

In *dslop*(), the function arg *dsn* is a pointer-to-pointer-to-char that points to no array. So we use a local buffer, *hold*[], to collect what will go into the array that *dsn* points to with double indirection. Starting in line *a,* the pointer *phold* indicates where the next character is to be placed in *hold*. Then in line *b* the string is dynamically saved and its address is assigned to the pointer variable whose address is the value of *dsn*.

We define *dsn* as a PTRADR, not as a STRING, to ensure that the value assigned it in *dslop*() sticks. Compare this to the definition of *dsn* in *pspslop*() in method 4 in Section 3.7.2.2, where the STRING *dsn* represents the predefined array that will hold the daughter string. There, *dsn* is used to access the single elements of the preexisting array, a task well within its capability.

```
STRING dslop(STRING str, int ndd, PTRADR dsn)
/*
*str:  pointer to the original string.
ndd: from the beginning of str for ndd chars.
dsn: unassigned char pointer.
*/
    {/*BP*/
    int        bgn = 0;
    char       hold[TTYSZE] = {SNUL};
    STRING     phold = hold;   /*phold is a local pointer set to traverse the array hold.*/

    for (bgn = 1; bgn <= ndd && *str; bgn++)                        /*a*/
        *phold++ = *str++;
    *phold = SNUL;
    *dsn = dssave(hold);                                           /*b*/
     return(str);               /*str indicates where in the mother string*/
    }/*EP*/                     /* the next substring will begin.*/
```

With slight modification, *dslop*() can be rewritten so that the part of the original string that is copied to the daughter string is destroyed during processing. To do this efficiently, the mother string is defined as a PTRADR.

dsdslop() does not need to return a pointer to where in the mother string the next substring will start, because the mother string is rewritten as part of the processing. By line *a*, it is completely gone. Note that this is a different version that the *dsdslop*() routine in LIST-INGS\include\comlib.c.

```
void callingfct(void)
    {
    int        i = 0;
```

```
STRING    pbuf = NULL;
STRING    pnew[5] = {NULL};

pbuf = dssave(keep);
for (i = 0; *pbuf; i++)
    {
    dsdslop(&pbuf, 7, &pnew[i]);
    PS(pnew[i]);     /*i is 0. PrintProduct: pnew[i] = [ABCDEFG];*/
    PS(pbuf);        /*i is 0. PrintProduct: pbuf[i] = [HIJKLMNOPQRSTUVWXYZ];*/
    PS(pbuf);        /*i is 4. PrintProduct: pbuf = []*/             /*a*/
    }
}
```

As before, *hold* in *dsdslop*() stores the emerging daughter string. But in this next version, it does double duty. At the end of the for() loop that starts on line *b*, *pstr*, representing the pointer referenced by *str*, has stopped at the character that begins the part of the mother string not copied to **dsn*. In line *c* we permanently save its contents in a place accessed by **dsn*. So *hold* can be used to delete the part of the original string In line *d*, *hold* is given a copy of the unexamined part of the mother string to hold temporarily. In line *e*, the pointer that accesses the mother string is freed, thereby 'erasing' the entire string. Finally, in line *f*), the copy of the unexamined part of the mother string stored temporarily in *hold* is permanently saved and its location is assigned to **str*.

```
void dsdslop(PTRADR str, int ndd, PTRADR dsn)
    {/*BP*/
    int       bgn = 0;
    char      hold[TTYSZE] = {SNUL};
    STRING    phold = hold;
    STRING    pstr = *str;

    for (bgn = 1; bgn <= ndd && *pstr; bgn++)        /*b*/
        *phold++ = *pstr++;
    *phold = SNUL;
    *dsn = dssave(hold);                             /*c*/
    hold[0] = SNUL;
    stcpy(pstr,hold);                                /*d*/
    NULLIT(*str);                                    /*e*/
    *str = dssave(hold);                             /*f*/
    return(pdsn);
    }/*EP*/
```

3.7.2. CHANGING THE STARTING ADDRESS OF A PRESET STRING

3.7.2.1.   Using A Pointer-To-Char.

In the previous section, the pointer-to-char was the contact point to a dynamically stored string. Our major concern was how to retain its value across functions without jeopardizing the system's knowledge of the string's whereabouts. But it was also the case that we did not need to worry about the location of the string as an entity independent of the pointer.

Preset strings are different. Once the char array containing the string is defined, there is no way physically to change the location of the start of the array or its extent, except by terminating the function in which it resides. Conceptually, however, the array and its resident string can be treated as semi-independent entities, where the string is the portion of the array under view and the rest of the string is ignored. We achieve virtual redefinition of the string by addressing it through a pointer. If we view the string through the lens of our chosen pointer, then by changing the value of the pointer, we effectively change the location of the string within the array or its size or its character.

In the next set of examples, as in the previous section, *keep*[] permanently accesses the text: **ABCDEFGHIJKLMNOPQRSTUVWXYZ**. Whenever we need a fresh copy of this text, we take it from *keep*.

A copy of the text is placed in *a*[]. Suppose, as in the first example below, we wish to delete the first 10 elements of *a*; i.e., to wipe out the contents of *a*[0] to *a*[9] so that the revised string will read: **KLMNOPQRSTUVWXYZ**. This next example does NOT do what we want.

```
static STRING keep = "ABCDEFGHIJKLMNOPQRSTUVWXYZ";

void callingfct(void)           /*THIS VERSION IS WRONG.*/
    {
    char    a[SZE(26+1)] = {SNUL};   /*A char array to hold the text.*/      /*a*/
    int     i = 0;
    char    *p = &a[0];      /*A pointer to the first element of the char array.*///*b*/

    stcpy(keep, a);
    delchar(p, 10);                                                          /*c*/
    PS(p);   /*The array appears empty because we SNUL'ed a[0] in delchar.*/  /*d*/
    PS(p+1); /*PrintProduct: p+1 = [BCDEFGHIJKLMNOPQRSTUVWXYZ]*/  /*e*/
    }

void delchar(STRING str, int howmany)
    {
    STRING    pstr= str;

    str[0] = SNUL;                                                           /*f*/
    pstr = (pstr+howmany);
    PS(pstr);               /*PrintProduct: pstr = [KLMNOPQRSTUVWXYZ]*/   /*g*/
    }
```

Recall from Section 3.2.3.2 that we can, inside a function, create a virtual string by temporarily changing the value of the pointer-to-char serving as function arg. In the present example, *p*, a pointer to *a*[0], is transmitted as a function arg to *delchar* in line *c*, where it is reset to point to the 11th element in the string. If we display the string beginning at the pointer, the screen, in line *g*, reads: **KLMNOPQRSTUVWXYZ**. Moreover, we've made some rain dance gestures to encourage permanent change in the string, including: (1)

defining an independent pointer in line *b*; starting with an empty array in line *a*; and SNUL'ing the first char of the string in line *f*. When control returns to *callingfct*(), if we print the string starting at *a*[0] (line *d*), the string appears empty, but printing the string beginning at *a*[1] (line *e*) demonstrates that all the values are intact. The string does NOT read: **KLMNOPQRSTUVWXYZ**.

No matter what we do to *p* in *delchar*(), we are working with a copy of the pointer's value as taken from the memory location where the pointer is stored. If in *callingfct*() we use *p* again, as in line *d*, the compiler goes to *p*'s home address, and the unmodified value at that location is taken as the address of the array and the string starts at *a*[0] as before.

We don't have the power to redefine the array, i.e., re-storage it within the context of the other information stored in memory. We can, however, change the address of the string resident in this array—providing we have a way to modify the at-home value of its associated pointer. And, unlike the case of the dynamic string, there is no penalty in 'losing' the original starting address.

As one way to change the start of the array using a pointer-to-char, we can modify *delchar*() so that it returns a pointer that is assigned to the relevant pointer-to-char. This is done next in Method 1.

Method 1.   Revalues the pointer with the address of the substring.

```
STRING delchar(STRING str, int howmany)
    {
    return(str += howmany);
    }
```

And we revise line *c* in *callingfct*() to read:

p = delchar(p, 10);

The initial characters in *a*[] would of course still be **ABCDEFGHIJ....** because there has been no shift in the physical location of the string. But the string we need to process, **if referenced through *p***, now starts at **K** for the duration of *callingfct*().

This is a relatively fast way to create a substring for the life of the calling function. It has no particular disadvantage unless we attempt to add chars at the end of the substring; in which case, we may, depending on array size, overrun the buffer.

Method 2.   Overwrites the array with the substring.

Alternatively, we can copy the substring to the start of the string's array. The starting address is not modified. The substring overwrites some of the space occupied by the original string, starting at the top of the array. *delchar*() does not need to return a pointer to secure the text of the new string.

```
void callingfct(void)
    {
    char      a[SZE(26)+1] = {SNUL};       /*A char array to hold the string.*/

    stcpy(keep, a);
```

```
    delchar(a,10);
    PS(a);                          /*PrintProduct: a = [KLMNOPQRSTUVWXYZ]*/
    stcat("abcdefghij",a);          /*There's room in a to add text to the tail      /*a*/
                                    of the first string.*/
    PS(a);                          /*PrintProduct: a =
    }                               [KLMNOPQRSTUVWXYZabcdefghij]*/
```

```
void delchar(STRING str, int howmany)
    {
    STRING   p = str;               /* p is a local pointer to the start of the array.*/
    p += howmany;                   /*Defines the start of the substring.*/
    stcpy(p,str);                   /*Copies the substring to the top of the array.*/ /*b*/
    }
```

Rewriting the text (line *b*) means this is a relatively slow technique. But shunting the substring to the top of the array leaves the rest of the array available for adding more text. Hence, as shown in line *a*, this method is suitable when additional material will be added to the end of the substring.

3.7.2.2.   Using A Pointer-To-Pointer-To-Char.

A certain way to delete the first part of a string permanently is to make use of the address of the associated pointer-to-char to re-address the start of the string. Like Method 4 in Section 3.7.1.2, the technique is efficient and fast, because we change only a single value instead of rewriting all the elements of what could be a long string. When a dynamic string was involved, we had to be careful to save the original start of the string, so the string space could eventually be freed. This is not a concern with preset strings. By definition, they are not freeable.

The original characters at the beginning of the array are still resident. But they won't hamper use of the newly-devised string if it is invoked solely through the pointer that holds its changed address. The technique of using the address of the pointer-to-char has the advantage that the value of the pointer is changed permanently without *delchar*() needing to return its value.

Method 1.   Directly re-values the pointer-to-the pointer-to-char with the address of the substring.

Most of the examples illustrate shifting the string by a specific number of characters. But a major reason for eliminating the start of a string is in preprocessing to clean the start of the string of white space and/or specific characters, where the start of the new string is calculated on-line, as in this simple function that cleans up the beginning of a string and changes the address of the string permanently to that of the first significant char.

clean() is written using the address of the pointer-to-char as arg. In consequence, we are able to manipulate addresses directly. Procedurally, we decide what the substring should be, place its starting address in the home of the pointer we initially associated with the string (line *c*) and decree that the value of this pointer is hereafter, as shown in line *a*, the starting address of the string. We need go no further to have an acceptable string for further processing. We may choose not to return a function value. Or we can use the return value as an indicator for other purposes.

The amount of space laid down for the array during compilation does not change because of runtime modifications to the text in the array. So, while this is an excellent way to rearrange or permanently convert a string to one of its possible substrings, it is less suitable, given a less than capacious array, as a way to concatenate a newly formed substring with new material. The original string is still in place.

```
void callingfct(void)
      {
      char      a[MEDSZE] = {SNUL};
      char      *p = a;

      stcpy("        \n    ABCDEFG",p);
      PS(p);          /*PrintProduct:  p = [
                                                  ABCDEFG]*/

      PS(a);          /*PrintProduct:  a = [
                                                  ABCDEFG]*/

      p = clean(&p);
      PS(p);          /*PrintProduct: p = [ABCDEFG]*/              /*a*/
      PS(a);          /*PrintProduct: a = [
      }                                        ABCDEFG]*/   /*b*/
```

The value of *s*, a pointer-to-pointer-to-char, is the address of a pointer. Note that the cleaned string is 'defined' in line *c* by replacing the value stored in *s* with the address of the first significant char. Viewed through *p* as in line *a*, the string is cleaned. The original string, however, is unaffected (line *b*).

```
STRING clean(PTRADR s)
      {/*BP*/
      STRING   cs = NULL;

      for (cs = *s; *cs; cs++)
            if (*cs == '\t' || *cs == '\40' || *cs == '\n')
                  continue;
            else break;
      return(*s = cs);                                         /*c*/
      }/*EP*/
```

Method 2.   Overwrites the array with the substring.

This is a variant of method 2 in Section 3.7.2.1, in that it first successfully reassigns the pointer with the address of the substring n delchar(). (See lines a and b.) It then transfers the substring that starts at *p* to *a*[0] in line *c*. As shown in line *d*, this changes the value of the first char of the array. In 'sliding' the substring to the top of the array, some of *p* is overwritten. What is left is shown in line *e*; i.e., *p* is still 10 characters beyond the start of the string.

```
void callingfct(void)
    {
    char     a[SZE(26)+1] = {SNUL};        /*A char array to hold the string.*/
    char     *p = &a[0];                   /*A pointer to the first element of the char array.*/

    stcpy(keep, a);
    delchar(&p, 10);
    PS(p);     /*PrintProduct: p = [KLMNOPQRSTUVWXYZ]*/            /*a*/
    PS(a);     /*PrintProduct: a = [ABCDEFGHIJKLMNOPQRSTUVWXYZ]*/  /*b*/
    stcpy(p,a);                                                    /*c*/
    PS(a);     /*PrintProduct: a = [KLMNOPQRSTUVWXYZ]*/            /*d*/
    PS(p);     /*PrintProduct: p = [UVWXYZ]*/                      /*e*/
    p = a;     /*p can now be used to represent a.*/
    }

void delchar(PTRADR pa, int howmany)
    {
    *pa += howmany;     /* *pa references the pointer-to-char, whose address is*/
                        /* the value of pa.*/
    PS(*pa);            /*PrintProduct: *pa = [KLMNOPQRSTUVWXYZ]*/
    }
```

Method 3.   Accesses the address of the pointer.

In this technique, *pa*, the address of the pointer-to-char, is a separate variable defined in *callingfct*() and transmitted as function arg to *alarm*(), which checks whether the string contains a CTRLg. Finding a CTRLg is a signal to delete the previous section of the string and, when control returns to *callingfct*(), do some special processing. Otherwise, when *alarm*() terminates, *p* snaps back to its original position, pointing to *a*[0]. In this example, the view through *p* is the text that follows the CTRLg. The original string is of course still in place.

```
void callingfct(void)
    {
    BOOL     YorN = NO;
    char     a[MEDSZE] = {SNUL};           /*A char array to contain text.*/
    char     *p = &a[0];                   /*A pointer to the first element of the char array.*/
    char     **pa = &p;                    /*A pointer-to-pointer-to-char.*/

    stcpy("Stand-in\07for a string.",p); /*Demo text is copied to a.*/
    YorN = alarm(pa);
    if (YorN)                              /*Longer form: if (YorN == YES) */
            DoSpecialStuff(p);
    else DoRegularStuff(p);
    PS(p);                                 /*PrintProduct: p = [for a string.]*/
    PS(a);                                 /*PrintProduct: a = [Stand-infor a string.]*/
    }

BOOL alarm(PTRADR pa)
    {
```

/*It is not necessary but it is somewhat clearer to assign to a local pointer the value of the pointer referenced by the PTRADR acting as function arg. In line a below, it is as if p, a local pointer-to-char, were given memory residence at the address that is the value of pa. Hence, p contains the address of the first element of the array a, and so can access the entire array.*/

/*Without it, the while (*p ..) would be written: while (**pa..). In either case, the notion is that processing is done if the specific char at the location pointer has a non-SNUL value. Similarly, either if (*p ..) or if (**pa) in lines b and c convey the idea that processing depends on a specific value, CTRLg.*/

```
     STRING p = *pa;                          /*a*/

     while (*p != SNUL)                       /*b*/
          {
          if (*p == '\07')                    /*c*/
               {
               p++;
               printf("\nHALT. Problem.\n");  /*In the current example, it would */
                                              /* display this message.*/
```

/*A CTRLg was found. The value of the dummy PTRADR variable, pa, is the permanent address of a pointer that is not identified in *alarm*(). (In *callingfct*(), the PTRADR *pa* holds the address of the pointer variable, *p*.) In line d, this unnamed pointer is re-valued with the value of the local pointer, *p*. The value of a character pointer is the address of an array element. In our example, in line *d* when control is returned to callingfct(), *pa is pointing to the 'f' after the CTRLg.*/

```
               *pa = p;                        /*d*/
               return(YES);
               }
          p++;
          }
     return(NO);          /*No CTRLg was found. The string was not modified.*/
     }
```

In line *d*, we effected a permanent change in the pointer-to-char *p* in *callingfct*() that is the analog of the local pointer-to-char *p*. Changing the value of *pa* assigns the current address of the local variable *p* to a copy of *pa*. We can not change *pa* itself this way because we don't have access to *its* home address. But the value of a copy of *pa* is an address, specifically, the address of the pointer-to-char that points to the start of the string. So, within *alarm*(), if we change this address, it indeed does change the value of the start of the *string* permanently, which is what we want. The *array* containing the string remains intact.

Less of the char array *a*[] is used when the address of the substring is substituted for that of the initial string in *pa*. However, the local variables will be trashed anyway when *callingfct*() terminates. So no harm is done, unless, of course, the array serves as a mold into which enough new text pieces are poured to overflow its limits.

<u>Method 4.</u>   Uses TXT library routines.

pspslop() is a static string version of *dsdslop*(), shown in Method 5 in Section 3.7.1.2. It chops a preset string from the first char of the referenced array for the number of chars given by the second arg of *pspslop*(); it stores the substring in a preset buffer.

The first arg is the address of the pointer to the start of the string. By indirectly accessing the string through the address of the associated pointer, *pspslop*() is able to rewrite the string minus its lopped chars, and make this modification permanent. It writes the text deleted from the string to preset storage that is referenced through a pointer-to-char, the third arg. The original string is modified. Although somewhat ungainly, the procedure can be used in a loop to fill several daughter strings and completely eliminate the mother string, starting with a string in *buf* and several empty receiving buffers, *new1* to *new4*. But confronted with the need to handle several preset arrays at once, 2D arrays, such as those discussed in Chapter 5, are preferable.

```
void callingfct(void)
    {
    int       i = 0
    char      buf[TTYSZE] = {SNUL};
    STRING    pbuf = buf;
    char      new1[TTYSZE] = {SNUL};
    char      new2[TTYSZE] = {SNUL};
    char      new3[TTYSZE] = {SNUL};
    char      new4[TTYSZE] = {SNUL};
    STRING    p[5];

    p[1] = new1;
    p[2] = new2;
    p[3] = new3;
    p[4] = new4;
    stcpy("ABCDEFGHIJKLMNOPQRSTUVWXYZ.",buf);
    for (i = 1; i <= 4; i++)
        {
```

/*The next statement is read as: lop the first 7 characters from buf. Put these chars in new[i]. In the first cycle, ABCDEFGHIJ would be placed in new[1] and the rest of the text would replace the original string in buf. In the fourth iteration, buf would be empty and new[4] would read: VWXYZ.*/

```
        pspslop(&pbuf, 7, p[i]);
        }
```

pspslop() creates permanent changes in the string by shifting what's left of the string to the starting address of the array in which it resides; e.g., **stcpy(pstr,*str);** in line *a*. Recall that shifting text to the start of the array is relatively slow but maximizes the amount of space left in the bottom of the array for adding more text.

This method of finding a substring or eliminating the first part of the string is particularly effective with preset strings. If the original string were stored dynamically, this would still work, because less of the occupied space is now used. But it would be poor management of dynamic storage space.

void pspslop(PTRADR str, int ndd, STRING dsn)
```
/*
str:   address of the pointer to the original string, whose front end will be lopped.
ndd: from the beginning of *str for ndd chars.
dsn: preset storage where the front end of the string will be stored.
*/
```

```
{/*BP*/
int       bgn = 0;
STRING    pstr = *str;      /*A local pointer to set to the value of str.*/

dsn[0] = SNUL;
for (bgn = 1; bgn <= ndd && *pstr; bgn++)
      *dsn++ = *pstr++;
*dsn = SNUL;           /*A daughter string is completely cloned.*/
stcpy(pstr,*str);      /*The original string minus the 1st ndd chars is shifted*/
                       /* to the top of the array.*/           /*a*/
}/*EP*/
```

The analysis on the positional notation is as follows: *str* points at an address, not at an array. To put it another way, the value of *str* is the address of a pointer. The local pointer *pstr* is assigned this value in line *a*. In turn, it then points to a char, specifically, it points to the first char of *buf*, the variable pointed to by *str* with double indirection. This is equivalent to setting *pstr* equal to the pointer to *buf*. As *pstr* travels down the array, the array is copied to *dsn*, char by char. When *bgn* exceeds *ndd* (7 in our example), the loop terminates, leaving *pstr* pointing to the 8th element of the array; i.e., *buf*[7]. The final statement, line *a*, assigns the address of this char to the pointer whose address is the value of *str*. This attachment is permanent.

This is consistent with C's method of sending args by value. What was sent was a copy of the address of *pbuf*. But a copy of a value that is an address is an address. In this case, it is the address of a pointer. So when the copy of the address of the pointer is accessed, the change in contents at that address affects the actual pointer. The change in pointer value is permanent.

3.8. SUMMARY

How to effect permanent changes in a string used as a function arg:

- To change a single character within an array, send its address as function arg. This will allow a permanent change to be made in the character resident at that location.

- To change the contents of a sequence of chars within an array, reference them through the address of the first element of the sequence or through a pointer variable that is assigned the address of the first element of the sequence. The other characters of the sequence are accessed using pointer arithmetic.

- To delete the first characters of a string permanently, i.e., to affect the starting address of the text, it is efficient to work with its pointer's address. The value assigned to the pointer indirectly through the PTRADR becomes the new starting address of the string. When the string is system-stored, we don't know (or care) where the string is. But we need to reallocate space for the revised text and return the address of this space to where the pointer resides in memory; this also is facilitated by working through the address of the pointer to the sequestered string.

What these statements amount to can be stated as a single Rule of Thumb. If char, char array, pointer-to-char and pointer-to-pointer-to-char represent a logical hierarchy, then:

**To effect a permanent change in the variable under examination
go up one level in the hierarchy.**

To make local changes in the text, without changing the place in memory where it resides, work with the text or a pointer to the text. But to change a text permanently, work through its pointer's address.

We started with a small bag of tricks. Save a string in a preset buffer. This buffer can be local or global. It may need a separate pointer to act as its representative in processing or the array's name may suffice. Or save a string dynamically. The pointer to where it is in memory can be local or global. Strings can be copied from dynamic storage areas to preset storage areas, and visa versa. Pointers can be set and reset to point to different parts of the text. Pointers themselves have addresses, which provide alternative indirect access to the string. The repertoire is small. But variations in other conditions and task requirements guarantee that decision-making will often not be easy. When several choices are possible, the programmer determines which solution is best for a given situation based on the types of string shapings and substring development that are required. He needs to recognize when the situation allows for personal preference; and when a favorite technique has troublesome side-effects. And always, he needs to consider the pragmatic limitation of memory size and stack space on most small machines. The permutations are such that the task confronting the programmer can be compared to that confronting the golfer. He has a limited number of sticks and a little ball to drop into a series of targets. Sounds simple.

CHAPTER 4

THE SETBREAK UTILITY AND BITMAPPING

4.1. INTRODUCTION

This chapter deals with the re-creation of the *setbreak*, a built-in facility provided by the Sail language to simplify string processing. Each call to the setbreak function constructs an individual and complete setbreak table.

A table controls the traffic of characters between disk file and memory as well as the manipulation of a string already in memory. For incoming strings, the setbreak utility regiments what is let into the string in the first place. For strings in memory, it provides a simple way to state detailed rules on how to transfer or copy the whole or a part of the string to a daughter string. It is a general purpose facilitator in the reconstruction of strings. Tables can be customized to chop strings at precise locations; to shrink them by forcing specific omissions; to expand them by halting the stream to enable the pooling of substrings with fixed text; and to concatenate them by aiding the merging of strings previously shaped or structured by the same or by other setbreak tables.

In a sense, a setbreak table can be regarded as a very complex but very concise switch or case statement that governs the character content of a string that passes through its control.

Each setbreak table embodies a particular and specific set of string processing instructions. In one compact statement, a setbreak table:

- references characters by type (e.g., as digits or punctuation marks) or by idiosyncratic clustering

- compresses a mass of instructions on how to handle data entry, character by character

- stops entry at any of a specified list of Break characters

- refuses entry to any of a specified list of Omit characters

- issues instructions on how to dispose of the character that halts data entry; i.e., include it or exclude it from the evolving string

- is capable of changing the case of characters allowed entry

- provides a simple means of identifying itself so these manipulations may be carried out from within other functions.

This chapter has several purposes.

First: it explains the setbreak table, which, added to the programmer's repertoire, should gain him considerable flexibility in processing strings.

Second: it illustrates a data structure, twinned matrices, that can handle the infra-structure of the setbreak table.

Third: it provides a case study of how to use bitmapping in string processing.

Fourth: it considers the general problem of conflicting rules—how to assign priorities and to customize a utility.

Fifth: it presents specific code and functions to implement the setbreak table.

Sixth: it contrasts the setbreak concept with some C library string manipulating functions.

Because they represent essential steps in string processing, two major functions dependent on the setbreak facility—*psin*() for bringing strings in from file and *pspsscan*() for disarticulating a string already in memory—are listed in this chapter (see Section 4.11) as well as in LISTINGS\include\comset.c.

The programmer [1] uses a function appropriately called *setbreak*() to construct an individual setbreak table. A large number of unique tables can be constructed, each having a precise effect on strings under its jurisdiction. Once written, the same setbreak table can be used by procedures that manipulate a string of chars streaming in from a database on disk and by procedures that operate on strings already stored in memory. A setbreak table gives these procedures the capability of stopping at particular chars rather than at fixed intervals or by position, the methods used by most lop, copy or substringing procedures. The setbreak facility frees the programmer from the need to refer to ordinal positions within a string in

---

[1] For Sailors: The implementation of setbreak tables in C requires some reformulation consequent on the differences between C and Sail. First, the string is not a primitive type in C. So at a minimum, additional information is needed to deal with the revised char array; specifically, is it to be dynamically stored or is it preset? Second, arrays in Sail may begin at any value, not just at array element zero, so Sail could provide a set of pre-formed numbered tables, without interfering with how the Sail programmer identified his tables within a specific program. To prevent conflict between setbreak tables required by some TXT utilities and those used by programmers, in the current version table identifiers are always variables. One of the tasks performed by *setbreak*() is to give the table the value of an empty BitColumn. Modes C and L are not in Sail. On the other hand, Sail's line number disposition modes—P, N, L, E and D—are not supported.

defining operations that determine the fate of the individual chars in the character stream during string construction or restructuring.

Storage for multiple setbreak tables has been implemented as sister bitmapped matrices, one for characters to be included, the other for characters to be omitted. A single table occupies the same BitColumn in each matrix. By means of one's and zero's, a BitColumn explicitly maps the disposition of all the ASCII characters when its associated table is in force. One of these columns declares which characters halt the character stream, the other of which declares which characters are specifically disqualified from migrating to the new file or string. Together they instruct functions that call *setbreak*() directly or indirectly in what to do with each and every ASCII char when that particular table is in control of processing the string.

4.2.   A PRELIMINARY EXAMPLE

The characteristics of a table are completely determined by the directives contained in the four args of the *setbreak*() statement that creates the table.

setbreak() is prototyped as:

extern void setbreak(BITMAP *ptbl, STRING BreakChars, STRING OmitChars, STRING options);

It has four arguments:

Arg 1:   a pointer to an unsigned int or long (whichever is 32 bits for the particular machine in use) variable that serves to reference the table name in other functions. BITMAP is typedef'ed as int or long, depending on int size on the particular machine.

Arg 2:   a pointer to a string variable or a string literal that holds the characters that compose the BreakChars list. Any and all these characters stop data entry and string examination.

Arg 3:   a pointer to a string variable or a string literal that contains the characters that constitute the OmitChars list. These characters are not allowed into the entry string and/or daughter string. A member of OmitChars does not halt data entry or string examination, unless it is also on the BreakChars list.

Arg 4:   a pointer to a string variable that lists various logic, case, BreakChars and OmitChars options.

As example:

```
#define ALLVOWELS "aeiouAEIOU"
BITMAP Tcommonpunc = 0;
setbreak(&Tcommonpunc, ",.;", ALLVOWELS, "ua");
```

would establish a setbreak table called *Tcommonpunc*. The table will stop the movement or the processing of a string when a function using the setbreak table encounters either a comma, a period or a semicolon (arg 2). The table directs the function to omit all vowels from the receiving buffer or the daughter string (arg 3). and to change the entry text to upper case (the **u** option in arg 4). The actual BreakChar is to be appended to the resultant string (the **a** option in arg 4).

As a preliminary example[2], we illustrate how a function we call *inputchars*() might use the setbreak table to control data entry from a file. The setbreak table, *Tcommonpunc*, is written outside *inputchars*() for two reasons. First, although it is not critical in this small example, in a realistic program the table could be shared with other functions called in *main*(). The second and more important reason is that input functions are characteristically used in a loop to bring in database records or individual strings one at a time. Were *Tcommonpunc* resident within *inputchars*(), it would be demolished and reconstructed each time *inputchars*() was called, thus adding avoidable processing time.

inputchars() opens a file and calls *psin*() to handle the traffic flow from the file to an array in memory, *dsn* in this example. *psin*() streams chars into memory. It can be made to either overwrite the current text in the buffer or append to it. (See examples in Section 4.7.)

psin() is an actual function that resides in *comset.c*. Its code is reproduced in Section 4.11.1. It is prototyped as:

STRING psin(FILE *ifptr,BITMAP tbl, int *pbrk, int lim, STRING pdsn);

Arg 1:   The source of the data is an opened ASCII file that is referenced by the pointer-to-FILE that was uniquely linked to it when the file was opened. (See Section 1.2.4.) In this example, *fin* is the pointer-to-FILE variable associated with the data file *dbnov* as long as the file remains open.

Arg 2:   A particular setbreak table. *Tcommonpunc*, the example table, is, as is usual, defined as a global variable.

Arg 3:   A pointer to the int that will eventually store the particular BreakChar at which the input flow stopped; in this case, it will be a comma, a semicolon or a period. (If information on the specific halting character is never needed, the *setbreak*() and related functions can be written omitting this arg.)

Arg 4:   The size of the buffer transmitted as Arg 5.

Arg 5:   A pointer to the char array that holds the resultant string.

In the example in Table 4.1, first the setbreak table *Tcommonpunc* is created in *main*(). Then a string is read in from *dbnov* to a preset array called *dsn*. After processing, the table is cleared using *relbreak*(). Note that the only setbreak functions directly accessible to the

---

2   Other examples, illustrating the setbreak and comparing it to some C string library functions, are to be found in Sections 4.6 and 4.7.

programmer are *setbreak*(), *relbreak*() and *DULcase*(). They and their supporting procedures reside in *comset.c*.

The input stream: **This will write a phone book.**
The text in dsn: **THS WLL WRT PHN BK.**

Layout of inputchars() in context:

```
#include "DEFINE.H"      /*File of macro definitions.*/
#include "GLOBALS.H" /*File declaring global variables.*/
#include "COMLIB.H"     /*File declaring string utilities.*/
#include "COMSET.H"     /*File declaring setbreak functions.*/

BITMAP Tcommonpunc = 0L;
#define ALLVOWELS "AEIOUaeiou"

extern int       main(void);
extern void      inputchars(void);

void inputchars()
    {
    int        brk = 0;
    FILE       *fin = read1("dbnov");
    char       dsn[LRGSZE] = {SNUL};

    psin(fin, Tcommonpunc, &brk, LRGSZE, dsn);
    }

main()
    {
    setbreak(&Tcommonpunc, ",.;", ALLVOWELS, "ua");
    inputchars();
    relbreak(&Tcommonpunc);
    return(0);
    }
```

Table 4.1.   Layout of a program that selectively brings in chars
             from disk to memory.

4.3. THE SETBREAK ARGS

4.3.1. SETBREAK ARG 1: THE TABLE IDENTIFIER

The first arg in the *setbreak*() function is a pointer to a setbreak table, i.e., the first arg is the
address of an integer variable such as *tbl20* or *Tdelnoise* or whatever. The name of the table

is a global or (rarely) a local 32-bit int and is chosen by the programmer. Its value is assigned by *setbreak*().

The setbreak function finds the first empty BitColumn in *bChar*, the matrix storing the information on which characters halt entry. The corresponding BitColumn in *oChar*, the matrix that stores information on what characters to omit is simultaneously reserved for this table. All the information supplied by the setbreak statement is coded into these two BitColumns. The integer variable pointed to by arg 1 (i.e., the table name) is assigned the BitColumn number.

A table name should be initialized to zero before it is used as an arg in *setbreak*(). Otherwise, if the variable has by chance the value of an already preset table or if the programmer absentmindedly uses the same name for more than one table, the existing table will be deleted. The program's initial reaction depends on a variable called *barf*, a short int defined in a file of global variables (*globals.c* in this book) and given a default value of FALSE. If *barf* is set to TRUE, the program will notify the programmer whenever he is about to delete an existing table before it overwrites the BitColumn. If *barf* is set to FALSE, the program overwrites the table without alerting the programmer. It is useful to turn *barf on* when debugging a program, even if it is turned off after the program is permanently compiled.

A table can be released by using *relbreak*(), a function whose single arg is a pointer to the same table identifier as that used in *setbreak*(). If a table is released, the table is cleared out and the name may be reused for a differently structured setbreak table without arousing the barf alert.

4.3.2. SETBREAK ARG 2: THE BREAKCHARS LIST

The second argument is a string comprising the list of BreakChar characters; for example, **aAbC** means that the BreakChars are a lower and upper case **a**, a lower case **b** and an upper case **c**. If the fourth arg contains the **I** option (for 'Include'), then the program will stop input whenever an **a, A, b** or **c** is encountered. **I** is the default, so it does not need to be written into the fourth arg. If an option in arg 4 is **X** (for 'eXclude'), then the program will break on any char except those listed in the arg 2; in:

setbreak(&TXvowel, ALLVOWELS, "", "x");

the character stream would stop on any character that was NOT a vowel.

When a BreakChar is trapped, its disposition is determined by the SAR option of arg 4, which informs the program to forget about the BreakChar (**S** for skip) or to append it to the characters already in the buffer (**A** for append) or to return it to the data source (**R** for return), so that it is the first char in line in the next cycle.

There need not be a BreakChars string. An empty set would mean that all chars are to be accepted into the buffer. The empty set is written "", with no space between the quotes. " " is interpreted as the space char and a procedure using that setbreak table would break when it encountered a space. We might expect NULL to be acceptable as empty set indicator, but its use often produces peculiar effects—the interaction of bit manipulation and NULL makes for unpredictable results with some compilers.

As said, the information on which characters are BreakChars for the different setbreak tables is stored in *bChar*, a matrix that is 132 rows long and $32*WD^3$ BitColumns wide. Each row has the information about a single ASCII char. Each BitColumn has the bit pattern for a single table. If there is a 1 in Row 121, BitColumn 75, this would mean that **y** (decimal ASCII 121) is a BreakChar in the table stored by the program in BitColumn 75.

4.3.3. SETBREAK ARG 3: THE OMITCHARS LIST

The program will omit from the stream of chars allowed into the working area the list of chars of the third arg, if the fourth arg option is **O** (for 'Omit'). **O** is the default and does not need to be explicitly written into Arg 4. If a fourth arg option is **C** (for 'exClude'), the program will omit every char except those listed in the third arg. Thus:

(1) setbreak(&TXvowel, "\n", ALLVOWELS, "o");
(2) setbreak(&TXvowel, "\n", ALLVOWELS, "c");

(1) would omit all vowels, stopping data entry at the end of a line. (2) would only allow in vowels, stopping data entry at the end of a line.

A pair of double quote marks, **""**, indicates that there are no characters that are to be left out of the buffer collecting the incoming characters. **" "** can not be used, because the space would mean that spaces are to be omitted. As with the BreakChars list, it is not a good idea to use NULL to indicate the empty set.

If a character is both a BreakChar and an OmitChar (i.e., it appears in both the second and third args), the program will both erase the OmitChar (i.e., not allow it into the collecting buffer) and stop data entry. The rules of precedence are articulated in Section 4.4.1.

4.3.4. SETBREAK ARG 4: THE OPTIONS LIST

The options are set by the fourth arg in the setbreak function. These determine BreakChar disposal, change case and reverse the meaning of the second and/or third args. Only one option can be selected from each group. If no option from the group is explicitly written, the default option rules. If several options from a single group are requested, the program uses the last one.

The option groups are listed in Table 4.2.

------

3 The width of a matrix is the number of WD's allocated by the user for the matrix, where each unit is 32 bits wide.

```
GROUP 1 = BreakChar specification
    "I" =    Include any char listed in arg 2. DEFAULT.
    "X" =    EXclude any char listed in arg 2. Break on all other chars.

GROUP 2 = OmitChar specification
    "O" =    Omit any char listed in arg 3. DEFAULT.
    "C" =    ExClude any char not listed in arg 3.

GROUP 3 = Case conversion specification
    "D" =    Do not change case for (a-z) OR (A-Z). DEFAULT.
    "U" =    Convert all alphabet letters to upper case: (a-z) to (A-Z)
    "L" =    Convert all alphabet letters to lower case: (A-Z) to (a-z).

GROUP 4 = BreakChar disposition
    "S" =    Skip the BreakChar. Throw away the BreakChar. DEFAULT.
    "A" =    Append the BreakChar to the end of the string collected in the buffer.
    "R" =    Return the BreakChar with ungetc(c,ifptr). It will start the next input.
```

Table 4.2.   List of setbreak options.

Option letters may be in any order and in either case. **SUOX** is the same as **xous**. If a meaningless letter is in the options list, it is ignored. If arg 4 is empty, (i.e., ""), the defaults will be operative.

An arg 4 string reading **IOUS** would tell the program to include all the chars listed in the second arg, omit all the chars listed in arg 3, convert all the accepted chars to upper case before storing them in the buffer and throw away the char that was the actual BreakChar.

A fourth arg string reading **cdr** would tell the program to omit all chars except all those listed in the third arg, leave case unchanged and return the char that was the actual BreakChar to the database file.

The *setbreak*() function handles a good many tasks in string shaping all at one time. Once the concept is mastered, it is not difficult to write a setbreak function that expresses what you wish done.

Just remember:

- ALWAYS set the table identifier to zero just before writing a setbreak function statement. Otherwise, by chance, the variable might contain the value of another table, which would cause the program to believe the new name is already in use. (A table of the same name may have been assigned in another function, and not cleared.) This would cause the program to destroy the resident table and install the new one in its stead.

- If the BreakChars string is empty, write "" for the empty string, not NULL and not " ". An arg of " " is interpreted as the space char. Similarly, if the OmitChars string is empty, write arg 3 as "", not NULL and not " ".

- ALWAYS do a *relbreak*() promptly on the table name when the setbreak table is no longer needed for more inputs or scans. This will free space for another table. Like a dynamic variable, the table does not disappear when it is no longer accessible.

4.4.   PRIORITIES IN THE SEQUENCE OF OPERATIONS GOVERNED BY SETBREAK

The setbreak facility can be considered as a collection of string filters that operate in a context-dependent manner to perform almost any conceivable characterwise operation on the stream of characters flowing within or into or out of memory. This section will examine some of the interactions that can occur among the setbreak arguments.

4.4.1.   INTERACTIONS AMONG THE SETBREAK ARGS

A character may be designated in many ways. The char **x** may be called as itself or as a consonant or as not-a-vowel or as one of the group of chars greater than octal ASCII 127, and so forth. Hence, it is not surprising, as in any complex function, that a character with several memberships may simultaneously appear on both the BreakChars and OmitChars lists and, in addition, say, be subject to the change-to-upper-case option. Consequently, functions employing a setbreak table need an explicit and uniform set of priorities on what operation(s) take precedence when a character appears on more than one list.

The particular rules described next apply to the package of TXT input and scan utilities resident in *comset.c* and to functions that expand or customize these utilities. They are reasonably consonant with the Sail setbreak rules.

If a char is a BreakChar but not an OmitChar, it is skipped, appended or returned to the input file, depending on the SAR option. But if a char appears on both the BreakChars list and the OmitChars list, the OmitChar instruction overrides the SAR instructions on what to do with a BreakChar; i.e., instructions to erase it, to append it or to return it to its file of origin are ignored. The character is immediately eliminated and the stream stopped.

Case is handled last. The rationale is this: suppose only lower case characters are on the BreakChars list and the options string instructs the program to change characters to upper case. Obviously, if case is changed early, the program would not know it had trapped a BreakChar. It would allow the data stream to continue. A similar logic applies to a character that is on the OmitChars list and is to have a case change. Again, if case is changed early, a lower case character that should be eliminated would, instead, be sent out to the receiving buffer in upper case. (As things stand, if a lower case char is to be eliminated, any appearance in the database of that character in upper case would clearly indicate that the char was upper case in the original database; it was not changed by *setbreak*().)

The scan and input programs used in this book use this general set of rules when a character is a BreakChar and/or OmitChar and/or a case change is requested: bring in a character in whatever case it is written. Then

- If this character is both a BreakChar and an OmitChar, don't send it to the output buffer. Throw it away. Stop character entry.

- If this character is both a BreakChar and an OmitChar and is to have a case change, don't change its case and don't send it to the output buffer. Throw it away. Stop character entry.

- If this character is a BreakChar and not an OmitChar but is to have a case change, then: (1) for the Return condition, return the character to the input string in its original case; (2) for the Skip condition, throw it away; (3) for the Append condition, change case and send it to the output string. Stop character entry.

Other sequences responsive to other priorities are obviously possible. *psin*() could be revised, depending on what the programmer might wish to emphasize. Examples are:

- Treat the entering BreakChar according to the SAR option. For the **A** option, make the requisite case change and append it to daughter string. Ignore the OmitList.

- Treat the entering BreakChar according to the SAR option, but ignore case change. Ignore the OmitList.

- Bring in a char and first change its case if the DUL calls for a case change. Then check the char to see whether it is a BreakChar. Then check whether it is an OmitChar. If it is not an OmitChar but is a BreakChar, treat the BreakChar according to the SAR option.

- Check whether the entering char is an OmitChar. If so, delete it, ignoring whether it is a BreakChar and ignoring the DUL and SAR options. Continue to the next incoming char.

Table 4.4 describes in pseudo-language the segment of the *psin*() function that deals with transmitting a single char from a database file to a buffer in memory. It takes into account that a char may be an OmitChar and also a BreakChar and also require case change. Interactions are handled in accordance with the setbreak rules just described. If the char is both a BreakChar and an Omitchar, the program will stop data entry, but it will ignore instructions on case change and the disposition of the break char.

4.4.2. HANDLING THE SAR OPTION

The Skip and Append modes are straight-forward. Rmode, where the BreakChar is returned to the input buffer and becomes the first char the next time out, is difficult to implement in a useful fashion, because the program could go into an infinite loop, beginning with the second input string.

```
if char is an OmitChar                        /*Level 1:*/
   {
   if char is a BreakChar                     /*Level 2:*/
         break the input stream;
   else if char is not a BreakChar            /*Level 2:*/
         fetch next char;
   }
else if char is not an OmitChar               /*Level 1:*/
   {
   if char is a BreakChar                     /*Level 2:*/
      {
      if S Condition (the BreakChar is not admitted to the receiving buffer)
            break the input stream;
      else if A condition (the BreakChar is appended to the string)
            {
            change case if a L or U condition is TRUE;
            add char to receiving buffer;
            break the input stream;
            }
      else if R condition (the BreakChar is returned to the input)
            {
            return char to input file without changing case;
            break the input stream;
            }
      }
   else if char is not a BreakChar            /*Level 2:*/
      {
      change case if L or U condition is TRUE;
      add char to receiving buffer;
      fetch next char;
      }
   }
```

Table 4.4.   The way the program decides if a char may enter memory.

To counteract this, the first versions of the scan and input functions were written in an officious fashion. All TXT program establish a struct of type in_stat when a read file is first opened to monitor the characteristics of the text stream; i.e., the members of the struct collect statistics, whenever the file is used: how many chars are input, how many are omitted, and so forth. An additional member, *Rsw*, was added to this struct. *Rsw* switched ON whenever a char was returned to the input file. The next time through the loop, the char was accepted as an ordinary char and was sent to the receiving buffer. The Rsw was switched OFF. The stream continued until stopped by another BreakChar.

in_stat doesn't work on strings already in memory, so a local switch was installed for scanning strings, using this rule: a Rmode BreakChar that was also the first char of the string being scanned was treated as an ordinary char, not as a reserved char. If this char occurred later in the same string, it was a BreakChar that was reserved, so that in the scan after that, it was again the first char and again it became an ordinary char.

These measures prevented an infinite loop, but ran into usage problems. Ordinarily, after a Rmode BreakChar is returned to the data file or buffer, there is some follow-up text processing controlled by a second setbreak table, which might well pull in the reserved BreakChar together with other chars until stopped by the new directive. The returned BreakChar may in fact no longer be in the database or in the mother string by the time the setbreak table keyed to the Rmode BreakChar is again in control.

In the current version, a Return directive returns the BreakChar to the input file or string. It is left to the user to change the returned BreakChar somehow or move past it or remove it some other way before the next time the source file or string is controlled by the setbreak table with the Return directive. As an actual example, Rmode is shown as used in *intscan*(), a function that extracts decimal integer values from text. *intscan*() is prototyped as

int intscan(STRING s, int *pbrk);

where *s* is a pointer to the string examined by *intscan*() and *pbrk* is a pointer to the eventual BreakChar. This BreakChar value is returned by *intscan*().

The code starting in line *a* below is the loop in *intscan*() that marches past non-digit text until it gets to the start of what might be an integer value. The examined text is deleted from the string. Scanning stops at a significant character; i.e., a digit or a plus sign or a minus sign. We use Return mode so that the character that halts processing can be returned to the start of what's left of the string. It become the first character in the modified string, ready for the next step in processing. If we were to use Skip mode, the plus, minus or digit would be lost to future processing. If we were to use Append mode, we would be attaching the character to the end of text that is trashed.

There are three possibilities for what the BreakChar might be:

- The BreakChar is a digit. We are dealing with a single digit or, more likely, the first digit of the set of digits that constitute the text representation of an integer value. The **while (TRUE)** loop terminates and the program goes immediately to the next process- ing step, where it deals with the discovered integer.

- The BreakChar is a + or -. The cursor moves past the BreakChar to examine the next character in the string. If this next character is a digit, then again, as in the first case, the while() loop can be terminated.

- The + or - is part of unwanted letter text. The loop continues, searching for the next candidate integer. In pseudo-language, this is the game plan, as the next char in the string is scanned:

```
while (TRUE)
    {
    if (sign or digit)
        {
        if (digit)
            break;
```

```
        if (sign && (nextchar == digit))
            break;
        else continue;
        }
    }
```

The Return BreakChar mode allows us to handle these possible conditions efficiently. In *intscan*(), it is imbedded in the next table, which directs the program to move past white space or ordinary text, both of which are to be junked, and to stop at a digit or + or -. The examined portion of the string is erased in *pspsscan*() and the BreakChar becomes the first character in the modified string.

```
    setbreak(&_zzt0,"0123456789+-","\n","IR");

    while (*s)            /*This begins the loop under discussion.*/
        {                                                          /*a*/
        *pbrk = 0;        /*Initializing the BreakChar.*/
```

/*This next line of code searches a string. It will break on a digit or plus sign or minus sign. It destroys the part of the string that has been examined and uses the BreakChar as the start of what remains of the string. pbrk is pointer to the BreakChar.*/

```
        ptemp = pspsscan⁴(&s, _zzt0, pbrk, MEDSZE, nbrstr);
        if (ITDIGIT(*pbrk) || *pbrk == '-' || *pbrk == '+')         /*b*/
            {
```

/*Next, if BreakChar is not a plus or minus, it must be the start of an integer. So break.*/

```
            if (! (*pbrk == '+' || *pbrk == '-') )
                break;
```

/*If the program gets this far, then the BreakChar must be a + or -. s has to be incremented, because if we don't move past the plus or minus BreakChar, the program will keep breaking on +/- in an unending loop.*/

```
            s++;
```

/*Next we check the char after the +/-. If it is a digit, we can terminate the while() loop and go on to the next processing step. If not, the program will recycle, bringing in the next part of the string up to a + or - or digit.*/

```
            if ( ITDIGIT(*s) )
                break;
            }
        }
```

---

4 As discussed in the last paragraph of Section 2.5.3.2, if processing shortens the string and it is not known whether the string is dynamic or predefined, assume it to be preset and modify the original by sliding the modified string to the beginning of the original string. If the string is dynamic, it can still be freed by the system.

Usage for *intscan()*:

```
STRING    pstr = "Look--i.e., scan--for the 1st number, 23, + the 2nd, -54.9";

void intuse(void)
    {
    int    dbrk = 0;
    int    i = 0;
    int    numb[SZE⁵(50)] = {0};

    for (i = 1; *pstr; i++)
        {
        numb[i] = intscan(pstr, &dbrk);
        printf("\nNumber %d = %d.", i, numb[i]);
            /*Number 1 = 1.
            Number 2 = 23.
            Number 3 = 2.
            Number 4 = -54.      /*intscan is working properly. It doesn't deal */
            Number 5 = 9.*/      /* with non-integer numbers. Floatscan() does.*/
        }
    }
```

4.5. WHERE SETBREAK TABLES SHOULD BE INSTALLED

The *bChar* and *oChar* matrices are permanent for the life of the program, no matter where or when a specific setbreak table is written. They are global static variables (in TXT, they reside in *comset.c*) and accessible to functions such as *setbreak()*, which creates a table, and *relbreak()*, which deletes an existing table. Hence, once a table is constructed, it remains in effect unless NULL'ed or overwritten. So it is usually more practical to construct all the tables that will be needed for the whole program just once at the beginning of *main()*.

With similar reasoning, table names, the only way of accessing the tables, should be defined as global variables. If the tables are not needed by included utility files, they can be defined at the top of the main file (i.e., the file containing *main()*). If there are many setbreak tables scattered in many files, whose routines are active the life of the program, both the names and setbreak statements can be gathered into a single utility file. To ensure that the tables are accessible to all functions in all files while the program is running, a sister file of extern declarations is then made known to all the program modules by way of include statements.

---

5 **SZE(x)** is #define'd as **x**. It is a convenience in finding and modifying values in the program. See Section 2.2.2.1.

For example:

file1.c

```
BITMAP        T1 = 0;
BITMAP        T2 = 0;
BITMAP        T3 = 0;

void DoSetbreaks(void)
      {
      setbreak(&T1,..............);
      setbreak(&T2,..............);
      setbreak(&T3,..............);
      }
```

file1.h

```
extern     BITMAP T1;
extern     BITMAP T2;
extern     BITMAP T3;

extern     void  DoSetbreaks(void);
```

file2.c

```
include "file1.h"
```

main.c

```
include "file1.h"
include "file2.h"
......................
main()
      {
      DoSetbreaks();
      ......process input....
      relbreak(&T1);
      relbreak(&T2);
      relbreak(&T3);
      }
```

The exception to making a table name known to several or all files is if the table is used in a function that is called only once in the program; e.g., decoding some interactive material at the beginning of the program. Here the table space should be released once the procedure terminates, so that the space can be used by some other table.

The gray area is: if a particular route is followed, the table might be used by a procedure many times, but the route is not a likely one. In this case, it might be as simple to construct the table within a particular procedure, even though the *setbreak*() function will reconstruct the table each time the procedure is called. If the table is explicitly deleted with a *relbreak*() command before vacating the function, the table may be reconstructed the next time the function is entered in a different location. If the table is not deleted with a *relbreak*() command, the table is first deleted and then rewritten in the same location by the program, with or without notification, each time the function is entered. To destroy a table and then reconstruct it each time is time-consuming, but it does prevent a table that is unlikely to be used from holding on to valuable space. An alternative solution for writing tables for the unlikely path is to tuck the procedures that are used only when that particular path is traversed in a separate file. Setbreak table construction can be done in a single function within this separate file. For example:

file1.c

```
BITMAP   Tnovowels = 0;
BITMAP   Tparse = 0;
BOOL     Oddball = FALSE;

void DoUnlikelyTables(void)
    {
    setbreak(&Tnovowels,"","aeiouAEIOU","is");
    setbreak(&Tparse,"\40","","ia");
    }
```

file1.h

```
externBITMAPTnovowels, Tparse;
externvoidDoUnlikelyTables(void);
externBOOLOddball;
```

mainfile.c

```
include "file1.h"

void SetUpFct(options)
    {
    .........start complicated setup, which may trigger Oddball...
    if (Oddball == TRUE)
        DoUnlikelyTables();
    ........ continue to carry out tasks...
    }

main()
    {
    ...........
    SetUpFct(options);
    }
```

4.6. COMPARING THE SETBREAK UTILITY AND C STRING LIBRARY FUNCTIONS

To compare some library string functions and the setbreak utility, assume the text we will handle is read into a preset character array called *buf*. In these example we ignore I/O. We write text in *keep* and copy it to *buf* as needed.

 keep is defined as:

static STRING keep = "This\t\40\tis\40a\t\40\t\nrecord\40to\n\t\tcut\40and\40redo.";

We will use the program format shown in Table 4.5.

4.6.1. CLEANING TEXT. CHANGING DELIMITERS

The next program operates on an ASCII-delimited file. It does two jobs: it cleans each field of white space; and it changes field and record delimiters.

The second job is occasioned by the need to merge records sidewards from separate databases. It is used as a preprocessor when delimiters differ in the two databases. It is also used when adding a database with alien delimiters to a database repertoire with established delimiters.

The record is copied into *buf* for processing. Initially, the period is the record delimiter and the space is the field delimiter. The new record and field delimiters are **!** and **#**, respectively.

4.6.1.1.   Using strtok().

strtok() is prototyped as:

STRING = strtok(STRING str, const STRING set);

strtok() examines the string that is its first arg. It stops at any of the characters in the set that is its second arg, which, in setbreak terminology, is skipped. *strtok* returns a pointer to the beginning of the substring terminated by the break character. If this substring has no content, *strtok* continues until it has a substring to present. It returns NULL when it runs out of string.

If *strtok*() is run in a loop as in line *a* of *callingfct*() below, the elements of the pointer array *field* keep track of where the articulated substrings begin within the string.

```
void callingfct(void)
     {
     stcpy(keep,buf);
     pbuf = buf;
     for (i = 0; field[i] = (strtok(pbuf,"\40.\t\n")); i++)        /*a*/
          pbuf = NULL;              /*Necessary for strtok to work properly.*/   /*b*/
     PS(buf);                       /*PrintProduct: buf = [This]*/               /*c*/
```

```
num = i;
for (i = 0; i < num; i++)        /*The first 4 substrings are:*/              /*d*/
    PS(field[i]);                /*    field[i] = [This]
                                      field[i] = [is]
                                      field[i] = [a]
                                      field[i] = [record]*/

}
```

```
#include <\INCLUDE\STRING.H>
#include "DEFINE.H"
#include "COMLIB.H"
#include "COMSET.H"

static char  buf[TTYSZE] = {SNUL};   /*A preset array where the mother string resides.*/
static int    brk = 0;               /*brk will have the value of the halting char.*/
static STRING  field[20] = {NULL};   /*An array of pointers-to-char.*/
static int       i = 0;
static int       num = 0;
static STRING  pbuf = buf;
static STRING  set = NULL;           /*This will point to a user-selected set of characters.*/

static BITMAP  Tstop = 0;            /*Generic name for a setbreak table.*/

static STRING  keep = "....";        /*Some suitable illustration text.*/

STRING calledfct() {}                /*Any specialized function called by callingfct().*/

void callingfct(void) { }

main()
   {
   setbreak(&Tname, BreakChars, OmitChars, Options);   /*The format of a setbreak
table.*/
   callingfct();
   }
```

Table 4.5.   Test program for comparing ways of processing strings.

When the loop terminates (in line *c*), only the first token is directly accessible in the mother string, and the rest of the string appears erased. This is because, after the first time through the loop, the advancing pointer that will constitute the first arg in the next cycle (*pbuf* in line *b*) must, by *strtok*() syntax, first be NULL'ed.

The substrings can be treated as daughter strings only if the contents of the character buffer remain unchanged. They can be displayed separately, as in line *d*, but they do NOT exist independently of the character buffer where the original string is housed. Reconstructing the record with new delimiters by simple concatenation of the fields is not possible, because we would overwrite whatever was in the buffer, and hence we would overwrite where the separate words originally began. To preserve the words as separate entities, in this next version, we save them dynamically in line *a*. The record can then, beginning in line *c*, be reconstructed with different delimiters.

```
void callingfct(void)
    {
    stcpy(keep,buf);
    pbuf = buf;

    for (i = 0; p = strtok(pbuf,"\40.\t\n"); i++)  /*PART 1.*/
        {
        field[i] = dssave(p);                                        /*a*/
        pbuf = NULL;   /*Necessary for strtok to work properly.*/
        }
    num = i;
    for (i = 0; i < num; i++)
        PS(field[i]);                                                /*b*/
    buf[0] = SNUL;                        /*PART 2.*/
    for (i = 0; i < num-1; i++)                                      /*c*/
        {
        strcat(buf,field[i]);
        strcat(buf,"#");
        }
    strcat(buf,field[i]);   /*C library function, which adds arg to tail of arg 1.*/
    strcat(buf,"!");

    for (i = 0; i < num; i++)
        NULLIT(field[i]);
    PS(buf);                    /*PrintProduct: buf = [This#is#a#record#to#cut#and#redo!]
    }
```

4.6.1.2.   Using A Setbreak Table.

pspsscan() copies a preset string into another preset string until a halt character is found. The portion of the original string that was copied is deleted and the string is rewritten. The code for *pspsscan*() is presented in Section 4.11.2.

pspsscan() is prototyped as:

extern STRING pspsscan(PTRADR pstr, BITMAP tbl, int *pbrk, int lim, STRING dsn);

The specific setbreak table used by *pspsscan*() in this example is written in *main*(); see Table 4.5. It is:

setbreak(&Tstop, "\40.", "\40\n.\t", "is");

Tstop instructs *pspsscan*() that the stream is to be stopped at a space or a period. And the contents of the third arg of *Tstop*, which include the space and the period, are to be omitted from the daughter substring. Whenever *pspsscan*() encounters a BreakChar, it saves the accepted stream of characters, if the array is not empty. Part 2 of the program—changing field and record delimiters—can be done as shown in the previous *callingfct*(). And the results are exactly the same.

```
void callingfct(void)
    {
    char temp[TTYSZE] = {SNUL};

    stcpy(keep,buf);
    pbuf = buf;
    for (i = 0; *pbuf; i++)
        {
        pspsscan(&pbuf,Tstop, &brk, TTYSZE, temp);
        if (*temp != SNUL)
            field[i] = dssave(temp);
        else i--;
        }
    num = i;
    for (i = 0; i < num; i++)
        PS(field[i]);       /*PrintProduct is the same as on line b above, using strtok.*/
    }
```

Suppose, however, that the original field delimiter was the NewLine—or any other character that would ensure that the field contained more than a single word. *Tstop* would becomes

setbreak(&Tstop,"\n.", "\n.\t","is");

which would clean the substring of the indicated characters before the function halts.

The results would be:

field[i] = [This is a]
field[i] = [record to]
field[i] = [cut and redo]

and

buf = [This is a #record to# cut and redo!]

The closest we could come to this with *strtok*() in one operation would be to use **"\n."** as the second arg. The words would then be the same in each field

buf = [This   is a #   record to#   cut and redo!]

It would take an additional directive to clean the fields of tabs.

4.6.2. DELETING BRACKETED TEXT

Commentaries are often interspersed in text inside of brackets. Annotations, on-line coding, hypertext hooks and temporary notes—gloss material—are kept as bracketed text, 'color-coded' by type of bracket. The task is to eliminate this gloss material from the string; i.e., to delete the bracketed text. In this version, the program can delete different types of brackets in any order in one excursion through the text. If, say, a left square bracket is found, all the text is removed through the right square bracket before the program resumes its search for another left bracket.

The global variables are the same as in Table 4.5. These are the test strings. Note that *keep1* has partially commingled {- and [-bracketed material. The program will find the [-bracketed text, delete the left { as part of the [-bracketed text, and hence will treat **iggle}** as ordinary text. Detecting these errors should be handled in preprocessing.

static STRING keep = "<OUT>Delete [the]bracket[ed string].";
static STRING keep1 = "<Out>Delete[ERROR{squ]iggle} [the]bracket[ed string].";

4.6.2.1. Using Setbreaks.

In this version, the program constructs a setbreak table, *Tstop* to stop at whatever brackets the user interactively specifies (See line *g* in *main()*). Arg 2 of the setbreak is a global buffer for temporary storage of whatever *ttyin()* takes in (see Section 2.3.1). *Tstop* itself becomes the second arg of a specialized function, *psremovebracket()*, that searches a preset array. Whenever a left bracket is found, the function constructs a setbreak table specific for halting at the corresponding right bracket. When the right bracket is found, the table is dismantled. If the end of the string has not been reached, the program recycles, constructing a new setbreak table if and when the same or another left bracket is found. The procedure destroys the original string.

/*PROCEDURE*/ STRING psremovebracket(PTRADR s, BITMAP Tbr)[6]
/*

        *s   - the address of the pointer to the source string.
        Tbr - setbreak table number.

RULE: If the left bracket is greater than or equal (in ASCII) to '<', then the right bracket is the char ASCII value plus 2. Otherwise the right bracket is ASCII value plus 1. A left bracket can be any ASCII char; '0' and '1' are a bracket pair. As are ':' and ';'.
*/

    {/*BPbracket*/
    int   lftbrk = 0,   /*Will store the left bracket or halt char.*/
        rtbrk = 0;   /*Will store the right bracket or halt char.*/
    char ibrack[HUGESZE] = {SNUL}; /*To store bracketed material temporarily.*/
    char obrack[HUGESZE] = {SNUL}; /*To store text outside brackets temporarily.*/
    STRING   pobrack = &obrack[0];

/*Setbreak table syntax requires a char array, not a char constant. The array, rightstr, which is needed in line c, is defined in the next line as a minimum-sized string to contain a single bracket symbol. Starting at line b, this single right bracket is determined following the rule that a right bracket is ASCII plus 2 more than its corresponding left bracket with a value of '<' or more. Otherwise, the right symbol is ASCII value 1 greater than its corresponding left symbol.*/

    char   rightstr[SZE(2)] = {SNUL};

---

6 A different version of this procedure is listed in LISTINGS\include\comlib.c as psremibracket(). psremibracket() returns notification if an error was found.

```
    BITMAP   Trtbr = 0;  /*The name of the break table for finding a right-side bracket.*/
    while (**s)
        {/*bracks*/
        lftbrk = rtbrk = 0;
```

/*Examining the next two lines, the next statement, line a, scans the string and halts if it encounters any of the left brackets listed by the user interactively in main(). All the text until the halt is to be kept; i.e., it is non-bracketed text. When pspsscan() halts, it appends this text to obrack. In the line that follows line a, the pointer to obrack is incremented by the size of the text that was just installed. The left-side pobrack now indicates where in obrack the program can append more text, if unbracketed text is encountered in the next cycle.*/

```
        ptemp = pspsscan(s, Tbr, &lftbrk,HUGESZE, pobrack);              /*a*/
        pobrack += stlen(pobrack); /*Left-side pobrack is in terminal SNUL position*/
        if (lftbrk != 0)                              /*of obrack.*/
            {/*FoundBracket*/
            CLRCHAR(i,rightstr,2);
            if (lftbrk >= '<')                                        /*b*/
                rightstr[0] = (char)(lftbrk + 2);  /*Turns char into string for arg2*/
                                                   /* in line d below.*/
            else rightstr[0] = (char)(lftbrk + 1);
            Trtbr = 0;
```

/* A left-side bracket chosen by the user has been found. Next Trtbr is constructed to find the corresponding right-side bracket.*/

```
            setbreak(&Trtbr,rightstr,"","is" );                       /*c*/
```

/*Once a left-side bracket is found in the text, the program will determine what the matching right bracket is and use that as the BreakChar in a table that will control pspsscan() in line d. If no corresponding right bracket is in the text (an error), the rest of the string is deleted.*/

/*ibrack is an array used to store the text inside the brackets. This text will be trashed, so any bracketed text overwrites whatever text is in ibrack. There is no need to append to the end of previously written text.*/

```
            pspsscan(s,Trtbr,&rtbrk,HUGESZE,ibrack); /*To store trash.*/ /*d*/
            relbreak(&Trtbr);      /*The setbreak table is trashed.*/
            }/*FoundBracket*/
        }/*bracks*/
    stcpy(obrack,*s);
    return(*s);
    }/*EPbracket*/


callingfct(void)
    {
    stcpy(keep,buf);
    pbuf = buf;
    psremovebracket(&pbuf,Tstop);                                      /*e*/
    PS(buf);/*PrintProduct for the line f example using keep[]: buf = [Delete bracket.]*/
    stcpy(keep1,buf);
    pbuf = buf;
```

```
        psremovebracket(&pbuf,Tstop);
        PS(buf);          /*PrintProduct for the line f example using keep1[]:*/
        }                 /* buf = [Deleteiggle} bracket.]*/

main(void)
        {/*BP*/
        printf("\nTO DELETE MATERIAL IN BRACKETS:\n"
        "\nType the set of left bracket(s) -- [(\n\n");
        ttyin("t");               /*In this example, we type: {[< */      /*f*/
        Tstop = 0;
        setbreak(&Tstop,ttystr,"", "is" );                                /*g*/
        callingfct();
        }/*EP*/
```

4.6.2.2.   Using Library Functions.

strpbrk() is an elaboration of *strchr*(), the library function that finds the first occurrence of a specified character in a string and returns its address. *strpbrk*() returns the address of any one of a set of characters that it first finds in the string. If none of the characters is present, it returns NULL. Associated with *strpbrk*() are *strcspn*() and *strspn*(). *strcspn*() returns the number of array elements examined before an element in the character set was found. Conversely *strspn*() returns how many elements were examined before an element not in the character set was found; it is the analog of the X mode in setbreak. Recall that size_t is an unsigned integer of a size set by the particular compiler/machine; it is usually an insigned int in DOS machines. Given *s*, a pointer to a character array, and *set*, a pointer to a read-only string, these functions are prototyped as:

```
STRING strchr(const STRING s, int c);        /*Returns address of 1st c in s or NULL.*/
STRING strpbrk(const STRING s, const STRING set);    /*Returns address of s[i], when
                            /*s[i] is first occurrence of any-char-of-set or NULL.*/
size_t strcspn(const STRING s, const STRING set);      /*Returns i when s[i] is first*/
                            /*occurrence of any char-of-set.*/
size_t strspn(const STRING s, const STRING set);  /*Returns i when s[i] is the first*/
                            /*occurrence of not-a-char-of-set.*/
```

Except for *strspn*(), these functions are used in the next program. The program also illustrates *strcat*(), *strcpy*() and *strncat*(). *strcat*() appends the string that is arg 2 to the tail of the string that is arg 1. *strcpy*() overwrites the string that is arg 1 with the string that is arg 2. *strncat*() appends n chars of s2 to the tail of s1. They all return s1. They are prototyped as:

```
STRING strcat(STRING s1, const STRING s2);
STRING strcpy(STRING s1, const STRING s2);
STRING strncat(STRING s1, const STRING s2, size_t n);
```

Not used is *strstr*(), which finds the first occurrence of the second arg in the first. It is similar to *stmfind*() in 3.2.4.2. Other useful functions not used in the program are *strlen(const STRING s1)*(), which counts the number of elements in s1 upto the NULL; *strncpy*(), which copies n chars of arg s2 to arg s1 and returns s1; *strcmp*(), which compares arg s1 to arg s2

ASCII element by ASCII element and returns < 0 if s1 is the lesser string, > 0 if s1 is the greater one and 0 if they are the same; and *strncmp*(), which compares up to n characters of two strings, again returning < 0, 0, or > 0.

They are prototyped as:

```
STRING strstr(const STRING s1, const STRING s2);
 size_t strlen(const STRING s1);
STRING strncpy(STRING s1, const STRING s2, size_t n);
STRING strcmp(const STRING s1, const STRING s2);
STRING strncmp(const STRING s1, const STRING s2, size_t n);
```

The same program format is used as with the setbreak format, except that *main* creates no setbreak table and *callingfct*() calls a different bracket-removing function. The C library file string.h must be included. And line *e* is written: **psremovebracket(&pbuf,"{[<");** The results are the same as with the setbreak-based function in Section 4.6.2.1.

```
/*PROCEDURE*/ STRING psremovebracket(PTRADR s, STRING set)
    {/*BPbracket*/
    int        lftbrk = 0,        /*Will store the left bracket or halt char*/
               rtbrk = 0;         /*Will store the right bracket or halt char*/
    int        i = 0;
    char leftstr[SZE(2)]; = {SNUL}
    char rightstr[SZE(2)]; = {SNUL}
    char obrack[HUGESZE] = {SNUL};   /*To store  text outside the brackets.*/
    STRING   p = NULL;

    while (**s)
        {/*bracks*/
        lftbrk = rtbrk = 0;
        if ((p = strpbrk(*s,set)) != NULL)     /*Finds a left bracket at p.*/
            {/*FoundBracket*/
            CLRCHAR(i,rightstr,2);
            CLRCHAR(i,leftstr,2);
            lftbrk = *p;
            leftstr[0] = (char) lftbrk;
            if (i = strcspn(*s,leftstr))   /*Determines if and how many chars there are*/
                {                          /* in *s before the left bracket.*/
                strncat(obrack,*s,i); /*Append the 1st part of *s up to the left /
                                      /* bracket in obrack.*/
                strcpy(*s,*s+i);      /*Copy string starting at the*/
                }                     /* left bracket to top of the array.*/
            if (lftbrk >= '<')
                rtbrk = lftbrk + 2; /*For grammatical reasons, copy char to a string.*/
            else
                rtbrk = lftbrk + 1;
            rightstr[0] = (char) (rtbrk);
            if (p = strchr(*s,rtbrk))         /*Check that there's a right bracket*/
                {                             /* before using its position.*/
                i = strcspn(*s,rightstr);     /*Find out how many chars further */
                                              /* the right bracket is.*/
```

```
                    strcpy(*s+0,*s+i+1); /*Write the string starting 1 char beyond*/
                    }                              /* the right bracket to top of the array.*/
            else                                   /*If there is no right bracket,*/
                    {
                    strcpy(*s+0,*s+i+1); /* pull the rest of *s to the top of the array.*/
                    break;
                    }
            }/*FoundBracket*/
        else
            {
            strcat(obrack,*s);            /*If there's no more bracketed text,*/
                                          /* concatenate whatever is left of the string.*/

            break;
            }
        }/*bracks*/
    strcpy(*s,obrack);
    return(*s);
    }/*EPbracket*/
```

4.7. EXAMPLES USING THE DIFFERENT SETBREAK OPTIONS

The next is a complete program illustrating various options: Smode, Amode, Rmode, Xmode and Cmode. The setbreak functions reside in *comset.c* as does *psin*(), which brings in characters from a file to a char array. *psin*() returns a pointer to the SNUL terminus of the character string in the array. Each example brings in a short strip of text and breaks it into strings in accordance with the operative setbreak table. Note that *psin*() can write the text starting on the terminal SNUL of the previous text.

```
#include "DEFINE.H"
#include "GLOBALS.H"
#include "COMLIB.H"
#include "COMSET.H"

extern void     init(STRING filename, BITMAP Tdummy);
extern int      main(void);

FILE       *ChanIn = NULL;      /*ChanIn, buf and pbuf are global variables,*/
                                        /* reused by the different examples.*/
char       buf[LRGSZE] = {SNUL};
STRING     pbuf = buf;
```

/*The next function, init, opens a new file and initializes the parameters to zero. ChanIn is reused each time, with different files. example is the dummy arg for a file name; Tdummy represents the setbreak table in charge.*/

```
void init(STRING example, BITMAP Tdummy)
    {
```

```
        ChanIn = fopen(example,"r");
        brk = 0;                /*brk is defined as an int in globals.c.*/
        buf[0] = SNUL;
        pbuf = buf;
        Tdummy = 0;
        }

main()
        {
        char            temp[SZE(100)];
        BITMAP          Tappend  =   0,      /*Initializing the setbreak tables.*/
                        Tretain  =   0,
                        Tmoveit  =   0,
                        Tskip    =   0;
```

/*EXAMPLE 1 Smode (skip BreakChar): The input text breaks at a hatchmark (\43), which is deleted. *psin()* returns a pointer to the SNUL terminus of the storage buffer. So *buf* need not be overwritten each loop. Instead, it collects the chopped pieces, loop by loop, as shown below by the text after **OUTPUT:**. After looping, the string is a copy of the original sentence without hatchmarks.*/

```
        printf("\n\nEXAMPLE 1\n\n");
        init("example1.db", Tskip);
        setbreak(&Tskip, "\43", "", "is");
        printf("INPUT: This #sentence #will #be #chopped #at #hatch #marks.\n");
        while (TRUE)
                {
```

/*Initially, pbuf is assigned to point to the top of buf. It returns a pointer to the terminal SNUL. The next time through the loop, this pointer to the terminal SNUL becomes the right pointer and indicates where in buf to put the text that is coming in from the file. After the text is laid down, the left pbuf points to the SNUL terminus of the newly placed string in buf. And so forth.*/

```
                pbuf = psin(ChanIn, Tskip, &brk,LRGSZE,pbuf);
                printf("OUTPUT: %s\n",buf);                           /*a*/
                if (brk == EOF )
                        break;
                }
        fclose(ChanIn);
```

/*EXAMPLE 1

```
INPUT:    This #sentence #will #be #chopped #at #hatch #marks
OUTPUT: This                 /*Each line is a separate printout of line a above.*/
OUTPUT: This sentence
OUTPUT: This sentence will
OUTPUT: This sentence will be
OUTPUT: This sentence will be chopped
OUTPUT: This sentence will be chopped at
OUTPUT: This sentence will be chopped at hatch
OUTPUT: This sentence will be chopped at hatch marks.
*/
```

/*EXAMPLE 2 Amode (append BreakChar): This differs from Example 1 in three ways: (1) The input strings are upper-cased and vowels are deleted; (2) The BreakChar (#) is appended to the end of each input string; and (3) *buf* doesn't collect the incoming strings but is overwritten each time at line a below. This is accomplished by using buf[0] as the 5th arg rather than a pointer to buf that is shifted in *psin*() each time to the SNUL terminus as in example 1.*/

```
printf("\n\nEXAMPLE 2\n\n");
init("example2.db",Tappend);
setbreak(&Tappend, "\43", ALLVOWELS, "iua");
printf("INPUT: This #sentence #will #be #chopped #at #hatch #marks.\n");
while (TRUE)
      {
      pbuf = psin(ChanIn,Tappend, &brk, LRGSZE,buf);              /*a*/
      printf("OUTPUT: %s\n",buf);
      /*...realistically, something would be done with the piece of text at this point.*/
      if (brk == EOF ) break;
      }
fclose(ChanIn);
```

/*EXAMPLE 2

INPUT: This #sentence #will #be #chopped #at #hatch #marks.
OUTPUT: THS #
OUTPUT: SNTNC #
OUTPUT: WLL #
OUTPUT: B #
OUTPUT: CHPPD #
OUTPUT: T #
OUTPUT: HTCH #
OUTPUT: MRKS.
*/

/*EXAMPLE 3 Rmode (retain BreakChar): Tretain breaks text intake at digits and retains the BreakChar digit to attach it to the beginning of the next input string. It also doesn't let the # into the daughter string. However, if we continued just to put the BreakChar back in the file and then stop data entry on it, we would be in an endless loop. Hence, the second table, *Tmoveit*, sees to it that the string breaks at /. For *Tmoveit*, digits are ordinary chars. Note that buf collects the pieces one after the other, just as in example 1. ALLDIGITS is #defined as: **#define ALLDIGITS "0123456789"**.*/

```
printf("\n\nEXAMPLE 3\n\n");
init("example3.db",Tretain);
setbreak(&Tretain, ALLDIGITS, "\43", "ir");
setbreak(&Tmoveit, "/","","is");
printf("INPUT:1/#This2/#sentence3/#will4/#be5/#chopped6/#at7/#digits.\n");
while (TRUE)
      {
      pbuf = psin(ChanIn, Tretain, &brk, LRGSZE, pbuf);
      pbuf = psin(ChanIn, Tmoveit, &brk, LRGSZE, pbuf);
      printf("OUTPUT: %s\n",buf);
      if (brk == EOF ) break;
```

```
        }
    fclose(ChanIn);
```

/*EXAMPLE 3

```
INPUT: 1/#This2/#sentence3/#will4/#be5/#chopped6/#at7/#digits.
OUTPUT: 1
OUTPUT: 1This2
OUTPUT: 1This2sentence3
OUTPUT: 1This2sentence3will4
OUTPUT: 1This2sentence3will4be5
OUTPUT: 1This2sentence3will4be5chopped6
OUTPUT: 1This2sentence3will4be5chopped6at7
OUTPUT: 1This2sentence3will4be5chopped6at7digits.
*/
```

/*EXAMPLE 4 Xmode (don't break on chars listed): This demonstrates Xmode, where the program breaks on any char except the ones listed in the BreakChar string, *temp*, which is a concatenation of letters and numbers. So it will break on hatchmarks and the period, which are skipped. It continuously overwrites the previous text in *buf.*/

```
    printf("\n\nEXAMPLE 4\n\n");
    init("example4.db",Tskip);
    relbreak(&Tskip);              /*When rewriting a table, release previous version.*/
```

/*The next two lines illustrate a way to create a multi-char setbreak function arg; i.e., ALLDIGITS and ALLLETTS are macros spelling out all the digits and all the alphabet letters, respectively. ALLDIGITS is copied into temp. ALLLETTS is then written to the tail of ALLDIGITS in temp.*/

```
    stcpy(ALLDIGITS, temp);
    stcat(ALLLETTS,temp);
    Tskip = 0;
```

/*Tskip will stop on any char that is NOT a digit or alphabet letter; i.e., it will stop on hatchmarks and the period.*/

```
    setbreak(&Tskip, temp, "", "x");
    printf("INPUT:1#This2#sentence3#will4#be5#chopped6#at7#digits.\n");

    while (TRUE)
        {
        pbuf = psin(ChanIn,Tskip, &brk, LRGSZE, buf);
        printf("OUTPUT: %s\n",buf);
        if (brk == EOF) break;
        }
    fclose(ChanIn);
```

/*EXAMPLE 4

```
INPUT:     1#This2#sentence3#will4#be5#chopped6#at7#digits.
OUTPUT: 1
OUTPUT: This2
OUTPUT: sentence3
OUTPUT: will4
```

```
OUTPUT: be5
OUTPUT: chopped6
OUTPUT: at7
OUTPUT: digits
*/
```

/*EXAMPLE 5: Cmode (omit all chars but those listed): This demonstrates Cmode, where the program won't allow any chars into the stored strings except the ones listed in the OmitChars string, ALLDIGITS. There is no BreakChars list. The sentence in brought in in one iteration.*/

```
        printf("\n\nEXAMPLE 5\n\n");
        init("example5.db",Tskip);
        relbreak(&Tskip);                  /*When rewriting a table, release previous version.*/
        Tskip = 0;
        setbreak(&Tskip, "", ALLDIGITS, "c");
        printf("INPUT:1#This2#sentence3#will4#be5#chopped6#at7#digits.\n");
        while (TRUE)
            {
            pbuf = psin(ChanIn, Tskip, &brk, LRGSZE, buf);     /*To collect, last arg*/
                                                               /*would be pbuf.*/

            printf("OUTPUT: %s\n",buf);
            if (brk == EOF) break;
            }
        fclose(ChanIn);
        }
```

/*EXAMPLE 5

INPUT: 1#This2#sentence3#will4#be5#chopped6#at7#digits.
OUTPUT: 1234567*/

4.8. IMPLEMENTATION OF THE SETBREAK TABLE

The characteristics of all the setbreak tables created in a program are stored in sister matrices, *bChar* and *oChar*, each a 2-dimensional (2D) integer array, whose elements initially are all zeros. The *bChar* and *oChar* matrices are defined as static global variables (in *comset.c* in the TXT system). They are not accessible to the programmer except by way of the *setbreak()* and *relbreak()* functions. However, once a table is created by *setbreak()*, it remains for the life of the program, unless the user closes the table with *relbreak()*. In both *setbreak()* and *relbreak()*, the table is referenced by its name, an integer variable. Table accessibility depends on whether the name variable is global or local, and when it is defined (see Section 4.5).

bChar records which ASCII characters are BreakChars and which are not. *oChar* records which ASCII characters are OmitChars and which are not. Table information is bitmapped, meaning that each setbreak table is allocated a single bit within each row of the matrix, rather than a single byte. The bit-wide column has the same bit position in each of the rows.

An individual setbreak table occupies a single BitColumn in *bChar* and a similarly located single BitColumn in *oChar*. Based on the directions given by the setbreak args that constructed that table, each and every bit in the BitColumn is individually marked **1** or **0**. A 1 in a BitColumn position means that row-BitColumn element is significant. In *bChar*, a 1 bit indicates that the character that 'owns' the row is a BreakChar. In *oChar*, a 1 bit indicates that the row character is to be filtered out and not permitted into the text that is being collected. A 0 in a row-BitColumn cell in either matrix means the character is an ordinary char for that particular setbreak table. Together, the *bChar* and *oChar* matrices explicitly list what to do with all the ASCII chars for all the tables that the user constructs.

Each matrix has 132 rows, where the first 128 rows correspond with encoded ASCII values listed in their usual order from decimal 0 to decimal 127 (octal 177). The first row contains instructions on how to handle SNUL (\0) in all the tables, the 59th row refers to the semicolon (ASCII decimal 59) across all the tables, and so forth. More generally, within any BitColumn of *bChar*, reading up and down the rows, if a cell (a row-BitColumn intersection) is 1, then the corresponding ASCII char (the char whose decimal ASCII value is the same as the row number) is a BreakChar for that table. Similarly, a 1 bit in some row within the BitColumn in the *oChar* matrix indicates that the corresponding ASCII value is an OmitChar for that table. Rows 129 to 131 in *bChar* contain information on how to dispose of the BreakChar; rows 129 to 131 in *oChar* contain instructions on handling case.

BitColumn numbering begins at 0 and continues for the number of bits across the width of the matrix. So BitColumn 12 is the 13th bit from the right. If in *bChar* the bit in BitColumn 12, row 37 is a 1, that would mean that the asterisk (decimal ASCII 37) is a BreakChar in the table stored in BitColumn 12. If the bit in BitColumn 2, row 65 is a 1, input will break on **A** when the table stored in BitColumn 2 is in charge of stream traffic. *oChar*, the sister table to *bChar*, describes the disposition of all the OmitChars for all the tables. A 1 in BitColumn 12 row 33 would mean that the exclamation mark is not to appear in the final text whose input is controlled by the table stored in BitColumn 12. A character may appear on both the *bChar* and *oChar* lists for a particular table.

Suppose this set of setbreak statements, written one after the other in a program. BitColumn 0 is not used. No earlier tables were created, so the first table, *Tcommonpunc*, is given the value **1** and placed in BitColumn 1, *T2* is given the value **2** and placed in BitColumn 2, and so forth.

```
setbreak(&Tcommonpunc, ",.;",ALLVOWELS,"ua)";      /*See Section 4.2.*/
setbreak(&T2, ALLDIGITS, "", "ir"); /*The stream will stop at any digit.*/
setbreak(&T3, "", "", "");           /*The stream won't stop until it runs out of chars.*/
setbreak(&Tvow, ALLVOWELS, "", "L");  /*The stream will stop at any vowel, upper or*/
                                      /* lower case.*/
setbreak(&T5, "<>AEC", "", "is");     /*The stream will stop at triangular brackets,*/
                                      /* 'A', 'E' or 'C'.*/
setbreak(&T6,"ABCDEFG", ALLDIGITS, "or"); /*The stream will stop at any letter*/
                                      /* between A and G.*/
```

setbreak(&TBool, "01", "", "is"); /*The stream will stop at zero or 1.*/

where ALLDIGITS is #defined as: **#define ALLDIGITS "0123456789"**

Table 4.6 is a small segment of a bChar matrix, showing the BitColumn values for the tables that occupy BitColumns 1:7. For example, *T2* occupies BitColumn 2. Any digit will break the char flow. So ASCII values from zero to 9 are marked 1. To simplify, we will use a 8-bit wide matrix, sufficient bits for a single char value, not the 32-bit wide words actually used. Rows 48 to 73 are presented; these correspond to the ASCII values for the digit zero to the letter I.

ROW #	ASCII VALUE	7	6	5	4	3	2	1	0	BYTE VALUE IN DECIMAL
					BITCOLUMN					
48	0	1	0	0	0	0	1	0	0	bChar[48] = 132
49	1	1	0	0	0	0	1	0	0	bChar[49] = 132
50	2	0	0	0	0	0	1	0	0	bChar[50] = 4
51	3	0	0	0	0	0	1	0	0	bChar[51] = 4
52	4	0	0	0	0	0	1	0	0	bChar[52] = 4
53	5	0	0	0	0	0	1	0	0	bChar[53] = 4
54	6	0	0	0	0	0	1	0	0	bChar[54] = 4
55	7	0	0	0	0	0	1	0	0	bChar[55] = 4
56	8	0	0	0	0	0	1	0	0	bChar[56] = 4
57	9	0	0	0	0	0	1	0	0	bChar[57] = 4
58	:	0	0	0	0	0	0	0	0	bChar[58] = 0
59	;	0	0	0	0	0	0	1	0	bChar[59] = 2
60	<	0	0	1	0	0	0	0	0	bChar[60] = 32
61	=	0	0	0	0	0	0	0	0	bChar[61] = 0
62	>	0	0	1	0	0	0	0	0	bChar[62] = 32
63	?	0	0	0	0	0	0	0	0	bChar[63] = 0
64	@	0	0	0	0	0	0	0	0	bChar[64] = 0
65	A	0	1	1	1	0	0	0	0	bChar[65] = 112
66	B	0	1	0	0	0	0	0	0	bChar[66] = 64
67	C	0	1	1	0	0	0	0	0	bChar[67] = 96
68	D	0	1	0	0	0	0	0	0	bChar[68] = 64
69	E	0	1	1	1	0	0	0	0	bChar[69] = 112
70	F	0	1	0	0	0	0	0	0	bChar[70] = 64

Table 4.6. A section of a bChar matrix for 7 setbreak tables.

To the right in each column is the corresponding byte value for the row in decimal. *bChar*[48] is 132 (octal 204) and **bChar**[60] is 32 (octal 40).

The number of tables that can be written in bChar, or in its sister matrix oChar, depends on the number of available BitColumns, which, in turn, depends on the width of the array. Array width depends on the number of word strips that are set aside for the array, where a word is 32 bits or 4 bytes. So, ultimately, the number of tables that can be stored in either of the sister matrices is determined by (re)setting a value called WD, which defines the number of words to be allocated to matrix width. In TXT, WD is currently set to 4, sufficient for holding 32*WD -1 or 127 tables[7] as residents in WORD 0 to WORD 3. Put another way, a WD of 4 words provide 127 BitColumns, where each BitColumn is capable of storing all the BreakChar (or OmitChar) information of a single *setbreak()* instruction.

A single 32-bit word extended down the 132 rows provides 32 BitColumns, sufficient to store 32 tables, counting the lowest bit position as 0 and the highest bit position as 31. Because BitColumn 0 is not used, the instructions for the first table, Table #1, are captured in BitColumn 1 (the second bit from the right in WORD 0), and table #31 corresponds to BitColumn 31 in WORD 0. Table #32 information will be found in BitColumn 32, which corresponds to bit 0 of WORD 1, and table #63 will be in BitColumn 63, which corresponds to bit 31 of WORD 1. More generally, if the bit positions in a 32-bit word are bit 0 to bit 31, as in the first line of the table, then Table 4.7 illustrates the relationship of 4 such WORDS.

To summarize, a 32-bit (4-byte) word by 132-row matrix can hold complete information on 31 bitmapped tables and two 32-bit words can hold 63 tables. Presented with a directive to create a setbreak table, the program finds the first unoccupied BitColumn, starting with BitColumn 1. The integer value of this BitColumn is assigned to the table as a unique identifier. A particular row in the table indicates a particular ASCII char across all tables. The table is said to be bitmapped because each element in the table (i.e., a row-BitColumn location) is either a 0 or a 1 and each bit element has independent meaning. A 1 in one of the bit elements of the *bChar* matrix indicates that that ASCII char is a BreakChar in that particular setbreak table. Similarly, a 1 in the same element of the *oChar* matrix means that that ASCII char is an OmitChar in that particular table.

4.9.　BITMAPPING THE SETBREAK TABLE

As discussed above, the location of a particular table is a single BitColumn within the 132-row by 32*WD -1 column *bChar* matrix and within its sister *oChar* matrix. So the setbreak utility depends heavily on bit operations. This section discusses these operations.

Earlier, in Section 1.7.2.5, we presented all the ways that an 1-byte mask can contain a single 1 bit. The bit AND'ing operation results in a 1 if and only if both operands contain a 1 in the same position. Hence, AND'ing an integer with a mask that has a 1 bit in a particular location is a practical means of quickly isolating that particular location in that integer. AND'ing *MASK8*[2], which is valued at 00000100 (decimal value of 4), with an ordinary integer can affect only BitColumn 2 in the integer. Referring to the previous Chart, by using a loop, we could traverse the rows of the matrix, AND'ing each row with *MASK8*[2]. In each row, BitColumn 2 would be 'pulled out' for inspection from the rest of the BitColumns.

7　BitColumn 0 is not used; i.e., the zeroth bit in WORD 0 is not used to avoid ambiguity with NULL.

The result of the AND'ing will be 1 if bit 2 in the integer is 1 (as it is in rows 48 to 54) and zero otherwise. A setbreak table that halted input on digits might look like BITCOLUMN 2 in Table 4.6. BITCOLUMN 3 in Table 4.6 would facilitate the entry of any and all characters into memory in that there is no BreakChar.

---

31 30 29 28 27 26 25 24 23 22 21 20 19 18 17 16 15 14 13 12 11 10 9 8 7 6 5 4 3 2 1 0

The relationship of four such WORD's visualized across any row of the matrix:

WORD LAYOUT:	WORD 3	WORD 2	WORD 1	WORD 0
BITCOLUMN LAYOUT:	31...0	31...0	31...0	31...0

then in a 4-word matrix, the 127 tables that could reside in the matrix would be assigned the integer values that follow:

WORD 0 BitColumn values:	31	30	29................ 5	4	3	2	1
WORD 1 BitColumn values:	63	62	61................36	35	34	33	32
WORD 2 BitColumn values:	95	94	93............. 68	67	66	65	64
WORD 3 BitColumn values:	127	126	125............ 100	99	98	97	96

Table 4.7. Showing how break tables would occupy four 32-bit words.

A similar set of masks is used to isolate bit positions in a 32-bit word, where each mask is an element in a long int array. However, for larger sized masks, listing all the zeros becomes hard to read and harder to write. So the bit patterns are usually written in octal or in hexadecimal. The hexadecimal representations of all the patterns in a 32-bit word (i.e., 4 bytes in a word) in which one of the bits is 1 and the rest are zero is:

```
long tblmask[32] =
    {
    0x1, 0x2, 0x4, 0x8, 0x10, 0x20, 0x40, 0x80, 0x100, 0x200, 0x400,
    0x800, 0x1000, 0x2000, 0x4000, 0x8000, 0x10000, 0x20000, 0x40000,
    0x80000, 0x100000, 0x200000, 0x400000, 0x800000, 0x1000000, 0x2000000,
    0x4000000, 0x8000000, 0x10000000, 0x20000000, 0x40000000, 0x80000000
    }
```

4.9.1. BIT AND'ing

If we AND *tblmask*[4] with a number, n, it is guaranteed to isolate the 5th lowest bit in n for examination.

Applied to setbreak utilization, suppose that in Table 4.6 the disposition of the input stream is under control of the table resident in BitColumn 5 and that the incoming char is **M**, ASCII 77. Our task is to determine whether **M** is a BreakChar for that table. For simplicity, suppose the *bChar* matrix is 1-word wide, i.e., it has 32-bit columns. We can examine the bit that is located at the intersection of *bChar*[77] and BitColumn 5 thus:

```
tblmask[4] = 0x10 = 00000000000000000000000000010000;
if (bChar[77] & tblmask[4]) break;
```

Read the previous two lines as:

BitColumn 4 and only BitColumn 4 of tblmask[4] is 1. If AND'ing row 77 and tblmask[4] is TRUE, it must be that bit 4 of row 77 is a 1. So M is a BreakChar for that table.

When more than one 32-bit word is involved, we need to locate a table's actual position within the set of words that constitute the *bChar* matrix, rather than its Tablenumber (i.e., BitColumn) position in the 'virtual' matrix *bChar*. A setbreak table's real location is found by first determining which word it is in and then finding which bit within that word—a two-stage operation.[8]

Locating the word: To determine the word in which the table resides, the table number (i.e., the value of the integer variable that identifies the table) is divided by 32, using integer arithmetic[9]. This gives us the particular 32-bit word that holds the table. For example, if *Tpunc* is valued at 68, then the *Tpunc* table is resident in word 68/32, which is 2 and a fraction. *Tpunc* resides in WORD 2. Similarly, if *Tbool* is valued at 7, then the *Tbool* is in 3/32, which is zero and a fraction. *Tbool* is in WORD 0.

Locating the BitColumn: Then to determine where *Tpunc* is located within WORD 2, we turn to modulus arithmetic: 68 % 32 is 2 and 4/32. The fraction is 4. Given that bits are numbered in any word from bit 0 to bit 31, *Tpunc* is bit 4; it is located in the fifth bit from the right in WORD 2. To determine if **M** is a BreakChar when *Tpunc* is in control, we would AND *bChar*[77][2] & *tblmask*[4], thus:

tblmask[4] = 0x10 = 00000000000000000000000000010000;
if (bChar[77][2] & tblmask[4]) break;   /*If M is a BreakChar, stop.*/

This is to be read as: The 32-bit mask has a 1 in its 5th lowest position, the same BitColumn as the table of interest. It is AND'ed with the integer that embodies row 77, WORD 2 of *bChar*. If the result of the AND'ing is TRUE (i.e., 1), it can only mean that bChar[77][2] must contain a 1 in that bit position.

The arithmetic calculations for deriving the bit-in-word address are shown in the following loop from *getbreak*(), the function that finds the first available empty BitColumn. When *setbreak*() writes a table, it sets the bit at row 128 of the newly-occupied BitColumn to 1. This fact can later be used as in the following loop to query whether a BitColumn is occupied by a previously written table. *getbreak*() traverses the BitColumns across row 128,

---

8 A 32-bit mask can only be applied to 32-bit integers; in our terminology, to a single word at a time, not to all the columns of a multi-word *bChar* or *oChar* matrix. Alternatively, we could have spelled out the combinatorics of a 64-element (2 words) mask array or a 96-element (3 words) mask and needed only a single arithmetic operation to locate the BitColumn. But the mask matrix would need to be redone any time WD, which controls *bChar* matrix width, was changed.

9 In integer division, the integer result is retained and the fraction is thrown away. The symbol for integer arithmetic is /. In modulus division, the fractional part is kept and the integer result deleted. Its symbol is %.

starting at bit 1, WORD 0 looking for a BitColumn that contains a zero. A zero in a BitColumn would indicate that the BitColumn is available and can be occupied by a new setbreak table.

```
for (i = 1; i <= WD*32-1; i++)
    {                              /*find_empty_table*/
    waddr = (BITMAP) i / 32;    /*Determines which word holds the ith BitColumn
                                    of the bChar matrix.*/
    baddr = (BITMAP) i % 32;    /*Determines which bit in waddr corresponds to the ith
BitColumn.*/
    if ( bChar[SZE(128)][waddr] & tblmask[baddr] )     /*Result of AND'ing is TRUE.*/
                                                        /* BitColumn is occupied.*/

        continue;
    else
        {
        *ptbl = (BITMAP) i;
        return(*ptbl);          /*This BitColumn is free. Send back the table number.*/
        }
```

4.9.2. BIT OR'ing

If two integers are OR'ed, the result is a 1 in any bit position where that bit in either of the two integers is a 1. In the previous example, suppose that we found that when i was 25, we had free table space. To mark that table 25 is available and can be occupied by a new table, we would write: **bChar[SZE(128)][0] |= tblmask[25];** to put a 1 in BitColumn 25 in WORD 0. No other bit value in row 128 would be changed.

More generally, we start by locating the WORD and the BitColumn within that WORD that corresponds to a specific table value. The WORD is the vertical strip in the array within which our table resides. The appropriate mask is determined by the relative BitColumn value (a value between zero and 31). The horizontal coordinate, a row, depends on the task. Suppose, as in the next example, we wish to mark a table for a particular char, whose arg is c. If the mask appropriate for the particular BitColumn is OR'ed with the integer value of the correct WORD in the row 'belonging' to that particular char, the result will be a 1 that can be assigned to that row-BitColumn position. The other 1's and 0's already written in the row will be undisturbed.

In the code that follows, the result of the OR operation marks the particular cell that is the intersection of the char row and the BitColumn within the appropriate WORD strip. It will in consequence mark a particular row in a particular table with a 1. Thereafter, that 1 will indicate that, for that particular table, that particular character is a BreakChar. As in this example:

```
waddr = BitColumnValue / 32;
baddr = BitColumnValue % 32;
static void lbrkbit(int c)
    {
    bChar[c][waddr] |= tblmask[baddr];
    }
```

Read this as: *tblmask*[baddr] has a 1 in the same bit position as the BitColumn that holds the table. It is OR'ed with the row-word of bChar in which the row corresponds to the input char and the WORD contains the table. The result is a 1 in the targeted BitColumn, no matter what was previously written there. BitColumns containing information for other tables are not affected.

If, for example the function arg of *Ibrkbit* is **B**, a 1 would be written into the cell corresponding to the BitColumn where the particular table in *bChar* intersected row 66. If the table is valued at 62, its BitColumn would be the one to the right of the highest bit position in the second word, i.e., in bit 30 of WORD 1. In BitColumn terms, the 1-bit cell *bChar*[66][1][30] will contain a 1 in the 31st bit of the second word as the result of OR'ing whatever was at that position in *bChar*[66][1] with *tblmask*[30]. The other bits in row 66 are undisturbed, because *tblmask*[30] has only that single bit set to 1.

All the chars that are listed in arg 2 of the setbreak statement as a BreakChar can be assigned by calling *Ibrkbit*() inside a loop.

4.9.3. BIT XOR'ing

In addition to the ordinary OR, there is the exclusive OR. If two integers are logically XOR'ed, the result is 1 if only one of the integers has a 1 in that position. If both integers are 1 or if both integers are 0, the result is 0. The 32-bit mask selected is the one that has a single 1 positioned in the same BitColumn as the target table and is otherwise zero. So XOR'ing it row by row with the matrix word containing the particular table is a way to change the 1's in the table to zero. Conversely, if the cell contained a 0 bit, the same 1-bit mask will result in a 1 being written into that cell. No other table will be affected.

What we are describing is the usefulness of the exclusive OR mask for reversing 1's and zero's in a specific BitColumn. This is what is needed for the Xmode option, which reverses the sense of the BreakChars list.

If ALPHANUMS is the set of all letters and digits

#define ALPHANUMS
"ABCDEFGHIJKLMNOPQRSTUVWXYZabcdefghijklmnopqrstuvwxyz0123456789"

then

setbreak(&T1, ALPHANUMS,"","I");

would instruct the program to break a text stream at any letter or digit. In table terms, if T1 is valued at 11, this would amount to putting a 1 in each BitColumn 11 of each row that corresponds to an ASCII letter or digit and a 0 in each row corresponding to a control char or punctuation mark. If, however, the function was written with the Xmode option:

setbreak(&T1, ALPHANUMS,"","X");

then the sense of ALPHANUMS would be reversed. The text stream would halt at control chars and punctuation marks, i.e., at any symbol that was not a letter or number.

Similarly,

setbreak(&T1, "", ALPHANUMS, "O")

would bar all letters and digits from the string that was written. And

setbreak(&T1, "", ALPHANUMS, "C")

would bar any symbol that was NOT a letter or digit.

In practice, to record the X option for the target table, the program first marks those BreakChars listed in arg 2. It then reverses the entire BitColumn in *bChar*, so that the chars previously marked 1 are zeroed and the previously neutral chars are now possible BreakChars. For Cmode, the operation is also two-stage. First the OmitChars listed in arg 3 are marked 1 in the table and then the 1's and 0's of the entire table are reversed. To reverse each and every cell in a particular table, the XOR operation sweeps down the table, as in these pieces of code from *setbreak()*. *ptbl* is a BITMAP pointer to the BitColumn containing the table whose bits are to be reversed.

waddr = (*ptbl)/32;
baddr = (*ptbl)%32;

if (Xmode) for (i = 0; i <= SZE(127); i++) (bChar[i][waddr] ^= tblmask[baddr]);

if (Cmode) for (i = 0; i <= SZE(127); i++) (oChar[i][waddr] ^= tblmask[baddr]);

The exclusive OR can also be used to write a swap macro for two integers that employs just two variables, unlike the typical swap macro, which requires an additional variable as a temporary hold for one of the variables. Thus:

#define SWAP(x,y) { ((x) ^= (y)); ((y) ^= (x)); ((x) ^= (y));}

4.9.4. BIT REVERSAL

This is a unary flip-flop operation, reversing all bits within an integer—not down a BitCol as in Section 4.9.3. Bits set to 1 are reset to 0. Bits set to 0 are reset to 1. In this piece of code from *zerotable()*, bit reversal is the first operation in a two-stage process that clears out an entire BitColumn. A mask with a 1 in the position of the target table is reversed, so it now contains 1's in all positions except in the requisite BitColumn. In the second operation, a mask with a zero corresponding to the BitColumn is AND'ed with the table. The zero of the mask ensures that, in traversing the BitColumn, all cells are forced to zero. Because all other bits of the mask are 1, the AND'ing operation does not affect the bits of any of the other tables written into the *bChar* word; 1's remain 1's and 0's remain 0's.

for (i = 0; i <= SZE(131); i++)
**   bChar[i][waddr] &= ~tblmask[baddr];**   /*Clears brktable BitColumn.*/

As an aside, the unary reversal characteristic is the basis of this fast way of determining the two's complement of a number.

- To obtain the bit equivalent of a negative number, note that the negative of an octal number plus the complement of the number equal minus 1. For example, -16 and ~(+15) == 1111111111111111 which is -1. This is the same as this operation: (1) subtract 1 from a negative number; (2) make the 2nd number positive; and (3) ~ the 2nd number. To know what the bit pattern means: (1) complement the bit pattern; (2) add 1; and (3) add minus.

4.10. THE BASIC SETBREAK TABLE FUNCTIONS

4.10.1. ALPHABETIC LIST OF GLOBAL VARIABLES AND A GLOSSARY OF TERMS

static BITMAP baddr = 0;

baddr is the bit position of the specified setbreak table resident in the domain of *word #*. **baddr = tbl MOD 32;**, where tbl is the setbreak table number. *baddr* ranges between 0 and 31 except for the tables assigned to WORD 0, where it ranges between 1 and 31.

extern BOOL barf;

If barf is set to TRUE, a warning will be issued should an attempt be made to invade space set aside for another table.

static BITMAP bChar[ROW][WD] = {0};

bChar is a matrix where, conceptually, each bit across the first row marks the beginning of a separate column capable of containing a setbreak table. Each BitColumn is a separate map indicating which chars terminate data entry for the particular setbreak table assigned to that BitColumn. If a row-BitColumn element bit is set to 1, it means: **halt on this char when this table is in control**.

For each setbreak table (a BitColumn #), rows 0:127 are for the ASCII chars. The row 128 bit shows whether the table was constructed. The last three rows determine how to dispose of the BreakChar.

if *bChar*[128][BitColumn#] is 1, the table exists.
if *bChar*[129][BitColumn#] is 1, Smode is true; i.e., throw away the BreakChar.
if *bChar*[130][BitColumn#] is 1, Amode is true; i.e., append the BreakChar.
if *bChar*[131][BitColumn#] is 1, Rmode is true; i.e., return the BreakChar to the input stream or mother string.

BreakChars List

The second arg of *setbreak*() lists all the characters that can act as a BreakChar for that particular setbreak table. A BreakChar stops data entry. An option in the fourth arg of *setbreak*() determines whether to throw the BreakChar away (**S** for skip), append it as the last data entry char (**A** for append) or return it to the incoming data stream (**R** for return) so it can become the first char of the next incoming string. The sense of the BreakChars list is reversed if arg 4 contains **X**; i.e., the program will stop at all chars eXcept those listed in arg 2.

static BITMAP oChar[ROW][WD] = {0};

This is sister matrix to *bChar*. It contains information for all the active setbreak tables. A single BitColumn is capable of detailing all the chars that are to be omitted for a single setbreak table. If a row-BitColumn element bit is set to 1, it means: **Throw this char away. Do not send it to the collecting buffer.**

For each setbreak table (a BitColumn #), rows 0:127 are for the ASCII chars. The last rows describe case change information.

oChar[128][#] is not used.
oChar[129][#] is 1 if Umode is true; i.e., change accepted chars to upper case.
oChar[130][#] is 1 if Dmode is true; i.e., do not change case.
oChar[131][#] is 1 if Lmode is true; i.e., change chars to lower case.

OmitChars List

The third arg of *setbreak*() lists all the chars that can act as OmitChars for that particular setbreak table. A char on the OmitChars list is not allowed into the string that is being assembled. There are two complementary options in arg 4 of *setbreak*(): **O** says that the chars listed in arg 3 are to be omitted; **C** says that all chars exCept the chars listed in arg 3 are to be omitted.

Options:

```
static BOOL Smode = FALSE;
static BOOL Amode = FALSE;      /*Disposing of the BreakChar.*/
static BOOL Rmode = FALSE;

static BOOL Dmode = FALSE;
static BOOL Umode = FALSE;      /*Changing case.*/
static BOOL Lmode = FALSE;

static BOOL Imode = FALSE;      /*The BreakChar arg.*/
static BOOL Xmode = FALSE;

static BOOL Omode = FALSE;      /*The OmitChar arg.*/
static BOOL Cmode = FALSE;
```

The #modes are set by the fourth arg in a setbreak function. They are various clustered options. They set case, determine what to do with the BreakChar, and so forth.

SAR: The Smode, Amode and Rmode group controls the treatment of the BreakChar: **S** (the default): Skip or erase it; **A**: Append it as last char to the others chars in the buffer; **R**: Return it to the file or to the mother string until the next time.

DUL: The **Dmode, Umode** and **Lmode** group controls case change of incoming chars: **Umode**: change to upper case; **Dmode** (the default): leave case alone; **Lmode**: change to Lower case.

IX: Imode and **Xmode** are complements for BreakChars. **I** (the default): Include all the chars on the BreakChars list; **X**: eXclude all the chars on the BreakChars list.

OC: Omode and **Cmode** are complements for OmitChars. **O** (the default): Omit all the chars on the OmitChars list; **C**: exClude all the chars except those on the OmitChars list.

#define ROW 132

There are 132 rows, numbered from 0:131, in either the *bChar* or *oChar* matrix.

In *bChar*: rows 0:127 are each for a different ASCII char in the ordinary ASCII order. A bit set to 1 indicates the char is a BreakChar. Row 128 has bits set to 1 for all the existing tables; if the column bit in row 128 is 0, there is no table in that BitColumn. Row 129 has bits set to 1 in all tables using Smode; Row 130 has bits set to 1 in all tables using Amode; and Row 131 has bits set to 1 for all tables using Rmode.

In *oChar*: Rows 0:127 are used for the ordinary ASCII chars just as in *bChar*. A bit set to 1 indicates the char is an OmitChar. Row 129 sets bits for Umode; Row 130 is set for Dmode; and Row 131 will have the bit set to 1 in tables where the Lmode is in effect.

Setbreak Table

Setbreak tables are designed by the user and created using *setbreak()*. The contents of the setbreak args give a table an identifier; and determine which chars are BreakChars and/or OmitChars and how to treat the character that halted processing.

A setbreak table holds information on how to treat every incoming char when that setbreak table is in effect. The program stores this information in the twin matrices, *bChar* and *oChar*.

32 tables may be stored per word (except for WORD 0, which holds 31 tables) and the number of words to allocate to setbreak tables is determined by the value of WD in *define.h*. A WD of 4 will support the instructions for 4*32-1 or 127 tables, beginning with Table 1.

static BITMAP tblmask[32L] =

```
{
0x1, 0x2, 0x4, 0x8, 0x10, 0x20, 0x40 ,0x80, 0x100, 0x200, 0x400,
0x800 ,0x1000, 0x2000, 0x4000, 0x8000, 0x10000, 0x20000, 0x40000,
0x80000 ,0x100000, 0x200000, 0x400000, 0x800000, 0x1000000, 0x2000000,
0x4000000 ,0x8000000, 0x10000000, 0x20000000, 0x40000000, 0x80000000
};
```

tblmask[32] is a long integer array, where each element of the array is a different pattern composed of zeros except for a single 1-bit. For example, *tblmask*[2] is 4, which is written in binary as 00000000000000000000000000000100. One of the set of patterns is guaranteed to match the bit position of a specific setbreak table, within the word in which it is resident.

static BITMAP waddr = 0;

waddr = tbl DIV 32, where tbl is a table number.

The program integer divides the table BITMAP value by 32 (the number of bits in a word) to determine which word of the matrix contain the setbreak table. Within the domain of this word, the particular BitColumn that represents the particular setbreak table is determined by the *baddr* value.

WD

WD sets the number of words to be allocated to each of the twin matrices; i.e., it determines the width of the *bChar* matrix and of the *oChar* matrix. Because each word has 32 bits, the number of setbreak tables that can be stored in *bChar* (or *oChar*) is equal to WD*32. Thus, WD, currently set to 4, will provide 127 tables, numbered from 1 to 127. The zeroth BitColumn is not used. WD is to be found in *define.h*. It can be redefined and the modules recompiled.

4.10.2. SETBREAK FUNCTIONS: DESCRIPTION AND CODE

Table 4.8 lists the procedures that constitute the set of functions that make the setbreak utility work.[10]

setbreak(), *DULcase*() and *relbreak*() are directly accessible to other programs. The other functions are only callable by *setbreak*() or *relbreak*(). They are listed in alphabetical order.

```
extern   int      DULcase(int c);
static   BITMAP   getbreak(BITMAP *ptbl);
static   void     lbrkbit(int c);
static   void     lomitbit(int c);
static   void     parsemode(STRING psrc);
extern   void     relbreak(BITMAP *ptbl);
extern   void     setbreak(BITMAP *ptbl, STRING BreakChars,STRING OmitChars,
                           STRING options);
static   void     zerotable(BITMAP *ptbl);
```

Table 4.8.   The setbreak functions listed alphabetically.

4.10.2.1. DULcase.

USE: *DULcase*() changes incoming characters to upper or lower case or leaves case as is, depending on which of the three case possibilities was set in arg 4 of the *setbreak*() statement that established the table. If **L** was part of the arg 4 string, then *oChar*[131][Bit-

---

10 Note that files 4-8.c and 4-9.c in LISTINGS\chap4 use a modified version of comset.c, where all functions are extern so that you can display the operations. You can examine all the procedures discussed in the next sections by accessing *comdo.c* and inserting print statements.

Column] was set to 1 by *setbreak*(), as indicator that incoming characters controlled by that setbreak table are to be changed to lower case by *DULcase*(). If **U** was chosen, then (*oChar*[SZE(129)][waddr] was set to 1; during string entry, *DULcase*() changes incoming chars to uppercase. A 1 in BitColumn row 130 is the default and indicates that case is not to be changed.

ARGS: a single char whose case will be changed if that case change
                    option was chosen
CALLS: none
CALLED BY: any scan or input function that uses a setbreak table()
W/B EVAL: no[11]
RETURNS: Returns char, with/without its case changed

EXAMPLE: **c = DULcase(c);**

PROCEDURE: *DULcase*() first determines the type of case change requested by examining the BitColumn cells in rows 129 and 131 of *oChar*. It changes the char's case appropriately.

```
int DULcase(int ch)
    {/*BP*/
    if (oChar[SZE(129)][waddr] & (tblmask[baddr]) )      /*If the bit is set to 1, chars are
        {                                                    to be uppercased.*/
        if (islower(ch)) ch = toupper(ch);        /*If the char is lower case, uppercase it.*/
        }
    else if (oChar[SZE(131)][waddr] & (tblmask[baddr])) /*If the bit is set to 1,*/
        {                                                /*chars are to be lowercased.*/
        if (isupper(ch)) ch = tolower(ch);
        }       return(ch);            /*If neither the cell in row 129 nor in row 131 is 1,*/
                                       /*the char is transmitted as is.*/

    }/*EP*/
```

4.10.2.2. getbreak.

USE: *getbreak*() is used by *setbreak*() to find an empty BitColumn in which to store a new setbreak table. The *getbreak*() arg is the pointer to the table identifier that is the first arg in *setbreak*(). For tables that are about to be stored, the setbreak table identifiers should be set to zero before *setbreak*() is called. *getbreak*() gets the first available integer (an empty BitColumn) from 1 to 32*WD-1 to assign to the setbreak table. It exits if there is no free table space.

ARGS: a pointer to the BITMAP variable that serves as table identifier
CALLS: *zerotable()*
CALLED BY: *setbreak()*

---

11 W/B EVAL: whether *waddr* and *baddr* have to be computed by the function.

W/B EVAL: yes, definitely. Needs to find an empty table.
RETURNS: a table number || exit(2) if there are no free tables in bChar
EXAMPLE:

BITMAP Tword = 0;
setbreak(&Tword, "\40", "", "");   /*getbreak() is the first operation done in setbreak;*/

PROCEDURE:

static BITMAP getbreak(BITMAP *ptbl)

/*Note that ptbl is a pointer-to-BITMAP so that the table value returned by getbreak() to setbreak() is by reference.*/

```
{/*BP*/
unsigned i = 0;

waddr = (*ptbl)/32;
baddr = (*ptbl)%32;
```

/*IMPORTANT: If a table name is reused without first doing a relbreak() or NULL'ing the variable, the program will assume the table is still in use, as it may well be. Nevertheless, when getbreak() returns the old value, setbreak() will zero out the bChar and oChar columns for that table to avoid residue from previous use of the table name with possibly different BreakChars and OmitChars. If the previous table is no longer needed, there is no harm reusing the name with a new table, but it is cleaner to erase obsolete tables using relbreak().*/

```
if (bChar[SZE(128)][waddr] & tblmask[baddr])
    {/*found_a_repeat*/
    if (barf)          /*If the alarm variable is set to YES.*/
        {
        printf("\nCAUTION. bChar table number %ld may have been in use.\n"
            "It will be (re)assigned.\n",*ptbl);
        printf("This setbreak instruction erases the previous configuration.\n");
        }
    return(*ptbl);
    }/*found_a_repeat*/
for (i = 1; i <= WD*32-1; i++)
    {/*find_empty_table*/
    waddr = (BITMAP) i / 32;
    baddr = (BITMAP) i % 32;
    if ( bChar[SZE(128)][waddr] & tblmask[baddr] )/*tbl num is taken. Move on.*/
        continue;
    else
        {/*found_vacancy*/
        *ptbl = (BITMAP) i;
        if (barf)
            printf("\nIn getbreak(). bChar table number %ld"
                "has just been assigned.\n",*ptbl);
        return(*ptbl);
        }/*found_vacancy*/
    }/*find_empty_table*/
```

```
    printf("\nIn getbreak(). All %d tables have been used."   /*none free*/
        "Increase WD in define.h.\n", WD*32-1);
    exit(2);                                          /*Terminates program.*/
    }/*EP*/
```

4.10.2.3. lbrkbit.

USE: This is a table building function. *lbrkbit*() marks a BreakChar cell for a BitColumn in *bChar*. *setbreak*() traverses the entire BreakChars list, handling one BreakChar at a time. Using *lbrkbit*(), it marks the row-BitColumn cell that represents that BreakChar with a 1 bit by means of the bit OR operation.

ARGS: a single char
CALLS: none
CALLED BY: *setbreak( )*
W/B EVAL: no
RETURNS: none
EXAMPLE: **setbreak(&NewTbl, "\40", "", "a");**
If *NewTbl* occupies BitColumn 31 (the highest bit position in word 0), say, then *lbrkbit* will place a 1 in the cell that is the intersection of BitColumn 31 and row 32 (the space is ASCII decimal 32). This table will direct any function that uses it to stop incoming data only when a space is entered.

PROCEDURE:

```
static void lbrkbit(int c)
    {/*BP*/
    bChar[c][waddr] |= tblmask[baddr];
    }/*EP*/
```

4.10.2.4. lomitbit.

USE: *lomitbit*() is the sister function to lbrkbit. *setbreak*() examines one OmitChar at a time with *lomitbit*(), which puts a 1 in the row-BitColumn cell corresponding to that OmitChar for this setbreak table.

ARGS: a single char
CALLS: none
CALLED BY: *setbreak( )*
W/B EVAL: no
RETURNS: none
EXAMPLE:

```
#define ALLCCHARS                          /*The control characters.*/
"\1\2\3\4\5\6\7\10\t\n\13\14\15\16\17\20\21\22\23\24\25\26\27\30\31\32\33\34\35\36\37\177
"

setbreak(&NewTbl, ".", ALLCCHARS, "i");
```

The setbreak table directs any function that uses it to filter out all control chars from the incoming data stream. All other chars will be accepted and the stream will be stopped when a period is encountered. *setbreak()* will send each OmitChar to Iomitbrk() in turn, starting with ASCII 1. If the table occupies BitColumn 32 (the lowest bit position in WORD 1), Ibrkbit will place a 1 in the cell that is the intersection of BitColumn 32 and row 1 (ASCII 1).

PROCEDURE:

```
static void Iomitbit(int c)
    {/*BP*/
    oChar[c][waddr] |= tblmask[baddr];
    }/*EP*/
```

4.10.2.5. parsemode.

USE: *parsemode()* decodes Arg 4 of the setbreak table, which determines options in 4 groups: DUL (case), IX (include/exclude the BreakChars list), OC (include/exclude Omit-Chars), and (SAR) how to dispose of the BreakChar. Within a group, a single option is allowed. We can not instruct the table to both include the BreakChars list and exclude it; it's one or the other.

ARGS: a single string that lists the options requested (arg 4)
CALLS: none
CALLED BY: *setbreak()*
W/B EVAL: no
RETURNS: none
EXAMPLE:

```
#define ALPHANUMS
"ABCDEFGHIJKLMNOPQRSTUVWXYZabcdefghijklmnopqrstuvwxyz0123456789"
setbreak(&Toptions,"\n",ALPHANUMS,"sticla");
```

A program that uses Toptions will stop incoming data at line breaks (option **i**). It will exclude all chars except letters and digits (option **c**). It will change incoming letters to lower case (option **l**). The **s** option tells the function to throw the BreakChar, \n, away. But later, the **a** option tells it to append the \n to the end of the incoming data stream. The last one sticks. Note there is a non-option character, **t**, on the option list. It is ignored.

PROCEDURE:

```
static void parsemode(STRING cond)
    {/*BP*/
    char ch = SNUL;

    Dmode = Imode = Omode = Smode = TRUE;          /*Defaults for each group*/
    Amode = Cmode = Lmode = Rmode = Umode = Xmode = FALSE;
    while ( (ch = *cond++) != SNUL)
        {
        if (ch == 'A' || ch == 'a')
```

```
        {
        Amode = TRUE;
        Smode = FALSE;
        Rmode = FALSE;
        }
else if (ch == 'S' || ch == 's')
        {
        Smode = TRUE;
        Amode = FALSE;
        Rmode = FALSE;
        }
else if (ch == 'R' || ch == 'r')
        {
        Rmode = TRUE;
        Amode = FALSE;
        Smode = FALSE;
        }
else if (ch == 'I' || ch == 'i')
        {
        Imode = TRUE;
        Xmode = FALSE;
        }
else if (ch == 'X' || ch == 'x')
        {
        Xmode = TRUE;
        Imode = FALSE;
        }
else if (ch == 'U' || ch == 'u')
        {
        Umode = TRUE;
        Dmode = FALSE;
        Lmode = FALSE;
        }
else if (ch == 'D' || ch == 'd')
        {
        Dmode = TRUE;
        Umode = FALSE;
        Lmode = FALSE;
        }
else if (ch == 'L' || ch == 'l')
        {
        Lmode = TRUE;
        Dmode = FALSE;
        Umode = FALSE;
        }
else if (ch == 'O' || ch == 'o')
        {
        Omode = TRUE;
        Cmode = FALSE;
        }
```

```
    else if (ch == 'C' || ch == 'c')
        {
        Cmode = TRUE;
        Omode = FALSE;
        }
    }
}/*EP*/
```

4.10.2.6. relbreak.

USE: *relbreak()* cleans out a setbreak table BitColumn, resetting all bits to zero. The table is released and available for storing a new setbreak table.

ARGS: Pointer-to-BITMAP table identifier.
CALLS: *zerotable()*.
CALLED BY: any function that needs to clear a setbreak table
W/B EVAL: No.
RETURNS: none.
EXAMPLE:

```
setbreak(&Ttemp, "\n", "", "isd");
oneshot(&ifile, Ttemp, &ofile);
    {
    .................
    }
relbreak(&Ttemp);
```

PROCEDURE:

```
void relbreak(BITMAP *ptbl)
    {/*BP*/
    if (*ptbl == 0)
        {
        printf("\n\nFATAL ERROR. In relbreak().\n"
            "The argument should be a pointer to an int.\n");
        exit(2);
        }
    waddr = (*ptbl)/32;
    baddr = (*ptbl)%32;
    if (bChar[SZE(128)][waddr] & tblmask[baddr] )
        {
        zerotable(ptbl);
        *ptbl = 0;
        }
    else if (barf)
        {
        printf("\n\nCAUTION: In relbreak().\n");
        printf("\nTable assigned as number %ld was not found."
            " Typo? Check.\n",*ptbl);
        }
```

        }/*EP*/

4.10.2.7. setbreak.

USE: *setbreak*() is the function that creates a setbreak table from the information supplied by setbreak's args. In setting up a setbreak table, *setbreak*() will perform this sequence of tasks:

(1) It will search using *getbreak*() until it find an empty slot for the table in the *bChar* matrix. It will clean out this BitColumn using *zerotable*() and then mark *bChar*[128][BitColumn] with a 1 to indicate the space is taken.

(2) It sets all the options demanded by arg 4. If no option is listed for one of the four option groups, the default option is used.

(3) It marks the BreakChars with a 1. If the Exclude (**X**) switch is on, marking the BreakChars is performed in two steps. The final bitmap for the table is an Include BreakChars list; i.e., the chars marked 1 are possible BreakChars.

(4) It marks the OmitChars with a 1 . *oChar* holds the OmitChar instructions for ALL setbreak tables. The Exclude (**C**) switch is performed in two steps, so the final bitmap is the actual OmitChars list for the table.

(5) It marks one of the cells in rows 129:131 of *bChar* to indicate how the BreakChar is to handled. A 1 in *bChar*[129][BitColumn] means the BreakChar is thrown away. A 1 in *bChar*[130][BitColumn] means the BreakChar is appended to the end of the text that was taken in. *bChar*[131][BitColumn] means the BreakChar is returned to the input file. It will be the first char out the next time.

(6) Similarly, it marks one of the cells in rows 129:131 of *oChar* to indicate the case of the chars in the newly assembled text. A 1 in *oChar*[129][BitColumn] means that incoming chars are to be changed to upper case. If a 1 is inserted into *oChar*[130][BitColumn], chars will not be changed in case. A 1 in *oChar*[131][BitColumn] will direct functions to change incoming chars to lower case.

ARGS   ARG 1: a pointer to the table identifier; i.e., a pointer to an integer
              ARG 2: a list of BreakChars
              ARG 3: a list of OmitChars
              ARG 4: a list of options
CALLS: *getbreak( ), zerotable( ), parsemode( ), Ibrkbit( ), Iomitbit( )*
CALLED BY: any function requiring a setbreak table
W/B EVAL: yes
RETURNS: none
EXAMPLE: See scan and input functions in Section 4.11.
PROCEDURE:

void setbreak(BITMAP *ptbl, STRING BreakChars, STRING OmitChars, STRING options)
        {/*BP*/

```
int       c = 0 ;
unsigned i = 0;

*ptbl = getbreak(ptbl);                    /*getbreak finds an empty table column*/
waddr = (*ptbl)/32;
baddr = (*ptbl)%32;

zerotable(ptbl);/*Cleans out the BitColumn, just in case relbreak() wasn't called.*/
bChar[SZE(128)][waddr] |= tblmask[baddr];
parsemode(options);                        /*Set arg 4 Mode flags.*/
while ((c = *BreakChars++) != SNUL)        /*To mark BreakChars.*/
    lbrkbit(c);
if (Xmode)
    for (i = 0; i <= SZE(127); i++)
        (bChar[i][waddr] ^= tblmask[baddr]);
while ((c = *OmitChars++) != SNUL)         /*Now shove OmitChars into sister array.*/
    lomitbit(c);
if (Cmode)       /*Not standard in Sail. Need this for Complementing OmitChars.*/
    for (i = 0; i <= SZE(127); i++)
        (oChar[i][waddr] ^= tblmask[baddr]);
if (Smode)
    bChar[SZE(129)][waddr] |= tblmask[baddr];
else if (Amode)
    bChar[SZE(130)][waddr] |= tblmask[baddr];
else if (Rmode)
    bChar[SZE(131)][waddr] |= tblmask[baddr];
else printf(" error in SAR. Check \n");
if (Umode)
    oChar[SZE(129)][waddr] |= tblmask[baddr];
else if (Dmode)
    oChar[SZE(130)][waddr] |= tblmask[baddr];
else if (Lmode)
    oChar[SZE(131)][waddr] |= tblmask[baddr];
else printf(" error in DUL. Check \n");
}/*EP*/
```

4.10.2.8. zerotable.

USE: *zerotable*() clears the BitColumn in bChar and the BitColumn in *oChar* that represent the setbreak table. A pointer to the table is the arg to zerotable.

ARGS: pointer to table identifier
CALLS: none
CALLED BY: *relbreak( ), setbreak*()
W/B EVAL: yes
RETURNS: none
PROCEDURE:

void zerotable(BITMAP *ptbl)

```
{/*BP*/
BITMAP i = 0 ;

waddr = (*ptbl)/32;
baddr = (*ptbl)%32;
for (i = 0; i <= SZE(131); i++)
    {
    bChar[i][waddr] &= ~tblmask[baddr];        /*Clears brktable BitColumn.*/
    oChar[i][waddr] &= ~tblmask[baddr];        /*Ditto on omit array.*/
    }
}/*EP*/
```

4.11. AN INPUT FUNCTION AND A SCAN FUNCTION

4.11.1. PSIN()

USE: *psin*() brings in chars one by one from a file to a buffer in memory in accordance with instructions held in the setbreak table that is *psin*'s second arg. The table must be installed before *psin*() is called. The function assumes a preset char array is available to store the incoming stream; the array dummy is the fifth arg.

ARGS: Arg 1:   pointer-to-FILE that acts as file ID;
               Arg 2:   the setbreak table ID;
               Arg 3:   a pointer-to-int that holds the char that halts the stream;
               Arg 4:   the size of the buffer referenced in Arg 5;
               Arg 5:   pointer to the buffer that holds the incoming text.

CALLS: The file has to be open before *input*() can be open.
CALLED BY: Any function.
W/B EVAL: yes
RETURNS: pointer to terminal SNUL of the buffer in which the text is input.
EXAMPLE: See Section 4.2.
PROCEDURE:

```
STRING psin(FILE *ifptr, BITMAP tbl, int *pbrk, int lim, STRING dsn)
    {/*BP*/
    int       c = 0;       /*Make it an int rather than a char to allow for negative EOF.*/
    STRING    pdsn = dsn;

    *pbrk = 0;
```

/*dsn[0] doesn't have to be the actual first character in the destination array. It can begin at an interior character. Where ever it begins, the beginning character is SNUL'ed, which functionally erases the collecting buffer.*/

```
        dsn[0] = SNUL;
        if (ifptr == NULL)      /*ifptr is a pointer-to-FILE returned by an file-opening function.*/
                {
                printf("\n\nFATAL ERROR. In psin(). Usage: ifptr = fopen(ifile,\"r\")\n");
                exit(2);
                }
        waddr = tbl/32; /*Finding the WORD in the array.*/
        baddr = tbl % 32;      /*Finding the BitColumn in the WORD.*/
        if (! (bChar[SZE(128)][waddr] & tblmask[baddr]) ) /*If the cell is not 1, the table */
                {                       /* was never installed.*/
                printf("\n\nFATAL ERROR in psin(). There is no setbreak \
                 table number %ld.\n",tbl);
                exit(2);
                }
        while (c = getc(ifptr))          /*All input is done in this loop.*/
                {/*char_in*/
                if ( c == EOF )          /*If the End of File is reached, break.*/
                        {
                        *pbrk = EOF;          /*The value of the BreakChar is *pbrk.*/
                        *pdsn = SNUL;
                        break;
                        }
/*L1:*/if (oChar[c][waddr] & tblmask[baddr])     /*Char is an OmitChar.*/
                {/*do_omtlst_first*/
/*L2:*/                if (bChar[c][waddr] & tblmask[baddr])      /*Char is an*/
                                                /* OmitChar and also a BreakChar.*/
                        {/*brkchar*/
                        *pbrk = c;
                        *pdsn = SNUL;
                        break;
                        }/*brkchar*/
/*L2:*/        else
                        {/*not_brkchar*/      /*Char is an OmitChar but not a BreakChar.*/
                        *pdsn = SNUL;
                        *pbrk = 0;                /*When there's no BreakChar.*/
                        continue;
                        }/*not_brkchar*/
                }/*do_omtlst_first*/
/*L1:*/ else      /* if ( ! (oChar[c][waddr] & tblmask[baddr]) ) */ /*Char is not an OmitChar.*/
                {/*c_not_on_omtlst*/
/*L2:*/                if (bChar[c][waddr] & (tblmask[baddr]) )

/*Char is a BreakChar. Three options for disposing of the char follow:*/

                        {/*is_brkchar*/
/*S:*/                        if (bChar[SZE(129)][waddr] & (tblmask[baddr]) )
                                {/*in_Smode*/  /*Skip mode. Throw char away. Button up.*/
                                *pbrk = c;
                                *pdsn = SNUL;
                                break;
                                }/*in_Smode*/
```

```
/*A:*/                    else if (bChar[SZE(130)][waddr] & (tblmask[baddr]) )
                              {/*in_Amode*/ /*Append the char to the last char in the buffer.*/

/*In this next line, pdsn MUST be an exact match of the address.*/

                          if (pdsn == &dsn[lim - 1])
                              {
                              printf("\nln psin(). Must stop record input."
                              "Can't accept more than %d chars at a time.",lim -1);
                              ungetc(c,ifptr);
                              *pbrk = 0;  /*pbrk holds the BreakChar. Here, it's a '\0'.*/
                              pbrk = NULL; /*This is the test for an oversized record.*/
                              *pdsn = SNUL; /*Terminating dsn. This is done each */
                                            /* time to be on the safe side.*/
                              break;
                              }
                          *pbrk = c;
                          c = DULcase(c);      /*Check out if a case change is required.*/
                          *pdsn++ = (char) c;

/*Add the char to the buffer and move the pointer one ahead to pointer where the next char
will be copied.*/

                          *pdsn = SNUL;       /*Terminate the array with a SNUL.*/
                          break;
                          }/*in_Amode*/
/*R:*/      else /*if (bChar[SZE(131)][waddr] & (tblmask[baddr]))*/
                          {/* in_Rmode*/      /*Return char to file.*/
                          *pbrk = c;
                          ungetc(c,ifptr);
                          *pdsn = SNUL;
                          break;
                          }/*in_Rmode*/
                      }/*is_brkchar*/
/*L2:*/     else                              /*Char is an ordinary char.*/
                      {/*is_not_brkchar*/
                      if (pdsn == &dsn[lim - 1])                        /*a*/
                          {
                          printf("\nln psin(). Must stop record input."
                          "Can't accept more than %d chars in a single input.",lim -1);
                          ungetc(c,ifptr);
                          *pbrk = 0;      /*pbrk holds the BreakChar. Here, it's a '\0'.*/
                          pbrk = NULL;   /*This is the test for an oversized record.*/
                          *pdsn = SNUL; /*Terminating dsn. This is done each time */
                          break;         /* to be on the safe side.*/
                          }
                      c = DULcase(c);
                      *pdsn++ = (char) c;
                      *pdsn = SNUL;
                      *pbrk = 0;      /*When there's no BreakChar,*/
                      continue;       /*Continue loop. Will fetch the next char in the file.*/
                      }/*is_not_brkchar*/
```

```
/*L1:*/          }/*c_not_on_omtlst*/
          }/*char_in*/
```

/*The temporary buffer dsn has accumulated the text. The text is now copied to the actual buffer. pdsn is reused as return pointer to the end of dsnstr, the actual buffer, so if the function is used again, it can write starting on the tail of the present string.*/

```
          return(pdsn);
          }/*EP*/
```

4.11.2. PSPSSCAN()

pspsscan() is very similar to *psin*(), except that it operates on text already in memory. It transfers the text in the mother string char by char to the daughter string in accordance with the instructions in the setbreak table that is *pspsscan*'s second arg. Note that reference to the source string is by way of a pointer to a pointer-to-char. So changes in the string are permanent. The chars transferred are permanently deleted from the string. If the first arg were defined as a STRING rather than a PTRADR, then changes would not be permanent; i.e., the address of the start of the text would not change.

USE: *pspsscan*() removes the first part of a predefined string up to the BreakChar. The deleted portion is written to a predefined local char array, the daughter string.

ARGS: a pointer to the variable containing the address of the source string; the setbreak table ID; the int that will hold the BreakChar; the daughter string's size and name
CALLS: none
CALLED BY: *relbreak*(), *setbreak*()
W/B EVAL: yes
RETURNS: none
EXAMPLE: See Section 4.6.2.1.
PROCEDURE:

```
/*PROCEDURE*/ STRING pspsscan(PTRADR s, BITMAP tbl, int *pbrk, int lim,
STRING dsn)
     {/*BP*/
     int          c = (int) SNUL;          /*Make it an int to allow for EOF.*/
     STRING       pdsn = dsn;
     STRING       ps = *s;
     *pbrk = 0;
     dsn[0] = SNUL;
     waddr = tbl/32;
     baddr = tbl % 32;
     if (! (bChar[SZE(128)][waddr] & tblmask[baddr]) )
          {
          printf("\n\nFATAL ERROR. In pspsscan(). \
          There is no setbreak table number %ld.\n",tbl);
          exit(2);
          }
     while (c = *ps)
```

```
                {/*char_in*/
/*L1:*/         if (oChar[c][waddr] & tblmask[baddr])
                    {/*do_omtlst_first*/
/*L2:*/              if (bChar[c][waddr] & tblmask[baddr])
                    {/* is_brkchar*/
                    *pbrk = c;
                    *pdsn = SNUL;
                    ++ps ;
                    break;
                    }/*is_brkchar*/
/*L2:*/         else
```

/*The next code is to cover the case where there is no BreakChar but the program runs out
of string after the current char. Without this, we would lose characters.*/

```
                    {/*not_brkchar*/
                    if (*++ps == SNUL)
                        {
                        *pbrk = 0;
                        *pdsn = SNUL;
                        break;
                        }
                    else
                        {
                        *pdsn = SNUL;        /*SNUL's ahead without moving pointer*/
                        *pbrk = 0;           /*No BreakChar as of now.*/
                        continue;
                        }
                    }/*not_brkchar*/
                }/*do_omtlst_first*/
/*L1:*/ else /* if (!(oChar[c][waddr] & tblmask[baddr]))*/
            {/*c_not_on_omtlst*/
/*L2:*/         if (bChar[c][waddr] & (tblmask[baddr]) )
                    {/*is_brkchar*/
/*S:*/          if (bChar[SZE(129)][waddr] & (tblmask[baddr]) )
                        {/*in_Smode*/
                        *pbrk = c;
                        *pdsn = SNUL;
                        ++ps ;
                        break;
                        }/*in_Smode*/
/*A:*/          else if (bChar[SZE(130)][waddr] & (tblmask[baddr]) )
                        {/*in_Amode*/
                        if (pdsn == &dsn[lim - 1])
                            {
                            printf("\nCan't accept more than %d chars in a "
                            "single input.",lim-1);
                            *pbrk = 0;
                            pbrk = NULL;          /*The test for an oversized record.*/
                            *pdsn = SNUL;
                            break;
```

```
                              }
                       *pbrk = c;
                       c = DULcase(c);
                       *pdsn++ = (char) c;
                       *pdsn = SNUL;
                       ++ps;
                       break;
                       }/*in_Amode*/
/*R:*/            else /* if (bChar[SZE(131)][waddr] & (tblmask[baddr])) */
                       {/*in_Rmode*/
                       *pbrk = c;
                       *pdsn = SNUL;
                       break;
                       }/*in_Rmode*/
                    }/*is_brkchar*/
/*L2:*/       else
                  {/*if_not_brkchar*/        /*Covers case where there is no special break*/
                    if (pdsn == &dsn[lim - 1])
                           {
                           printf("\nCan't accept more than %d chars in a "
                               "single input.",lim-1);
                           *pbrk = 0;
                           pbrk = NULL;   /*The test for an oversized record.*/
                           *pdsn = SNUL;
                           break;
                           }
                    c = DULcase(c);        /*But program may run out of string.*/
                    *pdsn++ = (char) c;
                    if (*++ps == SNUL)
                           {
                           *pbrk = 0;
                           *pdsn = SNUL;
                           break;
                           }
                    else
                           {
                           *pdsn = SNUL;
                           *pbrk = 0;        /*No BreakChar as of now.*/
                           continue;
                           }
                  }/*if_not_brkchar*/
               }/*c_not_on_omtlst*/
           }/*char_in*/
     stcpy(ps, *s);
     return(pdsn);
     }/*EP*/
```

CHAPTER 5

CLUSTERING A GROUP OF STRINGS

5.1. INTRODUCTION

Until now we have been talking of strings in the singular: one string stored in a preset buffer or in memory space obtained on the fly. The name of a data file is the prototypic example. But strings most often are associated in clusters, grouped chronologically or alphabetically or by user-defined category. Typically, an initial step in using a business database is to separate records into chronological groups: all sales recorded in September, all those in October, and so forth. Or into geographic groups by regions or countries or counties or cities. Or alphabetized by customer. Or by a feature such as *paid, unpaid*. A simple way to organize all members of the same subgroup so that they can be simultaneously in memory to be processed as a unit is to provide them with collective storage. In this chapter we will examine techniques for storing a group of strings as a composite entity; i.e., the strings physically coexist as a unit or, if they are stored in discrete areas in memory, the pointers to their locations are grouped.

5.2. MULTIPLE STRINGS IN A TWO-DIMENSIONAL CHAR MATRIX

5.2.1. FIXED-SIZE PREDEFINED ARRAYS

The most obvious way to keep a set of strings together is to store them as rows in a 2-dimensional (2D) character matrix. Thus, char *mat*[SZE(26)] can only store a single string of up to 25 characters plus a terminal SNUL, but char *mat*[SZE(100)][SZE(26)] can store up to 100 such strings, from row zero through row 99. The last element of the filled matrix is *mat*[99][25] just as in an integer matrix. But in a character matrix, it is a terminal SNUL, not another char. In fact, in each row *i* of a completely filled matrix, *mat*[*i*][25]== SNUL.

A matrix can be cleared at definition. In a function and after use, to clear this matrix before it is used again, we can do this:

```
int i, j;

for (i = 0; i < SZE(100); i++)
        for (j = 0; j < SZE(26) ; j++)
                mat[i][j] = SNUL;
```

or this:

```
LOOP(i,100)
    LOOP(j,26)
        mat[i][j] = SNUL;
```

where LOOP is a macro #defined[1] as:

```
#define LOOP(i,x) for (i = 0; i < (x); i++)
```

If rows are filled one after the other in an initially cleared matrix, then to print the strings up to the first empty row, we would write:

```
for (i = 0; mat[i][0] && i < 100; i++)
        printf("\n%s", mat[i]);
```

or

```
LOOP(i,100)
    if (mat[i][0])
        printf("\n%s", mat[i]);
    else break;
```

When the exact number of strings to be pooled is not known in advance so the space allocated has to be large enough to fit the largest size string that might possibly or reasonably be entered, multidimensional character matrices can be enormously wasteful of space. On the other hand, visualization of each string in the entire set is uncomplicated and so the structure lends itself to the storage of related strings. As example, the names of the twelve cranial nerves, where we know the exact number and sizes of the strings with which we will be dealing, can be kept as a sequence of string constants in a predefined global matrix. Defined in this way, they are accessible to multi-file functions.

```
char nerves[][20] = {"", "olfactory", "optic", "oculomotor", "trochlear",
"trigeminal", "abducens", "facial", "auditory vestibular", "glossopharyngeal",
```
(char nerves[][2][20][3])

---

1 It was differently defined in Section 2.2.1.

2 It is not necessary to fill in the first dimension. See Section 1.5.3.

3 The longest string, **auditory vestibular**, contains 19 characters. The programmer must provide space in the definition for the terminal SNUL, so the size is set to 20 as in any ordinary definition. Given that the system takes care of the terminal SNUL for single global string constants (see Section 2.2.1), we might expect that this would also be true for a matrix of strings; i.e., that the size could be set at 19. It is not.

"vagus", "spinal accessory", "hypoglossal"};

Note that we started the actual list from *nerves*[1]—*nerves*[0] is empty—so *one* and *first* refer to the same array element. To list the nerves, we write

for (i = 1; i < 13; i++) printf("\n%s", nerves[i]);

To define the matrix of cranial nerves as a local variable

char nerves[13][20];

stcpy("optic", nerves[1]);
stcpy("ophthalmic", nerves[2]);
stcpy("oculomotor", nerves[3]);

and so forth.

The *stcpy*() function performs the very necessary chore of terminating the string occupying a matrix row with a SNUL. The requirement that the character elements of a row terminate in a SNUL sets the character matrix, global or local, apart from the integer matrix. In a character matrix, despite the fact that the system 'knows' the maximum extent of each row in the matrix, it is still necessary to provide space for the string's terminal SNUL to identify the end of a string. This is not just the case for strings such as **optic** that do not fill the entire space given it. It is just as true for the longest string, **auditory vestibular**. To demonstrate, suppose we change *nerves*[8][19], which currently contains a SNUL, to **Z** and print out *nerves*[8]. The program would display

auditory vestibularZglossopharyngeal

indicating that, lacking a terminal SNUL, the string continued into the next string in the sequence.

The next program, which constructs a quiz on the cranial nerves, illustrates usage of the fixed-sized character array. We begin by storing a set of questions and answers in a global matrix, to which new questions can be added at any time. For a low level quiz (in the sense that questions are simple, not compound, and are not dependent on integrating information), a single string can hold both question and answer, thus:

```
static char qz[][100] =
    {
    "Which nerve controls salivation?9",
    "Which nerve controls equilibration?8",
    "Which nerve originates in the thalamus?2",
    .
    .
    .
    }
```

Suppose we add the requirement that no question is used more than once in a session. To keep track of which questions have been asked, we set up a global int array *tick* with as many elements as there are in *qz*. These are initially set to zero. As example, when *qz*[21] is asked, *tick*[21] is set to 1, and thereafter question #21 is not used. The tick array can be used with varying rules. The level of *tick* might be set to 3, which would allow a question to be asked up to three times in a session.

The time to interrogate *tick* to find an unused question becomes progressively longer as more questions are asked. One solution is to stop when inspection time becomes noticeable. In the next example, we use a 29 question database and stop the program after 23 different questions are asked: **if (total == 4*NUM/5) ...** If the rules were changed so each question can be asked twice, this would become: **if (total == 2*4*NUM/5)....** The session is terminated before all the questions available have had their moment on the screen.

A very simple way to select questions is to make use of the library functions *rand*() and *srand*(), prototyped in *stdlib.h* as:

extern void = srand(unsigned int);
extern int rand(void);

Given some initial number by the user or program, *srand*() creates a seed, a starting integer, for *rand*(), which uses this seed number to initiate the creation of a sequence of pseudo-random integers between 0 and 32767. A starting number of 24, as in this piece of code:

```
int    i = 0;
int    numb = 24;
srand(numb);
for (i = 0; i < 5; i++)
      printf("%d\t",rand());
```

would with MSC invariably produce

116   3537   23994   22900   27029

The program uses the address of a local variable as seed to *srand*(). To keep the numbers generated in the range of *qz*[0] to *qz*[28], we do modulus division of the random number by NUM.

The program contains no graphics; a minimal addition would be a box to the side on the screen with a key to the names and their corresponding numbers. What follows is the complete program file.

```
#include "DEFINE.H"          /*This file includes a #include <stdlib.h> statement to access*/
                             /*srand() and rand().*/

#include "GLOBALS.H"
#include "COMLIB.H"


extern void        blurb(STRING rightans, STRING response);
extern int         main(void);
static BOOL        stfind(STRING str, STRING wrd, int *pbgnsrch);
```

/*The next set of variables are defined as static global. NUM is the number of questions in the database. Because we do modulus arithmetic, this should preferably be a prime number. Or at least an odd one. LEVEL sets the number of times a question can be asked. tick keeps track of which questions have been asked. numb, the seed number that starts generating random numbers, is defined globally; but its value each cycle is determined by *rand*(). *numright* is the number of questions answered correctly and *total* is the total number of questions asked.*/

#define NUM 29
#define LEVEL 1

```
int   numb = 0;
int   numright = 0;
int   out = 0;
int   tick[NUM] = {0};
int   total = 0;
```

char nerves[][20] = {"", "olfactory", "optic", "oculomotor",
"trochlear","trigeminal","abducens", "facial", "auditory vestibular",
"glossopharyngeal", "vagus", "spinal accessory", "hypoglossal"};

char qz[4][NUM][100] = {
```
    "Which nerve controls salivation?9",      /*A question mark separates*/
                                              /* the question and answer.*/
    "Which nerve controls equilibration?8",
    "Which nerve originates in the thalamus?2",
    .....
    .....
};
```

void blurb(STRING rightans, STRING response)
```
    {
    total++;
    if (EQU[5](rightans,response))
        {
        numright++;
        printf("\nFine. Let's try another one.");
        }
```

/*In the next line, atoi() converts the ASCII version of the number to an integer. nerves[int], of course, is a string.*/

---

4 In theory a large number of questions can be kept in *qz*. But in a DOS environment, it is difficult to maintain a large number without multiple modifications, castings, changing the environment size, and so forth. A way around system limitations is to store the database of questions in a separate file, and as an initial step before displaying the questions, determine the start and stop positions of each question in the file, using *ftell*(), a C library function discussed in Chapter 6.5.1. By storing the locations of all the questions in the database in a simple integer array, questions could be pulled into memory as required using *fseek*, a library function.

5 EQU is a macro defined as: **EQU(x,y) (stcmp((x),(y)) == 0)**, where *stcmp*() is the same as the library function *strcmp*(), which compares two strings. If arg 1 and arg 2 are equal, *stcmp*() returns zero.

```
else printf("\nThe answer is %s, nerve #%s. Let's try another one.",
    nerves[atoi(rightans)],rightans);
}
```

/*stfind() is a general purpose 'match text' function. stfind() attempts to find the sequence of characters pointed to by wrd within the char array pointed to by str. It begins its search at str[*pbgnsrch], where pbgnsrch is the address of an int given a value outside stfind(). Transmitting the address of the int as function arg means that the function has the opportunity of permanently changing the value of the int; i.e., the changed value is returned to the function that called stfind().*/

/*Typically, the first pass through str starts at str[0], but it need not be so.*/

/*If wrd isn't in str, stfind() resets the int referenced by pbgnsrch to zero and returns FALSE. If wrd is found, pbgnsrch will be set to point to the char in str that follows wrd. If the analog for str is 'thematic' and wrd is 'the', pbgnsrch will be revalued to the address of 'm'. If wrd is found and stfind() is called again, the search resumes at the character in str pointed to by the revalued pbgnsrch; 'm' in this instance.*/

/*stfind() differs from stmfind() in Section 3.2.4.2 only in that stfind() makes a single match instead of scouting all possible matches in a single function call. Its advantage is that processing of the found substring can be done in the calling function before a second match is attempted. Or the second match may be by a different rule than was the first match. In this program, it provides a way to obtain a virtual separation between question and answer in the elements of qz[][].*/

```
BOOL stfind(STRING str, STRING wrd, int *pbgnsrch)
    {/*BPSrch*/
    int   ls = stlen(str);
    int   lw = stlen(wrd);
    int   srchptr = 0;

    if (ls >= lw)
        for (srchptr = *pbgnsrch; srchptr <= ls-lw; srchptr++)
            {/*SLIDE*/
            if ( str[srchptr] == wrd[0] && (stequ⁶(&str[srchptr],wrd) == TRUE) )
                {
                *pbgnsrch = srchptr + lw;
                return(TRUE);
                }
            }/*SLIDE*/
    *pbgnsrch = 0;          /*If wrd isn't found, *pbgnsrch is reset to zero.*/
    return(FALSE);
    }/*EPSrch*/

main()
    {/*BPmain*/
```

6 *stequ*() is shown in Section 3.2.4.2.

```
char hold[SZE(100)];     /*Will hold the question.*/
char rightans[SZE(3)];   /*Allows for 2-digit answers.*/
int   qm = 0;            /* qm is used to track the position of the question*/ /*a*/
                         /* mark in the current question.*/

int   *p = &qm;
int r = (int) &qm;
```

/*The local variable, p, is an address, which can be negative. But srand() demands an unsigned int. So the value of p is copied into r, which can be kept positive.*/

```
if (r < 0) r = -r;
srand(unsigned int) r);

printf("\nThis is a quiz on the cranial nerves."
       "\nType the number corresponding to the nerve and <Carriage Return>."
       "\nWhen you want to quit, type <CTRLd> instead of an answer.\n\n");
while (TRUE)
    {
    numb = rand();
    out = numb % NUM;        /*MOD division to obtain a number*/
                             /* between zero and NUM-1*/
    if (tick[out] == LEVEL)  /*question[out] has been asked too often.*/
        continue;
    else
        {
        qm = 0;
```

/*The right answer follows the question in each database entry. We wish to display the question by itself. In the next line, if the question mark is found, stfind() will set qm one character position beyond the question mark, thus marking the end of the question. Note that the first arg is a string constant, referenced by its row position. It functions as a pointer arg.*/

```
        stfind(qz[out],"?",&qm);
```

/*The next line of code is similar to the substringing function, pssubst(), shown in Section 2.5.2.3. This version differs in that it uses array notation, rather than sentence notation (see Section 2.4.). In the previous line, stfind() set qm one position beyond the question mark. Next, pssubat() will copy the piece of the original string that is between zero and qm-1 into hold. Hence, the substring in hold will include the question and question mark but not the numerical answer. This is a way to non-destructively divide question and answer, leaving qm pointing to the answer.*/

```
        pssubat(qz[out],0,qm-1,hold);  /*qm-1 contains the question mark.*/
        printf("\n\n%s\t\t",hold);      /*This displays the question.*/
```

/*Next tick[out]'s value is incremented to show that the question has been asked. The number of times a question can be asked is set by LEVEL.*/

```
        tick[out] += 1;
        ptemp = ttyin("T");
        if (ttystr[0] == '\004') /*Recall that ttyin() places keyboard information*/
            break;               /* in ttystr; see Section 2.3.1.*/
```

/*This next produces a substring starting after the question mark and continuing to the end of the string. rightans contains the answer in ASCII format.*/

```
            pssubat(qz[out],qm,stlen(qz[out]),rightans);   /*This dissects out the*/
                                                           /* right answer.*/
            blurb(rightans,ttystr);          /*And this compares it to the answer*/
                                             /* coming in from the keyboard.*/
            if (total == LEVEL * 4*NUM/5)
                {
                printf("\n\nYou've done %d questions.\n "
                    "Restart program for another session.",total);
                break;
                }
            }
        }
    printf("\nYour score was %d out of %d. Bye now.", numright, total);
    return(0);
    }/*EPmain*/
```

5.2.2. VARIABLE-SIZED DYNAMIC ARRAYS

Space in the matrix can be saved by implementing a variable-width string matrix, where the space set aside for any member string is exactly enough for it, rather than being precut to accommodate the largest string in the matrix. This more efficient matrix is not a char matrix; it is implemented as an a set of variables: an array of pointers, each of which is assigned to point to a separate string. In the usage discussed in Section 2.2, when the array of pointers references a set of string constants, the character contents of the strings are part of the definition. When the pointers reference variable strings, an unassigned pointer will be bonded to one of the strings only when storage is requested for that string. In either case, the space that is eventually set aside for any string is just right for that string.

For string constants, the number of pointers can be deduced by the system from the strings listed in the definition. For string variables, the number of pointers needs to be specified in the definition; and, as with any other preset quantity, the size of the pointer array will determine the maximum number of strings that can be considered as a group held together by that set of array pointers. There is also, of course, the inconvenience, as with any system-stored string, of needing to free string space when it is no longer needed and of needing to reallocate space if string size changes.

5.2.2.1.   String Constants.

In Section 5.2.1, we defined a matrix of strings: *nerves[][20]*, where each array is large enough to hold the largest of the strings and the strings are physically contiguous in that they are stored consecutively in matrix formation. The notion of contiguity can also be applied to a set of string constants that are stored separately but are to be manipulated as members of a unit. By using as data structure an array of pointers-to-char, we ensure positional relationships among the pointers. This in turn provides the sequence of (possibly) physically unrelated strings with virtual contiguity.

If a set of different-sized strings is known in advance, as in our cranial nerves example, they can be economically stored by way of a set of pointers-to-char. Section 2.2.1 showed a common example—the error message that is partitioned into a sequence of short strings.

In the present case, we can redefine *nerves* as a set of pointers:

static STRING nerves[] =
```
    {
    "", "olfactory", "optic", "oculomotor", "trochlear","trigeminal", "abducens",
    "facial", "auditory vestibular", "glossopharyngeal", "vagus",
    "spinal accessory", "hypoglossal"
    };
```

where each pointer in turn points to the first char of the next string literal. *nerves*[1] points to **olfactory**, *nerves*[2] pointers to **optic**, and so forth. The number of pointers need not be stated and is deduced from the number of strings referenced by the pointer array. Defining *nerves* as a set of pointers-to-char rather than as a set of string constants would require no modification in the quiz program of Section 5.2.1.

Given that *nerves* is a set of pointers-to-char, we can, in addition, employ a single pointer to this array of pointers. For example

static PTRADR pn = nerves;

defines a new pointer, a pointer-to-pointer-to-char, and assigns it to the first element of the array of pointers; i.e., **pn* contains the address of *nerves*[0]. **(pn + 1)* references the pointer to **olfactory** and **(pn + 2)* is a way of writing the pointer to **optic**.

The pointer-to-pointer-to-char can be used to ripple down the array of pointers-to-char, printing each string in the list in turn. Thus:

LOOP(i,13)
```
    printf("\nCranial nerve %d is %s", i, *(pn + i));
```

In this program, however, we make little use of the constant string or the string literal except to display it on the screen. So adding another pointer adds overhead without concomitant benefit. Nor can we use the PTRADR to make permanent alterations in the string, because string constants should not be altered.

5.2.2.2.   String Variables.

To retain the flexibility of the string variable, pointers, which are members of an array of character pointers, can be assigned to point to a set of strings, which are dynamically stored in (possibly) unrelated locations in memory. In this example, the pointers are global static, so the strings are accessible to all the functions in the same file. The assignments are made at compile time.

static STRING nerves[13];

```
nerves[1] = dssave⁷("optic");
nerves[2] = dssave("ophthalmic");
nerves[3] = .....
```

Or the elements of an array can be filled in from the keyboard at run time.

In this next example, **ttyin("DT");** brings typed entry temporarily into a global array, strips out initial white space and then dynamically stores the result as the i th string, with $p[i]$ pointing to it. Keyboard entry is suited to "calculator query", where a small set of strings are entered 'by hand' and the result of processing them—alphabetizing them or finding similar strings within some fixed database or matching some crossword substring—is instantly displayed.

If the number of pointers is set to some high (for the expected number of strings) value, the user does not have to be warned what the upper limit is. But some way of halting the loop must be devised; in this case, it's CTRLd.

```
int       i;
STRING    p[SZE(100)];

for (i = 1; i < SZE(100); i++)
    {
    printf("\nType in phrase #%i\t", i);
        ptemp = ttyin("T");
    if (*ttystr == '\04')
        break;
    else p[i] = dssave(ttystr);
    }
```

Typically, however, elements of an array are filled from a text or database file, and the contents of the input are not usually known ahead of run time. The TXT system is representative of programs that bring in a record at a time from an ASCII-delimited read-only database and separate the record into its constituent data fields. The pertinent data fields are processed. And the modified record is written to a file.

ASCII-delimited files can not rely on size of field as do fixed-size records. Instead, delimited files designate a specific character to terminate each record, another specific character to terminate each field, and, if there are (sub)subfields, other specific characters to whatever depth the record is divided. The generic name for the record delimiter in the TXT system is *ter* (for inter record); and the name of the field delimiter is *tra* (for intra record)[8].

---

7 Recall that *dssave()* is based on *calloc()*, a library routine that calls on the system to find a specified amount of space in memory. It adds a SNUL to the end of the string.

8 The setbreak tables in lines *b* and *c* are simplified and made specific for the listed delimiters. See the example in Section 5.2.2.3 for the general case.

In this next example, a complete record is brought into a temporary memory buffer, *buf*, using some input functions such as *psin*(), to stop the text stream at the record delimiter; in this case, a ~. Usage for *psin*() is illustrated in Sections 4.2 and 4.7; its code is to be found in Section 4.11.1. A complete program using the segments shown in this section is in LISTINGS\chap5\5-2-2-2b.c. Its organization is:

Determine the order in which the fields of a record are to be output.
Bring in a record.
Cut it into its fields.
Output the fields in the requested order.

Once the record is installed in *buf*, it is chopped into its component fields and these are dynamically stored in system-obtained locations. Each data field is associated with a different element of the pointer array *field*, which is defined globally as:

STRING   field[MAXFIELDS+1] = {NULL};

If *field*[0] is not used, *field* can reference up to MAXFIELDS fields. If MAXFIELDS is set, say, at 50, this array of char pointers can be used by any database with records of 50 fields or less. In the present example, the setbreak table, *RecordTbl*, will stop flow from disk to memory at ~, the record delimiter. The setbreak table, *FieldTbl*, will extract the part of the mother string that stops at /, the field delimiter. These global variables are:

```
extern int      ter = '~';                /*The record delimiter is the value of ter.*/
extern int      tra = '/';                /*The field delimiter is the value of tra.*/

BITMAP    FieldTbl = 0;
BITMAP    RecordTbl = 0;
BITMAP    Tcomma = 0;
FILE      *inchn = NULL;
int       shuffle[2 * LIM] = {0};

main()
      {
      int       brkN = 0;
      char      buf[LRGSZE];
      int       i = 0;
      STRING    pbuf = buf;                                        /*a*/

      inchn = fopen("may.db","r");
      setbreak(&RecordTbl "~", "\n", "s");                         /*b*/
      setbreak(&FieldTbl, "/", "", "is");                          /*c*/
      setbreak(&Tcomma, ",", "","");
      ptemp = psin(inchn, RecordTbl, &brkN, LRGSZE, buf);   /*Brings a single record*/
                                                            /* into buf.*/
```

/*In line d, one field is resettled each cycle of the scanning loop using psdsscan(), a version of pspsscan() that chops a string resident in a preset array and stores the pieces dynamically. (pspsscan() is the scan and chop function presented in the last chapter.) psdsscan() rewrites the unexamined part of the mother string to the top of the array. So halting on an empty first element in the mother string is an appropriate way to stop the for()

loop. Note that in line a, a separate pointer, pbuf, was defined because psdsscan() demands the address of a pointer-to-char as arg and &&buf is unacceptable.*/

```
    for (i = 1; i <= MAXFIELDS && *buf; i++)
        field[i] = psdsscan(&pbuf,FieldTbl,&brk);                /*d*/
    ......
    exit(0);
    }
```

The procedure is ultimately destructive to the record residing in *buf*, deleting a field of chars from it each cycle. Thus if the 6-field record:

Englander/Sam/12 Rue Vavin/Paris/France/Company Name: MplusS~

is stripped of its terminator upon input and deposited in *buf*, then after the first cycle, *field*[1] will be:

Englander

and *buf* will read

Sam/12 Rue Vavin/Paris/France/Company Name: MplusS

Given control of each field by its ability to manipulate the pointers to these fields, the program has the flexibility, say, to allow the user to update a field while viewing one or more of the other fields and then to output some or all of the fields in rearranged order.

/*This next piece of code is a very simple way to determine the order in which the fields are to output. Note that interact has space for twice as many field numbers as there are fields, so a field can be output more than once; e.g., 1,2,1,3,1,4,1,5.*/

```
void interact(void)9
    {
    int i;
    int brk;
    char buf[MEDSZE] = {SNUL};
    char hold[SMLSZE] = {SNUL};
    STRING pbuf;

    PJ(Write field sequence with commas in between.\t);
    pbuf = ttyin("T");
    for (i = 0; i <= 2*LIM  && *ttystr; i++)
        {
        pspsscan(&pbuf,Tcomma,&brk,SMLSZE,hold);
        shuffle[i] = atoi(hold);
        }
    }
```

---

9 A struct-based method is presented in Section 6.7.

/*To rearrange records, the program is directed by the user-determined choices spelled out in interact(). In our sample record, a response in interact() of 2,1,4,5 would, in rearrange(), result in the display of fields 2,1,4,5; e.g., **Sam, Englander, Paris, France**.*/

```
void rearrange(void)
    {
    int i = 0;
    PJ(\n);
    for (i = 0; shuffle[i] != 0; i++)
        printf("\n%s%c",field[shuffle[i]],'\54');
    }
```

5.2.2.3.　　Command Line Args.

The command line args associated with the special C program function called *main*() are a special case of system storage of multiple strings. Like most dynamic strings, these are input at run time. Like string literals, they are stored by the system with no need for specific instructions by the programmer. By C conventional syntax, the first arg of *main*(int argc, STRING argv[]) records the number of words typed in. The second arg, again by convention, is a list of char pointers, where each pointer references a single and separate command line word, with argv[0] dedicated to the name of the running program. And by operating system convention, except for the first word typed, each command line word, which usually act to parameterize the running program with user-chosen options, will begin with a - or /. As example, if the command line typed by the user at runtime reads

write -may.db -temp.may

to summon a program filed as *write.exe*, this code will put the string **may.db** into *InputFile* and **temp.may** into *OutputFile*. Because there is no way to identify which is input file and which output, the program syntax will usually insist that the input file be listed before the output file and that both be present.

```
int main(int argc, STRING argv[])
    {
    char InputFile[SMLSZE];
    char OutputFile[SMLSZE];
    ............................
    stcpy(argv[1]+1,InputFile);
    stcpy(argv[2]+1,OutputFile);
    }
```

Note the second command line word, *argv[1]*, is copied into *InputFile* starting at the second char, the first char being a hyphen. This is also true for *argv[2]*.

Command line instructions can be made more flexible. As examples

- Options are listed in any order.

- The end user is given the choice of supplying none, some or all of the important parameters; vital missing information is elicited later by menu/interaction. Or the command line syntax may include a *D* option that instructs the program to use defaults for all information not supplied.

- A *word* may itself be a compound phrase that will be decoded in accordance with some agreed-upon syntax.

- If the program keeps log information on program usage, an indirect mode can be made available, whereby, for example, **-ipi** is interpreted as **the input file is the file used for input the last time the program was run**; and **-ipo** means **the input file is the previous output file**, and so forth.

A single function can be written to take care of all the acceptable command line words. In the next example, *argmode*() accepts command line instructions that detail the characteristics of the input file, the name of the output file, which task is to be done and the degree of help the user desires. When, for example, the program called *txtadd* is run, the user might type:

txtadd -imay.db,5,~,#,[10] **-t1 -otemp.may -f**

meaning:

-imay.db,5,~,#,	Information about the database.
-t1	Run task 1 of the txtadd menu.
-otemp.may	Put the results of running txtadd in temp.may.
-f	Use fast mode. Help in choosing options is not needed.

Order is unimportant because the first letter after the hyphen signals which option is meant.

-imay.db,5,~,#, supplies information about the database, with the last character—in this case, it is the comma—acting to partition the items of information. The database file is called *may.db*. Each record has 5 fields; and the record delimiter is ~. The field delimiter is #.

As noted earlier, the record delimiter is stored as an int variable called *ter*; the field delimiter is named *tra*. In the present example:

int ter = '~';
int tra = '#';

The following is a simplified version of *argmode*(), a function used by *txtadd.c* to interpret command line options. The indirect mode is not shown.

If argc is 1, no command line directives have been provided. If a program needs guidance before it can run, it will usually provide alternative ways for the user to supply the required

---

10 The final comma is needed by the program when it parses the compound information contained in this single 'word'. The separator may be any delimiter, not necessary a comma.

information—command line, menu and interactive query. Or oft-run routines with canned initialization parameters can be introduced from a parameter file by redirection (e.g., txtadd < interact). Or command pipes will send the output of some program to *txtadd* (e.g., txtsort I txtadd).

In a program with multiple possibilities, even if the user takes full advantage of command line availability, he is likely to be confronted with additional queries before the program can begin. Below, F for Fast mode means these additional requests for information will be tersely stated, H for Help mode means he will be provided with more or less extensive essays on what each option means.

An OK option switch is set to YES when information is provided for that option. OKjab sets the Fast-Help mode, OKin means the program knows what file it is to process, and so forth. If one or more of the options aren't set, the program will initiate interactive query to elicit user choices for these parameters.

Note that the function args, *inchan* and *outchan* are addresses of pointers-to-char. See Section 3.6.2 for a previous example: a pointer-to-pointer-to-FILE serves as function arg to *majorfile()*. Using the address of a pointer-to-FILE as arg guarantees that the value of the pointer-to-FILE will be permanent; i.e., it will be retained when the function terminates. Similarly, *infile* and *outfile* represent addresses of pointers that will be permanently assigned to the dynamically-stored file names. maxtask is the number of different tasks the program can do.

```
/*PROCEDURE*/ void argmode(int argc, STRING argv[], int maxtask, FILE **inchan,
char **infile, FILE **outchan, char **outfile)
    {/*BP*/
    int       i = 0;
    STRING   parg = NULL;

    if (argc > 1) for (i = 1; i < argc; i++)
        {
```

/*In line a, parg initially points to the second word in the command line (because i is initially valued at 1). In each cycle it moves to the start of the next word on the line. Once in a word, it moves forward one place (line c) and examines the character at this new pointer position (line d). */

/*Alternatively, dispensing with parg, i in the previous line can be valued at zero and argv defined as a PTRADR; i.e., main(int argc, PTRADR argv). Then *argv is the pointer to a single command line word. The equivalent of line a can be written as: *++argv, which first moves argv one past the first word, which is always the name of the program. Line b, which tests the first character of a word, can be written as: if (**argv == '-' || **argv == '/'). To interrogate the second character in a word, we could write: *(*argv+1). */

```
        parg = argv[i];                                                      /*a*/
        if (*parg == '-' || *parg == '/')                                    /*b*/
            {
            stuc(argv[i]);        /*Upper-case the command line word.*/
            parg++;               /*Move the pointer past the initial - or / */   /*c*/
            switch (*parg)        /* *parg is the character pointed to by parg.*/  /*d*/
```

```
{
case 'F': jabber = 0; OKjab = YES; break;/*Use Fast mode for*/
                                         /* further information.*/
case 'H': jabber = 1; OKjab = YES; break;/*Help comments are to*/
                                         /* be provided.*/
case 'I' : parg++;              /*Have input file information.*/
                               /* Decode it right away.*/
```

/*majorfile()—described in Section 3.6.2—is a special purpose function that decodes the information the user supplies about the database file: its name, the number of fields per record, the field and record delimiters and (sub)subfield delimiters, if any. If it is successful in assigning the input file name to *infile and the channel number to *inchan, it will then assign the user-selected delimiters to tter, ttra, Tterstop and Ttrastop.*/

```
           if (majorfile(parg,inchan,infile))
              {
```

/*tter and ttra are 2-element char arrays whose only purpose is to hold the record delimiter and field delimiter, respectively, whenever these delimiters are needed to serve as setbreak table args or as function args that require a char array rather than a single char. */

/*Tterstop and Ttrastop are setbreak tables created to stop the text stream at record delimiters and at field delimiters, respectively.*/

```
           tter[1] = ttra[1] = SNUL;
           tter[0] = (char) ter;
           ttra[0] = (char) tra;
           setbreak(&Tterstop,tter,"","s");
           setbreak(&Ttrastop,ttra,"","s");
```

/*In the next line of code, a YES OKin signals that data on the input file and its characteristics have been obtained. The program won't have to drag out its query and menu modes for this information.*/

```
           OKin = YES;
           break;
           }
       else               /*majorfile failed.*/
           {
           printf("\nInput file information is incorrect. Redo.");
           exit(2);        /*There's not much you can do to */
           }               /* salvage command line input.*/
       break;
```

/*The compiler automatically terminates an argv string at the following space. So this next line is safe.*/

```
case 'O': parg++;    /*The name of the output file has been
                       received. Save it.*/
*outfile = dssave(parg);   /*dssave() stops the program if there's */
                           /* not room to store the output name.*/
OKout = YES;         /*A sign the outfile file name is now*/
                     /* known to the program.*/
```

/*In the next line the output file name is assigned to outfile and its channel number to outchan. If the assignments can't be made, the user is alerted and the program ends.*/

```
if ((*outchan = io¹¹(*outfile,apend0)) == NULL)
        {
        printf("\nOutput File information is incorrect. Redo.");
        exit(2);
        }
break;
```

/*Next the program determines which job in its repertoire is to be done. txtadd.c, for example, upgrades the text in a field, replaces a set of phrases, inserts canned phrases, adds an accession number. statoi() converts a string of digits into a numerical value. If the user requests a task whose number is greater than the number of tasks available, an error message is issued. */

```
case 'T': parg++;
task = statoi(parg);
if (task <= 0 II task > maxtask)
        {
        printf("\nTask information is incorrect. Redo.");
        exit(2);
        }
else
        {
        OKtask = YES;
```

/*OKtask means the program now knows the task. It will not have to elicit this information by query.*/

```
        break;
        }
break;
default: printf("OPTIONS: -F<ast>-H<elp> -I<nput file info>"
" -O<utput Filename> -T<asknumber>");
exit(2);
        }
    }

else /*incorrect initial char */
    {
    printf("OPTIONS: -F<ast> -H<elp> -I<nput file info>"
        "-O<utput Filename -T<ask number>");
    exit(2);
    }
}
```

---

11 *io*() is a class function, in that it groups together such I/O functions as *apend0*, *read1* and *write1*, each of which is an independent function whose single arg is a pointer to the name of a file.

```
}/*EP*/
```

The variable-sized array takes less space than a comparable fixed-size array. Storage is now not an array in the sense that char follows char, string follows string in some system-devised sequence. Nevertheless, because the pointer array provides a communality for the group of strings no matter where they actually reside, the set of strings can be conceptualized as members of a list.

5.3. MULTIPLE STRINGS IN A SINGLE ARRAY

5.3.1. EXTRACTING THE INDIVIDUAL STRINGS

A less familiar way to store multiple strings is to chain them one after the other in a single large array. This works particularly well with strings that won't be undergoing size and content changes during the life of the program.

As aid to the typist inputting data via keyboard, a customized Question-Answer program (QAP) requests answers to specific items of information in some fixed order. Even the least sophisticated QAP used to compose a simple bibliographic file would likely include a set of questions designed to elicit information on author, title, journal, year, volume, and page. These questions might all be positioned simultaneously at different locations on the screen. Or each might be displayed on the screen as soon as the typist had finished typing the answer to the previous question, e.g.:

Enter Author's name. (Example: Brown AT, Green LM, Black CM)   Landis, C

Enter Year of publication (Example: 1972)   1964

Enter Name of the article (Example: The Retina) Visual Responses as Indicators of Neurological Damage.

Enter pages (Example: 12:24)   6:20

Enter Abbreviated Name of Journal (Example: JOSA) J Psychophys

Enter VOLume number (Example: 7)   56

The QAP typically offers options, the previous list of questions for the novice, and, for the experienced user of the QAP, a much shortened list such as this:

Author(s)?
Year?
Title?
Pages?
Journal?

Volume?

To store a question cycle, a possible structure would be a string constant, such as this:

char keep[] = "\nAuthor(s)?Year?Title?Pages?Journal?Volume?";

In this format, though storage is simple, extracting the individual questions is not.

Method 1.

One solution is to combine a search function such as *stfind*() and a virtual chopper such as *pssubat*(), both used previously in Section 5.2.1.

A simple program employing these functions is shown next. *stfind*() finds the position in *keep* of the first **?**, and sets *start* to that value plus one. The next time through the loop, the program will search the string for another **?**, starting at *keep[start]*.

Note that the array of questions is a static local variable in *main*(). Moreover, the program is specifically designed to handle bibliographic records whose field delimiter is I and record delimiter is ~. The last field in the record terminates with a record delimiter, not a combination of field and record delimiters; e.,g., the answer to **Volume?** is terminated with the record delimiter.

The program appends each response immediately to a file called *new.bib*. A new cluster of questions is output with an initial **\n** to ensure that a record begins on a new line. The program runs until it's halted by a CTRLd.

```
main(void)
    {/*BPmain*/
    FILE        *fout = NULL;
    int         i = 0;
    int         j = 0;
    static      char keep[] = "\nAuthor?Year?Title?Pages?Journal?Volume?";
    char        question[SZE(20)];
    int         start = 0;

    fout = io("NEW.BIB",apend0);
    while (TRUE)
        {
        j = 0;
        start = 0;
        for (i = 1; i <= 6 ; i++)
            {
            stfind(keep,"?",&start);
            pssubat(keep,j,start-1,question);
            printf("%s\t",question);
            ptemp = ttyin("T"); /*The keyboard input is cleaned and placed in ttystr.*/
            if (ttystr[0] == '\004')
                break;
            if (i == 1)
                fprintf(fout,"\n%sI",ttystr);
            else if (i == 3)
```

```
              fprintf(fout,"\"%s\"|",ttystr);
         else if (i == 4)
              fprintf(fout,"pp %s|",ttystr);
         else if (i < 6)
              fprintf(fout,"%s|",ttystr);
         else fprintf(fout,"VOL %s~",ttystr);
         j = start;
         }
    if (ttystr[0] == '\004')
         {
         fclose(fout);
         break;
         }
    }
return (0);
}/*EPmain*/
```

This would produce a record such as this:

Landis, C|1954|"Visual Responses As Indicators of Neurological Damage"|pp 6:20|J Psychophys|VOL 56~

Method 2.

This next example demonstrates an alternative to a virtual dissection of the display questions. In this version, the separate questions are 'cut' out as needed. *pspsscan*() is destructive, so *keep*[] is first copied to *cpykeep*[]. In line *a* below, each scan of *cpykeep*[] lops the initial portion of *cpykeep*[] up to a **?** and stores it in *question*[].

pspsscan() requires a pointer-to-pointer-to-char as first parameter, hence the need for a separate character pointer, *pcpykeep*, which points to the start of *cpykeep*[]. The address of *pcpykeep* is used as the first arg to *pspsscan*().

Although of little utility in this example, in other circumstances, creating a temporary copy of a string has its uses. For example, a copy of the string can be destroyed during a test for various halting conditions or grammatical errors. If the results are satisfactory, the untouched original is immediately available for processing.

In addition, this example collects all the text for a record before outputting it. The reciprocal task of chopping a record by informational field is accumulating it in a buffer by informational field, a lengthier process than in the previous program, where the individual fields were immediately output. Accumulating a string has the advantage, however, that it may be subjected to additional processing prior to outputting. In this next example, using *psnext*(), the developing record is accumulated answer by answer in *ansbuf*[]. Recall that *psnext*() copies the string of arg 1 to the string of arg 2 and returns a pointer to the terminal SNUL of the just copied string in string 2 (see Section 3.2.4.4). In this example, the terminal SNUL is immediately overwritten with a |, the field delimiter, or, if it is the last question in the series, with a ~, the record delimiter.

CTRLd is used to terminate typing at any time.

```
main()
    {
    char      ansbuf[LRGSZE];
    int       brk = 0;
    char      cpykeep[SZE(60)] = {SNUL};
    FILE      *fout = NULL;
    int       i = 0;

    static    char keep[] = "\nAuthor?Year?Title?Pages?Journal?Volume?";
    BOOL      mark = 0;
    STRING    pbuf = ansbuf;
    STRING    pcpykeep = cpykeep;
    char      question[SZE(20)] = {SNUL};
    BITMAP    Tcut = 0;
    setbreak(&Tcut, "\?", "", "is");
    fout = io("new.bib", apend0);
    while (TRUE)
        {
        stcpy(keep,cpykeep);
        pcpykeep = cpykeep;
        pbuf = ansbuf;
        ansbuf[0] = SNUL;
        for (i = 1; i <= 6; i++)
            {
            ptemp = pspsscan(&pcpykeep, Tcut, &brk,SZE(20), question); /*a*/
            printf("%s\t", question);
            ptemp = ttyin("T");
            if (ttystr[0] == '\04')
                {
                mark = 1;
                break;
                }
            if ( ( i == 1 || i == 3) && stlen(ttystr) > 50 )
                {
                printf("\nThis is too long as a citation. Redo it.\n");
                printf("\n----/----/----/----/----/----/----/----/----/----/\n");
                ptemp = ttyin("T");
                }
            pbuf = psnext(ttystr,pbuf);       /*The fields are accumulated in ansbuf.*/
            if (i < 6)
                    *pbuf++ = 'l';
            else *pbuf++ = '~';
            }
        if (mark == 1)
            break;
        *pbuf = SNUL;
        fprintf(fout,"\n%s",ansbuf);
        }
    PJ(The citations are in NEW.BIB);
```

```
      fclose(fout);
      return(0);
      }
```

A completed file of 3 records from this QAP might be:

Grant, TMI1980IComputerized Bibliographic Methodsl60:84IComputerl14~
Brown RM, Blackwell RS :1934ICollectingBibliographiesl1234:1240IJBibl134~
Muse RRI1935IAids to Compiling Biographiesl14:25IJBibl136~

5.3.2. AUGMENTING THE SINGLE ARRAY

If we indicate the start of each question in the question buffer, the continuous need to search out the end of one string to determine where the next begins is obviated. A basic technique for tagging the start of each individual string without disturbing the contents of the char array is to augment the question buffer with a sister array of character pointers. Two arrays are established, a pointer array and a single char array; in the next example, *q* and *buf*, respectively. Each pointer in turn points to the address of the first letter of the next string in the sequence, making it easier to chart where in the array each string is located.

As illustration, with some hand work we could simply assign to the elements of a pointers-to-char array called *q*[] the starting positions of the individual questions in the constant string *keep* of Section 5.3.1, thus:

```
static char      keep[] = "\nAuthor?Year?Title?Pages?Journal?Volume?";
static STRING   q[6] = {NULL};

q[0] = &keep[0];          /*keep[0] is \n, keep[7] is ?, keep[8] is Y, and so forth.*/
q[1] = &keep[8];
q[2] = &keep[13];
q[3] = &keep[19];
q[4] = &keep[25];
q[5] = &keep[33];
```

This has the defect that small changes in wording the question force one to 'count the stitches' individually. The more general method for ganging pointers and questions is to copy string constants individually or string literals into a single variable char array, using *psnext*(), as in the second example in Section 5.3.1.

In this example, *qbuf* is a string buffer and *p* is a pointer that, as it is incremented, will reference different locations in *qbuf*. *q*[] is an array of pointers that mark the starting positions of the individual questions.

```
int             i = 0;
char            qbuf[MEDSZE];        /*A single array.*/
STRING          p = NULL;            /*A single pointer that will traverse qbuf.*/
STRING          q[7];                /*An array of pointers-to-char.*/
```

In the code that follows, in line *a*, *p* is assigned the address of the first char in the array. As is *q*[0]. In line *b*, the phrase **\nAuthor?** is copied to the start of *qbuf* and hence referenced by $q[0]$. *psnext* returns the address of the terminal SNUL of the string **\nAuthor?**. This new address is assigned both to the revalued p and to $q[1]$, even though there is not yet text at that position. In line c, the phrase **Year?** is copied to that address, while $q[2]$ and p shift to the next empty spot in *qbuf*. And so forth. At completion, $q[6]$ points to the terminal SNUL of the full set of questions.

```
q[0]=p= qbuf;                        /*a*/
q[1] = p = psnext("\nAuthor?",p);    /*b*/
q[2] = p = psnext("Year?",p);        /*c*/
q[3] = p = psnext("Title?",p);
q[4] = p = psnext("Pages?",p);
q[5] = p = psnext("Journal?",p);
q[6] = p = psnext("Volume?",p);
```

It is as if we had filled *qbuf* with the set of questions and then assigned:

```
q[0] = &qbuf[0];                     /*Author?*/
q[1] = &qbuf[8];                     /*Year?*/
..........
 q[5] = &qbuf[33];                   /*Volume?*/
```

qbuf itself would read:

```
qbuf[0] =

qbuf[1] = A
qbuf[2] = u
qbuf[3] = t
qbuf[4] = h
qbuf[5] = o
qbuf[6] = r
qbuf[7] = ?
qbuf[8] = Y
qbuf[9] = e
.......
```

This version has the disadvantage that the individual questions don't have SNUL terminations to delimit the ends of strings for functions such as *printf*(). So if we were to write:

```
LOOP(i,6)
     printf("\n%s", q[i]);
```

we would not obtain a list of the individual questions. Instead, the first line would read: **Author?Year?Title?Pages?Journal?Volume?**, the second **Year?Title?Pages?.....** and so forth.

To remedy this, we need to slide the pointer p one position down past the SNUL terminus before copying the next question. In addition, while it doesn't matter that the strings are stored beginning at *qbuf[0]*, it is easier to keep track of the strings if the question is referenced by the pointer with the same index number as the question. Hence, we modify the code so that $q[1]$ points at the first question. This requires an additional element in q.

```
STRING q[8];
q[1] = p = qbuf;
p = psnext("\nAuthor?",p);
q[2] = ++p;
p = psnext("Year?",p);
q[3] = ++p;
p = psnext("Title?",p);
........
q[6] = ++p;
p = psnext("Volume?",p);
q[7] = p++;
```

printf("\ns",q[3]); would display: **Title?**

and *qbuf* would read:

qbuf[0] =

qbuf[1] = A
qbuf[2] = u
qbuf[3] = t
qbuf[4] = h
qbuf[5] = o
qbuf[6] = r
qbuf[7] = ?
qbuf[8] =
qbuf[9] = Y
qbuf[10] = e
qbuf[11] = a
qbuf[12] = r
qbuf[13] = ?
qbuf[14] =
qbuf[15] = T
....

In the next example, we write code for developing a bare-bones general QAP, where each question is typed in from the keyboard and stored sequentially in a single array, *qbuf*. The location of an individual question is assigned to one of the elements of a pointers-to-char array, *q*. The series of questions is immediately accessible by looping through *q*.

The first half of the program collects the questions that will be eventually displayed on the screen into a single buffer. As a variation on how to 'string beads', *stcpy()* is used instead of *psnext()* and an int called *next* marks the current array locations. In line *a*, the starting location of the next question is calculated, preserving the terminating SNUL for the current question. The second half of the program displays each question in turn, and creates a ASCII-delimited database record from the responses by adding field (|) and record (~) delimiters before sending the record to disk.

```
#include "DEFINE.H"
#include "GLOBALS.H"
#include "COMLIB.H"
```

```
#include "COMSET.H"

extern int main(void);
```

/*The next line set the size of q, the pointer-to-char array, to 26. Because the first question is referenced by q[1], not q[0], in effect LIM sets the maximum number of questions at 25 and, by extension, the maximum number of fields per record in any database it generates. Increase LIM to produce databases where records are sized at 26 fields or more.*/

```
#define LIM 25 + 1

int main(void)
    {/*BPmain*/
    char     ansbuf[LRGSZE];    /*The buffer that collects the growing record.*/
    FILE     *fout = NULL;      /*The pointer-to-FILE for the output.*/
    STRING   fname = NULL;      /*The name of the output file.*/
    int      i = 0;
    BOOL     mark = 0;
    int      next = 0;
    STRING   p = ansbuf;
    STRING   q[LIM];            /*The array of pointer-to-char.*/
    char     qbuf[MEDSZE];      /*The single array.*/
    int      tot = 0;

    printf("\nPlease list questions for the database, one at a time." /*PART 1.*/
        "\nWhen you are finished, push <CTRLd>.\n\n");
    for (q[i = 1] = &qbuf[next = 0]; i < LIM; i++, q[i] = &qbuf[next])
        {
        printf("\nType question %d.\t",i);
        ptemp = ttyin("T");
        if (ttystr[0] == '\04') break;
        stcpy(ttystr, &qbuf[next]);
        next += stlen(ttystr) + 1;    /*Skip 1 so the terminating SNUL*/   /*a*/
        }                             /* is not overwritten.*/
    tot = i-1;                        /*Each record will have tot fields.*/
    printf("\n\nThe records you type are to be added to which file?\t"); /*PART 2.*/
    fname = ttyin("D");        /*Here a pointer-to-char is necessary to point to*/
                              /* the dynamically stored file name.*/
    fout = io(fname,apend0);  /*APPEND the new records to a possibly existing file.*/
                              /* So old material won't be clobbered.*/
    printf("\nPlease start typing in the data."
        "\nYou may stop at any point by pushing <CTRLd>.\n\n");

    while (TRUE)¹²            /*Starts the outer loop that accumulates a single record.*/
        {
        ansbuf[0] = SNUL;
```

---

12 This last part has the same format as Method 2 in Section 5.3.1.

```
          p = ansbuf;

          for (i = 1; i <= tot; i++)          /*Starts the inner loop that acquires the fields*/
                {                               /* for the single record.*/
                if (i == 1) printf("\n");       /*So that each record will begin on a new line.*/
                printf("%s\t", q[i]);
                ptemp = ttyin("T");
                if (ttystr[0] == '\04')
                     {
                     mark = 1;                  /*To stop typing. This sets a flag for the outer loop.*/
                     break;                     /*This breaks out of the inner loop.*/
                     }
                p = psnext(ttystr,p);
                if (i < tot ) *p++ = 'l';
                else *p++ = '~';
                }
          if (mark == 1) break;
          *p = SNUL;                            /*It's essential that the end of the record*/
                                                /* terminates in a SNUL.*/
          fprintf(fout,"\n%s",ansbuf);
          }
     fclose(fout);
     exit(0);
     }/*EP*/
```

2D matrices, variable-sized matrices and multiple strings in a single buffer are useful methods of string unification. But in the general case, each of the strings may have links to associated data. So we often need a structure that not only maintains the string's contacts with its peer strings but also provides for the baggage each string carries. In the next section, the 2D array for clustering a set of strings is amplified to provide expanded space for these additional data. The emphasis is on the different ways to mimic the true 2D array or what in C would be a 3D character array.

5.4. SIMULATING A 2-COLUMN 2D STRING ARRAY IN C

An unrestricted string matrix would allow, as example, the set of QAP records shown in Section 5.3.1

Grant, TM|1980|Computerized Bibliographic Methods|60:84|Computer|14~
Brown RM, Blackwell RS :1934|CollectingBibliographies|1234:1240|JBib|134~
Muse RR|1935|Aids to Compiling Biographies|14:25|JBib|136~

to be stored as a 3 by 5 two-dimensional character matrix, each field constituting an element in the matrix, each element immediately accessible from knowledge of its row-column coordinate.

C hasn't the capability of doing this in the general case. So we are forced to device ways to represent particular formats. Specifically, we would like to represent in simple fashion what, for string processing, is the most popular subset of the general matrix—the two-column 2D matrix. For example, an alphabetized index may be thought of as a 2D string or as a record composed of two fields, where the string is the first field, the set of pages where the string is found the second.[13]

reclaim/	**3,5,10,20~**
recompile/	**12,14,15,20~**
reorganize/	**5,11,13,25-27,30~**

Similarly, keywords and their links to other text can be thought of as 2-field records or as 2D strings.

A true two-column 2D string matrix—i.e., a set of strings and their retinues—can not be directly implemented in C. Recall that a char array holds a single string, not a group of strings; a column of the array is a char, not a string. Nor can we easily construct, as substitute, a 3D matrix in C, where what is the second field of a 2-field record is stored in the third dimension. As shown in Section 1.5.3, accessing higher dimensions becomes progressively more cumbersome, particularly if we need to change the contents often, even when we deal with numerical elements. For strings, it becomes impossible, except by establishing a set of restrictions on what elements of the array can be filled with actual characters. We can illustrate this by attempting to rewrite the 3 by 4 by 2 array of Section 1.5.3 as a character array. This is shown in Table 5.1.

As Table 5.1 indicates, we can not hang higher dimension text from any SNUL that ends any string, hence the space available is more and more constricted with each higher dimension. Searches on higher dimensions would need to take this into account, making certain that no character overwrote a SNUL, yet ensuring than a terminal SNUL in dimensions greater than two does not block the writing and exploration of the string of the next higher dimension starting at that location. Alternatively, we might restrict string entry, so that the second field can be grafted, say, only to the first element of the first field. For example, **12,24,15** would be tied to the **c** of **cat**, beginning one character beyond it. These are not attractive solutions.

row 0:	c	a	t	\0	
row 1:	d	o	g	\0	
row 2:	r	a	t	\0	
					\0

Table 5.1. An example of a 3 by 4 by 2 array.

---

[13] Technically, the second field is composed of an indefinite number of subfields delimited by commas.

5.4.1. A PROGRAM THAT DEMONSTRATES 2D VIRTUAL EQUIVALENTS

This section will demonstrate ways of constructing virtual equivalents of true 2D strings by mixing and matching the several clustering data structures discussed in the first part of this chapter. In what follows, these formats are embodied in variations of a single program that stores a group of strings and the information associated with them.

Programs quite often start within an existing framework that contains a slew of necessary (and unnecessary) I/O, preprocessing and cleanup functions. Much of this is dead code that, in the press of writing a new routine, it was too much trouble to remove. After a while, it seems easier simply to use the cludge as a harmless lump than to trim it, for that would mean going through the hard work of trying to remember what the particular pieces of code were supposed to do. And then there's the superstitious fear that the code might contain a nugget or two needed by some other procedure. (When one reads that 90-95% of the DNA 'strings' in the human genome are meaningless in that they do not translate into RNA, one begins to wonder if cluttered programming is really such a new phenomenon.) At any rate, unexamined accretion seems to happen in any large program as more and more abilities and features are added.

The demonstration program, *Pnames*, (from ProcedureNames) was first written to determine procedure utilization as an aid in translating programs to C. As a general utility to characterize procedure utilization it has several basic characteristics.

• It examines program code and list the names of all the procedures in the program.

• It lists the functions called by each procedure.

• It counts how often each procedure is called.

Routines that are never called can safely be deleted. Run iteratively, *Pnames* will spot routines used exclusively by functions deleted in the previous run.

The original *Pnames* was written in Sail to operate on Sail code and took advantage of several Sail features. The versions presented in this segment are C language translations of the Sail program. As such, they analyze C programs that are styled like Sail programs.

As a case in point, in Sail and disregarding concurrency, as we read a program from top to bottom, we note that procedures written at the beginning of the file can be called by later ones but the reverse is not true; i.e., procedure D can call procedure A, B, C, and D, but not E, F, and beyond. So if we jot down the procedures in the order they are listed in the program, we can stop the search for functions called by D when we reach D. The same is true if it is a computer program reading down the ordered list. The assumption that functions are defined, not just declared, before they are used carries through to the C versions of *Pnames*.

To facilitate distribution, programs were mostly self-contained; i.e., except for general utilities for string processing, input/output and scanning, programs had no #include files.

The possibly unnecessary functions all resided within the file under examination. Mimicking this, the C *Pnames* versions assume they are operating on single-file programs.

Maintaining Sail style, each C source code procedure is labeled /*PROCEDURE*/. This lends itself happily to simple pattern matching. There are of course other ways to show *Pnames* where each function begins in the program under examination. A general-purpose parser would determine the domain of each new procedure. Or we could make assumptions about programming style as does Brief[14] to determine where C routines begin. Adding a marker, however, is simple and ensures accurate detection of the start of all functions and only functions.

In Sail, a two-dimensional string array such as the one shown in Table 5.2 was a convenient and simple way to list procedures and the indices of procedures they call. In any row of the array, the first element (the first column) contains the name of a procedure. While this function is under scrutiny, the row numbers of the procedures called inside the function are written in character format in the second column. The string in column 2 grows in size as the program identifies other called procedures. When the function terminates, the name of the next function is inserted into the first column of the next available row of the array.

When all the functions have been examined, the program uses the information in the array to print out a listing of procedures and the procedures they call. Suppose, as in Table 5.2, we have a 2D matrix called *Sname* and a group of procedures: AA, BB, CC and DD. Each procedure occupies a row in *Sname*. Suppose the first procedure in the file, AA, calls itself; the second, BB, calls no procedure; CC calls AA and BB; and DD calls BB, AA, CC and BB in that order.

Eventually, *Sname* would look like this:

String Array Sname[100,2]		
index # **(row #)**	**column 1** **value**	**column 2** **value**
(1)	AA	1
(2)	BB	
(3)	CC	1,2
(4)	DD	2,1,3,2
(5)	...	......

Table 5.2.   Coordinating functions and the index numbers of functions they call.

To determine from *Sname* what procedures were called by CC, we would find the names that correspond to the index numbers of the rows; in this case, row 1 and row 2: AA and BB.

---

14 A text editor developed by UnderWare, Inc. and marketed by Borland, Inc.

The program does much the same. It cuts the string in row 3, column 2 at commas and treats each piece as an index number of a row in the matrix.

As an added feature, to ensure that each procedure called inside a particular function is listed only once, no matter how many times that procedure is actually called, the index numbers for a procedure can be filtered, using an int vector called *filter*. This is illustrated in Table 5.3. Each procedure in column 1 of *Sname* is separately examined and the elements of the array are reset to zero before dealing with the next procedure. For any particular procedure—DD, say—the elements that correspond to the index numbers of procedures called by DD—column 2 values in *Snames*—are incremented each time they occur in the procedure. When DD is the procedure of interest, *filter* would look like this:

---

int filter[100]

filter[1] = 1
filter[2] = 2
filter[3] = 1
filter[4] = 0

Table 5.3.   Filtering out extra copies of functions that are called by a single function.

For each procedure, the program outputs function names corresponding to the indices listed in Column 2 of *Sname* after they have been filtered. For procedure DD, the value of *filter*[1] is greater than zero. The program 'looks up' *Sname*[1] and finds AA. The value of *filter*[2] is also greater than zero. The program 'looks up' *Sname*[2] and finds BB, and so on. The procedures called by DD would be output as AA, BB, CC, not as BB, AA, CC, BB. Note that the values of the elements of filter can also serve to indicate how many times a particular function was called by another function.

The three C variations of Pnames simulate a 2D matrix of function names and indices in different ways. Pnames1 uses twin 2D character matrices, one to list the procedures, the other to record the indices of the functions these procedures call. Pnames2 uses a large 1D array to list the procedure names and a pointer array to locate these procedure names; a 2D integer array holds the indices. Pnames3 uses two large 1D character buffers to hold names and indices.

The generic program can only analyze a limited subset of C programs, but does have the virtue of simplicity. This makes it easier to compare the different ways the three C versions simulate the 2D matrix. The programs also exhibit some useful string-handling procedures. *procname*(), a less restricted struct-based version of Pnames, is presented in LIST-INGS\chap6\procname.c. It is better suited to analyzing real C programs.

5.4.2. FORMAT OF THE NAME TRACKING PROGRAM

Except for the data structures in *main*() and the differences they make in how a file is examined, all the procedures are the same for all three versions of the program. They are listed and annotated in Section 5.4.3.

Each version examines source code from a C program that can be compiled and run.

This is the general strategy:

- Bring in a line of code from a file containing C source code. *Pnames* won't work on undebugged code where the problem is an unmatched { } pair.

- Pattern match on **/*procedure*/** within the first 15 chars of the line. If TRUE, this must be the start of a procedure.

- The name of the procedure is on the same line as the label **/*procedure*/**. *getname*() finds this name and write it into the first row of the name matrix. Note that *getname*() is written with a TRUE-FALSE return, so it is usable later in the general case to identify procedures called by the procedure we are currently examining.

- While in a procedure block, increment a counter called *procblock* for each { and decrement it for each }. A *procblock* of zero signals the end of the procedure block.

- While in the procedure, bring in one line of code at a time. Comments necessarily have to be deleted by the program; it might otherwise be led astray by a { or } within a comment. So if the line of text contains a comment, delete the comment entirely, even if this necessitates bringing in more lines.[15]

- Determine what procedures the current function contains. A candidate procedure name is any set of characters followed by a left parens, ignoring ordinary C keywords such as *return* or *while*. As the string is scanned, each candidate is checked against the procedure names previously written in the names matrix. If there is a match, the index number of the matched name is converted to character format and written (or, if there are previous matches, appended) in space linked to the current procedure.

- When the file has been completely examined, starting with the first procedure that was examined, write out the procedure name.

- Filter the index numbers of the functions this procedure calls to delete name repeats. Convert the index to the names of the called procedures and output them.

---

15 Except for deleting comments, the C versions of Pnames do not handle other string literals that can also contain braces. In consequence, a program will get into trouble if it encounters an unpaired { inside a string literal in a print statement or in a setbreak statement.

- Continue writing out each procedure in turn, together with the filtered names of the procedures each particular procedure calls.

5.4.3. PNAMES1: TWO 2D CHARACTER ARRAYS

To mimic a true 2D string array, we may set up two 2D char buffers. The list of procedure names is housed in a 2D string array, *Sname*[SMLSZE][2*SMLSZE]. The indices of the functions associated with each procedure are housed in another 2D string array, *Sindex*[SMLSZE][2*SMLSZE]. There is implicit linkage of the two matrices by row number.

SMLSZE is set at 40 in *define.h*. So defined, *Sname* can hold 40 procedure names listed in rows 0 to 39, with each string as long as 79 ASCII characters plus a terminal SNUL. The first row of the matrix is not used, so the first name found is stored in row 1. If *NEWPROC* were the 7th procedure listed in the file examined, row 7 would hold the char array N E W P R O C. **N** would be located in *Sname*[7][0], **E** would be in *Sname*[7][1], **W** in *Sname*[7][2], and so forth.

Sindex, the sister array to *Sname*, uses row 1 to store index numbers for the first procedure. The zeroth row is not used. The index numbers are stored as characters in a string array, separated by commas. *Sindex*[10][0] to *Sindex*[10][78] can store indices to the procedures called by the 10th procedure written in the file. Similarly, *Sindex*[2][0] points to the start of the index buffer affiliated with the second procedure.

```
/*FILE: pnames1.c*/
#include "DEFINE.H"
#include "GLOBALS.H"
#include "COMLIB.H"
#include "COMSET.H"
```

/*LIST OF PROCEDURES*/

```
static void        delcomment(PTRADR str);
extern void        psscoopat(PTRADR str, int bgn, int ndd, STRING dsn);
static BOOL        getname(PTRADR s,STRING pwrd);
static void        endgame(void);
static void        interactive(void);
extern int         main(void);
```

/*ALPHABETIZED LIST OF GLOBAL VARIABLES*/

```
static int         bgnsrch = 0;
extern int         brk = 0;
static int         current = 0;
static char        delo[] = "!@#$%^&*)-+=[]{}\96~|:;',.<>?";
static int         linecnt = 0;

static STRING      pa[SZE(5)] = {NULL};
static PTRADR      ppa = NULL;
static int         procblock = 0;
```

static BITMAP	**Tcomma = 0;**
static BITMAP	**Tcomment = 0;**
static BITMAP	**Teol = 0;**
static BITMAP	**Tquote = 0;**
static BITMAP	**TTokenOmit = 0;**

/*stfind() is discussed in Section 5.2.1.*/

/* delcomment() is a special purpose routine to delete comments from a line of text. delcomment() determines whether the string contains a comment and marks the location of the comment by using stfind(), in lines a and b, to find /* and */ diphthongs. The position of a found comment is relative to the input string; i.e., from the bgn th char of the string to the ndd th char of the string.*/

/*psscoopat() in line c does the actual extracting of the comment. Comment deletion is destructive in that the original string is rewritten without its bgn to ndd th elements. To make this change in the string permanent, psscoopat() is given the address of the pointer whose value is the address of the char array containing the string.*/

/*psscoopat() writes the unwanted comment into its fourth arg, a trash buffer. It may seem odd to make the dump a separate arg defined over all of delcomment() rather than a local variable within psscoopat(). But there are possible complications because code is taken in one line at a time but a comment can run over several lines. If, as in line d, the end of the comment is not found within that line, delcomment() takes over and brings in lines of code—line e is part of a loop—until it finds the end of the comment. The halting rule is written into the Tcomment setbreak table, which is set in interactive().*/

static BOOL   stfind(STRING str, STRING wrd, int *pbgnsrch);

/*PROCEDURE*/ static void delcomment(PTRADR s)

```
      {/*BP*/
      char      comment[HUGESZE] = {SNUL};
      char      rcd[LRGSZE] = {SNUL};          /*Used to gather the additional lines of*/
                                               /* extended comments in line e.*/
      STRING    prcd = rcd;          /*pspsscan in the line after f requires a pointer*/
                                     /*address. So rcd can't be used as the function arg.*/
      int       pl = 0;              /*Marks the last element of an additional line of*/
                                     /*entry text. (See line g.)*/
      int       start = 0;
      STRING    str = *s;            /*str is set to the address held in s, delcomment's arg.*/

      bgnsrch = 0;
```

/*stfind() begins the search for the start of a comment by looking for a /* combination. It always starts the search at the bgnsrch th array element. Initially bgnsrch is zero. If a /* is found, bgnsrch is reset by stfind just past the asterisk, and stfind proceeds to search for the end of the comment. If a complete comment exists within the line, i.e., if a */ is found, then bgnsrch is reset to point just after the slash.*/

```
      if (stfind(str,"/*",&bgnsrch) == TRUE)    /*If no /* is found,*/              /*a*/
            {/*FoundStartOfComment*/            /* the string isn't changed.*/
            start = bgnsrch-2;                  /*We also want to get rid of the / and */
                                                /* the * that start the comment.*/

            if (stfind(str,"*/",&bgnsrch))                                          /*b*/
```

```
        {/*CommentWithinStr*/
        psscoopat(s,start,bgnsrch-1,comment); /*The whole comment*/   /*c*/
        }/*CommentWithinStr*/          /* is within the confines of a single line.*/
    else
        {/*CommentNotWithinStr*/
```

/*The start of the comment is within the input line and can be deleted using psscoopat() in the next statement. But the comment runs beyond the single line. So the next line(s) of the program will be brought into memory from disk until the end of the comment is found and the entire comment deleted.*/

```
        psscoopat(&str,start,stlen(str),comment); /*If the program got*/
                            /* here, we have an extended comment.*/      /*d*/
        while (TRUE)
            {/*CommentRunsOver2orMoreLines*/
            comment[0] = SNUL;
```

/*In line e, under the control of the Teol setbreak table, psin() reads a line at a time from the source code file into rcd, stopping entry on the NewLine. Then (in the line that follows line f) the text in rcd is scanned under Tcomment, which stops processing on a /, the last char in a comment. If the slash is not found, the whole line must be part of the comment, so it is dumped into the array called comment. The next line is then fetched. But if pspsscan() traps a / that is preceded by an asterisk, the end of the comment has been reached. In line h, what is left of the entry line that contained the end of the comment is added to the beginning of the line up to the start of the comment.*/

```
            psin(inchan[1],Teol,&brk,LRGSZE,rcd);                    /*e*/
            linecnt++;
            if (linecnt % 100 == 0)
                printf("\nHave examined %d lines.\n",linecnt);

            if (rcd[0] == SNUL)      /*The line is empty except for an EOL.
                                     Go fetch another.*/
                continue /*CommentRunsOver2orMoreLines*/;       /*f*/
            ptemp = pspsscan(&prcd,Tcomment,&brk,HUGESZE,comment);
            pl = stlen(comment)-1;                                   /*g*/
            if (brk == '/' && comment[pl] == '*')
                {/*FoundEndOfComment*/
                stcat(rcd,str);                                     /*h*/
                break /*CommentRunsOver2orMoreLines*/;
                }/*FoundEndOfComment*/
            }/*CommentRunsOver2orMoreLines*/
        }/*CommentNotWithinStr*/
    }/*FoundStartOfComment*/
}/*EP*/
```

/*The next function, psscoopat(), is a general purpose function for extracting a substring identified by its position in the mother string, the analog to the first arg. It is used in this program to delete the comment from the string, sending it to dsn, the dummy for a preset collecting buffer. psscoopat() is similar to pssubat() in Section 5.2.1, except that it deletes the piece of the string that it copies to the daughter string. In deleting a part of the mother string, it behaves like pspsscan(), except that the portion erased is identified by its position in the string, whereas pspsscan() erases all characters from the top of the string to a defined halt character.*/


```
/*PROCEDURE*/ void psscoopat(PTRADR s, int bgn, int ndd, STRING dsn)
    {/*BP*/
    char        buf[HUGESZE] = {SNUL};        /*To accumulate the resultant string */
                                              /*stripped  of comments.*/
    int         cpybgn = 0;
    int         i = 0;
    STRING      pbuf = buf;
    STRING      str = *s;         /*The value assigned to str is the address stored in s.*/
    int         ls = stlen(str);

    dsn[0] = SNUL;
    if (bgn < 0)
        bgn = 0;
    if (ndd >= ls)
        ndd = ls - 1;            /*Because array[ls] is reserved for the terminal SNUL.*/
    cpybgn = bgn;                /*cpybgn will retain the position of the bgn th char of the*/
                                /* original string.*/
```

/*Next, if the bgn th and ndd th chars of the source string are within range of the string, the program is ready to copy the bgn th to ndd th chars of the string to another array, dsn. In the present example, because the position of the comment was ascertained before psscoopat() is called, this is an unnecessary step. But psscoopat() is a general utility that can be used to extract any position-defined substring from a preset string.*/

```
    if (ls != 0 && ndd >= 0 && bgn <= ndd)
        {
        while (bgn <= ndd)
            *dsn++ = str[bgn++];       /*One char of the comment is written to dsn.*/
```

/*When the loop finishes, dsn is pointing to what is or what will be the terminal SNUL of the accumulating substring that was scooped out of the original string. dsn will snap back to the beginning of this substring WHEN control returns to the calling function.*/

```
        *dsn = SNUL;
        }
```

/*Now that the comment substring has been copied to dsn, the parts of the string that surround the comment need to be combined. buf will serve to collect the reconstructed string.*/

```
    bgn = cpybgn;
    if (ls != 0 && ndd >= 0 && bgn <= ndd)/*The first part of the string is copied to buf.*/
        {
        for (i = 0; i < bgn; i++)
            {
            *pbuf = str[i];
            pbuf++;
```

```
        }
    for (i = ndd+1; i < ls; i++ )          /*The last part of the string is copied to buf.*/
        {
        *pbuf = str[i];
        pbuf++;
        }
    *pbuf = SNUL;
```

/*The next line of code copies the revised string that was collected in buf to the address contained in s. This overwrites the original string, starting at the top of the array. This is most efficient when used with preset arrays, which are trashed by the system when the function terminates, but can be used on dynamic strings. In this program, we can trace the original string from psscoopat() through delcomment() to its origin as a local char array in main().*/

```
        stcpy(buf,*s);
        }
    }/*EP*/
```

/*The first arg of the next function, getname(), is the address of the pointer to a string that is a line of code. Within the function, the value of s is assigned to a local variable, ps, in line a. In this way, the original value of the pointer *s is retained, while ps traverses the string. In line b, the string is cleaned of all the characters written into delo[]. In line c, pspsscan() chops the string into words. Candidate function names are words that end in '(' or ' ('. If the 1st letter of the word is a '(', it is stripped off. If the word ends in a ' (', the '(' is deleted before the rest of the sentence is returned for possible further inspection; i.e., fctName(fctName(....), ...) Common library utilities and control statements are ignored.*/

```
/*PROCEDURE*/ static BOOL getname(PTRADR s, STRING pwrd)
    {/*BP*/
    int        brk = 0;
    STRING     pon = NULL;
    STRING     ps = *s;                                          /*a*/
    char       w[SZE(100)] = {SNUL};
```

/*NOTE: It is necessary to SNUL the first char contents of pwrd, even if it was preNULL'ed in the calling routine.*/

```
    pwrd[0] = SNUL;
    ps = sttidy(s,"\40",delo,"","FED");                         /*b*/
    while (*ps)
        {/*DeleteWords*/
        w[0] = SNUL;
        pon = w;
        brk = 0;
```

/*pspsscan() stops at a space or a (. pspsscan() demands a pointer-to-pointer-to-char. Note that initially the address of ps (&ps) is the same as s, the first function arg of getname().*/

```
        ptemp = pspsscan(&ps,TTokenOmit,&brk,SZE(100),w);   /*c*/
        if ( w[0] == SNUL    || EQU(w,"if")       || EQU(w,"for")
        || EQU(w,"while")    || EQU(w,"return")   || EQU(w,"fopen")
        || EQU(w,"fclose")   || EQU(w,"fprintf")  || EQU(w,"printf")
```

```
        || EQU(w,"sprintf")  || EQU(w,"getchar")
        || EQU(w,"putchar") || EQU(w,"getc")     || EQU(w,"putc")
        || EQU(w,"calloc")   || EQU(w,"malloc")  || EQU(w,"fseek")
        || EQU(w,"fread")    || EQU(w,"scanf")    || EQU(w,"fscanf")
        || EQU(w,"sscanf"))
            continue /*DeleteWords*/;
        else if (brk == '(')
            {
            if (*pon == '(')
                pon++;
            stcpy(pon,pwrd);
            return(TRUE);                     /*This returns a candidate name.*/
            }
        else if ( brk == '\40' && *ps == '(' )   /*There's a gap between the function*/
            {                                     /* name and function body.*/
            if (*pon == '(')
            pon++;
            stcpy(pon,pwrd);
            ps++;
```

/*Given that ps now points to the start of the procedure candidate, we can write: *s = ps;, which instantly revalues s with the address of the start of the candidate, erasing the original value (the address of a char array) contained in s. This is Method 1 of Section 3.7.2.2. It is a short cut that is only safe with preset arrays, not dynamically stored arrays, which can not be freed if the original starting address is lost.*/

```
            *s = ps;
            return(TRUE);                     /*This returns a candidate name.*/
            }
        else continue /*DeleteWords*/;
        }/*DeleteWords*/
    return(FALSE);
    }/*EP*/


/*procedure*/ void endgame(void)
    {
    printf("The program counted %d procedures",current);
    printf("\nThe procedures are listed in %s.\n",outfile[1]);
    printf("\nThere were %d records searched.\n",linecnt);
    fclose(inchan[1]);
    fclose(outchan[1]);
    }
```

/*The next procedure, interactive(), obtains the name of the file to examine. Usually a database program needs information about the input file's record and field delimiters or, for fixed-size fields and records, the number of chars in each field. However this program brings in a line at a time, so only the name of the file needs to be supplied. The output name is fixed by the program.*/

```
/*PROCEDURE*/ static void interactive()
    {/*KeyboardInitiation*/
    while (TRUE)
        {/*LoopUntilFileCanBeOpened*/
        printf("\nWhat database should be examined:\n");
        infile[1] = ttyin("DUT");
        if (inchan[1] = io(infile[1],read1))
            break /*LoopUntilFileCanBeOpened*/;
        }/*LoopUntilFileCanBeOpened*/
    outfile[1] = dssave("pname.out");
    outchan[1] = io(outfile[1],write0);
    stuc(infile[1]);
    fprintf(outchan[1],"\n\n\t\t%s\t\t\n\n",infile[1]");
    fprintf(outchan[1],"times          \11\11procedures\n");
    fprintf(outchan[1],"used    PROCEDURE\11\11it calls\n\n");
    setbreak(&Tcomma,",", "\40\n", "is");
    setbreak(&Tcomment, "/", "" ,"is");
    setbreak(&Teol,"\n", "\13\14", "isu");
    setbreak(&Tquote,"\42","","is");
    setbreak(&TTokenOmit,"(\40\11","*!\13\14","is");   /* * is for indirect pointing.*/
    }/*KeyboardInitiation*/
```

```
/*PROCEDURE*/ main()
    {/*MAIN*/
```

/* **SEGMENT A.** These variables are common to the three versions of Pnames.*/

Marked segments will not be repeated in Pnames2 and Pnames3.

char	cpyrcd[SZE(1000)] = {SNUL};
STRING	expr = NULL;
int	freq[SMLSZE] = {0}; /*The number of times each procedure is used.*/
int	i = 0;
int	ii = 0;
STRING	pcpyrcd = cpyrcd;
char	rcd[SZE(1000)] = {SNUL};/*rcd must be defined before prcd.*/
STRING	prcd = rcd;
int	zz = 0;

Table 5.4.   Segment A, PNames.

```
    char      junk[SZE(1000)];
    int       filter[SMLSZE];
    STRING  Pindex = NULL;
```

/*Two 2D arrays are defined: Sname to hold the names of the procedures in the file, Sindex to hold the index numbers of the procedures called by the procedures in Snames. Note that the index numbers will be stored in character mode.*/

```
    char      Sname[SMLSZE][2*SMLSZE]; /*Char buffer for names of procedures.*/
    char      Sindex[SMLSZE][2*SMLSZE]; /*Holds index nos of procedures*/
                                        /* called by Sname procedures.*/
```

```
for (i = 0; i < SMLSZE; i++)
    for (ii = 0; ii < 2*SMLSZE; ii++)
        {
        Sname[i][ii] = SNUL;
        Sindex[i][ii] = SNUL;
        }
```

```
/* SEGMENT B. This is common to the three versions of Pnames.*/

interactive();
while (TRUE)
    {/*SrchFile*/
    psin(inchan[1],Teol,&brk,SZE(1000),rcd);   /*Each cycle brings in */
                                                /* a line of code.*/
    if (brk == EOF)
        break /*SrchFile*/;
    linecnt++;
    if (rcd[0] == SNUL)
        continue /*SrchFile*/;
    pssubat(rcd,0,SZE(15),cpyrcd);    /*Copies the 1st 15 chars.*/
                                      /* It will be matched against: /*Procedure*/
```

Table 5.5.   Segment B, Pnames.

/*If there is a match to the phrase /*Procedure*/ this is a start of procedure code. An integer variable called procblock is incremented whenever a left brace is encountered. procblock is decremented when a right brace is encountered. A procblock of zero signals the end of the function. The text /*procedure*/ found inside function code is taken as a comment.*/

```
if (keyfind(cpyrcd,"/*PROCEDURE*/"))      /*The start of*/              /*a*/
    {/*ExamineAProcedure*/                /*a procedure block.*/
    prcd = rcd;
    current++;                            /*Starts with 1.*/
    getname(&prcd,Sname[current]);        /*Assumes PROCEDURE label */
                                          /*and name of the procedure are on same line.*/
```

/*The general game plan is to determine what procedures—whose code was written earlier in the program—are called in the current procedure. In the next segment, while procblock is positive (i.e., the program is in a block of code that is a procedure), each potential name is matched against the procedure names already found. If there's a match, the row number is changed to character mode and is added to the previously stored index numbers. freq is incremented in line g.*/

```
/* SEGMENT C. This is common to the three versions of Pnames.*/

        while (TRUE)          /*Inside a procedure block.*/
            {/*WhatProcsDoesThisProcCall*/
            rcd[0] = SNUL;
            prcd = rcd;
            psin(inchan[1],Teol,&brk,SZE(1000),rcd); /*Brings*/
                            /* in lines from the procedure body.*/
            linecnt++;
            delcomment(&prcd); /*Lest a comment contain a brace.*/
            if (rcd[0] == EOF)
                break/*WhatProcsDoesThisProcCall*/;
            if (rcd[0] == SNUL)
                continue/*WhatProcsDoesThisProcCall*/;
            if (keyfind(rcd,"{")) procblock++;  /*Assumes*/
                            /* there won't be 2 braces on 1 line.*/
            if (keyfind(rcd,"}")) procblock--;
            while (TRUE)
                {/*CheckIfLineHasACandidate*/
                cpyrcd[0] = SNUL;
                pcpyrcd = cpyrcd;
                prcd = rcd;
```

Table 5.6.   Segment C, Pnames.

/*The program is still within the block begun in line a. It is seeking out names of procedures called in this procedure block. The name of a possible called function is uncovered by getname() in line b below. The program runs down the list of authentic procedure names stored from row 1 to the current row.*/

/*If the candidate name matches a name on this list, the index number of the matched procedure is added to the list of index numbers for the current procedure. To add the characters representing an index number to the string in Sindex, the string must be enlarged. This is done using stmcat (see line f), a multi-arg concatenating function.*/

/*A set of pointers-to-char, the elements of the array pa in this case, point to the strings to be concatenated. In line c, the index numbers of the called functions previously called in this function are copied to pa[0]. pa[1]—line d—holds a comma. pa[2] in line e is the row number of the candidate found by getname(). ppa is a pointer to pointer-to-char that points to each of these 3 pointers in turn as stmcat() ties these strings together, storing the merged product in dynamically obtained space pointed to by expr in line f. */

/*The enlarged string is then copied to the row of Sindex associated with the procedure currently under examination, erasing the previous material. For example, if we are using PNames1 on itself and the procedure under examination is the third function in the file, delcomment(), then Sindex[3] would be 1,2 because delcomment() calls stfind() and psscoopat(), the first two functions in the file.*/

/*A major programming consequence of keeping indices in character mode is the need to convert them and open up space for them. An alternative method to using stmcat() would be to determine the string's size with stlen(). Then the new material is added at the terminal SNUL with simple concatenate statements. Or an array of pointers-to-char could be defined, where a pointer element stores the location where new material should be added for a particular Sindex string.*/

```
            if (getname(&prcd,pcpyrcd))                        /*b*/
                {/*MayBeAFct*/
                for(ii = 1; ii <= current; ii++)
                    {/*CheckEachFctName*/
```

/*Next if pcpyrcd is a listed name, then find the next vacant position.*/

```
            if (EQU(pcpyrcd,&Sname[ii][0]))
                {/*MatchedAFunction*/
                Pindex = &Sindex[current][0];
                pa[0] = Pindex;                        /*c*/
                pa[1] = ",";                           /*d*/
                stitoa(ii,ttystr);       /*ttystr is a global array for*/
                                         /*temporary storage.*/
                pa[2] = ttystr;                        /*e*/
                ppa = pa;
                expr = stmcat(ppa,3);                  /*f*/
                stcpy(expr, Pindex);     /*Copy the phrase to*/
                                         /* permanent storage.*/
                NULLIT(expr);
                freq[ii]++;                            /*g*/
```

```
+--------------------------------------------------------------------+
|       /* SEGMENT D. This is common to the three versions of Pnames.*/ |
|                                                                    |
|                    break/*CheckEachFctName*/;                      |
|                    }/*MatchedAFunction*/                           |
|                }/*CheckEachFctName*/  /*For*/                      |
|                        /*fctnam(fctname(param)) cases.*/           |
|                }/*MayBeAFct*/                                      |
|            if (rcd[0])                                             |
|                continue/*CheckIfLineHasACandidate*/;               |
|            else break /*CheckIfLineHasACandidate*/;                |
|            }/*CheckIfLineContainsACandidate*/                      |
|                                                                    |
|                                                                    |
| /*Next, if procblock is zero, we're at the end of the procedure block. This falls through |
| and continues SrchFile because ExamineAProcedure is an IF statement, not a loop.*/ |
|                                                                    |
|            if (procblock == 0)                                    |
|                break/*WhatProcsDoesThisProcCall*/;                 |
|                /*If program gets here, then continue SrchFile.*/   |
|            }/*WhatProcsDoesThisProcCall*/                          |
|        }/*ExamineAProcedure*/                                      |
|    }/*SrchFile*/                                                   |
|                                                                    |
| **Table 5.7.** Segment D, Pnames.                                 |
+--------------------------------------------------------------------+
```

/*The procedures in the file examined are listed in order in Sname, beginning with Sname[1]. If Pnames1 were set to examine itself, stfind would be written in Sname[1]. The program outputs the number of times the function is called and the function name; in our example, stfind() is called twice in delcomment(). The program then determines what functions are called by stfind(), then in this loop examines the index numbers for each of the other functions in turn.*/

```
for (ii = 1; ii <= current; ii++)
    {/*output*/
    fprintf(outchan[1],"\n(%d)        ",freq[ii]);
    fprintf(outchan[1], "[%s]\n",&Sname[ii][0]);
```

/*In our example, stfind is in Sname[1], so its index number would be 1, psscoopat is in Sname[2], so its index number is 2, and so forth. All the procedures called by a given function are maintained as a string; for example, the third function, delcomment(), calls stfind() twice and psscoopat() twice. Sindex[3] would be 1,1,2,2. The ProcCalled block below chops one value out at a time using pspsscan(), converts it from char to integer mode with statoi() and increments the related element in the int array called filter. Initially, all the values in filter are set to zero. Using our example, the first value in Sindex[3] is 1 and so filter[1] would be incremented from 0 to 1. If the value was 10, filter[10] would be incremented from 0 to 1.*/

```
for (zz = 0; zz <= ii; zz++)
    filter[zz] = 0;                    /*This was explained in Section 5.4.1*/
while (stlen(&Sindex[ii][0]) != 0)
    {/*FillFilterArray*/
    junk[0] = SNUL;
    Pindex = &Sindex[ii][0];
    ptemp = pspsscan(&Pindex,Tcomma,&brk,SZE(1000),junk);
    if (stlen(junk) != 0)
        filter[statoi(junk)]++;
    }/*FillFilterArray*/
```

/*If filter[1] is greater than zero, then the procedure name in Sname[1] is output; in our example stfind. If filter[2] is greater than zero, psscoopat, the name listed in Sname[2], is output. This method guarantees that only one copy of each called function is output, even though the function may have been called several times within that procedure block.*/

```
for(zz = 0; zz <= ii; zz++)
    {/*ProcsCalled*/
    if (filter[zz] > 0)
        fprintf(outchan[1],"\t\t\t\t%s\n",Sname[zz]);
    }/*ProcsCalled*/
    }/*output*/
endgame();
exit(0);
}/*MAIN*/
```

Using *Pnames1* to examine *Pnames1.c*, the output is presented in Table 5.8.

```
┌─────────────────────────────────────────────────────┐
│                    PNAMES1                           │
│                                                      │
│   times                         procedures           │
│   used    PROCEDURE             it calls             │
│                                                      │
│   (2)     [STFIND]                                   │
│   (2)     [PSSCOOPAT]                                 │
│   (1)     [DELCOMMENT]                                │
│                                 STFIND                │
│                                 PSSCOOPAT             │
│   (2)     [GETNAME]                                   │
│   (1)     [ENDGAME]                                   │
│   (1)     [INTERACTIVE]                               │
│   (0)     [MAIN]                                      │
│                                 DELCOMMENT            │
│                                 GETNAME               │
│                                 ENDGAME               │
│                                 INTERACTIVE           │
└─────────────────────────────────────────────────────┘
```

Table 5.8.   Which procedures call which procedures.

The type of data structure used by *Pnames1* has a major disadvantage. The program must set aside 40 by 80 chars of storage even though little of this may be filled. This can become costly on a small machine with limited space. It is also obviously not a habitable data structure in C. It does, however, have the advantage of logical simplicity. All the evolving information on procedure names is contained in two matrices. No additional arrays are required.

5.4.4.   PNAMES2: A 1D CHAR ARRAY; A 1D POINTER ARRAY; AND A 2D INT ARRAY

The next version, *Pnames2*, uses less space, because it stores all the names sequentially in a single large buffer. Like *Pnames1*, *Pnames2* finds each procedure, indicates the number of times it is called and which procedures it itself calls. Each procedure must be labeled **/*PROCEDURE*/**. And all the pertinent user-created functions are in the file under examination. Include files are not examined. Each function calls itself or functions preceding it. *main*() is the final procedure block.

As a variation, if a procedure is called more than once within a function block, it is listed in that block as often as it is called.

Pnames2 uses a large 1D char buffer (*Sname*) to hold all the procedure names. A sister array of pointer-to-char (*Pname*) lists the start addresses of the names in *Sname*; e.g., if *Sname*[37] stores the start of the name of the third procedure; **Pname[3] = 37;**.

As in Section 5.3.2, an integer variable called *next0* determines the starting position of the next procedure name to be written into *Sname* relative to the current procedure name.

```
int next0 = 0;
next0 = next0 + 1 + strlen(Sname[#]);
```

next0 does the same as the function *psnext()*, except that it leaves the cursor pointing to where the next string should start, rather than on the SNUL terminus of the current string. Suppose *next0* is 10 and the function name *ttyin* of length 5 were written into *Sname* starting at *Sname*[10]. *next0* becomes 16, indicating that the starting address of the next string name will be at *Sname*[16].

```
Sname[10] = t
Sname[11] = t
Sname[12] = y
Sname[13] = i
Sname[14] = n
Sname[15] = \0
Sname[16] =
```

Each starting position is stored as an element in an array of char pointers: Pname[SMLSZE];

where *Pname*[1] is the starting address of the first name and *Pname*[current] holds the address of the latest *next0*; i.e., **Pname[current] = &Sname[next0];**.

In *Pnames1*, procedure indices were stored in a 2D char array. In contrast, in *Pnames2*, the procedures called inside a procedure block are stored by their index numbers in a multi-column 2D integer array. *Sindex*[SMLSZE][2*SMLSZE] is large enough to store up to 80 indices for each of 40 procedures. *Sindex*[10] stores indices to the procedures called by the tenth procedure, say procedures 3,4,1. In this case, *Sindex*[10][1] would be 3, *Sindex*[10][2] would be 4 and *Sindex*[10][3] would be 1. *Sindex*[0] is not used.

Note that *Sname*[ii][0] is a the first character in the string, not the string. *Sname*[ii], &*Sname*[ii][0] and &*Sname*[ii] may all be used when the function arg calls for a pointer-to-char to represent the string. In line *a*, getname(&prcd,*Pname*[current]) stores the name in *Sname*[next0], in that it writes the name at *Pname*[current], an address that happens to be part of *Sname*'s turf. *getname()* assumes the label PROCEDURE and the procedure's name are on same line.

Except for *main()*, the procedures in the file are exactly those in *Pnames1.c* and will not be listed here. Differences in *main()* are due to: (1) addressing procedure names in Sname indirectly through addresses stored in Pname; and (2) the difference in using an int buffer to store indices directly. Using an integer array has the advantage that numerical values are kept as readily accessible numbers. They do not have to be converted from character mode.

```
/*FILE: pnames2.C*/
/*PROCEDURE*/ main()
     {/*MAIN*/
```

```
          ┌─────────────────┐
          │ SEGMENT A HERE  │
          └─────────────────┘
```

```
     BOOL     flagout = FALSE;
     int      next0 = 0;
     STRING   Pname[SMLSZE];          /*The array of pointers to procedure names.*/
```

```
char       Sname[SZE(1000)] = {SNUL};/*Chararray  for the names of procedures.*/
int        Sindex[SMLSZE][2*SMLSZE]; /*A buffer for index numbers of*/
                                     /* procedures called by procedures in Sname.*/

for (i = 0; i < SMLSZE; i++)              /*It's essential to preclear the array.*/
    for (ii = 0; ii < 2*SMLSZE; ii++)
        Sindex[i][ii] = 0;
```

> SEGMENT B HERE

```
if (keyfind(cpyrcd,"/*PROCEDURE*/"))          /*The start of*/
    {/*ExamineAProcedure*/                    /* a procedure block.*/
    prcd = rcd;
    next0 += stlen(Pname[current]) + 1;       /*next0 points to
                                              /* where in Sname*/
                                              /* to write the next name.*/
    current++;        /*Moving to next pointer to the next string.*/
    Pname[current] = &Sname[next0];
    getname(&prcd,Pname[current]);                                    /*a*/
```

> SEGMENT C HERE

```
        if (getname(&prcd,pcpyrcd))
            {/*MayBeAFct*/
            flagout = FALSE;
```

/*Next, if pcpyrcd is a listed name, find the next vacant position in the index associated with
the procedure being examined.*/

```
            for(ii = 1; ii <= current; ii++)
                {/*CheckEachFctName*/
                if (EQU(pcpyrcd,Pname[ii]))
                    {/*MatchedAFunction*/
                    for (zz = 1; zz < 2*SMLSZE; zz++)
                        {/*FindNextVacantCell*/
                        if (Sindex[current][zz] == 0)
                            {/*FillVacantCell*/;   /*Add the
                    index number of the procedure matched.*/
                            Sindex[current][zz] = ii;
                            freq[ii]++;
                            flagout = TRUE;        /*A contortion
                                to avoid GOTO sinning.*/
                            break /*FindNextVacantCell*/;
                            }/*FillVacantCell*/;
                        }/*FindNextVacantCell*/
                if (flagout == TRUE)
```

> SEGMENT D HERE

```
fprintf(outchan[1],"[%s]\n",Pname[ii]);
for (ii = 1; ii <= current; ii++)
    {/*output*/
```

```
            fprintf(outchan[1],"\n(%d)        ",freq[ii]);
            fprintf(outchan[1],"[%s]\n",Pname[ii]);
            for (zz = 1; Sindex[ii][zz]; zz++)
                {/*ProcsCalled*/
                fprintf(outchan[1],"\t\t\t\t%s\n",Pname[Sindex[ii][zz]]);
                }/*ProcsCalled*/
            }/*output*/
        endgame();
        exit(0);
        }/*MAIN*/
```

The output, shown in Table 5.9, differs from *Pnames1* and *Pnames3* in that repetitions of called functions are allowed.

PNAMES2		
times used	PROCEDURE	procedures it calls
(2)	[STFIND]	
(2)	[PSSCOOPAT]	
(1)	[DELCOMMENT]	
		STFIND
		STFIND
		PSSCOOPAT
		PSSCOOPAT
(2)	[GETNAME]	
(1)	[ENDGAME]	
(1)	[INTERACTIVE]	
(0)	[MAIN]	
		INTERACTIVE
		GETNAME
		DELCOMMENT
		GETNAME
		ENDGAME

Table 5.9.   What procedures are called by what procedures.

5.4.5. PNAMES3: TWO 1D CHAR ARRAYS AND TWO 1D POINTER ARRAYS

The next version is called *Pnames3*. Like *Pnames1*, *Pnames3* stores the indices in a char array. And the output is the same as from *Pnames1*.

Like *Pnames2*, *Pnames3* uses a single buffer (*Sname*) for all the procedure names. Similarly, a sister array of pointer to char (*Pname*) lists the start addresses of the names in *Sname*; e.g., if *Sname*[37] stores the start of the name of the third procedure; **Pname[3] = 37;**. And the starting position of the next name in the buffer is determined by a variable called *next0* such that **next0 = next0 + 1 + strlen(Sname[#]);**

A similar arrangement holds the group of index numbers, representing the procedures called in a given function block.

next1 determines where the next string will be positioned in the buffer.

(1) **next1 += 1 + strlen(Pindex[current]);**   /*Find the next empty cell in Sindex.*/
(2) **current++;**   /*Increment current by 1.*/

Now assign to the current Pindex the address of the empty cell determined in (1).

(3) Pindex[current] = &Sindex[next1];

The procedures called are stored by their index numbers in a char buffer called *Sindex*. For example, suppose, beginning with *Sindex*[1], *Sindex*[1] read:

Sindex[1] = \0
Sindex[2] = 1
Sindex[3] = ,
Sindex[4] = 1
Sindex[5] = ,
Sindex[6] = \0
Sindex[7] = 2
Sindex[8] = ,
Sindex[9] = 1
Sindex[10] = ,
Sindex[11] = 1
Sindex[12] = ,
Sindex[13] = 2
Sindex[14] = ,
Sindex[15] = \0
Sindex[16]...

And

Pindex[1] = \0
Pindex[2] = 2
Pindex[3] = 7
Pindex[4] = 16

Or written as a string: **\0,1,1,\0,2,1,1,2,\0...**

This would indicate that the first procedure written in the file called no procedures. Indices to routines called by the second procedure are stored beginning at *Sindex*[2]. The second procedure called the first procedure twice. The third procedure in the file called Procedure 2, Procedure 1, Procedure 1, and finally Procedure 2. Its index string starts at *Sindex*[7]. The string holding the indices to the fourth procedure begins at *Sindex*[16]. This version of *Pnames* assumes, as do the previous ones, that once a set of index numbers is set down, it doesn't need to be enlarged; i.e., a procedure may call functions written early in the file or itself but not later functions.

/*FILE: pnames3.c*/
/*PROCEDURE*/ int main()
    {/*MAIN*/

SEGMENT A HERE

```
char      junk[SZE(1000)];
int       next0 = 0;
int       next1 = 0;
STRING    Pindex[SMLSZE] = {NULL};    /*Array of pointers to index of called procedures.*/
STRING    Pname[SMLSZE] = {NULL};     /*Array of pointers to procedure names.*/
char      Sindex[SZE(1000)] = {SNUL}; /*Buffer for index numbers of procedures*/
                                      /*called by procedures in Sname.*/
char      Sname[SZE(1000)] = {SNUL};  /*Char buffer for the names of all the*/
                                      /* procedures in the file.*/
int       filter[SZE(100)] = {0};
```

SEGMENT B HERE

```
if (keyfind(cpyrcd,"/*PROCEDURE*/"))   /*The start of*/            /*a*/
    {/*ExamineAProcedure*/             /*a procedure block.*/
    prcd = rcd;
next0 += stlen(Pname[current]) + 1;
```

/*The address of the Current Name is in Pname[current] next0 points to where in Sname to
write the next Name.*/

```
    next1 += stlen(Pindex[current]) + 1; /*The first time, current is 0.*/
                                /*There is no Pname[0].*/
    current++;                  /*This is to start all arrays at 1, not zero.*/
    Pname[current] = &Sname[next0];
    Pindex[current] = &Sindex[next1];
    getname(&prcd,Pname[current]);    /*Assumes the label PROCEDURE*/
                                /* and the procedure name are on the same line*/
```

SEGMENT C HERE

```
        if (getname(&prcd,pcpyrcd))
            {/*MayBeAFct*/
            for(ii = 1; ii <= current; ii++)
                {/*CheckEachFctName*/
                if (EQU(pcpyrcd,Pname[ii]))
                    {/*MatchedAFunction*/
                    pa[0] = Pindex[current];
                    pa[1] = ",";
                    stitoa(ii,ttystr);
                    pa[2] = ttystr;
                    ppa = pa;
                    expr = stmcat(ppa,3);
                    stcpy(expr, Pindex[current]);
                    NULLIT(expr);
                    freq[ii]++;
```

SEGMENT D HERE

```
        for (ii = 1; ii <= current; ii++)
            {/*output*/
            fprintf(outchan[1],"\n(%d)        ",freq[ii]);
            fprintf(outchan[1],"[%s]\n",Pname[ii]);
        for (zz = 0; zz <= ii; zz++)
             filter[zz] = 0;              /*To clear out an int array.*/
            while (stlen(Pindex[ii]) != 0)
            {/*FillFilterArray*/
            junk[0] = SNUL;
            ptemp = pspsscan(&Pindex[ii],Tcomma,&brk,SZE(1000),junk);
            if (stlen(junk) != 0)
                filter[statoi(junk)]++;
            }/*FillFilterArray*/
        for(zz = 0; zz <= ii; zz++)
            {/*ProcsCalled*/
            if (filter[zz] > 0)
                fprintf(outchan[1],"\t\t\t\t%s\n",Pname[zz]);
            }/*ProcsCalled*/
            }/*output*/
    endgame();
    exit(0);
    }/*MAIN*/
```

CHAPTER 6

STRUCTS AND LINKED LISTS

6.1. INTRODUCTION

Previous chapters dealt with both the simple and compound character array. The character array, constructed of elements of a single data type, was shown to be a data structure well-adapted to the decomposition and concatenation of strings. This chapter deals with a radically different data structure: the struct *per se* and in context of the linked list. The salient feature of the struct is its ability to contain a membership of different data types. The implications of this attribute are explored in this chapter.

Aside from an initial discussion of struct syntax, the chapter reduces to three themes: (1) using the struct both to map database records and to control text processing; (2) chaining structs using the linked list data structure; and (3) dealing with some of the disadvantages of working with the struct.

The section on utilizing the struct is built around the struct's natural isomorphism to many kinds of database record formats. A single struct is a compact entity we can jam pack with diverse data items. So it is both simple and effective to use the struct to house whatever segments of the original text or record are involved in a particular text processing task. This ability of the struct to store multiple and different data items can also be exploited to hold the essential information for controlling multiple string processing tasks in accessible form. The discussion of some problems in working with a set of structs is deferred until after the section on the linked list and the array of linked lists, data structures that extend the usability of the struct. The section on linked lists includes details about hash coding, a technique that speeds up the search for a particular struct in a set of structs.

Like the ordinary primitive data types, the entire struct may be assigned as a single unit. It functions as a compound data type in that it is itself composed of independent members, which may be ordinary C variables or string constants or complete structs or pointers to different data types. A struct is stylized in that its members must be the particular data types in the particular order set forth in the pattern that characterizes all structs of that template type. Because of the flexibility permitted the struct at incorporation, almost any set of diverse data constructions can be gathered within a struct, including structs within structs or pointers to structs within structs.

Choosing between character array and struct is often dictated by the task at hand. Individual preferences may, instead, prevail.

As general guidelines to choosing the 'right' data structure:

- The substring and concatenation derivatives of the character array are usually themselves character arrays. Integral to the notion of *struct* is its ability to hold together a set of different data types, giving each type its special place within the whole unit. And each of these data types has its own way to 'add' or 'subtract' portions of the variable.

- Array syntax is uniform in dealing with char elements, in that only very few—SNUL, EOL, EOF and, occasionally, control characters—need special handling. Struct syntax forces us to pay attention to order and to the requirements of each member of the struct.

- The array structure is familiar and can be handled by simple library string functions. The struct is more flexible but to use it efficiently requires familiarity with various other data structures such as the linked list and the array combined with linked lists.

- Given scan, strip and concatenate functions such as those discussed in the next chapter, the single array is sufficient for most kinds of manipulations on one or even a fair number of strings. The struct is more efficient for coordinating a large group of strings and for storing information about each of the individual strings of the group, information that can remain in memory in accessible form throughout the program run.

In previous chapters, we showed that the single character array is reliable initial storage for ordinary ASCII strings entering memory. Subdividing the string according to certain parsing schemes can yield substrings that are semantically recognizable. As example, controlling the disarticulation of a string by a setbreak table that breaks on spaces and omits punctuation will likely result in a set of individual dictionary words. Partitioning a document by halting at periods will produce mostly complete sentences, with the occasional disjoint **Ph** and **D**'s or **M** and **D**'s. Interim substrings, on the other hand, are likely to look like nonsense syllables, as when we halt string entry at vowels to make changes at these points. In all cases, if we maintain or expand array size so that it remains adequate, we can, with the aid of temporary ancillary storage buffers, reconstitute the string from its substrings within the original buffer or amplify these substrings with add-on 'boilerplate' text or conjoin them with other strings by means of a concatenation function or reduce the original string by deleting some parts of it[1].

Much of this manipulation holds true if the entering string is a database record and the subsidiary strings are fields. Typically, the initial steps in processing a database record are to bring the record from file into a single large array in memory, subdivide it into its component fields and subfields and house these substrings within their own separate arrays. This is usually sufficient for tasks where a single record is input, the text from one or more fields is examined and manipulated, the results immediately output to another data file and

---

1 Chapter 7 contains various functions for doing these tasks.

the next record brought into memory; e.g., rearranging fields in the record of a citations database to conform to a particular journal's style and filing each revised record as an ordinary sentence shorn of database delimiters and glosses.

The compound character array is a suitable alternative for storing separated components of the string. The large 1D buffer is particularly useful for storing 'final copy' components, recognizable entities that are fixed for the life of the program; for example, the separate questions of a QAP. The 2D array can store a set of strings. Either can be used in harness with other such structures to store a set of 2-field records, as for example, an index.

Like the character array, the struct can also be made to catch all or selected individual strings or database fields as they enter memory. But the struct, with its ability to store all data types not just strings, is especially useful as a permanent container when the characters of some fields of the database record are to serve as integers, other field characters are to be floating point numbers, the text of some fields is to be used as is and the text in other fields is to be modified from the original.

The struct has some advantages over the array, either conferred by the C language or integral to the notion of struct in any language or because of the availability of utility functions. As examples:

- The entire struct can serve as function arg, not just the pointer to the beginning of the struct.

- The methods for incrementing information in a member or for adding and subtracting related structs are well developed and far less kludgy than adding collateral information in 2D arrays.

- In manipulating database records, the struct has the capability of keeping informational fields extracted from the record in whatever order the user finds flexible and immediately accessible. This additional capability comes into its own when we need to deal with a set of records rather than a single record, either because we are comparing these records in some way or because we need pooled data from multiple records in our processing; e.g., if field 1 of record A AND field 3 of record B are equal, output field 2 of record C.

More generally—and this is to be emphasized—the struct's unique qualities suit it for multi-string chores. Just as the array is intrinsically adapted for dealing with the many ways a string can produce substrings and superstrings, so is the struct ideal for extracting essential data from a group of strings and substrings. Because it can summarize a large amount of information in compact but accessible space, it is the data structure of choice for job control; i.e, it can control operations by storing the sequence of which tasks are to be done on what parts of what strings from what files. Moreover, it can maintain the history of what happens to particular data objects during processing.

As a major simplification, both array and struct handle 'operands'—the objects of string processing and manipulation. The struct is efficient at handling their operators.

6.2. STRUCT SYNTAX

Section 1.5.6 demonstrated how to set up a struct pattern and create actual structs cut from that pattern. Chapter 1 also showed how a struct template can contain structs or pointers-to-structs. Almost any data type can be a member of a struct. As an exception, a struct template may not contain a struct of its own type as member; it can, however, contain a pointer to itself. A function may not be a member of a struct; a pointer-to-function may.

Chapter 3 focused on the relationship of the character array and the pointer-to-char; and how to use them in function statements and as function args. Much of the interaction of array and pointer is applicable to the struct and pointer-to-struct. Some syntactic differences are consequent on how they are defined by the C language: an array is a compound object, a struct is allowed some operations that characterize the primitive data types.

6.2.1. DEFINITIONS AND DECLARATIONS

A struct template is declared, not defined. An actual struct modeled on that template is defined—given storage—as is any variable; i.e., by naming it and declaring it to be of that template type. The first statement shown next declares a struct template of type ranking; the struct type is also known as the *struct tag*. In the second statement, the variable *grp1* is defined as a struct of type ranking.

DECLARATION: **struct ranking {char first[SZE]; char mid[SZE]; char last[SZE];};**
DEFINITION: **struct ranking grp1;**

Template and structs and affiliated variables can be consolidated into a single statement. Note that members of the struct template are enclosed in braces and separated by semicolons; even the final member is terminated by a semicolon. Variables associated with the template are separated by commas; the last variable has no comma. There is a final semicolon that ends the struct description.

struct ranking { char first[SZE]; char mid[SZE]; char last[SZE]; } grp1, grp2, *pgrp, **ppgrp, group[10] ;

If the template and all the struct variables that will ever be modeled on it during the program run and all the pointers that will be affiliated with it are written as a unit, the template tag can be omitted.

struct {char first[SZE], char mid[SZE], char last[SZE];} grp1, grp2, *pgrp, **ppgrp, group[10];

Struct members are automatically defined when the struct is defined.

For readability, struct template and pointers-to-struct data types can be given nicknames using typedef statements:

typedef struct ranking RANK;   RANK is the struct template.

typedef RANK   *PRANK;   PRANK is defined as a pointer-to-struct of type ranking.
typedef PRANK *ADRPRANK;   ADRPRANK is a pointer-to-pointer-to-struct of type
                                              ranking.

and variables can be defined in terms of these nicknames:

RANK grp;   is equivalent to: **struct ranking grp;**
PRANK pgrp;   is equivalent to: **struct ranking *pgrp;**
ADRPRANK ppgrp is equivalent to: **struct ranking **ppgrp;**

6.2.2. INITIALIZATION

Storage for a struct, as for any data object, can be global or global static or local or local static. Structs—not struct templates—can be defined and initialized in a single operation. Or the struct can be defined at one time and its members given values individually afterwards.

For the most part, initializing the struct or any of its members follows C rules for initializing any variable. When members of a struct are initialized with string literals the rules are the same as initializing any array with a string literal (see Section 2.2). Member arrays can be legally rewritten in C without interfering with the string literals.

```
struct phone {char name[20]; char tel[20]; char fax[20];}
    call = {"Steve", "011 331 4527 0434", "011 331 4527 2345"} ;        /*a*/
stcpy("011 331 555 1450", call.tel);
```

Along the same line, a pointer member initialized with a string literal should not be rewritten with a string copy function as in line *b* because this directly affects the string literal.

```
main()
    {
    struct ptr {STRING p;} newstr = {"Keep"};
    newstr.p = "Change";      /*Repointing newstr.p to another string literal is legal.*/
    stcpy("new", newstr.p);   /*This is illegal.*/                        /*b*/
    }
```

Dynamic memory space can not be requested for pointer members as part of initialization, even if the struct is a local variable. This is in contrast to initializing ordinary local pointers as in line *c*.

```
main()
    {
    struct nogood  {STRING p; }
        ng = {(STRING) calloc(stlen("Keep")+1, sizeof(char));}   /*WRONG*/
    STRING p = (STRING) calloc(stlen("KeepThis")+1, sizeof(char));    /*c.*/
    }
```

The boundary conditions for struct storage are rule-based but not intuitive. The struct treated as a single variable introduces still another factor. To avoid problems, it may be sensible to treat structs that are initialized when they are defined as virtual constants and make no changes in the original values. To define a subsequent struct of the same type, do not copy it complete with member values from the global initialized struct. Define the later struct separately and assign values for the members individually. As Section 6.2.5.1 will show, this is particularly true if one of the members is a pointer to text.

6.2.3. ACCESSING THE STRUCT AND STRUCT MEMBERS

Section 1.5.6 made the point that a struct member is accessed through its specific struct or through a pointer to that struct. If, as shown next, *pngrp* and *ppngrp* are pointers-to-structs of type ranking and assigned to *newgrp*, then

RANK grp, *pgrp, **ppgrp;
pgrp = &grp;   NOT   **pgrp = grp;**^{2}
ppgrp = &pgrp;   NOT   **ppgrp = pgrp;**

To anticipate, if *group* is an array of structs and *pgroup* an array of pointers-to-struct:

RANK group[10], *pgroup[10];
pgroup[0] = group; OR pgroup[0] = &group[0];   NOT **pgroup = &group[0];**
          NOT **pgroup = &group; NOT pgroup = group;**
ppgroup = pgroup; OR ppgroup = &pgroup[0];   NOT **ppgroup = &pgroup;**

Using the definitions beginning at line *a*, ways of referencing the second member of *newgroup* or one of its elements start at line *b*:

void callfct(void)
          {
          RANK grp, *pgrp, **ppgrp, copy;   /*a*/
          pgrp = &grp;
          ppgrp = &pgrp;

          stcpy("Shira",grp.mid);   /***Shira** is written into the array grp.mid.*/   /*b*/
          if (grp.mid[0] == 'S')   /*If the 1st letter in grp.mid is S,*/
                    PD^3(&grp);   /*display grp's address.*/

          stcpy(pgrp->mid, copy.first);   /***Shira** is copied to a member in another struct.*/
          if (stlen((*pgrp).mid))   /*If grp.mid isn't empty, display text.*/
          PS((*pgrp).mid);   /*PrintProduct: **(*pgrp).mid = [Shira]***/

          PS((**ppgrp).mid);   /*PrintProduct: **(**ppgrp).mid = [Shira]**.*/
          PS((*ppgrp)->mid);   /*PrintProduct: **(*ppgrp).mid = [Shira]**.*/
          PC((*ppgrp)->mid[2]);   /*PrintProduct: **(*ppgrp)->mid[2] = i**.*/
          }

Even though the values for the list of members of a struct can be written in pseudo-matrix fashion (see line *a* in Section 6.2.2), we can not row-column label a struct and its members.

---

2 There is no idiom similar to that which assigns a pointer to a character array.

3 Several print macros are used: PD prints the value in decimal; PC prints the value as a char: PS prints the string; PJ is a comment.

In simple structs, members are accessed through the particular struct that contains them. In complex structs—those that themselves contain structs—struct members are accessed hierarchically, from struct to member to submember to subsubmember, and so forth. As illustration, using the next template, **stru.x.y[2]** would access the letter **C**, the third element of the first member of the second member of *stru*, a struct of type KitchenSink.

```
struct XX
    {
    char y[10];
    int   z;
    } xgrp, *pxgrp;

struct KitchenSink
    {
    int   i;
    struct XX  x;
    struct KitchenSink  *pk;
    STRING   ps;
    struct XX *px;        /* px is within KitchenSink but it points to a struct of type XX*/
    } stru = {5,{"ABCDEFGHI",3},NULL,NULL,NULL}, *pf,*pstru, **ppstru;
```

Note that in initializing *stru*, the values for the submembers of a member struct are enclosed in separate braces. *pstru* and *pf* are defined as unassigned pointers that can be assigned to any struct of type KitchenSink and only to structs of type KitchenSink; e.g.

pf = &stru;

stores the address of *stru* in *pf*.

The pointer *pk* is a member of the struct; it also can be assigned to any struct of type KitchenSink and only to structs of type KitchenSink. If *pk* is a member of *stru*, then

stru.pk = &stru;

is self-referencing: the address of the struct *stru* is stored in *stru.pk*.

Note that any struct of type KitchenSink MUST have *pk* as a resident member. Pointers-to-structs of type KitchenSink can be defined outside the struct and assigned the same values as pointer members, as is *pf*, but they are not syntactically necessary to the struct construction.

Given that *pstru* and *ppstru* are assigned to *stru* as pointer and pointer address, respectively

```
pstru = &stru;
ppstru = &pstru;
```

then these are equivalent ways to access the second char in the first member of the second member of stru. In this example, they each target **B** from the text **ABCDEFGHI**.

stru.x.y[1];	or	stru.x.y[0]+1;
(*pstru).x.y[1];	or	(*pstru).x.y[0]+1;
pstru->x.y[1];	or	pstru->x.y[0]+1;
(**ppstru).x.y[1];	or	(**ppstru).x.y[0]+1;

(*ppstru)->x.y[1];   or   **(*ppstru)->x.y[0]+1;**

Structs can not be compared one to the other in a single statement; e.g., this is NOT grammatical: **if (stru1 == stru2)....** Only individual and eligible members can be compared. Also, because of the assorted members a struct carries, it would make no sense assigning the struct to another data type either directly or by casting.

This next example compares two structs of type KitchenSink member for member, writing the smaller value per member into a third struct that is created as part of the function. The address of the new struct does not need to be returned, because it is a global variable. Note that values for pk, ps and px are not returned. Comparing pointers isn't what is intended. And the structs indirectly referenced by pk, ps and px can't be compared directly. These structs could perhaps be recursively compared, but it is not clear to what purpose.

```
typedef struct KitchenSink KS;
KS stru1 = {5,{"ABC",3},NULL,NULL,NULL};
KS stru2 = {7,{"abc",1},NULL,NULL,NULL};
KS *pstru3;

void comp(KS s1, KS s2, KS *pnew)
    {
    pnew = (KS *) calloc(1, sizeof(KS));

    if (s1.i < s2.i)
        pnew->i = s1.i;
    else pnew->i = s2.i; PD(pnew->i);              /*PrintProduct: pnew->i = 5*/
    if (LESS(s1.x.y, s2.x.y))
        stcpy(s1.x.y, pnew->x.y);
    else stcpy(s2.x.y, pnew->x.y); PS(pnew->x.y); /*PrintProduct: pnew->x.y = [ABC]*/
    if (s1.x.z < s2.x.z)
        pnew->x.z = s1.x.z;
    else pnew->x.z = s2.x.z; PD(pnew->x.z);        /*PrintProduct: pnew->x.z = 1*/
    pnew->pk = NULL;
    pnew->ps = NULL;
    pnew->px = NULL;
    }
```

6.2.4. ASSIGNING VALUES TO THE STRUCT

Members of a struct receive values: (1) as part of initialization; (2) when the struct itself is assigned the value of another struct; or (2) by direct assignment. Initialization was discussed in Section 6.2.2. Assignment via the whole struct is discussed in Section 6.2.5.1. In this section, we will discuss direct assignment.

The ordinary rules of assignment hold for the members of the struct; i.e., assigning values to the individual members of the struct is done as if they were independent entities. (They are accessed, however, by their relative positions within the struct.) Thus:

```
struct KS *pf2, stru2;
stru2 = stru;              /*See Section 6.2.3 where stru is defined.*/
```

pf2 = &stru2;   /*Assigns pf2 to a specific struct, *stru2*.*/
stru2.x.y[2]='m';   /*The char 'm' becomes the value of the 3rd element of the */
                                    /* arrray, stru2.x.y. y now reads: **[ABmDEFGHI]***/
pf2->x.y[0] = SNUL;   /*Virtually clears stru2.x.y by clearing its first element.*/
(*pf2).x.z = 40;   /*Assigns the value of 40 to the second member of stru2.x.*/

Integers and floats are directly assigned. Incoming characters intended as numerical values are assigned using some letter-to-number conversion function such as the library function *atoi*(). If the array *buf* is the temporary repository of ASCII digits,

stru2.i = atoi(buf);

Additional conversions between integer and ASCII are not necessary during the program run. If a set of digits is sometimes to be treated as characters and sometimes as a numerical value, this is a liability; but in most cases specifying the data type early is efficient. Moreover, the case of the ambiguous data type can be handled by a union format; and a union can serve as struct member.

Strings are filled char by char. Preset char arrays are filled, as shown in Section 1.5.5.1, by streaming from a file, entry from keyboard or by some *strcpy*() function. Storing text in presized arrays has the usual disadvantages of fixed size: an unusually long name will have be chopped to avoid overflow; conversely, most of the space set aside to accomodate very long fill-ins will likely be unused.

An independent pointer-to-struct can be defined and later assigned to an array of the proper type. Just as the pointer-to-char contains the address of the first element of its associated character array, the independent pointer-to-struct of type whatever will contain the address of the first byte of the struct to which it is assigned. Or the independent pointer can be assigned a value during the process of acquiring memory storage dynamically. The struct and the pointer assigned to it have independent storage.

A pointer-to-struct of type A can be cast to a pointer-to-struct of type B or to any other type pointer, whether pointer-to-struct, pointer-to-int or pointer-to-char. Referring to the example in the previous section:

    PD(stru.pk = &stru);   /*PrintProduct: **stru.pk = &stru = 134***/
    PD(pxgrp = &xgrp);   /*PrintProduct: **pxgrp = &xgrp = 4836***/
    pxgrp = (struct XX *) stru.pk;
    PD(pxgrp);   /*PrintProduct: **pxgrp = 134***/

Be careful that casting a pointer assigned to a dynamically-obtained struct to some other type pointer does not affect the system's knowledge that it has allocated a certain number of bytes stored at the address that is the pointer's value. To reuse the pointer, the stored string should first be freed. Otherwise, what has been created is a home-made union-style dump for data types, whose use is likely to lead to unpredictable results.

Pointers intended for dynamically acquired strings should be initialized as NULL. The associated string gets space as needed by way of one of the library allocation functions. Storing text dynamically with access to it through a pointer-to-char struct member is sparing of space but the memory space must be freed before it is reallocated.

Syntactically similar mantras obtain system space for struct and for character array. Space for a string is obtained for the number of characters, including the terminal SNUL, in the string. Space for the struct and its members is obtained as a single unit, even if its members are strings. In both cases, the pointer returned by the allocation function must be cast to the proper pointer type.

Using the struct formed above:

```
static char keep[] = "ABCDEFG";
stru2.ps = (char *) calloc(stlen(keep)+1, sizeof(char));
stru2.pk = (struct KS *) calloc(1, sizeof(struct KS));
```

The address of a pointer-to-char and the address of a pointer-to-struct may be members of the struct or assigned to a struct type without initial value (except for NULL) or to a specific struct.

Freeing a struct depends on its storage type. If it is acquired as a local struct, it disappears when the function in which it resides terminates. It can no more be freed by programmer manipulation than can a preset character array, although all of its members can be NULL'ed or SNUL'ed or zeroed, depending on data type. A dynamically-acquired struct can be deleted with a **free(pointer-to-struct);** statement. The struct will appear to exist after it is freed and so it partakes of all the hazards of any variable that is deassigned but not erased. (Section 2.5.2.1). A dynamic struct that contains dynamic strings should not be cleared in a single operation. The member strings should be freed first in separate operations. More generally, given a dynamically-created struct that contains pointers to any type of dynamically stored entity (string, struct, 2D int array, and so forth), the dynamic member(s) should be freed before the struct is deallocated.

A macro such as *NULLP* prototyped as

```
#define NULLP(x) if (x) {free((x)); (x) = NULL;}
```

will reset the pointer-to-struct to NULL. Unlike NULLIT() (see Section 2.5.2.1), it can not generally zero out the first byte of the struct, the struct being an assortment of members, not a list of identical elements.

A struct member that is a pointer to a preset char array can be re-valued; techniques for virtual relocation of a string were shown in Section 3.7.1.1. A pointer to a dynamically stored character array should not change its link to the address of the beginning of the array, because this is needed by the system to free the string. However, as in Sections 3.6 and 3.7, the contents of the string can be changed passively; e.g., the last part of the string can overwrite the first part. Or the string can be changed dynamically—space can be reallocated to the modified string.

6.2.5. MANIPULATING THE STRUCT AS A VARIABLE

Considered as a single variable, a struct can be used as an lvalue in an assignment statement where appropriate. It can be copied to another struct of the same type. And it can serve as function arg.

6.2.5.1.   Assigning Values By Copying the Struct.

Some implications of the rule that the struct is itself an assignable variable should be examined. A struct can be assigned to another struct of the same type in a single statement and its members are automatically assigned. When one struct is written to another, as in line *a*, the two structs have separate addresses and are independent data objects. Members are stored in sequential locations within the struct domain.

```
RANK grp = {"Mari", "Jon", "Shira"}, *pgrp = &grp;

void callfct(void)
    {
    RANK copy = grp;                                                    /*a*/

    PD(&copy);                 /*PrintProduct: &copy =-7618*/
    PD(&copy.first);           /*PrintProduct: &copy.first = -7618*/

    PD(&copy.mid);             /*PrintProduct: &copy.mid = -7578*/
    PD(&copy.last);            /*PrintProduct: &copy.last = -7538*/
    PD(&grp);                  /*PrintProduct: &grp = 192*/
    PD(&grp.first);            /*PrintProduct: &grp.first = 192*/
    PD(&grp.mid);              /*PrintProduct: &grp.mid = 232*/
    PD(&grp.last);             /*PrintProduct: &grp.last = 272*/
    }
```

In this next example, the global struct *grp* contains a pointer to dynamic material, which in line *d* is assigned the address of some text. It passes the address of the dynamically-stored string to *copy.p* inside *callfct()* in line *a*. In consequence, even though *grp.p* and *copy.p* are independent entities, they share the same value (lines *b* and *f*. So when the text at *copy.p* is rewritten (line *c*), the modification is imparted to *grp.p* (see line *g*). Unless the string is physically shifted in memory, this will occur even if *copy.p* is reallocated space. Copying an entire struct from a global struct is not encouraged. Copying a global struct with a member that is a pointer to a dynamically-stored string is still riskier. It has the hazards associated with accessing a global variable through multiple, independent routes and the hazards of multiple pointer accesses to the same dynamic string.

```
typedef struct dyna {STRING p;} DYN;
DYN grp;

void callfct(void)
    {
    DYN copy = grp;            /*PrintProduct: copy = 612*/          /*a*/
    PD(copy.p);                /*PrintProduct: copy.p = 612*/        /*b*/
    PS(copy.p);                /*PrintProduct: [Words]*/
    stcpy("NEW", copy.p);      /*Wrong thing to do. Should realloc.*/ /*c*/
    PS(copy.p);                /*PrintProduct: copy.p = [NEW]*/
    }
```

```
main()
    {
    grp.p = (STRING) calloc(stlen("Words")+1,sizeof(char));          /*d*/
    stcpy("Words",grp.p); PS(grp.p); /*PrintProduct: grp.p = [Words]*/  /*e*/
    PD(grp.p);              /*PrintProduct: grp.p = 612*/            /*f*/
    callfct();
    PS(grp.p);              /*PrintProduct: grp.p = [NEW]*/          /*g*/
    }
```

6.2.5.2. The struct as function arg.

The struct can serve as function arg and is passed by value as is any lvalue data object (see line *a*). And it can be returned to the calling function as in line *b*. When a character array is a function arg, what is transmitted to the called function is the address of the first element of the array; so changes in the individual elements of the array are permanent. The struct in contrast is treated as a variable and what is passed is the 'value' of the struct. (Strictly speaking the struct gestalt has no value; only its members do.) Hence, changes made in member values in the called function are not permanent (see lines *c*, and *d*). As with any ordinary variable, the value the struct receives in the called function can be returned and assigned to another variable. (see in lines *e* and *f*.

Example 1.

```
struct XX
    {
    char y[10];
    int   z;
    } ;

extern struct XX calledfct(struct XX x1);
extern int main(void);

struct XX calledfct(struct XX x1)                               /*a*/
    {
    stcpy("XYZ",x1.y);  PS(x1.y);      /*PrintProduct: x1.y = [XYZ]*/
    x1.z = 100;         PD(x1.z);      /*PrintProduct: x1.z = 100*/
    return(x1);                                                 /*b*/
    }

main()
    {
    struct XX xgrp = {SNUL}, xgrp1;
    PS(xgrp.y);         /*PrintProduct: xgrp.y = []*/
    PD(xgrp.z);         /*PrintProduct: xgrp.z = 0*/
    xgrp1 = calledfct(xgrp);
    PS(xgrp.y);         /*PrintProduct: xgrp.y = []*/            /*c*/
    PD(xgrp.z);         /*PrintProduct: xgrp.z = 0*/            /*d*/

    PS(xgrp1.y);        /*PrintProduct: xgrp1.y = [XYZ]*/        /*e*/
```

```
    PD(xgrp1.z);          /*PrintProduct: xgrp1.z = 100*/                /*f*/
    }
```

Note also the order in example 1: struct definition, function prototypes, procedures codings, rather than the more usual: function prototypes, struct definition, procedure codings. If the function is prototyped before the struct is defined, the compiler issues an error message that the struct is undefined. To use normal order, use the prototype with the data types of the args, but no struct ID. In this case:

extern struct XX calledfct(struct XX);

Example 2.

In this example, a pointer-to-struct, *pxgrp*, is assigned the address of a struct, *xgrp* in line *c*. When a pointer to a predefined struct serves as function arg (see line *a*), modifications in member values within the called function are permanent, (see lines *f* and *g*). The pointer, itself, however, is passed by value and returns to its original value or whatever garbage is in that location when released from the function; as in line *e*. The called function can also return a pointer-to-struct. In this example, these returned values are assigned to a separate struct, *xgrp1* through its pointer *pxgrp1* at lines *h* and *i*.

```
struct XX *pcalledfct(struct XX *x1)                                     /*a*/
    {
    stcpy("XYZ",x1->y);
    x1->z = 100;
    PS(x1->y);              /*PrintProduct: x1->y = [XYZ]*/
    PD(x1->z);              /*PrintProduct: x1->y = */
    return(x1);                                                          /*b*/
    }

int main(void)
    {
    struct XX xgrp = {SNUL}, xgrp1 = {SNUL};
    struct XX *pxgrp = &xgrp;                                            /*c*/
    struct XX *pxgp1 = &xgrp1;
    PD(pxgrp);              /*PrintProduct: pxgrp = 0*/                   /*d*/
    PS(pxgrp->y);           /*PrintProduct: pxgrp->y = []*/
    PD(pxgrp->z);           /*PrintProduct: pxgrp->z = 0*/
    pxgrp1 = pcalledfct(pxgrp);
    PD(pxgrp);              /*PrintProduct: pxgrp = 22872*/               /*e*/
    PS(pxgrp->y);           /*PrintProduct: pxgrp->y = [XYZ]*/            /*f*/
    PD(pxgrp->z);           /*PrintProduct: pxgrp->z = 100*/             /*g*/
    PS(pxgrp1->y);          /*PrintProduct: pxgrp1->y = [XYZ]*/           /*h*/
    PD(pxgrp1->z);          /*PrintProduct: pxgrp->z =100*/              /*i*/
    }
```

Example 3.

A pointer-to-struct can serve as function arg even when no specific struct of that particular type exists. A struct can be acquired dynamically during the function run and its members given permanent values. Two ways to retain the address of the new struct beyond the called function are shown: (1) the address of the pointer-to-struct is used as function arg in *calling1fct*(); and (2) in *calling2fct*(), the pointer in the calling function is revalued with the value returned by the called function.

```
struct XX
    {
    char y[10];
    int    z;
    } keep = {"ABC", 14};

void called1fct(struct XX **pf)
    {
    *pf = (struct XX *) calloc(1, sizeof(struct XX));
    stcpy(keep.y, (*pf)->y);
    (**pf).z = keep.z;
    }

void calling1fct(void)
    {
    struct XX *pdyn;
    calledfct(&pdyn);
    PS(pdyn->y);          /*PrintProduct: pdyn->y = [ABC]*/
    PD(pdyn->z);          /*PrintProduct: pdyn->z = 14*/
    }

struct XX *called2fct(struct XX *pf)
    {
    pf = (struct XX *) calloc(1, sizeof(struct XX));
    stcpy(keep.y, pf->y);
    (*pf).z = keep.z;
    return(pf);
    }

void calling2fct(void)
    {
    struct XX *pdyn;
    pdyn = calledfct(pdyn);
    }
```

Aside from these operations on the whole struct—copying it, assigning to it and using it as a function arg or a return arg—all operations on the struct involve one or more of its members. These operations are those that would apply to the members if they were independent variables. As with assignments, each individual member of a struct is dealt with according to its data type: arithmetic operations are performed on int or float members, strings are examined or copied char by char and the rules of automatic conversions and casting apply.

6.3. THE ARRAY OF STRUCTS; THE ARRAY OF POINTERS-TO-STRUCT

As useful as individual named structs can be, nevertheless, given that a set of structs may contain and/or model the contents of a multi-record database, it is more than likely that a struct will not be individually named but be part of a set of structs of the same kind, each devoted to a separate record.

6.3.1. THE ARRAY OF STRUCTS

The simplest such collective is the array of structs. In analogy to the fixed-size 2D character array, where each row holds a string, each row in an array of structs can be regarded as a separate record or, reading from left to right, as the sequence of values of the members of the struct defined in that row.

As a simple example, suppose stylized records in a database dealing with major authors. The database record has five fields; ~ is the record delimiter; | is the field delimiter; the comma is the subfield delimiter. These are two possible records:

Dickens, Charles|England|1812|novel|David Copperfield~
Shakespeare, William|England|1564|dramatic play|Hamlet~

The analogous struct array is:

```
struct fiction
    {
    char author[30];          /*A char array of size 30*/
    char country[SMLSZE];     /*A char array of size SMLSZE.*/
    int birthyear;            /*A ordinary int*/
    char genre[MEDSZE];       /*A char array of size MEDSZE.*/
    char majorwork[SZE(30)];  /*An array of size 30*/
    } writers[SZE(100)], *pwrite;
```

The struct array *writers* provides space sufficient to store the information for 100 writers, from row zero through row 99, where each struct is patterned on the template tagged as *fiction*. Record and field delimiters are stripped out; they aren't necessary.

Since we have just defined *writers*, we couldn't initialize the struct as we did *grp* in Section 6.2.5.1. Instead, we would fill the fields individually with a string copy function. The structs could be represented as:

writers[1] = {"Dickens, Charles","England",1812,"novel","David Copperfield"}
writers[2] = {"Shakespeare, William","England",1564,"dramatic play","Hamlet"}

6.3.2. USING THE POINTER-TO-STRUCT IN AN ARRAY OF STRUCTS

The ability of the pointer-to-struct to move flexibly among array elements and subelements is as valuable in dealing with the individual structs in an array of structs as the pointer-to-char was in locating individual chars within a simple character array. As example, *pwrite*, when defined as pointer-to-struct of type fiction, can point to any individual struct in the array and to any member of that struct. It can also be assigned to any other struct of type fiction or to any other array of structs of type fiction. It can NOT be assigned to a struct modeled after a different struct template without casting.

Assigned to a specific struct, it can immediately target any member of the struct; e.g., until the pointer is reassigned, it refers only to the struct. We would first assign the pointer:

pwrite = writers; /*Idiomatic for pwrite = &writers[0];*/ /*a*/

Then, either

stcpy("England", pwrite->country); or: **(*pwrite).country;**

would write the text **England** into the second member of this struct. Which form is used is a matter of personal preference. In either case, it is as if we had written:

stcpy("England",writers[0].country);.

Similarly, for dynamic storage, **pwrite->author = dssave("Dickens, Charles");** has exactly the same effect as **writers[0].author = dssave("Dickens, Charles");**. It would copy the text into a memory location within the domain of the first struct in the array.

To copy a string member such as the country name to some other struct requires the *stcpy()* function, thus: **stcpy(writers[0].country, writers[10].country);**. But, treating the struct as a single unit, **writers[10] = writers[0];** would immediately fill all the fields of the 11th struct in the array with the text of all the members of the first struct in the array, including the contents of the second member, *writers[10].country*.

To point it to the final struct, either **pwrite = &writers[99];** or **pwrite = writers + 99;** will do. The first statement assigns the address of the struct in the last row directly to *pwrite* as its value. The second is written in offset mode. It uses pointer arithmetic to leap from the address of the very beginning of the array of structs to the beginning of the last struct in the array.

If the pointer is to be used in a loop to move down the entire array, it would be assigned to the first struct in the array, as in line *a*. Then, as with any other type of pointer, incrementing a struct pointer thus:

pwrite++;

will cause *pwrite* to point to the next struct. As with the pointer-to-char, the pointer-to-struct is incremented by one—one struct in this case—and its value is the address of its associated variable. The loop stops when the address of the incremented pointer equals the address of the last struct in the array.

```
for (pwrite = writers; pwrite <= writers+99; pwrite++)
    stcpy("DefaultText",pwrite->genre;
```

These next are other ways to sweep through an array. In the example starting at line *a*, *writers*, the name of the array, serves as a constant and unmoving pointer to the top of the *writers* array. In each cycle, *i* is increased by 1 and *pwrite* moves one struct down the array. Looping stops when a birthyear within the 1890 to 1920 range is found. Starting at line *b*, the sequence of genre fields for the entire array is displayed. Each struct is accessed directly, one struct per cycle. The example starting at line *c* compares cycles. In each case, the loop continues until: (1) one exact address is the same as another exact address; or (2) a particular cycle count is triggered.

```
for (i = 0; i < 100; i++)                               /*a*/
    {
    pwrite = writers + i;
    if (pwrite->birthyear > 1890 && pwrite->birthyear < 1920) break;
    }

for (i = 0; i < 100; i++)                               /*b*/
        PS( writers[i].genre);

for (pwrite = writers; (pwrite - writers) < 100; pwrite++)    /*c*/
    PS((*pwrite).genre);
```

6.3.3. STORING/IDENTIFYING TARGET STRUCTS IN THE ARRAY

Suppose this sorting task (chosen to make a point about storing structs in an array rather than illustrating efficiency in comparing multiple keys): several files are searched record by record for a particular phrase. Records containing the phrase are converted to structs, stored in memory and processed. As a result of the processing, some of the structs are deleted. The files are read in a second time, structs with the second text phrase are processed, and some are kept. We do this several time for different keywords. So by the time we reread the files a few times, the structs are not necessarily in the original sequence and certainly not systematically arranged.

We stipulate that at no time is there to be more than one copy of any record. Text from a repeat entry record is added to the already stored struct that represents that record.

An array of structs would serve admirably to accomodate the multiple structs that are created. And because each struct can be uniquely identified by its position in the array, we are absolved from the chore of needing to name them individually.

When order can not be easily maintained, or when there is no simple way to maintain structs in a particular order in the array (e.g., chronologically or by date), this next is a general procedure that can be used to find a particular struct. (Later in the chapter we will examine a more efficient method for accessing a particular struct in an array.)

It is assumed each record has some specific ID that differentiates it from all others. We call this identifier its PSI—for Positive Specimen Identifier. The PSI can stay with the record no matter how often and in what manner it is grouped with records of its own file or other files in later processing. The PSI is particularly useful when a composite database comes from many different sources. It can be elaborated so that it succintly stores a coded reference to the file, the position of the record in the file and what general category of record it embodies. Well-designed PSI formats guarantee a record or portions of the record never encounter a doppelganger, not matter how large the domain.

We begin by crafting space for TOT structs within an array called *KEY*, where TOT is suffient to store all the records in the files, if necessary. As a matter of preference we don't use the zeroth element of the array, so the array KEY can hold TOT-1 structs.

```
struct text
    {
    char ID[SMLSZE];
    char key1[MEDSZE];
    char key2[SMLSZE];
    char key3[MEDSZE];
    int FREQ1;
    int FREQ2;
    int FREQ3;
    }KEY[TOT];
```

Each struct provides us with one unique member, the PSI, acquired when it was brought in from disk. If a struct is dropped from the group, we clear its ID to mark that the row is available to hold some other struct.

The only difficulty is in making the identification robust enough so that:

*   The first time a new record is used, its ID, its PSI, is written into the first available array position.

*   The record does not 'own' more than one array position if, as is likely, it is read in again.

*   The correct struct row is found quickly each time a repeat record is read into memory.

With only the ID to go on, the procedure interrogates each row in *KEY* until the PSI is matched or until all rows have been examined.

If the record's ID is already listed in *KEY*, the struct is immediately ready to accumulate more key words or change member values. As *findslot*() looks down *KEY*, the program takes note of the first vacancy it encounters. If it can't match the incoming record's ID by the time it reaches the end of *KEY*, then the empty slot is immediately available to the program to assign to the current record. The record's ID is written into the first member of this struct.

The arg to *findslot*() is, in this case, the PSI of the current entry record.

```
struct text *findslot(STRING PSI)
```

```
{/*BP*/
```

/*Next, a pointer-to-struct of type text is defined: pstr will traverse the entire array if necessary; hold, a long integer (for larger databases with more than 32K records), will index the first not-in-use row. A short int, sw, will become 1 if a vacancy is found or 2 if the record referenced by this struct is already stored in the array.*/

```
struct text *pstr = NULL;
long hold = 0L;
long i = 0L;
BOOL sw = 0;
```

/*Procedure Logic: In finding a slot in KEY[], the program can not assume that a record is not already stored in the array. So all the array elements must be checked. To save time, however, the first time that the program encounters an empty slot, it makes a note of its position with hold and sets sw to 1. Then if all the possible slots have been checked without finding that the record is a repeater, the whole set of elements does not have to be traversed again. The new record struct is installed in the KEY[hold] row.*/

```
for (i = 1; i < TOT; i++)
    {/*check_if_record_struct_is_already_stored*/
    pstr = KEY + i;
    if (sw == 0)
        {/*need a vacancy*/        /*In case we will need an empty struct*/
                                   /* for the record.*/

        if (pstr->ID[0] == SNUL)
            {/*found_a_vacancy*/
            hold = i;
            sw = 1;                /*If a vacancy is found, we make note of it.*/
            }/*found_a_vacancy*/
        }/*need a vacancy*/
```

/*Next, the code handles the case where the record has been read from previously. It already has a struct. There's no need to check out any more rows. Mission accomplished.*/

```
        if (EQU(PSI, pstr->ID))
            {/*Record struct is already stored.*/
            sw = 2;
            return(pstr);
            }/*record struct was already stored*/
    }/*check_if_record_struct_is_already_stored*/
```

/*All the rows have been searched and there is no struct with the current accession number. The next piece of code provides for the contingency that all structs are in use. In the scenario for this example, we know how many records there are in the databases. But in the general case, with an unknown number of entry strings, this next piece of code protects the array from overrun. In this version, we stop the program. But it is just as simple to terminate entry and send a message to the calling function.*/

```
    if (i > TOT-1 && sw == 0)
        {/*slots_are_all_filled*/
        printf("\nOnly %d records can be stored.\n",TOT-1);
        exit(2);
```

```
        }/*slots_are_all_filled*/
```

/*If sw is 1, the program has looked down all the rows, of the incoming record and has
determined the record has not been read from previously. So it will use the empty row it
had indexed in hold.*/

```
    else if (sw == 1)
        {/*install_new_record*/
        pstr = KEY + hold;
        stcpy(PSI, KEY[hold].ID;
        return (pstr);
        }/*install_new_record*/
    }/*EP*/
```

Usage.

See LISTINGS\chap6\6-3-2.c for a small program that finds vacancies for data, simulating
a partially emptied array and several pass throughs.

Actually, this is not a bad routine, particularly for a small number of input calls to a few
hundred records. If only a single database is accessed, the record's accession number can
be used as ID. The time for targetting a repeater record can be reduced by having an
auxiliary integer vector holds the inverse listings of each record's ID and its corresponding
array position.

8
16
5
... and so forth

would indicate that the record with an ID of 1 (the first record in the database) was in row
8; the record with an ID of 2 (the second record) was in row 16; the third record was in row
5; and so forth.

6.3.4. THE ARRAY OF POINTERS-TO-STRUCT

In the previous examples demonstrating arrays of structs, the number of files or tasks was
fairly small. But as the number of structs increases, or if the structs contain many large-sized
char arrays as members, maintaining the set of structs becomes a burden. An economical
solution to storing a set of structs is to begin with an array of pointers-to-structs, not an array
of structs, and create structs only as needed. This cuts down on the overhead of keeping a
static amount of storage—only the space for pointers is maintained permanently.

Returning to Section 6.3.3, if, instead of an array of structs (**struct text KEY[TOT]**), we
define **struct text *KEY[TOT] = {NULL};** as an array of TOT pointers-to-structs of type
text, with, again, the first element unused. This would require little modification in the
previous function.

```
struct text *findslot(STRING PSI);
    {/*BP*/
    struct  text *pstr = NULL;
```

```
long hold = 0L;
long i = 0L;
BOOL sw = 0;

for (i = 1; i < TOT; i++)
    {/*check_if_record_struct_is_already_stored*/
    pstr = KEY[i];
    if (sw == 0)
        {/*need a vacancy*/
        if (KEY[i] == NULL || pstr->ID[0] == SNUL) /*There may not be a struct.*/
            {/*found_a_vacancy*/
            hold = i;
            sw = 1;          /*If a vacancy is found, we make note ofit.*/
            }/*found_a_vacancy*/
        }/*need a vacancy*/
    if (EQU(PSI, pstr->ID))
        {/*Record struct is already stored.*/
        sw = 2;
        return(pstr);
        }/*record struct was already stored*/
    }/*check_if_record_struct_is_already_stored*/
if (i > TOT && sw == 0)
    {/*slots_are_all_filled*/
    printf("\nOnly %d records can be stored.\n",TOT-1);
    exit(2);
    }/*slots_are_all_filled*/
else if (sw == 1)
    {/*install_new_record*/
    KEY[hold] = (struct text *) calloc(1, sizeof(struct text));
    stcpy(PSI,KEY[hold]->ID);
    return (KEY[hold]);
    }/*install_new_record*/
}/*EP*/
```

6.4. CONVERTING THE DATABASE RECORD TO A STRUCT

A major use of the struct is storing the literal text of defined units of the database record. This section focuses on mapping the text to struct, for several different types of records.

The struct is a cubbyhole capable of holding and handling the fields of a database record such as the one shown in Section 6.3.1 and the very different one in Table 6.1. More generally, it is a flexible data structure and a useful resource for implementing a variety of record schemes. The struct as record holder is particularly useful when a set of records need to be compared and/or pooled before they can be output. When only some of the components of the decomposed record are to be used, the struct format makes it easy to salvage particular fields, subfields and/or subsubfields.

It is beyond the scope of this book to compare theoretical database models and the techniques appropriate to the different database models. Instead, we treat the database record as a string brought into memory as a whole. It is then decomposed by a procedure that 'knows' how to identify a (sub)(sub)field; see, for example, *inandchop*() in Section 6.5.2. Depending on task type, particular fields or parts of fields are retained as members of the struct. The descriptors for the types of database records are just that: descriptions of the design of database records, without theoretical implications.

As a general procedure to extract the particular fields or subfields that are currently significant, the record is first streamed into a temporary buffer. Then depending on the struct pattern and on what information is needed for processing, it is decomposed; i.e., some fields are kept as received, some fields are parsed to the (sub)subfield level, some are thrown away. Alternatively, the entry record is halted at field delimiters until the required field(s) are located; the fields that aren't essential for processing the record are ignored. The others are immediately converted to their permanent data types. And ancillary non-record information such as pointers to other records or comments can be stored in still other members of the struct. The entire record can be recovered as long as its file position is one member of the struct describing the record.

For want of a better term, we will define as a **personal database** any database that allows the user to write records in a way that suits him and which he can manipulate, using 'canned' database programs or programs he writes or customizes. The record style may but does not have to conform to the particular set of formal rules that by convention characterize and differentiate database types. Records may range from the chaotic to the rigidly stylized. Typically, the record is multi-field and mostly structured[4]

There may be no limit (except to conform to machine limitations) to the size of any field or any record. Alternatively, the maximum number of characters in each field may be predetermined. When field size is unconstrained, the usual ploy is to terminate the field by a character that is used exclusively to signal the End-of-Field. The End-of-Record, similarly, is another unique character that is not used in the body of the record. Records with subfields employ a third unique character not used in the body of the record.

---

4 By structured we mean that if record 1 contains five fields, all records contain five fields. If field 1 of record 1 is the name of a person, field 1 of every record is a name of some person. Similarly, field 2 will contain the same type of information in all records, and so forth. If field 2 of record 1 contains subfields, then field 2 of subsequent records may contain subfields. Subfields and subsubfields tend not to have a fixed number; there may be many or none in a field. But each (sub)subfield, if it is present, will be partitioned by a character reserved for the (sub)subfield delimiter. Appended note fields may have looser construction.

This section suggests servicable structs for different record styles. This implies considera-tion of these major factors: (1) what parts of the record are needed for the particular operation or task; (2) the particular hypothesis tested; and (3) frequency of use.

The first and second factors are the heart of the matter. Task type and test hypothesis are the major considerations in designing the appropriate struct template. As in Section 6.5.1, an alphabetization scheme might need only a single field plus information outside the record. Alternatively, attaching the same identification number to all the fields as a first step in indexing requires all the fields. For our present purposes, it is sufficient to note that these factors determine how to dissect the record and how to rearrange the units for incorporation into the struct.

The last factor is important in deciding when to create the set of structs. As one possibility, we can keep the records as read-only and in ASCII on disk, mapping fields into structs as needed under the direction of the programs that do the sorting and collating of the individual records. If we will be querying the database at irregular intervals, the layout of the particular struct constructed will depend on what information is required, which in turn will depend on what hypothesis we are testing.

Alternatively, we might wish to have the database always set in oracle mode; i.e., once the records are converted to structs, the program is kept running. This implies that all the data items in the record are retained as struct members or submembers. This format may be overly rich for any particular query, but everything is readily available. The set of structs can be responsive to a variety of queries.

In this section, we assume that all the fields are to be mapped to the struct. What follows is descriptive of the sorts of records a personal database might contain[5]

The chaotic or random or manuscript text.

These records can be a list of phrases or sentences or the start of an outline or more or less random jottings. A record can be defined as all the material up to a NewLine. Or a record can be defined as all the material up to two NewLines in a row or up to a period or up to a paragraph mark. In the example shown, because the name stamp begins with a hyphen, the hyphen can be used as delimiter, providing it does not appear in the body of the 'record'.

The notes can be handled by a struct with a single member, a pointer-to-char that will hold the address of the text when it is dynamically stored.

struct chaos {STRING ptext;}

When laboratory notes for several on-going experiments are typed on-line into a single file, with hotkeys for PSI, date and time, they can become valuable adjuncts to the experimental values obtained. In some settings, a note can automatically be stamped with the address or name of the file that is collecting the data on-line. These notes can help reconstruct the

---

5 Thanks are due to Libbe L. Englander and Nadine C. U. Lipkin for helpful suggestions on record construction and examples.

context in which the data are taken. What follows is a few lines of notes on three nerve-muscle preparations in a study of acetyl choline receptor clustering over time. 30 dishes of muscle cultures, 6 days after plating, were divided randomly into 3 sets called NM1, NM2 and NM3. All the notes for a single set are later output to one file, the notes on another set are sent to a separate file. To compare time sequences, the time data will be converted from absolute time to relative time in minutes or hours from time zero using procedure whose prototypes are in the library file *time.h.*

-NM1: 10:05	**15 ug of acetylcholine receptor clustering factor/MEM added**
-NM2: 16:05	**Added factor**
-NM1: 20:30	**add rhodamine alpha-bugarotoxin**
-NM2: 20:32	**add rhodamine alpha-bugarotoxin**
-NM3: 20:35	**add rhodamine alpha-bugarotoxin**
-NM3: 21:00	**add factor**
-NM1: 21:55	**cells look slightly less dense than in the other preps**
-NM1: 22:00	**Rinse 3X with 2% horse serum. fix with 2% paraformaldehye/lysine. Label with DAP.**
-NM2: 22:10	**Rinse 3X with 2% horse serum. fix with 2% paraformaldehye/lysine. Label with DAP.**
-NM3: 22:17	**Rinse 3X with 2% horse serum. fix with 2% paraformaldehye/lysine. Label with DAP.**

The record composed of an indefinite number of informational fields.

Unlike the random record, in this style, each record has distinguishable components. But the individual records in the database have variable numbers of fields. Manuscripts are the prototypic example, where breaking down the document into specific units is used in a variety of tasks from counting keystrokes to making elaborate judgments on style. To examine a speech, say, the paragraph symbol is declared to be the record delimiter and the period is the field; fields are individual sentences. Juxtaposing the first and last 'fields' are useful for speeches that follow the traditional: 'tell them what you are going to say', say it, 'tell them what you've said'. Determining the average number of fields in a record can be used as an index of the space devoted to a topic.

Or the sentence can be taken as the record unit and commas used to divide the record into fields. Words become the subfields. This division is useful in determining the average size of a sentence and can be declared to be an indicator of 'crispness' or 'runon score' or 'intelligence-of-user level' or 'boredom measure' or any other silly label the program creator decides to give the index.

Programs that decode database information, such as *majorfile()*, discussed in Sections 3.6.2 and 5.2.2.3, can easily make provision for indefinite records. In *majorfile()*, the second field of the user-supplied information about the database is either a **I** for indefinite, an 'S' for semidefinite (see the section on the semi-stylized record below) or a specific number for a structured database. Indefinite and semidefinite database records are arbitrarily given a cap of MAXFIELDS fields per record, where MAXFIELDS can be redefined in *define.h.*

The record composed of a definite number of simple informational fields.

The records in Sections 6.3.1 are examples of simple records. Obviously records in this styled fit the relational database model. Such records have in common with commercial relational databases a fairly shallow structure; i.e., records are divided into fields but fields are not subdivided into subfields. Queries can relate to specific text. Complex boolean search instructions can be handled in C with nested case statements or if-else conditionals.

This format lends itself to a variety of uses and is particularly well suited to static data such as bibliographic entries and name-address lists. The record type is one in which the informational fields that compose the record relate to a common entity: a person, an event, a product, or whatever. The individual attributes about the key item that constitute the separate fields of the record become the sequential members of the struct. This is a popular format, if only because there exist a number of commercial database programs for entering the data, updating them and querying them. Most if not all of these programs have import/export utilities that allow the user to store his database in ASCII-delimited format, using his own field and record delimiters. The record can be converted to whatever data types are permitted by the database language. Using Paradox as representative, some data types found in the commercial databases can be readily represented in C: very long numbers by floats; shorter numbers by integers; alphanumeric characters by the single-byte character set; and memos by finding storage for text collected initially in a HUGESZE array. Date and time and money data types can be written using formats available in the library file *locale.h*. Blobs, on the other hand, can not be immediately mapped into C data types. Blobs begins to deal with the demand for amalgamating data from different media: text, graphics, still images, video and sound. The blob has no primitive representation in a language designed for characters and numbers but must be constructed from the available resources. Fundamental building blocks including a grid for the coordinates of a displayed image are available as language extenders in a number of compilers. Pointers to the applications programs dealing with the construction and handling of the blob can be kept in the struct.

The string-mapped hierarchical record.

A record is viewed as a hierarchy of informational fields that may be divided into subfields and these subfields into subsubfields, the whole stretched out as a string. Note that *hierarchy* as used here describes a style of record; it is not related to the hierarchical database model. The record is considered the root of a 'tree', each field a major branch, the subfields and their subsubfields the smaller branches. In theory, there is no restriction on subfield depth. In practice, a depth greater than the subsubfield is unusual. The entire record is stored as a string, where field 1 precedes field 2 as in the relational database. Within field 1, subfield 1 of field 1 (if it exists) precedes subfield 2 of field 1 (if it exists), which, in turn, precedes subfield 3 of field 1. The subfield and the subsubfield must have unique delimiters that: (1) are not used within the body of the record; and (2) are not the field and record delimiters. Typically, even if the fields are well structured, the subfields are not. In the present example, there may be none or a few or many notes.

Though little advantage is taken of this feature by relational databases, the struct has the ability to store and the syntax to reference subsubmembers within submembers within members; we thread down the levels of the hierarchy to the specific unit. Hence, the struct with its stylized ordering of members where a member can itself be a struct or a pointer to a struct can rewrite the compound record in a way that makes it accessible to text manipulation procedures.

```
struct name {char ln[30]; char fn[20];} ;
struct address {int snum; char st[30]; char city[30]; char ST[2]; char zip[10];};
struct TELE {int tel; int fax;};
struct contacts {char *when[20]};
struct money {int cde[5]; int YN;}

struct charitydrive
        {
        struct name n;
        struct address a;
        struct TELE t;
        struct when w;
        struct money m;
        STRING NOTES[10];
        }
```

The major problem is handling as indefinite number of subfields or subsubfields, as expected for structs such as *when*. One solution is to set a fixed but high limit to the number of subfields or subsubfields. Another, to anticipate, is to use the linked list (see Section 6.8) to add (sub)subfields as necessary.

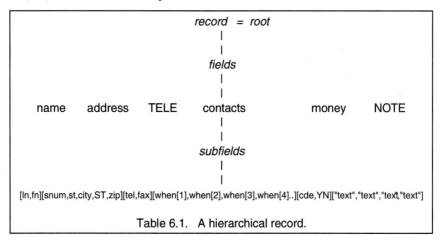

Table 6.1. A hierarchical record.

The semi-stylized record.

The semi-stylized record is one that has some rigidly formatted fields, and then a set of *ad hoc* notes of varying lengths. So the first part of the record looks like the simple record style. The prototypic example is the patient's chart, where most of the patient's history and diagnosis can be written in a stylized format, but chart notes need constant updating in a non-rigid format.

For example:

```
struct chart
    {
    char lastname[30];
    char firstname[20];
    char SocSec[10];
    char Attending[20];
    STRING DX[5];
    struct NextofKin {char Name[30]; char addr[30];} ;
    char street[30];
    char city[20];
    char STATE[2];
    int    zip[10]
    int    TEL[10]
    int    FAX[10];
    STRING CHARTNOTES;
    }
```

The struct can be made to collect these additional data differently than does the amplified 2D array discussed in Section 6.5.2. For example, the semi-stylized record can utilize the linked list of structs discussed below; semi-stylized TIDBYTE's[6] of fixed length are reserved for unsystematic notes.

As a variant of the semi-stylized record, the indefinite portion of the record is a number of pointers that 'hook' into records in the same or other databases. These pointers and some keywords constitute subsidiary links in a chain (see Section 6.8 below).

Using an expanding number of links is also a way of handling those versions of the hierarchical model that fit the semi-structured model; i.e., the informational fields are properly structured, but subfields within a field or subsubfields within a subfield vary in number for different records. Or the number of (sub)subfields are incremented or contracted during processing for some records but not for others.

---

6 A buffer containing TIDBYTE characters (a preset and fixed number of bytes) is maintained to display a memo or note. Or text multiples of the TIDBYTE are entered into memory at one time. Refinements include displaying up to a number of characters on both sides of particular text. Or displaying as many complete sentences as possible without overflowing the TIDBYTE.

6.5. STORING ESSENTIAL INFORMATION ABOUT A STRING IN A STRUCT

Section 6.4 focused on how structs could represent actual database records by accommodative mappings of the original file records. This section examines structs that also hold some text from the record. But usually the struct keeps only selected portions of the text. And the struct augments what it keeps with other information. An example of this type of struct is shown in the next section.

6.5.1. KEEPING THE NECESSARY AND THE SUFFICIENT

Suppose a record format such as:

Stevens, Alfred@Canada@1955@~

consisting of a name, a country and a date. Were we to alphabetize these records by country (field 2), this next struct template would, in a compact representation, hold: (1) the necessary key text from the record; (2) the starting location of this particular record on disk, which is necessary to recall the record for an alphabetized printout as well as to arbitrate chronologic sequence when two records have the same key; and (3) some positive specimen identifier (PSI). In this case, given a simple sort in a single database, concatenating a reminder of what the database is about and the record number is more than sufficient.

```
static struct alpha
    {
    STRING key2;
    long locate;
    char PSI[MEDSZE];
    } ;
```

These next operations would collect information about the first 25 records of the database stored in alphafile.db. It would save the essential information for a record in a dynamically-acquired struct. The address of the struct is kept in an element of pa, an array of pointers-to-struct. Only field 2 is needed, so only the text of field 2 is stored. The other fields are read into memory only so that at the start of the next cycle, the file cursor will point to the start of the next record.

```
#define LIM 2
#define TOP 25

struct alpha *pa[TOP];
static FILE *inch = NULL;
static BITMAP Trcd = 0;
static BITMAP Tfld = 0;
```

```
void store(void)
      {
      int      brk = 0;
      int      count = 0;      /*This will count fields chopped until field 2 is reached.*/

      char     dump[SZE(100)];    /*Where the unnecessary parts of the record*/
                                  /* will be dumped.*/
      int      i = 0;
      inch = fopen("alphafil.db","r");/*Opens a file called alphafile.db for reading.*/
      for (i = 0; i < TOP; i++)     /*This will bring in the first 25 records from alphafile.db.*/
           {                        /*storing them in pa[0] to pa[24].*/
           pa[i] = (struct alpha *) calloc(1, sizeof(struct alpha)); /*This buys us a*/
                                                                     /*struct of type alpha.*/
```

/*Just before we stream another record into memory, we can interrogate ftell(), a library file utility prototyped in stdio.h. ftell() tells us the position of the file cursor in number of bytes into the file.*/

```
           pa[i]->locate = ftell(inch);
           for (count = 1; count <= LIM; count++)
                {
```

/*This next halts at field delimiters. When it brings in the second field, at line a, it secures space for a struct, saves the text of field 2, and, in line b, brings in the rest of the record for dumping by forcing entry to halt at the record delimiter. This prevents the unneeded end of the present record from blocking the next record in the file.*/

```
                ptemp = psin(inch,Tfld,&brk,SZE(100),dump);
                if (count == LIM)                                          /*a*/
                     {
                     pa[i]->key2 = dssave(dump);   /*This obtains dynamic storage*/
                                                   /* for the text of field 2.*/
                     ptemp = psin(inch,Trcd,&brk,SZE(100),dump);        /*b*/
                                                   /*To bring in the rest of the record.*/
                     stitoa(i, pa[i]->PSI);
                     stcat("-Authors",pa[i]->PSI);
                     }
                }
           }
      }

void recall(void)
        {
        int i;
        char dump[MEDSZE];

        for (i = 0; i < TOP; i++)
          {
          fseek(inch,pa[i]->locate,0);
          dump[0] = SNUL;
          psin(inch,Trcd,&brk,100,dump);
          printf("\nRecord %ld = %s@%s@ %s~", i,pa[i]->key2, pa[i]->PSI, dump);
```

```
            }
        }

main()
    {
    setbreak(&Tfld,"@","","");       /*This will halt entry at each field delimiter.*/
    setbreak(&Trcd,"~","","");       /*This will halt entry at the end of a record.*/
    store();
    recall();
    }
```

After the structs are sorted by country using some alphabetic program such as *quicksort()* (see K&R, p. 87), the actual records can be brought into memory in sort sequence under the direction of the second member of the struct, which contains the record's file position. In this simple example, in *recall()* we write out the records from the disk in the original order, but, nevertheless, we find the particular record in the database by using the information kept in the second member of the associated struct.

The library functions, *ftell()* and *fseek()* are used to interrogate and handle the file pointer. *ftell()* tells where the file cursor is pointing in the disk file, *alphafile.db* in the example. As each new record is read in, the cursor shifts position further into the file. *fseek()* positions the file cursor to the location that is its second arg. *fseek()* has no control on how much of the file is then read into memory. In the example shown, reading the file is halted at the record delimiter. Alternatively, for fixed-sized records the storage struct could contain an additional member to indicate the byte position of the end of the record in the file, thus:

```
static struct alpha
    {
    STRING key2;
    long locate;
    long endn;
    char PSI[MEDSZE];
    } *pa[TOP+1];
```

And the code in *store()* would be modified to read:

```
for (i = 0; i <= TOP+1; i++)  /*This will bring in the first 26 records from.*/
    {                          /*alphafile.db, storing them in pa[0] to pa[24].*/
    pa[i] = (struct alpha *) calloc(1, sizeof(struct alpha));
    pa[i]->locate = ftell(inch);
    if i > 0)
        pa[i-1]->endn = ftell(inch)-1;
    }
```

Note that we need an additional struct, pa[26], so we can acquire endn for pa[25];

endn would store the end position of the record in the file and the data would be read back in *recall()* with

fgets(dump, (int) pa[i]-endn, inch);

This latter format is suitable for fixed-field records and the UNIX system, which stores text lines with a NewLine terminator. Unfortunately, under DOS and other systems that store the EOL as a CRLF and convert incoming CRLF's to C NewLine's, *fseek()* is unreliable.

6.5.2. CONSTRUCTING 2D STRING ARRAYS WITHIN A STRUCT

This section illustrates how the struct solves the problem of storing specific text phrases or specific fields taken from a sequence of (or a set of) database records.

It also illustrates another aspect of the struct's versatility. The struct can envelop a set of 2D arrays, a feat that, recalling the previous chapter, is hard to do with ordinary 2D array representation. This is shown using a mailmerge program, which saves name-address fields until the labels that are to printed side by side have been collected.

Mailmerge programs merge a database file of names-addresses and a letter file, so that the same letter, suitably modified, can be sent to each name in the address file. These program output customized letters and envelop labels. (Of course a mailmerge program can be designed to write the name and address immediately and directly on an envelop. But then it wouldn't illustrate the storage struct.)

A mailmerge program can be written comprehensively to accommodate a variety of printers, fonts and label sizes, at the expense of the time it takes to choose among the many options. At the other extreme, as shown here, a program can be customized for a single printer and text formatter combination. Variants of the program can be written for other printer-formatter combinations, each callable by a different program name.

The program is fairly general for letters, in that it can work with any stylized ASCII-delimited database, no matter what the record and field delimiters are. Using | as the signal character[7], it replaces any |**<digit>**| expression in the letter with the text of that field number from the person-address record currently under examination.

For example, suppose this database format and sample record. The field delimiter is a comma. The record delimiter is a ~. Subfield notes terminate in a /.

1	Alphabet Name: LAST, FIRST,	MIRIAM, Esther,
2	Dear Name,	Meem,
3	Envelop name,	Professor E Miriam,
4	Street Address,	99 3rd Street,

---

7 If | is a character in the database or letter, use some other character that is NOT an ordinary character in the file. Control chars—chars whose ASCII representation is octal 37 or less—are good alert chars in that they are less likely to be used as ordinary symbols in the database or letter. (CtrlA seems to work under almost any text processor or editor.) However, this book was formatted by Ventura, which has no provision for printing control characters. If another character is used, the statement **if (brk == |) ...** in line *a* should also be changed.

5 City,	Bethesda,
6 ST,	MD,
7 ZIP,	20333,
8 Office Tel,	301 555 7890,
9 FAX Tel,	301 555 3220,
10 Home Tel,	301 555 1234,
11 Title,	Associate Professor,
12 Institution,	New University,
13 Notes ~	App't 1990/Specialty: The 2nd Temple Period/
	Summer address: Liberty Marina, Dale, MD, 21345~

A portion of a sample letter using this record might be:

|3|,<R>[8]
|4|,<R>
|5| |6| |7|

Dear |2|,

The next meeting of the |12| special panel will take place at 6pm, November 2nd. It should last about 2 hours.

When the letter is processed by the mailmerge program, it will read:

Professor E Miriam,
99 3rd Street,
Bethesda MD 20333

Dear Meem,

The next meeting of the New University special panel will take place at 6pm, November 2nd. It should last about 2 hours.

The only real problem in such programs comes when we print multiple labels; i.e., the paper has more than one label across a row, where a row is modulo single label. The start of a 3-label by 10-label format is shown in Table 6.2. We need to collect the text for the three labels that compose a row. When all the fields for the two labels are in from disk, we can output line 1 of the first label, line 1 of the second label, line 1 of the 3rd label, EOL; then in the second print line, we output line 2 of the first label, line 2 of the second label, line 2 of the third label, EOL, and so forth. Then we can reuse the storage space to collect the text for row 2.

The label output is NOT general. The program shown assumes a laser printer and Ventura formatting and printing. These next are the parameters that need changing depending on paper and font size. They are set as #define's on top of the program.

•   LABELSACROSS   Number of COLUMNS: the number of labels across the page. Three columns are used in Table 6.2.; three are used in the program.

---

8 The <R> serves as EOL marker in Ventura.

- LABELSDOWN   Number of ROWS: the number of labels down the page. Two rows out of ten are shown in Table 6.3; ten rows are used in the program.

- MAXLINESPERLABEL   The number of lines in a label plus the inter label line (a total of 6 in this example). The number of lines that can contain text is one less than MAXLINESPERLABEL. Label size and font size determine this parameter.

- LINESPERLABEL   The number of actual lines in the current label. In this example three lines out of a possible five have text.

Each label is treated as a row-column element

	Label 1	Label 2	Label 3
	[---/----/----/----/----/----/-]-[----/----/----/----/----/----/-]-[----/----/----/----/----/----/-]		
Field 3:	Prof E Miriam	Dr RM Morris	Dr Bill Toll<R>
Field 4:	99 3rd Street	1234 Camp Drive	35 Conn Avenue<R>
Fields 5,6,7:	Bethesda MD 20333	Bethesda MD 20333	SS MD 20333<R>
line 4			
line 5			
interline 6			
	Prof Joel Sturn	Dr Rickie Viener	Dr Steven Lander<R>
	2638 Morency Drive	12 Lone Ave Road	7 Michael Street<R>
	Bethesda MD 20333	Bethesda MD 20333	SS MD 20333<R>
line 5			
interline 6			

Table 6.2.   Two rows and 3 columns of a 3 by 10 label sheet.

- MAXCHARSPERLABELLINE   The largest amount of characters in a label, as shown on the ruler. In this example it is 32: the brackets and the text they include. The inter label character is at position 33. Label size and font size determine this parameter. Fields 5,6,7 make up the text of line 3 of any label. If City, field 5, is very long, it might be advisable to put field 7 on line 4, and change LINESPERLABEL to 4.

/*The program code assumes a 3 labels across by 10 labels down (30 labels per page) printout on 8.5 by 11 inch laser label paper, with up to 5 lines per label plus an interline for a MAXLINESPERLABEL of 6. Assuming a font size of 10, the concatenation of fields 5, 6 and 7 can not be longer than 32 chars. Trimming is done by a preliminary program such as pslinechop() (see Chapter 7). */

/*The stylized Ventura tag @LBLHEIGHT was given these values: PARAGRAPH font: Swiss 10. PARAGRAPH Spacing: .05" Above, .95" Below, .12 fractional points Interline. PARAGRAPH Alignment: Left Justify. PARAGRAPH Break: After. PARAGRAPH Tabs: tab 1 = 2.96". tab 2 = 5.84" (i.e., 2 x 2.96"). tab 3 = 3 x 2.96". FRAME Margin & Columns: 1 column. Set margins: top and bottom .5"; left and right .2".*/

labcrew[1]	Prof E Miriam 99 3rd Street Bethesda MD 20333
labcrew[2]	Dr RM Morris 1234 Camp Drive Bethesda MD 20333
labcrew[3]	Dr Bill Toll 35 Conn Avenue SS MD 20333

Table 6.4.   Three 'elements' in an array of labels.

/*The program prints out enough labels per LABELHEIGHT tag to fill a page. Then it puts out another complete batch to fill the next page.*/

/*To remove Ventura-specific format, delete lines beginning with @. Remove the <R>'s at the end of lines; these represent line—not paragraph—breaks. Print statements are also Ventura-specific.*/

/*For Ventura and 24-pin printers: Set FRAME Margin & Columns to 1 column and zero for all margins (top,bottom,left,right). Set PARAGRAPH font to 10. The difference in margin sizes is very necessary. Laser printers requires 3 dead lines on top, whereas pin printers don't.*/

/*The three initation and initialization functions—*inarg*(), *init*() and *initiation*()—are in LISTINGS\chap6\6.5.2.c. The user has the option of entering the names of the files that hold the letter and the names-address database on the command line or interactively. *inarg* a condensed version of *argmode*(), discussed in Section 5.2.2.3, handles command line input. If the database and letter files are not announced at run time, *init*() obtains the information interactively. Both *inarg*() and *init*() set setbreak tables to trap incoming text on the field and record delimiters. *initiation*() opens four output files. It sends the envelop labels as a print-ready unit ready to *mail.lbl*, completed letters as a print-ready unit to *mail.out*, error messages to *mail.err* and log information to *mail.trl*.*/

```
#include "DEFINE.H"
#include "GLOBALS.H"
#include "COMLIB.H"
#include "COMSET.H"
```

```
/* ALPHABETIZED LIST OF PROCEDURES*/
static void    inarg(int argc, STRING argv[]);
static void    init(void);
static void    initiation(void);
extern int     main(int argc, STRING argv[]);
extern void    printstrip(void);
```

```
static BOOL    OKL = NO;            /*This becomes YES if the letter file*/
                                   /*is named on the command line.*/
static BOOL    OKA = NO;            /*This becomes YES if the address file is*/
                                   /* named on the command line.*/
static BITMAP  TEOL = 0;
static BITMAP  Talert = 0;

#define LINESPERLABEL        3     /*The actual number of lines in a label.*/
#define MAXLINESPERLABEL 6        /*The most lines that can be written in*/
                                   /* this label size plus 1 for the interline.*/
#define LABELSDOWN          10    /*The most labels that can be written down a page.*/
#define MAXCHARSPERLABELLINE 32 /*The most chars per individual label line.*/
#define LABELSACROSS        3     /*The number of labels across a page.*/
```

/*The following template has a single member: a 2D char array that is large enough to hold all the lines in a single label (LINESPERLABEL), where each line can be up to MAXCHARSPERLABELLINE chars in size. (It is LINESPERLABEL + 1 because the zero th element isn't used. It is MAXCHARSPERLABELLINE + 1 to provide space for an interlabel space.) The array labcrew is big enough to store LABELSACROSS structs to enable the program to access the individual fields of LABELSACROSS records. (It is LABELSACROSS+1 because the count starts on 1.*/

/*The structure can perhaps best be visualized as an array of arrays. Each label is itself a 2D array. But the ENTIRE label becomes the text of one element of the array labcrew. This is shown in Table 6.4.*/

```
static struct lab
    {
    char f[LINESPERLABEL+1] [MAXCHARSPERLABELLINE+1];
    } labcrew[LABELSACROSS+1];
```

/*In printstrip(), the program outputs the string that will be the first line of the first label, then the string that is the first line of the second label up to the first line of the LABELSACROSS th label, then the second line of the first label, then the second line of the second label and so on. Once a group of LABELSACROSS labels is output, the structs are virtually cleared and reused to prepare the next row of labels for output.*/

```
extern void printstrip(void)
    {/*BP*/
    int i,ii;
    for (ii = 1; ii <= LINESPERLABEL; ii++)
        {
        for (i = 1; i <= LABELSACROSS; i++)
            {                                    /*Don't tab last label in the row.*/
            if (i == LABELSACROSS)
                fprintf(outchan[4],"%s",labcrew[i].f[ii]);
            else                                /*Tab to next label across.*/
```

/*Shifting to the next label on the right is done by building in a tab. Note that if formatting/printing is done by other than Ventura, this next line should be used instead. It puts out a set of spaces to pad the label:

```
for (iii=stlen(labcrew[i].f[ii])+1; iii <= MAXCHARSPERLABELLINE; iii++)
    fprintf(outchan[4]," "); */
```

```
                fprintf(outchan[4],"%s\t",labcrew[i].f[ii]);
                labcrew[i].f[ii][0] = NULL;
                }
        fprintf(outchan[4],"<R>\n");           /*Ventura's EOL is a <R>.*/
        }
    for (i = LINESPERLABEL + 1; i <= MAXLINESPERLABEL; i++)
        fprintf(outchan[4],"<R>\n");
    }/*EP*/


/*PROCEDURE*/ int main(int argc, STRING argv[])
    {/*MAIN*/
    char buf[HUGESZE] = {SNUL};
    int   endf = 0;
    int   i = 0;
    int   ii = 0;
    int   iii = 0;
    int   LABgroup = 0;
    int   mod = 0;          /*For modulo. It counts the number of labels across the page.*/
    char rcd[HUGESZE] = {SNUL};
    STRING   prcd = rcd;
    int    task = 1;

    setbreak(&TEOL,"\n", "\13\14", "is");
    setbreak(&Talert,"|", "\13\14", "is");
    inarg(argc,argv);
    initiation();
    dbreccnt = 0;
    fclose(inchan[2]);
    fprintf(outchan[4],"\n\n@LBLHEIGHT = "); /*Uses Ventura stylesheet: label.sty.*/
    while (TRUE)
        {/*ExamineARecord*/
        /*Bring in an address*/
        endf = 0;
        endf = inandchop(inchan[1],Tterstop,Ttrastop,pf0,nfields,&infields,
                    outchan[2],dbreccnt);
        if (endf == EOF)
            {
            dbreccnt-- ;
            printstrip();
            break;
            }
        mod++;
        for (i = 1; i <= infields; i++)
            sttidy(&field[i],"","","\n","FE");
```

/*ATTENTION: Assigning record fields to label fields has to be redone for other record formats. In this example, the third label line is concatenated from fields 5, 6 and 7 with spaces in between them.*/

```
            stcpy(field[3],labcrew[mod].f[1]);
            stcpy(field[4],labcrew[mod].f[2]);
```

```
    stcpy(field[5],labcrew[mod].f[3]);
    stcat("\40",labcrew[mod].f[3]);
    stcat(field[6],labcrew[mod].f[3]);
    stcat("\40",labcrew[mod].f[3]);
    stcat(field[7],labcrew[mod].f[3]);

    if (mod == LABELSACROSS)   /*Time to output LABELSACROSS labels*/
        {
        printstrip();
        mod = 0;
        LABgroup += 1;      /*MAXLINESPERLABEL have been printed out.*/
        if (LABgroup == LABELSDOWN)
            {
```

/*LABELSDOWN has been reached. No more labels can be printed on the page. The next
instruction sets up a style tag that contains a page break for the next page of labels.
@LBLHEIGHT is derived from the Ventura stylesheet:fax.sty. For non-Ventura formatters
that can handle the form feed symbol, use this instead:
fprintf(outchan[4],"\014"); */

```
            fprintf(outchan[4],"\n\n@LBLHEIGHT = ");
            LABgroup = 0;
            }
        }
    dbreccnt++;
    if (dbreccnt % 100 == 0)
        printf("\nLetter number %ld is being processed.\n",dbreccnt);
    inchan[2] = io(infile[2],read0);
    while (TRUE)
        {/*BringInTheLetterALineAtATime*/
        psinput(inchan[2],TEOL,&brk,HUGESZE,rcd);
        if (brk == EOF || brk == 0)       /*brk is defined in globals.c*/
            break;
        prcd = rcd;
    while (*rcd)
        {
        pspsscan(&prcd,Talert,&brk,HUGESZE,buf);
        if (buf[0] != NULL)
            fprintf(outchan[1],"%s",buf);
        if (brk == 'l')                          /*a*/
            {
            pspsscan(&prcd,Talert,&brk,HUGESZE,buf);
            fprintf(outchan[1],"%s",field[atoi(buf)]);
            continue;
            }
        }
    fprintf(outchan[1],"\n");
    }/*BringInALetterALineAtATime*/
```

/*Ventura destroys the form feed symbol. So to start a new letter, the program outputs a
Ventura style tag @PAGEBREAK to separate letters, where @PAGEBREAK sets
PARAGRAPH Page Break before, PARAGRAPH Line Break before and after. For other

formatters and printers, use this instead.
    fprintf(outchan[1],"\014"); */

```
    fprintf(outchan[1],"\n@PAGEBREAK = \n");
    fclose(inchan[2]);
    for (i = 1; i <= infields; i++)
        NULLIT(field[i]);
    }/*ExamineARecord*/
    closeup();
    exit(0);
    }/*MAIN*/
```

6.6.   ASSOCIATING THE INFORMATION IN DISPARATE STRUCTS

With this section, we begin discussing the struct's second major role: the repository of meta information. In this role it can establish linkages among disparate struct systems, it can store information that cuts through a set of structs and it can store a sequence of instructions that control processing.

There are several ways by which linkage between differently constructed structs in made. For example, the availability of a member-in-common can create or maintain contact between differently constructed structs or between the records from which they were formed. Or a commonality can be created artificially around some variable of common interest or some common locus of activity.

6.6.1. A MEMBER IN COMMON

The virtual linking of disparate structs is simple if, serendipidously, both types of structs (or the records they map) have a member in common. If particular fields in a record from database A match particular fields in a record from database B, selected fields from the two records can be concatenated into a new type of struct and later output to database C. Or matching fields might be used to select the record either from A or from B; e.g., if (field2-database A > field1-database B)...

Suppose we expect several members from each of a group of camps for a super camp GetTogether. We have several lists—digitized, of course.

- A list of the attendees and their home addresses.

- A list from each participating camp of ALL its campers; the list includes names of children not coming to the GetTogether.

Each record on each list can be converted to a struct of type A.

static struct A {char name[MEDSZE]; STRING address;};

In this example, when the name field in two records from the two lists match, one of the databases (the camp list) acts to supply a critical piece of information about the common member; namely, what camp is the attendee from. A new struct is created, which uses the member in common as one member of the struct; the rest of the struct is composed of ancillary information not resident in either struct.

As part of preparing for the festivities, we need a list of the essential information about each attendee; i.e.

* Who is arriving when. If we know the attendee's camp group, we know when he arrives, experience having taught us to stagger arrival times.

* Who to call for help. If we know the camp group, we know who to contact should we need to know more about the little darling than was recorded on paper or floppy.

In other words, we would like to create records modeled on a struct of type B.

static struct B {char name[MEDSZE]; char contact[MEDSZE]; float TIMEcode;};

If we can match an attendee name against a name on one of the camp lists, we can use some ancillary information we have about that camp to create a record of type B. To keep things simple, in this version, happily, no two campers have the same names. Realistically, more than one field would have to be matched to assure a match. And the field and record delimiters are fixed at | and ~, respectively. Note that most of the material that will be updated for the next Get Together group is stored in the procedure called *match*().

```
#include "DEFINE.H"
#include "GLOBALS.H"
#include "COMLIB.H"
#include "COMSET.H"

#define PARTICIPATINGCAMPS 5
#define NUMATTENDEES 53

struct A {char name[MEDSZE]; char address[LRGSZE];};
struct B {char name[MEDSZE]; char contact[MEDSZE]; float TIMEcode;};
struct B *p[NUMATTENDEES+1];     /*An array of pointers-to-structs of type B.*/

extern BOOL match(STRING Aname, STRING Cname, int j);
extern int main(void);

FILE *camp[PARTICIPATINGCAMPS+1] = {NULL};
FILE *fAttend = NULL;
FILE *outch = NULL;
BITMAP Trecord = 0;
BITMAP Tfield = 0;
long current = 0L;
long rcdcnt = 0L;
```

/*Aname is the dummy for an Attendee name; Cname represents a name from one of the Camp lists. j is the # of the specific camp. current is the next type B struct to be created. Specific info is here. Reminder: ter and tra may need to be changed.*/

```
BOOL match(STRING Aname, STRING Cname, int j)
    {/*BP*/
    if (EQU(Aname, Cname))                    /*If there's a match...*/
        {
        current++;
        p[current] = (struct B *) calloc(1, sizeof(struct B));/*Creates a type B struct.*/
            stcpy(Aname, p[current]->name);
        switch(j)
            {
            case 1: {stcpy("Sam Smith 215 555 1213", p[current]->contact);
                    p[current]->TIMEcode = 8.30F; break;}
            case 2: {stcpy("Suki Jones 914 555 0927", p[current]->contact);
                    p[current]->TIMEcode = 10.30F; break;}
            case 3: {stcpy("Chuck Brown 703 555 3212 ", p[current]->contact);
                    p[current]->TIMEcode = 1.00F; break;}
            case 4: {stcpy("Hal Green 212 555 1245", p[current]->contact);
                    p[current]->TIMEcode = 2.30F; break;}
            case 5: {stcpy("Jimbo Blue 301 555 1897", p[current]->contact);
                    p[current]->TIMEcode = 4.30F; break;}
            default: break;
            }
        fprintf(outch,"(%.3ld) %-25sl %-25sl %.2f~\n",rcdcnt,p[current]->name,
        p[current]->contact,p[current]->TIMEcode);  /*To change delimiters,*/
                                                    /*change lines a and b below.*/

        return(TRUE);
        }
    return(FALSE);
    }/*EP*/


int main(void)
    {/*MAIN*/
    int brk = 0, brk1 = 0;
    int i, j;
    BOOL goA = 0;
    struct A tempA;      /*Temporary dumps for an Attendee name*/
    struct A tempC;      /*Temporary dumps for a Camplist name.*/
    STRING pa = tempA.name;
    STRING pc = tempC.name;

    fAttend = fopen("attendees.cmp","r");
    outch = fopen("arrivals.cmp","w");
    setbreak(&Trecord,"~","","");                        /*a*/
    setbreak(&Tfield,"|","","");                         /*b*/
    fprintf(outch,"\nGet Together. Weekend: August 13\n\n");
    for (i = 1; i <= NUMATTENDEES; i++)                  /*c*/
        {/*MainLoop*/
        goA = 0;
        psin(fAttend,Tfield, &brk, MEDSZE, tempA.name);
        if (brk == EOF)
            break;
```

```
sttidy(&pa,"","","\n","FEM");
psin(fAttend,Trecord,&brk, LRGSZE, tempA.address); /*garbage*/
rcdcnt++;
for (j = 1; j <= PARTICIPATINGCAMPS; j++)                        /*d*/
    {/*OpenaClist*/
    switch (j)        /*If campfile is not listed in directory, program will bomb.*/
        {/*which camp*/
        case 1:    camp[j]= fopen("Hiawatha.cmp","r"); break;
        case 2:    camp[j] = fopen("CompSci.cmp","r"); break;
        case 3:    camp[j] = fopen("GirlGuides.cmp","r"); break;
        case 4:    camp[j] = fopen("BadBears.cmp","r"); break;
        case 5:    camp[j] = fopen("BlueHills.cmp","r"); break;
        default: ;
        }/*which camp*/
    while(TRUE)                                        /e*/
        {/*bring in name from current Clist*/
        psin(camp[j], Tfield, &brk, MEDSZE, tempC.name);
        sttidy(&pa,"","","\n","FEM");   /*the first field of a record
                                           (an attendee) from Camp[j].*/
        psin(camp[j], Trecord, &brk1, LRGSZE, tempC.address);/*Bring*/
                                           /*in the last field.*/
        if (brk == EOF II brk1 == EOF)
            {
            fclose(camp[j]);
            break;                 /*Will fall through to line g and do*/
            }                      /* the loop starting on line d again.*/
        if (match(tempA.name, tempC.name, j))
            {
            goA = 1;               /*Will fall through to line g,*/
                                   /* where it will break out*/        /*f*/
            break;   /*of OpenaClist loop and go to loop starting on line a.*/
            }
        }/*bring in name from current Clist*/
    if (goA == 1) break;                                        /*g*/
    }/*OpenaClist*/
}/*MainLoop*/
printf("\nNew list is filed in ARRIVALS.CMP");
printf("\nExpected Number of Attendees = %d;\n "
 "Number that could be traced to a Participating Camp = %ld",NUMATTENDEES,
        current);
printf("\nIf numbers don't match, check lists.");
fprintf(outch,"\nExpected Number of Attendees = %d;\n";
 "Number that could be traced to a Participating Camp = %ld",NUMATTENDEES,
        current);
fprintf(outch,"\nIf numbers don't match, check lists.");
fclose(fAttend);
fclose(outch);
exit(0);
}/*MAIN*/
```

Typically, stringent matching of member fields needs to be weakened. Instead of insisting on a perfect match, given some preliminary preprocessing—uppercasing letters and eliminating punctuation and white space except for single space separators between words—a 'fuzzy' similarity may be more attainable; e.g., **if (A.name == Sm*th*)...**, where any set of letters can fill in the asterick: Smith, Smithson, Smythe, and so forth. (A function such as *stwildsearch*() in Chapter 7 is suitable for such a search.) Or the presence of two more or less similar informational fields may be acceptable; e.g., **if (EQU(field1,Sm*th*) && ((EQU(field5,"Boston") || EQU(field5,"Brookline") || EQU(field5,"Newton"))....** Or the commonality may be within a range of chronological dates rather than a single year; e.g., **if (year > 1982 && year < 1992) ...**

As an aside on program construction, this program is complicated in that loops are nested and the if-else conditionals lead to different loops. In pseudo-code:

/*Alist is the attendee list; Clist is any Camp list. AA is a struct of type A to hold information on a kid on the Alist. CC is a struct of type A to hold information on a kid on one of the Clists. A:, B: and C: are where the three loops begin.*/

```
LOOP: for the number of attendees on Alist              A:
        bring in a name from Alist to AA.name
            if EOF(Alist)
                program is done
            LOOP: else open a Clist                      B:

        LOOP: bring in a name from open Clist to CC.name   C:
            if EOF(Clist)
                close Clist

            if get to EOF(last Clist) without a match
                can't match attendee and a camp      [go back to A:]
            else open another Clist                  [go back to B:]

            if AA.name matches CC.name
                create a new struct of type B
                send new struct's values to output file
                get another name from Alist          [go back to A:]
            else  fetch another name from Clist       [go back to C:]
```

Two ways are used to eliminate gotos in the actual program code: (1) at line *d*, the break command causes the loop to terminate and fall through into the right loop; and (2) the return value of the independent function, *match*(), can be used to set a switch, *goA*, that can thread through several levels of nested loops.

6.6.2. A VARIABLE IN COMMON

The importance of a struct linked to an important variable or process can be considerable. As example, a single struct maintains much of the information the system needs to control access to a disk file during the running of a C program, including information on whether the file is transferring bytes from memory or sending bytes to memory and which byte in the file is currently ready for transport. This kind of struct, a struct of type _iobuf—FILE for short—is created whenever a file is opened by way of the library *fopen*() function. And the function returns a pointer-to-FILE that can serve as file identifier for the particular file. When you consider that most programs have only a few files open at a time, the controlling capability of such a single struct is impressive.

Other types of structs are often constructed to monitor opened files for different purposes. For example, a statistical struct such as that mentioned in Section 2.3.1. can be designed to keep track of the types of characters that stream from file to memory. This struct can record whatever information the programmer considers important: how many chars are sent from a particular file to memory, how many are accepted under the particular setbreak table then in control, how many separate strings enter, what characters are omitted, how many characters of ASCII decimal 128 or higher are encountered, how often the NewLine and the space/tab are encountered, and so forth.

The usefulness of unrelated structs designed for different purposes can often be amplified by exploiting a mutual interest in some independent variable. In this case, if the statistical struct is linked to the system-created FILE struct, information on what type of character is entering memory can, for example, be augmented with information on where the character is located in the file. To do so, when opening a particular file for reading text to memory, it is efficient to provide these unrelated structs a common file identifier. In that the system will create a pointer-to-FILE no matter, the statistical struct 'coattails' on the work done by the system struct; one of its members stores the value of the pointer-to-FILE that identifies the newly-opened file to the system.

By way of this common pointer-to-FILE, any input function built on the library routine *fopen*() can: (1) access the specific file associated with the channel number; (2) contribute information on the different kinds of data moving between file and memory to the associated struct of type stat; and (3) determine where the file cursor is at any moment.

The statistical struct continues to accumulate statistics as long as the file remains open. Typically, as in this example, we declare it a global variable. Note that a struct template can NOT be initialized; nor do we, as yet, have an actual statistical struct.

struct stat/*struct stat is declared in comset.c to take advantage of the setbreak utility.*/

```
    {
    FILE *file_ID;    /*The pointer to a system struct; it will act as the file's identifier,*/
                      /* as its channel number.*/
    long rcd_cnt;    /*Counts records; is incremented when char is a record delimiter.*/
    long line_cnt;    /*Counts each newline; is incremented when char is a newline.*/
    long space_cnt;    /*Counts non-run tab/spaces. (Space_cnt + line_cnt) is a rough*/
                       /*measure of the number of words input.*/
    } *pstat;          /*pstat is an unassigned pointer-to-struct of type stat.*/
```

/*Section 2.3.1 presented some file-opening utilities that included the creation of a statistical struct. As shown in *read1*(), in example 2, the first time the referent file is opened for reading, we can create a viable statistical struct dynamically and associate it with the file's pointer-to-FILE. read1() assumes that several files will be open simultaneously and part of its effort is directed to ensuring that each open file has no more than one statistical struct associated with it.*/

/*When only one input and one output file are needed, the statistical struct can be linked as part of a simple file-opening procedure such as the one shown next. *IOstruct*() opens two files: a user-determined file for reading and a program-named output file, whose previous contents are erased when the file is (re)opened. In contrast to *init*() in Section 2.3.1, *IOstruct*() has to create the statistical struct separately from the basic file-opening instructions. But only a single file is opened during the program run, so it does not, as does *init*() in Chapt 2 or the function in Section 6.9.2, need to concern itself with storing this struct *vis a vis* the stored statistical structs of the other open files.*/

/*Note that the args to *IOstruct*() are pointers to pointers-to-FILE; i.e., we transmit the *addresses* of the pointers-to-FILE so that the values will be permanently available. The function returns a pointer-to-struct of type stat.*/

```
char OutFile[MEDSZE] = {SNUL};    /*To hold the file name. This is a string variable,*/
                                  /* not a constant, so its contents can be changed.*/
struct stat *IOstruct(FILE **infileptr, FILE **outfileptr)
     {/*BP*/
     struct stat *pstr = NULL;        /*Local pointer-to-struct of type stat.*/
     while (TRUE)                     /*This will cycle until an accessible file is named.*/
          {
          printf("\nEnter input file name.\t");
          ttyin("T");                 /*See Section 2.3.1.*/
          if ( ( *infileptr = fopen(ttystr,"r") ) != NULL)
               break;
          }
```

/*Next, the struct is given storage dynamically if space is available. pstr is the dummy for the pointer whose value is the address of the stored struct.*/

```
     pstr = (struct stat *) calloc(1, sizeof(struct stat));
     if (pstr == NULL)
          {
          printf("\n. There is no more calloc() space available.\n");
          exit(2);
          }
     else
```

/*This next block initializes values for the newly-created struct. The first statement ties the struct to the channel number of the input file.*/

```
          {
          pstr->file_ID = *infileptr;
          pstr->rcd_cnt = 0L;
          pstr->line_cnt = 0L;
          pstr->space_cnt = 0L;
          }

     while (TRUE)        /*This will recycle until an accessible output file is named.*/
          {/*OK_to_overwrite*/
          *outfileptr = fopen(OutFile,"w");    /*It is *outfileptr, because the arg is the*/
                                               /*address of the pointer-to-FILE*/
          if (*outfileptr == NULL)    /*In case the user is barred from writing to the file.*/
               {
```

```
                printf("\nI am not able to open %s. Name another file.",OutFile);
                ttyin("T");
                stcpy(ttystr,OutFile);              /*OutFile now contains another */
                }                                   /* candidate output filename.*/
            else break;
            }/*OK_to_overwrite*/
        return(pstr);
        }/*EP*/
```

Usage.

In *main*(), the *IOstruct*() function activates *pstat*, a pointer-to-struct of type stat for the just opened file. The value of *readchan* is the first member of the struct and a pointer to the file name is the second member.

```
int main(void)
        {
        FILE *readchan = NULL;          /*The pointer-to-FILE for the input file.*/
        FILE *writechan = NULL;         /*The pointer-to-FILE for the output file.*/
        BITMAP Table = 0;               /*This setbreak table controls traffic from the file. */
        int BrkChar = 0;                /*This will record the halt char.
        char buf[LRGSZE];

        ter = '/';          /*Change this if the end-of-record delimiter is different.*/
        tra = '@';          /*Change this if your database has a different end-of-field delimiter.*/
        setbreak(&Table,"/","",""); /*Input from the file will stop at the slash.*/
        stcpy("out.tmp",OutFile);       /*This is a string variable not a string constant, */
                                        /* in case it needs to be changed.*/
        pstat = IOstruct(&readchan,&writechan);
        while (BrkChar != EOF)    /*The loop will stop when it encounter the EOF mark.*/
            {
```

/*Data are read in by psone(), which brings text in from a file to memory as does *psinput*(). The statistical struct used for psinput() is more elaborate than the one shown in this section. It is defined as a struct of type in_stat and the struct for each open file is stored in an array of structs called *IN_KEEP*.*/

/*The function is prototyped as: **extern STRING psone(FILE *ifptr, struct stat *pstr, BITMAP tbl, int *pbrk, int lim, STRING dsn);**. The first arg is the pointer-to-FILE representing the file from which the text is read in. The second arg is very special purpose: the arg is a pointer-to-struct of type stat. The third and fourth args relate to the setbreak table that will halt entry. The last arg is the buffer into which the input text is read; and the next to last arg is the capacity of that buffer.*/

```
                ptemp = psone(readchan,pstat,Table,&BrkChar,LRGSZE,buf); /*c*/
                if ( pstat->line_cnt % 100 == 0)/*Query the line counter every 100 lines.*/ /*a*/
                    PD(pstat->line_cnt);
            }
        fclose(readchan);
        fclose(writechan);
        exit(0);
        }
```

Whenever *psone*() operates, these values are incremented.

```
if (c == '\n')                    /*The current input char, c, is a Newline.*/
        pstr->line_cnt++;
if (c == ter)                     /*The current input char is a record delimiter.*/
        pstr->rcd_cnt++;
if (c == TAB || c == SPACE)       /*This will add to the word count, if it's not one of*/
                                  /* a run of spaces/tabs.*/
if (*(pdsn-1) != TAB && *(pdsn-1) != SPACE)
                pstr->space_cnt++;
```

The programmer may of course ignore the struct. But its member values are accessible and the struct can be queried at any time while the file is open (see line *a*. Individual values can also be used as switches or traffic controllers dictating one of several options; for example, if the break char is a vowel, the string would be subjected to *fct1*, otherwise it would be processed by *fct2*.

```
if (ITVOWEL(pstat->brk_char))
        fct1(pstat->file_ID);
else fct2(pstat->file_ID);
```

Or input can be terminated when a certain number of lines have been entered; e.g.,

```
if (pstat->line_cnt == 500)
        break;
```

6.6.3. CREATING META ASSOCIATIONS

Pointers-to-struct associations can be used to link a phrase, a keyword, a comment, a class name to similar items in the same file or other files. Or, in browsing mode, they link ideas whose association is meaningful to the user, but which do not contain the ordinary clues—identical ASCII characters, a range of integer values, etc.—for the program.

At some point, the database(s) have to be searched to determine the absolute or relative locations of the linked information. A step in composing the index to this book for example consisted of adding an otherwise not-used character 'by hand' to the end of each to-be-printed page, effectively making each page a record. The record accession number was added to all the words on the page except conjunctions, prepositions and most three-letter words. An alphabetizer sorted the words. A squish module combined the accession numbers. So **processing|16@**, **processing|18@**, **processing|25@** and **processing|29@** became **processing|16,18,25,29@**. Unwanted items were deleted 'by hand'.

The most direct way is to store the set of file locations in a linked list (see below) and save the first address of the list in a member of the struct. This simplifies displaying the associations; i.e., the end user can ask for one link or a specific number or all possible links. Or a single member (such as the last fields of the record in each database in the next example) acts like an index, retaining all the relevant links, either as sequential record count, or by location on hard disk, etc.

This example outlines a way a gallery can connect each of its paintings to information on the painter and to schools of painting. It also points out that without a specific query or set of queries, a group of interrelated databases can grow enormously to little purpose—except, perhaps, as a computerized art history compendium.

For a specific painting, what we will call the PAINTING STRUCT might have the following items of information. A set of structs could be stored in an array or in a linked list.

1. Painter's name (if known, else School)
2. Name of Painting (if known, else some brief description)
3. Year of Painting (if known, else 'circa ...', 'blue period', 'late 17th cent')
4. Type painting (Landscape, Portrait, Religious,etc.)
5. Medium (oil assumed if not specified)
6. Canvas, wood, etc (Canvas assumed if not specified)
7. Size (entered/recovered either in mm or inches; stored canonically in mm.)
8. Authentication: Certain, Anectodal, Circumstantial, Expert confirmation, Gallery Backstop.
9. Last known selling price
10. Comments: Other information such as previous owner, uniqueness, state of preservation, what group the painter belonged to, etc.
11: Pointer list to locations in PAINTER structs.
12: Pointer list to locations in SCHOOL structs.

Fields 11 and 12 are a set of index numbers either to record number or to absolute location.

A second struct, the PAINTER struct, would have biographical information on the painter, some chronological, some that focus on relationships, such as: friend of, student of, teacher of, member of what school, painted in what period. Also, for a prolific painter, his various painting styles or phases classified by year.

1: LastName/FirstName/MiddleInitial/Jr or Sr
2: Nickname
3: Birthdate
4: Death date
5: Country he is identified with
6: General class or school
7: Buddylist
8: Students
9: Teachers
10: Patrons
11: Periods and their dates.
12: Pointer list to locations in PAINTING structs.
13: Pointer list to locations in SCHOOL structs.

Because schools of painting are so important, we might add a SCHOOL STRUCT, which includes data on:

1: What year(s) the school was in existence
2: What country or countries
3: Members of the school
4: Pointer list to locations in PAINTING structs.
5: Pointer list to locations in PAINTER structs.

To be useful, queries have to phrased in terms of the data. Relational databases for inventories are popular because we can ask direct concrete questions that are easily mapped to the information in the record. As questions become more general or more abstract, and linkages more diffuse, query strategy becomes more difficult. And it is not a problem that becomes easier by throwing more data at it.

6.7. STRUCTS THAT COORDINATE INFORMATION AND CONTROL ACTIVITY

The stat struct is passive in the sense that it collects data that can serve if and when needed as switches and controllers. Structs can have a more active role, such that members of the struct need to be consulted at each stage of a running program, because the struct stores information essential to the running of the program. A program with multiple task options needs to keep track of the set of fields affected by each task. The sets of fields affected by two separate operations may be identical; one may overlap the other; they may intersect or be completely separate. When a program has a menu in which several tasks can run simultaneously, it is essential the program knows:

- what fields are to be processed? Is the task to operate on several or on all the fields in each record?.

- in what order are these fields to be processed or output?

An array provides an excellent medium for holding the critical information for each of the current jobs performed by the program module. In this example, we use an array of structs of type menustr.

Suppose each job is given a different number:

enum whatjob{MSSFORMAT = 1, MSSFORMAT, PERMUTE, REARRANGE, LNKFLD, FLDCHOP, INVERT..[9] } job;

for NUMJOBS type of jobs. Each type of job is handled by a separate struct of type menustr.

---

9 The example is taken from *txtio.c*, which creates diverse output formats: tidying ASCII-delimited records so they look like ordinary sentences, permuting word sequences, rearranging field order, chopping field text into equal-sized strips, inverting fields and records in matrix fashion and so forth.

```
struct menustr
    {
    int maxfld;
    int *pfldlst;
    } menu[NUMJOBS+1];
```

The array *menu* holds NUMJOBS structs of type menustr. *menu[task]* references the struct in a particular row. REARRANGE is defined by enum syntax as 3. So if *task* is REAR-RANGE, menu[task] would be the element in row 3. Each struct has two members:

- *maxfld* indicates how many fields in each record are to be examined or output[10]

- *pfldlst* is defined as a pointer to an int array that will be dynamically obtained and that will hold the actual field numbers, where fields are numbered from 1 to MAXFIELDS (currently set at 50). It indicates the actual order in which the affected fields are examined or output.

By means of an array of this type of struct, in a large program that combined several string processing tasks, each task can be set to operate on a different group of fields—fields and field sequence per task is determined by the end user at the time the program is run. If record size is 10 fields and the program is requested to do tasks 1,3 and 5, then in pseudo code:

```
menu[MSSFORMAT]        = { 5, pfldlst->1,2,8,9,10}
menu[REARRANGE1]       = { 10, pfldlst->3,1,2,7,9,8,10,4,6,5}
menu[FLDCHOP]          = { 2, pfldlst->4,6}
```

The first task, MSSFORMAT, which corresponds to the first struct in the array, will operate on five fields; specifically fields 1,2,8,9,10. REARRANGE will work on ten fields; specifically it will rearrange and output fields in the order shown. The order in which the different jobs are listed is not necessarily the order in which they are done. It is likely, for example, that REARRANGE would be the last task done because it not only rearranges fields, it outputs them.

Almost independent of task, there is usually a general method—a plot, a story line—for most multifaceted programs. In the TXT system, after a small interactive session when the end user selects among the options available for each of the tasks, usually the program runs without monitoring until it has completed its work. With few exceptions, the program operates on one record at a time. Data files are read-only; the processed data are sent to newly-created files. One advantage of this uniformity in that the same control struct template can be used in different program modules without modification, except for changing int *maxtasks*, in accordance with the number of jobs performed in the particular module.

---

10 This is particularly useful for a relational database with a fixed number of fields. A more complex struct may be needed when the program has to deal with databases with an indefinite numbers of fields and with semi-structured databases, where several fields follow a stylized sequence and the rest do not.

The general procedure in bringing in a string or record for processing is:

1. Find out what tasks are to be done. Do which options for these tasks? Jobs can be selected on the command line, or a menu list. In this example, a single task, REARRANGE, is illustrated.

2. Store the pertinent information in structs in the menu array. The user's response on which fields are to be rearranged and output is interpreted by *fillmenuitem*(), a procedure that fills the menu[] struct allocated to the particular job.

3. Bring in a record and chop it into (sub)fields.

4. Process the record according to what jobs are to be done.

5. Output the record in the original order or in the rearranged order.

In one way or another, the job struct is involved in all these operations. Some of the options query is handled by the *fillmenuitem*() function, which is prototyped as:

extern BOOL fillmenuitem(int item, STRING msg);

where the first arg is an alias for the numbered job and the second is the query that is displayed on the screen. The full initiation involves obtaining the information needed for running the program: the name of the database, the number of fields in the database, the End-of-Field delimiter, the End-of-Record delimiter. In this example, we will fill them with values appropriate to the demonstration database, demo.db, which has 5 fields. Its End-of-Field delimiter is '/'; its End-of-Record delimiter is '~'. These are the procedures in the program.

/*This next is a large chunk of *fillmenuitem*(). MAXFIELDS is the largest number of fields a record can have. (As personal choice, the zeroth element in fldnos[] is not used.)*/

```
/*PROCEDURE*/ BOOL fillmenuitem(int item, STRING msg)
    {/*BP*/
    int        i = 0;
```

/*fldnos will collect the sequence of which fields are to be processed. Once it is known how much int space has to be provided then it can be obtained from the system and pointed to by menu[TASK#].pfldlst.*/

```
    int        fldnos[MAXFIELDS+1];
    int        *pf = NULL;     /*This will represent pfldlst for the particular task.*/

    while (TRUE)
        {/*CheckWhichFields*/
        menu[item].maxfld = 0;
        printf("\n%s (a OR $,$,$:$) [a]\n", msg);
        ptemp = ttyin("TU");
        if (ttystr[0] == SNUL || ttystr[0] == 'A')
            {/*all fields are to be processed*/
            menu[item].maxfld = nfields;   /*nfields is the maximum number of*/
                                    /* fields. It's defined in globals.c.*/
            menu[item].pfldlst = (int *) calloc((unsigned) nfields+1,
                    (unsigned) sizeof(int));  /*Gets space for an int array*/
```

```
                                                          /* of size nfields*/
        if (menu[item].pfldlst == NULL)
            {
            printf("\nln fillmenuitem(). No more calloc space is available.");
            exit(2);
            }
        pf = menu[item].pfldlst;                 /*This will fill the int array*/
        for (i = 0; i <= nfields; i++, pf++)
            *pf = fldnos[i] = i;
        return(TRUE);
        }/*all fields are to be processed*/

        else if (menuintdecode(item,ttystr)) /*If only several fields are processed.*/
            return(TRUE);
        else continue;
        }/*CheckWhichFields*/
    return(TRUE);
    }/*EP*/
```

/*When selected fields are to handled, *fillmenuitem*() calls *menuintdecode*, which has two args: item is the job number and s is the input string of numbers. This is a portion of menuintdecode(), which decodes the number string. Numbers can be separated by commas (e.g., 5,6,4) or be written as a range (e.g., 1:4). Formats can be mixed (e.g., 1:4,7,9,11:14).*/

```
/*PROCEDURE*/ BOOL menuintdecode(int item, STRING s)
    {/*BPDecodeints*/
    int        brk = 0;
    int        brk2 = 0;
    int        fldnos[MAXFIELDS+1] = {0};
    int        i = 0;
    int        j = 0;
    int        numb = 0;
    int        numb2 = 0;
    int        *pf = NULL;

    for (i = 1; *s; )                           /*Start field count at field 1.*/
        {/*ConvertIntsIntoArrayElements*/
        brk = 0;
        numb = intscan(s,&brk);
        fldnos[i] = numb;                  /*Takes care of single # or #,#*/
        menu[item].maxfld++;
        if (brk == ':')                     /*Range notation.*/
            {
            brk2 = 0;
            numb2 = intscan(s,&brk2);
            if (numb2 >= numb) for (i++, j = numb+1; j <= numb2; j++,i++)
                {
                fldnos[i] = j;
                menu[item].maxfld++;
                }
```

```
        else for (i++, j = numb-1; j >= numb2; j--, i++)
                {
                fldnos[i] = j;
                menu[item].maxfld++;
                }
            }
    else if (brk == ',')
            i++;
    }/*ConvertIntsIntoArrayElements */
if (menu[item].maxfld == 0)
    {
    printf("\nERROR. Please check. You need at least one field number.");
    return(FALSE);
    }

menu[item].pfldlst = (int *) calloc((unsigned) menu[item].maxfld+1, (unsigned)
    sizeof(int));       /*Obtains enough space to store the int array dynamically.*/
if (menu[item].pfldlst == NULL)
    {
    printf("\nIn menuintdecode(). No more calloc space is available.\n");
    exit(2);
    }
pf = menu[item].pfldlst;
for (i = 0; i <= menu[item].maxfld; i++, pf++)
    *pf = fldnos[i];  /*Fill the dynamic storage with the list of field numbers.*/
return(TRUE);
}/*EPDecodeints*/
```

/*Once the initialization period is over, processing begins under control of the appropriate struct. Output is just another task handled by the struct.*/

/*REARRANGE rearranges and outputs whatever fields were selected. Usually rearrange is combined with one or more other tasks. This output version is simplified to highlight how the values in a menu[] struct are tapped to control field output. ter is the record delimiter for the database; tra is the field delimiter.*/

```
void out(void)
    {
    int ii;
    int *pf;

    for (ii = 1, pf = menu[REARRANGE].pfldlst+1;
        ii <= menu[REARRANGE].maxfld; ii++,pf++)
    if (*field[*pf])
        fprintf(outchn,"%s%c", field[*pf], (ii == upto) ? ter : tra);
        else fprintf(outchn,"\40%c", (ii == upto) ? ter : tra);
    for (ii = 1; ii <= infields; ii++)
        NULLIT(field[i]);
    }
```

Usage.

```
main()
    {     char buf[LRGSZE] = {SNUL};
    int i = 0;
    int pbuf = buf
    int *pf = NULL;

    nfields = 5;      /*Set to the number of fields in the demo database.*/
    ter = '~';        /*Set to End-of-Record delimiter for the demo database.*/
    tra = '/';        /*Set to End-of-Field delimiter for the demo database.*/
    inchn = fopen("demo.db","r");
    outchn = fopen(demo.tmp","w");
    setbreak(&Trcd, "~", "\n","is");
    setbreak(&Tfld, "/", "\n","is");
    fillmenuitem(REARRANGE, "Output All fields? Or list which fields?");

    while (TRUE)
        {
        psin(inchn, Trcd, &brk, LRGSZE, buf); /*...The tasks would be done here...*/
        if (brk == EOF)
            {
            dbreccnt--;
            break;
            printf("\n\n%d  processed records are in demo.tmp.", dbreccnt);
            }
        else for (i = 1; i <= nfields; i++)
            field[i] = psdsscan(&pbuf, Tfld, &brk);
        out();
        }
    return(0);
    }
```

6.8.   THE LINKED LIST

A list of records can be read in and stored as independent structs; and even though they are
not tied to a preset array of pointers they retain disk order. This is accomplished by having
each struct 'know' the memory address of the next struct in the series. A new struct is created
when a record is brought into memory. It is affixed by an address link to the previous struct.

Only the address of the first struct in the series needs to be stored as an independent preset
variable. In the example that follows, only *pfirst* needs to be defined to be able to recover
all the structs that are created

Suppose a database whose first three records are:

Bill Brown ,Washington ,1945~
Harry Jones ,Boston ,1935~
Joe Smithers ,New York ,1955~

As each record is brought into memory, it is translated into a struct of the type tagged as *birthplace*.

```
#include "DEFINE.H"
#include "GLOBALS.H"
#include "COMLIB.H"
#include "COMSET.H"

static struct birthplace
     {
     char person[SMLSZE];
     char city[SMLSZE];
     int year;
     struct birthplace *NEXT;
     } *pfirst = NULL;
```

/*The first three members are obvious. The last provides the link between the separate structs. Its mission is to keep track of the address of the next struct stored.*/

```
BITMAP Tfld = 0;
BITMAP Trcd = 0;
FILE *inchn = NULL;

void chain(void)
     {
     struct birthplace *p, *pprev;
     char dump[SMLSZE];
     for (p = pfirst = pprev = NULL; ; pprev = p)          /*a*/
          {
          p = (struct birthplace *) calloc(1, sizeof(struct birthplace));     /*b*/
```

/*A local pointer, p, has just been given the address of a newly-created struct of type birthplace. The first time through the loop, pfirst is NULL. So it is valued at the address of the local pointer, p. p will be revalued with the creation of each new struct and it will disappear when the procedure terminates. pfirst will keep the address of the first struct in the chain. The member NEXT of the first struct will be the address of the second struct, and so on. */

/*At the end of the first cycle of the loop, pprev, another temporary pointer-to-struct of type birthplace, is set to the value of p (in the third term of the for() loop in line a). Immediately after that, p hooks on the newly-created struct (line b) and changes value. But pprev continues to point to what is now the previous struct. At the start of the second cycle, pprev and pfirst will point to the same struct. The statement—pprev->NEXT = p—assigns the latest value of p to the previous struct's NEXT member. So the NEXT member of the previous struct will point to the address of this latest struct. Conceptually, this is similar to a procedure that swaps two variables; i.e., we need a temporary store for the current value of a variable that is about to receive a new value.*/

```
        if (pfirst == NULL)          /*Only used for the first cycle.*/
            pfirst = p;
        else pprev->NEXT = p;
        ptemp = psin(inchn,Tfld, &brk, SMLSZE, p->person);
        if (brk == EOF)
            {
```

/*The program creates a struct in line a before it knows it has reached the end of the input file. So the next line of code puts a NULL in the member NEXT of the previous completed struct. Then it frees the current struct.*/

```
            pprev->NEXT = NULL;
            free(p);
            break;
            }
        ptemp = psin(inchn,Tfld,&brk,SMLSZE, p->city);
        ptemp = psin(inchn,Trcd,&brk,SMLSZE, dump);
        p->year = atoi(dump);
        p->NEXT = NULL[11]*/;
        }
    }
```

/*To read the membership of the list of structs, we would start reading at the only address we have saved: *pfirst. pfirst->NEXT* is the address of the second struct. In the for() loop, *p*, the probe pointer, traverses the chain of structs; i.e., it is re-valued each cycle to the address of the next struct in the series. The loop stops when p is assigned the value of a (struct).NEXT which is NULL. When p becomes NULL, it has reached past the last struct in the series.*/

```
void retrieve(void)
    {
    struct birthplace *p;

    for (p = pfirst; p != NULL; p = p->NEXT)
        {
        PS(p->person);
        PS(p->city);
        PD(p->year);
        PD(p->NEXT);
        }
    }

main(void)
    {
```

---

11 In a double linked list, each struct stores not only the address of the next struct but also the address of the previous struct as an additional struct member. In this example, if the member is called PREV, say, then **p->PREV = pprev;**. Double links have the advantage that both neighbor structs are immediately accessible from the target struct.

```
setbreak(&Tfld, ",", "\t\n", "");      /*Stops at commas. Deletes NewLines,tabs.*/
setbreak(&Trcd, "/", "\t\n", "");      /*Stops at /. Deletes NewLines, tabs.*/
inchn = fopen("place.db","r");
chain();
retrieve();
fclose(inchn);
return(0);
}
```

p and *pprev* are temporary variables. Only *pfirst*, the pointer assigned the address of the first struct, is permanent. Conceptually, starting with the address stored in *pfirst*, we jump from one struct to the next following the trail of addresses stored in the NEXT member of each successive struct, thus:

pfirst->NEXT->NEXT->NEXT->NULL

As applied to the first records of our database:

pfirst is NULL, so there is no *pprev*. The first struct is created and *pfirst* points to where in the system it is stored; for example:

pfirst = 12;
pfirst->person: Bill Brown
pfirst->city: Washington
pfirst->year: 1945
pfirst->NEXT: NULL

The next time,

pprev is 12; p is 614; pprev->NEXT is 614.

and the struct is:

pfirst->NEXT->person: Harry Jones
pfirst->NEXT->city: Boston
pfirst->NEXT->year: 1935
pfirst->NEXT->NEXT: NULL

At the third iteration, pprev is 614; p is 702; pprev->NEXT is 702; and struct 3 is:

pfirst->NEXT->NEXT->person: Joe Smithers
pfirst->NEXT->NEXT->city: New York
pfirst->NEXT->NEXT->year: 1955
pfirst->NEXT->NEXT->NEXT: NULL

At each stop of retrieve(), some member of the struct can be interrogated. In this example, we simply displayed the structs. But the same technique can be used to identify some particular struct(s) we seek. Or we can wait until we reach the end of the chain and then add another link. We can of course break into the series anywhere to add a struct.

Suppose, for example, we wished to add:

Jay Marr; Philadelphia, 1946~

after the Harry Jones struct.

To do so, we need to:

STEP 1: find the Harry Jones struct, so we can add a new one just after it.

STEP 2: create a new struct for Jay Marr and fill its first 3 members with the data from the record's fields.

STEP 3: take the address of the Joe Smithers struct that is stored in the Harry Jones struct and write it in the NEXT member of the newly created Jay Marr struct.

STEP 4: place the address of the Jay Marr struct in the NEXT member of the Harry Jones struct.

void addalink[12](STRING ID, STRING f1, STRING f2, int f3)
```
                                      /*In this case, ID is "Harry Jones"*/

    {
    struct birthplace *p, *pnew;

    for (p = pfirst; p != NULL; p = p->NEXT)
    if (EQU(p->person,ID))          /*We have found the Harry Jones struct*/
        {
        pnew = (struct birthplace *) calloc(1, sizeof(struct birthplace));
            /*pnew points to a brand new struct.*/
        stcpy(f1,pnew->person);
        stcpy(f2,pnew->city);
        pnew->year = f3;
        pnew->NEXT = p->NEXT;
        p->NEXT = pnew;
        }
    }
```

Our chain of structs now links Bill Brown to Harry Jones to Jay Marr to Joe Smithers.

To delete a link, such as the Harry Jones struct, we need to

STEP 1: find the Harry Jones struct in the chain

STEP 2: write the address of the Jay Marr struct (which is written into the Harry Jones NEXT member) into the Bill Brown struct NEXT member

STEP 3: free the space holding the Harry Jones struct

void deletealink(STRING f1)   /*In this case, f1 is "Harry Jones"*/
```
    {
    struct birthplace *pprev, *p;

    for (p = pfirst; p != NULL; pprev = p, p = p->NEXT)
```

---

12 The addalink() function in LISTINGS\chap6\6-8.c is a variant. It obtains space for a new struct, then copies the members of the new struct from an existing struct. It places the struct it has created in the appropriate place in the chain as does this version.

```
if (EQU(p->person,f1))
    {
    pprev->NEXT = p->NEXT;
    free(p);
    }
}
```

The linked list is a general solution to reducing the investment in space based on anticipated need for storing structs. Unlike the array of structs or the array of pointers-to-structs, it is not restricted to sequential rows. Structs with dynamic storage, where the actual residences are unknown to the user and which have no specific independent pointers, may still be joined in a coherent linkage. To repeat: only the starting address must be retained as an independent variable. This is usually a global variable, because obviously losing the starting address forfeits the entire set of structs, yet they continue to take memory space—the worst of both possible worlds.

6.9.   THE ARRAY-OF-LINKED-LISTS

Using either the array of pointers-to-struct of Section 6.3.4 or a linked list of structs saves space. Of the two, the array of pointers-to-struct format has the advantage of random access; if the location of the struct to be fetched is known, we can access it immediately from its row, without needing to traverse intermediary structs. The linked list, on the other hand, is a railroad flat: we must always go a particular route, starting from the first struct in the series, to fetch any struct in that series. But if the structs have some unifying feature so that any struct with that feature is guaranteed to be in the list and if we know the starting address of the list, the linked list becomes a drawer in which we can rummage systematically with the certainty that the struct we want is somewhere inside.

Marrying the array of pointers and the linked list into a single data structure would combine the ease of accessing any 'row' with the tidyiness of having a related group of structs all together in a list. The array-of-linked-lists structure does just that. A single linked list can be visualized as attached through one of its members to a particular 'row' of the array. The first member of another linked list occupies its own and different row in the array. But if structs had to be examined in a fixed order starting with row 1 each and every time a particular struct was to be fetched, querying the array and sets of structs would be annoyingly slow. How to speed up the process is the subject of the next section.

6.9.1. HASH CODING

Hash coding is a general address-generating technique. In a sense, it is a magical way to select the correct row of an array of pointers-to-structs. It is sufficiently important to have given rise to a multitude of papers on how to select the 'best' scheme under different conditions[13]. The objective in most hashing schemes is to spread out the values of the stored pointers, so that ideally each pointer occupies a separate row and doesn't need to share space with any other pointer. To map the values created by a hash function to the rows of the array, hashing typically includes a MOD division, where the denominator is the number of rows in the array. Recall that MOD division keeps the remainder of the result of dividing A by B, so resultant values are between 0 and B-1. Making the denominator a prime number and large relative to the number of storable elements increases the ability of the hash function to avoid collisions and assign each pointer-to-struct to a separate row.

A hash code scheme utilizes some feature of the struct or of one or more of its members or of the text from which the struct will be constructed. For example, in the *birthplace* type struct in Section 6.8, we might simply add the ASCII values of the letters in the name listed in the first field of the data base record. And MOD divide the result by a suitable prime number. Or we could take the nearest previous prime to the summed ASCII values, and MOD divide that by some other prime number. Or we can apply a log function or some Fourier transform. Or we can create a hash value that allots, say, 4 digits for each of several hashed member values; i.e., RecordHash = [hashed member1][hashed member2][hashed member3]. This is a composite of three separate values, depending under which key we wish to organize the structs. In any run, the correct hash value is uncovered by masking the values for the other members. Whatever the scheme, simple or complicated, once chosen, we would apply it to each and every struct that we handle within that project.[14]

Given the coding scheme, the hash function operating on a particular struct returns a value that targets a particular row in the array. Conversely, given a hashed value, we immediately are directed to one and only one row of the array, the position of the address of structs with this particular coded value.

In practice, finding a particular struct from its address in the pointers-to-struct array is complicated by the tendency of multiple struct identifiers to hash to the same value. If our scheme is **add the ASCII values of the letters of the identifier and divide by the size of the array**, there is no way to separate **c a t** from **a c t** or **t a c**. These would all hash to the same row of the array. Here is where we utilize the linked list: if several identifiers hash to the same 'row', their associated structs can be chained in a single list, with the starting

---

13 An early one, and still useful, is **Hashing Functions** by Gary D. Knott, *British Computer Journal*, August, 1975, Vol. 18, pp. 265-278.

14 Hash values can be made resistant to white space by eliminating white space and punctuation (if not relevant) and control characters before determining the hash value.

address of the list written into that row of the array. Then, if we are in a particular row and the first struct searched is the wrong one, we would examine the next linked struct and so forth. We are guaranteed by the way the structs were installed that the identifier we are looking for is among the group that has a common hash value. In simpler though somewhat imprecise language, if an identifier hashes to a particular row of the array, its struct will be found in that row or not at all.

This array is NOT a set of structs. It is defined as a set of pointers to structs. The actual structs often do NOT as yet exist—as when the struct is constructed from some incoming text—or at least have not as yet been stored in the array.

Suppose we want to store a set of incoming records as structs. We use, say, a string hash function on the first 20 significant characters of each record. Initially, the row targetted by the hash scheme contains nothing; i.e., the hash code has only found an apartment. There is no inherent connection between the selection of the particular element in the array and the struct that will be composed from the text of the record. It is up to some other operation to create this connection. At this point, we can ask the system for storage space for a new struct, using one of the system allocation functions. As usual, the system returns the address where the struct can be stored. It is this address that is installed in the particular array row. Its function is to locate the struct when it is needed.

In the next sections, we pick a simple hash scheme and devote attention to how hashing can enrich the use of the array-of-linked-lists structure to contain or find or reject one of a related group of structs. Hashing solves the problem of how to point immediately to the exact row holding the first of a set of linked structs.

6.9.2. THE FILE_STAT PROGRAM

Many programs operate with only one input file open at a time, so usually only a single struct needs to be created to accumulate statistics on the characters that are read into memory from that file. But when multiple files are open simultaneously, an array such as *IN_KEEP* to store the multiple pointers-to-structs of type in_stat becomes very useful. Functions in *comset.c* that open a file for reading also create a statistical struct of type in_stat. The in_stat struct is also the one that is used by the psinput functions that are expanded versions of psin() in Section 4.11.1. (See *comset.c*.)

When a new file is opened, the read functions make use of *i_lookup* and *i_install()* to determines it is indeed a new file. For programs in which different files are open and shut at various times, there is also a function, *i_remove()* that can be used to remove the file. As in the previous example, a new struct is added at the end of the chain of associated structs if more than one file_ID hashes to the same value.

typedef struct in_stat FSTAT;
typedef FSTAT *PALFSTAT;

(FSTAT is short for file statistics. PAL is a reminder that the **P**ointers are stored in an **A**rray, where each element of the array gathers together **L**inked structs, i.e., structs with the same hashcode value.)

```
struct in_stat
    {
    FILE *file_ID ;         /*STREAM, file identification, channel number.*/
    struct in_stat *next ;/*Points to next linked struct in this array slot*/
    STRING fname;           /*Name of the input file.*/
    long tot_cnt;           /*Counts all chars. Should = in_cnt + omt_cnt.*/
    long in_cnt;            /*Recycles. Counts # chars input to file, including 'A' brkchar*/
    long omt_cnt;           /*Counts # chars skipped, including S and O chars.
                            Defers counting Rmode chars.*/
    int brk_char;           /*Current brk_char.*/
    long rcd_cnt;           /*Counts records (incremented when char is a record delimiter)*/
    long line_cnt;          /*Counts each newline (incremented when char is a newline)*/
    long space_cnt;         /*Counts significant tab/spaces.*/
                            /*Space_cnt + line_cnt is a rough measure of # words*/
    } *IN_KEEP[MAXIF];  /*See Section 2.3.1 for a discussion of MAXIF.*/
```

This differs from the statistical struct in Section 6.6.2 in that it handles more text features and has two new types of members:

- *next* is a pointer to the address of the next struct in the chain.

- *fname* is the name of the file associated with the file ID. It provides an additional handle on the file of use when a set of MAXIF files out of a very large group of files are opened, closed (to allow another group of MAXIF files to be opened) and reopened. Each time a file is forced to close, it sends its member information to a file in the form of a record or a set of records. The file_ID will change when the file is reopened, but the collected information is not lost.

The prototypes of the functions are:

extern PALFSTAT i_install(FILE *ifptr, PALFSTAT opnfiles[], int hashsize, STRING filename);
extern PALFSTAT i_lookup(FILE *ifptr, PALFSTAT opnfiles[], int hashsize);
extern PALFSTAT i_remove(FILE *ifptr, PALFSTAT opnfiles[], int hashsize);

In each function, the first arg is the file_ID value. The second arg is an array of pointers-to-struct. The third arg is the size of the array.

To prevent creating multiple structs for the same file, read1() uses i_lookup()—see Example 2, Section 2.3.1—to search through IN_KEEP to determine whether it already holds a struct with the current file's ID (in this case, the value of fileptr). A positive value of pstr is returned by *lookup*() if the file has been installed. If no such struct exists (because the file has just been opened and not yet assigned a struct) then *i_lookup*() returns NULL. The NULL return acts as a signal to install a new struct, referencing it through pstr.

The in_stat structs have a member called *next*, which, unless it is the last of the series, will point to the address of the next struct in that row of the array. To install a new struct, the program examines IN_KEEP[MAXIF]. If this is vacant, it is filled with the PALFSTAT to the file struct. Otherwise, the program starts with the address to the first struct in the appropriate 'hash row' and threads its way through the 'next' address to the 'next' address much as it would in an ordinary linked list. It ties the new struct's address to the last 'next' in the series of linked struct keys for that row of the array. A similar strategy is part of *i_lookup()*, which is used to prevent multiple installations of a given struct. Again, starting with the hashcode value of the struct under examination, the program threads its way from 'next' address to 'next' address, inquiring whether any of the structs that share the hashcode number has the right ID. If none do, the lookup function returns a NULL. With *i_remove()*, again, the function threads through the *next* members until it comes upon the correct struct to remove from the chain.

6.9.2.1. Lookup.

i_lookup() finds out if the struct for a particular file has been created and is pointed to by a member of the array of pointers-to-struct. *i_lookup()* returns a zero if the file_ID of the file of interest isn't stored. Otherwise it returns the value of the pointer-to-struct corresponding to the file of interest.

```
/*PROCEDURE*/ PALFSTAT i_lookup(FILE *ifptr, PALFSTAT opnfiles[], int hashsize)
    {/*BP*/
    PALFSTAT        pstr = NULL;
    if (ifptr == NULL)
        {
        printf("\nUsage: ifptr = fopen(ifile,\"r\")\n");
        exit(2);
        }
    for (pstr = opnfiles[inthash(ifptr,hashsize)]; pstr != NULL; pstr = pstr->next)
        if ( pstr->file_ID == ifptr)
            return(pstr);
    return(NULL);              /*ifptr is NOT stored. Therefore file isn't stored*/
    }/*EP*/
```

6.9.2.2. Install.

i_install() creates a struct for a new file and adds its address to the appropriate row of the array. It is a good idea first to check whether the struct aready exists by using *i_lookup()*. The *i_install()* function should be done right after a file is opened by any Open-A-File function. *i_install()* is used AFTER it is ascertained using *i_lookup()* that this is indeed a new file. *i_install()* returns zero if no calloc space is available. Otherwise, for the new file, *i_install()* returns a pointer to where the struct is. Note that MAXIF is the size of *opnfile*, or, in this example, the size of *IN_KEEP*, where pointer values can be assigned to *IN_KEEP[0]* to *IN_KEEP[MAXIF-1]*. *IN_KEEP[0]* is not used—the hash function is rigged not to return a value less than 1.

```
/*PROCEDURE*/ PALFSTAT i_install(FILE *ifptr, PALFSTAT opnfiles[], int hashsize,
STRING filename)
    {/*BP*/
    int            hashval = 0;
    PALFSTAT        opstr = NULL;
    PALFSTAT        pstr = NULL;
```

```
if (ifptr == NULL)
    {
    printf("\nIn i_install(). Usage: ifptr = fopen(infile,\"r\")\n");
    exit(2);
    }
hashval = inthash(ifptr, hashsize);
opstr = pstr = NULL;
for (pstr = opnfiles[hashval] ; pstr != NULL; opstr = pstr, pstr = pstr->next)
    {/*determine-opstr-location*/
    if (pstr->file_ID == ifptr)           /*Unlikely. Ruled out by lookup*/
        {
        printf("\nFile %s is already installed."
            " Install request is ignored.\n",filename);
        return(pstr);
        }
    }/*determine-opstr-location*/
pstr = (PALFSTAT) calloc(1, sizeof(FSTAT));
if (pstr == NULL)
    {
    printf("\nThere is no more calloc space available.\n");
    /*return (NULL);*/ exit(2);        /*No more calloc space is left.*/
    }
```

/*The new struct is linked to the previous struct unless it is first time opnfiles[hashval] is used. If it is the first time (NULL is returned), then opnfile[hashval] is filled with a start index.*/

```
if (opnfiles[hashval] != NULL)
        opstr->next = pstr;
else opnfiles[hashval] = pstr;

pstr->file_ID = ifptr;
pstr->fname = dssave(filename);        /*dssave() will exit if there's no calloc space.*/
pstr->tot_cnt = 0L;
pstr->in_cnt = 0L;
pstr->omt_cnt = 0L;
pstr->brk_char = 0;
pstr->rcd_cnt = 0L;
pstr->line_cnt = 0L;
pstr->space_cnt = 0L;
return(pstr);
}/*EP*/
```

6.9.2.3.   Remove.

When a file is closed, *i_remove*() is used to delete the associated struct and its pointer-to-struct. *i_remove*() returns the value of the initial pointer of the group of structs linked by a common hash value, *(opnfiles[hashval])*, if it has removed the struct. Otherwise it returns NULL to indicate that the struct was NOT installed, hence could not be removed; it alerts the user if *barf* is on.

```
/*PROCEDURE*/ PALFSTAT i_remove(FILE *ifptr, PALFSTAT opnfiles[], int hashsize)
    {/*BP*/
    int           hashval = 0;
    PALFSTAT      opstr = NULL;
    PALFSTAT      pstr = NULL;

    if (ifptr == 0)
        {
        printf("\nUsage: ifptr = fopen(infile,\"r\")\n");
        exit(2);
        }
    hashval = filehash(ifptr, hashsize);
    for (pstr = opnfiles[hashval]; pstr != NULL; opstr = pstr, pstr = pstr->next)
        {
        if (pstr->file_ID == ifptr)
            {
            if (pstr == opnfiles[hashval])
                opnfiles[hashval] = pstr->next;
            else opstr->next = pstr->next;
            NULLIT(pstr->fname);
            free(pstr);
            return(opnfiles[hashval]);
            }
        }
    if (pstr == NULL)
        {
        if (barf == TRUE)
            printf("\nFile struct was not installed."
                "Delete request will be ignored.\n");
        return(NULL);
        }
    }/*EP*/
```

Usage.

```
#define TOP 13

int main()
    {
    char buf[LRGSZE] = {SNUL};
    int i;
    FILE *inchn[TOP];
    STRING pkeep[TOP];
    BITMAP Trcd = 0;
    char t[SMLSZE];

    setbreak(&Trcd,"!", "\n", "");
    for (i = 1; i < TOP; i++)
        {
        buf[0] = SNUL;
```

```
        stitoa(i,t);
        stcat("temp.db",t);
        inchn[i] = io(t,read1);
        if (inchn[i] == NULL)
            PJ(File isn't open.);
        else PS(t);
        psinput(inchn[i], Trcd, &brk, LRGSZE, buf);
        pkeep[i] = dssave(buf);
        }

    for (i = 1; i < TOP; i++)
        PS(pkeep[i]);

    for (i = 1; i < TOP; i++)
        NULLIT(pkeep[i]);    /*Free dynamically allocated space.*/

    for (i = 1; i < 5; i++)        /*Delete structs associated with the first 4 files opened.*/
        {
        i_remove(inchn[i];, IN_KEEP, MAXIF);
        fclose(inchn[i]);
        }
```

6.9.2.4.   Inthash And HashSize.

The size of a PALFSTAT array is some prime number which, once determined, becomes the third arg to the lookup, install and remove functions. It is also the second arg to *filehash()*, which is the function used to determine the row in which to seek a particular struct. *filehash()* is prototyped as:

extern int filehash(FILE *numb, int prime);

The hash value returned by the hash routine points to a particular row in the array of pointers, the only possible row of the array that can hold the relevant struct. What we do with the knowledge depends on conditions in the chain of structs. For example, given some value returned by *filehash()*, the possibilities for installing a struct are:

• *IN_KEEP[hashval]* is NULL. Therefore, there are no structs hanging from this row. So the file from which we are about to read text MUST be a new file (one that is open but that has not yet transmitted data to memory). So we create a new struct and install in it the ID of this new file. We also set *IN_KEEP[hashval]->next* equal to NULL to indicate that there was no other file that hashed to the same spot. And we return the pointer to the hash row.

• There is a struct connected with the hashval pointer and its File_ID is filled. Moreover, it is the same ID as the channel number we are checking. This tells us that we have received input from this file previously. We can immediately assign pstr the value of this pointer: *pstr = IN_KEEP[hashval]* and make no modifications in the struct. We certainly do not need to create another struct for the file.

- *IN_KEEP[hashval]->File_ID* is filled but the ID is different from our current file ID. This means we may have a hash collision; two or more structs share the same row of the array. We examine *next* of the struct whose address is in *IN_KEEP[hashval]* and it is NULL; i.e., until now, there is only a single struct that that occupies that row. At this point, we ask the system to create storage for a new struct, and place its address in *IN_KEEP[hashval]->next*.

- As in the previous possibility, *IN_KEEP[hashval]->File_ID* is filled and the ID is different from our current file ID, BUT *IN_KEEP[hashval].next* is not NULL. This means we have at least two structs already sharing the row. We search the chain of addresses linked to the hash value. If we find the file ID, we don't have to create a new file—it is like possibility 2. If, however, we complete the chain without finding the ID, the file does not yet have an associated struct, so we create it and place its address into what was previously the last member of the chain.

```
/*PROCEDURE*/ int filehash(FILE *numb, int prime)
    {/*BP*/
    long j = (long) numb;
    return( (int) MAX(1, (j % prime) ) );   /*prime MUST match the size*/
    }/*EP*/                                  /*of the PAL array.*/
```

Surprisingly, deciding on a prime number to spread the keys to the input files around in an efficient manner (i.e., where the number of structs in any row is as close to one as possible yet the number of rows is not excessively high) is not simple; it is somewhat of an artform dependent on what we know about the array and its elements. As two examples:

Case 1:

Our system allows us 16 files open at a time and we wish to store information about these files. We wish to come close to having just one PALSTAT per array row. We know that the numbers to identify each file (the channel numbers) are handed out sequentially and that these numbers are small positive integers, so using an integer value a little larger than 16 should come close to achieving our goal. Hence we find the next prime after 16 (17) and use this for our MOD factor in a hash scheme based on the file ID. If we wish a less dense array, we could find the next few primes after 17; using. 19 or 23 as our hash divisor would give us a bit more latitude. This should also work nicely in the general case if we begin by TYPEDEF'ing the maximum number of files that can be simultaneously open under the different operating systems and/or compilers.

Case 2:

We base the identification of structs on strings, not integers. We know we have around 16 files but they are identified by filenames assigned by individual users, so these identifiers can be considered as randomly assigned. We use the rule of thumb that no more than 1/2 to 3/4 of the spaces in an array should be assigned to cut down on the number of pointers-to-struct that share an array row. We can use *nxtprime*() to obtain the first prime larger than 16 times 4/3 or the first prime larger than 16 time 2. For the first, *nxtprime*() returns 23; for the second, 37. Requesting the primes midway between these values gets us the primes 29 and 31, which are also reasonable sizes.

In both these cases, we are trying to cut down on 'collisions', i.e., the number of pointers or structs that have the same hashcode value and hence share an array row. If the collision rate is high, the array is too dense. If the collision rate is likely to be low or, as in example above, memory space tight, the array can be reduced in size.

$nxtprime$[15]() will compute up to 1000 primes, so the largest prime it can compute is 7901. Given any number up to 7900, $nxtprime$() will return the previous prime and the number itself if it is a prime OR the next prime.

```
/*PROCEDURE*/ int nxtprime(int topvalue)
     {/*BP*/
     int          i,
                  is_prime = NO,
                  p,
                  primes[SZE(1000)] = {SNUL},
                  prime_index = 2 ;

     if (topvalue > PRIMEMAX)
          {
          printf("\nThe largest number NXTPRIME can handle is 7900."
               " Its prime is 7901.\n");
          exit(2);
          }
     primes[0] = 2;
     primes[1] = 3;
     for ( p = 5; ; p += 2 )
          {
          is_prime = YES;
          for (i = 1; is_prime && p / primes[i] >= primes[i]; ++i)
               if ( p % primes[i] == 0)
                    is_prime = NO;
          if (is_prime)
               {
               primes[prime_index] = p;
               if (p >= topvalue)
                    break;
```

/*This will return topvalue if topvalue is a prime. Otherwise it will return the prime just larger than topvalue.*/

```
               ++prime_index;
               }
          }
     printf("\nPrevious prime = %d",primes[--prime_index]);
     printf("\nCurrent prime = %d",primes[++prime_index]);
```

---

15 $nxtprime$() is adapted from a program to generate prime numbers on page 89 of Stephen G. Kochen, "Programming in C", published by Hayden Book Company in 1983 and now distributed by Prentice Hall, Indianapolis, IN.

```
    return(primes[prime_index]);
    }/*EP*/
```

6.10. OVERCOMING SOME DISADVANTAGES OF THE STRUCT FORMAT

6.10.1. USING COLLISIONS TO GROUP SUBSETS AND OPTIONS

Typically in developing a hash function, we try to obtain conditions to avoid collisions. But this is not usually possible and often not even desirable when trying to gather all the pieces of information that 'belong' together. We can often take advantage of the fact that the chain has stores all identical keys within a single linked group. To simplify, suppose we are matching two data bases, A and B, both membership lists. Each database has two fields: a name and a city. (We will pretend that the name field also has an address and telephone number and so forth, so that it is usable.) A is the list of new members; B is the list of old members. Each record in B is hashed on the text in city and forced into a struct, whose address is installed in a row of an array-of-linked-lists. (The complete program to install and match two sample databases is in LISTINGS\chap6\6-10-1.c.)

```
typedef struct membership MEM;
typedef MEM *PMEM;

MEM{
    PMEM next;
    char name[MEDSZE];
    char city[SMLSZE];
    long recnum;
    } *oldmembers[PRIMOLD];
```

All the Boston's will be found within the same chain (together, of course, with any other city names having the same hash value), all the NYC's in another, and so forth. Then records from A are brought in to be matched, one record at a time.

Consider the options should we match the city name in an A record:

1.   We find a match and write the corresponding record numbers out. The B struct is not removed. It is available for possible matches to later records in A. This is a useful technique if we want to give the new member the name of some old member familiar with the organization. It doesn't matter if the old member is linked with other new members. (It might be a town with very few old members but a recent membership drive.)

2.   If there is a match, the corresponding record numbers are written out and the B struct is deleted from the chain. It will not be available for matching to a later

record in A. This is useful with a large pool of old members in each town, so that we can have a one-on-one buddy system for new members.

3.   We plan to supply each new member with a membership list of all the old members in the same city.

4.   We supply the list of old members in the city to a single new member—a foreman type. It is this person's responsibility to be the temporary go-between the new members and the old members until some future time—when we get organized.

In summary, for each A record, given that it can be matched:

1.   Only a single match is made. The B struct matched is retained for future examination.

2.   Only a single match is made. The B struct matched is removed from future examination.

3.   Multiple matches are made. Matched B structs are retained for future examination.

4.   Multiple matches are made. Matched B structs are removed from future examination.

m_match checks the A field, (*city*), for possible matches to the B struct member named *city*. As in earlier examples, possible matches must be among the structs with the same hashval as *city*. If there is a match, the record number(s) of the B match is recorded in an array called *where*. The struct is retained or removed according to the value of *reuse*. Also single or multiple matches are done according to *reuse*. The function returns a zero if no match is made.

```
/*PROCEDURE*/ static int m_match(STRING city, long *where, int hashsize, PMEM
memfile[])
     {/*BP*/
     int       hashval = 0;
     int       hit = 0;
     PALITEM pstr = NULL;
     PALITEM opstr = NULL;

     *where = 0;
     hashval = sthash(city,hashsize);

     for (pstr = memfile[hashval]; pstr != NULL;)
         {/*SearchLinkedListForHashValue*/
         if (EQU(pstr->city, city))
             {/*Match*/
             *where = pstr->recnum;
             where++;
             hit++;
             if (reuse == 2 || reuse == 4)
                 {/*DeleteMatchedRecordFileB*/
                 if (pstr == memfile[hashval])
```

```
                              {
                              memfile[hashval] = pstr->next;
                              NULLP(pstr); /*If any struct member was dynamically*/
                                      /* obtained, free it first before NULLing the struct.*/
                              pstr = memfile[hashval];
                              }
                      else
                              {
                              opstr = pstr->next;   /*opstr functions just to hold*/
                                                     /*the next address temporarily*/
                              NULLP (pstr);
                              pstr = opstr;
                              }
                      }/*DeleteMatchedRecordFileB*/
                  else
                      {/*OKToReuseMatchedRecord*/
                      opstr = pstr;
                      pstr = pstr->next;
                      }/*OKToReuseMatchedRecord*/
                  if (reuse == 1 || reuse == 2)
                          return(hit);
                  continue/*SearchLinkedListForHashValue*/;
                  }/*Match*/
              opstr = pstr; pstr = pstr->next;
              }/*SearchLinkedListForHashValue*/
      return(hit);
      }/*EP*/
```

6.10.2. TREATING THE LINKED LIST AS AN ARRAY

Typically, when a record is entered from the database, its sort key is shaped, memory to hold the key[16] (and perhaps the record) is set aside and, if the data structure is an array of pointers-to-char, the address to this memory area is placed in the next available array element, which is, of course, a pointer. These pointers will be rearranged, so that the reference keys are in alphabetical order, so that A[0] will address **at**, A[1] will hold the pointer to **bat**, and so on. There is no need for defining separate pointers, p1,p2,p3.., as we have done here. They are simply an aid to visualizing the chronological entry of the different keys.

Suppose four keys have been examined and their pointers placed thus:

A[0] = p3 = 111110	*p3 = at;
A[1] = p4 = 7864	*p4 = bat;
A[2] = p2 = 6890	*p2 = cat;
A[3] = p1 = 12345	*p1 = hat;

16 The part of the record on which the record is alphabetized is called the key word or key.

A nice way to alphabetize a set of records is by way of a log comparison of keys. Suppose, we start with an ordinary array of pointers, where each pointer references a separate text key This array of pointers is built up, one entry at a time, such that the reference keys are ALWAYS in alphabetical order. Pointers are moved within the array to maintain alphabetization.

If the next key, whose pointer is p5, is **hat**, then where to locate p5 in the array can be determined by continuous halving of the array. If the key is less[17] than *p3, its pointer is placed in A[0], after the other pointers are pushed down by 1 element. If the key is more than *p1, it is placed directly in A[4]. Otherwise, the array is halved; the midpoint in this example is A[3]-A[0]/2 or A[2]. If *p5 is more than the key pointed to by the contents of A[2], (*cat*, the top half of the array can be ignored. The location of the key will be somewhere in the bottom half. The array is again halved until Top-Bottom/2 is 0 or 1. In this case, p5 would be placed in A[4], after p1 was moved to A[5]. A log sort of structs, manipulating an array of pointers-to-struct is similar, provided: (1) the array of pointers is constantly updated as each key is examined; and (2) Each row of the array holds a single pointer; hashing and chaining are not allowed. The chief problem is that each time a key has to be fitted into the array, an entire group of pointers needs to be shifted up or down by one element, an expensive operation. Shifting pointers is particularly irksome as the list grows large.

In contrast, introducing a struct into a chain of linked structs is simple (see Section 6.8). Unfortunately, structs in a linked list have no special 'physical' relationship to each other. It is only by storing the address of the next in line in each struct that the next struct in the virtual chain can be accessed. Hence, a log sort, which depends on knowing which struct is 'first', which is 'last', which is the 'middle' struct, while simple in an array representation, is impossible in a linked list.

The following example demonstrates an alphabetizing technique that finesses the problem of knowing the actual locations of the members of the linked list.

- It keeps track of the number of structs added to date.

- It keeps two permanent 'goal post' structs. The first, *pA*, holds down the 'A'th position; it has the address of the struct that contains the current topmost key in the alphabetized list. The second, *pZ*, pins down the 'Z'th key; it holds the address of the struct holding the current last key in the list.

---

17 **less** means that the key is closer to the **A** end of the alphabet; **more** means the key is closer to the **Z** end of the alphabet.

As each record comes in for placement, the program dynamically allocates it a struct, one member of which holds the sort key (whether the key is alphabetic or numeric is user-determined). Another member *begrec* retains where the record is located in the database file and another is the familiar pointer to the location of the next struct (i.e., the struct that contains the next key in the alphabetized list). The struct contains one more member, *pprev*, which contains the address of the previous key in the list[18]

Structs are sequenced in alphabetical order from the very beginning. If the second struct is less than the first, it becomes the first struct in the series; if it is greater than the first, it becomes the second struct in the series. As each struct is brought in, its key can compared to the chain of existing structs, and its proper position determined. In this example, we simplify the program by using a 1-field record, no key shaping, and a particular file. The struct is usable by either alphabetic or numeric sorts. Only the alphabetic sort is shown.

```
#include "DEFINE.H"
#include "GLOBALS.H"
#include "COMLIB.H"
#include "COMSET.H"


typedef struct alpnum ALPNUM;


struct alpnum                          /*struct type for keeping statistics on input files*/
     {
     union
          {
          STRING   akey;               /*The key for the record.*/
          float nkey;
          } key;
     long rec;                         /*Where the record begins as offset in db file.*/
     ALPNUM *pnext;                    /*Points to next linked struct in this array slot.*/
     ALPNUM *pprev;                    /*Points to previous linked struct in this array slot.*/
     } ;

FILE *inchn = NULL;
BITMAP Table = 0;
int reccnt = 0;



int main(void)
 {
 char buf[MEDSZE];
 register long i;
 register long bottom = 0L;      /*Toward Zth end of alphabet or toward largest number*/
```

18 This is another example of a double linked list. If the addresses of the top and bottom structs are known, then from the top the list is traversed from pA->pnext->pnext->pnext to pZ. From pZ->pprev->pprev->pprev, the list is read backwards to pA.

```
register long med = 0L;        /* (bottom+top/2) from p->pnew-> on starting at top*/
register long top = 0L;        /*Toward Ath end of alphabet or toward smallest number*/


ALPNUM      *p = NULL;         /*Non-assigned pointer*/
 ALPNUM     *pnew = NULL;      /*Pointer to struct created for current key*/
ALPNUM      *pold = NULL;      /*Pointer to struct previous to one being examined*/
ALPNUM      *pA = NULL;        /*Pointer to 1st struct in list of structs*/
ALPNUM      *pZ = NULL;        /*Pointer to last struct in list of structs*/


inchn = fopen("alpha.db","r");
setbreak(&Table, "~", "\n", "");      /*Change this for different record delimiters.*/
```

/*The comparison algorithm places the new struct alphabetically (or numerically) in its proper place among the list of structs, using the *pprev* and *pnext* pointers, which contain the addresses of the previous and next structs in the list, respectively. So the keys are always in alphabetic order traversing the list of structs by pA->pnext->pnext->pnext.*/

/*The program makes use of two macros for comparing keys.*/

- **#define GREQU(x,y) (stcmp((x),(y)) >= 0)**

- **#define LESS(x,y) (stcmp((x),(y)) < 0)**

/*Both of these depend on the library function *strcmp*, written here as *stcmp*, to maintain compatibility with the other string functions in the TXT library.*/

/*To illustrate with the alphabetic sort, structs are maintained in alphabetical order from the very beginning. If the second struct examined is less than the first, it becomes the first struct in the series; if it is greater than the first, it becomes the second struct in the series. As each struct is brought in, its key is compared to the chain of existing structs, and its proper position determined by using this pseudo-log sorting scheme.*/

/*If the key is less than the current topmost key, three operations take place: its address is placed in the Ath goalpost, its *pnext* is assigned the address of the previous first struct in the chain and the *pprev* of the previous first struct is given the address of the latest struct.*/

/*Similarly, if the key is the same or greater that the bottommost key: its address is placed in the Zth goalpost, its *pprev* is given the address of the previously final struct and the previous final struct's *pnext* now points to the newest struct.*/

/*More than likely, the program will need to determine where in the body of the list the struct belongs. It knows the Ath key. It knows the number of keys, so it knows how many jumps from one struct to the next struct in line it takes to get midway through the chain, traversing the chain of linked addresses. Once arrived at the midway struct, as in any ordinary log comparison, it can see whether the new key is less than the midpoint struct or more than it.*/

/*pA is permanent for a list of structs. Its pnext holds address of 1st struct. Its key is == to top key. pZ is permanent for a list of structs. Its pprev hold address of last struct. Its key is == to bottom key.*/

```
pA = (ALPNUM *) calloc(1, sizeof(ALPNUM));
pZ = (ALPNUM *) calloc(1, sizeof(ALPNUM));


while (TRUE)
```

```
{/*ExamineARecord*/
psin(inchn,Table,&brk,MEDSZE,buf);
PS(buf);
if (brk == EOF)
  break;

  pnew = (ALPNUM *) calloc(1, sizeof(ALPNUM));        /*Starts new struct.*/
  pnew->key.akey = dssave(buf);      /*In a general program, the key would be
                                      shaped from the data.*/


{/*AlphabeticSort*/
 if (reccnt == 0)                      /*Special case: 1st record.*/
 {/*SpecialCase,1stRecord*/
 pA->pnext = pnew;                     /*pA->pnext ALWAYS stores address of*/
                                       /*TopKey struct (start of list of structs).*/
 pA->key.akey = dssave(pnew->key.akey);/*pA->key ALWAYS stores TopKey*/
 }/*SpecialCase,1stRecord*/

 else if (reccnt == 1)                 /*Special case: 2nd record*/
 {/*SpecialCase,SecondRecord*/
 if (GREQU(pnew->key.akey,pA->key.akey))    /*If latest key is greater or*/
     {                                       /*equal to 1st key.*/
     pA->pnext->pnext = pnew;          /*The struct pointed to by the top */
                                       /* struct-its pnext holds the address of pnew*/
         pnew->pprev = pA->pnext;      /*The pprev of the latest struct points*/
                                       /* back to the 1st struct*/
         pZ->pprev = pnew;             /*pZ->pprev ALWAYS stores the address of*/
                                       /*BottomKey struct.*/
         pZ->key.akey = dssave(pnew->key.akey); /*pZ->key ALWAYS stores*/
         }                             /*BottomKey.*/
     else /*If the latest key is less (more to top, more to A) than previous topkey*/
         {
         pZ->pprev = pA->pnext;        /*Address of BottomStruct is Address*/
                                       /* of previous TopStruct*/
         pZ->key.akey = dssave(pA->key.akey);   /*Key from 1st record/
                                       /* become BottomKey*/
         pnew->pnext = pA->pnext;      /*Newest TopKey struct stores*/
                                       /*previous TopKey address in pnext*/
         pA->pnext = pnew;             /*pA->pnext ALWAYS stores address/
                                       /*of TopKey struct*/
         NULLIT(pA->key.akey);
         pA->key.akey = dssave(pnew->key.akey);/*pA->key ALWAYS*/
         }                             /* stores TopKey*/
     }/*SpecialCase,SecondRecord*/

 else if (LESS(pnew->key.akey,pA->key.akey)) /*Latest key is Topmost key;*/
     {                                       /*i.e., within top struct in list.*/
     pA->pnext->pprev = pnew;          /*The last Topkey now is pprev to the*/
                                       /* latest TopKey.*/
     pnew->pnext = pA->pnext;          /*Newest TopKey.pnext stores previous*/
```

```
                                      /* TopKey address.*/
       pA->pnext = pnew;   /*pA->next ALWAYS stores address of TopKey struct.*/
       NULLIT(pA->key.akey);
       pA->key.akey = dssave(pnew->key.akey);
       }


   else if (GREQU(pnew->key.akey,pZ->key.akey)) /*Latest key is Bottommost key */
            {                             /*within last struct in list. */
       pZ->pprev->pnext = pnew;       /*The previous Zth struct is now just before*/
                                      /*the latest BottomStruct.*/
       pnew->pprev = pZ->pprev;       /*Latest BottomKey->pprev stores address of*/
                                      /*the previous BottomKey struct address.*/
       pZ->pprev = pnew;              /*pZ->pprev ALWAYS stores address*/
                                      /* and key of Bottom Struct.*/

       NULLIT(pZ->key.akey);
       pZ->key.akey = dssave(pnew->key.akey);
       }

   else /*MOSTCASES*/
       {/*Latest Key is somewhere inside the list of structs*/
       top = 1;
       bottom = reccnt;
       med = (top + bottom)/2;
       p = pA->pnext;        /*So start at top (Ath) struct and go to*/
                             /*the middle of the list for 1st search.*/

       while (TRUE)           /*First compare Key to Top Half of List Keys.*/
            {
            for (i = top; i < med; pold = p, p = p->pnext, i++)
                 ;                     /*Breaks after (i < med), so p and i are set to med, */
                                       /*pold is at med-1.*/

            if (LESS(pnew->key.akey,p->key.akey))   /*If new key is less than*/
                 {                                  /* key at med.*/
                 if (GREQU(pnew->key.akey,pold->key.akey)) /*But more*/
                                                    /* than key at med-1.*/
                      {/*FoundAHome. Key is >= (med-1 key) and < (med key)*/
                      pold->pnext = pnew;
                      pnew->pprev = pold;
                      p->pprev = pnew;
                      pnew->pnext = p;
                      break;
                      }/*FoundAHome. Key is >= (med-1 key) and < (med key)*/
                 else
                      {/*key must be closer to top (KT)*/
                      bottom = med-1;
                      med = (bottom + top)/2;
                      p = pA->pnext;
                      if (top != 1)
```

/*To guarantee that the loop starts with right key. This leaves p at current top which is the ith struct.*/

```
            for (i = 1 ; i < top; p = p->pnext, i++)
                    ;
            continue;
            }                    /*Key must be closer to KT.*/
        }


    else                         /*Key must belong in bottomer half.*/
        {
```

/*pnew's key is equal to or > than med struct's key. p is pointing at med struct, which will now become the top struct*/

```
            if(LESS(pnew->key.akey,p->pnext->key.akey))
                {/*FoundAHome. Key is >= (med key) and < (med+1 key)*/
                pnew->pnext = p->pnext;
                pnew->pprev = p;
                p->pnext->pprev = pnew;
                p->pnext = pnew;
                break;
                }*FoundAHome. Key is >= (med-1) and < (med) key*/
            else
                {
                top = med+1;
                med = (bottom + top)/2;
                p = p->pnext;   /*So loop will start at the med+1 th struct.*/
                continue;
                }
            }
        }
    }/*Latest Key is somewhere inside the list of structs*/
}/*AlphabeticSort*/

reccnt++;
}/*ExamineARecord*/

for (p = pA->pnext, i = 1; i <= reccnt; pold = p, p = p->pnext, i++)
        printf("\n%s%c",p->key.akey,ter);
return(0);
}
```

CHAPTER 7

STRING MANIPULATION ROUTINES

7.1. INTRODUCTION

This chapter is devoted to ways of doing some generally useful string processing tasks.

LISTINGS*include\comlib.c* and LISTING*include\comset.c* contain a select group of working string manipulation functions taken from TXT. Many of them have been used throughout the book as basic utilities by other functions and programs, which are themselves to be found in the chapter subdirectories in LISTINGS[1]. The full source code of each of these basic utilities is provided in LISTINGS, along with a formal description of each argument. In addition, many of the individual programs in LISTINGS\chap7 have expanded examples of usage and are extensively commented.

This chapter is a selective commentary on string functions. On one level, it acts as a guide in choosing the appropriate routine from among a family of similar functions available in LISTINGS; it highlights the particular characteristics that make a particular routine the most suitable for the task at hand. On a different level, it uses these functions as instantiators of features that can influence the utility and utilization of any string function. In this chapter we address the general question of how the fine structure of a string processing procedure affects its integration into larger functions or programs. For example, to what extent does the presence or absence of a local collecting buffer determine the degree to which a string can overwrite itself?

Ways to acquire and manipulate strings have been discussed in the previous chapters; Sections 1.5.5.1 and 2.2, in particular, talked about general methods of acquiring a string. To work with partially or fully structured databases, functions such as *majorfile*() (see Sections 3.6.2 and 5.2.2.3) can be used to determine user task preferences and to inform the

---

[1] Any of the \chap#\<name>.c programs in LISTINGS can be run directly under DOS or with minimal 'hookup' to Windows. In principle, these programs should run under UNIX with little or no modification. Instructions that swap CRLF's and NewLine's should be checked. No hooks to graphics are provided, but packages are available with the different compilers. Error messages and boiler plate use string constants and can be displayed on the screen immediately or sent to an error file.

system about the characteristics of the database. Initialization information for guiding program activity can be brought in through the keyboard using functions such as *ttyin()*. Instructions can also be written on the command line using functions such as *argmode()*.

Functions such as *psin()* and *psinput()* bring in a string to a preset memory buffer. *inandchop()*, used in Sections 2.3.2 and 6.5.2, brings in a record at a time and splits it into its component fields, which are immediately stored dynamically by the system. Section 6.5.1 illustrates how to convert incoming text to struct format directly. Some of the programs in LISTINGS illustrate how these procedures work together.

Alternatively, when strings create other strings dynamically through some scan or lop procedure, *dssave()* is available to request dynamic space, make sure such space exists, or terminate the program if no space if available. These is also *dsresave*, which reallocates dynamic space.

Now that we know how to acquire a string and store it, what do we do with it? Essentially, string processing procedure, including the ones highlighted in previous chapters, can be divided into three general areas. They:

1. modify the single string.

- These include operations that clean and tidy a string; pad it, change its case; substitute individual characters; delete parts of the string or add to it; and convert strings to numerical values.

2. derive substrings and clones.

- These include creating substrings by chopping a string into fixed-sized chunks; or by scooping out section(s) anywhere within the confines of the original string. Or an existing string can be broken into irregular-sized segments under the direction of a setbreak table. Clones can be created that duplicate the string in whole or in part. In these operations, the original string may remain intact or be destroyed in the process.

3. handle multiple strings.

- These include joining a set of string into a larger one, matching strings and swapping strings. The original strings are retained or eliminated, as the occasion requires. The new string may or may not have the same name as one of the original group.

These are separations of convenience. There are no hard and fast rules defining group membership. An operation that modifies a single string can become a substringing operation by copying the modification to a separate string.

Often, a number of these operations are done in sequence: the string is cleaned, cut into pieces; some of the pieces are merged, text from other buffers are added, and the string is reassembled, complete with modifications and additions. To create a complex record identifier, a record is chopped into (sub)(sub)fields, several of its segments are abbreviated and then concatenated into a single badge with some intermingled constant text. This can be added as a separate field to the beginning of the reassembled record.

In this chapter, ways of implementing an algorithm are compared but issue of function design are skirted. Is it better to develop a stack of well-tested functions, each doing a very small task or to write a larger one with multiple options and contingencies? When no small functions are available, is it better to use an available function that does more than what is needed but that is reliable? Or is it better to reinvent a specific manipulation tailored just for the situation? The functions presented here say yes to all these. Many of them incorporate well-tested scan functions, which may or may not do more than is necessary in the particular case. Others do just one job. It is also possible to take a compound function such as *sttidy*() and incorporate it into a still larger routine such as *ttyin*(), which is designed to handle a number of input conditions.

It is self evident that it is hard to manipulate a region of the string without some way of pointing to it. The procedures presented rely on alphanumeric identification and easy parsings—bracketed text, coded text, commented text—and counting elements in the array—the 5th character, or the last character, and so forth. The intention is to demonstrate fundamental operations on strings, manipulations that can be built into more complex functions. This chapter ignores the general problem of data identification, particularly complex ways of identifying parts of the string.

The emphasis is on what must be attended to when writing procedures: the type of storage space for both the source and destination strings; whether the function will be used to copy a string to itself, how to prevent overflow and if the function's grammar feel right. I hate to go against the general tendency to increase procedure efficiency at all costs, but if the more efficient method goes against the general way you expect things to be done and where you expect variables to be placed when a function has finished its operations, it's probably not worth using it. Even the sequence in which function args are listed make a difference in programmer efficiency, even if it doesn't affect the operation of the function. Writing all function prototypes so they follow the same Source to Sink sequence or Sink to Source, or whatever, can be, over all, an enormous savings in time.

Most of the functions shown are twinned, one for preset strings, one for dynamic strings. As noted in Section 2.5.3.2, a cluster of functions such as *pssubaf*(), *pssubat*, *dssubat*(), and so forth, can be condensed into a single function, with a case statement that attends to how and where the modified string is sent. There would be an additional arg to indicate whether the function outputs to preset or dynamic storage and to denote the range. This would have the advantage of reduced library overhead.

In addition to the functions shown here, there are macros available in *define.h* that clear arrays, show the octal representation of invisible chars, and determine if a char is a delimiter, upper case, vowel, etc.

7.1.1. NAMING FUNCTIONS

As shown in Table 1, function name notation deals with several parameters:

1.   whether the output is to predefined or dynamic storage and whether the original string is destroyed by the processing

ST: A prefixed *st* indicates a procedure without reference to storage type. These procedures usually modify characters inside the string. But they do not twin, split, copy, enlarge or otherwise form a new string in addition to the source string. *stlen*() returns an integer whose value is the size of the string, whether preset or dynamic; *streverse*() reverses character order; it does not require additional storage space.

PS: Function names with a *ps* prefix write the new string to preset storage. They operate on either predefined or dynamic strings. For example, *psreverse*() will write a copy of any type of string in reversed order to some predefined char array. The original string is not modified by the routine.

DS: Names of routines that create storage dynamically either to store new strings or to store expanded versions of old strings begin with the prefix *ds*. *dsreverse*(), for example, will obtain dynamic space for the copy of a string written in reversed order. The original string may be dynamic or preset; it is unmodified by the procedure.

When the original string is modified, names begin with a double prefix. *psdsscan*() indicates the mother string has preset storage, the daughter string dynamic storage. *pspsscan*() indicates both the input and output strings have preset storage, and the input string is modified or destroyed.

2.   whether the operation is on a single or on multiple strings. s is implied, if the m is not present. Multiple string involvement begin with STM as in *stmcat*().

3.   The root name

4.   whether the results are expressed in sentence or array notation

5.   whether the range of characters included is absolute or relative

1	2	3	4	5	EXAMPLES		
st	m	root	a	f	st-m-find()	st-char-a()	st-m-cat()
ps		name	s	t	ps-sub-s-t()	ps-reverse()	ps-scoop-a-t()
ds					ds-scoop-a-f	ds-lop()	ps-input()
psps					ps-ps-scan()	st-reverse()	ps-remicode()
psds					ps-ds-scan()	ds-sub-a-f()	ds-tidy()
dsps					ds-ps-scan()	ds-sub-a-t()	ps-next()
psps					ds-ps-scan()	ds-sub-s-f()	st-swap()

Table 7.1 Parsing a string name.

4 and 5 are used by a limited number of functions. Some substring operations—the *sub* group, which create a substring specified by location in the original string and the *scoop* group, which delete string sections—indicate both sentence-array notation and the inclusion range by suffix.

•   *AF* is array notation and the range is read: "from the bgn th character in the string FOR ndd chars".

•   *AT* is array notation an the range is read: "from the bgn th character TO the ndd th character".

- *SF* is sentence notation and the range is read: "from the bgn th character in the string FOR ndd chars".

- *ST* is sentence notation and the range is read: "from the bgn th character TO the ndd th character".

The FOR range is one char longer than the TO range. Array notation counts 0, 1, 2. Sentence notation counts first, second, and so forth. *pssubat()* determines the substring using array notation and the TO range and writes it to predefined storage. *dssubsf()* determines the substring using sentence notation and the FOR range and writes it to dynamic space. The original string is unmodified in either of these procedure.

7.1.2. NAMING FUNCTION ARGS

The prototypes use these pseudo-names for args:

src:=   A pointer to the source string. src may be a separately defined pointer variable, or the name of the string can serve as its own pointer.

dsn:=   A pointer to the array destined to be the home of the created or output string.

psrc:=   A pointer to the pointer to the source string. This is the address of the pointer-to-char or a separate variable defined as the address of the pointer-to-char.

Reserved alias for data types and special zeros are:

BOOL:=   The function returns TRUE/FALSE. (typedef short BOOL).
BITMAP:=   typedef unsigned int or long int, whichever is 32 bits long.
              Used exclusively for constructing setbreak tables.
INTEGER:=   typedef int or long, whichever is 32 bits long.
NULL:=   zero. Pointers with value NULL point to no address.
PTRADR:=   Pointer-to-pointer-to-char (typedef: char **).
SNUL:=   '\0'. The char byte whose every bit is zero.
STRING:=   A pointer to a char array. (typedef char *)

The ordering of the args in a procedure is fairly well standardized. The first arg is most likely the source string. A set of other parameters, specific to the procedure, follows. If the source string gives rise to a second string that is to be stored in a preset buffer, the last arg is: STRING dsn. To maintain consistency (and not be forced to write variables as consts), even heavily used library functions were rewritten; i.e., *strcpy()*, *strcmp()*, *strcat()*. The library function *strcpy(STRING dsn, STRING src)* writes TO the destination string FROM the source string. The rewritten version, *stcpy(STRING src, STRING dsn)* writes FROM the source string TO the destination string.

Full code for most of the procedures is to found in LISTINGS\include\comlib.c. The scan functions are in LISTINGS\include\comset.c.

7.1.3. PSEUDO-SYSTEM PROCEDURES

7.1.3.1. Isolating Utility Setups From the Actions of the Calling Functions.

There is a problem in writing utilities that require special handling in any language that doesn't permit the programmer to isolate them from the procedures that use the utility. Procedures such as *intscan* are of interest in that they write setbreak tables independent of the setbreak tables written by the programmer who utilizes *comset.c* and *comlib.c* functions; i.e., these can be regarded as pseudo-system operations, or at least as meta-program functions.

The points of interest are: (1) how to handle tables that may or may not need to be written, depending if their associated procedures are called during a program run; and (2) how to handle these tables so they won't need to be written more than once if they are called several times during a program run. The solution used here is not to write the setbreak tables for a function until the function is initially called. Once the table is written, a global switch is set, so that the table is not rewritten the next time the function is called during the run.

For example, the first time *intscan()* is called by any function, it writes two permanent tables that remain the life of the program. Once the switch is set, these tables can not be overwritten by other tables except by random error—overwriting could happen if some new table id is not set to zero before it is used as an arg in writing a new *setbreak()* table and by chance the table id has the value assigned the table written by *intscan()*. **BOOL intset** is defined as a global variable.

```
if (intset == 0)
    {
    _zzt0 = _zzt1 = 0;                              /*The table ID's.*/
    setbreak(&_zzt0,"0123456789+-","\n","IR");      /*To junk whitespace.*/
    setbreak(&_zzt1,"0123456789","\n","XR");        /*To break at integers*/
    intset = 1;
    }
```

Several other functions such as *floatscan()* and those that delete lines and chop lines into segments contain permanent setbreak tables. They are handled as is *intscan()* The process is user-transparent.

An alternative is to let—or force—the user revamp the particular procedures he will be calling in a particular program.

As example, the *stdel()* function, which deletes lines that begin with any one of the set of characters listed in arg 2, could have been written this way:

```
/*PROCEDURE*/ void stdel(PTRADR pstr, STRING omitstr)
    {/*BP*/
    int    brk = 0;
    char collect[HUGESZE] = {SNUL};
    BOOL  dump = 0;
```

```
    char line[LRGSZE] = {SNUL};
    STRING   pcollect = collect;
    STRING   pom = omitstr;
    STRING   ps  = *pstr;       /* pstr is the address of ps which in turn points to the */
                               /* char array.*/
```

/***ATTENTION:** *If this procedure will be called more than once in the running program, it is advisable to relocate the next two lines. Reposition Tdel as a global variable and put setbreak at the beginning of main().**/

```
    BITMAP   Tdel = 0;
    setbreak(&Tdel, "\n", "\13\14", "is");
    while (*ps)                                    /*While there is any char left in the array.*/
         {/*bring in whole string*/
         ptemp = pspsscan(pstr,Tdel,&brk,LRGSZE,line);    /*Split off a line.*/
         pom = omitstr;                            /*pom points to the 1st of the 'omitchars.'*/
         while (*pom)
              {/*check_1st_char_in_line*/
              if (*line == *pom || (*line == SNUL && *pom == '\n')) /*Line begins*/
                                                   /* with an omitchar. Will want to dump it.*/

                   {
                   dump = 1;                       /*Anything to avoid a goto.*/
                   break;                          /*Break out of while loop.*/
                   }
              else
                   pom++;                          /*Go try the next omitchar.*/
              }/*check_1st_char_in_line*/
         if (dump == 1)
              dump = 0;                            /*Turn off switch*/
         else
              {
              pcollect = psnext(line, pcollect);/*collect collects the accepted lines*/
              if (brk == '\n' || ter == '\n')
                   pcollect = psnext("\n",pcollect);
              *pcollect = SNUL;
              }
         }/*bring in whole string*/
```

/***ATTENTION:** *Move the next line, relbreak(&Tdel), to the end of main() if setbreak() is repositioned.**/

```
relbreak(&Tdel);
    stcpy(collect, *pstr);
    }/*EP*/
```

Usage.

```
BITMAP Tdel = 0;               /*Repositioned from stdel().*/
main()
    {
    char      buf[LRGSZE] = {SNUL};
    STRING   pbuf = buf;
```

```
setbreak(&Tdel, "\n", "\13\14", "is"); /*Repositioned from stdel()*/
PJ(EXAMPLE: Omit lines beginning with semicolon or period.);
stcpy(";Delete 1.\nKeep 2.\n;Delete 3.\nKeep 4.\n",buf);
stdel(&pbuf,";.");
PS(buf);                /*PrintProduct: buf = Keep 2.\nKeep 4.\n*/
relbreak(&Tdel);        /*Repositioned from stdel().*/
}
```

As shown, the programmer would: (1) define each associated table id (e.g., **BITMAP Tdel = 0;**) as a global external; (2) remove the permanent table(s) to the beginning of *main*(); (3) set *relbreak*() statements at the end of his program; and (4) recompile *comlib.c* and *comset.c*. If this is done, the switch variables are not necessary and can be deleted.

These pseudo-system functions differ from all the other functions that write setbreak tables for the life of the program. The args in the tables written by procedures such as *initforfile*(), *argmode*(), *instruction*() and *majorfile*() depend on the information supplied by the user and, usually, are called just once. In contrast, *intscan*(), *floatscan*(), *stdel*() and the linechop functions write invariant tables independent of outside information but they can be called many times in a running program.

They also differ from *controllog*(), a procedure that brings in the log file for the program, adds information about the current run and sends the file out. *controllog*() also writes a specific setbreak table. But it is used just once and the table is released before the function terminates.

The set of procedures that keep or remove bracketed/coded text also require a setbreak table. This must be written by the user, because the second arg is a list of the left-side brackets (or codes) that the user wants the procedure to handle. Section 7.2.3.3 below shows an example.

7.1.3.2.   Pseudo-system Variables.

In any large system, there are variables that are integrated with functions and that frame the processing domain. In the programs and functions in this book, these global variables are contained in *globals.c*. Many of them are used in working with databases: (*nfields* for the maximum number of fields in a record, *infields* for the actual number and an array of pointers called *field[ ]* to address the fields of a record. *globals.c* provides a descriptor to identify the database as structured, semi-structured or variable. It includes generic names for database delimiters. *ter* (derived from inTER record) is the generic name for record delimiter. *tra* (derived from inTRA record) is the generic name for field delimiter. Identifiers for setbreak tables for stopping entry on these delimiters are provided. These variables are used directly in entry decoding functions—*majorfile*() and *initforfile*. They are used indirectly as function args in *instruction*().

Structs are provided for identifying which fields are to processed (*struct menustr menu[ ]*) and for keeping statistics on incoming characters (*struct in_stat *IN_KEEP[ ]*)—these were discussed in chapter 6. An in_stat struct is automatically produced by the *read0*() and *read1*() functions.

Setbreak table construction is an integral part of the scan functions and of most of the input functions. Many of the string processing functions illustrated in this chapter also use setbreak tables. They can be rewritten with C library functions as was done for *psremibracket()* in Section 4.6.2.2.

7.2. OPERATIONS THAT MODIFY THE SINGLE STRING

Each function category is usually preceded by the prototype of those procedures that will be discussed.

7.2.1. STRING CLEANING

**STRING sttidy(PTRADR pstr, STRING nchar, STRING changestr, STRING omitstr,
       STRING feuldm)**
**STRING dstidy(PTRADR pstr, STRING nchar, STRING changestr, STRING omitstr,
       STRING feuldm)**
STRING endbyperiod(STRING src);

Preprocessing functions are used to ensure that incoming strings do not contain characters that will disrupt processing. These routines clean the string of invisible characters or delimiters or specific contents that should be eliminated so that later string operations behave properly. It is ironic that most of the effort in writing text-handling functions is devoted to trimming the running time of complex functions, yet often efficiency is most improved when the text is cleaned of complications before the function is used.

Special-purpose preprocessing functions can take advantage of some string feature to make the string more robust in string hashing operations. Or, when length of line is important, they can dispose of tabs and hyphens in a particular way. If tabs are preprocessed—reduced to one space or written as the equivalent number of spaces or kept as a tab, with the understanding that some lines will look longer than the particular line length when the tab is active—functions such as the linechopper function below would not need to handle them. Special-purpose preprocessors are helpful in handling text containing formating, graphic and other non-standard characters; e.g., stripping e-texts to simplify searches. *endbyperiod()*, shown in Section 3.4.3, is an example of a special purpose routine. Note that it prevents a run of the punctuation character. Another function might always reproduce a run of spaces but change tabs to a specified number of spaces.

Alternatively, general utilities, such as setbreak tables, can be customized to clean text; e.g., white space or control characters are written as omit characters. The *tidy()* function shown here is an example of an all-purpose routine for accomplishing various tasks. Aspects of its usage were illustrated in Section 2.2.2.3. Two versions of the the function are in *comlib.c*. *dstidy()* is specifically for dynamic strings. *sttidy()* works on either dynamic or preset strings. If you aren't absolutely certain the source string is dynamically stored, use *sttidy()*. It can handle these tasks:

- Cleaning the front of the string. Removing whitespace, etc.

- Cleaning the end of the string. Removing whitespace, etc.

- Changing one or more characters into a particular character. For example, newlines and punctuation should be changed to spaces if individual words are to be compared or alphabetized.

- Changing record and file delimiters to a particular character. Changing delimiters to commas is useful in creating a ordinary manuscript version of a citation.

- Eliminating some characters altogether. For example, control chars may interfere with the next stage of processing.

- Making the text upper case.

- Making the text lower case.

- Not allowing a run of a particular character; e.g., eliminating a string of spaces.

STTIDY ARGS:

arg 1: the address of the pointer-to-char. If the string is stored in a preset char array, define a separate pointer to the array and use its address as first arg.

arg 2: Arg 3 characters are changed to the arg 2 single character, which is written in as a character array only for consistency with the other args. The second arg is declared empty ("") when no characters are to be changed or omitted (args 3 and 4), as when the function only changes delimiters and cleans the outsides of the string.

arg 3: This is a string constant or string literal. It is case sensitive; **D** is not **d**. Each character in the string is changed to the character that is arg 2.

arg 4: This is a string literal or string constant. These characters are omitted from the cleaned string; this is case sensitive.

arg 5: a set of switches written as a string literal or a string constant. **F** cleans the front of the string of white space, **E** the end of the string. **M** changes the record and (sub)(sub)field delimiters to nchar. **L** changes the string to lower case. **U** changes it to upper case. **D** checks that there is no run of nchars; it allows in only the first nchar of the sequence.

Usage.

```
main()
    {
    char buf[LRGSZE] = {SNUL};
    STRING pbuf = buf;

    ter = '!';    /*ter and tra are defined in globals.c, but not initialized.*/
    tra = '#';
stcpy("\05\07\40\40\40The\tauthor\05\07\40\40is\tDickens.\t#Book\40is\n\"Tale\tof\t
Two\tCities\"!",buf);
    pbuf = sttidy(&pbuf, "\40", ",?:\t\n", "\05\07", "dfeum");        /*a*/
```

PS(buf);   /*PrintProduct: **buf = [THE AUTHOR IS DICKENS. BOOK IS\
"TALE OF TWO CITIES"]***/
}

In this example, line *a* will change all commas, colons and question marks and NewLines to spaces. Contrl E and Contrl G are omitted from the revised string. Runs of spaces are not allowed (**D**). White space is eliminated from the front of the string (**F**). White space is eliminated from the end of the string (**E**). The record is written upper case (**U**). Record and (sub)(sub)field delimiters are changed to spaces (**M**), providing they are defined before the function is used.

As usual, the sequence of operations in the function makes a difference in the results. In this version, tasks are done in this order:

1.   If a char is to be omitted, don't use it. Get the next char.

2.   If the char is a record/field/subfield char to be changed to nchar (the 2nd char), make the change.

3.   If an ordinary char is to changed to nchar, make the change.

4.   If a string of nchar is to be avoided, and this is the second nchar in a row, delete the char.

5.   If the char is to be changed to UPPER/lower case, make the change.

After the characters in the string have been examined, then:

6.   Clean the end of the string of white noise.
7.   Clean the front of the string of white noise.
8.   Return a pointer to the beginning of the modified string.

7.2.2. CHANGING INDIVIDUAL CHARACTERS

```
 extern void stcpy(STRING src, STRING dsn);
extern void streverse(STRING src);
extern void stlc(STRING src);
extern void stuc(STRING src);
extern void stcvtchar(STRING src, char new, char old, char neighbor,
     char beforeaft);
extern void stlcpy(STRING src, STRING lim, STRING  dsn);
extern void stccpy(STRING src, STRING lim, STRING dsn);
```

7.2.2.1.   Overwriting the string.

stcpy() can be used to overwrite a part of the string from an external source, or with another section of the same string.

stcpy(&s[5],s);

writes the portion of the string starting with the sixth character to the top of the string. This was shown in Section 3.2.4.3 as a way of reducing a string to a part of itself. Overwriting a string at its tail end can be done, but the string can not be allowed to go beyond its boundaries. This next rewrites *stcpy*() so that it can be used to write to the tail of another string. *lim* is the address of the element that is one beyond the array. If the array is defined as a[20], lim is &a[20]. This is done as a matter of human factors, in that most functions that utilize the dimension of the array as a function arg use array size; i.e., lim is an int. Writing lim as a STRING turns it into an address, albeit an impossible element in the array. So the procedure subtracts one in line *a* to ensure that copying stops on the SNUL terminal.

```
void stlcpy(STRING src, STRING lim, STRING dsn)
    {/*BP*/
    while ((*dsn++ = *src++) != SNUL)
        {
        if (dsn == lim-1)              /*a*/
            {
            *dsn = SNUL;
            break;
            }
        }
    }/*EP*/
```

/*stlcpy() prevents overflow, but it can not be used to copy to the end of the same string; the characters interfere with each other as shown in the example below. This next version armorplates this fundamental procedure. Again, lim is the address of a[sizeof(a)].*/

```
/*PROCEDURE*/ void stccpy(STRING src, STRING  lim, STRING dsn)
    {/*BP*/
    char buf[HUGESZE];
    STRING pbuf = buf;
    long K = lim-1 - dsn;/*The size of the offset; i.e., the difference in bytes between*/
                        /* the first and last elements of dsn.*/
    STRING L = pbuf + K;      /*K is used to map dsn information to buf. L is the */
                        /* address that is K bytes past the first element of buf.*/

    if (K >= HUGESZE)
        {
        PCD(String is too long. It has been cut to , HUGESZE-1);
        L = &buf[HUGESZE-1]);
        }
    while ((*pbuf++ = *src++) != SNUL)
        {
        if (pbuf == L)
            {
            *pbuf = SNUL;
            break;
            }
        }
    stcpy(buf,dsn);
    }/*EP*/
```

Usage.

The three copy functions will produce the same results copying one string to the start of another string, or to the beginning of itself. Difference appear when a string is copied to a position further into itself.

```
int main(void)
    {
    STRING keep = "ABCDEFGHIJKLM";
    char old[SZE(36)] = {SNUL};

    stcpy(keep,old);
    PS(&old[5]);          /*PrintProduct: &old[5] = [FGHIJKLM]*/
    PS(&old[10]);         /*PrintProduct: &old[10] = [KLM]*/

    PJ(USING STCPY: copy to tail of same string);
    stcpy(&old[5],&old[10]);  /*Don't try this. It produces an infinite loop.*/

    PJ(USING STLCPY: copy to tail of same string);
    stlcpy(&old[5],&old[36],&old[10]);
```

/*The destination position becomes a moving target. As copying continues the string grows. It is stopped only when the end of the string is reached.*/

```
    PS(old);   /*PrintProduct: old = [ABCDEFGHIJFGHIJFGHIJFGHIJFGHIJFGHIJ]*/
    PD(stlen(old));        /*PrintProduct: stlen(old) = 35*/

    PJ(USING STCCPY: copy to tail of same string);
    stccpy(&old[5], &old[36], &old[10]);
    PS(old);               /*PrintProduct: old = [ABCDEFGHIJFGHIJKLM]*/
    PD(stlen(old));        /*PrintProduct: stlen(old) = 18*/
    return(0);
    }
```

7.2.2.2.   Reversing the contents of the string

streverse() rewrites the string from right to left. It stuffs the reversed string back into the space holding the original string, destroying the original. *streverse*() acts on both dynamic or predefined strings. Unlike its sister functions *psreverse*() and *dsreverse*() (see Section 2.5.3.1), it is written as a straightforward three-way swap of characters, thus:

```
/*PROCEDURE*/ void streverse(STRING str)
    {/*BP*/
    char      c = SNUL;
    STRING    p = str + stlen(str)-1;

    while (str < p)
        {
        c = *str;
        *str++ = *p;
```

```
            *p-- = c;
            }
    }/*EP*/

main()
    {
    STRING   p = NULL;

    while (TRUE)
        {
        printf("\n\nType a phrase for streverse. Break by pushing <CTRLd>.\n");
        p = ttyin("T");
        if (*p == '\04') break;
        streverse(p);
        printf("\n\np = [%s]\n",p);
        }
    }
```

/* Note that in *streverse*(), we operated directly on the text *str*, which resides in the array *str*. It is transmitted, of course, as a pointer, but the system can readily figure out its length by counting characters in the original up to the SNUL. Contrast this with, for example, line *a*, Section 4.11.1. There, we could not halt input at the length of a string, because the length of the string was a moving target, incremented as characters enter the array. We could not use sizeof(array) because what was transmitted is a pointer-to-char, and a sizeof() query would tell us the 2- or 4- or 8-byte size of the pointer, not the size of the array. So we needed an additional function arg, the size of the array.*/

7.2.2.3.   Case changes

stuc() and *stlc*() change the case of the original string. They are easy to use and general. They are often used as part of a preprocessing function so that user responses are made case-resistant. They are built on library macros that identify upper and lower case letters. *stuc*() changes the string to upper case; *stlc*() changes it to lower case. NOTE: There are also macros in *define.h* that define case or change case. Also *sttidy*() can be used to change upper and lower case.

```
main()
    {
    char new[MEDSZE];

    stcpy("words and WORDS.", new);
    stlc(new);      /*PrintProduct: [words and words.]*/
    stuc(new);      /*PrintProduct: [WORDS AND WORDS.]*/
    }
```

7.2.2.4.   Context-dependent changes in string content

stcvtchar() is a specialized routine to change a specific char or not, depending on its nearest neighbor. It is a way to modify a character in context; for example, adding a subfield delimiter after specific characters in a database field. Its converse can be written, so that changes are made only if particular characters are neighbors. It can be amplified so that *neighbor* is a phrase, rather than a character. It can be expanded so that there are both before and after neighbors, so the final arg is unnecessary. The program can also be rewritten to define classes of character types—punctuation, digits, vowels, control characters—using a string in place of the single character *old* or in place of the arg *neighbor*. Essentially, this type of function can become the equivalent of finding and substituting regular expressions in word processing programs, with the added advantage that the end user can describe the target material in his own terms.

The algorithm is: change trapchar to newchar unless omitchar is just before trapchar or just after trapchar, depending on the value of ba. If ba is **b**, stcvtchar() changes trapchar to newchar if the character immediately BEFORE trapchar is not omitchar. If ba is **a**, stcvtchar() changes trapchar to newchar if trapchar is not followed immediately AFTER by omitchar.

The source string may be either dynamic or predefined; both types are treated by the routine as predefined. The starting address and the length of the string do not change.

```
void stcvtchar(STRING s, char new, char old, char neighbor, char beforeaft)
    {/*BP*/
    STRING cs = NULL;

    for (cs = s; *cs; ++cs)
        {
        if (beforeaft == 'b') if (*cs == old && *(cs-1) != neighbor)
            *cs = new;
        if (beforeaft == 'a') if (*cs == old && *(cs+1) != neighbor)
            *cs = new;
        }
    }/*EP*/


main()
    {
    STRING keep = "The cat sat curled on the couch.";
    char new[MEDSZE] = {SNUL};

    stcpy(keep,new);
    stcvtchar(new,'~','\40','c','a');
    PS(new);        /*PrintProduct: new = [The cat~sat curled~on~the couch.];*/
    }
```

7.2.3. DELETING IDENTIFIABLE PARTS OF THE STRING

```
extern void         stdel(PTRADR pstr, STRING omitstr);
extern void         delcomment(PTRADR pstr);
extern STRING       dsremibracket(PTRADR psrc, BITMAP table, BOOL *nortbr);
extern STRING       dsremobracket(PTRADR psrc, BITMAP table, BOOL *nortbr);
extern STRING       dsremicode(PTRADR psrc, BITMAP table, BOOL *nortbr);
```

extern STRING	**dsremocode(PTRADR psrc, BITMAP table, BOOL *nortbr);**
extern STRING	**psremibracket(PTRADR psrc, BITMAP table, BOOL *nortbr);**
extern STRING	**psremobracket(PTRADR psrc, BITMAP table, BOOL *nortbr);**
extern STRING	**psremicode(PTRADR psrc, BITMAP table, BOOL *nortbr);**
extern STRING	**psremocode(PTRADR psrc, BITMAP table, BOOL *nortbr);**
extern void	**psscoopaf(PTRADR str, int bgn, int ndd, STRING dsn);**
extern void	**psscoopat(PTRADR str, int bgn, int ndd, STRING dsn);**

These functions delete pieces of the original string but do not make a copy of the new version. The size of the source string is reduced. *stdel*() deletes lines that begin with specific characters. The bracket and code functions delete the text inside or outside brackets or codes. They can, as example, remove glosses from citation databases or delete private information in public/private databases prior to outputting the database.

7.2.3.1. Removing Lines From a String

stdel() deletes all lines from a string that begin with any of the characters contained in the second arg. The first arg is a pointer to the address of the string. This is necessary so that the program can change the starting address of the string, if the beginning of the string is deleted. The string is reconstructed from the lines that remain. *stdel*() can also delete empty lines in a record or in a manuscript.

The routine runs as a loop, where in each cycle a line (i.e., all the chars up to a newline mark) is cut out of the string. If the line begins with any one of the chars that force line omission, the program throws the line away and examines the next line segment of the string. It accumulates the lines that are to be kept in a large temporary buffer. It then recopies this new string to the old starting address of the original string. The original string can be either preset or dynamic. It should be recognized, however, that the reconstituted string might be much smaller than it was originally; so it would be reasonable to rewrite the function to reallocate space for the revised dynamically-stored string.

In contrast to the version shown in Section 7.1.3.1, *stdel*() in *comlib.c* writes a setbreak table transparently; it is defined in *comlib.c* as Tdel.

Usage.

```
FILE      *inchn = NULL, *outchn = NULL;
BITMAP   Trec = 0;

int main()
   {
   char      buf[LRGSZE] = {SNUL};
   STRING   pbuf = buf;
```

/*The record delimiter is usually given a value by decoding user instructions at the beginning of a large program. The delimiter is not really necessary for running stdel() UNLESS the record delimiter is the NewLine. Then the delimiter value must be available to stdel(), so that it will know to reinstate a NewLine to the strings that are kept. Otherwise, records will be output in one long string.*/

```
ter = '~';
```

```
setbreak(&Trec,"~","","");
PJ(EXAMPLE: Omit empty lines from database records.);
inchn = fopen("demo.db","r");
outchn = fopen("demo.db","a");

while (TRUE)
    {/*BringInARecord*/
    psin(inchn, Trec, &brk, LRGSZE buf);
    if (brk == EOF ) break;
    stdel(&pbuf,"\n");
    fprintf(outchn, "%s%c", buf,ter);
    }/*BringInARecord*/
relbreak(&Trec);
fclose(inchn);
fclose(outchn);
}
```

Elaborations to the basic routine include keeping just the lines that has a particular first character, and keeping/deleting lines that begin with a particular phrase.

When each line (or field or subdivision, etc) that is kept also needs to be reshaped, an effective alternative strategy is to use *stmcat*() (see below). First bring in a line at a time, reshape it and store it dynamically with a pointer to it. When all the lines have been redone, *stmcat*() reconstitutes the string from the array of pointers. The individual pointers can be freed.

7.2.3.2.   delcomment()

delcomment() was discussed in Section 5.4.3. Its use there is fairly typical—it removed comments from text because a comment could contain an unpaired brace that would throw off the count that pairs braces. More generally, *delcomment*() is an example of a 'wrapper' function: (1) it locates a commented section of the string using *stfind*() and (2) it relies on *psscoopat*() to do the actual removal. The major reason for using *delcomment*() as a unit, rather than simply running *stfind*() and *psscoopat*() in sequence is that it also acts a traffic controller. If the entire comment is not within a single string, it can pull in strings until the end of the comment is found.

7.2.3.3.   Removing Brackets and Codes from a String

A bracket pair is a pair of coordinated delimiters; for example, '[' and ']' or '<' and '>'. The rule for determining what the right hand bracket is for any left hand symbol is this:

RULE: If the left bracket is greater or equal (in ASCII value) to '<', then the right bracket is the char ASCII value plus 2. For example, the left bracket of '<' is '>'. Otherwise the right bracket is ASCII value plus 1. NOTE that a left bracket does not have to be an ordinary bracket. Any ASCII char will do; '0' and '1' are a bracket pair. ':' and ';' are a pair. So are 'a' and 'c', but not 'A' and 'c'. 'A' and 'C' are also a pair of brackets. The difference between brackets and codes is that a code uses the same char to mark the start and end of the 'coded' text.

The routines that deal with text containing bracketed or coded material assume an ASCII character set and a single symbol, so they are unsuitable for EBCDIC or wide-char representation.

If the function is given a list of different bracket types to delete, the function can be written to delete text that is inside the first bracket in the list, then to rescan the text to delete text inside the second bracket type and so on. This would give priority to one type of bracket over another, a very useful feature in many cases. Or the function can be written to delete only one bracket at a time. The functions shown here are one-pass. They attend to any of the list of left-side brackets they find as they scan the contents of the string from left to right. The bracketed-text removers of Section 4.6.2.1 and 4.6.2.2 were of this kind. In the present terminology, given that they operated on preset strings, they would be named *psremibrack-et*(). They also provide an example of usage.

Customized functions can be written with attention to whether: (1) the text to be deleted is bracketed or coded; (2) the text to be retained is bracketed or coded; and (3) the string is dynamic or preset. The group in *comset.c* also have a function arg that returns an indication whether the each left-bracket was paired or not. *psremibracket*() removes the text Inside bracketed pairs and the bracket symbols in preset text; *psremocode*() removes the text Outside coded preset text; *dsremobracket*() removes any text Outside a bracketed dynamic string; and *dsremicode*() removes text Inside a coded pair and the code symbols in a dynamic string. The format of anyone of these procedures is:

STRING FunctionName(PTRADR pstr, BITMAP SetbreakTable, BOOL *nortbr)

The first arg is a pointer to the address of the start of the string to be processed. The original string may be either dynamic or predefined. It may remain unchanged, but more likely it will shrink because some of its contents will be deleted. A PTRADR is necessary because it is possible that the first part of the string is some of the text that should be deleted.

The second arg is the name of a setbreak table, which MUST be defined before the procedure is called. Its second arg is one or more characters; for example, <[(. Each of these is treated as the left-side of a bracket or code pair. The *psremibracket*() procedure used as the next example will eliminate all the text found inside <> brackets or [] brackets. The third arg is user-determined but it is essential that the fourth arg of the setbreak table use the Skip ("S") option for the disposition of the breakchar and the Include ("I") option for including all the chars on the breakchar list. Both these options are the default for their mode type. Acceptable fourth args are: "" (same as "IS") or "ISU" (which turns the string into upper case) or "IS" (which uses the defaults) or "ISCL" (which omits all chars except those written as part of the third arg string and make those lower case). So an example setbreak table is:

BITMAP &Trem = 0; /*This is best positioned as a global extern at the top of the file.*/
setbreak(&Trem, "A[", "",""); /*This looks at text between A and B, and [] */

The third arg, nortbr (for: no right bracket), is a signal that all left-hand bracket or code symbols were or were not paired. If no right-hand bracket is found, nortbr becomes TRUE, meaning that the bracket pair is defective. The need for a signal can be eliminated by preprocessing to find and correct defective strings.

```
main()
    {
    BOOL    brackerror = FALSE;
    STRING  pold = NULL;
    STRING  pnew = NULL;
    BITMAP  Tobr = 0;    /*OK here because main() is the whole program.*/

    setbreak(&Tobr,"[<", "", "is");
    pold = dssave
            ("Remove everything [outside] [] brackets [<from>] this <sentence>.");
    pnew = dsremobracket(&pold,Tobr,&brackerror));  /*PrintProduct:
                                            [outside][][<from>]<sentence>*/
    if (brackerror) PJ(BracketError);
    relbreak(&Tobr);
    }
```

There is some risk in examining a string for multiple brackets at one time, unless it is certain that the different brackets are never confounded. Otherwise, the function might unintention-ally delete some text that should have been saved. A text-cleaning function that checks that all brackets and codes in the database are paired should be run before glosses are eliminated.

To preserve particular text linked to a bracket type, brackets can be double wrapped; for example:

.......<...[...]... >....[..]... where the dots represent text.

dsremobracket() with a breakchar arg of "<" would protect the text surrounding the left-most []-bracketed text. In contrast, *dsremibracket*() with a breakchar arg of "<" would delete all the material inside the left-most []-bracketed text. Doublewrapping can be used as an additional discriminator of text types.

7.2.3.4.   Scooping out a portion of the string identified by location.

psscoopat() was demonstrated in Section 5.4.3, where it was used to eliminate comments. A portion of the string is identified by location of its first to last characters. *psscoopat*() extracts it. There is also a version, *psscoopaf*, which locates a segment that is from a particular spot in the string for a certain number of characters. The extracted portion is copied to a separate file; so scoop routines can function as substring extractors. On the other hand, they modify the original string by deleting an identifiable segment.

7.2.4. CHANGING DATA TYPES

Shifting between single characters and character arrays was discussed in Section 2.2.2.4. Converting a pointer of one type to a pointer of another type is handled by casting. Similarly, shifts between integer types and between integer and floating point numbers can be done by automatic assignment or by specific casts. The printf and scanf functions do reciprocal shifts between numbers and strings. Primarily, they are used to input and output data, but *sscanf()* operates on variables in memory.

For the most part, the procedures presented here change numbers to strings and strings to numbers, operations that can not be done by casting. Some of the functions examine strings to find numbers. Some of them work out the string representations for the same number in different bases. Many do a specific task. Some, such as *menuintdecode()*, which stores job information, are customized to handle certain types of databases.

7.2.4.1. Strings to Numbers

extern int   statoi (STRING src);
extern long statol (STRING src);
extern float floatscan(STRING psrc, int *pbrk);
extern int   intscan(STRING psrc, int *pbrk);
extern BOOL menuintdecode(int item, STRING s);
extern BOOL stintarray(STRING src, int maxval, int maxnum, int *howmany,
**   int *parray);**

Both *statoi()* and *statol()* are rewrites of system library functions except that the pointer arg is not a const. *statoi()* converts a string representation of a number to an int; *statol()* converts it to a long int. They can operate on variables in memory. A major use is to change a string to a number when data come in through the keyboard. They clean initial white space and non-integer symbols but they are not particularly robust. As this example shows, they can not recover from a plus or minus sign that is not followed by an number. And they expect only a single numeric value; buf is not changed as a result of using the functions.

char buf[SMLSZE] = {SNUL};
int num = 0;

stcpy("#+ -43",buf);
PD(statoi(buf));   /*PrintProduct: **statoi(buf) = 0***/
PS(buf);   /*PrintProduct: **buf = [#+ -43]***/

intscan() also converts a string characters to an integer. It has two advantages over *statoi()* and *statol():*

(1) It is resilient and can ignore plus and minus symbols that are not followed by a numerical symbol.

(2) It finds a single value at a time. But it extracts the value from the string, so it can be used in a loop to extract all the numeric values in the string.

It can be used for either preset or dynamic strings, because it utilizes *pspsscan()*, which rewrites a shortened string to the top of its array. Hence, even if a dynamic string is shortened, its address is not lost, so it can be eventually freed by the system. This is true even if the entire string is destroyed.

Arg 1 in either function is a string; arg 2 is an integer variable whose value is the character that stopped the scan. Arg 2 is minus 1 if no number is found. It returns a numerical value.

Usage.

```
main()
    {
    char buf[LRGSZE] = {SNUL};
    int    num = 0;
    int    nbrk = 0;

    stcpy("THIS is a + and - string with 3 values: 12.3 45E+6 78.9", buf);
    num = intscan(buf, &nbrk);
    PD(num);        /*PrintProduct:  num = 3; */
    PD(nbrk);       /*PrintProduct:  nbrk = 32 (space in decimal ASCII)*/
    while (*buf)
        {
        PD(intscan(buf, &nbrk));        /*Program correctly sees 12.3 as 2 numbers.*/
        PS(buf); PD(nbrk);              /*Ditto with 45 and 6. And 78 and 9.*/
        }
    return(0);
    }
```

Functions to extract numbers from strings can be elaborated and customized. *menuintdecode*(), which builds on *intscan*(), was discussed in Section 6.7. It is a straightforward way to store a set of numbers entered as a string into an integer array. The numbers can be written either as n,n,n (as in **6,9,2**) or as n1:n2 (as in **6:9**). But it contains some customized features that limit its use to *fillmenuitem*(), a procedure that determines which fields of the database are to be processed by which of several routines (see Section 6.7.) *stintarray*() is a neutral procedure for writing a string of numbers into an integer array. It checks that the array isn't overfilled, that the value was within some permitted range and returns the number of values that were accepted. The version presented here expects single numbers punctuated by any non-digit values, so it is suitable for extracting numbers from ordinary sentences. It returns NO if an error is found.

stintarray() is prototyped as

extern BOOL stintarray(STRING s, int maxval, int possibles, int *actuals, int *parr);

where:

arg 1: the input string which contains the numbers
arg 2: 0 <= n <= maxval (highest value allowed)
arg 3: how many numbers can fit into the int array; i.e. size of the array
arg 4: how many numbers were actually in the input string
arg 5: a pointer to the integer array

Usage.

```
BOOL YorN = NO;
    int counts[SMLSZE] = {0};
    int *pcounts = counts;
```

```
int total = 0;
STRING ptemp = NULL;

while (YES)
{
printf("\n\nType in up to 10 calibrations. Max value is 25.\n");
ptemp = ttyin("T");        /*The numbers are written into ttystr (see globals.c).*/
```

/*The int array holds 10 numbers. If a value larger than 25 is entered, the numbers would need to be reentered.*/

```
if ((YorN = stintarray(ttystr, 25, 10, &total, pcounts)) == YES)
    break;
else continue;
}
```

A general package would check value range, count values, accept numbers scattered in manuscript text as well as numbers written with specific delimiters. It would differentiate between the colon that is a way of writing a set of numbers and the colon that is an ordinary text symbol. It would differentiate between the times 23,345 is equivalent to 23345 and when it was two separate numbers. Given all the quirks in real text data, it is probably simpler—and safer—to write several text-to-numbers procedures, each designed for a different situation—stylized stylized databases versus free text, bookkeeping versus scientific notetaking, and so forth.

floatscan() finds floating point numbers in a string and returns a float value. It can handle numbers written, say, as 23.4 or 2e-4 or 2E+4.

This example uses the demonstration string for *intscan*():

```
main()
    {
    char buf[LRGSZE] = {SNUL};
    float  fnum = 0;
    int    nbrk = 0;

    stcpy("THIS is a + and - string with 3 values: 12.3 45E+6 78.9", buf);
    fnum = floatscan(buf, &nbrk);
    PF(fnum);        /*PrintProduct: num =  3.000000; */
    PD(nbrk);        /*PrintProduct: nbrk = 32 (space in decimal ASCII)*/
    while (*buf)
        {
        fnum = floatscan(buf, &nbrk); PF(fnum); /*Consecutive values for
                fnum are: 12.300000, 45000000.000000 and 78.900002.*/
        }
    return(0);
    }
```

7.2.4.2. Numbers to Strings

These routines convert numbers into string equivalents. For most of these, there is no source string, just a numerical value. *stitoa*() writes the string representation of a 2-byte (16 bit) integer. It is the same as *itoa*() in K&R, except that it doesn't use a const char arg. It differs from the MSC version in that the MSC *stitoa*() has three args. *stltoa*() operates on a long integer, returning its string equivalent. The other routines in the series return a string equivalent of other numerical types based on a 32-bit number. They do arithmetic conversions of decimal, binary, octal and hexadecimal numbers. They write a string analogue most typically into a predefined string, at least 11 elements in length in order to accept the ASCII representation of the maximum number allowed in a single word on a 32-bit word machine. It is possible to write into a dynamically allocated string, provided the string is large enough.

```
extern void    stbd32(INTEGER num, STRING pdsn);
extern void    stdb32(INTEGER num, STRING pdsn);
extern void    stdd32(INTEGER num, STRING pdsn);
extern void    stdh32(INTEGER num, STRING pdsn);
extern void    stdo32(INTEGER num, STRING pdsn);
extern void    sthd32(INTEGER num, STRING pdsn);
extern void    stitoa(int num, STRING pdsn);
extern void    stltoa(long num, STRING pdsn);
extern void    stod32(INTEGER num, STRING pdsn);
```

```
        stdd32 is the same as stitoa, but for 4-byte long integers
        stdh32 returns the hex string of a decimal long integer number
        stdo32 returns the octal string of a decimal long integer number
        stbd32 returns the decimal string of a binary long integer number
        sthd32 returns the decimal string of a hex long integer number
        stod32 returns the decimal string of an octal long integer number
```

The third character in the name is the 'from' number. 'd' is a decimal number; 'h' indicates that the given number is a hex number; 'b' is a binary number; and 'o' is an octal number. The fourth char of the function name indicates the type of string produced; i.e., a 'd' is a decimal string; a 'h' indicates a hex string, and so forth. Thus, *stdb32*() is a routine that will produce a string holding the binary equivalent of a given decimal number, assuming 32 bits or 4 bytes of storage for the number. *sthd32*() is read as: write this Hex number as a Decimal in string format. *stdd32*() is the same as *stitoa*(), except that it uses 32-bit 4-byte numbers.

These procedures use *ppower*() to change base prior to creating a string equivalent. *ppower*() returns b raised to the e th power, where b is a positive digit.

```
/*PROCEDURE*/ INTEGER ppower (INTEGER b, INTEGER e)
    {/*BP*/
    INTEGER p = 0;
    INTEGER i = 0;
    for ( i = 1, p = 1; i <= e; ++i)
        p *= b;
    return(p);
    }/*EP*/
```

stdo32() is representative of how the functions are written. It creates an Octal string representation of a Decimal integer.

```
/*PROCEDURE*/ void stdo32(INTEGER num, STRING pdsn)
    {/*BP*/
    INTEGER i = 0;
    INTEGER pvalue = 0;

    if (num >= MAXS32 || num <= -MAXS32)
        {
        printf("\n Number is too large or too small.");
        exit(2);
        }
    if (num  0)
        {
        *pdsn = '-'; pdsn++;
        num = -num;
        }
```

/*Determine the largest power of 8 yielding an antilog just smaller than num. This way, we won't have to reverse the string.*/

```
    while (ppower(8L,i) <= num) ++i;
        --i; /*Corrects overshoot.*/
    for ( ; i >= 0; --i)
        {
        pvalue = ppower(8L,i);
        *pdsn++ = (char) (num / pvalue + '0');
        num %= pvalue;
        }
    *pdsn = SNUL;
    }/*EP*/
```

Usage.

```
main()
    {
    char buf[SMLSZE] = {SNUL};
    int num = 426;
    INTEGER lnum = 426L;

    stitoa(num,buf);
    PS(buf);            /*PP: buf = [426]*/
    stdb32(num,buf);
    PS(buf);            /*PP: buf = [110101010]*/
    stdd32(lnum,buf); /*This is the same as stitoa*/
    PS(buf);            /*PP: buf = [426]*/
    stltoa(lnum,buf);
    PS(buf);            /*PP: buf = [426]*/
    stdh32(lnum, buf);
    PS(buf);            /*PP: buf = [1AA]*/
    stdo32(lnum, buf);
```

```
PS(buf);              /*PP: buf = [652]*/
stbd32(lnum, buf);
PS(buf);              /*PP: buf = [26]*/
sthd32(lnum, buf);
PS(buf);              /*PP: buf = [1062].*/
stod32(lnum, buf);
PS(buf);              /*PP: buf = [278]*/
return(0);
}
```

7.2.5. AUGMENTING A STRING

extern void   stpad(STRING str, int padwidth, int lim);
extern void   stpadleft(STRING str, int padwidth, int padchar, int lim);
extern void   stpadright(STRING str, int padwidth, int padchar, int lim);

7.2.5.1.   Padding Functions

Padding functions are needed for fixed-field databases or to pad a string that is displayed or printed in some particular-sized format such as a label or a column in multicolumn text output. It can ensure that a complex accession number has a standard size. *stpad()*, *stpadleft()* and *stpadright()* are related functions. They pad the characters in an array, either on the left or right. They are most often used to pad a number for format consistency. But they will pad any set of alphanumeric characters or punctuation marks.

stpad() will pad a set of characters in a char array with zeros on the left. For example, if the chars are the string representation of the number '57', and the desired width is 5, stpad() will overwrite the char array with '00057'. The minus sign counts as part of the padding; i.e., '-57' padded to width 5 is '-0057'.

stpadleft() and *stpadright()* are similar to *stpad()* but more general. *stpadleft()* will pad a char array on the left (i.e., the topmost chars of the source char array) with any alphanumeric character or punctuation mark. *stpadright()* will pad a char array on the right (the tail chars) with any alphanumeric character or punctuation mark. *stpadleft()* and *stpadright()* can also be used to create a row of repeating chars; e.g., if the string contents are "*", then a request to *stpadleft()* for a 20 char minimum size using '*' as the pad char will result in a 21 char string: '*********************'.

In all three functions, if the requested size would overflow the available local space, the function truncates the padding width to fit the available char array size and send a message to the screen that it has done so. It returns a pointer, so if the string storage was not predefined large enough (i.e., if it was created dynamically), the return pointer must be pointing to space large enough to hold the expanded string. Hence, to use the stpad functions with dynamically acquired strings, previously acquired ample space is necessary.

stpad() has three args: (1) strnum is a character array containing an integer; (2) padwidth is the minimum required width for the number; and (3) lim is the size of the character array.

stpadleft() and *stpadright*() have an additional arg: (1) strnum is a character array containing an integer; (2) padwidth is the minimum required width for the number; (3) padchar is the filler character; (4) lim is the size of the character array.

Examples of Usage:

```
STRING keep = "ABC";
STRING keep2 = "\01";
void f1(void)
    {
      char buf[SMLSZE];
      PJ(Example 1: Using stpad. It left pads with zeros.);
      while (TRUE)
          {
          stcpy(keep,buf);
          PJ(\n\nType in minimum width required.\t);
          PJ(Stop interaction with a CTRL D\t\t);
          ttyin("T");
          if (*ttystr == '\04') break;
          stpad(buf, atoi(ttystr), SMLSZE);
          PS(buf);
          }
    }

void f2(void)
    {
    char buf[SMLSZE];
    int num;
    PJ(Example 2: Using stpadright. It pads right with a user-selected character.);
    while (TRUE)
        {
        stcpy(keep2,buf);
        PJ(\n\nType in minimum width required.\t);
        PJ(Stop interaction with a CTRL D\t\t);
        ttyin("T");
        if (*ttystr == '\04') break;
        else num = atoi(ttystr);
        PJ(Pad with what character?);
        ttyin("T");
        if (*ttystr == '\004') break;
        else  stpadright(buf, num, (int) *ttystr, SMLSZE);
        PS(buf);
        }
    }
```

7.2.5.2. AddCode boilerplate

These functions augment a string by adding stylized text.

extern STRING dsaddcode(STRING src, BITMAP Tnum, STRING pref,STRING postf);

extern STRING psaddcode(STRING src, BITMAP Tnum, STRING pref,
    STRING postf, STRING dsn);

Arg 1: the source string, either predefined or dynamic.

Arg 2: the setbreak table that will isolate the part of the string from its beginning to any of the breakchars that are the second arg of the setbreak table.

Arg 3: the character or characters that will prefix the portion isolated. Use "" to indicate the empty string.

Arg 4: The character or characters that will postfix the portion isolated. Use "" to indicate the empty string.

Return: A pointer-to-char that points to the destination area. This is essential when a dynamic string is created and unnecessary when the destination string is preset.

The complete string is examined. Each piece is isolated, copied with its prefix and suffix to a storage area and the original part of the string is destroyed. Deliberately, this version adds the post text to the final piece of string, even if the last bit of text did not end in a break character. The function can be refined so that it adds boilerplate only if the piece of text broke on the break character.

Within the routine, a HUGESZE buffer is provided to reconstitute the string, where HUGESZE is as large as the system will allow. If the new string grows to HUGESZE-1, the program terminates and send a message to the terminal that some of the string has been lost. The local buffer is always necessary for collecting the components that will then be given dynamic permanent storage. But if the routine is to be used to create strings only in predefined storage other than in the original array, a version can be written that transmits directly to the daughter string, bypassing local storage. In this latter case, an additional arg providing the procedure with the size of the daughter array would guarantee the string doesn't overflow the destination space.

Addcode functions intersperse text in the string. Such functions are useful for adding specific characters such as codes and brackets, new field and subfield delimiters, stylized phrases or boiler plate to parts of a string. They are useful functions for generating bracket and code symbols within a field or record. Either one operates on both predefined or dynamically obtained source strings. They scan a copy of the source string, decomposing it in a loop according to the setbreak table that is the second arg. They affix prefix and postfix expressions, and eventually write out the augmented version of the string to new storage. The versions shown here collect the evolving string in a local array, which acts, as in *stccpy*() in Section 7.2.2.1 above, to prevent interference between the characters being output and the characters being input. So the string can be copied into itself.

Technically, in that add routines compose augmented string clones, they should be classified with substringing and cloning operations. Usually, however, the modified string is used in lieu of the original string. They can, of course, be used to create new strings, where the original text is destroyed. If the original string was dynamically obtained, it is still capable of being freed and should be released.

The functions differ in how they obtain storage for the reconstituted string. *dsaddcode()* requests space using calloc() and returns a pointer to the start of the new string. *psaddcode()* writes the reconstituted string to a predefined char array pointed to by dsn. This must be large enough to contain the new string. *psaddcode()* returns a pointer to the SNUL terminus of the new string. In this example of *dsaddcode()*, the predefined string new is the source string. The function will leave the original string intact. It will obtain new space dynamically for the reworked string and return a pointer to the start of its storage address.

Usage.

```
int main(void)
    {
    BITMAP Tspace = 0;
    char new[300] =  "The string is very short.";
    STRING psecond = NULL;
    setbreak(&Tspace,"\40","","is");
    PJ(\n\nAn EXAMPLE OF A PRESET STRING COPIED TO A DYNAMIC STRING.);
    psecond = dsaddcode(new,Tspace,"[","/] " ); /*PrintProduct:
                    psecond = [The/] [string/] [is/] [very] [short./]*/
    PS(psecond);
    }
```

7.3. SUBSTRINGING AND CLONING

Substringing does not necessarily reduce size. What it does do is to create at least one new string. Depending on the particular algorithm, the original string may remain as it was or it may be destroyed. The fundamental operation in creating a substring is scanning a string beginning at some position and ending at some position. The various algorithms for substringing are different ways and means of determining the start and stop positions.

The difference between substringing and cloning is conceptual, not operational. Substringing is usually thought of as a reduction process, whereby some part of the string is actually or virtually extracted. Cloning suggests duplication, with perhaps minor changes in content. The same operations, with differences in location parameters, do either substringing or cloning.

7.3.1. SCANNING: CREATING SUBSTRINGS BY CHARACTER CONTENT

```
extern STRING dsdsscan(PTRADR psrc, BITMAP tbl, int *pbrk);
extern STRING dspsscan(PTRADR psrc, BITMAP tbl, int *pbrk, int lim,
          STRING pdsn);
extern STRING psdsscan(PTRADR psrc, BITMAP tbl, int *pbrk);
extern STRING pspsscan(PTRADR ptrpsrc, BITMAP tbl, int *pbrk, int lim,
```

STRING pdsn);

These functions always start examining the string at its beginning. They utilitize the setbreak facility to determine where to stop. Halting depends on encountering a character that is one of the break characters in the setbreak table. To make sure there's no overflow, the fourth arg is the size of the array that will hold the projected substring. Section 7.2.2.1 above discussed the need for a function to contain a local buffer to collect the evolving string, if the substring is to occupy the quarters of the original string. The preset scan functions do not provide this buffer; they send the characters destined for the substring directly to the substring array. So they can not be used to scan a string and immediately have it converted into its substring.

The intent was to have the facility to scan a string for a substring, perhaps do something with the substring, then scan the source string some more for the same type or another type of substring. To provide this flexibility, the functions delete the part of the original string that has been examined. They rewrite the rest of the string to the top of its array. Therefore, the programmer must always direct the substring to a separate array.

Examples of usage can be found in Sections 3.6.3 and on. A discussion on the relationship of scanning to string processing is to be found in Section 3.7.

7.3.2. CHOPPING A STRING INTO UNIFORM-SIZED SUBSTRINGS

```
extern void      stpad(STRING str, int padwidth, int lim);
extern void      stpadleft(STRING str, int padwidth, int padchar, int lim);
extern void      stpadright(STRING str, int padwidth, int padchar, int lim);
extern STRING dslop(STRING str, int ndd, PTRADR dsn);
extern STRING dsdslop(PTRADR ppstr, int ndd);                    /*In comlib.c*/
extern void      ds1dslop(PTRADR ppstr, int ndd, PTRADR dsn); /*In Section 3.7.1.2.*/
extern STRING dspslop(PTRADR ppstr, int nnd, int lim, STRING dsn);
extern void      pspslop(PTRADR str, int ndd, STRING dsn);      /*In comlib.c*/
extern STRING dslinechop(STRING src, int linewidth, int tabsize);
extern STRING pslinechop(STRING src, int linewidth, int tabsize, STRING dsn);
```

Used in a loop, lop cuts off uniform-size pieces from the beginning of the string; pad adds characters to a string to create a string of a certain size. The linechop functions chop a string into a set of lines of uniform size.

7.3.2.1.   Padding Functions

The stpad functions in Section 7.2.5.1 can be used to create uniform-sized substrings. Usually the procedure is to cut the original string into components—fields, or to a specific character, or by matches to phrases. The pad functions then operate on these substrings. The pad functions can be a finishing touch even when a string is chopped into substrings by size, in that not all the substrings may be that size; e.g., the string runs out of characters and the last substring hasn't the size of the other substrings. Alternative methods of producing same-sized substrings are to use the lop functions, and, specific for lines, the linechop functions. These are discussed next.

7.3.2.2. LOP Functions

The prototypic lop function is the macro LOP, which lops characters one at a time, starting at the head of the string. The macro in *define.h* does a virtual deletion of the string as in Section 3.3.3. In contrast, most of the lop functions, with the exception of *dslop*(), destroy the part of the original string that is examined, while creating a substring (see LIST-INGS\chap7\7-3-2-2.c).

The lop routines chop a string from the first char of the char array referenced for the number of chars given by the 2nd arg. The lop routines are like the scan routines in that they modify the original string. They write out the chopped portion of the original string as a new string, and rewrite the original string without the lopped chars. They differ in that they target a fixed number of characters, while the scan routines halt on a specific character or set of characters.

The original string in either *dsdslop*() or *dspslop*() is dynamic. The routines differ in how they store the newly created string. *dspslop*() writes the chopped text to a predefined storage destination. *dsdslop*() writes the chopped text to dynamically obtained storage and returns a pointer to this stored string.

It is easy to chop a string into fixed size pieces by doing incremental lops in a loop with *dspslop*(). It is more difficult to do incremental lops with dsdslop(), without extensive *realloc*() calls. When the function is done repeatedly in a loop, the entire string is eventually deleted, because each time the remaining part of the string is shifted to the top of the array. The segments lopped may be concatenated into a single string, or they be saved as individual strings.

arg 1: the address of the mother string. The 1st arg is the address of the pointer to the string. We use the address of the pointer in order to effect a permanent change in the original string.

arg 2: a number of characters starting from the first element in the array. The lop routines do not differentiate array versus sentence mode. However, because they start at the beginning of the string FOR ndd char, there is little chance of confusion.

arg 3: When present, it is the address of the destination string.

The lop functions presented are not simply different because they operate on preset or dynamic strings. They also use return functions or not. Thus they demonstrate different ways to formulate a basic concept. I don't advocate they all be used. For the TXT functions, for example, *dslop*() is anomalous, because grammatically, return pointers are usually to the created string, not to the string of origin. In point of fact, many of functions presented can be recast to suit a particular idiom or style of programming.

dslop() creates a substring but does not destroy the original string. To aid in splitting off some more of the string in a later cycle through a loop, the function returns a pointer to the start of the unexamined part of the string. *dslop*() was shown and discussed in Method 5, Section 3.7.1.2. *pspslop*() returns no pointer, in that the substring is collected into a preset array and the original string is reduced to its unexamined portion. *pspslop*() was demonstrated in Method 4, Section 3.7.2.2. Similarly, the function labeled here as *ds1dslop*(), which was also discussed in Method 5, Section 3.7.1.2, returns no pointer. It and *dsdslop*(), which is in *comlib.c* do exactly the same jobs. *ds1dslop*() writes the address of the substring into the PTRADR, which is one of the function args, so it doesn't need to return a pointer. The other functions uniformly return a pointer to the substring. When the substring is copied into preset space, this is unnecessary, except that I find it easier to remember one rule than a set of rules. And it is easier to compose functions patterned on a generally similar format.

In one way or another, this is what the lop functions do. Given that pnew points to the character array, new, and pbuf points to the char array, buf, the expression

pnew = GenericLop(&pbuf, 8, lim, pnew)

is read as: 'permanently lop the 1st 8 characters from buf and put them in the char array called new at the position pointed at by pnew. Make sure the assignment is permanent.'

7.3.2.3.   Chopping a string into uniform-sized lines

dslinechop() and *pslinechop*() are sister routines that chop a string into lines of a size indicated by the second arg. *dslinechop*() creates a dynamic substring; *pslinechop*() sends the revised string to a preset array. The original string, which can be dynamic or predefined in either of the sister routines, is destroyed in the process. If the original string, the first arg, was dynamic, it should be freed formally with a free() statement by the user, after the routine is finished. If the modified string is sent to a preset array, the program prevents overflow in the local buffer, but it is the user's responsibility to see to it that the char array that will receive the recreated string is ample. This should not be a difficult assignment in that the new string should be about the same size of the old, with the addition of some spaces substituting for tabs and some newline characters.

A linechop routine breaks on tabs, spaces and newlines. It restores spaces faithfully. It rewrites the tab with the number of spaces specified by function arg 4. If the tab were treated as a single character, it would produce variable length lines. Alternatively, tab size can be set to 1 and the original string prelaundered through *sttidy*() to change tabs to spaces and to disallow a run of spaces prior to running a linechop routine

The program seals up a word at the end of the line that is hyphenated by appending the first word in the next line. It assumes the first part of the hyphenated word is followed by the rest of the word on the next line, NOT by tabs or spaces prior to the rest of the word. The program does no ordinary hyphenation or right justification. It writes as many words into the line as possible, and then starts a new line. If it is impossible to fit even one word into the requested line width, then the word is chopped, a hyphen is added at the chop point, and notification bells are sounded.

The reconstituted string is built up in buf. The program counts the number of chars per word exactly, adds one character after each word for a space and an EOL every linewidth chars. This may be a slight overestimate of the number of chars in buf because when the word is a space or tab, the program does not add a space after the word. The local buffer stops accepting chars at HUGESZE-1. The program reports the word it choked on.

In the routine, lc points directly at the spot on the line where the next char will be written. lc starts numbering the chars in a line at 1, numbers up to the requested linewidth, and recycles to 1 to write the next line.

Usage.

```
/*This would read in a database, a record at a time and output them at the requested
linewidth. The function is robust, so that the a string can be immediately written back into
itself by changing line a thus: pslinechop(buf, 15, 5, buf);*/
FILE *inchn = NULL, *outchn = NULL;
BITMAP Trcd = 0;

main()
    {
    char buf[HUGESZE];
    char final[HUGESZE];
    STRING pbuf = buf;
    inchn = fopen("demo.db","r");
    outchn = fopen("demo.tmp","a");
    setbreak(&Trcd,"~","","");

    while (TRUE)
        {
        psin(inchn, Trcd, &brk, LRGSZE, buf);
        if (brk == EOF) break;
        pslinechop(buf,15,5,final);        /*a*/
        fprintf(outchn,"%s\n", final);
        }
    return(0);
    }
```

7.3.3. CREATING A SUBSTRING BASED ON ITS LOCATION IN THE STRING

These functions find the char which is in a particular position in the string; The subset operations are a way of determining the text in a particular part of the string. They are similar to the lop functions except that the original string is not changed.

```
extern STRING dssubaf(STRING str, int bgn, int ndd);
extern STRING dssubat(STRING str, int bgn, int ndd);
extern STRING dssubsf(STRING str, int bgn, int ndd);
extern STRING dssubst(STRING str, int bgn, int ndd);
extern STRING pssubaf(STRING str, int bgn, int ndd, STRING dsn);
```

extern STRING pssubat(STRING str, int bgn, int ndd, STRING dsn);
extern STRING pssubsf(STRING str, int bgn, int ndd, STRING dsn);
extern STRING pssubst(STRING str, int bgn, int ndd, STRING dsn);
extern STRING sbstr(STRING (*fctname)(STRING , int, int), STRING str, int bgn, int ndd);

The first eight functions all reproduce a part of a given string as a separate entity, without destroying the original string. They can of course be written as a single entity, using case statements for the different conditions, and an additional function arg to identify the condition. Or the last function, *sbstr()*, a class function that calls one of the eight functions, can be used. It is a matter of personal preference.

The major reason for function proliferation is that the different functions provide for different conditions: (1) Sentence versus array mode; (2) TO and FOR notation; and (3) whether the substring is dynamic or preset.

The substring procedures differentiate between sentence notation—an **s** in the fourth character of the name of the functions and array notation—an **a** in that position. Array position notation is the more likely to be used for actual programming; sentence notation is useful for interactive discourse with the end user.

They distinguish between TO and FOR notation; i.e., string[# TO #] or string[# FOR #]. Given the phrase: *nowadays*

The substring made in sentence mode from string[2 TO 4] is: **owa** The substring made in sentence mode from string[2 FOR 4] is: **owad**

Functions ending in *t* produce string[# TO #] substrings. Functions ending in *f* produce string[# FOR #] substrings.

Any of the functions can be used either by preset or dynamic mother strings, because the string is not modified. The ds (dynamic string) functions return a pointer to a substring saved dynamically via calloc() and stored somewhere by the system. When no longer needed, these substrings need to be specifically freed by free() to regain the used space. The only link to one of these substrings is by a predefined pointer.

As well as creating a substring, the ps (predefined string) functions return a pointer to the SNUL terminus of the substring, stored in some predefined char array. This predefined char array may be 'above' the functions that use it; in which case the substring remains accessible for the life of the program unless some other text is written into the char array. Or the predefined char array may be within another function; in which case the substring ceases to exist when the function terminates and its space can be reused by the program with no specific command by the programmer.

GENERAL FORMAT for substring functions:

There are 4 components to the function name: (ds,ps) (sub) (a,s) (t,f).

ds, ps:	denotes function returns dynamic substring (ds) or predefined one (ps).
sub:	indicates this is a function of the sub group
a, s:	'a' = array position; 's' = sentence. 'a' is the more likely.
t, f:	't' = 'to'; 'f' = 'for'. 'to' is the more often used.

Hence, the various function names are:

dssubat():ptr to dynamically stored string = str[bgn to ndd], array position.
dssubaf():ptr to dynamically stored string = str[bgn for ndd], array position.
dssubst():ptr to dynamically stored string = str[bgn to ndd], sentence position.
dssubsf():ptr to dynamically stored string = str[bgn for ndd], sentence position.
pssubat():ptr to prior stored string = str[bgn to ndd], array position.
pssubaf():ptr to prior stored string = str[bgn for ndd], array position.
pssubst():ptr to prior stored string = str[bgn to ndd], sentence position.
pssubsf():ptr to prior stored string = str[bgn for ndd], sentence position.

The function returns a NULL pointer if no substring can be composed as requested. This will happen if the last char position is less than the first; if the last char position is less than zero; or if the original string is empty.

sbstr(str, bgn, ndd) is a pass through function for substrings. *sbstr*() itself gets no new storage. It calls one of the substring functions.

The Sail language allowed the programmer to indicate end of string by 'INF', independent of the number of characters in the string. str[5 to inf -2] would describe the string from the 5th char to all but the last 2 chars. The same effect may be obtained with the present functions by:

substring_function(str, 5, stlen(str) -2), dsnstr).

The program will extract the correct chars from the array. Examples of usage can be found in Section 2.5.2.3. LISTINGS\chap7\7-3-3.c contains an example of each function.

7.3.4. CREATING SUBSTRINGS BY USING IDENTIFIABLE PARTS OF THE STRING

```
extern void        stdel(PTRADR pstr, STRING omitstr);
extern void        delcomment(PTRADR pstr);
extern STRING      dsremibracket(PTRADR psrc, BITMAP table, BOOL *nortbr);
extern STRING      dsremobracket(PTRADR psrc, BITMAP table, BOOL *nortbr);
extern STRING      dsremicode(PTRADR psrc, BITMAP table, BOOL *nortbr);
extern STRING      dsremocode(PTRADR psrc, BITMAP table, BOOL *nortbr);
extern STRING      psremibracket(PTRADR psrc, BITMAP table, BOOL *nortbr);
extern STRING      psremobracket(PTRADR psrc, BITMAP table, BOOL *nortbr);
extern STRING      psremicode(PTRADR psrc, BITMAP table, BOOL *nortbr);
extern STRING      psremocode(PTRADR psrc, BITMAP table, BOOL *nortbr);
extern void        psscoopaf(PTRADR str, int bgn, int ndd, STRING dsn);
extern void        psscoopat(PTRADR str, int bgn, int ndd, STRING dsn);
```

This uses the same functions as in Section 7.2.3 above. The difference is point of view. In Section 7.2.3, the intent was to modify the mother string. Here the intent is to use the extracted portion as a separate entity. Thus, the scoop functions that write the extracted portion to a separate string can be used directly. In the present context, the remove brackets and codes functions, which immediately rewrite the string, create immediate substrings in place of the original string. Or they could be written with an additional arg for an independent destination buffer. The *stdel()*, which deletes lines based on initial character in the line, could be modified to split output into two strings: one reconstructed string with lines deleted and another string that has just the rejected line.

7.3.5. CASE-CHANGED CLONES, REVERSE IMAGE CLONES AND EXACT COPIES

extern STRING dscase(STRING src, char mode);
extern STRING pscase(STRING src, char mode, STRING dsn);
extern STRING dsreverse(STRING src);
extern STRING psreverse(STRING src, STRING dsn);
extern void stcpy(STRING src, STRING dsn);
extern void stlcpy(STRING src, STRING lim, STRING dsn);
extern void stccpy(STRING src, STRING lim, STRING dsn);

7.3.5.1.   Case-Changed Clones

dscase() and *pscase()* are general procedures that effect different types of case change. They create a case-changed copy of the source string.

The first arg in either is the string that is copied. It may be a predefined char array, a string constant or a pointer to a char array, where the array was predefined or acquired dynamically.

The second arg is a char in single quotes that instructs the program to convert the copy to upper case, to lower case, to convert just vowels to lower case, to convert just first letters to upper case, etc. The second arg may be written upper or lower case.

dscase() makes a copy of the source string, changes the case of the copy, stores this copy dynamically, and returns a pointer to the copy. The source string is untouched. *dscase()* uses *calloc()* to obtain storage, so the space holding a string created by *dscase()* must eventually be freed using *free()*. To change the case of a dynamic string and store the changes immediately in the original string, use *pscase()*.

pscase() creates a string that it stores in pdsn, a predefined char array, so dsn must be at least the size of the source string. It returns a pointer to the terminal SNUL of the copy stored in dsn. The original string is not changed, unless str and dsn are the same. The procedure is sufficiently robust so that str and dsn can be the same string. These are the options:

c	changes consonants to upper case.
d	changes consonants to lower case.
f	changes the first letter of each word to upper, the other letters to lower.
l	changes every character to lower case.
s	switches chars from lower case to upper or upper case to lower, char by char.
u	changes every character to upper case.
v	change vowels to upper case.
w	changes vowels to lower case.

Usage.

```
    STRING   pd = NULL;
    pd = dssave("this is a dynamic string."); /*Create a dynamic string.*/
```

/*In the next statement, we use the dynamic string as the first arg in pscase to change the first letter in each word to upper case. Because it is also the last arg, the revision is copied back into the string pointed to by pd. This does no harm, because pscase() changes neither size of string or location. The print product will be: **This Is A Dynamic String.**/

```
    pscase(pd,'f',pd);
    }
```

Other examples of usage, including the ability to selectively change portions of a string, are shown in LISTINGS\chap7\7-3-5-1.c.

7.3.5.2.   Creating reverse image clones

Section 2.5.3.1 illustrated how to rewrite a function that works on preset strings to one that works on dynamic strings, using *psreverse*() and *dsreverse*().

They are versions of the same procedure: the reversing of a string, so that "ABCD" becomes "DCBA". They both expect to create substrings, leaving the original intact. *dsreverse*() obtains new storage space from the system and writes the reversed string into this new space, thus preserving the original. *psreverse*() writes the reversed string directly to predefined storage, not collecting the evolving string in a local buffer. So it should not be used to write the string back into itself; *streverse*() is available to do that.

```
void RevString(void)
    {
    char buf[SMLSZE] = {SNUL};
    char buf1[SMLSZE] = {SNUL};
    STRING  r = NULL, s = NULL;

    PJ(Type a phrase for dsreverse.\n);
    r = dsreverse(ttyin("T"));  /*Creates a dynamic substring that is reversed.*/
    PS(ttystr);
    PS(r);

    printf("\n\nType a phrase for psreverse.\n");
    stcpy(ttyin("T"),buf);
    s = psreverse(buf, buf1);  /*s points to buf1. It has no real use*/
                               /*except for the grammar.*/
    PS(buf); PS(buf1); PS(s);
    }
```

7.3.5.3.   Exact Copy Clones

These are easily done with a string copy procedure. See Section 7.2.2.1 for variations on constructing such a function.

7.4.   OPERATIONS ON TWO OR MORE STRINGS.

7.4.1. EXACT MATCHES

7.4.1.1.   Complete string matches

int strcmp(STRING s1, STRING s2);

This is the most stringent of string comparisons. Routines based on the library function *strcmp*() do pairwise ASCII comparisons on comparable elements of two strings; i.e., a[0] to b[0], A[1] to b[1], and so forth. The routine stops as soon as a comparison pair fails to match. The strings are considered equal only if they are of the same size and the same content. Using s1 as the fulcrum, the procedure returns a negative number to signal that s1 is the smaller string; i.e., in the last comparison that was made, the ASCII value of its element was less that the ASCII value of the comparison element. s1 is zero when the strings are the same and a positive number when s1 is the larger.

Variations answer the question of degree of sameness. We can count how many paired comparisons succeeded. Or how many succeeded relative to the number of characters in the smaller string. Or how many succeeded beyond some minimum value. Eliminating unnecessary white space and bracketed glosses usually increase the chances of matching. If case doesn't matter, changing both strings to the same case also increases the likelihood of a match.

An alternative way of formulating the match question is to ask: which of n possible words is this new word? In a restricted universe of strings, there are just so many named strings available—commands in the operating system or tokens in a program that parses user instructions. Beyond some criterion number, which differs in the different words, the string is known.(Implementing the larger string in binary tree format simplifies the process but doesn't change the principle.) Matching can stop. Typing can stop. Guessers work on this principle.

7.4.1.2.   An identical substring.

extern BOOL   stequ(STRING psrc, STRING keyword);
extern BOOL   keyfind(STRING str, STRING wrd);
extern BOOL   stfind(STRING str, STRING wrd, int *pbgnsrch);
extern int   stmfind(STRING str, STRING wrd, long *place);

Phrase-matching procedures match a substring within a larger-sized string, anywhere within the string. As such, they are usually less stringent than full-word comparisons. They do not fail at the first incorrect match. Rather they move on and try again. The ones presented here are all based on simple character matching, yet they exhibit different characteristics.

The basic operation requires a match function that can compare a substring to a sequence of characters in a string that is usually of longer length. The substring does not have to match the entire string. The major difference between a phrase matcher and a whole string match function is that the substring is matched only for its own length. The terminal SNUL of the substring is not part of the comparison; so if the comparison gets that far, it is a signal that the match has been successful.

This type of match can done by a function such as *stequ()*, which appear to be very similar to *strcmp()*, yet is significantly different. This is *stequ()* written so to be easily compared with *strcmp()*.

```
BOOL stequ(STRING s, STRING t)  /*s is the substring; t is the string*/
    {/*BP*/
    for ( ; *s ; s++, t++)                  /*Test up to but don't include the terminal SNUL of t*/
        if (*s != *t ) return(0);
            return(1);                      /*If it falls through loop, the substring is part of the string*/
    }/*EP*/
```

as compared to *stcmp* which is written as:

```
int stcmp(STRING s, STRING t)
    {/*BP*/
    for ( ; *s == *t; s++, t++)
        if (*s == SNUL) return(0);
    return(*s - *t);
    }/*EP*/
```

The find operator, shown here written in several versions, explores the string until it has a single successful match or until it runs out of string. *keyfind()* begins at the start of the string. *stfind()* begins at the position set by the third arg. If there is a match, the starting point shifts to the position in the string that is just after the end of the characters that match the substring. In section 5.2.1, it is shown being set by another procedure. It also more suitable for searching within a loop, where other operations take place after each successful match. *keyfind()*, on the other hand, can be used as a less constrained *strcmp()*. First, a procedure such as *pssubat()* constricts the match to a particular segment of the string, (e.g., pssubat(str, 10, 40) reduces the search space to the characters in positions 10 to 40). *keyfind()* then matches the substring against that limited section of the string. *stmfind()*, which was shown in Section 3.2.4.2, is an elaboration of the basic find operation. It differs from the other two in that it does not stop at a successful match but finds all the matches within the string and reports their locations.

7.4.2. FUZZY MATCHING

```
extern BOOL    stwildsearch(STRING sbstring, STRING word, int *pbgnsrch, int
                 *pfirst, int *plast);
extern BOOL    wildsearch(STRING str, STRING wrd);
```

In fuzzy matches, the substring can be a composite of different pieces of actual text that are to be matched in the string; these text units can be separated by text that is ignored. The positions of the text that doesn't matter is by convention indicated by the wildcard symbols: '?' for a single gap and '*' for any amount of irrelevent text. For example, ne*ates would match new plates, negates, network rates, etc. re?d would match reed or read. The particular implementation might state that there must be some text where ever '*' appears, or it may allow A*B to match AB.

The basic algorithm used here is *stwildsearch*(), which searches a string for matches to the fuzzy substring. Like *stfind*(), it begins the search as dictated by a separate variable that can be set in the calling function. If it finds matching text, it marks the position of the start and end of the text in the string. There is also a variant called *wildsearch* that always starts the search at the beginning of the string. It doesn't mark the location. It only answers the question: yes, there is a match or no, there is not.

Usage.

```
/*In this example, we open two output files, one to receive records that contain the fuzzy
phrase, the other to hold the records that do not.*/
FILE *inchn = 0;
FILE *outchn1 = 0;
FILE *outchn2 = 0;
BITMAP Trec = 0;
STRING fuz = "CA*mo";   /*This will extract 3 records from demo.db*/

main()
     {
     char  buf[LRGSZE];
     STRING pbuf = buf;
     char new[120] = {SNUL};
     int pfirst, plast;
     int start = 0;
     setbreak(&Trec,"~","","");
     inchn = fopen("demo.db","r");
     outchn1 = fopen("yes.tmp","w");
     outchn2 = fopen("no.tmp","w");
```

/* This brings in a record at a time. It will match records that contain: the fuzzy phrase. */

```
     while (TRUE)
          {
          psin(inchn, Trec, &brk, LRGSZE, buf);
          PS(buf);
          if (brk == EOF) break;

          if (stwildsearch(buf, fuz, &start, &pfirst, &plast))
               fprintf(outchn1,"%s~",buf);
          else fprintf(outchn2, "%s",buf);
          }
```

```
relbreak(&Trec);
fclose(inchn);
}
```

Elaborations increase the power of this type of match function.

The extent of the search space can become a parameter. For example, the search might extend over several fields of a record by ignoring delimiters or it might be confined to a single field. Or several of the fields might be concatenated in user-defined order and searched as a unit.

The pieces of text in the substring can be treated as OR booleans, in that the program tries to match as many of them as it can. It doesn't stop if the first one is not in the string. It might keep a running score of how many could be matched per substring, as a measure of success. Or, under another set of rules, it doesn't accept a string unless some minimum number of the pieces are matched.

Alternatively, they substring segments can be treated as AND booleans. This can be all-or-nothing. As another option, if the substring is not matched within a particular string, the search area is widened; from a sentence, say, to a paragraph.

NOT words can be introduced in a complementary substring. They can prevent the program from attempting to match the substring. For example: **if the NOT words appear in field 1 and 2, do not match the substring**. Or they can change stringency. For example, **if there are five or more strings that match the substring, reject the strings that have NOT words in field 1 and 2. Unless you are down to one match.**

In a different approach, the substring can sum up what you recall about an item. As example, in developing a list of references, you might remember **Smith*197?*Data*base*Designs**, meaning that *Smith* was one of the authors; the paper was written in the 70s, and it has the words *data*, *base* and *designs* in it. Order isn't important, because the informational items in the citations will be in whatever order is used by the digitized database. The direction to the program in this case is: **find a citation that has these pieces of text in whatever order they occur**.

7.4.3. SWAPPING STRINGS

```
extern  void stswap(STRING str1, STRING str2, int lim);
extern  void dsswap(STRING str1, STRING str2)
```

Swap routines exchange the the contents of two strings. For dynamic strings pointers are exchanged in a three-way switch involving a temporary pointer. Thus:

```
STRING ptemp;
ptemp = s1;
s1 = s2;
s2 = ptemp;
```

This is replicated in *dsswap()*, which can be used by *stmcat()* to rearrange substrings before concatenating them.

With preset strings, the actual contents are shifted. The first two args to *stswap*() are the strings that are to be swapped. The third arg is array size. It makes sense to use the size of the smaller array as this value. There remains the problem of swapping two strings, one obtained dynamically, one with preset storage. Several solutions are poor but adequate. If the strings are equal in size, *stswap*() can be used. It can also be used if the dynamically obtained string is initially larger than the preset string and if the dynamically obtained string is still small enough to be stored eventually in the predefined buffer. Alternatively, *realloc*() can be used to reallocate string space for the dynamic string(s), each time the swap occurs. A general solution is to do a single copy of the preset string to a dynamic string. Then swapping can be done by pointer switching. This is a heavy investment but is cleaner in programs that do a lot of string matching, where strings switch places depending on some ranking algorithm. Or when the same strings are often reconcatenated in different order with *stmcat*().

```
main()
    {
    char s1[2 * SMLSZE] = {SNUL};
    char s2[SMLSZE] = {SNUL};
    STRING ps1;
    STRING ps2;

    PJ(Example: exchange dynamic and preset strings of any sizes);
    ps1 = s1;
    PJ(Type a preset sentence\n);
    stcpy(ttyin("T"),s1);
    ps1 = dssave(s1); /*s1 has now been stored dynamically.*/
    PJ(Type a dynamic sentence.\n);
    ps2 = ttyin("d");
    dsswap(ps1,ps2);
    printf("\nps1: %s",ps1);
    printf("\nps2: %s",ps2);
    }
```

7.4.4. COMBINING MULTIPLE STRINGS

extern void   stcat(STRING str, STRING dsn);
extern STRING stmcat(PTRADR ppstr, int num);
extern STRING stmKat(PTRADR psrc, int num, FILE *outchan);
extern STRING psnext(STRING str, STRING dsn);

The system library function *stcat*() adds the source string to the tail of dsn. It can handle two strings at a time. Multiple string combination, when the number varies from run to run requires a different approach.

stmcat() works by joining the elements of a char pointer array, where each element of the array is a pointer to a string. The original strings are not modified in *stmcat*(), whereas one of the source strings is modified in *stcat*(). The cat functions work on the strings in one operation. In contrast, *psnext*() must be run in a loop to concatenate the source strings.

stcat() concatenates two strings; these may be variables, string constants or pointers to strings. *stmcat*() handles multiple strings, pointed to by an array of character pointers. The elements of the pointer array may point to particular locations in some large character array where new strings start (see Section 5.3.2). Or they may represent the row elements in a 2D char array with the same amount of fixed storage for each string; e.g., char names[20][100] to store 20 strings, Or they may be independent strings, created dynamically at different times. *stmcat*() returns a pointer to the newly concatenated and stored string.

It uses local storage to build up the new string. When the exact number of chars that need to be stored is known, stmcat() gets machine storage via calloc(), and returns a pointer to where the new string is stored. *stmcat*() uses *calloc*(), so strings created by *stmcat*() must be deallocated at some point using *free*().

arg 1: the address of the first element of the pointer array.

arg 2: the number of strings that are to be concatenated.

The array of pointers may point to any combination of strings: constant strings, literal strings, variable strings, pointers to preset arrays, pointers to dynamically stored strings. Single chars MUST be inserted as strings, not chars.

The procedure is simpleminded--it can not be made to skip pointer elements; it can not be made to concatenate them out of order. Usually, this will not create a problem in that the number of pointer elements examined is controlled by the second arg to stmcat(). So even if stmcat() first concatenates 5 strings (stmcat(ppa,5)) and then, using the same pointer array, is called on to concatenate the first two strings, (stmcat(ppa,2)), it will return a correct result.

If the 6th pointer of the previous run is to be the 2nd pointer this time, and visa versa, this will work:

```
dsswap(p6,p2);
stcat(ppa,5);
```

If the 3rd element, say, is not part of some later concatenation, then it can be emptied by writing **p[3] = ""**; for a pointer to a preset array or NULLIT(p) for a pointer to a dynamic string. (Alternatively, the pointer to the preset array can be cleared between runs using a macro such as CLRPTR.) An empty string does not halt the concatenation. The program skips over empty strings, but pointers to empty strings are added to the count of the number of pointers recorded in the second arg.

In this example, words or phrases are entered from the keyboard singly. Each phrase is immediately saved using dynamic storage. They are then assembled into a single new string. The component phrases are released from storage.

```
main ()
    {
    int i;
    STRING p;
    char *pa[10] = NULL;
    char **ppa = &pa[0];
```

```
PJ(Please type in some text.);
PJ(This will be a loop. Stop the loop with a CTRLd.\n);
for (i = 0; i < 10; i++)
        {
        if (*ttyin("T") == '\004')
                break;
        else pa[i] = dssave(ttystr);
        printf("\nPlease type in some more text.\n");
        }
printf("\n\nthis is i: [%d]",i);
p = stmcat(ppa, i);
printf("\n this is p: [%s]",p);
```

/*stmcat() returns a pointer to where the system has stored the newly concatenated string. If the parts composing the new string are no longer needed, they should be freed with free(). (This assumes the old strings were acquired with some routine that used calloc()).*/

```
        for ( ; i <= 0; i-- ) free(pa[i]);
        }
```

/*Running this program would give this kind of result:

Type something.	What
Type something.	Is
Type something.	It?
Type something.	'\04'

p = WhatIsIt?/*

Suppose a set of pointers are to be concatenated out of order; say, pa[5], pa[18], pa[0], pa[3]. A second array could constructed, thus:

```
STRING   newpa[4];
STRING   pa[20];
PTRADR   pnew = newpa;
STRING   p = NULL;

newpa[0] = pa[5];
newpa[1] = pa[18];
newpa[2] = pa[0];
newpa[3] = pa[3];
/*Suppose:
pa[0] = "GHI";
pa[3] = "JKL";
pa[5] = "ABC";
pa[18] = "DEF";
*/
p = stmcat(newpa,4);                   /*PrintProduct: [ABCDEFGHIJKL]*/
```

The new string may then be renamed to the same name as one of the concatenated strings.

The procedure assumes that a HUGESZE array is sufficient to gather together the chars comprising the new string in a temporary store. This is more than likely true, but it could fail. All the program does if the new string is more than HUGESZE bytes long is to notify the user that there isn't enough room Then it bombs. Instead of terminating the program, the function can be rewritten to concatenate what it could, and terminate the function. If HUGESZE is insufficient to merge the files, a version of *stmcat*() called *stmKat*() sends an error message to the file that is its arg 3. It then concatenates what it has built up to that point and stops the function, not the program.

In addition to the cat functions, there is *psnext*(), shown in Chapter 5. *psnext*() copies a string to an existing char array as does *stcpy*(). But *psnext*() returns a pointer to the SNUL termination of the copied string. Hence it is useful for plating a set of strings in a buffer. Used in a loop, *psnext*() provides an alternative to *stmcat*(), without the need to construct a pointer array to the individual strings.

psnext() is particularly useful when a string is scanned to dissect out separate phrases, which are modified before the string is reconstituted. It has the advantage that there is not the bother of freeing the string that is being concatenated and of regaining storage dynamically for the accumulating string. It has the disadvantage that individual parts of the string are not later available for manipulation.

As shown in Chapter 5, *psnext*() can also be used to store a group of strings in a buffer with a pointer to the start of each string maintained in a separate pointer array. STRING ptrarr[20] could serve as the array of pointers to the start of 20 separate strings stored sequentially in a large buffer, called buf. When the buffer acts as repository for a set of strings, the pointer pbuf should be incremented by one before psnext() is reused to position the next string. This array of pointer-to-char is useful in maintaining a permanent index to the stored set of strings. However, after the pointer array has been created, concatenations become more efficient using *stmcat*(), rather than *psnext*().

7.4.5. REARRANGING STRING SEGMENTS

There is no particular function, in that rearranging is context dependent. Section 6.7 demonstrated a way of storing output order so that records can be output in user-requested order. This can be used as a guide for rearrangement.

Index and Glossary

Functions and macros have the () logo appended.

SYMBOLS USED

Order is by precedence. (*see* Table 1.8, p. 55.)
id, *identifier*, name of variable.
rvalue, right side of an assignment statement.

()	function logo
[]	array logo
->	pointer-to-struct
.	struct.member operator
!	boolean unary NOT
~	bitwise complement
++	prefix/postfix increment by 1
--	prefix/postfix decrement by 1
+	addition operator
-	subtraction operator
*	indirect referent
&	address of
*	multiplication operator
/	ordinary division operator
%	modulus division operator
<<	bitwise shift to left
>>	bitwise shift to right
<	relational: is less than
<=	relational: is less than or equal to
>	relational: is greater than
>=	relational: is more than or equal to
==	relational: is equal to
!=	relational: is not equal to
&	bitwise AND
^	bitwise EXCLUSIVE OR (XOR)
I	bitwise INCLUSIVE OR (OR)
&&	boolean AND
II	boolean OR
?I	if-else triad
=	assignment operator
+=	id = id + rvalue; arithmetic plus
-=	id = id - rvalue; arithmetic minus
*=	id = id * rvalue; arithmetic multiply
/=	id = id / rvalue; arithmetic divide
%=	id = id % rvalue; arithmetic modulus divide
&=	id = id & rvalue; bitwise AND
^=	id = id ^ rvalue; bitwise XOR
I=	id = id I rvalue; bitwise OR
<<=	id = id << rvalue; bitwise shift left
>>=	id = id >> rvalue; bitwise shift right
,	comma operator

In addition

\0	SNUL, char zero
0	numerical zero
0	octal prefix
0x	hexadecimal prefix
NULL	pointer zero
'0'	zero as a character, ASCII decimal 60
'	bracket for char constant
"	bracket for string literal
#	preprocessor operator
##	token pasting preprocessor operator
_	underscore character in id
\a	backslash alert
\b	backslash backspace
\r	backslash carriage return
\v	backslash vertical tab
\'	backslash literal single quote
\f	backslash form feed
\	backslash line continuation
\\	backslash literal backslash
\t	backslash horizontal tab
\?	backslash question mark
\"	backslash literal double quote
\n	backslash NewLine

Trigraph Sequence

??=	represents #
??/	represents \
??'	represents ^
??(	represents [
??)	represents]
??!	represents I
??<	represents {
??>	represents }
??-	represents ~

A